The origins
of modern critical thought

The origins
of modern critical thought:
German aesthetic and literary
criticism from Lessing to Hegel

Edited by
David Simpson

The right of the
University of Cambridge
to print and sell
all manner of books
was granted by
Henry VIII in 1534.
The University has printed
and published continuously
since 1584.

Cambridge University Press

Cambridge
New York   New Rochelle
Melbourne   Sydney

Published by the Press Syndicate of the University of Cambridge
The Pitt Building, Trumpington Street, Cambridge CB2 1RP
32 East 57th Street, New York, NY 10022, USA
10 Stamford Road, Oakleigh, Melbourne 3166, Australia

First published 1988

Printed in the United States of America

Library of Congress Cataloging-in-Publication Data

The Origins of modern critical thought: German aesthetic and literary criticism from
Lessing to Hegel/edited by David Simpson.
p. cm.
Bibligraphy: p.
Includes index.
ISBN 0-521-35004-2. ISBN 0-521-35902-3 (pbk.)
1. Aesthetics, German – 18th century. 2. Aesthetics, German – 19th century.
3. Criticism—Germany. 4. Literature, Modern – 18th century – History and criticism –
Theory, etc. 5. Literature, Modern – 19th century – History and criticism – Theory, etc.
I. Simpson, David, 1951 -
BH221.G3075 1988
111'.85' 0943–dc19 88-23383 CIP

British Library Cataloguing in Publication Data

The origins of modern critical thought:
German aesthetic and literary criticism
From Lessing to Hegel
1. Aesthetics
I. Simpson, David
111'.85
ISBN 0-521-35004-2 hard covers
ISBN 0-521-35902-3 paperback

Contents

Citations and abbreviations

Most references give the name of the author and the date of the edition cited, so that the bibliography should be consulted for full details.

The following abbreviations have been used:

AE   Schiller, *On the Aesthetic Education of Man*
Ak.   *Kants gesammelte Schriften*, Akademie Edition
CJ   Kant, *Critique of Judgement*
DS   *German Aesthetic and Literary Criticism; Kant, Fichte, Schelling, Schopenhauer, Hegel*, ed. David Simpson
HBN   *German Aesthetic and Literary Criticism: Winckelmann, Lessing, Hamann, Herder, Schiller and Goethe*, ed. H. B. Nisbet
KFSA   *Kritische Friedrich–Schlegel–Ausgabe*
KMW   *German Aesthetic and Literary Criticism: The Romantic Ironists and Goethe*, ed. Kathleen M. Wheeler
SW   *Sämtliche Werke* (for Fichte and Schelling)
System Schelling, *System of Transcendental Idealism*

A note on selections and translations

This anthology reprints selections from the three previous volumes of German aesthetic and literary criticism published by Cambridge University Press, edited by H.B. Nisbet, David Simpson and Kathleen M. Wheeler. It also includes passages from Schiller's *On the Aesthetic Education of Man* (not to be found in the previous volumes). Translations and footnotes overseen and provided by the three original editors have been reprinted here, with only the minor alterations required by the new format. Fuller annotations, selections, and bibliographies are to be found in the three original volumes. The present editor (David Simpson) has provided a new introduction.

Introduction

I

It must at first sight seem implausibly grandiloquent to claim that the writers represented in this anthology constitute the originators of modern critical thought. Such a notion is likely to be treated skeptically by at least two different kinds of reader. On the one hand, there are many of us who are disposed to question the very idea of origins, and are inclined to suspect that the image of a foundational past is no more than a convenient projection intended to grant some undeserved authority to a version of the present, whether desired or disavowed. On the other hand, there are at least as many of us who take arguments about origins very seriously indeed. For such readers, it is likely that the case here proposed for the exemplary status of the generations of German critics from Lessing to Hegel will be disputed less in principle than in particular. Why offer these writers, rather than those of Greece, or Rome, or France, or Britain? Why Kant and Hegel rather than Plato, or Aquinas, or Rousseau, or Coleridge?

No simple and absolute answer to the objections of either of these two classes of readers can be given here; and these objections must indeed be acknowledged and assimilated as useful restraints upon any inclination toward arguing for the complete determination of any series of writings by any other set of writings, from whatever periods or national cultures. Two responses may, however, be offered. First, nothing written is alien to anyone. When we take seriously the genealogies of writing, we will find that to speak of 'Kant' is also to speak of the tradition of philosophical aesthetics, from Plato to Hume, that informs and particularizes the issues that are raised and the ways in which they are addressed. German critics and philosophers, being very aware of the relative paucity of precursors within their own language and culture, were as it happens especially eclectic and internationalist in their understanding of the tradition. To speak of this particular moment in the history of aesthetic theory is thus also and to an unusual degree to speak of the collective history of the subject itself. Ideals of Enlightenment universality only reinforced the tendency to look behind and beyond the immediate that must be seen to have informed even the inquiry into the characteristics of the Germanic itself.

There is a second response that does not so much negate as qualify the first: however much of the history of aesthetics is gathered into the discourse taking shape among German speakers in the late eighteenth and early nineteenth centuries, that discourse yet constitutes an address to a particular time and place. We might then wonder how a series of writings produced by and for a culture now almost two hundred years behind us could possibly be 'original' to the world we now inhabit. Much has of course changed since 1800, and various discontinuities will be immediately obvious to the reader of this volume. For Schelling, to take an extreme case, aesthetics was at the top of the philosophical pyramid, and philosophy itself encompassed nothing less than the whole of spiritual, intellectual, and natural life – past, present, and to come. Those of us working within the narrower subject disciplines of modern universities will tend to find such paradigms both ideologically and technologically unconvincing, whether or not we regret the passing of such inclusive aspirations. But, notwithstanding such distinctions – and there are many of them – there is yet an arguable continuity between the late eighteenth and the twentieth centuries. This is obvious in the shared conventions of their debates, and it may thus signal some corresponding continuity between the social and psychological experiences that give life and audience to those debates. These writers are very concerned about the growth of the reading public, about the place of literature and art within a commercial and early industrial economy, about the changing balance between work and leisure, and about the threatened status of the disinterested state of mind that they (mostly) felt to be essential to an authentically aesthetic experience. All of these questions, and others like them, have continued to be central, implicitly or explicitly, for twentieth-century critics. They are explicit in the work of the Frankfurt School, and of F.R. Leavis and Raymond Williams and Lionel Trilling; implicit, but equally powerful, in the theories of I.A. Richards, Cleanth Brooks, and Northrop Frye. The modern condition is not a simple historical unity, invented in the late eighteenth century and still alive today. But in limited and important ways – all the more important for being limited – we can recognize the exemplary status of these older writers for much of what is written about and discussed in the present.

The tracing of individual patterns of influence would require careful and exhaustive argument, well beyond the limits of this introduction (which does, however, end with a brief discussion of the subject, and some guidance for further reading). Coleridge alone, to take a famous example, has left his editors and critics the almost impossible task of plotting the quantity and quality of his assimilations of the German tradition, whether by plagiarism, purposive interpretation, unconscious absorption or downright misrepresentation. The transmission of ideas and arguments is often indirect, especially between different languages and through time. We have no trouble recognizing a source in Arnold's writings for Leavis' emphasis upon the 'free play of the mind'; but that phrase needs to be traced back to Kant and Schiller for an understanding of its fuller motives and resonances. These remain exemplary even when they are not acknowledged by those who evoke or refigure them in later years. In this way Kant, for example, remains a presence for generations of writers and critics who have never read him. Twentieth-century criticism in English bears along with it a tradition of which it is seldom consciously aware, and perhaps cannot even read. Coleridge, Carlyle, Arnold, and George Eliot all knew that they were responding to German predecessors and contemporaries; they engaged with them directly, through reading and translation. In the modern universities, where we work much more commonly within the confines of national literatures – so much so that the idea of a comparative literature has had to be reinvented as a discipline in itself – conscious awareness of these connections, and others like them, has been lost, even as we continue to reproduce them as habits and assumptions, and reinvent them as original to ourselves. Not the least of the virtues of a figure like Derrida is that he reminds us of the continued presence of these precursors, as he alerts us also to the implications of not questioning the degree to which we reproduce a continuous history with them. But a true critical internationalism, and a truly historical consciousness, are hard to achieve in a culture whose own interests seem to be antithetical to such developments. And this very struggle, between an Enlightenment ideal of universality and a nationalistic or Eurocentric discourse of special destiny, is played out within and between the writers represented in this anthology. Thus an understanding of their various positions can produce a revivified sense not of the uniformity but of the diversity of modern critical thought. The fact that it was Hegel rather than Schelling who became the 'origin' for successive generations of philosophers, historians, social scientists, and literary critics has had enduring consequences for theorists across the humanities and of all shades of political preference. One of the functions of the following selections, brief and incomplete as they are, is thus to reveal for critical inspection those parts of the map traversed by roads not often taken.

This volume should also, as I have implied, reveal that to an often surprising extent certain familiar routes were mapped long before the twentieth century invented the discipline of literary criticism as a special subject with procedures peculiar to itself. In anthologizing a series of historical precursors for deconstruction, for example, Mark Taylor reasonably includes texts by Kant and Hegel, but he also unwittingly quotes Friedrich Schlegel almost verbatim in contending for the literariness of philosophy and the philosophical identity of literature (1986, p. vii; see Schlegel's *Critical Fragments*, nos. 42, 115). Readers of Derrida and de Man may be surprised to come upon Schlegel's prescient contention that "words often understand themselves better than do those who use them", that incom-

prehension is the ghost in the machine of comprehension, and that no
better thing could happen than that "humanity will at last rise up in a mass
and learn to read" (see below, p. 180). Novalis similarly pointed out "the
absurd error people make of imagining they are speaking for the sake of
things; no one knows the essential thing about language, that it is concerned only with itself" (Monologue). In the same spirit, Jean Paul Richter's
whimsically presented remarks on linguistic determination are quite serious in their suggestion that much of German comedy must be understood
as a result of that culture's odd embarrassment over the placing of the
word ich. Readers familiar with the varieties of twentieth-century criticism
will discover all kinds of parallels and precursors in the following texts.
Even Trotsky, feeling the need to reconcile the new findings of psycho-
analysis with a revolutionary Marxist criticism, echoes Schiller in his assertion that "art is an expression of man's need for a harmonious and complete life, that is to say, his need for those major benefits of which a society
of classes has deprived him" (1972, p. 104).

II

Let me now move on to a brief exposition of the historical conditions
affecting the emergence of these writings, and of the thematic preoccupations that will be found to inform them. First, we must be aware of the
state of Germany and the German language. In fact, the entity known as
'Germany' as it existed at the beginning of World War II did not come
into being until the second half of the nineteenth century. Bismarck
brought together what had been a collection of principalities and duchies
of various sizes, each governing itself and deriving its models of taste and
behaviour as much from England and France as from any agreed-upon
notion of a unitary German identity. Goethe, in his autobiography,
described the situation as follows:

as no universal cultivation can pervade our fatherland, every place adheres to its
own fashion, and carries out, even to the last, its own characteristic peculiarities:
exactly the same thing holds good of the universities.   (1974), I, 270

Prussia was beginning to emerge as the strongest of the various states, and
it was at the forefront of the war of liberation carried on against Napoleon.
But the prospect of a single political identity for German speakers existed
at this time only as an ideal. When Lessing rehearses, successively, the various limitations of the French and English critics, we may sense the
urgency of a German alternative that can exist only as a critical and intellectual and not as a political identity. Philosophers and critics before the
late eighteenth century had written more often in French or Latin than in
German (see Blackall, 1959), and the relative unfamiliarity of the language
was to contribute decisively to the problems faced by the first foreign read-

ers (and indeed many German-speaking readers) of Kant and Hegel and their contemporaries. The political condition of the German-speaking world must have helped determine the emphasis of so many of its writers upon a unity that could only be envisaged at the level of the ideal, and achieved at the level of the individual mind. A.W. Schlegel wrote, in 1809, that "in the mental domain of thought and poetry, inaccessible to worldly power, the Germans, who are separated in so many ways from each other, still feel their unity" (1846, p. 6). Many of the writings in this volume were produced at a time when German speakers could reasonably fear, as Schlegel himself feared, that the descendants of the citizens of the Holy Roman Empire were "in danger of disappearing altogether from the list of independent nations" (p. 529).

Schlegel thus had ample justification for suggesting that being a German involved belonging to a "speculative people" (p. 36). For Schiller, the hegemony of speculation is the besetting syndrome of the modern condition itself. Nature and the sphere of reality have disappeared as the medium of experience and have been displaced into the medium of the ideal. The Kantian philosophy, he explains, could only have been developed within a culture predisposed to encourage "the most intense effort of abstraction" (AE, pp. 41–43; and below, p. 134). Marx and Engels, in a famous passage in The German Ideology, explained Kant's emphasis upon the subjective will as the expression of "the impotence, repression and wretchedness of the German burghers, whose petty interests were never capable of developing into the common, national interests of a class and who were, therefore, constantly exploited by the bourgeois of all other nations" (1970, p. 97). And Lukács, in a more complex but related argument, saw in the same philosophy a disabling commitment to the absolute distinction of gnosis from praxis, wherein the mind had set itself the task of analysing only the forms of its own consciousness, itself posited as all that we can know of the world (1971, pp. 110–49).

We cannot, of course, simply invoke the politics of preunification Germany as the single cause of a tendency toward speculative idealism. That tendency was not uncontested in itself, as the following selections will make clear. And there are other historical factors to be considered. The debate between the claims of the single and the social also took on an urgent polemical profile in the tension between Protestantism and Catholicism in German culture. The stress upon the aesthetic value of incompletion, evident for example in the Romantic ironists and the apologists of the fragment as an authentic art form, needs to be understood as an incorporation of Protestant theology into philosophical aesthetics. So too does Kant's categorical imperative and Hegel's model of history as recording the progress of spirit toward knowledge of itself outside the sphere of contingent experience. Schelling, conversely, refuses to see in Shakespeare the desirable ideal of the modern condition, precisely because Shakespeare is the poet of a Protestant culture founded by definition in the privileging of singleness and solitude. He offers the alternative paradigm of Calderón, the poet of a Catholic country wherein a metaphysically authentic consensus is still available to the writer. The variously complex ways in which these writers evaluate Greek art and culture may also be understood within the context provided by the theological debate. On the one hand, the Greek city states must have seemed ideal forerunners to a Germanic tradition that was itself founded upon a disjunction between political and linguistic unity. If Athens alone could produce a Plato and a Sophocles, then why not Jena, or Weimar, or Berlin? On the other hand, Greek life seemed to emanate from a state of affairs absolutely antithetical to the modern condition as it was defined by most of Goethe's contemporaries. As a pre-Christian culture, Greece had no sense of the schism between the real and the ideal that was seen to be the basic element of the Christian world view. It was also thought to have been innocent of all the other forms of social and psychic division affecting and defining modern life. In Greece all was simplicity and unity, creating conditions for the production of art and culture that were no longer available to the eighteenth-century mind. The ancients lived happily within the totality of a present that was not constantly undermined by awareness of the past and future. They had not invented desire, and the longing for another world. Many moments in the writings of Goethe, Schiller, Schelling and others will invite us to regret the passing of this happy period in the childhood of the species. At the same time, good Protestant ethics (which is not, of course, limited to self-declared Protestants) demands that this fall be deemed somehow fortunate. Schiller thus insists that it is neither possible nor desirable to duplicate Greek life in the modern world, although we must maintain the ideal of harmony as an imperative for the unrealized future. Hegel, with brilliant ingenuity, similarly argued that whereas Greek culture afforded the most perfect conditions for the production of art (depending as it does upon a synthesis of the ideal and the material in the sphere of representation), art itself will be superseded as spirit progresses through time to its goal in the completely dematerialized medium of self-conscious philosophical prose. By contrast, Schelling is much less committed to a Eurocentric teleology, describing instead a model within which the absolute is always already latent, and open to recognition as essentially beyond and outside time. Having no need to represent Greek or any other culture as primitive or prototypic, Schelling preserves a much greater respect for the intrinsic integrity of other periods and societies. And before Schelling, and with an even greater adherence to Enlightenment ideals of tolerance, there is Herder, who abjures anything resembling a master-narrative for history in favour of "the science of what is, not of what possibly may be according to the hidden designs of fate", or of what may be derived from "the philosophy of final causes" (1968, pp. 215, 266).

Hegel and Herder thus stand forth as the exponents of two quite different kinds of historical relativism. Both accept that art must be understood as the expression of its culture in a moment of time, that it can only come into being as the emanation of a particular *Weltanschauung* or *Mythologie* (Hegel's and Schelling's terms, respectively). Herder sees a single human species expressing itself in different ways, allowing space in his explanations for a high degree of materialist coincidence – climate, soil fertility and so on – as a causal principle. While of course not completely devoid of the prejudices and assumptions of his own particular culture, he sees no need to choose between different societies and epochs as superior or inferior to some common standard, or as obedient to some principle of ongoing development in the species or the race. The effect of critical analysis is thus to mitigate rather than to reinforce the idea of one's own culture as in any sense normative or inevitable. Hegel, conversely, is absolutely clear in his faith in history as the medium through which *Geist* evolves from primitive to more perfect states. His judgements about earlier or non-western cultures (and their art) thus inevitably take on the rhetoric of condescension, however cleverly disguised. Like the sun which is its metaphorical engine, Hegel's system moves from east to west, from prehistory to modernity, from the pagan past to the Protestant present. As the physical sun sets in the west, so it is in the west that "the inner sun of self-consciousness, which emits a higher radiance, makes its further ascent" (1980, p. 197). So pervasive has this Hegelian paradigm proved to be that even some Marxist arguments have accepted its Eurocentric legacy.

I have so far described two major conditions affecting the preoccupation with speculative idealism – whose exact forms have yet to be discussed – in German aesthetics: the political dispersal of German speakers, and the tension between Protestantism and Catholicism. We must add in at least a third condition, which emerges in the writers here anthologized as a concern with the negative results of divided labour. Even though the industrialization of western Europe was still at a very early phase in its development, there had been throughout the eighteenth century a growing debate about the positive and negative consequences of social inequality and occupational specialization. Drawing upon this debate, Kant coined the term "splendid misery" (*CJ*, §83) as a way of defining the oxymoronic necessity whereby the progress of the species as a whole could only occur through the exploitation of the many by the few. The same paradox was taken up by Schiller in his two major essays, *On the Aesthetic Education of Man* and *On Naive and Sentimental Poetry*. In order that society may develop, most of the individuals within it must suffer some form of alienation or self-division:

Everlastingly chained to a single little fragment of the Whole, man himself develops into nothing but a fragment; everlastingly in his ear the monotonous sound of the wheel that he turns, he never develops the harmony of his being, and instead of putting the stamp of humanity upon his own nature, he becomes nothing more than the imprint of his occupation or of his specialized knowledge.

(AE, p. 35; see below, p. 131)

Kant implies and Schiller explicitly proposes an origin for this experience of social and psychological alienation in the necessary development of communal life itself. Alienation is thus exacerbated rather than created by the conditions of modern culture. Nonetheless, in its particularly intense modern form this perceived syndrome is obviously quite conformable with the two other determinations, already discussed, impinging upon the phenomenon of speculative idealism. Each of these three conditions, the political reality, the theological debate, and the findings of political economy, may be assumed to have intensified the others. What emerges is thus a strongly maintained concern with the experience of division: division within the self, of self from others, and of present or worldly life from the past and from the realm of the eternal and the ideal.

III

We are now in a position to understand the immediate contexts of some of the thematic preoccupations of these writers, which otherwise must seem somewhat abstract and technical. For, with Kant and those who came after him, the role of art and the aesthetic experience is often to resolve problems raised by the perceived disjunction between personal and public spheres, and to offer alternatives to the negative determinations of social life. At the most general level, a number of these writers propose a definition of art, or philosophy – the terms often mutually define one another – that is inclusive rather than exclusive. The discipline of literary criticism in its modern form has, conversely, usually identified itself in contrast to other modes of inquiry – history, philosophy, even aesthetics. Even as literary criticism remains a necessarily eclectic practice, recognizing all sorts of data and incorporating elements of various methodologies, it has yet tried to declare a territory that is all its own. (The rhetoric of exclusion is very much under attack, but has by no means capitulated.) The German writers represented here had a quite different vision of their task, seeking to combat rather than pursue specialization. This was the case both in practice and in principle. In the practical sense, the direct personal contacts and exchanges between such figures as Schelling, Hegel, Schleiermacher, the Schlegels, Goethe, and Fichte (to name but a few) made for a high level of 'interdisciplinary' (as we must now say) writing. Poetry, drama, criticism and philosophy were all circulated and held within a coherent social circuit, to a degree that has probably never been matched in any period of British or American culture. And, in principle and as a matter of policy, the agreed goal of intellectual inquiry was often held to be a *whole* system that would explain and contain all its various parts. The grand systems of Schelling and Hegel are explicit in their attempts to account for the whole of life and history, and Kant's more refined propaedeutic method is no less totalistic in its project of describing the first principles according to which all questions must be asked and all forms of knowledge understood. The ambition toward wholeness appears in its most extreme form (though not in Kant) as an attempt to establish the ultimate identity of art and science, whose imminent disjunction was beginning to preoccupy these writers as it later preoccupied Richards and Leavis. Schopenhauer, for one, strongly denied this identity: science belongs the world of experience, governed by the fourfold principle of sufficient reason, and art by definition takes us outside it. But he is here reacting to the strong claims of those of his contemporaries who were touched by the spirit of the *Naturphilosophie*, those for whom self and world, art and science, the human and the natural, are all merely manifestations of a single, indwelling identity. Thus Schelling proposes that philosophy and science will return to the poetic origin from which they originally derived, and Friedrich Schlegel anticipates the eventual unity of science, poetry, and philosophy (*Critical Fragments*, no. 115).

The attempt to construct a totality out of the different forms of human knowledge and inquiry was matched, and for similar reasons, by an effort at healing the divisions within the individual mind. The aesthetic experience, particularly, provides for the psyche something completely different from what occurs when it engages with the empirical world, whether of objects or of other selves. There we are ruled by interest, needs and desires, the things that divide us from others and from our better selves. If our relation to the world is thus appetitive, we can only appreciate it in terms of the success or failure of gratification. And the priority or habit of an interested attitude to the world is encouraged rather than discouraged by a social contract founded in divided labour and by what Schiller called "specialized knowledge". This destroys both individual peace of mind and the prospect of social consensus. This is why Kant defines the judgement of taste in terms of the absence of any personal interest whatsoever (*CJ*, §2); it is this which allows us to assume or project its universality. Take away what divides one person from another, and what remains may be assumed to be common. Thus, in Schiller's words, "only the aesthetic mode of communication unites society, because it relates to that which is common to all" (*AE*, p. 215; and below, p. 146). A similar obsession with the value of disinterest appears throughout the writings in this volume. For Friedrich Schlegel, one can only write well about something when one is no longer "preoccupied" with it, when one can enter "the mood that surveys everything and rises infinitely above all limitations" (*Critical Fragments*, nos. 37, 42). Irony, at its most cultivated level, allows us to stand above and outside ourselves. Correspondingly, for Schlegel's brother August Wilhelm, that which brings about "universality of mind", and leads us beyond "all personal predilections and blind habits", is called "criticism" (see below, p. 254). Schopenhauer finds in art and genius the path beyond the abyss of particular desires governed by the will, and Hegel, who agreed with Schopenhauer about very little, agreed with him in this, that art frees us from the practical interests of desire, as it restrains and educates our passions and our impulses.

For almost all of these writers, those aspects of our lives that are subject to the determinations of interest are connected to our identities as material beings, as biological organisms and competitively situated social creatures. The aesthetic is thus almost by definition anti-materialistic, since it must remove us from the pressures of this part of our lives. It is because art is always at *some* level dependent upon material embodiment that it cannot, for Hegel, serve as the ultimate vehicle of spirit. This seems to present something of a problem for the writers who wanted to privilege the aesthetic. If art has to employ the very representational forms *(Vorstellungen)* that we also associate with things in the world, how can we be kept from confusing the two, in variously refined tendencies toward fetishism and the Pygmalion syndrome?

Again, it is Kant who offers the exemplary solution to this problem, developed by a number of those who came after. In the aesthetic judgement we experience a pleasure that must have nothing to do with the availability of the representations before us in empirical form. What we enjoy is pure representation, or form; and not form simply in and for itself (a qualification Kant's readers have often missed), but in its capacity for communication, *as* form, to others. This argument stands as the 'origin' of a great many later varieties of formalism which rely upon a psychological criterion of value (as opposed to those which proposed some access to an Ideal, as Schopenhauer, for example, did). It brings with it certain consequences and priorities. It requires the claim that true art cannot be didactic; or, that what we respond to properly as aesthetic is not that dimension of art that might happen to be didactic. As Schiller puts it, "subject matter . . . always has a limiting effect upon the spirit, and it is only from form that true aesthetic freedom can be looked for " (*AE*, p. 155; and below, p. 144). The same emphasis tends toward the idea that artistic excellence is the result of a perceived harmony *between* representations, i.e., a happy subsumption of parts within wholes, at least within the aesthetics of the beautiful (though not of the sublime). We derive pleasure from the structural integrity of a whole, not from its availability as an object of empirical consumption (which it may still of course resemble). Lessing's *Laocoon* contains a very important discussion of this topic, and argues that the perceived integration of parts into wholes in space may actually be impossible in poetry, which is committed to temporality and to sequence. The plastic arts are the true medium of the beautiful, and this explains why it is that

Kant also refers to spatial forms (mostly, in fact, the forms of nature) rather than to poetry in his own exposition of it, and why he is so careful to limit his account of organic form to natural organisms developing through time, wherein efficient and final causes must be thought to be operating simultaneously: the organization of nature "has nothing analogous to any causality known to us" (*CJ*, §65). Despite this cautious reservation, we can yet see how tempting such an analogy might have been to a generation of writers many of whom were committed to the search for a synthesis of art and nature, and who would thus be very keen indeed to propose an organic form for the the work of art. Strictly speaking, this proposition confuses the synchronic perception of parts-in-whole that characterizes the beautiful (as explained by Kant and Lessing) with the diachronic teleology of nature that even poetry, itself a temporal medium, cannot replicate, being made by men. The confusion nonetheless became quite popular. Coleridge's much-quoted definition of the "symbol" as "itself a living part in that Unity, of which it is the representative" (1972, p. 30) appears to have been immediately offered as a theological rather than an aesthetic discrimination, but it specifies a paradigm that has often been applied in the evaluation of works of art, and conspicuously so by Coleridge himself. Novels, plays, poems, literary characters all start to be judged according to whether they satisfy a standard of wholeness projected through both space and time. Here is a classic example from Friedrich Schlegel's essay *On Goethe's 'Meister'*:

> The differing nature of the individual sections should be able to throw a great deal of light on the organization of the whole. But in progressing appropriately from the parts to the whole, observation and analysis must not get lost in over-minute detail. Rather analysis must pause, as if the detail were merely a matter of simple parts, at those major sections whose independence is also maintained by their free treatment, and by their shaping and transformation of what they have taken over from the previous section; and whose inner, unintentional homogeneity and original unity the poet himself has acknowledged in using the most various, though always poetic, means, in a deliberate effort to shape them into a rounded whole. The development within the individual sections ensures the overall coherence, and in pulling them together, the poet confirms their variety. And in this way each essential part of the single and indivisible novel becomes a system in itself.
>
> (see below, pp. 201–2)

Seldom has the case been better made. Schlegel is well aware that even in an organic model, some parts are more important than others, and it is upon these that we must concentrate. At the same time, the rhetoric of total formation – never a word or an apostrophe out of place – is preserved, as it has been preserved as both the goal and the nightmare of much subsequent literary criticism. Jeal Paul Richter writes in a similar spirit when he claims that the imagination "unites all parts into wholes and transforms all parts of the world into worlds. It totalizes everything" (see

below, p. 293). Solger's discussion of the symbol obeys the same impera-
tives, uniting parts and wholes both in space and through time.

We have seen that it is representational rather than empirical form that
is at the heart of the aesthetic experience, which must always be preserved
from our tendencies to fetishize, to mistake our subjective and creative
responses for things in themselves, objects in the world. This explains
another prominent (though not uncontested) claim made in these writings:
the claim that poetry (or, sometimes, music) is superior to the other art
forms. This claim also has underwritten a great many of the assumptions
of twentieth-century critics. Lessing implies that poetry is a more flexible
and comprehensive art than sculpture, since it is not limited to the con-
straints of an atemporal, spatial form. While sculpture and painting must
always *show* what they mean to communicate, poetry can *imply*. Homer signals Helen's beauty by describing the responses of the Trojan elders rather
than by trying to picture it in itself, in which attempt he would inevitably
fall short. Kant even more emphatically places poetry at the top of the scale
of the fine arts, because it gives the most "freedom to the imagination"
and allows the mind to understand itself as "free, spontaneous, and independent of determination by nature" (*CJ*, §53). And for Hegel, even
though it is classical sculpture that stands as the highest embodiment of
art *as art*, it is poetry whose historical prominence in the modern period
signifies the imminent passage of *Geist* out of the realm of representation
as such. Poetry is more productive of self-consciousness than the other arts
because the conversion of verbal signs into representational images calls
for an effort on the part of a reader. Passive contemplation is less likely
than it might be in our response to sculpture or painting, where the forms
are already there before us. Of all the arts, except music, poetry is the
furthest from material form; unlike music (Schopenhauer's candidate for
superiority), it still preserves a semantic dimension, and thus has intellectual potential for the mind's coming to knowledge of itself.

The above commitment to the importance of self-consciousness is, of
course, very much in line with the mainstream of Protestant doctrine, and
it takes its most famous form in the various theories of irony to be deduced
from the writings of Friedrich Schlegel, Solger, Richter and others, where
the rhetoric of suspension and evasion is always veering toward its opposite
pole in absolute commitment, as Kierkegaard, for one, clearly understood.
Hegel psychologized the art-instinct itself as the result of "man's rational
need to lift the inner and outer world into his spiritual consciousness as
an object in which he recognizes again his own self" (see below, p. 361).
And it is this common foundation in self-consciousness that holds together
(though not as cause and effect) the aesthetic and the moral in Kant's critical system. In the aesthetic judgement, the mind experiences "a feeling of
the free play of the powers of representation" (*CJ*, §9), the same "free
play" that occupies the center of Schiller's argument. Schiller images the

human mind as always torn between two drives, one toward pure content (the real), the other toward pure form (the ideal). It is the aesthetic drive that profitably disturbs our exclusive focus upon either extreme, and keeps us from becoming either vulgar materialists or raving fanatics. As we pass from the sensuous to the rational in our habitual mental operations, we experience a "middle disposition" in which we are "momentarily *free of all determination* whatsoever" (*AE*, p. 141; see below, p. 141). This is the aesthetic moment, strictly defined, and the more we emerge out of it with any specific disposition toward a physical or ideal end, the less purely aesthetic that moment has been (*AE*, p. 153).

In these ways, by the positioning of form as something enjoyed purely as representation and for the communicability of that representation, and by the emphasis upon the process of free play, Kant and Schiller avoid locating the definition of the aesthetic either in fixed objects in the world or in fixed states within the individual mind. But this by no means solved the problem of consensus that was such a source of anxiety for the writers of their generation, as they themselves well knew. Kant insists that the agreement of others in the aesthetic judgement is by definition imputed but never postulated; that is, universality is a psychologically projected rather than an empirically demanded attribute. This judgement is not subsumed within the concepts of the understanding, but we behave instinctively as if it were. Schiller, for his part, is clear that among his own generation no poet or artist can entertain the hope of pleasing universally. The distinction between naive and sentimental poetry is based upon a profound tension within the human mind itself. Each takes both positive and negative forms, differently weighted at different times. But the dichotomy is always there, and those capable of experiencing or appreciating the brief moments of synthesis or indifference that the aesthetic moment affords are likely to be few and far between. The existence of authentic disinterest does not then guarantee consensus; it merely allows us to project it or to set an ideal example. In this way the very aspiration toward intersubjectivity is itself held within the psychology of the subject. This paradox suggests a covert continuity between Kant and Schiller and those writers who stressed the integrity of pure subjectivity. Friedrich Schlegel and Schopenhauer, for example, never imply that genius is to be sought among the many, even if it is in principle open to all. In this way they differ from Kant in degree rather than in kind; their skepticism about the passage from the private to the public is merely more emphatic than that of their precursor.

There was a further perceived threat to the achievement of consensus widely held to be a consequence of the general disposition of German thought toward speculative idealism: the threat of fanaticism (*Schwärmerei*), which Kant characterized as an "undermining disease" (*CJ*, remark following §29) transporting the subject beyond the normal spheres of experience into a pseudo-visionary state. At the end of *On Naive and Sentimental Poetry*

Schiller identified the "false idealism" of the "fantast" as an even more dangerous contemporary tendency than the vulgar empiricism of the materialist. Because it is completely uprooted from any base in the real world, it leads to "an infinite fall into a bottomless abyss and can only terminate in complete destruction" (see below, p. 173). This fear of fanaticism contributes to the fairly common assertion by these writers that "genius" must be understood as an intensification of the normal or potentially normal state of mind, rather than as some visitation from another world. Kant thus argues that in the true artist genius must co-exist with taste, and that genius without taste cannot produce exemplary forms. If sacrifices are to be made by one or the other, they should be made by genius – by the exceptional rather than by the normative determination (*CJ*, §§48–50). For Hegel, genius by definition gives form to that which is absolutely rational within its own historical moment, even though the artist is not consciously aware of that rationality. Even Schopenhauer, who is convinced that the productions of genius will almost never be understood as such, thanks to the disabling worldliness of our fellow beings, is quite clear that these productions are completely objective.

If, as I have suggested, many of these writers are aspiring, through the postulate of disinterest, toward a consensus that they simultaneously theorize as strictly beyond the reach of the aesthetic, then two questions arise, as they indeed arose for Kant and his successors. What is the relation of the aesthetic to the moral, and how can art function to regenerate society, if at all? The relation between the aesthetic and the moral is one of the most difficult and disputed arguments of the *Critique of Judgement*. Moral and aesthetic judgements are similar in that both involve the subject in the projection of a universality that cannot be empirically adjudicated; in neither case does the actual disagreement of others make us change our minds. But Kant is very skeptical about close causal connections between the two. First, it is the sublime rather than the beautiful that is closer to the moral experience, because it is further from contact with the ordinary concepts of the understanding, and thus depends upon a less secure assumption of universality (§§23, 29). The stoical nature of Kant's ethics demands a strong negative correlation between morality and interest; and, while the beautiful is merely independent of interest, the sublime may actually threaten it. Thus it is closer to the moral. Many among those writing after Kant were to miss or underplay this distinction, in an attempt to bring the beautiful and the moral closer together.

Second, if there is any potential causal sequence working between the aesthetic and the moral in Kant's exposition, then it is the moral that is prior to the aesthetic, rather than the other way around. Without the preparatory experience of moral culture, the sublime is likely to seem merely terrifying. In the sphere of the beautiful, he does allow that a sensitivity to the beauty of nature is "always a mark of a good soul", and may indicate a personality "favourable to the moral feeling" (*CJ*, §42). But, as we have seen, the beautiful allows for only a weak connection with the moral.

Kant's skepticism about the relation between the aesthetic and the moral was widely received as an adverse and divisive strategy. Again, it was Schiller who proposed the exemplary alternative. In his 1793 essay 'On Grace and Dignity' he developed the redefinition of the "beautiful soul" (*schöne Seele*) to embody precisely the synthesis between spontaneity and moral behavior that Kant had held in suspense (see Schiller, 1943–, XX, 287f.). Again, in *On Naive and Sentimental Poetry* he tried to strengthen the ties between the appreciation of nature and the moral idea, a connection that had only been tentatively affirmed by Kant. But Schiller is scrupulous in preserving the distinction between the moral potential of the aesthetic and anything like didacticism, though he does at times propose that art can heal or resolve the tensions generated by human nature in general, and by modern society in particular.

This leads us to the second question: what, if any, is the force of the aesthetic for social reform or general enlightenment? For Hegel, art records rather than resolves the necessary tensions immanent in the evolution of history throughout the past, even as it functions for the individual mind as the symptom of "man's rational need to lift the inner and outer world into his spiritual consciousness as an object in which he recognizes again his own self" (see below, p. 361). It is always the servant of *Geist* and the forerunner of philosophy, but it does operate to fulfil an urgent subjective need experienced as such at all times. Fichte, more enthusiastically, saw in poetry the potential for "flooding the life of all with the spiritual culture that has been attained" (1968, p. 68), but his extended remarks (selections from which are reprinted in this anthology) on the role of the author in disseminating that spiritual culture in the present are much more skeptical. Like Shelley and Schopenhauer, he suggests that the proper audience for the pure idea is likely to be discovered only in later generations. Friedrich Schlegel made the notorious and apparently extreme claim that the three great tendencies of his age were the French Revolution, Fichte's philosophy, and Goethe's *Meister* (*Athenäum Fragments*, no. 216), and opined that the function of art might include "exalting politicians and economists into artists" (*Ideas*, no. 54). But it is by no means clear what causal energies he saw in these tendencies, nor does it follow that politicians who had become artists would remain politicians in the usual sense of the word. Most affirmatively of all, the young Schelling saw in art the unique means for making the insights of philosophy available to the wider public, thanks to its dependence upon forms that can be represented in the world rather than merely thought or argued. This idea was always, however, more successfully articulated in theory than in any account of actual or potential practice.

The most detailed attempt at such a theory of practice is perhaps to be found in Schiller, who poses without solving (or intending to solve) the question of the relation of personal development to public welfare. It is "man's inner being" that must first be reformed by the aesthetic education (*AE*, p. 59; and below, p. 137). The effects of such reform, working through example and upon the leisure hours of others, can in theory rejuvenate at least a small class of fellow humans. But the very condition that preserves the purity of the aesthetic experience, its identity not as product but as a process or ideal that can never be fully realized in actuality – "for man can never escape his dependence upon conditioning forces" (*AE*, p. 153) – means that it is never likely to be available to large numbers of people. Few indeed are those who can achieve "a disinterested and unconditional appreciation of pure semblance" (*AE*, p. 205; and below, pp. 145– 6). The aesthetic state that Schiller describes at the end of his treatise must then exist in the everyday world more as a utopian imperative than as an anticipated social development. Similarly, it is the commitment to an ideal whose attainment is always deferred that characterizes the sentimental poet in the second of Schiller's great treatises; and it is the sentimental poet who is most representative of the modern condition. The properly balanced aspiration toward the ideal is always threatened by a tendency to decline into abstract enthusiasm, unless it is leavened by just enough of the naive to guarantee its hold on reality. Whether a significantly numerous class of poets and artists and readers, able to avoid the limitations of both the labouring and the intellectual classes, could ever come into being, is a question that Schiller deliberately refuses to answer. Coleridge's ideas about the role of an enlightened clerisy, and the self-definitions put about by the Cambridge Apostles, were both attempts to meet this perceived need in nineteenth-century culture. But Schiller himself, by ending his second essay with a discussion of the "psychological antagonism" between real and ideal drives that he proposes as basic to human nature (see below, p. 171), even as it is intensified by the particular circumstances of modern life, seems much less sanguine.

IV

The foregoing account is meant to offer at least a few major points of departure for readers approaching this material for the first time. It does not, of course, pretend to any completeness. No more is the anthology itself anything more than a radical selection from the broad field of German eighteenth- and nineteenth-century aesthetics and criticism. Some writers who were unarguably important are not represented at all – Baumgarten, Winckelmann, Tieck, Humboldt, Schleiermacher and so forth. And those who are represented are not represented in their entirety. Kant, for example, cuts a very different figure when read in his pre-critical and non-critical phases, that is, outside the three great *Critiques* for which he is principally known. Thus in the *Anthropology* he makes clear that "the field of our *obscure* representations is immeasurable, while our clear ones are only the infinitesimally few points on this map that lie open to consciousness: our mind is like an immense map with only a few points *illuminated*" (1974, p. 16). This conviction lends a kind of desperate dignity to the transcendental philosophy, concerned as it is to plot those few points with absolute precision. Without some knowledge of Kant's other writings, we will miss this dimension of its ambition.

A few words about the difficulty of much of the following material are also in place here. "People are always complaining that German authors write for such a small circle, and even sometimes just for themselves", says Friedrich Schlegel (*Athenäum Fragments*, no. 275). Some writers, like Schlegel himself, seem aware and even proud of this difficulty, whether as a means of preserving the strict integrity of their arguments, or as a technique for calling forth the co-creative energies of an engaged and perhaps even enraged reader. Kant claimed that he quite deliberately resorted to the "sheer force" of "insight" rather than to the "free play of mind and wit" (E. Cassirer, 1981, p. 140), wishing to avoid any suspicion that he might have been trying to "beguile the reader" into any unearned acquiescence. Kant's own *Critique of Judgement* is itself perhaps the most obvious example of a frequent tendency in these writers to avoid examples – empirical instances that might serve to distract our attention away from the *a priori* concerns of the transcendental method toward some expectation of a catalogue of good and bad works of art. Aware of the problems of this strict focus upon the subjective consciousness rather than the contingent vehicle, Fichte tried hard to write different versions of his system for the perusal of different audiences, one of which might be able to follow the sophisticated logic of philosophical argument, while another could only expect to comprehend an exoteric statement of its general conclusions. Hegel remains difficult for many modern readers, despite the degree to which so many of his general emphases and ideas have passed into common knowledge. These difficulties, and others like them, led to widespread misunderstandings and frustrations among the first generations of readers, especially in Britain. Crabb Robinson half complained of Schelling's "most profound abstraction & enthusiastick mysticism" (1929, p. 117), and Hazlitt attributed not a little of Coleridge's obscurity to his having "wandered into Germany and lost himself in the labyrinths of the Hartz Forest and of the Kantean philosophy, and amongst the cabalistic names of Fichte and Schelling and Lessing and God knows who" (1930, p. 732). Difficulty often generates mythology, and it is thus not entirely surprising to discover the widespread suspicion among British contemporaries that German philosophy was in some sense directly responsible for the principles and practices of the French Revolution.

The question of influences: a guide to further reading

Apart from the obvious case of the influence of the following philosophers
on each other, which has been dealt with specifically in the endnotes, there
are other points to be made about the general subject of influence. Neither
space nor the editor's competence permits any analysis of the relation of
the great Idealists to subsequent explorations in strictly philosophical aesthetics: Croce, Nietzsche, the Scottish Hegelians, Bradley, Dewey and so
forth. The very close relations subsisting between the philosophers and
their friends and contemporaries in German Romantic literature have
been indicated already. The major interest of the English-speaking reader
must lie, I assume, in the influence of these writers upon the literature of
Britain and America.

This is a difficult and complicated subject, and apart from describing a
few of the less obvious cases much of what I shall have to say will consist
of referring the reader to work already available. The contribution of German thought to the growth of the transcendentalist movement in nineteenth-century America is well known, and substantial efforts have been
made in recovering the details of its incorporation: see Vogel (1955), Pochmann (1957), and Wellek (1965). In the case of English literature the presence or absence of direct connections has been much harder to assess. The
easy cases are signalled by direct reference or translation, but in the crucial
case of Coleridge, for example, the whole question of the exact degree and
kind of assimilation of German thought remains an open one. We do not
yet have reliable modern editions of all the major works, and the task of
producing them is not made easier by Coleridge's tendency to avoid mention of his specific sources, a fact which itself has sparked off famous con-
troversies over whether or not we should consider him a 'plagiarist'. Moreover, in the first three decades of the nineteenth century Coleridge is
struggling to come to grips with a mode of thought hardly familiar to an
English speaker, much less popular. The general attitude to German philosophy before about 1830 seems to have been one of vaguely hostile curiosity. Curiosity, because many people had a sense that something important might be going on, but hostile because it was going on in an unstable
and unfamiliar language, and because such of its apparent conclusions as
did 'translate' were often felt to be at odds with British tastes.

Generally it is safe to assume that, with the exception of the well-known
cases, such influence as did pass over from Germany before 1830 was relatively indirect or coincidental. The reader familiar with English Romantic
writing will quite commonly find in what follows ideas or arguments teas-
ingly close to those discovered in English literature at the time; take, for
example, the similarity of some among Schelling's arguments and even his
images and metaphors to those evident in Shelley's *A Defence of Poetry*.
Shelley did read Black's translation of A.W. Schlegel's lectures, and Schle-

gel learned much from Schelling; and of course we may refer these connections to the *Zeitgeist* or "spirit of the age", a phrase Hazlitt and Shelley themselves used in explaining the relations of art and history. But in this period the spirit of the age in Germany had been significantly formed by a wholesale incorporation, through almost immediate translation, of all the important eighteenth-century British treatises on aesthetics, ethics, political theory, and philosophy at large (see Price, 1932, and Price and Price, 1934, 1955), as well as most of the significant novels and journals. Kant and his successors thus quite literally stand in the tradition of Hume, Shaftesbury, Addison, Hutcheson and so on, just as do the English Romantic writers. This adds to the difficulty of estimating exactly how much someone like Coleridge might have taken directly from the Germans, rather than from his own reading of the likes of Locke, Cudworth, and Berkeley, as well as of the enduring sources available to both cultures: Plato, Aristotle, Plotinus, Augustine and so forth. Perhaps the most probable general hypothesis would imagine a Coleridge who was already primed by his own readings to receive the maximum value from the arguments he found in the Germans, recognizing them as derived from and contributing to a common tradition. This would help explain why Coleridge might have seen the German influence as less significant than many of his later critics have argued it to be, and why he might have estimated its proponents in a surprising way, as when Crabb Robinson reports as follows:

He adheres to Kant, notwithstanding all Schelling has written, and maintains that from the latter he has gained no new ideas. All Schelling has said, Coleridge has either thought himself, or found in Jacob Boehme.   Robinson (1869), I, 388

Not that the originality of the German tradition should be slighted. It was a definite originality, and the gradual recognition of it was among the reasons for the increasing excitement about all things German noticeable in the later nineteenth century; or at least, some things German, as they suited the needs of the time. The most difficult period for the literary historian is the period of partial or possible assimilation, before German thought becomes unarguably fashionable and unashamedly celebrated. There is a considerable literature to help us through this period. Studies of Coleridge in particular have come more and more to recognize the question of the German influence: see Orsini (1969), McFarland (1969), Shaffer (1975), Wheeler (1980), among others. Even Shelley has received attention in this context: see Klapper (1975). Hirsch (1960) has written of a deliberately 'indirect' common ground between Wordsworth and Schelling, and there are a number of general books on the relation of German to English thought: see Wellek (1931, 1965), Stokoe (1926), and Ashton (1980). The direct and indirect legacy of Schiller is discussed in *AE*, pp. cxliv–clxxxi, and in Pick (1961). Important thematic studies emphasizing the continuities between German and English literature include M. Brown

(1979), Stockley (1929), and Handwerk (1985). See also the two books by
Abrams (1953, 1971) and the useful account of theories of the imagination
by Engell (1981).

There were several contemporary accounts of developments in German
philosophy: Drummond (1805) speaks scathingly of a popular vogue for
Kant among those who "know metaphysics *a priori,* who possess an intuitive faculty, who see visions of pure reason, and who carried the whole
science of geometry in their heads, before they even looked into Euclid"
(p. 358). He seems to be working largely with a French defence of Kant
written by Villars rather than with Kant himself, and finds his disciples
"unable to convey any clear idea of the meaning of their master" (p. 367).
Dugald Stewart, writing in the next decade, continues to rely largely on
French accounts of Kant, though he has seen enough German by 1827 to
suggest that its convoluted structures might be responsible for the confu-
sions in Kant's thoughts: see Stewart (1854), IV, 53. In 1815 Stewart had
claimed to be able to make nothing of Fichte, and to find in Schelling only
a "transcendental mysticism" (I, 418–19). Even where glimpses of the
authentic Kant do emerge in the English language before 1830 or so, they
are not much concerned with aesthetics, and it is safest to assume that any
parallels between the English and German traditions in this respect are a
result of the common tradition explained above. Stokoe (1926) argues that
there was a greater popular awareness of German literature in the 1790s
than one might have expected, but with the protracted state of war
between Britain and the continent such contacts could not have been easily
maintained, and anyway Wellek (1931) makes clear that they did not
involve much cognisance of the critical philosophy. The translation from
the French of Madame de Staël's *Germany,* in 1813, provided something of
a ready-reference guide to the subject, but few readers could have been
converted by the following summary of Kant's thoughts:

Kant wished to establish primitive truths and spontaneous activity in the soul, conscience in morals, and the *ideal* in the arts.   III, 73

There follows a quite extraordinary reading of the argument of the third
Critique:

Kant maintains, that there are in poetry, and in the arts which are capable, as
poetry is, of painting sentiments by images, two kinds of beauty: one which may be
referred to time and to this life; the other, to eternity and infinity.   III, 89

This second sort of beauty is "the realization of that image which is constantly present to the soul" (p. 89), and its universality is ensured by virtue
of all men having in their souls "sentiments of celestial origin, which
beauty awakens, and of which it excites the enjoyment" (pp. 90–1). Fichte
and Schelling fare a little better in their summarized identities, and, in fact,
Madame de Staël's account is intended to be a positive one. She regards it

as "infinitely better for the literature of a country, that its poetical system should be founded upon philosophical notions, even if they are a little abstract, than upon simple external rules" (p. 143). At the same time, she has to regret that such philosophical speculations "only place the ignorant and the enlightened at too great a distance from each other. There are too many new, and not enough common, ideas circulating in Germany, for the knowledge of men and things" (pp. 169–70).

In estimating the reaction to German thought in England, we must of course remember that we are faced with what is even more fundamentally a reaction to Germanically inclined Englishmen, like Peacock's Mr. Flosky (Coleridge) in *Nightmare Abbey* (published in 1818). Hazlitt, for example, never had much time for Kant and his kind, but he rises to heights of vituperation when the time comes to review Coleridge's *Biographia Literaria*, accusing Kant of publishing "the most wilful and monstruous absurdity that was ever invented": see Hazlitt (1930–4), XVI, 123. De Quincey, who himself translated Kant, offers a more reasoned view of the situation:

everything yet published on the subject of Kant in the English language errs by one of two defects. Either it is mere nonsense, in a degree possible only to utter and determined ignorance of the German language; or it is so close a translation of the *ipsissima verba* of Kant as to offer no sort of assistance to an uninitiated student, to say nothing of the barbarous effect produced by a German structure of sentence and a terminology altogether new.   De Quincey (1889–90), VIII, 87

This was written in 1830, by which time some of the wisdom of hindsight had come to be available. De Quincey details his own struggles with the Germans in the *Autobiography*, reporting how he found the "negative" spirit of the first *Critique* so hard to take (II, 86); like most readers of his generation he wanted more than sound Enlightenment advice about what *not* to believe. But he found positive things too: the harmony of philosophy with mathematics, the doctrine of the categories, and the account of the functions of practical reason (II, 106); and by 1823 he is blaming Coleridge for obfuscating doctrines that are much clearer in their original Kantian formulations (X, 77). De Quincey's later writings already reveal an interest in German Idealism for its potential availability in criticizing the condition of England, as he refers to "the unpopularity of *all* speculative philosophy whatsoever, no matter how treated, in a country where the structure and tendency of society impress upon the whole activities of the nation a direction almost exclusively practical" (IV, 324–5). Here, the very mysteries that had perplexed and were to continue to perplex even sympathetic readers are focussed as a criticism of utilitarian society, and German philosophy has entered the public debate in nineteenth-century Britain. When Morris speaks of the capacities of art to heal the disastrous psychic effects of the division of labour, and Arnold speaks of the "free play of the mind" at its healthiest moments (as Leavis was to do after him), neither of them sees any need to invoke Schiller, or Kant, or Fichte. The process of naturalization has already taken place, partly through the efforts of Carlyle and Coleridge (among others), partly because the terms of German Idealist aesthetics have been brought fully into the mainstream as a challenge to the spirit of the age in Victorian England.

General studies

Important surveys of the period containing discussions of German writers include E. Cassirer (1945, 1951), Gay (1966, 1969), and Nivelle (1955). Surveys and topic studies that are entirely devoted to Germany and its literature include Bell (1984), Bruford (1935, 1949, 1962), Hatfield (1964), Kohlschmidt (1975), Lange (1982), Menhennet (1973), Pascal (1953), Reed (1980), and Ward (1974).

Part 1

Lessing

Gotthold Ephraim Lessing

(1729–1781)

Lessing was born in 1729 at Kamenz in Saxony, the son of a Lutheran pastor. He seemed destined for a distinguished career in theology, for which he enrolled at Leipzig University, but his interests quickly moved to literature and the theatre, and he devoted himself increasingly to dramatic composition and to literary journalism. On his move to Berlin in 1748, Lessing became one of the first Germans to support himself by writing (mainly journalistic criticism for the growing educated public of largely middle-class readers). His greatest journalistic success was the periodical *Letters Concerning Recent Literature (Briefe, die neueste Literatur betreffend,* 1759–65), to which he and his friends Friedrich Nicolai and Moses Mendelssohn were the chief contributors. Their literary criticism set new standards in Germany, and did much to end the French domination of German literary culture. Lessing's championship of Shakespeare prepared the way for the Shakespeare cult of Herder and the *Sturm und Drang* movement of the 1770s.

Lessing's appetite for analytical criticism and polemics found new outlets in antiquarian studies during his sojourn in Breslau (1760–5) as secretary to a Prussian general. The chief fruit of these was the *Laocoon.* His years in Hamburg (1767–70) were chiefly devoted to dramatic criticism (*Hamburg Dramaturgy,* 1767–9), in which he attempted to reconcile Aristotelian and neo-classical models with the realism he was himself cultivating, under the influence of Diderot's dramatic theory, in his own dramas (*Minna von Barnhelm,* 1767; *Emilia Galotti,* 1772).

During the last phase of his life (1770–81) as librarian to the Duke of Brunswick in Wolfenbüttel, Lessing was able to develop his already formidable learning in numerous disciplines, including philosophy, history, philology, and theology. After 1777, he became embroiled in acrimonious polemics with various theologians as a result of his publishing the *Fragments* of the freethinker H.S. Reimarus, which criticised the Bible from a position of deistic rationalism. One positive result of the controversy was Lessing's last drama, *Nathan the Wise,* with its message of enlightened cosmopolitanism and religious tolerance.

Lessing's forceful personality and rigorous analytical intellect made him the dominant figure in German literary life before Goethe's rise to fame. His three major plays helped to end the provincialism of German literature, his work as a critic ended the hegemony of French literary models in Germany, and his *Laocoon* gave neo-classical poetics a new philosophical basis and a more secure foundation in the literature of ancient Greece – a foundation on which the Weimar classicism of Goethe and Schiller was to build in the closing decade of the century.

Further reading

The standard edition of Lessing's works is that of Lachmann and Muncker (1886–1924), which also contains Lessing's correspondence. There are less complete, but useful modern editions by Rilla (second edition, 1968) and Göpfert (1970–9). English translations include those by Steel (1930) of the *Laocoon, Nathan the Wise,* and *Minna von Barnhelm,* by Zimmern (1962) of the *Hamburg Dramaturgy,* and by Chadwick (1956) of selected theological writings. The standard biography is that of Schmidt (fourth edition, 1923). The best general accounts in English are Garland (second edition, 1962) and F.A. Brown (1971). Robertson (second edition, 1965) deals with the dramatic theory, Allison (1966) with philosophical aspects, and Wellbery (1984) with Lessing's aesthetics. See also Mitchell (1986) and Nisbet (1979).

HBN

From
Laocoon
or
On the Limits of Painting and Poetry[1]

1766

Translated by W.A. Steel (slightly modified).

German text in *Sämtliche Schriften,* edited by Lachmann and Muncker (1886–1924), IX, 1–177.

Preface

The first who likened painting and poetry to each other must have been a man of delicate perception, who found that both arts affected him in a similar manner. Both, he realised, present to us appearance as reality, absent things as present; both deceive, and the deceit of either is pleasing.

A second sought to penetrate to the essence of the pleasure and discovered that in both it flows from one source. Beauty, the conception of which we at first derive from bodily objects, has general rules which can be applied to various things: to actions, to thoughts, as well as to forms.

A third, who reflected on the value and the application of these general rules, observed that some of them were predominant rather in painting, others rather in poetry; that, therefore, in the latter poetry could help out painting, in the former painting help out poetry, with illustrations and examples.

The first was the amateur; the second the philosopher; the third the critic.

The two former could not easily make a false use either of their feeling or of their conclusions. But in the remarks of the critic, on the other hand, almost everything depends on the justice of their application to the individual case; and, where there have been fifty witty to one clear-eyed critic, it would have been a miracle if this application had at all times been made with the circumspection needful to hold the balance true between the two arts.

Supposing that Apelles and Protogenes[2] in their lost treatises upon painting confirmed and illustrated the rules of the same by the already settled rules of poetry, then one can certainly believe it must have been done with the moderation and exactitude with which we still find Aristotle, Cicero, Horace, Quintilian, in their writings, applying the principles and practice of painting to eloquence and poetry. It is the prerogative of the ancients, in everything to do neither too much nor too little.

But we moderns in several things have considered outselves their betters, when we transformed their pleasant little byeways to highroads, even if the shorter and safer highroads shrink again to footpaths as they lead us through the wilds.

The startling antithesis of the Greek Voltaire,[3] that painting is a dumb poetry, and poetry a vocal painting, certainly was not to be found in any manual. It was a sudden inspiration, such as Simonides had more than once; the true element in it is so illuminating that we are inclined to ignore what in it is false or doubtful.

Nevertheless, the ancients did not ignore it. Rather, whilst they confined the claim of Simonides solely to the effect of the two arts, they did not omit to point out that, notwithstanding the complete similarity of this effect, they were yet distinct, both in their subjects and in the manner of their imitation (ὕλῃ καὶ τρόποις μιμήσεως).[4]

But entirely as if no such difference existed, many of our most recent critics have drawn from that correspondence between painting and poetry the crudest conclusions in the world. Now they force poetry into the narrower bounds of painting; and again, they propose to painting to fill the whole wide sphere of poetry. Everything that is right for one is to be granted to the other also; everything which in the one pleases or displeases is necessarily to please or displease in the other; and, obsessed by this notion, they utter in the most confident tone the shallowest judgements; and we see them, in dealing with the works of poets and painters beyond reproach, making it a fault if they deviate from one another, and casting blame now on this side and now on that, according as they themselves have a taste for poetry or for painting.

Indeed, this newer criticism has in part seduced the virtuosos themselves. It has engendered in poetry the rage for description, and in painting the rage for allegorising, in the effort to turn the former into a speaking picture without really knowing what she can and should paint, and to turn the latter into a silent poem without considering in what measure she can express general concepts and not at the same time depart from her vocation and become a freakish kind of writing.

To counteract this false taste and these ill-founded judgements is the primary object of the pages that follow. They have come together incidentally, according to the order of my reading, instead of being built up by a methodical development of general principles.[5] They are, therefore, rather unordered *collectanea* for a book than themselves a book.

Yet I flatter myself that even as such they are not wholly to be despised. Of systematic books there is no lack amongst us Germans. Out of a few assumed definitions to deduce most logically whatever we will – this we can manage as well as any nation in the world.

Baumgarten[6] confessed that for a great part of the examples in his *Æsthetics* he was indebted to Gesner's Dictionary.[7] If my argument is not as conclusive as Baumgarten's, at all events my examples will taste more of the original sources.

As I started, as it were, from Laocoon and return to him several times, I have desired to give him a share in the superscription. Some other little digressions concerning various points in the history of ancient art contribute less to my purpose, and they only stand here because I cannot hope ever to find for them a more suitable place.

I would further remind the reader that under the name of Painting I include the plastic arts in general, and am not prepared to maintain that under the name of Poetry I may not have had some regard also to the other arts whose method of imitation is progressive.

I

The general distinguishing excellence of the Greek masterpieces in painting and sculpture Herr Winckelmann places in a noble simplicity and quiet greatness, both in arrangement and in expression. 'Just as the depths of the sea', he says,

always remain quiet, however the surface may rage, in like manner the expression in the figures of the Greek artists shows under all passions a great and steadfast soul.

This soul is depicted in the countenance of the Laocoon, and not in the countenance alone, under the most violent sufferings. The pain which discovers itself in every muscle and sinew of the body, and which, without regarding the face and other parts, one seems almost oneself to feel from the painfully contracted abdomen alone – this pain, I say, yet expresses itself in the countenance and in the entire attitude without passion. He raises no agonising cry, as Virgil sings of his Laocoon; the opening of the mouth does not permit it: much rather is it an oppressed and weary sigh, as Sadoleto[8] describes it. The pain of the body and the greatness of the soul are by the whole build of the figure distributed and, as it were, weighed out in equal parts. Laocoon suffers, but he suffers like the Philoctetes of Sophocles: his misery touches us to the soul; but we should like to be able to endure misery as this great man endures it.

The expression of so great a soul goes far beyond the fashioning which beautiful Nature gives. The artist must have felt in himself the strength of spirit which he impressed upon the marble. Greece had artist and philosopher in one person, and more than one Metrodorus.[9] Wisdom stretched out her hand to Art and breathed more than common souls into the figures that she wrought, etc., etc.[10]

The remark which is fundamental here – that the pain does not show itself in the countenance of Laocoon with the passion which one would expect from its violence – is perfectly just. This, too, is incontestable, that even in this very point in which a sciolist might judge the artist to have come short of Nature and not to have reached the true pathos of the pain: that just here, I say, his wisdom has shone out with especial brightness.

Only in the reason which Winckelmann gives for this wisdom, and in the universality of the rule which he deduces from this reason, I venture to be of a different opinion.

I confess that the disapproving side-glance which he casts on Virgil at first took me rather aback; and, next to that, the comparison with Philoctetes. I will make this my starting-point, and write down my thoughts just in the order in which they come.

'Laocoon suffers like the Philoctetes of Sophocles.' How, then, does the latter suffer? It is singular that his suffering has left us with such different impressions – the complaints, the outcry, the wild curses, with which his pain filled the camp and disturbed the sacrifices and all the sacred functions, resounded no less terribly through the desert island, as it was in part they that banished him thither. What sounds of anger, of lamentation, of despair, by which even the poet in his imitation made the theatre resound! People have found the third act of this drama disproportionately short compared with the rest. From this one gathers, say the critics, that the ancient dramatists considered an equal length of acts as of small consequence. That, indeed, I believe; but in this question I should prefer to base myself upon another example than this. The piteous outcries, the whimpering, the broken ἆ, ἆ, φεῦ, ἀτταταῖ, ὦ μοι, μοι! the whole long lines full of παπα, παπα,[11] of which this act consists and which must have been declaimed with quite other hesitations and drawings-out of utterance than are needful in a connected speech, doubtless made this act last pretty well as long in the presentation as the others. On paper it appears to the reader far shorter than it would to the listeners.

To cry out is the natural expression of bodily pain. Homer's wounded warriors not seldom fall to the ground with cries. Venus scratched screams loudly; not in order that she may be shown as the soft goddess of pleasure, but rather that suffering Nature may have her rights. For even the iron Mars, when he feels the spear of Diomedes, screams so horribly, like ten thousand raging warriors at once, that both hosts are terrified.

However high in other respects Homer raises his heroes above Nature, they yet ever remain faithful to her when it comes to the point of feeling pain and injury, and to the utterance of this feeling by cries, or tears, or abusive language. By their deeds they are creatures of a superior order, by their sensibilities mere men.

I am well aware that we Europeans of a wiser posterity know better how to control our mouth and our eyes. Politeness and dignity forbid cries and tears. The active fortitude of the first rude ages has with us been transformed into the fortitude of endurance. Yet even our own ancestors were greater in the latter than in the former. Our ancestors, however, were barbarians. To conceal all pains, to face the stroke of death with unaltered eye, to die smiling under the teeth of vipers, to bewail neither his sin nor the loss of his dearest friend, are the marks of the ancient Northern hero. Palnatoko[12] gave his Jomsburgers the command to fear nothing nor once to utter the word fear.

Not so the Greek! He both felt and feared; he uttered his pain and his trouble; he was ashamed of no human weaknesses; but none must hold him back on the way to honour or from the fulfilment of duty. What with the barbarian sprang from savagery and hardness, was wrought in him by principle. With him heroism was like the hidden sparks in the flint, which sleep quietly so long as no outward force awakes them, and take from the stone neither its clearness nor its coldness. With the barbarian, heroism was a bright devouring flame, which raged continually and consumed, or at least darkened, every other good quality in him. When Homer leads out the Trojans to battle with wild outcries, and the Greeks, on the other hand, in resolute silence, the commentators remark with justice that the poet in this wishes to depict those as barbarians and these as civilised people. I am surprised that they have not remarked in another passage a similar characteristic contrast. The opposing hosts have concluded a truce; they are busy with the burning of their dead, which on neither side takes place without hot tears: δάκρυα θερμὰ χέοντες.[13] But Priam forbids his Trojans to weep; οὐδ᾽ εἴα κλαίειν Πρίαμος μέγας.[14] He forbids them to weep, says Dacier,[15] because he dreads that they will weaken themselves too much and return to battle on the morrow with less courage. Good! But I ask, Why must Priam dread this? Why does not Agamemnon, too, give his Greeks the same command? The sense of the poet goes deeper. He would teach us that only the civilised Greek can at the same time weep and be brave, whilst the uncivilised Trojan in order to be so must first stifle all human feeling. Νεμεσσῶμαί γε μὲν οὐδὲν κλαίειν,[16] in another place, he puts in the mouth of the understanding son of wise Nestor.

It is worthy of remark that amongst the few tragedies that have come down to us from antiquity two pieces are to be found in which bodily pain is not the smallest part of the calamity that befalls the suffering hero: there is, besides the Philoctetes, the dying Hercules.[17] And even the latter Sophocles represents complaining, whining, weeping and crying aloud. Thanks to our polite neighbours, those masters of the becoming,[18] today a whimpering Philoctetes, a screaming Hercules, would be the most laughable, the most unendurable persons on the stage. It is true one of their latest dramatists has ventured on Philoctetes.[19] But would he venture to show them the true Philoctetes?

Amongst the lost dramas of Sophocles is numbered even a 'Laocoon'. Would that Fate had only granted us this Laocoon also! From the slight references made to it by some ancient grammarians it is not easy to gather how the theme was handled. Of one thing I feel sure: that the poet will not have depicted Laocoon as more of a stoic than Philoctetes and Hercules. All stoicism is untheatrical, and our pity is always proportionate to the suffering which the interesting subject expresses. If we see him bear his misery with greatness of soul, then indeed this greatness of soul will excite our admiration, but admiration is a cold emotion, whose passive wonder excludes every other warmer passion as well as every other more significant representation.

And now I come to the inference I wish to draw. If it is true that outcries on the feeling of bodily pain, especially according to the ancient Greek way of thinking, can quite well consist with a great soul; then the expression of such a soul cannot be the reason why, nevertheless, the artist in his marble refuses to imitate this crying: there must be other grounds why he deviates here from his rival, the poet, who expresses this crying with obvious intention.

II

[After establishing that "with the ancients beauty was the supreme law of the plastic arts", Lessing takes up the argument as follows.]

I will dwell a little longer on *expression*. There are passions and degrees of passion which express themselves in the countenance by the most hideous grimaces, and put the whole frame into such violent postures that all the beautiful lines are lost which define it in a quieter condition. From these, therefore, the ancient artists either abstained wholly or reduced them to lower degrees in which they were capable of a measure of beauty. Rage and despair disfigured none of their works. I dare maintain that they never depicted a Fury.[20]

Wrath they reduced to sternness: with the poet it was an angry Jupiter who sent forth his lightnings; with the artist the god was calmly grave.

Lamentation was toned down to sadness. And where this softening could not take place, where lamentation would have been just as deforming as belittling – what then did Timanthes?[21] His picture of Iphigenia's sacrifice, in which he imparted to all the company the peculiar degree of sadness befitting them individually, but veiled the father's face, which should have shown the supreme degree, is well known, and many nice things have been said about it. He had, says one, so exhausted himself in sorrowful countenances that he despaired of being able to give the father one yet more grief-stricken. He confessed thereby, says another, that the pain of a father in such events is beyond all expression. I, for my part, see here neither the impotence of the artist nor the impotence of art. With the degree of emotion the traces of it are correspondingly heightened in the countenance; the highest degree is accompanied by the most decided traces of all, and nothing is easier for the artist than to exhibit them. But Timanthes knew the limits which the Graces set to his art. He knew that such misery as fell to Agamemnon's lot as a father expresses itself by distortions which are at all times ugly. So far as beauty and dignity could be united with the expression of sorrow, so far he carried it. He might have been willing to omit the ugliness had he been willing to mitigate the sorrow; but as his composition did not admit of both, what else remained to him but to veil it? What he dared not paint he left to be guessed. In a word, this veiling was a sacrifice which the artist offered to Beauty. It is an example, not how one should force expression beyond the bounds of art, but rather how one must subject it to the first law of art, the law of Beauty.

And if we refer this to the Laocoon, the motive for which I am looking becomes evident. The master was striving after the highest beauty, under the given circumstances of bodily pain. This, in its full deforming violence, it was not possible to unite with that. He was obliged, therefore, to abate, to lower it, to tone down cries to sighing; not because cries betrayed an ignoble soul, but because they disfigure the face in an unpleasing manner. Let one only, in imagination, open wide the mouth in Laocoon, and judge! Let him shriek, and see! It was a form that inspired pity because it showed beauty and pain together; now it has become an ugly, a loathsome form, from which one gladly turns away one's face, because the aspect of pain excites discomfort without the beauty of the suffering subject changing this discomfort into the sweet feeling of compassion.

The mere wide opening of the mouth – apart from the fact that the other parts of the face are thereby violently and unpleasantly distorted – is a blot in painting and a fault in sculpture which has the most untoward effect possible. Montfaucon[22] showed little taste when he passed off an old, bearded head with widespread mouth for an oracle-pronouncing Jupiter. Must a god shriek when he unveils the future? Would a pleasing contour of the mouth make his speech suspicious? I do not even believe Valerius,[23] that Ajax in the imaginary picture of Timanthes should have cried aloud. Far inferior artists, in times when art was already degraded, never once allow the wildest barbarians, when, under the victor's sword, terror and mortal anguish seize them, to open the mouth to shrieking-point.

Certain it is that this reduction of extremest physical pain to a lower degree of feeling is apparent in several works of ancient art. The suffering Hercules in the poisoned garment, from the hand of an unknown ancient master, was not the Sophoclean who shrieked so horribly that the Locrian cliffs and the Euboean headlands resounded. It was more sad than wild. The Philoctetes of Pythagoras Leontinus[24] appeared to impart this pain to the beholder, an effect which the slightest trace of the horrible would have prevented. Some may ask where I have learnt that this master made a statue of Philoctetes? From a passage of Pliny which ought not to have awaited my emendation, so manifestly forged or garbled is it.

III

But, as we have already seen, Art in these later days has been assigned far wider boundaries. Let her imitative hand, folks say, stretch out to the whole of visible Nature, of which the Beautiful is only a small part. Let fidelity and truth of expression be her first law, and as Nature herself at all times sacrifices beauty to higher purposes, so also must the artist subordinate it to his general aim and yield to it no further than fidelity of expression permits. Enough, if by truth and faithful expression an ugliness of Nature be transformed into a beauty of Art.

Granted that one would willingly, to begin with, leave these conceptions uncontested in their worth or worthlessness, ought not other considerations quite independent of them to be examined – namely, why the artist is obliged to set bounds to expression and never to choose for it the supreme moment of an action?

The fact that the material limits of Art confine her imitative effort to one single moment will, I believe, lead us to similar conclusions.

If the artist can never, in presence of ever-changing Nature, choose and use more than one single moment, and the painter in particular can use this single moment only from one point of vision; if, again, their works are made not merely to be seen, but to be considered, to be long and repeatedly contemplated, then it is certain that that single moment, and the single viewpoint of that moment, can never be chosen too significantly. Now that alone is significant and fruitful which gives free play to the imagination. The more we see, the more must we be able to add by thinking. The more we add thereto by thinking, so much the more can we believe ourselves to see. In the whole gamut of an emotion, however, there is no moment less advantageous than its topmost note. Beyond it there is nothing further, and to show us the uttermost is to tie the wings of fancy and oblige her, as she cannot rise above the sensuous impression, to busy herself with weaker pictures below it, the visible fullness of expression acting as a frontier which she dare not transgress. When, therefore, Laocoon sighs, the imagination can hear him shriek; but if he shrieks, then she cannot mount a step higher from this representation, nor, again, descend a step lower without seeing him in a more tolerable and consequently more uninteresting condition. She hears him only groan, or she sees him already dead.

Further. As this single moment receives from Art an unchangeable continuance, it must not express anything which thought is obliged to consider transitory. All phenomena of whose very essence, according to our conceptions, it is that they break out suddenly and as suddenly vanish, that what they are they can be only for a moment – all such phenomena, whether agreeable or terrible, do, by the permanence which Art bestows, put on an aspect so abhorrent to Nature that at every repeated view of them the impression becomes weaker, until at last the whole thing inspires us with horror or loathing. La Mettrie, who had himself painted and engraved as a second Democritus, laughs only the first time that one sees him.[25] View him often, and from a philosopher he becomes a fool, and the laugh becomes a grin. So, too, with cries. The violent pain which presses out the cry either speedily relaxes or it destroys the sufferer. If, again, the most patient and resolute man cries aloud, still he does not cry out without intermission. And just this unintermitting aspect in the material imitations of Art it is which would make his cries an effeminate or a childish weakness. This at least the artist of the Laocoon had to avoid, if cries had not been themselves damaging to beauty, and if even it had been permitted to his art to depict suffering without beauty.

Among the ancient painters Timomachus[26] seems to have chosen by preference themes of the extremest emotion. His Frenzied Ajax, his Medea the child-murderess, were famous pictures. But from the descriptions we have of them it clearly appears that he understood excellently well, and knew how to combine, that point where the beholder does not so much see the uttermost as reach it by added thought, and that appearance with which we do not join the idea of the transitory so necessarily that the prolongation of the same in Art must displease us. Medea he had not taken at the moment in which she actually murders the children, but some moments earlier, when motherly love still battles with jealousy. We foresee the end of the fight. We tremble beforehand, about to see Medea at her cruel deed, and our imagination goes out far beyond everything that the painter could show us in this terrible moment. But for this very reason we are so little troubled by the continued indecision of Medea, as Art presents it, that rather we devoutly wish it had so continued in Nature itself, that the struggle of passions had never been decided, or had at least endured long enough for time and reflection to weaken rage and assure the victory to motherly feeling. To Timomachus, moreover, this wisdom of his brought great and manifold tributes, and raised him far above another unknown painter who had been misguided enough to represent Medea in the height of her rage, and thus to give to this transient extreme of frenzy a permanence that revolts all Nature. The poet who blames him on this account remarks, very sensibly, addressing the picture itself: 'Dost thou, then, thirst perpetually for the blood of thy children? Is there constantly a new Jason, always a new Creusa here, to embitter thee for evermore? To the devil with thee, even in picture!' he adds, with angry disgust.

Of the Frenzied Ajax of Timomachus we can judge by Philostratus' account.[27] Ajax appeared not as he rages amongst the herds and binds and slays oxen and goats for his enemies. Rather, the master showed him when, after these mad-heroic deeds, he sits exhausted and is meditating self-destruction. And that is actually the Frenzied Ajax; not because just then he rages, but because one sees that he has raged, because one perceives

the greatness of his frenzy most vividly by the despair and shame which he
himself now feels over it. One sees the storm in the wreckage and corpses
it has cast upon the shore.

IV

Glancing at the reasons adduced why the artist of the Laocoon was obliged
to observe restraint in the expression of physical pain, I find that they are
entirely drawn from the peculiar nature of Art and its necessary limits and
requirements. Hardly, therefore, could any one of them be made applicable to poetry.

Without inquiring here how far the poet can succeed in depicting physical beauty, so much at least is undeniable, that, as the whole immeasurable
realm of perfection lies open to his imitative skill, this visible veil, under
which perfection becomes beauty, can be only one of the smallest means
by which he undertakes to interest us in his subject. Often he neglects this
means entirely, being assured that if his hero has won our goodwill, then
his nobler qualities either so engage us that we do not think at all of the
bodily form, or, if we think of it, so prepossess us that we do, on their very
account, attribute to him, if not a beautiful one, yet at any rate one that is
not uncomely. At least, with every single line which is not expressly
intended for the eye he will still take this sense into consideration. When
Virgil's Laocoon cries aloud, to whom does it occur then that a wide mouth
is needful for a cry, and that this must be ugly? Enough, that *clamores hor-
rendos ad sidera tollit*[28] is an excellent feature for the hearing, whatever it
might be for the vision. Whosoever demands here a beautiful picture, for
him the poet has entirely failed of his intention.

In the next place, nothing requires the poet to concentrate his picture
on one single moment. He takes up each of his actions, as he likes, from
its very origin and conducts it through all possible modifications to its final
close. Every one of these modifications, which would cost the artist an
entire separate canvas or marble-block, costs the poet a single line; and if
this line, taken in itself, would have misled the hearer's imagination, it was
either so prepared for by what preceded, or so modified and supplemented by what followed, that it loses its separate impression, and in its
proper connection produces the most admirable effect in the world. Were
it therefore actually unbecoming to a man to cry out in the extremity of
pain, what damage can this trifling and transient impropriety do in our
eyes to one whose other virtues have already taken us captive? Virgil's Laocoon shrieks aloud, but this shrieking Laocoon we already know and love
as the wisest of patriots and the most affectionate of fathers. We refer his
cries not to his character but purely to his unendurable suffering. It is this
alone we hear in his cries, and the poet could make it sensible to us only
through them. Who shall blame him then, and not much rather confess

that, if the artist does well not to permit Laocoon to cry aloud, the poet does equally well in permitting him?

But Virgil here is merely a narrative poet. Can the dramatic poet be included with him in this justification? It is a different impression which is made by the narration of any man's cries from that which is made by the cries themselves. The drama, which is intended for the living artistry of the actor, might on this very ground be held more strictly to the laws of material painting. In him we do not merely suppose that we see and hear a shrieking Philoctetes; we hear and see him actually shriek. The closer the actor comes to Nature in this, the more sensibly must our eyes and ears be offended; for it is undeniable that they are so in Nature when we hear such loud and violent utterances of pain. Besides, physical pain does not generally excite that degree of sympathy which other evils awaken. Our imagination is not able to distinguish enough in it for the mere sight of it to call out something like an equivalent feeling in ourselves. Sophocles could, therefore, easily have overstepped a propriety not merely capricious, but founded in the very essence of our feelings, if he allowed Philoctetes and Hercules thus to whine and weep, thus to shriek and bellow. The bystanders could not possibly take so much share in their suffering as these unmeasured outbursts seem to demand. They will appear to us spectators comparatively cold, and yet we cannot well regard their sympathy otherwise than as the measure of our own. Let us add that the actor can only with difficulty, if at all, carry the representation of physical pain to the point of illusion; and who knows whether the later dramatic poets are not rather to be commended than to be blamed, in that they have either avoided this rock entirely or only sailed round it with the lightest of skiffs?

How many a thing would appear irrefragable in theory if genius had not succeeded in proving the contrary by actual achievement! None of these considerations is unfounded, and yet Philoctetes remains one of the masterpieces of the stage. For some of them do not really touch Sophocles, and by treating the rest with contempt he has attained beauties of which the timid critic without this example would never dream. The following notes deal with this point in fuller detail.

1. How wonderfully has the poet known how to strengthen and enlarge the idea of the physical pain! He chose a wound – for even the circumstances of the story one can contemplate as if they had depended on choice, in so far, that is to say, as he chose the whole story just because of the advantages the circumstances of it afforded him – he chose, I say, a wound and not an inward malady, because a more vivid representation can be made of the former than of the latter, however painful this may be. The mysterious inward burning which consumed Meleager[29] when his mother sacrificed him in mortal fire to her sisterly rage would therefore be less theatrical than a wound. And this wound was a divine judgement. A supernatural venom raged within without ceasing, and only an unusually severe

attack of pain had its set time, after which the unhappy man fell ever into a narcotic sleep in which his exhausted nature must recover itself to be able to enter anew on the selfsame way of suffering. Chateaubrun[30] represents him merely as wounded by the poisoned arrow of a Trojan. What of extraordinary can so commonplace an accident promise? To such every warrior in the ancient battles was exposed; how did it come about that only with Philoctetes had it such terrible consequences? A natural poison that works nine whole years without killing is, besides, more improbable by far than all the mythical miraculous with which the Greek has furnished it.

2. But however great and terrible he made the bodily pains of his hero, he yet was in no doubt that they were insufficient in themselves to excite any notable degree of sympathy. He combined them, therefore, with other evils, which likewise, regarded in themselves, could not particularly move us, but which by this combination received just as melancholy a tinge as in their turn they imparted to the bodily pains. These evils were – a total deprivation of human society, hunger, and all the inconveniences of life to which in such deprivations one is exposed under an inclement sky. Let us conceive of a man in these circumstances, but give him health, and capacities, and industry, and we have a Robinson Crusoe who makes little demand upon our compassion, although otherwise his fate is not exactly a matter of indifference. For we are rarely so satisfied with human society that the repose which we enjoy when wanting it might not appear very charming, particularly under the representation which flatters every individual, that he can learn gradually to dispense with outside assistance. On the other hand, give a man the most painful, incurable malady, but at the same time conceive him surrounded by agreeable friends who let him want for nothing, who soften his affliction as far as lies in their power, and to whom he may unreservedly wail and lament; unquestionably we shall have pity for him, but this pity does not last, in the end we shrug our shoulders and recommend him patience. Only when both cases come together, when the lonely man has an enfeebled body, when others help the sick man just as little as he can help himself, and his complainings fly away in the desert air; then, indeed, we behold all the misery that can afflict human nature close over the unfortunate one, and every fleeting thought in which we conceive ourselves in his place awakens shuddering and horror. We perceive nothing before us but despair in its most dreadful form, and no pity is stronger, none more melts the whole soul than that which is mingled with representations of despair. Of this kind is the pity which we feel for Philoctetes, and feel most strongly at that moment when we see him deprived of his bow, the one thing that might preserve him his wretched life. Oh, the Frenchman, who had neither the understanding to reflect on this nor the heart to feel it! Or, if he had, was small enough to sacrifice all this to the pitiful taste of his countrymen. Chateaubrun gives Philoctetes society. He lets a young Princess come to him in the desert island. Nor is

she alone, for she has her governess with her; a thing of which I know not whether the Princess or the poet had the greater need. The whole excellent play with the bow he set quite aside. Instead of it he gives us the play of beautiful eyes. Certainly to young French heroes bow and arrow would have appeared a great joke. On the other hand, nothing is more serious than the anger of beautiful eyes. The Greek torments us with the dreadful apprehension that poor Philoctetes must remain on the desert island without his bow, and perish miserably. The Frenchman knows a surer way to our hearts: he makes us fear the son of Achilles must retire without his Princess. At the time the Parisian critics proclaimed this a triumphing over the ancients, and one of them proposed to call Chateaubrun's piece '*La Difficulté vaincue*'.[31]

3. After the general effect let us consider the individual scenes, in which Philoctetes is no longer the forsaken invalid; in which he has hope of speedily leaving the comfortless wilderness behind and of once more reaching his own kingdom; in which, therefore, the painful wound is his sole calamity. He whimpers, he cries aloud, he goes through the most frightful convulsions. To this behaviour it is that the reproach of offended propriety is particularly addressed. It is an Englishman who utters this reproach;[32] a man, therefore, whom we should not easily suspect of a false delicacy. As we have already hinted, he gives a very good reason for the reproach. All feelings and passions, he says, with which others can only slightly sympathise, are offensive when they are expressed too violently.

> For this reason there is nothing more unbecoming and more unworthy of a man than when he cannot bear pain, even the most violent, with patience, but weeps and cries aloud. Of course we may feel sympathy with bodily pain. When we see that any one is about to get a blow on the arm or the shin-bone, and when the blow actually falls, in a certain measure we feel it as truly as he whom it strikes. At the same time, however, it is certain that the trouble we thus experience amounts to very little; if the person struck, therefore, sets up a violent outcry, we do not fail to despise him, because we are not at all in the mind to cry out with so much violence.
>
> (Adam Smith, *Theory of the Moral Sentiments*, Part I, sect. 2, chap. i., p. 41, London, 1761)

Nothing is more fallacious than general laws for human feelings. The web of them is so fine-spun and so intricate that it is hardly possible for the most careful speculation to take up a single thread by itself and follow it through all the threads that cross it. And supposing it possible, what is the use of it? There does not exist in Nature a single unmixed feeling; along with every one of them there arise a thousand others simultaneously, the very smallest of which completely alters the first, so that exceptions on exceptions spring up which reduce at last the supposed general law itself to the mere experience of a few individual cases. We despise him, says the Englishman, whom we hear shriek aloud under bodily pain. No; not always,

nor at first; not when we see that the sufferer makes every effort to suppress it; not when we know him otherwise as a man of fortitude; still less
when we see him even in his suffering give proof of his fortitude, when we
see that the pain can indeed force cries from him, but can compel him to
nothing further – that he will rather submit to the longer endurance of
this pain than change his opinions or his resolves in the slightest, even if
he might hope by such a change to end his agony. And all this we find in
Philoctetes. With the ancient Greeks moral greatness consisted in just as
unchanging a love to friends as an unalterable hatred to enemies. This
greatness Philoctetes maintains in all his torments. His pain has not so
dried his eyes that they can spare no tears for the fate of his old friends.
His pain has not made him so pliable that, to be rid of it, he will forgive
his enemies and allow himself willingly to be used for their selfish purposes. And this rock of a man ought the Athenians to have despised
because the surges that could not shake him made him give forth a cry? I
confess that in the philosophy of Cicero, generally speaking, I find little
taste; and least of all in that second book of his *Tusculan Disputations,*
where he pours out his notions about the endurance of bodily pain. One
might almost think he wanted to train a gladiator, he declaims so passion-
ately against the outward expression of pain. In this alone does he seem to
find a want of fortitude, without considering that it is frequently anything
but voluntary, whilst true bravery can only be shown in voluntary actions.
In Sophocles he hears Philoctetes merely complain and cry aloud, and
overlooks utterly his otherwise steadfast bearing. Where save here could
he have found the opportunity for his rhetorical outburst against the
poets? 'They would make us weaklings, showing us as they do the bravest
of men lamenting and bewailing themselves.' They must bewail themselves,
for a theatre is not an arena.The condemned or venal gladiator it behoved
to do and suffer everything with decorum. No complaining word must be
heard from him, nor painful grimace be seen. For as his wounds and his
death were to delight the spectators, Art must learn to conceal all feeling.
The least utterance of it would have aroused compassion, and compassion
often excited would have speedily brought an end to these icily gruesome
spectacles. But what here it was not desired to excite is the one object of
the tragic stage, and demands therefore an exactly opposite demeanour.
Its heroes must show feeling, must utter their pain, and let Nature work
in them undisguisedly. If they betray restraint and training, they leave our
hearts cold, and pugilists in the cothurnus could at best only excite admiration. This designation would befit all the persons of the so-called Seneca
tragedies,[33] and I firmly believe that the gladiatorial plays were the principal reason why the Romans in tragedy remained so far below the mediocre. To disown human nature was the lesson the spectators learned in the
bloody amphitheatre, where certainly a Ctesias[34] might study his art, but
never a Sophocles. The tragic genius, accustomed to these artistic death

scenes, necessarily sank into bombast and rodomontade. But just as little as such rodomontade could inspire true heroism, could the laments of Philoctetes make men weak. The complaints are those of a man, but the actions those of a hero. Both together make the human hero, who is neither soft nor hardened, but appears now the one and now the other, according as Nature at one time, and duty and principle at another, demand. He is the highest that Wisdom can produce and Art imitate.

4. It is not enough that Sophocles has secured his sensitive Philoctetes against contempt; he has also wisely taken precautions against all else that might, according to the Englishman's remark, be urged against him. For if we certainly do not always despise him who cries aloud in bodily pain, still it is indisputable that we do not feel so much sympathy for him as these outcries seem to demand. How, then, shall all those comport themselves who have to do with the shrieking Philoctetes? Shall they affect to be deeply moved? That is against nature. Shall they show themselves as cold and as disconcerted as we are really accustomed to be in such cases? That would produce for the spectator the most unpleasant dissonance. But, as we have said, against this Sophocles has taken precautions. In this way, namely, that the secondary persons have an interest of their own; that the impression which the cries of Philoctetes make on them is not the one thing that occupies them, and the spectator's attention is not so much drawn to the disproportion of their sympathy with these cries, but rather to the change which arises or should arise in their disposition and attitude from sympathy, be it as weak or as strong as it may. Neoptolemus and his company have deceived the unhappy Philoctetes; they recognise into what despair their betrayal will plunge him; and now, before their eyes, a terrible accident befalls him. If this accident is not enough to arouse any particular feeling of sympathy within them, it still will move them to repent, to have regard to a misery so great, and indispose them to add to it by treachery. This is what the spectator expects, and his expectations are not disappointed by the noble-minded Neoptolemus. Philoctetes mastering his pain would have maintained Neoptolemus in his dissimulation. Philoctetes, whom his pain renders incapable of dissimulation, however imperatively necessary it may seem to him, so that his future fellow-travellers may not too soon regret their promise to take him with them; Philoctetes, who is nature itself, brings Neoptolemus, too, back to his own nature. This conversion is admirable, and so much the more touching as it is entirely wrought by humane feeling. With the Frenchman,[35] on the contrary, beautiful eyes have their share in it. But I will say no more of this burlesque. Of the same artifice – namely, to join to the pity which bodily pain should arouse other emotion in the onlookers – Sophocles availed himself on another occasion: in the *Trachiniae*. The agony of Hercules is no enfeebling agony; it drives him to frenzy in which he pants for nothing but revenge. He had already, in his rage, seized Lichas and dashed him to

pieces upon the rocks. The chorus is of women; so much the more naturally must fear and horror overwhelm them. This, and the expectant doubt
whether yet a god will hasten to the help of Hercules, or Hercules succumb
to the calamity, form here the real general interest, mingled merely with a
slight tinge of sympathy. As soon as the issue is determined by the oracle,
Hercules becomes quiet, and admiration of his final steadfast resolution
takes the place of all other feelings. But in comparing the suffering Hercules with the suffering Philoctetes, one must never forget that the former
is a demigod and the latter only a man. The man is not for a moment
ashamed of his lamentations; but the demigod is ashamed that his mortal
part has prevailed so far over the immortal that he must weep and whimper
like a girl. We moderns do not believe in demigods, but our smallest hero
we expect to feel and act as a demigod.

Whether an actor can bring the cries and grimaces of pain to the point
of illusion I will not venture either to assert or to deny. If I found that our
actors could not, then I should first like to know whether it would be
impossible also to a Garrick,[36] and if even he did not succeed, I should still
be able to suppose a perfection in the stage-business and declamation of
the ancients of which we today have no conception.

V

[After pondering whether poet and plastic artist might have based their versions of
the Laocoon episode upon a prior, common source, Lessing goes on to explore
the consequences of the assumption that Virgil was in fact the source for the
sculptors.]

The poet has depicted the serpents as of a marvellous length. They have
enfolded the boys, and when the father comes to their aid, seize him also
(corripiunt). From their size they could not at once uncoil themselves from
the boys; there must therefore be a moment in which they had attacked
the father with their heads and foreparts, while they still with their other
parts enveloped the children. This moment is required in the development
of the poetic picture; the poet makes it sufficiently felt; only the time had
not yet been reached for finishing the picture. That the ancient commentators actually realised this appears to be shown by a passage in Donatus.[37]
How much less would it escape the artists in whose understanding eyes
everything that can advantage them stands out so quickly and so plainly.

In the coils themselves with which the poet's fancy sees the serpents
entwine Laocoon, he very carefully avoids the arms, in order to leave the
hands their freedom.

Ille simul manibus tendit divellere nodos.[38]

In this the artists must necessarily follow him. Nothing gives more life
and expression than the movement of the hands; in emotion especially the

most speaking countenance without it is insignificant. Arms fast bound to the body by the coils of the serpents would have spread frost and death over the whole group. For this reason we see them, in the chief figure as well as in the secondary figures, in full activity, and busiest there where for the moment there is the most violent anguish.

Further, too, the artists, in view of the convolutions of the serpents, found nothing that could be more advantageously borrowed from the poet than this movement of the arms. Virgil makes the serpents wind themselves doubly about the body and doubly about the neck of Laocoon, with their heads elevated above him.

> Bis medium amplexi, bis collo squamea circum
> Terga dati, superant capite et cervicibus altis.[39]

This picture satisfies the imagination completely; the noblest parts are compressed to suffocation, and the poison goes straight to the face. Nevertheless, it was not a picture for artists, who want to exhibit the effects of the pain and the poison in the bodily frame. For in order to make these visible the chief parts must be as free as possible, and no external pressure whatever must be exercised upon them which could alter and weaken the play of the suffering nerves and straining muscles. The double coil of the serpents would have concealed the whole body, so that the painful contraction of the abdomen, which is so expressive, would have remained invisible. What one would still have perceived of the body, over, or under, or between the coils, would have appeared under pressures and swellings caused not by the inward pain, but by the external burden. The neck so many times encircled would have spoiled completely the pyramidal tapering of the group which is so agreeable to the eye; and the pointed serpent heads standing out into the air from this swollen bulk would have made so abrupt a break in proportion that the form of the whole would have been repulsive in the extreme. There are doubtless draughtsmen who would nevertheless have been unintelligent enough to follow the poet slavishly. But what would have come of that, we can, to name no other instances, understand from a drawing of Franz Cleyn,[40] which can be looked on only with disgust. (This occurs in the splendid edition of Dryden's English Virgil.)[41] The ancient sculptors perceived at a glance that their art demanded an entire modification. They removed all the serpent coils from neck and body to thighs and feet. Here these coils, without injuring the expression, could cover and press as much as was needful. Here they aroused at once the idea of retarded flight and of a kind of immobility which is exceedingly advantageous to the artistic permanence of a single posture.

I know not how it has come about that the critics have passed over in perfect silence this distinction, which is exhibited so plainly in the coilings of the serpents, between the work of art and the poet's description. It exalts the artistic wisdom of the work just as much as the other which they mention, which, however, they do not venture to praise, but rather seek to excuse. I mean the difference in the draping of the subject. Virgil's Laocoon is in his priestly vestments, but in the group appears, with both his sons, completely naked. I am told there are people who find something preposterous in representing a prince, a priest, unclothed, at the altar of sacrifice. And to these people connoisseurs of art reply, in all seriousness, that certainly it is an offence against custom, but that the artists were compelled to it, because they could not give their figures any suitable attire. Sculpture, say they, cannot imitate any kind of cloth; thick folds would make a bad effect. Of two embarrassments, therefore, they had chosen the smaller, and were willing rather to offend against truth than to incur the risk of blame for their draperies. If the ancient artists would laugh at the objection, I really cannot tell what they would have said about the answer. One cannot degrade Art further than by such a defence. For, granted that sculpture could imitate the different materials just as well as painting, should then Laocoon necessarily have been clothed? Should we lose nothing by this draping? Has a costume, the work of slavish hands, just as much beauty as the work of the Eternal Wisdom, an organised body? Does it demand the same faculties, is it equally meritorious, does it bring the same honour, to imitate the former as to imitate the latter? Do our eyes only wish to be deceived, and is it all the same to them with what they are deceived?

With the poet a dress is no dress; it conceals nothing; our imagination sees through it at all times. Let Laocoon in Virgil have it or lack it, his suffering in every part of his body is, to the imagination, an evil equally visible. The brow is bound about for her with the priestly fillet, but it is not veiled. Indeed, it does not only not hinder, this fillet, it even strengthens yet more the conception that we form of the sufferer's misfortunes.

Perfusus sanie vittas atroque veneno.[42]

His priestly dignity helps him not a whit; the very symbol which secures him everywhere respect and veneration is soaked and defiled by the deadly venom.

But this accessory idea the artist had to sacrifice if the main work were not to suffer damage. Besides, had he left to Laocoon only this fillet, the expression would in consequence have been much weakened. The brow would have been partly covered, and the brow is the seat of expression. So, just as in that other particular, the shriek, he sacrificed expression to beauty, in the same way here he sacrificed custom to expression. Generally speaking, custom, in the view of the ancients, was a matter of little consequence. They felt that the highest aim of Art pointed to dispensing with the customary altogether. Beauty is this highest aim; necessity invented clothing, and what has Art to do with necessity? I grant you there is also a beauty of drapery; but what is it compared with the beauty of the human form? And will he who is able to reach the higher content himself with the lower? I am much afraid that the most finished master in draperies shows by that very dexterity in what it is he is lacking.

VI

My hypothesis – that the artists imitated the poet – does not redound to their disparagement. On the contrary, this imitation sets their wisdom in the fairest light. They followed the poet without allowing themselves to be misled by him in the slightest. They had a pattern, but as they had to transpose this pattern from one art into another, they found opportunity enough to think for themselves. And these thoughts of theirs, which are manifest in their deviation from their model, prove that they were just as great in their art as he in his own.

And now I will reverse the hypothesis and suppose the poet to have imitated the artists. There are scholars who maintain this supposition to be the truth. Whether they had historical grounds for that, I do not know. But when they found the work of art so superlatively beautiful, they could not persuade themselves that it might belong to a late period. It must be of the age when Art was in its perfect flower, because it deserved to be of that age.

It has been shown that, admirable as Virgil's picture is, there are yet various features of it which the artists could not use. The statement thus admits of being reduced to this, that a good poetic description must also yield a good actual painting, and that the poet has only so far described well when the artist can follow him in every feature. One is inclined to presume this restricted sense, even before seeing it confirmed by examples; merely from consideration of the wider sphere of poetry, from the boundless field of our imagination, and from the spiritual nature of the pictures, which can stand side by side in the greatest multitude and variety without one obscuring or damaging another, just as the things themselves would do or the natural signs of the same within the narrow bounds of space and time.

But if the less cannot include the greater, the greater can contain the less. This is my point – if not, every feature which the descriptive poet uses can be used with like effect on the canvas or in the marble. Might perhaps every feature of which the artist avails himself prove equally effective in the work of the poet? Unquestionably; for what we find beautiful in a work of art is not found beautiful by the eye, but by our imagination through the eye. The picture in question may therefore be called up again in our imagination by arbitrary or natural signs,[43] and thus also may arise at any time the corresponding pleasure, although not in corresponding degree.

This, however, being admitted, I must confess that to my mind the hypothesis that Virgil imitated the artists is far less conceivable than the contrary supposition. If the artists followed the poet, I can account for their deviations. They were obliged to deviate, because the selfsame features as the poet delineated would have occasioned them difficulties such as do not embarrass the poet. But what should make the poet deviate? If he had followed the group in every detail would he not, all the same, have presented to us an admirable picture? I can conceive quite well how his fancy, working on its own account, might suggest one feature and another; but the reasons why his imagination should think that beautiful features, already before his eyes, ought to be transformed into those other features – such reasons, I confess, never dawn upon me.

It even seems to me that if Virgil had had the group as his pattern he could scarcely have refrained from permitting the union together, as it were in a knot, of the three bodies to be at least conjectured. It was too vivid not to catch his eye, and he would have appreciated its excellent effect too keenly not to give it yet more prominence in his description. As I have said, the time was not yet arrived to finish this picture of the entwined group. No; but a single word more would perhaps have given to it, in the shadow where the poet had to leave it, a very obvious impression. What the artist was able to discover without this word, the poet, if he had seen it in the artist's work, would not have left unspoken.

The artist had the most compelling reasons not to let the suffering of Laocoon break out into a cry. But if the poet had had before him the so touching union of pain and beauty in the work of art, what could have so imperatively obliged him to leave completely unsuggested the idea of manly dignity and great-hearted endurance which arises from this union of pain and beauty, and all at once to shock us with the terrible outcries of Laocoon? Richardson says, 'Virgil's Laocoon must shriek, because the poet desires to arouse not so much pity for him as terror and horror in the ranks of the Trojans.'[44] I grant, although Richardson seems not to have considered it, that the poet does not make the description in his own person, but lets Aeneas make it, and this, too, in the presence of Dido, to whose compassion Aeneas could never enough appeal. It is not, however, the shriek that surprises me, but the absence of any gradation leading up to the cry, a gradation that the work of art would naturally have shown the poet to be needful, if, as we have supposed, he had had it for a pattern. Richardson adds, 'The story of Laocoon should lead up merely to the pathetic description of the final ruin; the poet, therefore, has not thought fit to make it more interesting, in order not to waste upon the misfortune of a single citizen the attention which should be wholly fixed on Troy's last dreadful night.' Only, this sets out the affair as one to be regarded from a painter's point of view, from which it cannot be contemplated at all. The calamity of Laocoon and the Destruction of the City are not with the poet pictures set side by side; the two together do not make a great whole which the eye either should or could take in at a glance; and only in such a case

would it be needful to arrange that our eyes should fall rather upon Laocoon than upon the burning city. The two descriptions follow each other
successively, and I do not see what disadvantage it could bring to the second, how greatly soever the preceding one had moved us. That could only
be, if the second in itself were not sufficiently touching.

Still less reason would the poet have had to alter the coiling of the serpents. In the work of art they leave the hands busy and bind the feet. This
disposition pleases the eye, and it is a living picture that is left by it in the
imagination. It is so clear and pure that it can be presented almost as effectively by words as by actual material means

> . . . Micat alter, et ipsum
> Laocoönta petit, totumque infraque supraque
> Implicat et rabido tandem ferit ilia morsu
> .   .   .   .
> At serpens lapsu crebro redeunte subintrat
> Lubricus, intortoque ligat genua infima nodo.[45]

These are the lines of Sadoleto,[46] which would, no doubt, have come from
Virgil with a more picturesque power if a visible pattern had fired his
fancy, and which would in that case certainly have been better than what
he now gives us in their place:

> Bis medium amplexi, bis collo squamea circum
> Terga dati, superant capite et cervicibus altis.[47]

These details, certainly, fill the imagination; but it must not rest in them,
it must not endeavour to make an end here; it must see now only the serpents and now only Laocoon, it must try to represent to itself what kind
of figure is made by the two together. As soon as it sinks to this the Vir-
gilian picture begins to dissatisfy, and it finds it in the highest degree
unpictorial.

If, however, the changes which Virgil had made in the pattern set before
him had not been unsuccessful, they would yet be merely arbitrary. One
imitates in order to resemble. Can resemblance be preserved when alterations are made needlessly? Rather, when this is done, the design obviously
is – not to be like, and therefore not to imitate.

Not the whole, some may object, but perhaps this part and that. Good!
But what, then, are these single parts that agree in the description and in
the work of art so exactly that the poet might seem to have borrowed them
from the latter? The father, the children, the serpents – all these the story
furnished to the poet as well as to the artists. Excepting the story itself,
they agree in nothing beyond the one point that they bind father and children in a single serpent-knot. But the suggestion of this arose from the
altered detail, that the selfsame calamity overtook the father and the children. This alteration, as has already been pointed out, Virgil appears to

have introduced; for the Greek legend says something quite different. Consequently, when, in view of that common binding by the serpent coils, there certainly was imitation on one side or the other, it is easier to suppose it on the artist's side than on that of the poet. In all else the one deviates from the other; only with the distinction that, if it is the artist who has made these deviations, the design of imitating the poet can still persist, the aim and the limitations of his art obliging him thereto; if, on the other hand, it is the poet who is supposed to have imitated the artist, then all the deviations referred to are an evidence against the supposed imitation, and those who, notwithstanding, maintain it, can mean nothing further by it than that the work of art is older than the poetic description.

[Sections VII–IX discuss in further detail the limitations of the critical tradition that judges the plastic and poetic arts by the same standards, and sees in them the same conventions. The British critics Spence and Addison[48] are the exemplary culprits in Lessing's narrative.]

From X

*   *   *

When the poet personifies abstract qualities, these are sufficiently characterised by their names and by what they do. To the artist these means are wanting. He must therefore attach symbols to his personifications by which they can be distinguished. By these symbols, because they are something different and mean something different, they become allegorical figures. A woman with a bridle in her hand, another leaning on a pillar, are in art allegorical beings. But Temperance and Steadfastness are to the poet allegorical beings, and merely personified abstractions. The symbols, in the artist's representation, necessity has invented. For in no other way can he make plain what this or that figure signifies. But what the artist is driven to by necessity, why should the poet force on himself when no such necessity is laid upon him?

What surprises Spence so much deserves to be prescribed to the poets as a law. They must not make painting's indigence the rule of their wealth. They must not regard the means which Art has invented in order to follow poetry as if they were perfections which they have reason to envy. When the artist adorns a figure with symbols, he raises a mere figure to a superior being. But when the poet makes use of these plastic bedizenments, he makes of a superior being a mere lay-figure.

And just as this rule is authenticated by its observance amongst the ancient poets, so is its deliberate violation a favourite weakness amongst their successors. All their creatures of imagination go in masquerade, and those who understand this masquerade best generally understand least the chief thing of all, which is to let their creatures act and to distinguish and characterise them by their actions.

Yet amongst the attributes with which the artists distinguish their abstract personalities there is one sort which is more susceptible and more worthy of poetic employment. I mean those which properly have nothing allegorical in their nature, but are to be regarded as implements of which the being to whom they are assigned would or might make use when acting as real persons. The bridle in the hand of Temperance, the pillar on which Steadfastness leans, are purely allegorical, and thus of no use to the poet. The scales in the hand of Justice are certainly less purely allegorical, because the right use of the scales is really a part of justice. But the lyre or flute in the hand of a Muse, the spear in the hand of Mars, hammer and tongs in the hands of Vulcan, are not symbols at all, but mere instruments, without which these beings could not effect the achievements we ascribe to them. Of this kind are the attributes which the ancient poets did sometimes weave into their descriptions, and which I on that ground, distinguishing them from the allegorical, would call the poetic. The latter signify the thing itself, the former only some likeness of it.[49]

[Sections XI–XIII take issue with the French critic Caylus'[50] similarly false attempts to make poetry and the plastic arts respond to common standards. Lessing argues that we deem poetry more difficult in the invention than in the execution; the opposite is the case with sculpture. Poetry can represent distinctions between the visible and the invisible without risking a decline of the sublime into the grotesque. Because of the differences between the two media, the excellence of a poet – Lessing gives examples from Homer – is not to be judged by the pictorial imitations that follow upon his writings.]

XIV

But if it is so, and if one poem may yield very happy results for the painter yet itself be not pictorial; if, again, another in its turn may be very pictorial and yet offer nothing to the painter; this is enough to dispose of Count Caylus' notion, which would make this kind of utility the criterion or test of the poets and settle their rank by the number of pictures which they provide for the artist.[51]

Far be it from us, even if only by our silence, to allow this notion to gain the authority of a rule. Milton would fall the first innocent sacrifice to it. For it seems really that the contemptuous verdict which Caylus passes upon him was not mere national prejudice, but rather a consequence of his supposed principle. 'The loss of sight', he says, 'may well be the nearest resemblance Milton bore to Homer.' True, Milton can fill no galleries. But if, so long as I had the bodily eye, its sphere must also be the sphere of my inward eye, then would I, in order to be free of this limitation, set a great value on the loss of the former. The *Paradise Lost* is not less the first epic poem since Homer on the ground of its providing few pictures, than the story of Christ's Passion is a poem because we can hardly put the point of a needle into it without touching a passage that might have employed a multitude of the greatest artists. The Evangelists relate the facts with all the dry simplicity possible, and the artist uses the manifold parts of the story without their having shown on their side the smallest spark of pictorial genius. There are paintable and unpaintable facts, and the historian can relate the most paintable in just as unpictorial a fashion as the poet can represent the least paintable pictorially.

We are merely misled by the ambiguity of words if we take the matter otherwise. A poetic picture is not necessarily that which can be transmuted into a material painting; but every feature, every combination of features by means of which the poet makes his subject so perceptible that we are more clearly conscious of this subject than of his words is called pictorial, is styled a picture, because it brings us nearer to the degree of illusion of which the material painting is specially capable and which can most readily and most easily be drawn from the material painting.

XV

Now the poet, as experience shows, can raise to this degree of illusion the representations even of other than visible objects. Consequently the artist must necessarily be denied whole classes of pictures in which the poet has the advantage over him. Dryden's Ode on St Cecilia's Day is full of musical pictures that cannot be touched by the paint-brush. But I will not lose myself in instances of the kind, from which in the end we learn nothing more than that colours are not tones and that eyes are not ears.

I will confine myself to the pictures of purely visible objects which are common to the poet and the painter. How comes it that many poetical pictures of this kind cannot be used by the painter, and, vice versa, many actual pictures lose the best part of their effect in the hands of the poet?

Examples may help us. I repeat it – the picture of Pandarus in the Fourth Book of the *Iliad* is one of the most finished and most striking in all Homer. From the seizing of the bow to the very flight of the arrow every moment is depicted, and all these moments are kept so close together, and yet so distinctly separate, that if we did not know how a bow was to be managed we might learn it from this picture alone.[52] Pandarus draws forth his bow, fixes the bowstring, opens his quiver, chooses a yet unused, well-feathered shaft, sets the arrow on the string, draws back both string and arrow down to the notch, the string is brought near to his breast and the iron head of the arrow to the bow; back flies the great bent bow with a twang, the bowstring whirs, off springs the arrow flying eager for its mark.

This admirable picture Caylus cannot have overlooked. What, then, did he find in it to render it incapable of employing his artist? And for what reason did he consider fitter for this purpose the assembly of the carousing gods in council? In the one, as in the other, we find visible subjects, and what more does the painter want than visible subjects in order to fill his canvas? The solution of the problem must be this. Although both subjects, as being visible, are alike capable of actual painting, yet there exists the essential distinction between them, that the former is a visible continuous action, the different parts of which occur step by step in succession of time, the latter, on the other hand, is a visible arrested action, the different parts of which develop side by side in space. But now, if painting, in virtue of her signs or the methods of her imitation, which she can combine only in space, must wholly renounce time, then continuous actions as such cannot be reckoned amongst her subjects; but she must content herself with actions set side by side, or with mere bodies which by their attitudes can be supposed an action. Poetry on the other hand –

XVI

But I will turn to the foundations and try to argue the matter from first principles.[53]

My conclusion is this. If it is true that painting employs in its imitations quite other means or signs than poetry employs, the former – that is to say, figures and colours in space – but the latter articulate sounds in time; as, unquestionably, the signs used must have a definite relation to the thing signified, it follows that signs arranged together side by side can express only subjects which, or the various parts of which, exist thus side by side, whilst signs which succeed each other can express only subjects which, or the various parts of which, succeed each other.

Subjects which, or the various parts of which, exist side by side, may be called *bodies*. Consequently, bodies with their visible properties form the proper subjects of painting.

Subjects which or the various parts of which succeed each other may in general be called *actions*. Consequently, actions form the proper subjects of poetry.

Yet all bodies exist not in space alone, but also in time. They continue, and may appear differently at every moment and stand in different relations. Every one of these momentary appearances and combinations is the effect of one preceding and can be the cause of one following, and accordingly be likewise the central point of an action. Consequently, painting can also imitate actions, but only by way of suggestion through bodies.

On the other hand, actions cannot subsist for themselves, but must attach to certain things or persons. Now in so far as these things are bodies or are regarded as bodies, poetry too depicts bodies, but only by way of suggestion through actions.

Painting, in her co-existing compositions, can use only one single moment of the action, and must therefore choose the most pregnant, from which what precedes and follows will be most easily apprehended.

Just in the same manner poetry also can use, in her continuous imitations, only one single property of the bodies, and must therefore choose that one which calls up the most living picture of the body on that side from which she is regarding it. Here, indeed, we find the origin of the rule which insists on the unity and consistency of descriptive epithets, and on economy in the delineations of bodily subjects.

This is a dry chain of reasoning, and I should put less trust in it if I did not find it completely confirmed by Homer's practice, or if, rather, it were not Homer's practice itself which had led me to it. Only by these principles can the great manner of the Greeks be settled and explained, and its rightness established against the opposite manner of so many modern poets, who would emulate the painter in a department where they must necessarily be outdone by him.

Homer, I find, paints nothing but continuous actions, and all bodies, all single things, he paints only by their share in those actions, and in general only by one feature. What wonder, then, that the painter, where Homer himself paints, finds little or nothing for him to do, his harvest arising only there where the story brings together a multitude of beautiful bodies, in beautiful attitudes, in a place favourable to art, the poet himself painting these bodies, attitudes, places, just as little as he chooses? Let the reader run through the whole succession of pictures piece by piece, as Caylus suggests, and he will discover in every one of them evidence for our contention.

Here, then, I leave the Count, who wishes to make the painter's palette the touchstone of the poet, that I may expound in closer detail the manner of Homer.

For one thing, I say, Homer commonly names one feature only. A ship is to him now the black ship, now the hollow ship, now the swift ship, at most the well-rowed black ship. Beyond that he does not enter on a picture of the ship. But certainly of the navigating, the putting to sea, the disembarking of the ship, he makes a detailed picture, one from which the painter must make five or six separate pictures if he would get it in its entirety upon his canvas.

If indeed special circumstances compel Homer to fix our glance for a while on some single corporeal object, in spite of this no picture is made of it which the painter could follow with his brush; for Homer knows how, by innumerable artifices, to set this object in a succession of moments, at each of which it assumes a different appearance, and in the last of which the painter must await it in order to show us, fully arisen, what in the poet we see arising. For instance, if Homer wishes to let us see the chariot of Juno, then Hebe must put it together piece by piece before our eyes. We see the wheels, the axles, the seat, the pole and straps and traces, not so much as it is when complete, but as it comes together under the hands of Hebe. On the wheels alone does the poet expend more than one feature, showing us the brazen spokes, the golden rims, the tyres of bronze, the silver hub, in fullest detail. We might suggest that as there were more wheels than one, so in the description just as much more time must be given to them as their separate putting-on would actually itself require.

> Ἥβη δ' ἀμφ' ὀχέεσσι θοῶς βάλε καμπύλα κύκλα,
> Χάλκεα ὀκτάκνημα, σιδηρέῳ ἄξονι ἀμφίς.
> Τῶν ἤτοι χρυσέη ἴτυς ἄφθιτος, αὐτὰρ ὕπερθεν
> Χάλκε' ἐπίσσωτρα προσαρηρότα, θαῦμα ἰδέσθαι·
> Πλῆμναι δ' ἀργύρου εἰσὶ περίδρομοι ἀμφοτέρωθεν·
> Δίφρος δὲ χρυσέοισι καὶ ἀργυρέοισιν ἱμᾶσιν
> Ἐντέταται, δοιαὶ δὲ περίδρομοι ἄντυγές εἰσι.
> Τοῦ δ' ἐξ ἀργύρεος ῥυμὸς πέλευ· αὐτὰρ ἐπ' ἄκρῳ
> Δῆσε χρύσειον καλὸν ζυγόν, ἐν δὲ λέπαδνα
> Κάλ' ἔβαλε, χρύσεια.[54]

If Homer would show us how Agamemnon was dressed, then the King must put on his whole attire piece by piece before our eyes: the soft under-vest, the great mantle, the fine laced boots, the sword; and now he is ready and grasps the sceptre. We see the attire as the poet paints the action of attiring; another would have described the garments down to the smallest ribbon, and we should have seen nothing of the action.

> Μαλακὸν δ' ἔνδυνε χιτῶνα,
> Καλὸν, νηγάτεον, περὶ δ' αὖ μέγα βάλλετο φᾶρος·
> Ποσσὶ δ' ὑπαὶ λιπαροῖσιν ἐδήσατο καλὰ πέδιλα,
> Ἀμφὶ δ' ἄρ' ὤμοισιν βάλετο ξίφος ἀργυρόηλον·
> Εἵλετο δὲ σκῆπτρον πατρώϊον, ἄφθιτον αἰεί.[55]

And of this sceptre which here is called merely the paternal, ancestral sceptre, as in another place he calls a similar one merely χρυσείοις ἥλοισι πεπαρμένον – that is, the sceptre mounted with studs of gold – if, I say, of this mighty sceptre we are to have a fuller and exacter picture, what, then, does Homer? Does he paint for us, besides the golden nails, the wood also and the carved knob? Perhaps he might if the description were intended for a book of heraldry, so that in after times one like to it might be made precisely to pattern. And yet I am certain that many a modern poet would have made just such a heraldic description, with the naive idea that he has himself so painted it because the painter may possibly follow him. But what does Homer care how far he leaves the painter behind? Instead of an image he gives us the story of the sceptre: first, it is being wrought by Vulcan; then it gleams in the hands of Jupiter; again, it marks the office of Mercury; once more, it is the marshal's baton of the warlike Pelops, and yet again, the shepherd's crook of peace-loving Atreus.

Σκῆπτρον ἔχων, τὸ μὲν Ἥφαιστος κάμε τεύχων.
Ἥφαιστος μὲν δῶκε Διΐ Κρονίωνι ἄνακτι,
Αὐτὰρ ἄρα Ζεὺς δῶκε διακτόρῳ Ἀργεϊφόντῃ
Ἑρμείας δὲ ἄναξ δῶκεν Πέλοπι πληξίππῳ,
Αὐτὰρ ὁ αὖτε Πέλοψ δῶκ' Ἀτρέϊ, ποιμένι λαῶν·
Ἀτρεὺς δὲ θνῄσχων ἔλιπε πολύαρνι Θυέστῃ,
Αὐτὰρ ὁ αὖτε Θυέστ' Ἀγαμέμνονι λεῖπε φορῆναι,
Πολλῇσι νήσοισι καὶ Ἀργεϊ παντὶ ἀνάσσειν.[56]

[Section XVI ends with a discussion of the allegorical potential realized by Homer's narratives.]

XVII

But, some will object, the signs or characters which poetry employs are not solely such as succeed each other; they may be also arbitrary;[57] and, as arbitrary signs, they are certainly capable of representing bodies just as they exist in space. We find instances of this in Homer himself, for we have only to remember his Shield of Achilles in order to have the most decisive example in how detailed and yet poetical a manner some single thing can be depicted, with its various parts side by side.

I will reply to this twofold objection. I call it twofold, because a just conclusion must prevail even without examples, and, on the other hand, thé example of Homer weighs with me even if I know not how to justify it by any argument. It is true, as the signs of speech are arbitrary, so it is perfectly possible that by it we can make the parts of a body follow each other just as truly as in actuality they are found existing side by side. Only this is a property of speech and its signs in general, but not in so far as it suits best the purposes of poetry. The poet is not concerned merely to be intelligible, his representations should not merely be clear and plain, though this may satisfy the prose writer. He desires rather to make the ideas awakened by him within us living things, so that for the moment we realise the true sensuous impressions of the objects he describes, and cease in this moment of illusion to be conscious of the means – namely, his words – which he employs for his purpose. This is the substance of what we have already said of the poetic picture. But the poet should always paint; and now let us see how far bodies with their parts set side by side are suitable for this kind of painting.

How do we arrive at the distinct representation of a thing in space? First we regard its parts singly, then the combination of these parts, and finally the whole. Our senses perform these various operations with so astonishing a swiftness that they seem to us but one, and this swiftness is imperatively necessary if we are to arrive at a conception of the whole, which is nothing more than the result of the conceptions of the parts and their combination. Provided, then, the poet leads us in the most beautiful order from one part of the object to another; provided he knows also how to make the combination of those parts equally clear – how much time does he need for that? What the eye sees at a glance, he counts out to us gradually, with a perceptible slowness, and often it happens that when we come to the last feature we have already forgotten the first. Nevertheless, we have to frame a whole from those features; to the eye the parts beheld remain constantly present, and it can run over them again and again; for the ear, on the contrary, the parts heard are lost if they do not abide in the memory. And if they so abide, what trouble, what effort it costs to renew their impressions, all of them in their due order, so vividly, to think of them together with even a moderate swiftness, and thus to arrive at an eventual conception of the whole. Let us try it by an example which may be called a masterpiece of its kind:[58]

> Dort ragt das hohe Haupt vom edeln Enziane
> Weit übern niedern Chor der Pöbelkräuter hin,
> Ein ganzes Blumenvolk dient unter seiner Fahne,
> Sein blauer Bruder selbst bückt sich und ehret ihn.
> Der Blumen helles Gold, in Strahlen umgebogen,
> Thürmt sich am Stengel auf, und krönt sein grau Gewand,
> Der Blätter glattes Weiß, mit tiefem Grün durchzogen,
> Strahlt von dem bunten Blitz von feuchtem Diamant.
> Gerechtestes Gesetz! daß Kraft sich Zier vermähle,
> In einem schönen Leib wohnt eine schönre Seele.
>
> Hier kriecht ein niedrig Kraut, gleich einem grauen Nebel,
> Dem die Natur sein Blatt im Kreuze hingelegt;
> Die holde Blume zeigt die zwei vergöldten Schnäbel,
> Die ein von Amethyst gebildter Vogel trägt.
> Dort wirft ein glänzend Blatt, in Finger ausgekerbet,
> Auf einen hellen Bach den grünen Widerschein;
> Der Blumen zarten Schnee, den matter Purpur färbet,
> Schließt ein gestreifter Stern in weiße Strahlen ein.
> Smaragd und Rosen blühn auch auf zertretner Heide,
> Und Felsen decken sich mit einem Purpurkleide.

Here are weeds and flowers which the learned poet paints with much art and fidelity to Nature. Paints, but without any illusion whatever. I will not say that out of this picture he who has never seen these weeds and flowers can make no idea of them, or as good as none. It may be that all poetic pictures require some preliminary acquaintance with their subjects. Neither will I deny that for one who possesses such an acquaintance here the poet may not have awakened a more vivid idea of some parts. I only ask him, how does it stand with the conception of the whole? If this also is to be more vivid, then no single parts must stand out, but the higher light must appear divided equally amongst them all, our imagination must be able to run over them all with equal swiftness, in order to unite in one from them that which in Nature we see united in one. Is this the case here? And if it is not the case, how could anyone maintain 'that the most perfect drawing of a painter must be entirely lifeless and dark compared with this poetic portrayal'?[59] It remains infinitely below that which lines and colours on canvas can express, and the critic who bestows on it this exaggerated praise must have regarded it from an utterly false point of view: he must have looked rather at the ornaments which the poet has woven into it, at the heightening of the subject above the mere vegetative life, at the development of the inner perfection to which the outward beauty serves merely as a shell, than at the beauty itself and at the degree of life and resemblance in the picture which the painter and which the poet can assure to us from it. Nevertheless, we are concerned here purely with the latter, and whoever says that the mere lines:—

> Der Blumen helles Gold, in Strahlen umgebogen,
> Thürmt sich am Stengel auf, und krönt sein grün Gewand,
> Der Blätter glattes Weiß, mit tiefem Grün durchzogen,
> Strahlt von dem bunten Blitz von feuchtem Diamant

— that these lines in respect of their impression can compete with the imitation of a Huysum,[60] can never have interrogated his feelings, or must be deliberately denying them. They may, indeed, if we have the flower itself in our hands, be recited concerning it with excellent effect; but in themselves alone they say little or nothing. I hear in every word the toiling poet, and am far enough from seeing the thing itself.

Once more, then; I do not deny to speech in general the power of portraying a bodily whole by its parts: speech can do so, because its signs or characters, although they follow one another consecutively, are nevertheless arbitrary signs; but I do deny it to speech as the medium of poetry, because such verbal delineations of bodies fail of the illusion on which poetry particularly depends, and this illusion, I contend, must fail them for the reason that the *co-existence* of the physical object comes into collision with the *consecutiveness* of speech, and the former being resolved into the latter, the dismemberment of the whole into its parts is certainly made easier, but the final reunion of those parts into a whole is made uncommonly difficult and not seldom impossible.

Wherever, then, illusion does not come into the question, where one has only to do with the understanding of one's readers and aims only at plain and as far as possible complete concepts, those delineations of bodies (which we have excluded from poetry) may quite well find their place, and not the prose-writer alone, but the didactic poet (for where he dogmatises he is not a poet) can employ them with much advantage. So Virgil, for instance, in his poem on agriculture, delineates a cow suitable for breeding from:—

> . . . Optima torvae
> Forma bovis, cui turpe caput, cui plurima cervix,
> Et crurum tenus a mento palearia pendent;

> Tum longo nullus lateri modus: omnia magna,
> Pes etiam, et camuris hirtae sub cornibus aures.
> Nec mihi displiceat maculis insignis et albo,
> Aut juga detractans interdumque aspera cornu
> Et faciem tauro propior, quaeque ardua tota,
> Et gradiens ima verrit vestigia cauda.[61]

Or a beautiful foal:–

> . . . Illi ardua cervix
> Argutumque caput, brevis alvus, obesaque terga,
> Luxuriatque toris animosum pectus, etc.[62]

For who does not see that here the poet is concerned rather with the setting forth of the parts than with the whole? He wants to reckon up for us the characteristics of a fine foal and of a well-formed cow, in order to enable us, when we have more or less taken note of these, to judge of the excellence of the one or the other; whether, however, all these characteristics can be easily gathered together into one living picture or not, that might be to him a matter of indifference.

Beyond such performances as these, the detailed pictures of physical objects, barring the above-mentioned Homeric artifice of changing the Co-existing into an actual Successive, has always been recognized by the best judges as a frigid kind of sport for which little or nothing of genius is demanded. 'When the poetic dabbler', says Horace, 'can do nothing more, he begins to paint a hedge, an altar, a brook winding through pleasant meads, a brawling stream, or a rainbow:–

> . . . Lucus et ara Dianae
> Et properantis aquae per amoenos ambitus agros,
> Aut flumen Rhenum, aut pluvius describitur arcus.'[63]

Pope, in his manhood, looked back on the pictorial efforts of his poetic childhood with great contempt. He expressly required that whosoever would not unworthily bear the name of poet should as early as possible renounce the lust for description, and declared a merely descriptive poem to be a dinner of nothing but soup.[64] Of Herr von Kleist I can avow that he was far from proud of his 'Spring': had he lived longer, he would have given it an entirely different shape.[65] He thought of putting some design into it, and mused on means by which that multitude of pictures which he seemed to have snatched haphazard, now here, now there, from the limitless field of rejuvenated Nature, might be made to arise in a natural order before his eyes and follow each other in a natural succession. He would at the same time have done what Marmontel,[66] doubtless on the occasion of his Eclogues,[67] recommended to several German poets; from a series of pictures but sparingly interspersed with sensations he would have made a succession of sensations but sparingly interspersed with pictures.

XVIII

And yet may not Homer himself sometimes have lapsed into these frigid delineations of physical objects?

I will hope that there are only a few passages to which in this case appeal can be made; and I am assured that even these few are of such a kind as rather to confirm the rule from which they seem to be exceptions. It still holds good; succession in time is the sphere of the poet, as space is that of the painter. To bring two necessarily distant points of time into one and the same picture, as Fr. Mazzuoli[68] has done with the Rape of the Sabine Women and their reconciling their husbands to their kinfolk, or as Titian with the whole story of the Prodigal Son, his dissolute life, his misery, and his repentance, is nothing but an invasion of the poet's sphere by the painter, which good taste can never sanction. The several parts or things which in Nature I must needs take in at a glance if they are to produce a whole – to reckon these up one by one to the reader, in order to form for him a picture of the whole, is nothing but an invasion of the painter's sphere by the poet, who expends thereby a great deal of imagination to no purpose. Still, as two friendly, reasonable neighbours will not at all permit that one of them shall make too free with the most intimate concerns of the other, yet will exercise in things of less importance a mutual forbearance and on either side condone trifling interferences with one's strict rights to which circumstances may give occasion, so it is with Painting and Poetry.

It is unnecessary here for my purpose to point out that in great historical pictures the single moment is almost always amplified to some extent, and that there is perhaps no single composition very rich in figures where every figure has completely the movement and posture which at the moment of the main action it ought to have; one is earlier, another later, than historical truth would require. This is a liberty which the master must make good by certain niceties of arrangement, by the position or distance of his *personae*, such as will permit them to take a greater or a smaller share in what is passing at the moment. Let me here avail myself of but one remark which Herr Mengs has made concerning the drapery of Raphael.[69] 'All folds', he says, 'have with him their reasons, it may be from their own weight or by the pulling of the limbs. We can often see from them how they have been at an earlier moment; even in this Raphael seeks significance. One sees from the folds whether a leg or an arm, before the moment depicted, has stood in front or behind, whether the limb has moved from curvature to extension, or after being stretched out is now bending.' It is undeniable that the artist in this case brings two different moments into one. For as the foot which has rested behind and now moves forward is immediately followed by the part of the dress resting upon it, unless the dress be of very stiff material and for that very reason is altogether inconvenient to paint, so there is no moment in which the dress makes a fold different in the slightest from that which the present position of the limb demands; but if we permit it to make another fold, then we have the previous moment of the dress and the present moment of the limb. Nevertheless, who will be so particular with the artist who finds his advantage in showing us these two moments together? Who will not rather praise him for having the intelligence and the courage to commit a fault so trifling in order to attain a greater perfection of expression?

The poet is entitled to equal indulgence. His progressive imitation properly allows him to touch but one single side, one single property of his physical subject at a time. But if the happy construction of his language permits him to do this with a single word, why should he not also venture now and then to add a second such word? Why not even, if it is worth the trouble, a third? Or, indeed, perhaps a fourth? I have said that to Homer a ship was either the black ship, or the hollow ship, or the swift ship, or at most the well-rowed black ship. This is to be understood of his manner in general. Here and there a passage occurs where he adds the third descriptive epithet: Καμπύλα κύκλα, χάλκεα, ὀκτάκνημα, round, brazen, eight-spoked wheels.[70] Even the fourth: ἀσπίδα πάντοσε ἴσην, καλήν, χαλκείην, ἐξήλατον, a completely polished, beautiful, brazen, chased shield.[71] Who will blame him for that? Who will not rather owe him thanks for this little exuberance, when he feels what an excellent effect it may have in a suitable place?

I am unwilling, however, to argue the poet's or the painter's proper justification from the simile I have employed, of the two friendly neighbours. A mere simile proves and justifies nothing. But they must be justified in this way: just as in the one case, with the painter, the two distinct moments touch each other so closely and immediately that they may without offence count as but one, so also in the other case, with the poet, the several strokes for the different parts and properties in space succeed each other so quickly, in such a crowded moment, that we can believe we hear all of them at once.

And in this, I may remark, his splendid language served Homer marvelously. It allowed him not merely all possible freedom in the combining and heaping-up of epithets, but it had, too, for their heaped-up epithets an order so happy as quite to remedy the disadvantage arising from the suspension of their application. In one or several of these facilities the modern languages are universally lacking. Those, like the French, which, to give an example, for καμπύλα κύκλα, χάλκεα, ὀκτάκνημα, must use the circumlocution 'the round wheels which were of brass and had eight spokes', express the sense, but destroy the picture. The sense, moreover, is here nothing, and the picture everything; and the former without the latter makes the most vivid poet the most tedious babbler – a fate that has frequently befallen our good Homer under the pen of the conscientious

Madame Dacier.[72] Our German tongue, again, can, it is true, generally translate the Homeric epithets by epithets equivalent and just as terse, but in the advantageous order of them it cannot match the Greek. We say, indeed, *'Die runden, ehernen, achtspeichigten';*[73] but *'Räder'*[74] trails behind. Who does not feel that three different predicates, before we know the subject, can make but a vague and confused picture? The Greek joins the subject and the first predicate immediately, and lets the other follow after; he says, *'Runde Räder, eherne, achtspeichigte'*. So we know at once of what he is speaking, and are made acquainted, in consonance with the natural order of thought, first with the thing and then with its accidents. This advantage our language does not possess. Or, shall I say, possesses it and can only very seldom use it without ambiguity? The two things are one. For when we would place the epithets after, they must stand *in statu absoluto;* we must say, *'Runde Räder, ehern und achtspeichigt'*. But in this *status* our adjectives are exactly like adverbs, and must, if we attach them as such to the next verb which is predicated of the thing, produce a meaning not seldom wholly false, and, at best, invariably ambiguous.

But here I am dwelling on trifles, and seem to have forgotten the Shield – Achilles' Shield, that famous picture in respect of which especially Homer was from of old regarded as a teacher of painting. A shield, people will say – that is surely a single physical object, the description of which and its parts ranged side by side is not permissible to a poet? And this particular Shield, in its material, in its form, in all the figures that covered the vast surface of it, Homer has described in more than a hundred splendid verses, with such exactness and detail that it has been easy for modern artists to make a replica of it alike in every feature.

To this special objection I reply, that I have replied to it already. Homer, that is to say, paints the Shield not as a finished and complete thing, but as a thing in process. Here once more he has availed himself of the famous artifice, turning the *co-existing* of his design into a *consecutive,* and thereby making of the tedious painting of a physical object the living picture of an action. We see not the Shield, but the divine artificer at work upon it. He steps up with hammer and tongs to his anvil, and after he has forged the plates from the rough ore, the pictures which he has selected for its adornment stand out one after another before our eyes under his artistic chiselling. Nor do we lose sight of him again until all is finished. When it is complete, we are amazed at the work, but it is with the believing amazement of an eye-witness who has seen it in the making.

The same cannot be said of the Shield of Aeneas in Virgil. The Roman poet either did not realise the subtlety of his model here, or the things that he wanted to put upon his Shield appeared to him to be of a kind that could not well admit of being shown in execution. They were prophecies, which could not have been uttered by the god in our presence as plainly as the poet afterwards expounds them. Prophecies, as such, demand an obscurer language, in which the actual names of persons yet-to-be may not fitly be pronounced. Yet these veritable names, to all appearance, were the most important things of all to the poet and courtier. If, however, this excuses him, it does not remove the unhappy effect of his deviation from the Homeric way. Readers of any delicacy of taste will justify me here. The preparations which Vulcan makes for his labour are almost the same in Virgil as in Homer. But instead of what we see in Homer – that is to say, not merely the preparations for the work, but also the work itself – Virgil after he has given us a general view of the busy god with his Cyclops:–

> Ingentem clypeum informant . . .
>   . . . Alii ventosis follibus auras
> Accipiunt redduntque, alii stridentia tingunt
> Aera lacu. Gemit impositis incudibus antrum.
> Illi inter sese multa vi brachia tollunt
> In numerum, versantque tenaci forcipe massam –[75]

drops the curtain at once and transports us to another scene, bringing us gradually into the valley where Venus arrives at Aeneas' side with the armour that has meanwhile been completed. She leans the weapons against the trunk of an oak-tree, and when the hero has sufficiently gazed at, and admired, and touched and tested them, the description of the pictures on the Shield begins, and, with the everlasting: 'Here is', 'and there is', 'near by stands', and 'not far off one sees', becomes so frigid and tedious that all the poetic ornament which Virgil could give it was needed to prevent us finding it unendurable. Moreover, as this picture is not drawn by Aeneas as one who rejoices in the mere figures and knows nothing of their significance:–

> . . . rerumque ignarus imagine gaudet,[76]

nor even by Venus, although conceivably she must know just as much of the future fortunes of her dear grandchildren as her obliging husband,[77] but proceeds from the poet's own mouth. The progress of the action meanwhile is obviously at a standstill. No single one of his characters takes any share in it; nor does anything represented on the Shield have any influence, even the smallest, on what is to follow; the witty courtier shines out everywhere, trimming up his matter with every kind of flattering allusion, but not the great genius, depending on the proper inner vitality of his work and despising all extraneous expedients for lending it interest. The Shield of Aeneas is consequently a sheer interpolation, simply and only intended to flatter the national pride of the Romans, a foreign tributary which the poet leads into his main stream in order to give it a livelier motion. The

Shield of Achilles, on the other hand, is a rich natural outgrowth of the fertile soil from which it springs; for a Shield had to be made, and as the needful thing never comes bare and without grace from the hands of the divinity, the Shield had also to be embellished. But the art was, to treat these embellishments merely as such, to inweave them into the stuff, in order to show them to us only by means of the latter; and this could only be done by Homer's method. Homer lets Vulcan elaborate ornaments because he is to make a Shield that is worthy of himself. Virgil, on the other hand, appears to let him make the Shield for the sake of its ornaments, considering them important enough to be particularly described, after the Shield itself has long been finished.

[Sections XIX and XX discuss the critical commentaries on Homer's description of the shield of Achilles, arguing that poetry proper cannot depict beauty, which depends upon the immediate perception of the relation of the parts to a whole. Great poets thus do not attempt this task.]

XXI

But does not Poetry lose too much if we take from her all pictures of physical beauty? Who wishes to do so? If we seek to close to her one single road, on which she hopes to achieve such pictures by following in the footsteps of a sister art, where she stumbles painfully without ever attaining the same goal, do we, then, at the same time close to her every other road, where Art in her turn can but follow at a distance?

Even Homer, who with evident intention refrains from all piecemeal delineation of physical beauties, from whom we can scarcely once learn in passing that Helen had white arms and beautiful hair – even he knows how, nevertheless, to give us such a conception of her beauty as far outpasses all that Art in this respect can offer. Let us recall the passage where Helen steps into the assembly of the Elders of the Trojan people. The venerable old men looked on her, and one said to the other:–

> Οὐ νέμεσις Τρῶας καὶ ἐϋκνήμιδας Ἀχαιοὺς
> Τοιῇδ' ἀμφὶ γυναικὶ πολὺν χρόνον ἄλγεα πάσχειν
> Αἰνῶς ἀθανάτηισι θεῆς εἰς ὦπα ἔοικεν.[78]

What can convey a more vivid idea of Beauty than to have frigid age confessing her well worth the war that has cost so much blood and so many tears? What Homer could not describe in its component parts, he makes us feel in its working. Paint us, then, poet, the satisfaction, the affection, the love, the delight, which beauty produces, and you have painted beauty itself. Who can imagine as ill-favoured the beloved object of Sappho,[79] the very sight of whom she confesses robbed her of her senses and her reason? Who does not fancy he beholds with his own eyes the fairest, most perfect form, as soon as he sympathises with the feeling which nothing but such a form can awaken? Not because Ovid shows us the beautiful body of his Lesbia part by part:

> Quos humeros, quales vidi tetigique lacertos!
>   Forma papillarum quam fuit apta premi!
> Quam castigato planus sub pectore venter!
>   Quantum et quale latus! quam juvenile femur! –[80]

but because he does so with the voluptuous intoxication in which it is so easy to awaken our longing, we imagine ourselves enjoying the same sight of exquisite beauty which he enjoyed.

Another way in which poetry in its turn overtakes art in delineation of physical beauty is by transmuting beauty into grace. Grace is beauty in motion, and just for that reason less suitable to the painter than to the poet. The painter can only help us to guess the motion, but in fact his figures are motionless. Consequently grace with him is turned into grimace. But in poetry it remains what it is – a transitory beauty which we want to see again and again. It comes and goes; and as we can generally recall a movement more easily and more vividly than mere forms and colours, grace can in such a case work more powerfully on us than beauty. All that still pleases and touches us in the picture of Alcina is grace. The impression her eyes make does not come from the fact that they are dark and passionate, but rather that they:–

> Pietosi à riguardar, à mover parchi –

'look round her graciously and slowly turn'; that Love flutters about them and from them empties all his quiver. Her mouth delights us, not because lips tinted with cinnabar enclose two rows of choicest pearls; but because there the lovely smile is shaped which in itself seems to open up an earthly paradise; because from it the friendly words come forth that soften the most savage breast. Her bosom enchants us, less because milk and ivory and apples typify its whiteness and delicate forms than because we see it softly rise and fall, like the waves at the margin of the shore when a playful zephyr contends with the ocean:–

> Due pome acerbi, e pur d'avorio fatte,
> Vengono e van, come onda al primo margo,
> Quando piacevole aura il mar combatte.[81]

I am sure such features of grace by themselves, condensed into one or two stanzas, will do more than all the five into which Ariosto has spun them out, inweaving them with frigid details of the fair form, far too erudite for our appreciation.

Even Anacreon himself would rather fall into the apparent impropriety of demanding impossibilities from the painter than leave the picture of his beloved untouched with grace:—

> Τρυφεροῦ δ' ἔσω γενείου,
> Περὶ λυγδίνῳ τραχήλῳ
> χάριτες πέτοιντο πᾶσαι.[82]

Her chin of softness, her neck of marble – let all the Graces hover round them, he bids the artist. And how? In the exact and literal sense? That is not capable of any pictorial realisation. The painter could give the chin the most exquisite curve, the prettiest dimple, *Amoris digitulo impressum*[83] (for the ἔσω appears to me to signify a dimple); he could give the neck the most beautiful carnation; but he can do no more. The turning of this fair neck, the play of the muscles, by which that dimple is now more visible, now less, the peculiar grace, all are beyond his powers. The poet said the utmost by which his art could make beauty real to us, so that the painter also might strive for the utmost expression in his art. A fresh example of the principle already affirmed – that the poet even when he speaks of works of art is not bound in his descriptions to confine himself within the limits of art.

XXII

Zeuxis[84] painted a Helen and had the courage to set under it those famous lines of Homer in which the enchanted Elders confess their emotions. Never were painting and poetry drawn into a more equal contest. The victory remained undecided, and both deserved to be crowned. For, just as the wise poet showed beauty merely in its effect, which he felt he could not delineate in its component parts, so did the no less wise painter show us beauty by nothing else than its component parts and held it unbecoming to his art to resort to any other method. His picture consisted in the single figure of Helen, standing in naked beauty. For it is probable that it was the very Helen which he painted for the people of Crotona.[85]

[The final sections, XXII–XXV, continue the discussion of part-whole relations as they apply to the aesthetics of ugliness in poetry and painting.]

Letter to Nicolai

26 May 1769[1]

Translated by Joyce P. Crick.

German text in *Sämtliche Schriften*, edited by Lachmann and Muncker (1886–1924), XVII, 289–92.

I can be well satisfied with the review of my *Laocoon* in the last issue of your *Bibliothek*.[2] And I think I know the name of the reviewer. But what do I care about names? After all, I shall not make the acquaintance of the person. If he goes on to read the continuation of my book,[3] he will probably find that his strictures do not apply. I grant, there are various things in it which are not sufficiently precise; but how can they be, when I have barely begun to consider the one distinction between poetry and painting which arises from the different use of their representational signs, insofar as the signs of the one exist in time, and of the other in space. Both can be either natural or arbitrary; consequently there must be two sorts of painting and two sorts of poetry, a higher and a lower kind. Painting requires co-existing signs, which are either natural or arbitrary; and this same distinction is also to be found in the consecutive signs of poetry. For it is not true that painting uses only natural signs, just as it is not true that poetry uses only arbitrary signs. But one thing is certain: the more painting departs from natural signs, or employs natural and arbitrary signs mixed together, the further it departs from its true perfection; just as conversely poetry draws all the closer to its true perfection, the closer it makes its arbitrary signs approach the natural. Consequently the higher kind of painting is that which employs only natural signs in space, and the higher kind of poetry is that which employs only natural signs in time. Consequently, neither historical nor allegorical painting can belong to the higher kind, for they can be understood only by means of their additional arbitrary signs. By arbitrary signs in painting I do not only mean the costuming and all that pertains to it, but also much of the bodily expressiveness itself. It is true that these things are not really arbitrary in painting; their signs in painting are also natural signs; but they are still *natural* signs of *arbitrary* things, which could not possibly produce that general understanding, that swift and immediate effect which *natural* signs of *natural* things can produce. Now if in this latter case the highest law is the law of beauty, and if my reviewer himself admits that the painter is in fact most fully painter when this is so, then we are in agreement, and, as I said, his strictures do not touch my argument. For everything I said about painting applied only to the effect of painting on the viewer at its highest and most painterly. I have never denied that it can also produce effects enough quite apart form this; I only wanted to deny that the name of painting was any the less appropriate then. I have never doubted the effect produced by historical and allegorical painting, still less wanted to banish these kinds from the world. I said only that in this respect the painter is less of a painter than in painting where his sole end and purpose is beauty. And does the reviewer concede me that? And now a word more about poetry, so that you do not misunderstand what I have just said. Poetry must endeavour absolutely to elevate its arbitrary signs into natural ones, for only thereby is it distinguished from prose and becomes poetry. The means it employs to do this are tone, choice of words, arrangement of words, metre, figures of speech, tropes, metaphors and so forth. All these things cause the arbitrary signs to approximate more closely to the natural; but they do not make them natural signs; consequently all the kinds of poetry that employ only these means are to be regarded as the lower kinds of poetry; and the highest kind of poetry is the one that turns the arbitrary signs wholly into natural signs.[4] Now that is dramatic poetry, for in drama the words cease to be arbitrary signs, and become the *natural* signs of arbitrary things. Aristotle already declared that dramatic poetry is the highest, indeed the only poetry, and he puts epic poetry into second place only insofar as it is, or can be, to a large extent dramatic. The reason he gives for this is not mine, it is true; but it can be reduced to mine, and only reducing it to mine ensures it against being applied falsely.

If you happen to have a half hour's conversation with Herr Moses[5] about it, pray let me know what he has to say. The third part of my *Laokoon* will constitute a further development of these ideas.[6]

Part 2

Herder

Johann Gottfried Herder

(1744–1803)

Herder was born in Mohrungen in East Prussia, and grew up in humble circumstances. He studied theology at Königsberg University from 1762 to 1764, and attended the lectures of the young Immanuel Kant, who had not yet emancipated himself from post-Cartesian rationalism and was keenly interested in the sciences. At the same time, he became friendly with the deeply religious Hamann.

Herder taught at a school in Riga for several years, and thereafter occupied posts of increasing seniority within the Lutheran church, at Riga (1767–9), Bückeburg (1771–6), and Weimar (1776–1803). He was a polymath and prolific writer from an early age. His early works deal mainly with literary and aesthetic theory, and are indebted to, among others, Lessing, Winckelmann, and Hamann. His prize-essay *On the Origin of Language* (1771) applied naturalistic, psychological methods to the problem of linguistic origins, and the essays on Ossian and on Shakespeare (1773) display a degree of imaginative historical understanding hitherto unprecedented in the German Enlightenment. The historical relativism already apparent in these essays is extended to history as a whole in his (ironically entitled) *Yet Another Philosophy of History* (1774), in which the then fashionable optimism of progress is rejected in favour of a more sympathetic view of primitive societies and of the Middle Ages.

After a series of theological works, some of them close in spirit to Hamann and often concerned with the poetic aspects of the Bible, Herder returned to history with his greatest work, the *Ideas on the Philosophy of History* of 1784–91. Human history is now placed in the context of the physical universe as a whole, and the determining influence of climate and geography is emphasised. Herder's earlier relativism is now modified by a belief in rational laws in both nature and human history. His late works, mainly collections of essays in periodical form, show an increasingly secular spirit. *God, a Series of Dialogues* (1787) expounds a form of nature pantheism strongly influenced by Spinoza, and anticipates the *Naturphilosophie* of Schelling. His last years were embittered by a feud with his former teacher Kant, whose critical philosophy seemed to Herder a new form of scholasticism divorced from experience, and by a breach in his long friendship with Goethe.

Herder was an unsystematic and eclectic thinker, but his fertile mind generated ideas which others, including Goethe, Schiller, Schelling, and Alexander von Humboldt, were to develop further. Perhaps his greatest contribution to German thought is his historical relativism, which taught his successors to assess each age and culture on its own terms and helped to discredit the linear and progressive model of history favoured by the rationalists of the *Aufklärung*.

Further reading

The standard edition of the works is that of Suphan (1877–1913), and the new edition of the letters by Hahn (1977–85) is now completed. Barnard (1969) contains a useful selection of English translations from the works, and there are complete translations of *On the Origin of Language* by Moran and Gode (1967), *God* by Burkhardt (new edition, 1962), and the *Reflections on the Philosophy of History* (= *Ideas on the Philosophy of History*) by Churchill (new edition, 1968). The standard biography is that of Haym (new edition, 1954), and there are shorter (Gillies, 1945) and longer (Clark, 1955) biographies in English. Berlin (1976) assesses Herder's stimulus to Romanticism, Wells (1959) and Barnard (1965) deal with social and political aspects, and Nisbet (1970) examines Herder's relationship with the sciences.

HBN

Extract from

*Correspondence on Ossian and
the Songs of Ancient Peoples*[1]

1773

Translated by Joyce P. Crick, with modifications by the editor.

German text in *Sämtliche Werke*, edited by Suphan (1877–1913), V, 159–207.

[Herder welcomes the appearance of a German translation of *Ossian*[2] – in whose authenticity he believes – but disputes the translator's use of the hexameter as anachronistic.]

Know then, that the more barbarous a people is – that is, the more alive, the more freely acting (for that is what the word means) – the more barbarous, that is, the more alive, the more free, the closer to the senses, the more lyrically dynamic its songs will be, if songs it has. The more remote a people is from an artificial, scientific manner of thinking, speaking, and writing, the less its songs are made for paper and print, the less its verses are written for the dead letter. The purpose, the nature, the miraculous power of these songs as the delight, the driving-force, the traditional chant and everlasting joy of the people – all this depends on the lyrical, living, dance-like quality of the song, on the living presence of the images, and the coherence and, as it were, compulsion of the content, the feelings; on the symmetry of the words and syllables, and sometimes even of the letters, on the flow of the melody, and on a hundred other things which belong to the living world, to the gnomic song of the nation, and vanish with it. These are the arrows of this barbarous Apollo with which he pierces our hearts and transfixes soul and memory. The longer the song is to last, the stronger and more attached to the senses these arousers of the soul must be to defy the power of time and the changes of the centuries – so which way does my argument turn now?

The Scandinavians, as we find them throughout Ossian too, were certainly a wilder, ruder people than the mild idealised Scots. I do not know of any Scandinavian song where a gentle feeling flows. They tread on rock and ice and frozen earth, and with regard to such treatment and culture, I do not know any Scandinavian poem that can be compared with Ossian's. But if once you look at their poems in the editions of Worm, Bartholin,

Peringskiöld, or Verel[3] – how many kinds of metre! how exactly each one
is determined by the ear's immediate susceptibility to rhythm! alliterative
syllables symmetrically arranged within the lines like signals for the metri-
cal beat, marching-orders to the warrior-band. Alliterative sounds as a call
to arms, for the bardic song to resound against the shields. Distichs and
lines corresponding! Vowels alike! Syllables harmonising – truly a rhyth-
mical pulse to the line so skilful, rapid, and exact that we study-bound
readers have difficulty apprehending it with our eyes alone. But those peoples in all their vitality who did not read it from the page but heard it,
heard it from childhood on and joined in singing it and adapted their ear
to it – do not imagine that they had any difficulty with the rhythm! Nothing
becomes habituated more strongly and enduringly, more rapidly and del-
icately than the ear. Once it has grasped a thing, how durably it retains it!
Once apprehended in our youth with stumbling speech, how vividly it
returns to us, and in swift association with every aspect of the living world,
how richly and powerfully it returns! If I were minded to psychologise, I
could relate you many a strange phenomenon from the realms of music,
song and speech![4]

*   *   *

And another thing. Read through Ossian's poems. In all the characteristics
of bardic song they resemble another nation which still lives and sings and
acts on earth today, and in whose history I have more than once recognised
without illusion or prejudice the living story of Ossian and his forebears.
They are the five Indian nations of North America: war-cry and lament,
battle-song and funeral dirge, historical paeans on their forefathers and to
their forefathers – all this is common to Ossian's bards and the North
American savages alike. I make an exception of the Indians' songs promising torture and revenge; instead the gentle Caledonians coloured their
songs with the tender blood of love. Now look at how all the travellers,
Charlevoix and Lafiteau, Rogers and Cadwallader Colden have described
the tone, the rhythm, the power of these songs even for strangers' ears.[5]
Examine how all the reports agree on how much these songs depend for
their effect upon living movement, melody, gesture, and mime. And when
travellers acquainted with the Scots who have also lived for long periods
among the American Indians – Captain Timberlake,[6] for example –
acknowledge the obvious similarity between the lays of both nations – you
can draw your own conclusions. With Denis' translation our feet are firmly
planted on dull earth: we can hear something of the content and meaning
conveyed in our own decently poetic idiom; but not a sound, not a tone
resembling all the barbarous tribes, not a single living breath from the
Caledonian hills to raise our hearts and set our pulses racing and bring us
the living sound of their songs. We sit and read with our feet firmly on dull
earth.

I once hoped deep in my heart that I might some day travel to England.

Dear friend, you cannot imagine how I counted on visiting these Scots too! First an insight, I thought, into the spirit of this nation, into its public institutions, into the English stage and the vast living drama of the English people to clarify my ideas about the history, philosophy, politics, and peculiarities of this marvellous nation which are so often obscure and confused in the mind of the foreigner. And then the great change of scenery – to the Scots, to Macpherson! There I wanted to hear a living performance of a living people's songs, see them in all their effectiveness, see the places that are so alive in all their poems, study in their customs the remains of that ancient world, become for a while an ancient Caledonian myself – and then back to England to increase my acquaintance with the living monuments of her literature, art collections, and the finer points of her national character – how much I looked forward to fulfilling this plan! And as a translator I would certainly have set about my task in a completely different way from Denis. For him, even the example of the original Gaelic offered by Macpherson was printed in vain.

. . . You mock my enthusiasm for these savages almost as Voltaire scoffed at Rousseau for wanting to go on all fours:[7] but do not think that this makes me despise the advantages of our own morals and manners, whatever they may be. The human race is destined to develop through a series of scenes in culture and customs; alas for the man who mislikes the scene on which he has to make his entrance, do his deeds, and live his life! But alas too for the philosopher of mankind and culture who thinks that his scene is the only one, and misjudges the primal scene to be the worst and the most primitive! If they all belong together as part of the great drama of history, then each one displays a new and remarkable aspect of humanity – and take care that I do not shortly afflict you with a psychology based on Ossian's poems! The ideas for one, at least, are stirring alive and deep in my heart, and would make very strange reading![8]

* * *

You know from travellers' accounts how vigorously and clearly savages always express themselves. Always with a sharp, vivid eye on the thing they want to say, using their senses, feeling the purpose of their utterance immediately and exactly, not distracted by shadowy concepts, half-ideas, and symbolic letter-understanding (the words of their language are innocent of this, for they have virtually no abstract terms); still less corrupted by artifices, slavish expectations, timid creeping politics, and confusing pre-meditation – blissfully ignorant of all these debilitations of the mind, they comprehend the thought as a whole with the whole word, and the word with the thought. Either they are silent, or they speak at the moment of involvement with an unpremeditated soundness, sureness, and beauty, which learned Europeans of all times could not but admire – and were bound to leave untouched. Our pedants who have to clobber everything

together in advance and learn it by rote before they can stammer it out
with might and method; our schoolmasters, sextons, apothecaries and all
the tribe of the little-learned who raid the scholar's house and come out
empty-handed until finally, like Shakespeare's gravediggers, his Lancelot
or his Dogberry, they speak in the uncertain inauthentic tones of decline
and death – compare these learned fellows with the savages! If you are
seeking traces of their firm clarity in our own time, do not go looking for
it among the pedants. Unspoiled children, women, folk of a sound natural
sense, minds formed less by speculation than by activity – these, if what I
have been describing is true eloquence, are the finest, nay the only orators
of our time.

But in ancient times, it was the poets, the skalds, the scholars who best
knew how to wed this sureness and clarity of expression to dignity, sonority, and beauty. And as they had thus united soul and voice and a firm
bond, not to confound each other but to be a support and an helpmeet,
thus it was that those (to us) half-miraculous works were composed by the
ἀοίδοις,[9] singers, bards, minstrels – for that is what the greatest poets of
ancient times were. Homer's rhapsodies and Ossian's songs were as it were
impromptus, for at that time oratory was known only in impromptu deliv-
ery. Ossian was followed, though faintly and at a distance, by the minstrels,
but still they did follow him, until finally Art arrived and extinguished
Nature. From our youth we have tormented ourselves learning foreign languages and spelling out the syllabic quantity of their verses, to which our
ear and nature can no longer respond; working according to rules virtually
none of which a genius would acknowledge as rules of Nature; composing
poetry about subject-matter that gives us nothing to think about, still less
to *sense,* and even less to imagine; feigning passions we do not feel; imitating faculties of the soul we do not possess – until finally it all turned false,
insipid, and artificial. Even the best minds were confounded, and lost their
sureness of eye and hand, their certainty of thought and expression and
with them their true vitality and truth and urgency – everything was lost.
Poetry, which should have been the most passionate, confident daughter
of the human soul, became the most insecure, weak and hesitant, and
poems turned into schoolboys' exercises for correction. And if that is the
way our time thinks, then of course we will admire Art rather than Nature
in these ancient poems; we will find too much or too little Art in them,
according to our predisposition, and we will rarely have ears to hear the
voice that sings in them: the voice of Nature. I am sure that if Homer and
Ossian were to come back to earth and hear their works read and praised,
they would all too often be astonished at what we add to them and take
away from them, at the artifices we apply to them, and at our lack of any
immediate feeling for them.

Of course our hearts and minds have been formed differently from
theirs by our education from youth and by the long intervening generations. We scarcely see and feel any longer: we only think and brood. Our

poetry does not emerge from a living world, nor exist in the storm and confluence of such objects and feelings. Instead we force either our theme or our treatment or both, and we have done so for so long and so often and from our tenderest years that if we attempted any free development, it would scarcely prosper; for how can a cripple get up and walk? That is why so many of our recent poems lack that certainty, that exactness, that full contour which comes only from the first spontaneous draft, not from any elaborate later revisions. Our ridiculous versifying would have appeared to Homer and Ossian as the weak scribbles of an apprentice would have appeared to Raphael, or to Apelles,[10] whose barest sketch revealed his mastery.

* * *

. . . You think that we Germans too probably had poems like the Scottish ballad I quoted.[11] I do not merely think so; I know it for certain. I know of folksongs, dialect songs, peasant-songs from more than one province which certainly yield nothing in the way of rhythm and liveliness, simplicity and vigour of language, to many such ballads. But who is there to collect them? to care about them? to care about the songs of the people, from the streets and alleys and fishmarkets? about the unsophisticated roundelays of country folk? about songs which often do not scan, whose rhymes are often false? who would take the trouble to collect them – who would bother to print them for our critics who are so clever at scansion and syllable-counting? We would rather read our prettily printed modern poets – just to pass the time, of course. Let the French collect their old *chansons*! Let the English publish their ancient songs and ballads and romances in splendid volumes! Let Lessing be the only one in Germany to bother about Logau and Scultetus and the old bardic lays![12] Our recent poets, of course, are better printed and more agreeable to read; at most we print extracts from Opitz, Fleming, and Gryphius.[13] Let the remnants of the old, true folk poetry vanish entirely with the daily advance of our so-called culture, just as many such treasures have already vanished – after all, we have metaphysics and dogmatics and bureaucratics – and we dream peacefully on –

And yet, believe me, if we were to go in search of our local songs, each one of us, in our own province, we might well gather poems together, perhaps half as many as in Percy's *Reliques,* but almost their equal in value! How often have I been reminded as I read poems from his collection, particularly the best Scottish pieces, of German customs and German poems, some of which I have heard myself. If you have friends in Alsace, in Switzerland, in the Tyrol, in Franconia or Swabia, then beg of them – first that they should not be ashamed of these poems – for the sturdy Englishmen were not ashamed of theirs, nor did they need to be.[14]

* * *

All the songs of these savage peoples move around objects, actions, events, around a living world! How rich and various are the details, incidents, immediate features! And the eye has seen it all, the mind has imagined it all. This implies leaps and gaps and sudden transitions. There is the same connection between the sections of these songs as there is between the trees and bushes of the forest; the same between the cliffs and grottoes of the wilderness as there is between the scenes of the event itself. When the Greenlander tells of the seal-hunt, he does not speak; he paints all the details with words and gestures, for they are all part of the picture in his mind. When he holds a graveside eulogy and sings a funeral dirge for his departed, he does not praise or lament, but paints, and the dead man's life, vividly portrayed with all the sudden leaps of the imagination, cannot but speak and cry.[15]

*   *   *

Look at the overloaded artificial Gothick style of the recent so-called philosophical and pindaric odes by the English poets Gray, Akenside, Mason,[16] etc., which they regard as masterpieces! Does the content or the metre or the wording produce the least effect of an ode? Look at the artificial Horatian style we Germans have fallen into at times – Ossian, the songs of the savage tribes and the old Norse skalds, romances, dialect poems could show us a better path, but only if we are ready to learn more than the form, the wording, or the language. But unfortunately this is only our starting-point, and if we stay there, we will get nowhere. Am I wrong, or is it not true that the most beautiful lyric poems we have now – and long have had – are consonant with this virile, firm, vigorous German tone, or at least approach it – so what can we not hope from the awakening of more of that kind![17]

Extracts from
Shakespeare[1]

1773

Translated by Joyce P. Crick, with modifications by the editor.

German text in *Sämtliche Werke,* edited by Suphan (1877–1913), V, 208–31.

If there is any man to conjure up in our minds that tremendous image of one 'seated high on the craggy hilltop, storm, tempest, and the roaring sea at his feet, but with the radiance of the heavens about his head',[2] that man is Shakespeare. Only with the addition that below him, at the foot of his rocky throne, there murmur the masses who explain him, apologise for him, condemn him, excuse him, worship, calumniate, translate, and traduce him – and to all of whom he is deaf!

*   *   *

It is from Greece that we have inherited the words drama, tragedy, comedy. And as the lettered culture of the human race has, in a narrow region of the world, made its way solely through tradition, a certain store of rules which seemed inseparable from its teaching has naturally been carried everywhere with it as in its womb and in its language. Since of course it is impossible to educate a child by way of reason, but only by way of authority, impression, and the divinity of example and of habit, so also entire nations are to an even greater extent children in all that they learn. The kernel will not grow without the husk, and they will never harvest the kernel without the husk, even if they have no use for it. That is the case with Greek and northern drama.

In Greece drama developed in a way in which it could not develop in the north. In Greece it was what it could not be in the north. Therefore in the north it is not and cannot be what it was in Greece. Thus Sophocles' drama and Shakespeare's drama are two things which in a certain respect have scarcely the name in common. I believe I can demonstrate these propositions from Greece itself and thereby decipher in no small measure the nature of northern drama and of the greatest northern dramatist, Shakespeare. We will perceive the origins of the one by means of the other, but at the same time see it transformed, so that it does not remain the same thing.

[Herder argues that the simplicity and unity of Greek drama was a direct reflection of the culture of the times, and not an imposed convention.]

77

As everything in the world changes, so the Nature which was the true creator of Greek drama was bound to change also. Their view of the world, their customs, the state of the republics, the tradition of the heroic age, religion, even music, expression, and the degrees of illusion changed. And in the natural course of things the material for plots vanished, the opportunity for their use, the incentive for using them. True, poets could work on old material and even take over their material from other nations and dress it in the accustomed manner. But that did not achieve the effect. In consequence it lacked the soul. In consequence it was no longer (why should we mince our words) the thing itself. Puppet, imitation, ape, image, in which only the most blinkered devotee could find the moving spirit which once filled the statue with life. Let us turn straight away (for the Romans were too stupid, or too clever, or too savage and immoderate to create a totally hellenising theatre) to the new Athenians[3] of Europe, and the matter will, I think, become obvious.

There is no doubt: everything that makes for this stuffed likeness of the Greek theatre has scarcely been more perfectly conceived and produced than in France. I do not only mean the rules of the theatre, so-called, which are laid at the good Aristotle's door: unity of time, place, action, connection between scenes, verisimilitude of setting, and so on. What I really want to ask is whether there is anything in the world possible beyond that glib classical thing that Corneille, Racine, and Voltaire have produced, beyond that sequence of beautiful scenes, of dialogue, of lines and rhymes with their measure, their decorum, their polish? The writer of this essay not only doubts it, but all the admirers of Voltaire and the French, especially those noble Athenians themselves, will deny it outright – they have done so often enough in the past, they are still at it, and they will go on doing so: 'There is nothing above it; it cannot be bettered!' And in the light of this general agreement, with that stuffed and stilted image there on the stage, they are right, and are bound to become more so, the more all the countries of Europe lose their heads to this glib smoothness and continue to ape it.

*   *   *

This in itself proves nothing as to its merit or lack of merit, but only raises the question of difference, which I think my previous remarks have established beyond doubt. And now I leave it to the reader to decide for himself whether a copy of foreign ages, customs, and actions which is only half true, with the entertaining purpose of adapting them to a two-hour performance on a wooden stage, could compare with, let alone be regarded as greater than, an imitation which in a certain sense was the epitome of a country's national identity? I leave it to the reader to judge (and a Frenchman will have to do his best to get round this one) whether a poetic drama which really has no purpose at all as a whole – for according to the best thinkers its greatest virtue lies only in the selection of detail – whether this

can be compared with a national institution in which each minute particular has its effect and is the bearer of the richest, deepest culture. Whether
finally a time was not bound to come when, with most of Corneille's most
artificial plays already forgotten, we will regard Crébillon[4] and Voltaire
with the same admiration with which we now look on d'Urfé's *Astrea*[5] and
all the *Clelias*[6] and *Aspasias*[7] from the times of chivalry: 'So clever, so wise,
so inventive and well-made, there might be so much to learn from them,
but what a pity it is in *Astrea* and *Clelia.*' Their entire art is unnatural,
extravagant, tedious! We would be fortunate if our taste for truth had
already reached that stage! The entire French repertory would have been
transformed into a collection of pretty lines, maxims, and sentiments – but
the great Sophocles would still stand where he is now!

So let us now assume a nation which, on account of circumstances which
we will not pursue, had no desire to ape ancient drama and run off with
the walnut-shell, but rather wanted to create its own drama. Then, I think,
our first question would still be: when, where, under what conditions, out
of what materials should it do so? And it needs no proof that its creation
can and will be the result of these questions. If it does not develop its
drama out of the chorus and the dithyramb, then it will not have any trace
of a choric, dithyrambic character. If its world did not offer such simplicity
in its history, traditions, domestic, political, and religious conditions, then
of course it will not display it either. If possible, it will create its drama out
of its own history, the spirit of its age, customs, views, language, national
attitudes, traditions, and pastimes, even if they are carnival farces or puppet-plays (just as the Greeks did from the chorus) – and what they create
will be drama, as long as it achieves the true purpose of drama among this
nation. Clearly, I am referring to the

toto divisis ab orbe Britannis[8]

and their great Shakespeare.
   That this was not Greece, neither then nor earlier, will not be denied by
any *pullulus Aristotelis,*[9] and so to demand that Greek drama should
develop naturally then and there (I am not speaking of mere imitation) is
worse than expecting a sheep to give birth to lion-cubs. Our first and last
question is solely: what is the soil like? what harvest has it been prepared
for? what has been sown in it? what is its most suitable produce? And great
heavens, how far we are from Greece! History, tradition, customs, religion,
the spirit of the time, of the nation, of emotion, of language – how far
from Greece! Whether the reader knows both periods well or but a little,
he will not for a moment confuse things that have nothing in common.
And if in this different time – changed for good or ill, but changed – there
happened to be an age, a genius who might create a dramatic œuvre out
of this raw material as naturally, impressively, and originally as the Greeks

did from theirs; and if this creation were to attain the same end, though
taking very different paths; and if it were essentially a far more complexly
simple and simply complex entity, that is (according to all the metaphysical
definitions) a perfect whole – then what fool would compare and condemn
because this latter was not the former? For its very nature, virtue, and perfection consist in the fact that it is not the same as the first; that out of the
soil of the age there grew a different plant.

Shakespeare's age offered him anything but the simplicity of national
customs, deeds, inclinations, and historical traditions which shaped Greek
drama. And since, according to the first maxim in metaphysics, nothing
will come of nothing, not only, if it were left to the philosophers, would
there be no Greek drama, but, if nothing else existed besides, there would
and could no longer be any drama at all. But since it is well known that
genius is more than philosophy, and creation a very different thing from
analysis, there came a mortal man, endowed with divine powers, who con-
jured out of utterly different material and with a wholly different approach
the self-same effect: *fear* and *pity*! and both to a degree which the earlier
treatment and material could scarcely produce. How the gods favoured his
venture! It was the very freshness, innovation, and difference that demonstrated the primal power of his vocation.

Shakespeare did not have a chorus to start from, but he did have puppet-plays and popular historical dramas; so out of the inferior clay of these
dramas and puppet-plays he shaped the splendid creation that lives and
moves before us! He found nothing like the simplicity of the Greek
national character, but a multiplicity of estates, ways of life, attitudes,
nations, and styles of speech. To grieve for the former would be labour
lost; so he concentrated the estates and the individuals, the different peoples and styles of speech, the kings and fools, fools and kings, into a splendid poetic whole! He found no such simple spirit of history, story, action:
he took history as he found it, and his creative spirit combined the most
various stuff into a marvellous whole; and though we cannot call it plot in
the Greek sense, we could refer to it by the middle-period term 'action',
or by the modern term 'event' *(événement)*, 'great occurrence' – O Aristotle, if you were to appear now, what Homeric odes you would sing to the
new Sophocles! You would invent a theory to fit him, such as his fellow
countrymen Home and Hurd,[10] Pope and Johnson have not yet created!
You would rejoice to draw lines for each of your plays on plot, character,
sentiments, expression, stage, as it were from the two points at the base of
a triangle to meet above at the point of destination – perfection! You
would say to Sophocles: 'Paint the sacred panel of this altar; and thou,
northern bard, paint all the sides and walls of this temple with thy immortal
fresco!'

Let me continue expounding and rhapsodising, for I am closer to Shakespeare than to the Greek. Whereas in Sophocles' drama the unity of a sin-

gle action is dominant, Shakespeare aims at the entirety of an event, an occurrence. Whereas Sophocles makes a single tone predominate in his characters, Shakespeare uses all the characters, estates, walks of life he requires to produce the concerted sound of his drama. Whereas in Sophocles a single ethereal diction sings as it were in the Empyrean, Shakespeare speaks the language of all ages, of all sorts and conditions of men; he is the interpreter of Nature in all her tongues – and in such different ways can they both be the familiars of the same Divinity? And if Sophocles represented and taught and moved and educated Greeks, Shakespeare taught and moved and educated northern men! When I read him, it seems to me as if theatre, actors, scenery all vanish! Single leaves from the book of events, providence, the world, blowing in the storm of history. Individual impressions of nations, classes, souls, all the most various and disparate machines, all the ignorant blind instruments – which is what we ourselves are in the hand of the creator of the world – which combine to form a whole theatrical image, a grand event whose totality only the poet can survey. Who can imagine a greater poet of mankind in the northern world, and a greater poet of his age?

*   *   *

Oh, if only I had words for the one main feeling prevailing in each drama, pulsing through it like a world soul. As it does in *Othello,* belonging as an essential part to the drama, as in his searching for Desdemona at night, as in their fabulous love, the sea-crossing, the tempest, as in Othello's raging passion, in Desdemona's manner of death, which has been so much derided, singing her willow-song as she undresses, while the wind knocks; as in the nature of the sin and passion itself, his entrance, his address to the candle – if only it were possible to comprehend all this in words, to express how it all belongs deeply and organically to *one* world, one great tragic event – but it is not possible. Words cannot describe or reproduce the merest most miserable painting, so how can they render the feeling of a living world in all the scenes, circumstances, and enchantments of Nature? Peruse what you will, gentle reader, *Lear* or the *Henries, Caesar* or the two *Richards,* even the magical plays and the interludes; *Romeo* in particular, the sweet drama of love, a romance indeed in every detail of time and place and dream and poetry – attempt to remove something of its quality, to change it, even to simplify it for the French stage – a living world in all the authenticity of its truth transformed into this wooden nullity – a fine metamorphosis! Deprive this plant of its soil, juices, and vigour, and plant it in the air, deprive this human being of place, time, individuality – you have robbed them of breath and soul, and you have a mere image of the living creature.

For Shakespeare is Sophocles' brother, precisely where he seems to be so dissimilar, and inwardly he is wholly like him. His whole dramatic illusion is attained by means of this authenticity, truth, and historical creativity. Without it, not merely would illusion be left unachieved, but nothing of Shakespeare's drama and dramatic spirit would remain – or else I have written in vain. Hence the entire world is but the body to this great spirit. All the scenes of Nature are the limbs of this body, even as all the characters and styles of thought are the features of this spirit – and the whole might well bear the name of Spinoza's giant god: Pan! Universum![11] Sophocles was true to Nature when he treated of *one* action in *one* place and at *one* time. Shakespeare could only be true to Nature when he rolled his great world events and human destinies through all the places and times – where they took place. And woe betide the frivolous Frenchman who arrives in time for Shakespeare's fifth act, expecting it will provide him with the quintessence of the play's touching sentiment. This may be true of many French plays, where everything is versified and paraded in scenes only for immediate theatrical effect. But here, he would go home empty-handed. For the great world-event would already be over. He would witness but its last and least important consequences, men falling like flies. He would leave the theatre and scoff: Shakespeare is an affront to him, and his drama the merest foolishness.

The whole tangled question of time and place would long ago have been unravelled if some philosophical mind had only taken the trouble to ask what time and place really mean in drama.[12] If the place is the stage and the length of time that of a *divertissement au théâtre,* then the only people in the world to have observed the unity of place and the measure of time and scenes are – the French. The Greeks, with a degree of illusion higher than we can conceive, whose stage was a public institution and whose theatre was a temple of worship, never gave the unities a thought. What kind of illusion is experienced by a spectator who looks at his watch at the end of every scene to check whether such an action could take place in such a span of time, and whose chief delight it is that the poet has not cheated him out of a second, but has showed him on the stage only what would take the same length of time in the snail's pace of his own life? What kind of creature could find this his greatest pleasure? And what kind of poet would regard this as his chiefest end, and pride himself on this nonsense of rules? 'How much pretty performance I have crammed so neatly into the narrow space of this pit made of boards, called *le théâtre français;* how elegantly I have fitted it all into the prescribed length of time of a polite visit! How I have sewed and stitched, polished and patched!' – miserable master of ceremonies, a theatrical posturer, not a creator, poet, god of the drama! The clock does not strike on tower or temple for you if you are a true dramatic poet, for you create your own space and time; and if you are capable of creating a world which can only exist in the categories of time and space, behold, your measure of space and duration is there within you, and you must conjure all your spectators to accept it, and urge it upon them – or else you are, as I have said, anything but a true dramatic poet.

Is there anyone in the world who needs to have it demonstrated that space and time are in themselves nothing, that in respect of being, action, passion, sequence of thought, and degree of attention within and without the soul, they are utterly relative? Has there never been any occasion in your life, good time-keeper of the drama, when hours seemed to you moments, and days seemed hours; and conversely times when hours turned into days and the watches of the night into years? Have you never known situations in your life when your soul dwelt sometimes outside you? Here, in your beloved's romantic chamber? there, gazing upon that frozen corpse? again, in the oppression of external shame and distress – or occasions when your soul fled far beyond world and time, overleaping the places and regions of the earth, unmindful of itself, to inhabit heaven, or the soul, the heart of the one whose being you feel so deeply? And if something of this kind is possible in your slow and sluggish, vermiculate and vegetable life, where there are roots enough to hold you fast to the dead ground, and each slow length you drag along is measure enough for your snail's pace, then imagine yourself for just one moment into another, poetic world, transpose yourself into a dream. Have you never perceived how in dreams space and time vanish? What insignificant things they are, what *shadows* they must be in comparison with action, with the working of the soul? Have you never observed how the soul creates its own space, world, and tempo as and where it will? And if you had experienced that only once in your life, and wakened after a mere quarter of an hour, the dark remnants of your actions in the dream would cause you to swear that you had slept and dreamed and acted whole nights away, and Mahomet's dream would not for one moment seem absurd to you.[13] And is it not the first and sole duty of every genius, of every poet, above all of the dramatic poet, to carry you off into such a dream? And now think what worlds you would be throwing into disarray if you were to show the poet your pocket-watch or your drawing-room, and ask him to teach you to dream according to their prescriptions!

The poet's space and time lie in the movement of his great event, in the *ordine successivorum et simulataneorum*[14] of *his* world. How and where does he transport you? As long as he sees to it that you are transported, you are in his world. However quickly or slowly he causes the course of time to pass, it is he who makes it pass; it is he who impresses its sequence upon you: that is his measure of time. And what a master Shakespeare is in this respect too! His grand events begin slowly and ponderously in his nature, as they do in Nature itself, for it is this which he renders, but on a smaller scale. How laborious his presentation, before the springs of action are set in motion! But once they are, how the scenes race by, how fleeting the

speeches, how winged the souls, the passion, the action, and how powerful
then the hastening movement, the pell-mell interjection of single words
when time has run out for everyone. And finally, when the reader is
entirely caught up in the illusion he has created, and is lost in the dark
abyss of his world and his passion, how bold he becomes, what trains of
events he commands! Lear dies after Cordelia! And Kent after Lear! It is
virtually the end of his world; the Last Judgement is upon us, when everything, the Heavens included, lurches and collapses, and the mountains fall!
The measure of time is no more. Not for our merry clock-watcher, of
course, who turns up unscathed for the fifth act to measure by his time-
piece how many died and how long it took. But Great Heavens, if that is
supposed to be criticism, theatre, illusion – so much the worse for criticism, theatre, illusion! What do all these empty words mean?

*   *   *

Part 3

Kant

Immanuel Kant

(1724–1804)

Kant is quite simply one of the half dozen or so most important figures in the history of philosophy. Although brought up in a Pietist household, his earliest preoccupations were in the natural sciences, and much of the point of the great *Critique of Pure Reason* (1781; second edition 1787) can be said to depend upon its inquiry into how the apparently original discoveries of the scientific method are both possible and intelligible.

The first *Critique* is Kant's most famous work, and is the founding text for the whole of what came to be known as the "critical" or "transcendental" philosophy. Roughly speaking, it is an investigation of the *a priori* element implicit though usually unnoticed in all empirical perception, which is governed by what Kant defines as the "understanding" [Verstand]. The model of the transcendental synthesis of apperception, which explains the conjunction of that which is in the mind *(a priori)* with that which is in the world, and their regular synthesis into habitual and communicable experience, is in fact a going behind and beyond the various versions of materialism and idealism Kant had inherited from his predecessors: it puts together elements of both approaches and explains the synthesis as the only reasonable explanation of experience. Thus experience must be thought of as a synthesis of concept [Begriff] and intuition [Anschauung], neither being open to self-consciousness without the assumption of the other. Without the concepts of the understanding, sense data would make no sense; and without the reception of such data, the concepts would never be deducible. This synthesis is operative all the time in ordinary experience – or, more strictly speaking, it is what must be supposed if the self-evident coherence of experience is to be explained.

Obviously I cannot try to do justice to the sophistications of the arguments of the first *Critique*, and various ones have exercised various kinds of readers. The distinction between analytic and synthetic judgements, for example, has been a popular stalking horse for philosophers but does not (as far as I can see) much impinge upon Kant's aesthetics. We should, however, register here Kant's use of the distinction between phenomena and noumena, things as they appear to us in experience and things as they must be thought to be in themselves. This was in itself controversial among Kant's immediate readers, and the dichotomy it introduces into epistemology is also crucial in the explanation of the nature and function of reason [Vernunft]. The understanding is the faculty governing our relations to the empirical world, and in fact the *Critique of Pure Reason* is mostly about the understanding. But behind it, and properly speaking the keystone of the whole transcendental philosophy, is reason, whose fuller articulation comes in the *Critique of Practical Reason* (1788) and whose operations are in the sphere of freedom and the moral law. Ethical behaviour, for Kant, depends on its very divorce from contingent (empirical) experience; no reference to such experience is called for in its validation. The laws of reason are self-imposed and self-subsisting.

The third of the great critical works, the *Critique of Judgement* (1790), was intended to mediate between the other two, and this explains in part the eagerness with which many of Kant's successors seized upon aesthetics (which is one of its two main subjects, along with teleology) as a way of healing what they thought to be a mind divided tragically between the independent realms of reason and understanding. This is discussed at greater length below.

As soon as there was Kant, there were myths of Kant. The most enduring among them project Kant the silent ascetic, by whose habits one could set one's watch. Herder set going a corrective myth of the enlivening Kant, the ideal host – polymath, raconteur, a perpetually diversifying intelligence. It is indeed the case that attention to the three great *Critiques* alone gives a very incomplete view of the range of Kant's opinions and approaches. I have discussed this, and the reasons for it, in the Introduction; suffice it to say here, once again, that to read the *Anthropology* or peruse the writings on history and civil society is to gain a very different sense of his total intellectual profile, and to recognize his engagement with many more ideas and problems than those with which he is most famously associated.

Further reading

There are many books on Kant. For general introductions and summaries see, among others, Ernst Cassirer (1981), Stephan Körner (1955), and Copleston (1964b). More specialized but very readable accounts and formulations, mostly of the epistemological arguments, may be found in Bennett (1966, 1974) and Strawson (1966). Studies of the aesthetics include the commentary by H.W. Cassirer (1938), and books by Coleman (1974), Crawford (1974), Guyer (1979), and Shaper (1979). On the English reception of Kant, Wellek (1931) is basic; see also the relevant sections of Orsini (1969), Stokoe (1926), Ashton (1980), among others. Finally, those interested in the deeper and more creative continuities might consult Gadamer (1975) and Ernst Cassirer (1953–57).

DS

Selections from
The Critique of Judgement
[Kritik der Urtheilskraft]

1790

Excerpts from the translation by James Creed Meredith, slightly modified.

German text in *Ak.* V, 167ff.

Introductory Note

Kant famously said of Hume that reading the Scottish philosopher had taken possession of him as if with a giant's hand and woken him from his slumbers. As a description of Kant's own effect on his immediate generation in Germany this might almost seem too modest. As the first two *Critiques* established the terms of the debates in epistemology and ethics for years to come, so the *Critique of Judgement* is the immediate inspiration and reference point for almost everything written by philosophers on aesthetics during the following half century. It was read eagerly though not always accurately by writers and critics – Goethe, Schiller, and the Schlegel brothers among them – and Fichte, Schelling, and Schopenhauer all saw themselves as in some sense true to the spirit of Kant even as they differed among themselves. In fact there are few arguments in Romantic aesthetics which cannot either be traced back directly to the *CJ* or intelligibly related to it in thematic terms, whether to its major arguments or to the hints and observations that arise with them or qualify them.

Kant was sixty-six when the *CJ* was published in 1790. It was not his first pronouncement on the subject of aesthetics. His early work of 1764, the *Observations on the Feeling of the Beautiful and Sublime* (see Kant, 1960), is of a very different character. It does indeed anticipate some of the concerns of the *Critique*, but as remarks rather than as methodical formulations. Thus there are comments on the relation of taste to virtue, and on the incompatibility of taste and interest, but the general assumption of the book is that no philosophically exact aesthetic theory is possible. This seems to have been Kant's conviction for much of his career.

There is an early draft of the introduction to *CJ*, translated under a different title by Humayun Kabir (see Kant, 1935), but this need not concern us here; readers interested in following up possible significant shifts of position between the early draft and the finished work should consult Crawford (1974), pp. 3–28.

The third of the great *Critiques*, which might more exactly be rendered into English as that of the "power of judging" [Urtheilskraft] and of the "faculty for making estimations" [Beurtheilungsvermögen], describes this power of judging as the "middle term between understanding and reason" (*CJ*, I, 4). Thus it complements and mediates the conclusions of the two earlier parts of the critical philosophy in epistemology (understanding) and ethics (reason). Understanding and reason coexist in the human subject but neither can interfere with the other; it is judgement that provides "the mediating concept between concepts of nature and concepts of freedom" (I, 13). As such, judgement is the "faculty of thinking the particular as contained under the universal" (I, 18), and it operates on transcendental principles, prescribing laws in an *a priori* fashion. Its estimations are however always only referable to subjective assumptions, albeit necessary ones. Thus, as applied to the two parts of the inquiry in *CJ*, aesthetics and teleology, we are compelled to assume that judgements about the beautiful are as universal *as if they were* containable under a concept (for Kant the guarantee of intersubjective experience), and that nature demonstrates a purposiveness, *as if it were* aiming at an end. But in each case there is strictly speaking only "a finality in respect of the subject's faculty of cognition" (I, 25).

Whilst aesthetic and teleological judgements are the exclusive subjects of the *CJ*, judgement properly speaking enters into every perception. However in ordinary experience the subsumption of intuitions under concepts is so habitual that we no longer distinguish the parts of the process (I, 27–8), and seldom therefore experience any feeling of pleasure or any other incentive to self-consciousness. It is in aesthetic experience and in teleological estimates of objects of nature that we most readily achieve such self-consciousness, because the pleasure is experienced independently of any confirmation of successful subsumption of intuition under concept: we react as if this had taken place at the same time as knowing that it cannot. There are no objective verifications of beauty, or of an end in nature, but we are somehow compelled to behave as if there were.

The second part of the *CJ*, the 'Critique of Teleological Judgement', is not very fully represented in the selections that follow, though it would have been possible to produce an anthology more heavily weighted toward theories of organic form based on longer extracts from this second part. Exemplary passages have been included, but most of what follows has been excerpted from the 'Critique of Aesthetic Judgement'. Even here, as might be expected, no complete coverage is possible, and certain important arguments simply cannot be followed through completely without reference to parts of the book not here reprinted. This is unavoidable given the demands of space, and I have tried to indicate important parallels or qualifications in the endnotes. Perhaps most regrettably, the whole of the dialectic of aesthetic judgement (§§55–60), which refines on the relation between judgements of taste and concepts, has been omitted; hence also the important §59, central as it is to any proper grasp of Kant's view of the relation of beauty to morality. It is here that the notion of beauty as the "symbol" of the moral is explored, along with the strong claim that this is our sole source of pleasure in the assumption of its communicability.

There is a more 'public' and less specialized exposition of some of the main points of *CJ* in the later *Anthropology*, and this too should be consulted (Kant, 1974, pp. 108–16; *Ak*. VII, 239–49). Here, for example, the relation of aesthetic and moral experience appears in a different form:

Ideal taste has a tendency to promote morality in an external way. Making a man *well-mannered* as a social being falls short of forming a *morally good* man, but it still prepares him for it by the effort he makes, in society, to please others (to make them love or admire him).   (Kant, 1974, pp. 111–12)

The *Anthropology*, it might be thought, can afford to explore the unconscious relation of uncontingent self-legislation to social approbation in a way that the critical philosophy cannot.

For detailed exposition and commentary, the reader should consult H.W. Cassirer (1938); and Meredith (1911) is especially useful for its comprehensive evidence of Kant's possible borrowings from British eighteenth-century writers on aesthetics.

Part I   Critique of Aesthetic Judgement

FIRST BOOK
ANALYTIC OF THE BEAUTIFUL

§2

The delight which determines the judgement of taste is independent of
all interest

The delight which we connect with the representation of the real existence of an object is called interest. Such a delight, therefore, always involves a reference to the faculty of desire [Begehrungsvermögen][1], either as its determining ground, or else as necessarily implicated with its determining ground. Now, where the question is whether something is beautiful, we do not want to know whether we or anyone else are, or even could be, concerned in the real existence of the thing, but rather what estimate we form of it on mere contemplation [Betrachtung] (intuition or reflection) . . . All one wants to know is whether the mere representation [bloße Vorstellung] of the object is to my liking, no matter how indifferent I may be to the real existence of the object of this representation. It is quite plain that in order to say that the object *is beautiful,* and to show that I have taste [Geschmack], everything turns on the meaning which I can give to this representation, and not on any factor which makes me dependent on the real existence of the object. Every one must allow that a judgement on the beautiful which is tinged with the slightest interest, is very partial and not a pure judgement of taste. One must not be in the least prepossessed of the real existence of the thing, but must preserve complete indifference in this respect, in order to play the part of judge in matters of taste.

[Kant goes on to distinguish "the beautiful" from two other forms of the relation of representations to pleasure and displeasure, the "agreeable" and the "good".

Unlike the "beautiful" they are dependent upon interest, and on a concern for the real existence of the object. This interest pre-empts freedom: "All interest presupposes a want, or calls one forth; and, being a ground determining approval, deprives the judgement on the object of its freedom" (§5).]

DEFINITION OF THE BEAUTIFUL DERIVED FROM THE FIRST MOMENT

Taste is the faculty of estimating an object or a mode of representation by means of a delight or aversion *apart from any interest*. The object of such a delight is called *beautiful*.

SECOND MOMENT OF THE JUDGEMENT OF TASTE: MOMENT OF QUANTITY

§6

The beautiful is that which, apart from concepts, is represented as the Object[2] of a UNIVERSAL *delight*

This definition of the beautiful is deducible from the foregoing definition of it as an object of delight apart from any interest. For where any one is conscious that his delight in an object is with him independent of interest, it is inevitable that he should look on the object as one containing a ground of delight for all men. For, since the delight is not based on any inclination of the subject (or on any other deliberate interest), but the subject feels himself completely *free* in respect of the liking which he accords to the object, he can find as reason for his delight no personal conditions to which his own subjective self might alone be party. Hence he must regard it as resting on what he may also presuppose in every other person; and therefore he must believe that he has reason for demanding a similar delight from every one. Accordingly he will speak of the beautiful as if beauty were a quality of the object and the judgement logical (forming a cognition of the Object by concepts of it); although it is only aesthetic, and contains merely a reference of the representation of the object to the subject; because it still bears this resemblance to the logical judgement, that it may be presupposed to be valid for all men. But this universality cannot spring from concepts. For from concepts there is no transition to the feeling of pleasure or displeasure (save in the case of pure practical laws, which, however, carry an interest with them; and such an interest does not attach to the pure judgement of taste).[3] The result is that the judgement of taste, with its attendant consciousness of detachment from all interest, must involve a claim to validity for all men, and must do so apart from universality attached to Objects, i.e. there must be coupled with it a claim to subjective universality.

§7

Comparison of the beautiful with the agreeable and the good by means of the above characteristic

As regards the *agreeable* [*Angenehmen*] every one concedes that his judgement, which he bases on a private feeling, and in which he declares that an object pleases him, is restricted merely to himself personally. Thus he does not take it amiss if, when he says that Canary-wine is agreeable, another corrects the expression and reminds him that he ought to say: It is agreeable *to me*. This applies not only to the taste of the tongue, the palate, and the throat, but to what may with any one be agreeable to eye or ear. A violet colour is to one soft and lovely: to another dull and faded. One man likes the tone of wind instruments, another prefers that of string instruments. To quarrel over such points with the idea of condemning another's judgement as incorrect when it differs from our own, as if the opposition between the two judgements were logical, would be folly. With the agreeable, therefore, the axiom holds good: *Every one has his own taste* (that of sense).

The beautiful stands on quite a different footing. It would, on the contrary, be ridiculous if any one who plumed himself on his taste were to think of justifying himself by saying: This object (the building we see, the dress that person has on, the concert we hear, the poem submitted to our criticism) is beautiful *for me*. For if it merely pleases *him,* he must not call it *beautiful*. Many things may for him possess charm and agreeableness – no one cares about that; but when he puts a thing on a pedestal and calls it beautiful, he demands the same delight from others. He judges not merely for himself, but for all men, and then speaks of beauty as if it were a property of things. Thus he says the *thing* is beautiful; and it is not as if he counted on others agreeing in his judgement of liking owing to his having found them in such agreement on a number of occasions, but he *demands* this agreement of them. He blames them if they judge differently, and denies them taste, which he still requires of them as something they ought to have; and to this extent it is not open to men to say: Every one has his own taste. This would be equivalent to saying that there is no such thing at all as taste, i.e. no aesthetic judgement capable of making a rightful claim upon the assent of all men.

Yet even in the case of the agreeable we find that the estimates men form do betray a prevalent agreement among them, which leads to our crediting some with taste and denying it to others, and that, too, not as an organic sense but as a critical faculty in respect of the agreeable generally. So of one who knows how to entertain his guests with pleasures (of enjoyment through all the senses) in such a way that one and all are pleased, we say that he has taste. But the universality here is only understood in a comparative sense; and the rules that apply are, like all empirical rules, *general* [*generale*] only, not *universal* [*universale*] – the latter being what the judgement of taste upon the beautiful deals or claims to deal in.[4] It is a judgement in respect of sociability so far as resting on empirical rules. In respect of the good it is true that judgements also rightly assert a claim to validity for every one; but the good is only represented as an Object of universal delight *by means of a concept,* which is the case neither with the agreeable nor the beautiful.

§8

. . . When one forms an estimate [beurtheilt] of Objects merely from concepts, all representation of beauty goes by the board. There can, therefore, be no rule according to which any one is to be compelled to recognize anything as beautiful. Whether a dress, a house, or a flower is beautiful is a matter upon which one declines to allow one's judgement to be swayed by any reasons or principles. We want to get a look at the Object with our own eyes, just as if our delight depended on sensation. And yet, if upon so doing, we call the object beautiful, we believe ourselves to be speaking with a universal voice, and lay claim to the concurrence of every one, whereas one private sensation would not be decisive except for the observer alone and *his* liking.

Here, now, we may perceive that nothing is postulated in the judgement of taste but such a *universal* [*allegemeine*] *voice* in respect of delight that is not mediated by concepts; consequently, only the *possibility* of an aesthetic judgement capable of being at the same time deemed valid for every one. The judgement of taste itself does not *postulate* the agreement of every one (for it is only competent for a logically universal judgement to do this, in that it is able to bring forward reasons); it only *imputes* this agreement to every one, as an instance of the rule in respect of which it looks for confirmation, not from concepts, but from the concurrence of others. The universal voice is, therefore, only an idea – resting upon grounds the investigation of which is here postponed.[5] It may be a matter of uncertainty whether a person who thinks he is laying down a judgement of taste is, in fact, judging in conformity with that idea; but that this idea is what is contemplated in his judgement, and that, consequently, it is meant to be a judgement of taste, is proclaimed by his use of the expression 'beauty'. For himself he can be certain on the point from his mere consciousness of the separation of everything belonging to the agreeable and the good from the delight remaining to him; and this is all for which he promises himself the agreement of every one – a claim which, under these conditions, he would also be warranted in making, were it not that he frequently sinned against them, and thus passed an erroneous judgement of taste.

§9

Investigation of the question of the relative priority in a judgement of taste of the feeling of pleasure and the estimating of [Beurtheilung] the object

The solution of this problem is the key to the critique of taste, and so is worthy of all attention.

Were the pleasure in a given object to be the antecedent, and were the universal communicability of this pleasure to be all that the judgement of taste is meant to allow to the representation of the object, such a sequence would be self-contradictory. For a pleasure of that kind would be nothing but the feeling of mere agreeableness to the senses, and so, from its very nature, would possess no more than private validity, seeing that it would be immediately dependent on the representation through which the object *is given.*

Hence it is the universal capacity for being communicated incident to the mental state in the given representation which, as the subjective condition of the judgement of taste, must be fundamental, with the pleasure in the object as its consequent. Nothing, however, is capable of being universally communicated but cognition [Erkenntniß] and representation [Vorstellung], so far as appurtenant to cognition. For it is only as thus appurtenant that the representation is objective, and it is this alone that gives it a universal point of reference with which the power of representation of every one is obliged to harmonize. If, then, the determining ground of the judgement as to this universal communicability of the representation is to be merely subjective, that is to say, is to be conceived independently of any concept of the object, it can be nothing else than the mental state that presents itself in the mutual relation of the powers of representation so far as they refer a given representation *to cognition in general.*

The cognitive powers brought into play by this representation are here engaged in a free play, since no definite concept restricts them to a particular rule of cognition. Hence the mental state in this representation must be one of a feeling of the free play of the powers of representation in a given representation for a cognition in general. Now a representation, whereby an object is given, involves, in order that it may become a source of cognition at all, *imagination [Einbildungskraft]* for bringing together the manifold of intuition, and *understanding [Verstand]* for the unity of the concept uniting the representations. This state of *free play* of the cognitive faculties attending a representation by which an object is given must admit of universal communication: because cognition, as a definition of the Object with which given representations (in any subject whatever) are to accord, is the one and only mode of representation which is valid for every one.[6]

As the subjective universal communicability of the mode of representation in a judgement of taste is to subsist apart from the presupposition of any definite concept, it can be nothing else than the mental state present in the free play of imagination and understanding (so far as these are in mutual accord, as is requisite for *cognition in general*): for we are conscious that this subjective relation suitable for a cognition in general must be just as valid for every one, and consequently as universally communicable, as is any determinate cognition, which always rests upon that relation as its subjective condition.

Now this purely subjective (aesthetic) estimating of the object, or of the representation through which it is given, is antecedent to the pleasure in it, and is the basis of this pleasure in the harmony of the cognitive faculties. Again, the above-described universality of the subjective conditions of estimating objects forms the sole foundation of this universal subjective validity of the delight which we connect with the representation of the object that we call beautiful.[7]

That an ability to communicate one's mental state, even though it be only in respect of our cognitive faculties, is attended with a pleasure, is a fact which might easily be demonstrated from the natural propensity of mankind to social life, i.e. empirically and psychologically. But what we have here in view calls for something more than this. In a judgement of taste the pleasure felt by us is exacted from every one else as necessary, just as if, when we call something beautiful, beauty was to be regarded as a quality of the object forming part of its inherent determination according to concepts; although beauty is for itself, apart from any reference to the feeling of the subject, nothing. But the discussion of this question must be reserved until we have answered the further one of whether, and how, aesthetic judgements are possible *a priori*.

At present we are exercised with the lesser question of the way in which we become conscious, in a judgement of taste, of a reciprocal subjective common accord of the powers of cognition. Is it aesthetically by sensation and our mere internal sense? Or is it intellecutally by consciousness of our intentional activity in bringing these powers into play?

Now if the given representation occasioning the judgement of taste were a concept which united understanding and imagination in the estimate of the object so as to give a cognition of the Object, the consciousness of this relation would be intellectual (as in the objective schematism of judgement dealt with in the Critique).[8] But, then, in that case the judgement would not be laid down with respect to pleasure and displeasure, and so would not be a judgement of taste. But, now, the judgement of taste determines the object, independently of concepts, in respect of delight and of the predicate of beauty. There is, therefore, no other way for the subjective unity of the relation in question to make itself known than by sensation. The quickening of both faculties (imagination and understanding) to an indefinite, but yet, thanks to the given representation, harmonious activity, such as belongs to cognition generally, is the sensation whose universal communicability is postulated by the judgement of taste. An objective relation can, of course, only be thought, yet in so far as, in respect of its conditions, it is subjective, it may be felt in its effect upon the mind, and, in the case of a relation (like that of the powers of representation to a faculty of cognition generally) which does not rest on any concept, no other consciousness of it is possible beyond that through sensation of its effect upon the mind – an effect consisting in the more facilitated play of both mental powers (imagination and understanding) as quickened by their mutual accord. A representation which is singular and independent of comparison with other representations, and, being such, yet accords with the conditions of the universality that is the general concern of understanding, is one that brings the cognitive faculties into that proportionate accord which we require for all congition and which we therefore deem valid for every one who is so constituted as to judge by means of understanding and sense conjointly (i.e. for every man).

DEFINITION OF THE BEAUTIFUL DRAWN FROM THE SECOND MOMENT

The *beautiful* is that which, apart from a concept, pleases universally.

[After further remarks on the pure judgement of taste, which has nothing to do with "empirical delight" (§14), Kant goes on to distinguish between "free" and "dependent" beauty (§16). The latter does presuppose a concept of what the object should be, and goes beyond the appreciation of pure form to consider ends and purposes. It is therefore not the "pure judgement of taste", though it may be combined with it to produce a harmony in the whole faculty of "representative power" (Vorstellungskraft).]

§17

The ideal of beauty

There can be no objective rule of taste by which what is beautiful may be defined by means of concepts. For every judgement from that source is aesthetic, i.e. its determining ground is the feeling of the subject, and not any concept of an Object. It is only throwing away labour to look for a principle of taste that affords a universal criterion of the beautiful by definite concepts; because what is sought is a thing impossible and inherently contradictory. But in the universal communicability of the sensation (of delight or aversion) – a communicability, too, that exists apart from any concept – in the accord, so far as possible, of all ages and nations as to this feeling in the representation of certain objects, we have the empirical criterion, weak indeed and scarce sufficient to raise a presumption, of the derivation of a taste, thus conformed by examples, from grounds deep-seated and shared alike by all men, underlying their agreement in estimating the forms under which objects are given to them.[9]

For this reason some products of taste are looked on as *exemplary* – not meaning thereby that by imitating others taste may be acquired. For taste must be an original faculty; whereas one who imitates a model, while showing skill commensurate with his success, only displays taste as himself a critic of this model.[10] Hence it follows that the highest model, the archetype of taste, is a mere idea, which each person must beget in his own consciousness, and according to which he must form his estimate of everything that is an Object of taste, or that is an example of critical taste, and even of universal taste itself. Properly speaking, an *idea* signifies a concept of reason, and an *ideal* the representation of an individual existence as adequate to an idea. Hence this archetype of taste – which rests, indeed, upon reason's indeterminate idea of a maximum, but is not, however, capable of being represented by means of concepts, but only in an individual presentation – may more appropriately be called the ideal of the beautiful. While not having this ideal in our possession, we still strive to beget it within us. But it is bound to be merely an ideal of the imagination, seeing that it rests, not upon concepts, but upon the presentation – the faculty of presentation being the imagination. Now how do we arrive at such an ideal of beauty? Is it *a priori* or empirically? Further, what species of the beautiful admits of an ideal?

First of all, we do well to observe that the beauty for which an ideal has to be sought cannot be a beauty that is *free and at large,* but must be one *fixed* by a concept of objective finality. Hence it cannot belong to the Object of an altogether pure judgement of taste, but must attach to one that is partly intellectual. In other words, where an ideal is to have place among the grounds upon which any estimate is formed, then beneath grounds of that kind there must lie some idea of reason according to determinate concepts, by which the end underlying the internal possibility of the object is determined *a priori*. An ideal of beautiful flowers, of a beautiful suite of furniture, or of a beautiful view, is unthinkable. But, it may also be impossible to represent an ideal of a beauty dependent on definite ends, e.g. a beautiful residence, a beautiful tree, a beautiful garden, &c., presumably because their ends are not sufficiently defined and fixed by their concept, with the result that their finality is nearly as free as with

beauty that is quite *at large*. Only what has in itself the end of its real existence – only *man* that is able himself to determine his ends by reason, or,
where he has to derive them from external perception, can still compare
them with essential and universal ends, and then further pronounce aesthetically upon their accord with such ends, only he, among all objects in
the world, admits, therefore, of an ideal of *beauty*, just as humanity in his
person, as intelligence, alone admits of the ideal of *perfection*.

Two factors are here involved. *First*, there is the aesthetic *normal idea*
[*Normalidee*], which is an individual intuition (of the imagination). This represents the norm by which we judge of a man as a member of a particular
animal species. *Secondly*, there is the *rational idea* [*Vernunftidee*]. This deals
with the ends of humanity so far as incapable of sensuous representation,
and converts them into a principle for estimating its outward form,
through which these ends are revealed in their phenomenal effect. The
normal idea must draw from experience the constituents which it requires
for the form of an animal of a particular kind. But the greatest finality in
the construction of this form – that which would serve as a universal norm
for forming an estimate of each individual of the species in question – the
image that, as it were, forms an intentional basis underlying the technic of
nature, to which no separate individual, but only the race as a whole, is
adequate, has its seat merely in the idea of the judging subject. Yet it is,
with all its proportions, an aesthetic idea, and, as such, capable of being
fully presented *in concreto* in a model image. Now, how is this effected? In
order to render the process to some extent intelligible (for who can wrest
nature's whole secret from her?), let us attempt a psychological
explanation.

[This "normal idea" is constructed in the imagination by the intuitive standardiza-
tion of separate mental images into a normative image, of course variable according
to whether we are Europeans, Chinamen, etc. But this is only a pre-condition and
not a definition of the archetype (Urbild) of beauty. The ideal of the beautiful, to
be sought only in the human figure, must involve a perception of the moral.]

. . . The visible expression of moral [sittlich] ideas[11] that govern men
inwardly can, of course, only be drawn from experience; but their combination with all that our reason connects with the morally good in the idea
of the highest finality – benevolence, purity, strength, or equanimity, &c.
– may be made, as it were, visible in bodily manifestation (as effect of what
is internal), and this embodiment involves a union of pure ideas of reason
and great imaginative power, in one who would even form an estimate of
it, not to speak of being the author of its presentation. The correctness of
such an ideal of beauty is evidenced by its not permitting any sensuous
charm [Sinnenreiz] to mingle with the delight in its Object, in which it still
allows us to take a great interest. This fact in turn shows that an estimate
formed according to such a standard can never be purely aesthetic, and

that one formed according to an ideal of beauty cannot be a simple judgement of taste.

DEFINITION OF THE BEAUTIFUL DERIVED FROM THIS THIRD MOMENT

Beauty is the form of *finality* in an object, so far as perceived in it *apart from the represenation of an end.*[12]

FOURTH MOMENT OF THE JUDGEMENT OF TASTE: MOMENT OF THE MODALITY OF THE DELIGHT IN THE OBJECT

§18

Nature of the modality in a judgement of taste

I may assert in the case of every representation that the synthesis of a pleasure with the representation (as a cognition) is at least *possible.* Of what I call *agreeable* I assert that it *actually* causes pleasure in me. But what we have in mind in the case of the *beautiful* is a *necessary* reference on its part to delight. However, this necessity is of a special kind. It is not a theoretical objective necessity – such as would let us cognize *a priori* that every one *will feel* this delight in the object that is called beautiful by me. Nor yet is it a practical necessity, in which case, thanks to concepts of a pure rational will in which free agents are supplied with a rule, this delight is the necessary consequence of an objective law, and simply means that one ought absolutely (without ulterior purpose) to act in a certain way. Rather, being such a necessity as is thought in an aesthetic judgement, it can only be termed *exemplary.* In other words it is a necessity of the assent of *all* to a judgement regarded as exemplifying a universal rule incapable of formulation. Since an aesthetic judgement is not an objective or cognitive judgement, this necessity is not derivable from definite concepts, and so is not apodictic. Much less is it inferable from universality of experience (of a thorough-going agreement of judgements about the beauty of a certain object). For, apart from the fact that experience would hardly furnish evidences sufficiently numerous for this purpose, empirical judgements do not afford any foundation for a concept of the necessity of these judgements.

[There follows (§§19–22) a description of "common sense" (Gemeinsinn), the assumption of which underlies the *supposition* of universality in judgements of taste. This is to be distinguished from the *sensus communis* which governs the operation of the understanding, which judges by concepts and not by feeling (Gefühl). In a general remark on the first book, the free imagination involved in the judgement of taste is defined as "productive . . . as originator of arbitrary forms of possible intuitions", rather than merely "reproductive".]

GENERAL REMARK ON THE FIRST SECTION OF THE ANALYTIC

... All stiff regularity (such as borders on mathematical regularity) is inherently repugnant to taste, in that the contemplation of it affords us no lasting entertainment. Indeed, where it has neither cognition nor some definite practical end expressly in view, we get heartily tired of it. On the other hand, anything that gives the imagination scope for unstudied and final play is always fresh to us. We do not grow to hate the very sight of it. *Marsden* in his description of Sumatra observes that the free beauties of nature so surround the beholder on all sides that they cease to have much attraction for him.[13] On the other hand he found a pepper garden full of charm, on coming across it in mid-forest with its rows of parallel stakes on which the plant twines itself. From all this he infers that wild, and in its appearance quite irregular beauty, is only pleasing as a change to one whose eyes have become surfeited with regular beauty. But he need only have made the experiment of passing one day in his pepper garden to realize that once the regularity has enabled the understanding to put itself in accord with the order that is its constant requirement, instead of the object diverting him any longer, it imposes an irksome constraint upon the imagination: whereas nature subject to no constraint of artificial rules, and lavish, as it there is, in its luxuriant variety can supply constant food for his taste. – Even a bird's song, which we can reduce to no musical rule, seems to have more freedom in it, and thus to be richer for taste, than the human voice singing in accordance with all the rules that the art of music prescribes; for we grow tired much sooner of frequent and lengthy repetitions of the latter. Yet here most likely our sympathy with the mirth of a dear little creature is confused with the beauty of its song, for if exactly imitated by man (as has been sometimes done with the notes of the nightingale) it would strike our ear as wholly destitute of taste.[14] ...

SECOND BOOK
ANALYTIC OF THE SUBLIME [DAS ERHABENE]

§23

Transition from the faculty of estimating the beautiful to that of estimating the sublime

The beautiful and the sublime agree on the point of pleasing on their own account. Further they agree in not presupposing either a judgement of sense or one logically determinant, but one of reflection. Hence it follows that the delight does not depend upon a sensation, as with the agreeable, nor upon a definite concept, as does the delight in the good, although it has, for all that, an indeterminate reference to concepts. Consequently the delight is connected with the mere presentation or faculty of presentation, and is thus taken to express the accord, in a given intuition, of the faculty of presentation, or the imagination, with the *faculty of concepts* that belongs to understanding or reason, in the sense of the former assisting the latter. Hence both kinds of judgements are *singular,* and yet such as profess to be universally valid in respect of every subject, despite the fact that their claims are directed merely to the feeling of pleasure and not to any knowledge of the object.

There are, however, also important and striking differences between the two. The beautiful in nature is a question of the form of the object, and this consists in limitation, whereas the sublime is to be found in an object even devoid of form, so far as it immediately involves, or else by its presence provokes a representation of *limitlessness,* yet with a super-added thought of its totality. Accordingly the beautiful seems to be regarded as a presentation of an indeterminate concept of understanding, the sublime as a presentation of an indeterminate concept of reason. Hence the delight is in the former case coupled with the representation of *Quality,* but in this case with that of *Quantity.* Moreover, the former delight is very different from the latter in kind. For the beautiful is directly attended with a feeling of the furtherance of life, and is thus compatible with charms and a playful imagination.[15] On the other hand, the feeling of the sublime is a pleasure that only arises indirectly, being brought about by the feeling of a momentary check to the vital forces followed at once by a discharge all the more powerful, and so it is an emotion that seems to be no sport, but dead earnest in the affairs of the imagination. Hence it is irreconcilable with charms [Reizen]; and, since the mind is not simply attracted by the object, but is also alternately repelled thereby, the delight in the sublime does not so much involve positive pleasure as admiration or respect, i.e. merits the name of a negative pleasure.

But the most important and vital distinction between the sublime and the beautiful is certainly this: that if, as is allowable, we here confine our attention in the first instance to the sublime of Objects of nature (that of art being always restricted by the conditions of an agreement with nature), we observe that whereas natural beauty (such as is self-subsisting) conveys a finality in its form making the object appear, as it were, preadapted to our power of judgement, so that it thus forms of itself an object of our delight; that which, without our indulging in any refinements of thought, but, simply in our apprehension of it, excites the feeling of the sublime, may appear, indeed, in point of form to contravene the ends of our power of judgement, to be ill-adapted to our faculty of presentation, and to be, as it were, an outrage on the imagination, and yet it is judged all the more sublime on that account.

From this it may be seen at once that we express ourselves on the whole inaccurately if we term any *object of nature* sublime, although we may with perfect propriety call many such objects beautiful. For how can that which is apprehended as inherently contra-final be noted with an expression of approval? All that we can say is that the object lends itself to the presentation of a sublimity discoverable in the mind. For the sublime, in the strict sense of the word, cannot be contained in any sensuous form, but rather concerns ideas of reason, which, although no adequate presentation of them is possible, may be excited and called into the mind by that very inadequacy itself which does admit of sensuous presentation. Thus the broad ocean agitated by storms cannot be called sublime. Its aspect is horrible, and one must have stored one's mind in advance with a rich stock of ideas, if such an intuition is to raise it to the pitch of a feeling which is itself sublime – sublime because the mind has been incited to abandon sensibility, and employ itself upon ideas involving higher finality.

Self-subsisting natural beauty reveals to us a technic of nature which shows it in the light of a system ordered in accordance with laws the principle of which is not to be found within the range of our entire faculty of understanding. This principle is that of a finality relative to the employment of judgement in respect of phenomena which have thus to be assigned, not merely to nature regarded as aimless mechanism, but also to nature regarded after the analogy of art. Hence it gives a veritable extension, not, of course, to our knowledge of Objects of nature, but to our conception of nature itself – nature as mere mechanism being enlarged to the conception of nature as art – an extension inviting profound inquiries as to the possibility of such a form. But in what we are wont to call sublime in nature there is such an absence of anything leading to particular objective principles and corresponding forms of nature, that it is rather in its chaos, or in its wildest and most irregular disorder and desolation, provided it gives signs of magnitude and power, that nature chiefly excites the ideas of the sublime. Hence we see that the concept of the sublime in nature is far less important and rich in consequences than that of its beauty. It gives on the whole no indication of anything final in nature itself, but only in the possible *employment* of our intuitions of it in inducing a feeling in our own selves of a finality quite independent of nature. For the beautiful in nature we must seek a ground external to ourselves, but for the sublime one merely in ourselves and the attitude of mind that introduces sublimity into the representation of nature. This is a very needful preliminary remark. It entirely separates the ideas of the sublime from that of a finality of *nature,* and makes the theory of the sublime a mere appendage to the aesthetic estimate of the finality of nature, because it does not give a representation of any particular form in nature, but involves no more than the development of a final employment by the imagination of its own representation.[16]

[There is a division in the analysis of the sublime, "namely one into the *mathematically* and the *dynamically* sublime" (§24). Unlike the restful contemplation characterizing the aesthetic, the sublime involves a mental movement, which may be referred either to the faculty of cognition or to that of desire, always bearing in mind that such reference to finality can involve no end or interest. Accordingly it is either mathematical or dynamical. There follows an elucidation of the mathematically sublime.]

§26

. . . Nature, therefore, is sublime in such of its phenomena as in their intuition convey the idea of their infinity. But this can only occur through the inadequacy of even the greatest effort of our imagination in the estimation of the magnitude of an object. But, now, in the case of the mathematical estimation of magnitude imagination is quite competent to supply a measure equal to the requirements of any object. For the numerical concepts of the understanding can by progressive synthesis make any measure adequate to any given magnitude in which we get at once a feeling of the effort towards a comprehension that exceeds the faculty of imagination for mentally grasping the progressive apprehension in a whole of intuition, and, with it, a perception of the inadequacy of this faculty, whch has no bounds to its progress, for taking in and using for the estimation of magnitude a fundamental measure that understanding could turn to account without the least trouble. Now the proper unchangeable fundamental measure of nature is its absolute whole, which, with it, regarded as a phenomenon, means infinity comprehended. But, since this fundamental measure is a self-contradictory concept (owing to the impossibility of the absolute totality of an endless progression), it follows that where the size of a natural Object is such that the imagination spends its whole faculty of comprehension upon it in vain, it must carry our concept of nature to a supersensible substrate (underlying both nature and our faculty of thought) which is great beyond every standard of sense. Thus, instead of the object, it is rather the cast of the mind in appreciating it that we have to estimate as *sublime*.

Therefore, just as the aesthetic judgement in its estimate of the beautiful refers the imagination in its free play to the *understanding*, to bring out its agreement with the *concepts* of the latter in general (apart from their determination): so in its estimate of a thing as sublime it refers that faculty to *reason* to bring out its subjective accord with *ideas* of reason (indeterminately indicated), i.e. to induce a temper of mind conformable to that which the influence of definite (practical) ideas would produce upon feeling, and in common accord with it.

This makes it evident that true sublimity must be sought only in the mind of the judging subject, and not in the Object of nature that occasions this attitude by the estimate formed of it. Who would apply the term 'sublime' even to shapeless mountain masses towering one above the other in wild disorder, with their pyramids of ice, or to the dark tempestuous ocean or such like things? But in the contemplation of them, without any regard to their form, the mind abandons itself to the imagination and to a reason placed, though quite apart from any definite end, in conjunction therewith, and merely broadening its view, and it feels itself elevated in its own estimate of itself on finding all the might of imagination still unequal to its ideas.

We get examples of the mathematically sublime of nature in mere intuition in all those instances where our imagination is afforded, not so much a greater numerical concept as a large unit as measure (for shortening the numerical series). A tree judged by the height of man gives, at all events, a standard for a mountain; and, supposing this is, say, a mile high, it can serve as unit for the number expressing the earth's diameter, so as to make it intuitable; similarly the earth's diameter for the known planetary system; this again for the system of the Milky Way; and the immeasurable host of such systems, which go by the name of nebulae, and most likely in turn themselves form such a system, holds out no prospect of a limit. Now in the aesthetic estimate of such an immeasurable whole, the sublime does not lie so much in the greatness of the number, as in the fact that in our onward advance we always arrive at proportionately greater units. The systematic division of the cosmos conduces to this result. For it represents all that is great in nature as in turn becoming little; or, to be more exact, it represents our imagination in all its boundlessness, and with it nature, as sinking into insignificance before the ideas of reason, once their adequate presentation is attempted.[17]

§27

Quality of the delight in our estimate [Beurtheilung] of the sublime

The feeling of our incapacity to attain to an idea *that is a law for us, is* RESPECT [ACHTUNG]. Now the idea of the comprehension of any phenomenon whatever, that may be given us, in a whole of intuition, is an idea imposed upon us by a law of reason, which recognizes no definite, universally valid and unchangeable measure except the absolute whole. But our imagination, even when taxing itself to the uttermost on the score of this required comprehension of a given object in a whole of intuition (and so with a view to the presentation of the idea of reason), betrays its limits and its inadequacy, but still, at the same time, its proper vocation of making itself adequate to the same as a law. Therefore the feeling of the sublime in nature is respect for our own vocation, which we attribute to an Object of nature by a certain subreption [Subreption] (substitution of a respect for the Object in place of one for the idea of humanity in our own self – the subject); and this feeling renders, as it were, intuitable the supremacy of our cognitive faculties on the rational side over the greatest faculty of sensibility.[18]

The feeling of the sublime is, therefore, at once a feeling of displeasure, arising from the inadequacy of imagination in the aesthetic estimation of magnitude to attain to its estimation by reason, and a simultaneously awakened pleasure, arising from this very judgement of the inadequacy of the greatest faculty of sense being in accord with ideas of reason, so far as the effort to attain to these is for us a law. It is, in other words, for us a law (of reason), which goes to make us what we are, that we should esteem as small in comparison with ideas of reason everything which for us is great in nature as an object of sense; and that which makes us alive to the feeling of this supersensible disposition [Bestimmung] of our being harmonizes with that law. Now the greatest effort of the imagination in the presentation of the unit for the estimation of magnitude involves in itself a reference to something *absolutely great*, consequently a reference also the law of reason that this alone is to be adopted as the supreme measure of what is great. Therefore the inner perception of the inadequacy of every standard of sense to serve for the rational estimation of magnitude is a coming into accord with reason's laws, and a displeasure that makes us alive to the feeling of the supersensible disposition of our being, according to which it is final, and consequently a pleasure, to find every standard of sensibility falling short of the ideas of reason.

The mind feels itself *set in motion* [*bewegt*] in the representation of the sublime in nature; whereas in the aesthetic judgement upon what is beautiful therein it is *restful* contemplation. This movement, especially in its inception, may be compared with a vibration, i.e. with a rapidly alternating repulsion and attraction produced by one and the same Object. The point of excess for the imagination (towards which it is driven in the apprehension of the intuition) is like an abyss in which it fears to lose itself; yet again for the rational idea of the supersensible it is not excessive, but conformable to law, and directed to drawing out such an effort on the part of the imagination: and so in turn as much a source of attraction as it was repellent to mere sensibility. But the judgement itself all the while steadfastly preserves its aesthetic character, because it represents, without being grounded on any definite concept of the Object, merely the subjective play of the mental powers (imagination and reason) as harmonious by virtue of their very contrast. For just as in the estimate of the beautiful, imagination and *understanding* by their concert generate subjective finality of the mental faculties, so imagination and *reason* do so here by their conflict – that is to say they induce a feeling of our possessing a pure and self-sufficient reason, or a faculty for the estimation of magnitude, whose pre-eminence can only be made intuitively evident by the inadequacy of that faculty which in the presentation of magnitudes (of objects of sense) is itself unbounded.[19]

Measurement of a space (as apprehension) is at the same time a description of it, and so an objective movement in the imagination and a progression. On the other hand the comprehension of the manifold in the unity, not of thought, but of intuition, and consequently the comprehension of the successively apprehended parts at one glance, is a retrogression that removes the time-condition in the progression of the imagination, and renders *coexistence* intuitable. Therefore, since the time-series is a condition of the internal sense and of an intuition, it is a subjective movement of the imagination by which it does violence to the internal sense – a violence which must be proportionately more striking the greater the quantum which the imagination comprehends in one intuition. The effort, therefore, to receive in a single intuition a measure for magnitudes which it takes an appreciable time to apprehend, is a mode of representation which, subjectively considered, is contra-final, but, objectively, is requisite for the estimation of magnitude, and is consequently final. Here the very same violence that is wrought on the subject through the imagination is estimated as final *for the whole province* [*Bestimmung*] of the mind.

The quality of the feeling of the sublime consists in its being, in respect of the faculty of forming aesthetic estimates, a feeling of displeasure at an object, which yet, at the same time, is represented as being final – a representation which derives its possibility from the fact that the subject's very incapacity betrays the consciousness of an unlimited faculty of the same subject, and that the mind can only form an aesthetic estimate of the latter faculty by means of that incapacity.

In the case of the logical estimation of magnitude the impossibility of ever arriving at absolute totality by the progressive measurement of things of the sensible world in time and space was cognized as an objective impossibility, i.e. one of *thinking* the infinite as given, and not as simply subjective, i.e. an incapacity for *grasping* it; for nothing turns there on the amount of the comprehension in one intuition, as measure, but everything depends on a numerical concept. But in an aesthetic estimation of magnitude the numerical concept must drop out of count or undergo a change. The only thing that is final for such estimation is the comprehension on the part of imagination in respect of the unit of measure (the concept of a law of the successive production of the concept of magnitude being consequently avoided). If, now, a magnitude begins to tax the utmost stretch of our faculty of comprehension in an intuition, and still numerical magnitudes – in respect of which we are conscious of the boundlessness of our faculty – call upon the imagination for aesthetic comprehension in a greater unit, the mind then gets a feeling of being aesthetically confined within bounds. Nevertheless, with a view to the extension of imagination necessary for adequacy with what is unbounded in our faculty of reason, namely the idea of the absolute whole, the attendant displeasure, and, consequently, the want of finality in our faculty of imagination, is still represented as final for ideas of reason and their animation. But in this very way the aesthetic judgement itself is subjectively final for reason as source of ideas, i.e. of such an intellectual comprehension as makes all aesthetic comprehension small, and the object is received as sublime with a pleasure that is only possible through the mediation of a displeasure.

B. THE DYNAMICALLY SUBLIME IN NATURE

§28

Nature as Might [*Macht*]

Might is a power which is superior to great hindrances. It is termed *dominion* [*Gewalt*] if it is also superior to the resistance of that which itself possesses might. Nature considered in an aesthetic judgement as might that has no dominion over us, is *dynamically sublime*.

[Nature is an object of fear, in the sublime, but yet we are not afraid of it.]

One who is in a state of fear can no more play the part of a judge of the sublime of nature than one captivated by inclination and appetite can of the beautiful. He flees from the sight of an object filling him with dread; and it is impossible to take delight in terror that is seriously entertained . . .

. . . Bold, overhanging, and, as it were, threatening rocks, thunder clouds piled up to the vault of heaven, borne along with flashes and peals, volcanoes in all their violence of destruction, hurricanes leaving desolation in their track, the boundless ocean rising with rebellious force, the high waterfall of some mighty river, and the like, make our power of resistance of trifling moment in comparison with their might. But provided our own position is secure, their aspect is all the more attractive for its fearfulness; and we readily call these objects sublime, because they raise the forces of the soul above the height of vulgar commonplace, and discover within us a power of resistance of quite another kind, which gives us courage to be able to measure ourselves against the seeming omnipotence of nature.

   In the immeasurableness of nature and the incompetence of our faculty for adopting a standard proportionate to the aesthetic estimation of the magnitude of its *realm*, we found our own limitation. But with this we also found in our rational faculty another non-sensuous standard, one which has that infinity itself under it as unit, and in comparison with which everything in nature is small, and so found in our minds a pre-eminence over nature even in its immeasurability.[20] Now in just the same way the irresistibility of the might of nature forces upon us the recognition of our physical helplessness as beings of nature, but at the same time reveals a faculty of estimating ourselves as independent of nature, and discovers a pre-eminence above nature that is the foundation of a self-preservation of quite another kind from that which may be assailed and brought into danger by external nature. This saves humanity in our own person from humiliation, even though as mortal men we have to submit to external violence. In this way external nature is not estimated in our aesthetic judgement as sublime as far as exciting fear, but rather because it challenges our power (one not of nature) to regard as small those things of which we are wont to be solicitous (worldly goods, health, and life), and hence to regard its might (to which in these matters we are no doubt subject) as exercising over us and our personality no such rude dominion that we should bow down before it, once the question becomes one of our highest principles and of our asserting or forsaking them. Therefore nature is here called sublime merely because it raises the imagination to a presentation of those cases in which the mind can make itself sensible of the appropriate sublimity of the sphere of its own being, even above nature.

This estimation of ourselves loses nothing by the fact that we must see ourselves safe in order to feel this soul-stirring delight – a fact from which it might be plausibly argued that, as there is no seriousness in the danger, so there is just as little seriousness in the sublimity of our faculty of spirit [Geistesvermögens]. For here the delight only concerns the *province* [*Bestimmung*] of our faculty disclosed in such a case, so far as this faculty has its root in our nature; notwithstanding that its development and exercise is left to ourselves and remains an obligation. Here indeed there is truth – no matter how conscious a man, when he stretches his reflection so far abroad, may be of his actual present helplessness.

[§29 pursues the connection of the sublime with the moral idea. Kant says quite explicitly that the development of the moral idea is the element in culture [Cultur] necessary for the experience of the sublime. Without it, such experience would be simply terrifying and not at all uplifting. Though preparatory culture is necessary for the appreciation of the sublime, it cannot yet *produce* it. The requisite faculty must be thought to be latent in the human mind "in that which, at once with common understanding, we may expect every one to possess and may require of him, namely, a native capacity for the feeling for (practical) ideas, i.e. for moral feeling" (*CJ*, I, 116). Thus it is a part of transcendental philosophy rather than of empirical psychology. In the "General Remark upon the Exposition of Aesthetic Reflective Judgements", Kant pursues the relation between the aesthetic and the moral (see my introduction for a discussion of this). In the following passage, he explains away any concern we might have about locating the sublime beyond sensuous representation.]

. . . We have no reason to fear that the feeling of the sublime will suffer from an abstract mode of presentation like this, which is altogether negative as to what is sensuous. For though the imagination, no doubt, finds nothing beyond the sensible world to which it can lay hold, still this thrusting aside of the sensible barriers gives it a feeling of being unbounded; and that removal is thus a presentation of the infinite. As such it can never be anything more than a negative presentation – but still it expands the soul. Perhaps there is no more sublime passage in the Jewish Law than the commandment: Thou shalt not make unto thee any graven image, or any likeness of anything that is in heaven or on earth, or under the earth, &c. This commandment can alone explain the enthusiasm which the Jewish people, in their moral period, felt for their religion when comparing themselves with others, or the pride inspired by Mohammedanism. The very same holds good of our representation of the moral law and of our native capacity for morality. The fear that, if we divest this representation of everything that can commend it to the senses, it will thereupon be attended only with a cold and lifeless approbation and not with any moving force or emotion, is wholly unwarranted. The very reverse is the truth. For when nothing any longer meets the eye of sense, and the unmistakable and ineffaceable idea of morality [Moralität] is left in possession of the field, there would be need rather of tempering the ardour of an unbounded imagination to prevent it rising to enthusiasm, than of seeking to lend these ideas the aid of images and childish devices for fear of their being wanting in potency. For this reason governments have gladly let religion be fully equipped with these accessories, seeking in this way to relieve their subjects of the exertion, but to deprive them, at the same time, of the ability, required for expanding their spiritual powers beyond the limits arbitrarily laid down for them, and which facilitate their being treated as though they were merely passive.[21]

This pure, elevating, merely negative presentation of morality [Sittlichkeit] involves, on the other hand, no fear of *fanaticism* [*Schwärmerei*], which is a *delusion* that would *will some* VISION *beyond all the bounds of sensibility;* i.e. would dream according to principles (rational raving). The safeguard is the purely negative character of the presentation. For *the inscrutability of the idea of freedom* precludes all positive presentation. The moral law, however, is a sufficient and original source of determination within us: so it does not for a moment permit us to cast about for a ground of determination external to itself. If enthusiasm [Enthusiasm] is comparable to *delirium,* fanaticism may be compared to *mania.* Of these the latter is the least of all compatible with the sublime, for it is *profoundly* ridiculous. In enthusiasm, as an affection, the imagination is unbridled; in fanaticism, as a deep-seated, brooding passion, it is anomalous [regellos]. The first is a transitory accident to which the healthiest understanding is liable to become at times the victim; the second is an undermining disease.[22]

Simplicity (artless finality) is, as it were, the style adopted by nature in the sublime. It is also that of morality. The latter is a second (supersensible) nature, whose laws alone we know, without being able to attain to an intuition of the supersensible faculty within us – that which contains the ground of this legislation.

One further remark. The delight in the sublime, no less than in the beautiful, by reason of its universal *communicability* not only is plainly distinguished from other aesthetic judgements, but also from this same property acquires an interest in society (in which it admits of such communication). Yet, despite this, we have to note the fact that *isolation from all society* is looked upon as something sublime, provided it rests upon ideas which disregard all sensible interest. To be self-sufficing, and so not to stand in need of society, yet without being unsociable, i.e. without shunning it, is something approaching the sublime – a remark applicable to all superiority to wants. On the other hand, to shun our fellow men from *misanthropy*, because of enmity towards them, or from *anthropophobia*, because we imagine the hand of every man is against us, is partly odious, partly contemptible. There is, however, a misanthropy (most improperly so called), the tendency towards which is to be found with advancing years in many right-minded men, that, as far as *good will* goes, is, no doubt, philanthropic enough, but as the result of long and sad experience, is widely removed from *delight* in mankind. We see evidences of this in the propensity to reclusiveness, in the fanciful desire for a retired country seat, or else (with the young) in the dream of the happiness of being able to spend one's life with a little family on an island unknown to the rest of the world – material of which novelists or writers of Robinsonades know how to make such good use. Falsehood, ingratitude, injustice, the puerility of the ends which we ourselves look upon as great and momentous, and to compass which man inflicts upon his brother man all imaginable evils – these all so contradict the idea of what men might be if they only would, and are so at variance with our active wish to see them better, that to avoid hating where we cannot love, it seems but a slight sacrifice to forego all the joys of fellowship with our kind.[23]

[Kant goes on to compare his own transcendental interest in the sublime and the beautiful with that of Burke, which for him is limited to the psychological and physiological sphere and therefore belongs to "anthropology". As such, it can never resolve the question of why it is that agreement about such responses is assumed by all subjects without empirical reference to what others think, which is the primary focus of Kant's interest. Only the transcendental method can address this question, by reference to the transcendental, *a priori* principles which Kant goes on to deduce (§§30–9), stressing once again that the very absence of proofs or objective principles in the determination of judgements of taste makes the presence of an inherited body of culture and art, a 'tradition', all the more important (cf. §§17–22). The job of the critic is not however to draw up a list of items for inclusion in such a canon, but to investigate the faculties which themselves make possible such judgements. In §34 Kant makes this the distinction between "art" (Kunst) and "science" (Wissenschaft), identifying himself firmly with the latter. The question of the deduction of judgements of taste belongs within the general problematic of the transcendental philosophy, already broached in the earlier *Critiques:* how are synthetic *a priori* judgements possible? §39 is an important restatement of the issues surrounding the assumption of universality in aesthetic judgements. It should be consulted, though it is not included here.]

§40

Taste as a kind of sensus communis

The name of sense [Sinn] is often given to judgement where what attracts attention is not so much its reflective act [Reflexion] as merely its result. So we speak of a sense of truth, of a sense of propriety, or of justice, &c. And yet, of course, we know, or at least ought well enough to know, that a sense cannot be the true abode of these concepts, not to speak of its being incompetent, even in the slightest degree, to pronounce universal rules. On the contrary, we recognize that a representation of this kind, be it of truth, propriety, beauty, or justice, could never enter our thoughts were we not able to raise ourselves above the level of the senses to that of higher faculties of cognition. *Common human understanding* which, as merely reliable (not yet cultivated) understanding, is looked upon as the least we can expect from any one claiming the name of man, has therefore the doubtful honour of having the name of common sense [Gemeinsinn] *(sensus communis)* bestowed upon it; and bestowed, too, in an acceptation of the word *common* (not merely in our own language, where it actually has a double meaning, but also in many others) which makes it amount to what is *vulgar* – what is everywhere to be met with – a quality which by no means confers credit or distinction upon its possessor.

However, by the name *sensus communis* is to be understood the idea of a *public* sense, i.e. a faculty of making estimations [Beurtheilungsvermögen] which in its reflection on the mode of representaton has regard in thought *(a priori)* to all others, in order, *as it were*, to weigh its judgement with the collective reason of mankind, and thereby avoid the illusion arising from subjective and personal conditions which could readily be taken for objective, an illusion that would exert a prejudicial influence upon its judgement. This is accomplished by weighing the judgement, not so much with actual, as rather with the merely possible, judgements of others, and by putting ourselves in the position of everyone else, as the result of a mere abstraction from the limitations which contingently affect our own estimate. This, in turn, is effected by so far as possible letting go the element of matter, i.e. sensation, in our general state of representative activity, and confining attention to the formal peculiarities of our representation or general state of representative activity. Now it may seem that this operation of reflection is too artificial to be attributed to the faculty which we call *common* sense. But this is an appearance due only to its expression in abstract formulae. In itself nothing is more natural than to abstract from charm and emotion where one is looking for a judgement intended to serve as a universal rule.

While the following maxims of common human understanding do not properly come in here as constituent parts of the critique of taste, they may still serve to elucidate its fundamental propositions. They are these: (1) to think for oneself; (2) to think from the standpoint of every one else; (3) always to think consistently. The first is the maxim of *unprejudiced* thought, the second that of *enlarged* thought, the third that of *consistent* thought. The first is the maxim of a never-*passive* reason. To be given to such passivity, consequently to heteronomy of reason, is called *prejudice* [*Vorurtheil*]; and the greatest of all prejudices is that of fancying nature not to be subject to rules which the understanding by virtue of its own essential law lays at its basis: i.e. *superstition* [*Aberglaube*].[24] Emancipation from superstition is called *enlightenment;*[25] for although this term applies also to emancipation from prejudices generally, still superstition deserves pre-eminently *(in sensu eminenti)* to be called a prejudice. For the condition of blindness into which superstition puts one, which it as much as demands from one as an obligation, makes the need of being led by others, and consequently the passive state of the reason, pre-eminently conspicuous. As the second maxim belonging to our habits of thought, we have quite got into the way of calling a man narrow (*narrow*, as opposed to being *of enlarged mind*) whose talents fall short of what is required for employment upon work of any magnitude (especially that involving intensity). But the question here is not one of the faculty of cognition, but of the *mental habit* of making a final use of it. This, however small the range and degree to which a man's natural endowments extend, still indicates a man of *enlarged mind:* if he detaches himself from the subjective personal conditions of his judgement, which cramp the minds of so many others, and reflects upon his own judgement from a *universal standpoint* (which he can only determine by shifting his ground to the standpoint of others). The third maxim – that, namely, of *consistent* thought – is the hardest of attainment, and is only attainable by the union of both the former, and after constant attention to them has made one at home in their observance. We may say: the first of these is the maxim of understanding, the second that of judgement, the third that of reason.[26]

[Though no interest can be the determining ground of a judgement of taste, interest can subsequently be combined with such a judgement in a secondary or tributary way (§41). "Empirical" interests of this sort are related to sociability, and to man's natural desire to communicate with others: there is a pleasure in communicability itself, though not one essential to judgements of taste since, after all, the assumption of universality does *not* determine that people *will* actually agree. There is also an "intellectual interest" in the beautiful, which Kant proceeds to relate to the moral faculty through a distinction between art and nature.]

§42

. . . Now I willingly admit that the interest in the *beautiful of art* (including under this heading the artificial use of natural beauties for personal adornment, and so from vanity) gives no evidence at all of a habit of mind attached to the morally good, or even inclined that way. But, on the other hand, I do maintain that to take an *immediate interest* in the beauty of *nature* (not merely to have taste in estimating it) is always a mark of a good soul; and that, where this interest is habitual, it is at least indicative of a temper of mind favourable to the moral feeling that it should readily associate itself with the *contemplation* [*Beschauung*] *of nature*. It must, however, be borne in mind that I mean to refer strictly to the beautiful *forms* [*Formen*] of nature, and to put to one side the *charms* [*Reize*] which she is wont so lavishly to combine with them; because, though the interest in these is no doubt immediate, it is nevertheless empirical.

[Kant goes on to assert that our preference for the forms made by nature over those made by artifice or imitation, and for the pure properties of art rather than those appealing to social vanity, is the true mark of the "beautiful soul" (schöne Seele) and similarly accordant with the moral feeling. He expands on ths analogy below.]

. . . We have a faculty of judgement which is merely aesthetic – a faculty of judging of forms without the aid of concepts, and of finding, in the mere estimate of them, a delight that we at the same time make into a rule for every one, without this judgement being founded on an interest, or yet producing one. – On the other hand we have also a faculty of intellectual judgement for the mere forms of practical maxims (so far as they are of themselves qualified for universal legislation) – a faculty of determining an *a priori* delight, which we make into a law for everyone, without our judgement being founded on any interest, *though here it produces one*. The pleasure or displeasure in the former judgement is called that of taste; the latter is called that of the moral feeling.

But, now, reason is further interested in ideas (for which in our moral feeling it brings about an immediate interest), having also objective reality. That is to say, it is of interest to reason that nature should at least show a trace or give a hint that it contains in itself some ground or other for assuming a uniform accordance of its products with our wholly disinterested delight (a delight which we cognize *a priori* as a law for everyone without being able to ground it upon proofs). That being so, reason must take an interest in every manifestation on the part of nature of some such accordance. Hence the mind cannot reflect on the beauty of *nature* without at the same time finding its interest engaged. But this interest is akin to the moral. One, then, who takes such an interest in the beautiful in nature can only do so in so far as he has previously set his interest deep in the foundations of the morally good. On these grounds we have reason for presuming the presence of at least the germ of a good moral disposition in the case of a man to whom the beauty of nature is a matter of immediate interest.[27]

[The interest in the beautiful in nature is not, for Kant, commonly found, but tends to be most possible for those who are already trained to an admiration of the good. To afford the fullest delight, the beautiful must properly inhere in nature: imitations are quite differently received. Whereas the imitation – Kant gives the example of a boy blowing a whistle in perfect replication of the song of the nightingale – derives its appeal from its proximity to nature, that of the truly natural demands relation to the sense of finality which we carry within ourselves, i.e. to the moral faculty. Art, that is, appeals most strongly when it has the appearance of nature. It must therefore not display the labour enacted in its creation.[28] Nature gives rules to art through what we call 'genius', whose products must be original and exemplary, and beyond the conscious control of the artist: "where an author owes a product to his genius, he does not himself know how the *ideas* for it have entered into his head, nor has he it in his power to invent the like at pleasure, or methodically, and communicate the same to others in such precepts as would put them in a position to produce similar products" (§46).[29] Though taste is responsible for the estimation of the products of genius (§48), in a sort of secondary way, it must coexist *with* genius in the true artist, as that which enables him to give form to his creations, and to turn them into something exemplary. One could have genius without taste: not all who have it are artists in the proper sense of the word. §49 continues with an analysis of "spirit".]

. . . *Spirit* [*Geist*] in an aesthetical sense, signifies the animating principle in the mind. But that whereby this principle animates the soul [Seele] – the material which it employs for that purpose – is that which sets the mental powers into a swing that is final, i.e. into a play which is self-maintaining and which strengthens those powers for such activity.[30]

Now my proposition is that this principle is nothing else than the faculty of presenting *aesthetic ideas*. But, by an aesthetic idea I mean that representation of the imagination which induces much thought, yet without the possibility of any definite thought whatever, i.e. *concept*, being adequate to it, and which language, consequently, can never get quite on level terms with or render completely intelligible. It is easily seen, that an aesthetic idea is the counterpart (pendant) of a *rational idea*, which, conversely, is a concept to which no *intuition* (representation of the imagination) can be adequate.

The imagination (as a productive faculty of cognition) is a powerful agent for creating, as it were, a second nature out of the material supplied to it by actual nature. It affords us entertainment where experience proves too commonplace; and we even use it to remodel experience, always following, no doubt, laws that are based on analogy, but still also following principles which have a higher seat in reason (and which are every whit as natural to us as those followed by the understanding in laying hold of empirical nature). By this means we get a sense of our freedom from the law of association (which attaches to the empirical employment of the imagination), with the result that the material can be borrowed by us from nature in accordance with that law, but be worked up by us into something else – namely, what surpasses nature.

Such representations of the imagination may be termed *ideas*. This is partly because they at least strain after something lying out beyond the confines of experience, and so seek to approximate to a presentation of rational concepts (i.e. intellectual ideas), thus giving to these concepts the semblance of an objective reality. But, on the other hand, there is this most important reason, that no concept can be wholly adequate to them as internal intuitions. The poet essays the task of interpreting to sense the rational ideas of invisible beings, the kingdom of the blessed, hell, eternity, creation, &c. Or, again, as to things of which examples occur in experience, e.g. death, envy, and all vices, as also love, fame, and the like, transgressing the limits of experience he attempts with the aid of an imagination which emulates the display of reason in its attainment of a maximum, to body them forth to sense with a completeness of which nature affords no parallel; and it is in fact precisely in the poetic art that the faculty of aesthetic ideas can show itself to full advantage. This faculty, however, regarded solely on its own account, is properly no more than a talent [Talent] (of the imagination).[31]

If, now, we attach to a concept a representation of the imagination belonging to its presentation, but inducing solely on its own account such a wealth of thought as would never admit of comprehension in a definite concept, and, as a consequence, giving aesthetically an unbounded expansion to the concept itself, then the imagination here displays a creative activity, and it puts the faculty of intellectual ideas (reason) into motion – a motion, at the instance of a representation, towards an extension of thought, that, while germane, no doubt, to the concept of the object, exceeds what can be laid hold of in that representation or clearly expressed.

... In a word, the aesthetic idea is a representation of the imagination, annexed to a given concept, with which, in the free employment of imagination, such a multiplicity of partial representations is bound up, that no expression indicating a definite concept can be found for it – one which on that account allows a concept to be supplemented in thought by much that is indefinable in words, and the feeling of which quickens the cognitive faculties and with language, as a mere thing of the letter, binds up the spirit also.[32]

The mental powers whose union in a certain relation constitutes *genius* [*Genie*] are imagination and understanding. Now, since the imagination, in its employment on behalf of cognition, is subjected to the constraint of the understanding and the restriction of having to be conformable to the concept belonging thereto, whereas aesthetically it is free to furnish of its own accord, over and above that agreement with the concept, a wealth of undeveloped material for the understanding, to which the latter paid no regard in its concept, but which it can make use of, not so much objectively for cognition, as subjectively for quickening the cognitive faculties, and hence also indirectly for cognitions, it may be seen that genius properly consists in the happy relation, which science cannot teach nor industry learn, enabling one to find out ideas for a given concept, and, besides, to hit upon the *expression* for them – the expression by means of which the subjective mental condition induced by the ideas as the concomitant of a concept may be communicated to others. This latter talent is properly that which is termed spirit [Geist]. For to get an expression for what is indefinable in the mental state accompanying a particular representation and to make it universally communicable – be the expression in language or painting or statuary – is a thing requiring a faculty for laying hold of the rapid and transient play of the imagination, and for unifying it in a concept (which for that very reason is original, and reveals a new rule which could not have been inferred from any preceding principles or examples) that admits of communication without any constraint of rules.[33]

§50

. . . Taste, like judgement in general, is the discipline (or corrective) of genius. It severely clips its wings, and makes it orderly or polished; but at the same time it gives it guidance, directing and controlling its flight, so that it may preserve its character of finality. It introduces a clearness and order into the plenitude of thought, and in so doing gives stability to the ideas, and qualifies them at once for permanent and universal approval, for being followed by others, and for a continually progressive culture [Cultur]. And so, where the interests of both these qualities clash in a product, and there has to be a sacrifice of something, then it should rather be on the side of genius; and judgement, which in matters of fine art bases its decision on its own proper principles, will more readily endure an abatement of the freedom and wealth of the imagination, than that the understanding should be compromised.[34]

[§§51–52 explore the division of the fine arts, which are then evaluated, with poetry at the top.]

§53

Comparative estimate of the aesthetic worth of the fine arts

Poetry [*Dichtkunst*] (which owes its origin almost entirely to genius and is least willing to be led by precepts or example) holds the first rank among all the arts. It expands the mind by giving freedom to the imagination and by offering, from among the boundless multiplicity of possible forms accordant with a given concept to whose bounds it is restricted, that one which couples with the presentation of the concept a wealth of thought to

which no verbal expression is completely adequate, and thus raises itself
aesthetically to ideas. It invigorates the mind by letting it feel its faculty –
free, spontaneous, and independent of determination by nature – of
regarding and estimating nature as phenomenon in the light of aspects
which nature of itself does not afford us in experience, either for sense or
understanding, and of employing it accordingly in behalf of, and as a sort
of schema for, the supersensible. It plays with semblance [Schein], which
it produces at will, but not as an instrument of deception; for its avowed
pursuit is merely one of play [Spiel], which, however, understanding may
turn to good account and employ for its own purpose.[35]

Part II   Critique of Teleological Judgement

[The second part of Kant's third *Critique* is less relevant to aesthetics than the first,
being concerned with finality in nature, and the logical status of judgements of
purposive phenomena. The following extract discusses what we have come to call
'organic form'. Kant is not here talking about art, except in so far as it provides a
partial analogy for what must be supposed in nature, i.e. a finality providing a cred-
ible basis for natural science to estimate its own processes according to ends. But
in what he says about reciprocal cause and effect, and about the relation of part to
whole, Kant is employing a model which was to be applied to works of art (as a
standard of excellence), and also to subsequent models of methodological and
social organization (Coleridge's notion of the 'symbol' being a case in point). In
insisting that "the organization of nature has nothing analogous to any causality
known to us", Kant may once again be meaning to pre-empt the tendency of speculative theology toward an argument from design, in which God becomes the "artist" of our world. As always, Kant's emphasis is on the articulation of our subjective
capacity to estimate finality.]

§4 (65)

Things considered as physical ends are organisms [organisierte Wesen]

Where a thing is a product of nature and yet, so regarded, has to be cognized as possible only as a physical end, it must, from its character as set
out in the preceding section, stand to itself reciprocally in the relation of
cause and effect. This is, however, a somewhat inexact and indeterminate
expression that needs derivation from a definite conception.

In so far as the causal connection is thought merely by means of understanding it is a nexus constituting a series, namely of causes and effects,
that is invariably progressive. The things that as effects presuppose others
as their causes cannot themselves in turn be also causes of the latter. This
causal connexion is termed that of efficient causes *(nexus effectivus)*. On the
other hand however, we are also able to think a causal connexion according to a rational concept, that of ends, which, if regarded as a series, would
involve regressive as well as progressive dependency. It would be one in

which the thing that for the moment is designated effect deserves none the less, if we take the series regressively, to be called the cause of the thing of which it was said to be the effect. In the domain of practical matters, namely in art, we readily find examples of a nexus of this kind.[36] Thus a house is certainly the cause of the money that is received as rent, but yet, conversely, the representation of this possible income was the cause of the building of the house. A causal nexus of this kind is termed that of final causes (*nexus finalis*). The former might, perhaps, more appropriately be called the nexus of real, and the latter the nexus of ideal causes, because with this use of terms it would be understood at once that there cannot be more than these two kinds of causality.

Now the *first* requisite of a thing, considered as a physical end, is that its parts, as to both their existence and form, are only possible by their relation to the whole. For the thing is itself an end, and is, therefore, comprehended under a conception or an idea that must determine *a priori* all that is to be contained in it. But so far as the possibility of a thing is only thought in this way it is simply a work of art. It is the product, in other words, of an intelligent cause, distinct from the matter, or parts, of the thing, and of one whose causality, in bringing together and combining the parts, is determined by its idea of a whole made possible through that idea, and consequently, not by external nature.

But if a thing is a product of nature, and in this character is notwithstanding to contain intrinsically and in its inner possibility a relation to ends, in other words, is to be possible only as a physical end and independently of the causality of the conceptions of external rational agents, then this *second* requisite is involved, namely, that the parts of the thing combine of themselves into the unity of a whole by being reciprocally cause and effect of their form. For this is the only way in which it is possible that the idea of the whole may conversely, or reciprocally, determine in its turn the form and combination of all the parts, not as cause – for that would make it an art-product – but as the epistemological basis upon which the systematic unity of the form and combination of all the manifold contained in the given matter becomes cognizable for the person estimating it.

What we require, therefore, in the case of a body which in its intrinsic nature and inner possibility has to be estimated as a physical end, is as follows. Its parts must in their collective unity reciprocally produce one another alike as to form and combination, and thus by their own causality produce a whole, the conception of which, conversely – in a being possessing the causality according to conceptions that is adequate for such a product – could in turn be the cause of the whole according to a principle, so that, consequently, the nexus of *efficient causes* might be no less estimated as an *operation brought about by final* causes.

In such a natural product as this every part is thought as *owing* its presence to the *agency* of all the remaining parts, and also as existing *for the sake of the others* and of the whole, that is as an instrument, or organ. But this is not enough – for it might be an instrument of art, and thus have no more than its general possibility referred to an end. On the contrary the part must be an organ *producing* the other parts – each, consequently, reciprocally producing the others.[37] No instrument of art can answer to this description, but only the instrument of that nature from whose resources the materials of every instrument are drawn – even the materials for instruments of art. Only under these conditions and upon these terms can such a product be an *organized* and *self-organized being*, and, as such, be called a *physical end*.

In a watch one part is the instrument by which the movement of the others is effected, but one wheel is not the efficient cause of the production of the other. One part is certainly present for the sake of another, but it does not owe its presence to the agency of that other. For this reason, also, the producing cause of the watch and its form is not contained in the nature of this material, but lies outside the watch in a being that can act according to ideas of a whole which its causality makes possible. Hence one wheel in the watch does not produce the other, and, still less, does one watch produce other watches, by utilizing, or organizing, foreign material; hence it does not of itself replace parts of which it has been deprived, nor, if these are absent in the original construction, does it make good the deficiency by the subvention of the rest; nor does it, so to speak, repair its own casual disorders. But these are all things which we are justified in expecting from organized nature. An organized being is, therefore, not a mere machine. For a machine has solely *motive power*, whereas an organized being possesses inherent *formative power* [*bildende Kraft*], and such, moreover, as it can impart to material devoid of it – material which it organizes. This, therefore, is a self-propagating formative power, which cannot be explained by the capacity of movement alone, that is to say, to mechanism.

We do not say half enough of nature and her capacity in organized products when we speak of this capacity as being the *analogue of art*. For what is here present to our minds is an artist – a rational being – working from without. But nature, on the contrary, organizes itself, and does so in each species of its organized products – following a single pattern, certainly, as to general features, but nevertheless admitting deviations calculated to secure self-preservation under particular circumstances. We might perhaps come nearer to the description of this impenetrable property if we were to call it an *analogue of life*. But then either we should have to endow matter as mere matter with a property (hylozoism) that contradicts its essential nature; or else we should have to associate with it a foreign principle standing in community with it (a soul). But, if such a product is to be a natural product, then we have to adopt one or other of two courses in order to bring in a soul. Either we must presuppose organized matter as the instrument of such a soul, which makes organized matter no whit more intelligible, or else we must make the soul the artificer of this structure, in which case we must withdraw the product from (corporeal) nature. Strictly speaking, therefore, the organization of nature has nothing analogous to any causality known to us.[38] Natural beauty may justly be termed the analogue of art, for it is only ascribed to the objects in respect of reflection upon the *external* intuition of them and, therefore, only on account of their superficial form. But *intrinsic natural perfection*, as possessed by things that are only possible as *physical ends*, and that are therefore called organisms, is unthinkable and inexplicable on any analogy to any known physical, or natural, agency, not even excepting – since we ourselves are part of nature in the widest sense – the suggestion of any strictly apt analogy to human art.[39]

The concept of a thing as intrinsically a physical end is, therefore, not a constitutive conception either of understanding or of reason, but yet it may be used by reflective judgement as a regulative conception for guiding our investigation of objects of this kind by a remote analogy with our own causality according to ends generally, and as a basis of reflection upon their supreme source. But in the latter connexion it cannot be used to promote our knowledge either of nature or of such original source of those objects, but must on the contrary be confined to the service of just the same practical faculty of reason in analogy with which we considered the cause of the finality in question.

Organisms are, therefore, the only beings in nature that, considered in their separate existence and apart from any relation to other things, cannot be thought possible except as ends of nature. It is they, then, that first afford objective reality to the conception of an *end* that is an end *of nature* and not a practical end.[40] Thus they supply natural science with the basis for a teleology, or, in other words, a mode of estimating its Objects on a special principle that it would otherwise be absolutely unjustifiable to introduce into that science – seeing that we are quite unable to perceive *a priori* the possibility of such a kind of causality.

[§22 (83) exposes the stoical side of Kant's thought about man's place in the world. Not only is he not an 'end' of physical nature: his own inner disposition also produces conflict. Culture (Cultur), or the *aptitude* for setting ends before *himself*, is the only final end of nature in man. Because its manifestation in 'skill' (Geschicklichkeit) is unequally distributed, Kant offers a somewhat gloomy analysis of the vocation of the human race.]

. . . external nature is far from having made a particular favourite of man or from having preferred him to all other animals as the object of its beneficence. For we see that in its destructive operations – plague, famine, flood, cold, attacks from animals great and small, and all such things – it has as little spared him as any other animal. But, besides all this, the discord of inner *natural tendencies* betrays him into further misfortunes of his own invention, and reduces other members of his species, through the oppression of lordly power, the barbarism of wars, and the like, to such misery, while he himself does all he can to work ruin to his race, that, even with the utmost goodwill on the part of external nature, its end, supposing it were directed to the happiness of our species, would never be attained in a system of terrestrial nature, because our own nature is not capable of it. Man, therefore, is ever but a link in the chain of physical ends. True, he is a principle in respect of many ends to which nature seems to have pre-determined him, seeing that he makes himself so; but, nevertheless, he is also a means towards the preservation of the finality in the mechanism of the remaining members. As the single being upon earth that possesses understanding, and, consequently, a capacity for setting before himself ends of his deliberate choice, he is certainly titular lord of nature, and, supposing we regard nature as a teleological system, he is born to be its ultimate end. But this is always on the terms that he has the intelligence and the will to give to it and to himself such a reference to ends as can be self-sufficing independently of nature, and, consequently, a final end. Such an end, however, must not be sought in nature.

. . . Skill can hardly be developed in the human race otherwise than by means of inequality among men. For the majority, in a mechanical kind of way that calls for no special art, provide the necessaries of life for the ease and convenience of others who apply themselves to the less necessary branches of culture in science and art. These keep the masses in a state of oppression, with hard work and little enjoyment, though in the course of time much of the culture of the higher classes spreads to them also. But with the advance of this culture – the culminating point of which, where devotion to what is superfluous begins to be prejudicial to what is indis-pensable, is called luxury – misfortunes increase equally on both sides. With the lower classes they arise by force of domination from without, with the upper from seeds of discontent within. Yet this splendid misery is con-nected with the development of natural tendencies in the human race, and the end pursued by nature itself, though it be not our end, is thereby attained.[41] The formal condition under which nature can alone attain this its real end is the existence of a constitution so regulating the mutual rela-tions of men that the abuse of freedom by individuals striving one against another is opposed by a lawful authority centred in a whole, called a *civil community*. For it is only in such a constitution that the greatest develop-ment of natural tendencies can take place. In addition to this we should also need a *cosmopolitan* whole – had men but the ingenuity to discover such a constitution and the wisdom voluntarily to submit themselves to its constraint. It would be a system of all states that are in danger of acting injuriously to one another. In its absence, and with the obstacles that ambi-tion, love of power, and avarice, especially on the part of those who hold the reins of authority, put in the way even of the possibility of such a scheme, *war* is inevitable. Sometimes this results in states splitting up and resolving themselves into lesser states, sometimes one state absorbs other smaller states and endeavours to build up a larger unit. But if on the part of men war is a thoughtless undertaking, being stirred up by unbridled passions, it is nevertheless a deep-seated, maybe far-seeing, attempt on the part of supreme wisdom, if not to found, yet to prepare the way for a rule of law governing the freedom of states, and thus bring about their unity in a system established on a moral basis. And, in spite of the terrible calamities which it inflicts on the human race, and the hardships, perhaps even greater, imposed by the constant preparation for it in time of peace, yet – as the prospect of the dawn of an abiding reign of national happiness keeps ever retreating farther into the distance – it is one further spur for developing to the highest pitch all the talents that minister to culture.

Part 4
Schiller

Friedrich Schiller

(1759–1805)

Schiller was born at Marbach in the Duchy of Württemberg, where his father held a commission in the Duke's army. From 1773 to 1780, he studied at the Military Academy in nearby Stuttgart, in whose running the despotic Duke Karl Eugen took a personal interest. After graduating in medicine, Schiller became a regimental physician. The Duke disapproved of the young Schiller's literary activities, and Schiller fled his domains in 1782 to Mannheim, at whose theatre his first drama, *The Robbers,* had already been successfully performed.

Schiller's early work, particularly *The Robbers* and his early tragedy *Intrigue and Love (Kabale und Liebe,* 1784), is characterised by social and political protest, in which the influences of Rousseau and of the *Sturm und Drang* movement of the 1770s are apparent. His historical tragedy *Don Carlos* (1787) defends the rights of the Dutch people under Spanish oppression, and Schiller's work on it prepared the way for his *History of the Revolt of the Netherlands* (1788), a work which gained him the Chair of History at Jena University. His *History of the Thirty Years War* followed in 1791–3.

In 1793, Schiller embarked on intensive studies of Kant, and wrote a series of essays on ethical and aesthetic subjects, several of them dealing with the theory of tragedy. Central to them is the concept of tragic sublimity, which is achieved by voluntary acceptance of suffering in the interests of a moral end. His *Aesthetic Letters* (1794–5) deal with the educative effects of aesthetic experience in promoting a balanced state of mind and an integral personality. This work, and *On Naive and Sentimental Poetry* (1795–6), in which Schiller distinguishes two basic types of poetry and poet (ancient and modern, spontaneous and reflective), benefited from his friendship with Goethe, which began in 1794.

Schiller's greatest historical tragedy, the trilogy *Wallenstein* (1797–8), was followed in quick succession by *Maria Stuart* (1800), *The Maid of Orleans* (1801), *The Bride of Messina* (1803), and *Wilhelm Tell* (1804). All are in verse, and all aspire to a universally representative or 'classical' character at the expense of merely local or contemporary relevance. (*The Bride of Messina* even employs a Greek chorus.)

As a critic, Schiller was much indebted to Kant's philosophy. But whereas Kant's moral rigorism could readily be accommodated to the theory of tragedy, Schiller felt the need to modify Kant's uncompromising dualism in presenting art as a means of harmonising conflicting impulses within the human psyche and restoring it to wholeness. The ideal of wholeness is fundamental in *On Naive and Sentimental Poetry,* which adopts a historical approach to the problem. Schiller defines and justifies the distinctive character of modern, as opposed to ancient, poetry; but he contends that the modern, reflective poet must ultimately overcome, by his own self-conscious methods, that division between ideal and reality which did not exist for the 'naive' poet of antiquity.

Further reading

The *Nationalausgabe* of the collected works (1943–) is still incomplete, but the edition by Fricke and Göpfert (1958–9) contains the principal writings. The letters have been collected by Jonas (1892–6). Biographical studies include those of Minor (1890) and the more modern account by von Wiese (fourth edition, 1978). Most of the plays have been translated into English, and Lamport's versions of *Maria Stuart* (1969) and of *The Robbers* and *Wallenstein* (1979) can be recommended. The bilingual edition of the *Aesthetic Letters* by Wilkinson and Willoughby (1967) is excellent. General studies in English include Garland (1949) and Witte (1949). Kerry (1961) deals specifically with the aesthetic writings. See also Carlyle (1845), Dewhurst and Reeves (1978), Ellis (1969), and Pick (1961).

HBN

From

On the Aesthetic Education of Man, in a Series of Letters
[Über die Ästhetische Erziehung des Menschen, in einer Reihe von Briefen]

1793–94, revised 1801[1]

Translated by Elizabeth M. Wilkinson and L.A. Willoughby.

Sixth Letter

1. Have I not perhaps been too hard on our age in the picture I have just drawn? That is scarcely the reproach I anticipate. Rather a different one: that I have tried to make it prove too much.[2] Such a portrait, you will tell me, does indeed resemble mankind as it is today; but does it not also resemble any people caught up in the process of civilization, since all of them, without exception, must fall away from Nature by the abuse of Reason before they can return to her by the use of Reason?

2. Closer attention to the character of our age will, however, reveal an astonishing contrast between contemporary forms of humanity and earlier ones, especially the Greek. The reputation for culture and refinement, on which we otherwise rightly pride ourselves *vis-à-vis* humanity in its *merely* natural state, can avail us nothing against the natural humanity of the Greeks. For they were wedded to all the delights of art and all the dignity of wisdom, without however, like us, falling a prey to their seduction. The Greeks put us to shame not only by a simplicity to which our age is a stranger; they are at the same time our rivals, indeed often our models, in those very excellences with which we are wont to console ourselves for the unnaturalness of our manners. In fullness of form no less than of content, at once philosophic and creative, sensitive and energetic, the Greeks combined the first youth of imagination with the manhood of reason in a glorious manifestation of humanity.

3. At that first fair awakening of the powers of the mind, sense and intellect did not as yet rule over strictly separate domains; for no dissension had as yet provoked them into hostile partition and mutual demarcation of their frontiers. Poetry had not as yet coquetted with wit, nor speculation prostituted itself to sophistry. Both of them could, when need

129

arose, exchange functions, since each in its own fashion paid honour to truth. However high the mind[3] might soar, it always drew matter lovingly along with it; and however fine and sharp the distinctions it might make, it never proceeded to mutilate. It did indeed divide human nature into its several aspects, and project these in magnified form into the divinities of its glorious pantheon; but not by tearing it to pieces; rather by combining its aspects in different proportions, for in no single one of their deities was humanity in its entirety ever lacking. How different with us Moderns! With us too the image of the human species is projected in magnified form into separate individuals – but as fragments, not in different combinations, with the result that one has to go the rounds from one individual to another in order to be able to piece together a complete image of the species. With us, one might almost be tempted to assert, the various faculties appear as separate in practice as they are distinguished by the psychologist in theory, and we see not merely individuals, but whole classes of men, developing but one part of their potentialities, while of the rest, as in stunted growths, only vestigial traces remain.

4. I do not underrate the advantages which the human race today, considered as a whole and weighed in the balance of intellect, can boast in the face of what is best in the ancient world. But it has to take up the challenge in serried ranks, and let whole measure itself against whole. What individual Modern could sally forth and engage, man against man, with an individual Athenian for the prize of humanity?

5. Whence this disadvantage among individuals when the species as a whole is at such an advantage? Why was the individual Greek qualified to be the representative of his age, and why can no single Modern venture as much? Because it was from all-unifying Nature that the former, and from the all-dividing Intellect[4] that the latter, received their respective forms.

6. It was civilization itself which inflicted this wound upon modern man.[5] Once the increase of empirical knowledge, and more exact modes of thought, made sharper divisions between the sciences inevitable, and once the increasingly complex machinery of State necessitated a more rigorous separation of ranks and occupations, then the inner unity of human nature was severed too, and a disastrous conflict set its harmonious powers at variance. The intuitive and the speculative understanding now withdrew in hostility to take up positions in their respective fields, whose frontiers they now began to guard with jealous mistrust; and with this confining of our activity to a particular sphere we have given ourselves a master within, who not infrequently ends by suppressing the rest of our potentialities. While in the one a riotous imagination ravages the hard-won fruits of the intellect, in another the spirit of abstraction stifles the fire at which the heart should have warmed itself and the imagination been kindled.

7. This disorganization, which was first started within man by civilization and learning, was made complete and universal by the new spirit of

government. It was scarcely to be expected that the simple organization of the early republics should have survived the simplicity of early manners and conditions; but instead of rising to a higher form of organic existence it degenerated into a crude and clumsy mechanism. That polypoid character of the Greek States, in which every individual enjoyed an independent existence but could, when need arose, grow into the whole organism, now made way for an ingenious clock-work, in which, out of the piecing together of innumerable but lifeless parts, a mechanical kind of collective life ensued. State and Church, laws and customs, were now torn asunder; enjoyment was divorced from labour, the means from the end, the effort from the reward. Everlastingly chained to a single little fragment of the Whole, man himself develops into nothing but a fragment; everlastingly in his ear the monotonous sound of the wheel that he turns, he never develops the harmony of his being, and instead of putting the stamp of humanity upon his own nature, he becomes nothing more than the imprint of his occupation or of his specialized knowledge. But even the meagre, fragmentary participation, by which individual members of the State are still linked to the Whole, does not depend upon forms which they spontaneously prescribe for themselves (for how could one entrust to their freedom of action a mechanism so intricate and so fearful of light and enlightenment?); it is dictated to them with meticulous exactitude by means of a formulary which inhibits all freedom of thought. The dead letter takes the place of living understanding, and a good memory is a safer guide than imagination and feeling.

8. When the community makes his office the measure of the man; when in one of its citizens it prizes nothing but memory, in another a mere tabularizing intelligence, in a third only mechanical skill; when, in the one case, indifferent to character, it insists exclusively on knowledge, yet is, in another, ready to condone any amount of obscurantist thinking as long as it is accompanied by a spirit of order and law-abiding behaviour; when, moreover, it insists on special skills being developed with a degree of intensity which is only commensurate with its readiness to absolve the individual citizen from developing himself in extensity – can we wonder that the remaining aptitudes of the psyche are neglected in order to give undivided attention to the one which will bring honour and profit? True, we know that the outstanding individual will never let the limits of his occupation dictate the limits of his activity. But a mediocre talent will consume in the office assigned him the whole meagre sum of his powers, and a man has to have a mind above the ordinary if, without detriment to his calling, he is still to have time for the chosen pursuits of his leisure. Moreover, it is rarely a recommendation in the eyes of the State if a man's powers exceed the tasks he is set, or if the higher needs of the man of parts constitute a rival to the duties of his office. So jealously does the State insist on being the sole proprietor of its servants that it will more easily bring itself (and

who can blame it?) to share its man with the Cytherean, than with the Uranian, Venus.[6]

9. Thus little by little the concrete life of the Individual is destroyed in order that the abstract idea of the Whole may drag out its sorry existence, and the State remains for ever a stranger to its citizens since at no point does it ever make contact with their feeling. Forced to resort to classification in order to cope with the variety of its citizens, and never to get an impression of humanity except through representation at second hand, the governing section ends up by losing sight of them altogether, confusing their concrete reality with a mere construct of the intellect; while the governed cannot but receive with indifference laws which are scarcely, if at all, directed to them as persons. Weary at last of sustaining bonds which the State does so little to facilitate, positive society begins (this has long been the fate of most European States) to disintegrate into a state of primitive morality, in which public authority has become but one party *more,* to be hated and circumvented by those who make authority necessary, and only obeyed by such as are capable of doing without it.[7]

10. With this twofold pressure upon it, from within and from without, could humanity well have taken any other course than the one it actually took? In its striving after inalienable possessions in the realm of ideas, the spirit of speculation could do no other than become a stranger to the world of sense, and lose sight of matter for the sake of form. The practical spirit,[8] by contrast, enclosed within a monotonous sphere of material objects, and within this uniformity still further confined by formulas, was bound to find the idea of an unconditioned Whole receding from sight, and to become just as impoverished as its own poor sphere of activity. If the former was tempted to model the actual world on a world conceivable by the mind, and to exalt the subjective conditions of its own perceptual and conceptual faculty into laws constitutive of the existence of things, the latter plunged into the opposite extreme of judging all experience whatsoever by one particular fragment of experience, and of wanting to make the rules of its *own* occupation apply indiscriminately to all others. The one was bound to become the victim of empty subtilties, the other of narrow pedantry; for the former stood too high to discern the particular, the latter too low to survey the Whole. But the damaging effects of the turn which mind thus took were not confined to knowledge and production; it affected feeling and action no less. We know that the sensibility of the psyche depends for its intensity upon the liveliness, for its scope upon the richness, of the imagination. The preponderance of the analytical faculty must, however, of necessity, deprive the imagination of its energy and warmth, while a more restricted sphere of objects must reduce its wealth. Hence the abstract thinker very often has a *cold* heart, since he dissects his impressions, and impressions can move the soul only as long as they remain whole; while the man of practical affairs often has a *narrow* heart, since his

imagination, imprisoned within the unvarying confines of his own calling, is incapable of extending itself to appreciate other ways of seeing and knowing.

11. It was part of my procedure to uncover the disadvantageous trends in the character of our age and the reasons for them, not to point out the advantages which Nature offers by way of compensation. I readily concede that, little as individuals might benefit from this fragmentation of their being, there was no other way in which the species as a whole could have progressed. With the Greeks, humanity undoubtedly reached a maximum of excellence, which could neither be maintained at that level nor rise any higher. Not maintained, because the intellect was unavoidably compelled by the store of knowledge it already possessed to dissociate itself from feeling and intuition in an attempt to arrive at exact discursive understanding; not rise any higher, because only a specific degree of clarity is compatible with a specific fullness and warmth. This degree the Greeks had attained; and had they wished to proceed to a higher stage of development, they would, like us, have had to surrender their wholeness of being and pursue truth along separate paths.

12. If the manifold potentialities in man were ever to be developed, there was no other way but to pit them one against the other. This antagonism of faculties and functions is the great instrument of civilization – but it is only the instrument; for as long as it persists, we are only on the way to becoming civilized. Only through individual powers in man becoming isolated, and arrogating to themselves exclusive authority, do they come into conflict with the truth of things, and force the Common Sense, which is otherwise content to linger with indolent complacency on outward appearance, to penetrate phenomena in depth. By pure thought usurping authority in the world of sense, while empirical thought is concerned to subject the usurper to the conditions of experience, both these powers develop to their fullest potential, and exhaust the whole range of their proper sphere. And by the very boldness with which, in the one case, imagination allows her caprice to dissolve the existing world-order, she does, in the other, compel Reason to rise to the ultimate sources of knowing, and invoke the law of Necessity against her.

13. One-sidedness in the exercise of his powers must, it is true, inevitably lead the individual into error; but the species as a whole to truth. Only by concentrating the whole energy of our mind into a *single* focal point, contracting our whole being into a single power, do we, as it were, lend wings to this individual power and lead it, by artificial means, far beyond the limits which Nature seems to have assigned to it. Even as it is certain that all individuals taken together would never, with the powers of vision granted them by Nature alone, have managed to detect a satellite of Jupiter which the telescope reveals to the astronomer, so it is beyond question that human powers of reflection would never have produced an analysis

of the Infinite or a Critique of Pure Reason, unless, in the individuals called to perform such feats, Reason had separated itself off, disentangled itself, as it were, from all matter, and by the most intense effort of abstraction armed their eyes with a glass for peering into the Absolute. But will such a mind, dissolved as it were into pure intellect and pure contemplation, ever be capable of exchanging the rigorous bonds of logic for the free movement of the poetic faculty, or of grasping the concrete individuality of things with a sense innocent of preconceptions and faithful to the object? At this point Nature sets limits even to the most universal genius, limits which he cannot transcend; and as long as philosophy has to make its prime business the provision of safeguards against error, truth will be bound to have its martyrs.

14. Thus, however much the world as a whole may benefit through this fragmentary specialization of human powers, it cannot be denied that the individuals affected by it suffer under the curse of this cosmic purpose. Athletic bodies can, it is true, be developed by gymnastic exercises; beauty only through the free and harmonious play of the limbs. In the same way the keying up of individual functions of the mind can indeed produce extraordinary human beings; but only the equal tempering of them all, happy and complete human beings. And in what kind of relation would we stand to either past or future ages, if the development of human nature were to make such sacrifice necessary? We would have been the serfs of mankind; for several millenia we would have done slaves' work for them, and our mutilated nature would bear impressed upon it the shameful marks of this servitude. And all this in order that a future generation might in blissful indolence attend to the care of its moral health, and foster the free growth of its humanity!

15. But can Man really be destined to miss himself for the sake of any purpose whatsoever? Should Nature, for the sake of her own purposes, be able to rob us of a completeness which Reason, for the sake of hers, enjoins upon us? It must, therefore, be wrong if the cultivation of individual powers involves the sacrifice of wholeness. Or rather, however much the law of Nature tends in that direction, it must be open to us to restore by means of a higher Art the totality of our nature which the arts themselves have destroyed.

Ninth Letter

1. But is this not, perhaps, to argue in a circle?[9] Intellectual education is to bring about moral education, and yet moral education is to be the condition of intellectual education? All improvement in the political sphere is to proceed from the ennobling of character – but how under the influence of a barbarous constitution is character ever to become ennobled? To this end we should, presumably, have to seek out some instrument not pro-

vided by the State, and to open up living springs which, whatever the political corruption, would remain clear and pure.

2. I have now reached the point to which all my preceding reflections have been tending. This instrument is Fine Art; such living springs are opened up in its immortal exemplars.

3. Art, like Science, is absolved from all positive constraint and from all conventions introduced by man; both rejoice in absolute *immunity* from human arbitrariness. The political legislator may put their territory out of bounds; he cannot rule within it. He can proscribe the lover of truth; Truth itself will prevail. He can humiliate the artist; but Art he cannot falsify. True, nothing is more common than for both, science as well as art, to pay homage to the spirit of the age, or for creative minds to accept the critical standards of prevailing taste. In epochs where character becomes rigid and obdurate, we find science keeping a strict watch over its frontiers, and art moving in the heavy shackles of rules; in those where it becomes enervated and flabby, science will strive to please, and art to gratify. For whole centuries thinkers and artists will do their best to submerge truth and beauty in the depths of a degraded humanity; it is they themselves who are drowned there, while truth and beauty, with their own indestructible vitality, struggle triumphantly to the surface.

4. The artist is indeed the child of his age; but woe to him if he is at the same time its ward or, worse still, its minion! Let some beneficent deity snatch the suckling betimes from his mother's breast, nourish him with the milk of a better age, and suffer him to come to maturity under a distant Grecian sky. Then, when he has become a man, let him return, a stranger, to his own century; not, however, to gladden it by his appearance, but rather, terrible like Agamemnon's son, to cleanse and to purify it.[10] His theme he will, indeed, take from the present; but his form he will borrow from a nobler time, nay, from beyond time altogether, from the absolute, unchanging, unity of his being. Here, from the pure aether of his genius, the living source of beauty flows down, untainted by the corruption of the generations and ages wallowing in the dark eddies below. The theme of his work may be degraded by vagaries of the public mood, even as this has been known to ennoble it; but its form, inviolate, will remain immune from such vicissitudes. The Roman of the first century had long been bowing the knee before his emperors when statues still portrayed him erect; temples continued to be sacred to the eye long after the gods had become objects of derision; and the infamous crimes of a *Nero* or a *Commodus* were put to shame by the noble style of the building whose frame lent them cover. Humanity has lost its dignity; but Art has rescued it and preserved it in significant stone. Truth lives on in the illusion of Art, and it is from this copy, or after-image, that the original image will once again be restored. Just as the nobility of Art *survived* the nobility of Nature, so now Art goes before her, a voice rousing from slumber and preparing the shape

of things to come. Even before Truth's triumphant light can penetrate the recesses of the human heart, the poet's imagination will intercept its rays, and the peaks of humanity will be radiant while the dews of night still linger in the valley.

5. But how is the artist to protect himself against the corruption of the age which besets him on all sides? By disdaining its opinion. Let him direct his gaze upwards, to the dignity of his calling and the universal Law, not downwards towards Fortune and the needs of daily life. Free alike from the futile busyness which would fain set its mark upon the fleeting moment, and from the impatient spirit of enthusiasm which applies the measure of the Absolute to the sorry products of Time, let him leave the sphere of the actual to the intellect, which is at home there, whilst he strives to produce the Ideal out of the union of what is possible with what is necessary. Let him express this ideal both in semblance and in truth, set the stamp of it upon the play of his imagination as upon the seriousness of his conduct, let him express it in all sensuous and spiritual forms, and silently project it into the infinity of time.[11]

6. But not everyone whose soul glows with this ideal was granted either the creative tranquillity or the spirit of long patience required to imprint it upon the silent stone, or pour it into the sober mould of words, and so entrust it to the executory hands of time. Far too impetuous to proceed by such unobtrusive means, the divine impulse to form often hurls itself directly upon present-day reality and upon the life of action, and undertakes to fashion anew the formless material presented by the moral world. The misfortunes of the human race speak urgently to the man of feeling; its degradation more urgently still; enthusiasm is kindled, and in vigorous souls ardent longing drives impatiently on towards action. But did he ever ask himself whether those disorders in the moral world offend his reason, or whether they do not rather wound his self-love? If he does not yet know the answer, he will detect it by the zeal with which he insists upon specific and prompt results. The pure moral impulse is directed towards the Absolute. For such an impulse time does not exist, and the future turns into the present from the moment that it is seen to develop with inevitable Necessity out of the present. In the eyes of a Reason which knows no limits, the Direction is at once the Destination, and the Way is completed from the moment it is trodden.

7. To the young friend of truth and beauty who would inquire of me how, despite all the opposition of his century, he is to satisy the noble impulses of his heart, I would make answer: Impart to the world you would influence a *Direction* towards the good, and the quiet rhythm of time will bring it to fulfilment. You will have given it this direction if, by your teaching, you have elevated its thoughts to the Necessary and the Eternal, if, by your actions and your creations, you have transformed the Necessary and the Eternal into an object of the heart's desire. The edifice of error and

caprice will fall – it must fall, indeed it has already fallen – from the moment you are certain that it is on the point of giving way. But it is in man's inner being that it must give way, not just in the externals he presents to the world. It is in the modest sanctuary of your heart that you must rear victorious truth, and project it out of yourself in the form of beauty, so that not only thought can pay it homage, but sense, too, lay loving hold on its appearance. And lest you should find yourself receiving from the world as it is the model you yourself should be providing, do not venture into its equivocal company without first being sure that you bear within your own heart an escort from the world of the ideal. Live with your century; but do not be its creature. Work for your contemporaries; but create what they need, not what they praise. Without sharing their guilt, yet share with noble resignation in their punishment, and bow your head freely beneath the yoke which they find as difficult to dispense with as to bear. By the steadfast courage with which you disdain their good fortune, you will show them that it is not through cowardice that you consent to share their sufferings. Think of them as they ought to be, when called upon to influence them; think of them as they are, when tempted to act on their behalf. In seeking their approval appeal to what is best in them, but in devising their happiness recall them as they are at their worst; then your own nobility will awaken theirs, and their unworthiness not defeat your purpose. The seriousness of your principles will frighten them away, but in the play of your semblance they will be prepared to tolerate them; for their taste is purer than their heart, and it is here that you must lay hold of the timorous fugitive. In vain will you assail their precepts, in vain condemn their practice; but on their leisure hours you can try your shaping hand. Banish from their pleasures caprice, frivolity, and coarseness, and imperceptibly you will banish these from their actions and, eventually, from their inclinations too. Surround them, wherever you meet them, with the great and noble forms of genius, and encompass them about with the symbols of perfection, until Semblance conquer Reality, and Art triumph over Nature.

Sixteenth Letter

1. We have seen how beauty results from the reciprocal action of two opposed drives and from the uniting of two opposed principles. The highest ideal of beauty is, therefore, to be sought in the most perfect possible union and *equilibrium* of reality and form. This equilibrium, however, remains no more than an Idea, which can never be fully realized in actuality. For in actuality we shall always be left with a preponderance of the one element over the other, and the utmost that experience can achieve will consist of an *oscillation* between the two principles, in which now reality, now form, will predominate. Beauty as Idea, therefore, can never be other

than one and indivisible, since there can never be more than one point of equilibrium; whereas beauty in experience will be eternally twofold, because oscillation can disturb the equilibrium in twofold fashion, inclining it now to the one side, now to the other.

2. I observed in one of the preceding Letters[12] – and it follows with strict necessity from the foregoing argument – that we must expect from beauty at once a releasing and a tensing effect: a *releasing* effect in order to keep both the sense-drive and the form-drive within proper bounds; a *tensing* effect, in order to keep both at full strength. Ideally speaking, however, these two effects must be reducible to a single effect. Beauty is to release by tensing both natures uniformly, and to tense by releasing both natures uniformly. This already follows from the concept of a reciprocal action, by virtue of which both factors necessarily condition each other and are at the same time conditioned by each other, and the purest product of which is beauty. But experience offers us no single example of such perfect reciprocal action; for here it will always happen that, to a greater or lesser degree, a preponderance entails a deficiency, and a deficiency a preponderance. What, then, in the case of ideal beauty is but a distinction which is *made* in the mind, is in the case of actual beauty a difference which *exists* in fact. Ideal Beauty, though one and indivisible, exhibits under different aspects a melting as well as an energizing attribute; but in experience there actually is a melting and an energizing type of beauty. So it is, and so it always will be, in all those cases where the Absolute is set within the limitations of time, and the ideas of Reason have to be realized in and through human action. Thus man, when he reflects, can conceive of Virtue, Truth, Happiness; but man, when he acts, can only practise *virtues*, comprehend *truths*, and enjoy *happy hours*. To refer these experiences back to those abstractions – to replace morals by Morality, happy events by Happiness, the facts of knowledge by Knowledge itself – that is the business of physical and moral education. To make Beauty out of a multiplicity of beautiful objects is the task of aesthetic education.

3. Energizing beauty can no more preserve man from a certain residue of savagery and hardness than melting beauty can protect him from a certain degree of effeminacy and enervation.[13] For since the effect of the former is to brace his nature, both physical and moral, and to increase its elasticity and power of prompt reaction, it can happen all too easily that the increased resistance of temperament and character will bring about a decrease in receptivity to impressions; that our gentler humanity, too, will suffer the kind of repression which ought only to be directed at our brute nature, and our brute nature profit from an increase of strength which should only be available to our free Person. That is why in periods of vigour and exuberance we find true grandeur of conception coupled with the gigantic and the extravagant, sublimity of thought with the most frightening explosions of passion; that is why in epochs of discipline and form

we find nature as often suppressed as mastered, as often outraged as tran-
scended. And because the effect of melting beauty is to relax our nature,
physical and moral, it happens no less easily that energy of feeling is stifled
along with violence of appetite, and that character too shares the loss of
power which should only overtake passion. That is why in so-called refined
epochs, we see gentleness not infrequently degenerating into softness,
plainness into platitude, correctness into emptiness, liberality into arbitrariness, lightness of touch into frivolity, calmness into apathy, and the
most despicable caricatures in closest proximity to the most splendid spec-
imens of humanity. The man who lives under the constraint of either matter or forms is, therefore, in need of melting beauty; for he is moved by
greatness and power long before he begins to be susceptible to harmony
and grace. The man who lives under the indulgent sway of taste is in need
of energizing beauty; for he is only too ready, once he has reached a state
of sophisticated refinement, to trifle away the strength he brought with
him from the state of savagery.

4. And now, I think, we have explained and resolved the discrepancy
commonly met with in the judgements people make about the influence of
beauty, and in the value they attach to aesthetic culture. The discrepancy
is explained once we remember that, in experience, there are two types of
beauty, and that both parties to the argument tend to make assertions
about the whole genus which each of them is only in a position to prove
about one particular species of it. And the discrepancy is resolved once we
distinguish a twofold need in man to which that twofold beauty corresponds. Both parties will probably turn out to be right if they can only first
agree among themselves which kind of beauty and which type of humanity
each has in mind.

5. In the rest of my inquiry I shall, therefore, pursue the path which
nature herself takes with man in matters aesthetic, and setting out from
the two species of beauty move upwards to the generic concept of it. I shall
examine the effects of melting beauty on those who are tensed, and the
effects of energizing beauty on those who are relaxed, in order finally to
dissolve both these contrary modes of beauty in the unity of Ideal Beauty,
even as those two opposing types of human being are merged in the unity
of Ideal Man.

From **Seventeenth Letter**

*   *   *

4. Melting beauty, so it was maintained, is for natures which are tense;
energizing beauty for those which are relaxed. I call a man tense when he
is under the compulsion of thought,[14] no less than when he is under the
compulsion of feeling. *Exclusive* domination by either of his two basic

drives is for him a state of constraint and violence, and freedom lies only in the co-operation of both his natures. The man one-sidedly dominated by feeling, or the sensuously tensed man, will be released and set free by means of form; the man one-sidedly dominated by law, or the spiritually tensed man, will be released and set free by means of matter. In order to be adequate to this twofold task, melting beauty will therefore reveal herself under two different guises. *First,* as tranquil form, she will assuage the violence of life, and pave the way which leads from sensation to thought. *Secondly,* as living image, she will arm abstract form with sensuous power, lead concept back to intuition, and law back to feeling. The first of these services she renders to natural man, the second to civilized man. But since in neither case does she have completely unconditional control over her human material, but is dependent on that offered her by either the form-lessness of nature or the unnaturalness of civilization, she will in both cases still bear traces of her origins, and tend to lose herself, in the one case, more in material life, in the other, more in pure and abstract form.

*   *   *

Twentieth Letter

1. That freedom cannot be affected by anything whatsoever follows from our very notion of freedom. But that *freedom is itself* an effect of *Nature* (this word taken in its widest sense) and not the work of Man, that it can, therefore, also be furthered or thwarted by natural means, follows no less inevitably from what has just been said. It arises only when man is a *complete* being, when *both* his fundamental drives are fully developed; it will, therefore, be lacking as long as he is incomplete, as long as one of the two drives is excluded, and it should be capable of being restored by anything which gives him back his completeness.

2. Now we can, in fact, in the species as a whole as well as in the individual human being, point to a moment in which man is not yet complete, and in which one of his two drives is exclusively active within him. We know that he begins by being nothing but life, in order to end by becoming form; that he is an Individual before he is a Person, and that he proceeds from limitation to infinity. The sensuous drive, therefore, comes into operation earlier than the rational, because sensation precedes consciousness, and it is this *priority* of the sensuous drive which provides the clue to the whole history of human freedom.[15]

3. For there is, after all, a moment in which the life-impulse, just because the form-impulse is not yet running counter to it, operates as nature and as necessity; a moment in which the life of sense is a power because man has not yet begun to be a human being; for in the human being proper there cannot exist any power other than the will. But in the

state of reflection into which he is now to pass, it will be precisely the opposite: Reason is to be a power, and a logical or moral necessity to take the place of that physical necessity. Hence sensation as a power must first be destroyed before law can be enthroned as such. It is, therefore, not simply a matter of something beginning which was not there before; something which was there must first cease to be. Man cannot pass directly from feeling to thought; he must first *take one step backwards,* since only through one determination being annulled again can a contrary determination take its place. In order to exchange passivity for autonomy,[16] a passive determination for an active one, man must therefore be momentarily *free of all determination whatsoever,* and pass through a state of pure determinability. He must consequently, in a certain sense, return to that negative state of complete absence of determination in which he found himself before anything at all had made an impression upon his senses. But that former condition was completely devoid of content; and now it is a question of combining such sheer absence of determination, and an equally unlimited determinability, with the greatest possible content, since directly from this condition something positive is to result. The determination he has received through sensation must therefore be preserved, because there must be no loss of reality; but at the same time it must, inasmuch as it is limitation, be annulled, since an unlimited determinability is to come into existence. The problem is, therefore, at one and the same time to destroy and to maintain the determination of the condition – and this is possible in one way only: *by confronting it with another determination.* The scales of the balance stand level when they are empty; but they also stand level when they contain equal weights.

4. Our psyche passes, then, from sensation to thought *via* a middle disposition in which sense and reason are both active *at the same time.* Precisely for this reason, however, they cancel each other out as determining forces, and bring about a negation by means of an opposition. This middle disposition, in which the psyche is subject neither to physical nor to moral constraint, and yet is active in both these ways, pre-eminently deserves to be called a free disposition; and if we are to call the condition of sensuous determination the physical, and the condition of rational determination the logical or moral, then we must call this condition of real and active determinability the *aesthetic.**

*For readers not altogether familiar with the precise meaning of this word, which is so much abused through ignorance, the following may serve as an explanation. Every thing which is capable of phenomenal manifestation may be thought of under four different aspects. A thing can relate directly to our sensual condition (to our being and well-being): that is its *physical* character. Or it can relate to our intellect, and afford us knowledge: that is its *logical* character. Or it can relate to our will, and be considered as an object of choice for a rational being: that is its *moral* character. Or, finally, it can relate to the totality of our various functions without being a definite object for any single one of them: that is its *aesthetic* character.

Twenty-second Letter

1. If, then, in one respect the aesthetic mode of the psyche is to be regarded as *Nought* – once, that is, we have an eye to particular and definite effects – it is in another respect to be looked upon as a state *of Supreme Reality*, once we have due regard to the absence of all limitation and to the sum total of the powers which are conjointly active within it. One cannot, then, say that those people are wrong either who declare the aesthetic state to be the most fruitful of all in respect of knowledge and morality.[17] They are entirely right; for a disposition of the psyche which contains within it the whole of human nature, must necessarily contain within it *in potentia* every individual manifestation of it too; and a disposition of the psyche which removes all limitations from the totality of human nature must necessarily remove them from every individual manifestation of it as well. Precisely on this account, because it takes under its protection no single one of man's faculties to the exclusion of the others, it favours each and all of them without distinction; and it favours no single one more than another for the simple reason that it is the ground of possibility of them all. Every other way of exercising its functions endows the psyche with some special aptitude – but only at the cost of some special limitation; the aesthetic alone leads to the absence of all limitation. Every other state into which we can enter refers us back to a preceding one, and requires for its termination a subsequent one; the aesthetic alone is a whole in itself, since it comprises within itself all the conditions of both its origin and its continuance. Here alone do we feel reft out of time, and our human nature expresses itself with a purity and *integrity*, as though it had as yet suffered no impairment through the intervention of external forces.

2. That which flatters our senses in immediate sensation exposes our susceptible and labile psyche to every impression – but only by rendering

A man can please us through his readiness to oblige; he can, through his discourse, give us food for thought; he can, through his character, fill us with respect; but finally he can also, independently of all this, and without our taking into consideration in judging him any law or any purpose, please us simply as we contemplate him and by the sheer manner of his being. Under this last-named quality of being we are judging him aesthetically. Thus there is an education to health, an education to understanding, an education to morality, an education to taste and beauty. This last has as its aim the development of the whole complex of our sensual and spiritual powers in the greatest possible harmony. Because, however, misled by false notions of taste and confirmed still further in this error by false reasoning, people are inclined to include in the notion of the aesthetic the notion of the arbitrary too, I add here the superfluous comment (despite the fact that these Letters on Aesthetic Education are concerned with virtually nothing else but the refutation of that very error) that our psyche in the aesthetic state does indeed act freely, is in the highest degree free from all compulsion, but is in no wise free from laws; and that this aesthetic freedom is distinguishable from logical necessity in thinking, or moral necessity in willing, only by the fact that the laws according to which the psyche then behaves *do not become apparent as such*, and since they encounter no resistance, never appear as a constraint.

us proportionately less fitted for exertion. That which tenses our intellectual powers and invites them to form abstract concepts, strengthens our mind for every sort of resistance – but only by hardening it and depriving us of sensibility in proportion as it fosters greater independence of action. Precisely because of this, the one no less than the other must lead to exhaustion, since material cannot for long dispense with shaping power, nor power with material to be shaped. If, by contrast, we have surrendered to the enjoyment of genuine beauty, we are at such a moment master in equal degree of our passive and of our active powers, and we shall with equal ease turn to seriousness or to play, to repose or to movement, to compliance or to resistance, to the discursions of abstract thought or to the direct contemplation of phenomena.

3. This lofty equanimity and freedom of the spirit, combined with power and vigour, is the mood in which a genuine work of art should release us, and there is no more certain touchstone of true aesthetic excellence. If, after enjoyment of this kind, we find ourselves disposed to prefer some one particular mode of feeling or action, but unfitted or disinclined for another, this may serve as infallible proof that we have not had a *purely aesthetic* experience – whether the cause lies in the object or in our own response or, as is almost always the case, in both at once.

4. Since in actuality no purely aesthetic effect is ever to be met with (for man can never escape his dependence upon conditioning forces), the excellence of a work of art can never consist in anything more than a high approximation to that ideal of aesthetic purity; and whatever the degree of freedom to which it may have been sublimated, we shall still leave it in a particular mood and with some definite bias. The more general the mood and the less limited the bias produced in us by any particular art, or by any particular product of the same, then the nobler that art and the more excellent that product will be. One can test this by considering works from different arts and different works from the same art. We leave a beautiful piece of music with our feeling excited, a beautiful poem with our imagination quickened, a beautiful sculpture or building with our understanding awakened. But should anyone invite us, immediately after a sublime musical experience, to abstract thought; or employ us, immediately after a sublime poetic experience, in some routine business of everyday life; or try, immediately after the contemplation of beautiful paintings or sculptures, to inflame our imagination or surprise our feeling – he would certainly be choosing the wrong moment. The reason for this is that even the most ethereal music has, *by virtue of its material,* an even greater affinity with the senses than true aesthetic freedom really allows; that even the most successful poem partakes more of the arbitrary and casual play of the imagination, *as the medium through which it works,* than the inner lawfulness of the truly beautiful really permits; that even the most excellent sculpture – the most excellent, perhaps, most of all – does, *by virtue of its conceptual*

precision,[18] border upon the austerity of science. Nevertheless, the greater the degree of excellence attained by a work in any of these three arts, the more these particular affinities will disappear; and it is an inevitable and natural consequence of their approach to perfection that the various arts, without any displacement of their objective frontiers, tend to become ever more like each other *in their effect upon the psyche*. Music, at its most sublime, must become sheer form and affect us with the serene power of antiquity. The plastic arts, at their most perfect, must become music and move us by the immediacy of their sensuous presence. Poetry, when most fully developed, must grip us powerfully as music does, but at the same time, like the plastic arts, surround us with serene clarity. This, precisely, is the mark of perfect style in each and every art: that it is able to remove the specific limitations of the art in question without thereby destroying its specific qualities, and through a wise use of its individual peculiarities, is able to confer upon it a more general character.

5. And it is not just the limitations inherent in the specific character of a particular art that the artist must seek to overcome through his handling of it; it is also the limitations inherent in the particular subject-matter he is treating. In a truly successful work of art the contents should effect nothing, the form everything; for only through the form is the whole man affected, through the subject-matter, by contrast, only one or other of his functions. Subject-matter, then, however sublime and all-embracing it may be, always has a limiting effect upon the spirit, and it is only from form that true aesthetic freedom can be looked for. Herein, then, resides the real secret of the master in any art: *that he can make his form consume his material;* and the more pretentious, the more seductive this material is in itself, the more it seeks to impose itself upon us, the more high-handedly it thrusts itself forward with effects *of its own,* or the more the beholder is inclined to get directly involved with it, then the more triumphant the art which forces it back and asserts its own kind of dominion over him. The psyche of the listener or spectator must remain completely free and inviolate; it must go forth from the magic circle of the artist pure and perfect as it came from the hands of the Creator. The most frivolous theme must be so treated that it leaves us ready to proceed directly from it to some matter of the utmost import; the most serious material must be so treated that we remain capable of exchanging it forthwith for the lightest play. Arts which affect the passions, such as tragedy, do not invalidate this: *in the first place,* they are not entirely free arts since they are enlisted in the service of a particular aim (that of pathos); and *in the second,* no true connoisseur of art will deny that works even of this class are the more perfect, the more they respect the freedom of the spirit even amid the most violent storms of passion. There does indeed exist a fine art of passion; but a fine passionate art is a contradiction in terms; for the unfailing effect of beauty is freedom from passion. Not less self-contradictory is the notion of a fine

art which teaches (didactic) or improves (moral); for nothing is more at variance with the concept of beauty than the notion of giving the psyche any definite bias.

6. But it is by no means always a proof of formlessness in the work of art itself if it makes its effect solely through its contents; this may just as often be evidence of a lack of form in him who judges it. If he is either too tensed or too relaxed, if he is used to apprehending either exclusively with the intellect or exclusively with the senses, he will, even in the case of the most successfully realized whole, attend only to the parts, and in the presence of the most beauteous form respond only to the matter. Receptive only to the *raw material,* he has first to destroy the aesthetic organization of a work before he can take pleasure in it, and laboriously scratch away until he has uncovered all those individual details which the master, with infinite skill, had caused to disappear in the harmony of the whole. The interest he takes in it is quite simply either a moral or a material interest; but what precisely it ought to be, namely aesthetic, that it certainly is not. Such readers will enjoy a serious and moving poem as though it were a sermon, a naïve or humorous one as though it were an intoxicating drink. And if they were sufficiently lacking in taste to demand *edification* of a tragedy or an epic – and were it about the Messiah himself – they will certainly not fail to take exception to a poem in the manner of Anacreon or Catullus.[19]

From **Twenty-seventh Letter**

1. You need have no fear for either reality or truth if the lofty conception of aesthetic semblance which I put forward in the last Letter were to become universal. It will not become universal as long as man is still uncultivated enough to be in a position to misuse it; and should it become universal, this could only be brought about by the kind of culture which would automatically make any misuse of it impossible. To strive after autonomous semblance demands higher powers of abstraction, greater freedom of heart, more energy of will, than man ever needs when he confines himself to reality; and he must already have left this reality behind if he would arrive at that kind of semblance. How ill-advised he would be, then, to take the path towards the ideal in order to save himself the way to the real! From semblance as here understood we should thus have little cause to fear for reality; all the more to be feared, I would suggest, is the threat from reality to semblance. Chained as he is to the material world, man subordinates semblance to ends of his own long before he allows it autonomous existence in the ideal realm of art. For this latter to happen a complete revolution[20] in his whole way of feeling is required, without which he would not even find himself *on the way* to the ideal. Wherever, then, we find traces of a disinterested and unconditional appreciation of pure sem-

blance, we may infer that a revolution[21] of this order has taken place in his nature, and that he has started to become truly human. Traces of this kind are, however, actually to be found even in his first crude attempts at *embellishing* his existence, attempts made even at the risk of possibly worsening it from the material point of view. As soon as ever he starts preferring form to substance, and jeopardizing reality for the sake of semblance (which he must, however, recognize as such), a breach has been effected in the cycle of his animal behaviour, and he finds himself set upon a path to which there is no end.

*   *   *

8. In the midst of the fearful kingdom of forces, and in the midst of the sacred kingdom of laws, the aesthetic impulse to form is at work, unnoticed, on the building of a third joyous kingdom of play and of semblance, in which man is relieved of the shackles of circumstance, and released from all that might be called constraint, alike in the physical and in the moral sphere.[22]

*   *   *

10. The dynamic State can merely make society possible, by letting one nature be curbed by another; the ethical State can merely make it (morally) necessary, by subjecting the individual will to the general; the aesthetic State alone can make it real, because it consummates the will of the whole through the nature of the individual. Though it may be his needs which drive man into society, and reason which implants within him the principles of social behaviour, beauty alone can confer upon him a *social character*. Taste alone brings harmony into society, because it fosters harmony in the individual. All other forms of perception divide man, because they are founded exclusively either upon the sensuous or upon the spiritual part of his being; only the aesthetic mode of perception makes of him a whole, because both his natures must be in harmony if he is to achieve it. All other forms of communication divide society, because they relate exclusively either to the private receptivity or to the private proficiency of its individual members, hence to that which distinguishes man from man; only the aesthetic mode of communication unites society, because it relates to that which is common to all. The pleasures of the senses we enjoy merely as individuals, without the genus which is immanent within us having any share in them at all; hence we cannot make the pleasures of sense universal, because we are unable to universalize our own individuality. The pleasures of knowledge we enjoy merely as genus, and by carefully removing from our judgement all trace of individuality; hence we cannot make the pleasures of reason universal, because we cannot eliminate traces of individuality from the judgements of others as we can from our own.[23] Beauty alone do we enjoy at once as individual and as genus, i.e., as *representatives* of the human genus. The good of the Senses can only make one man happy, since it is founded on appropriation, and this always involves exclu-

sion; and it can only make this *one* man onesidedly happy, since his Personality has no part in it. Absolute good can only bring happiness under conditions which we cannot presume to be universal; for truth is the prize of abnegation alone, and only the pure in heart believe in the pure will. Beauty alone makes the whole world happy, and each and every being forgets its limitations while under its spell.

From
On Naive and Sentimental Poetry[1]

1795–6

Translated by Julius A. Elias (slightly modified).

German text in *Schillers Werke. Nationalausgabe,* edited by Petersen and others (1943–), XX, 413–503.

There are moments in our lives when we dedicate a kind of love and tender respect to nature in plants, minerals, animals, and landscapes, as well as to human nature in children, in the customs of country folk, and to the primitive world, not because it gratifies our senses, nor yet because it satisfies our understanding or taste (the very opposite can occur in both instances), rather, simply *because it is nature.* Every person of a finer cast who is not totally lacking in feeling experiences this when he wanders in the open air, when he stays in the country, or lingers before the monuments of ancient times; in short, whenever he is surprised in the midst of artificial circumstances and situations by the sight of simple nature. It is this interest, not infrequently elevated into a need, which underlies much of our fondness for flowers and animals, for simple gardens, for strolls, for the country and its inhabitants, for many an artifact of remote antiquity, and the like; provided that neither affectation nor any other fortuitous interest plays a role. However, this kind of interest in nature can take place only under two conditions. First, it is absolutely necessary that the object which inspires it should be *nature* or at least be taken by us as such; second, that it be *naive* (in the broadest meaning of the word), i.e., that nature stand in contrast to art and put it to shame. As soon as the latter is joined with the former, not before, nature becomes naive.

Nature, considered in this wise, is for us nothing but the voluntary presence, the subsistence of things on their own, their existence in accordance with their own immutable laws.

This representation is absolutely necessary if we are to take an interest in such appearances. If one were able by the most consummate deception to give an artificial flower the similitude of nature, if one were able to induce the highest illusion of the naive in human behaviour by imitating it, the discovery that it was imitation would completely destroy the feeling of which we spoke.[a] From this it is clear that this kind of satisfaction in

148

nature is not aesthetic but moral; for it is mediated by an idea, not produced immediately by observation; nor is it in any way dependent upon beauty of form. For what could a modest flower, a stream, a mossy stone, the chirping of birds, the humming of bees, etc., possess in themselves so pleasing to us? What could give them a claim even upon our love? It is not these objects, it is an idea represented by them which we love in them. We love in them the tacitly creative life, the serene spontaneity of their activity, existence in accordance with their own laws, the inner necessity, the eternal unity with themselves.

They are what we were; they are what *we should once again become.* We were nature just as they, and our culture, by means of reason and freedom, should lead us back to nature. They are, therefore, not only the representation of our lost childhood, which eternally remains most dear to us, so that they fill us with a certain melancholy. But they are also representations of our highest fulfilment in the ideal, thus evoking in us a sublime tenderness.

Yet their perfection is not to their credit, because it is not the product of their choice. They accord us then, the quite unique delight of being our example without putting us to shame. They surround us like a continuous divine phenomenon, but more exhilarating than blinding. What determines their character is precisely what is lacking for the perfection of our own; what distinguishes us from them, is precisely what they themselves lack for divinity. We are free, they are necessary; we change, they remain a unity. But only if both are joined one with the other – if the will freely obeys the law of necessity, and reason asserts its rule through all the flux of imagination, does the ideal or the divine come to the fore. *In them,* then, we see eternally that which escapes us, but for which we are challenged to strive, and which, even if we never attain to it, we may still hope to approach in endless progress. *In ourselves* we observe an advantage which they lack, and in which they can either never participate at all (as in the case of the irrational) or only insofar as they proceed by *our* path (as with childhood). They afford us, therefore, the sweetest enjoyment of our humanity as idea, even though they must perforce humiliate us with reference to any particular condition of our humanity.

Since this interest in nature is based upon an idea, it can manifest itself only in minds which are receptive to ideas, i.e., in moral minds. By far the majority of people merely affect this state, and the universality of this sentimental taste in our times as expressed, particularly since the appearance of certain writings,[3] in the form of sentimental journeys, pleasure gardens, walks, and other delights of this sort, is by no means a proof of the universality of this mode of feeling. Yet nature will always have something of this effect even upon the most unfeeling, if only because that tendency toward the moral common to all men is sufficient for the purpose, and we are all without distinction, regardless of the distance between our actions and the simplicity and truth of nature, impelled to it in idea. Particularly powerfully and most universally this sensitivity to nature is given expression at the instance of such objects as stand in close connection with us, affording a retrospective view of ourselves and revealing more closely the unnatural in us, as, for example, in children and childlike folk. One is in error to suppose that it is only the notion of helplessness which overcomes us with tenderness at certain moments when we are together with children. That may perhaps be the case with those who in the presence of weakness are accustomed only to feeling their own superiority. But the feeling of which I speak (it occurs only in specifically moral moods and is not to be confused with the emotion that is excited in us by the happy activity of children) is humiliating rather than favourable to self-love; and even if an advantage were to be drawn from it, this would certainly not be on our side. We are touched not because we look down upon the child from the height of our strength and perfection, but rather because we *look upward* from the *limitation* of our condition, which is inseparable from the *determination* which we have attained, to the unlimited *determinability*[4] of the child and to its pure innocence; and our emotion at such a moment is too transparently mixed with a certain melancholy for its source to be mistaken. In the child *disposition* and *determination*[5] are represented; in us that *fulfilment* that forever remains far short of those. The child is therefore a lively representation to us of the ideal, not indeed as it is fulfilled, but as it is enjoined; hence we are in no sense moved by the notion of its poverty and limitation, but rather by the opposite: the notion of its pure and free strength, its integrity, its infinity. To a moral and sensitive person a child will be a *sacred* object on this account; an object, in fact, which by the greatness of an idea destroys all empirical greatness; one which, whatever else it may lose in the judgement of the understanding, it regains in ample measure in the judgement of reason.[6]

It is from just this contradiction between the judgement of reason and the understanding that the quite extraordinary phenomenon arises of those mixed feelings which the *naive* mode of thought excites in us. It connects *childlike* simplicity with the *childish;* through the latter it exposes its weakness to the understanding and causes that smile by which we betray our *(theoretical)* superiority. But as soon as we have cause to believe that childish simplicity is at the same time childlike, that in consequence not lack of understanding, not incapacity, but rather a higher *(practical)*[7] strength, a heart full of innocence and truth, is the source of that which out of its inner greatness scorns the aid of art, then that triumph of the understanding is set aside, and mockery of ingenuousness yields to admiration of simplicity. We feel ourselves obliged to respect the object at which we formerly smiled, and since we at the same time cast our glance upon ourselves, bemoan the fact that we are not likewise endowed. Thus arises the entirely unique phenomenon of a feeling in which joyous mockery, respect, and melancholy are compounded.[b]

To be naive it is necessary that nature be victorious over art,[c] whether this occur counter to the knowledge or will of the individual or with his full awareness. In the first case this is the naive of *surprise* and amuses us; in the second, it is the naive of *temperament* and touches us.

With the naive of surprise the individual must be *morally* capable of denying nature; with the naive of temperament this may not be the case, but we must not be able to think him *physically* incapable of doing so if it is to affect us as being naive. The actions and speech of children thus give us a pure impression of the naive only so long as we do not recall their incapacity for art and in any case only take into consideration the contrast between their naturalness and the artificiality in ourselves. The naive is *childlikeness where it is no longer expected,* and precisely on this account cannot be ascribed to actual childhood in the most rigorous sense.

But in both cases, in the naive of surprise just as in the naive of temperament, nature must be in the right where art is in the wrong.

Only by this last provision is the concept of the naive completed. The affect[9] is also nature, and the rule of propriety is something artificial; yet the victory of the affect over propriety is anything but naive. If, on the other hand, the same affect should triumph over artifice, over false modesty, over deceit, then we do not hesitate to call it naive.[d] Hence it is necessary that nature should triumph over art not by her blind violence as *dynamic greatness,* but by her form as *moral greatness,* in brief, not as *compulsion,* but as *inner necessity.* It is not the inadequacy of art but its invalidity that must have assured the victory of nature; for inadequacy is a shortcoming, and nothing that derives from a shortcoming can inspire respect. It is indeed the case with the naive of surprise that the superior power of the affect and a lack of awareness reveal nature; but this lack and the superior power by no means constitute the naive, rather they simply provide the opportunity for nature to obey unimpeded her moral character, i.e., the law of harmony.

[After distinguishing childlikeness, the truly naive trait, from mere childishness, Schiller continues as follows.]

Every true genius must be naive, or it is not genius. Only its naivety makes for its genius, and what it is intellectually and aesthetically it cannot disavow morally. Unacquainted with the rules, those crutches for weakness and taskmasters of awkwardness, led only by nature or by instinct, its guardian angel, it goes calmly and surely through all the snares of false taste in which, if it is not shrewd enough to avoid them from afar, the nongenius must inevitably be entrapped. Only to genius is it given to be at home beyond the accustomed and to *extend* nature without *going beyond* her. It is true that sometimes the latter befalls even the greatest geniuses, but only because even they have their moments of fantasy in which protective nature abandons them either because they are engrossed by the power of example, or because the perverted taste of their times misleads them.

The genius must solve the most complex tasks with unpretentious simplicity and facility; the egg of Columbus appears in every decision of genius. And only thus does genius identify itself as such, by triumphing over the complications of art by simplicity. It proceeds not by the accepted principles, but by flashes of insight and feeling; but its insights are the inspirations of a god (everything done by healthy nature is divine), its feelings are laws for all ages and for all races of men.

The childlike character that the genius imposes upon his works he likewise displays in his private life and morals. He is *chaste*, for this nature always is; but he is not *prudish*, for only decadence is prudish. He is *intelligent*, for nature can never be otherwise; but he is not *cunning*, for only art can be so. He is *true* to his character and his inclinations, but not so much because he possesses principles as because nature, despite all fluctuations, always returns to its former state, always revives the old necessity. He is *modest*, even shy, because genius always remains a mystery to itself; but he is not fearful, because he does not know the dangers of the path he travels. We know little of the private lives of the greatest geniuses, but even the little that is preserved, for example, of Sophocles, Archimedes, Hippocrates, and, in more recent times, of Ariosto, Dante, and Tasso, of Raphael, of Albrecht Dürer, Cervantes, Shakespeare, of Fielding, Sterne, etc., confirms this assertion.

Indeed, and this seems to present much more difficulty, even great statesmen and generals, if their greatness is due to their genius, will display a naive character. Among the ancients I cite only Epaminondas and Julius Caesar, among moderns only Henry IV of France, Gustavus Adolphus of Sweden, and Czar Peter the Great. The Duke of Marlborough, Turenne, and Vendôme all display this character. It is to the opposite sex that nature has assigned the naive character in its highest perfection. Woman's desire to please manifests itself nowhere so much as in seeking the *appearance of naivety;* proof enough, even if one had no other, that the greatest power of the sex depends upon this characteristic. But since the leading principles of feminine education are in perpetual conflict with this character, it is as difficult for a woman morally as it is for a man intellectually to preserve this magnificent gift of nature intact along with the advantages of a good education; and the *woman* who combines naivety of manner with a demeanour appropriate for society is as worthy of the highest esteem as the scholar who joins the genius's freedom of thought with all the rigours of the schools.

From the naive mode of thought there necessarily follows naive expression in word as well as in gesture, and this is the most important element in gracefulness. But this naive grace genius expresses its most sublime and profound thought; the utterances of a god in the mouth of a child. The understanding of the schools, always fearful of error, crucifies its words and its concepts upon the cross of grammar and logic, and is severe and stiff to avoid uncertainty at all costs, employs many words to be quite sure of not saying too much, and deprives its thoughts of their strength and edge so that they may not cut the unwary. But genius delineates its own thoughts at a single felicitous stroke of the brush with an eternally determined, firm, and yet absolutely free outline. If to the former the sign remains forever heterogeneous and alien to the thing signified, to the latter language springs as by some inner necessity out of thought, and is so at one with it that even beneath the corporeal frame the spirit appears as if laid bare. It is precisely this mode of expression in which the sign disappears completely in the thing signified, and in which language, while giving expression to a thought, yet leaves it exposed (whereas the other mode cannot represent it without simultaneously concealing it); and this it is we generally call a gifted style displaying genius.

*   *   *

Then ask of yourself, sensitive friend of nature, whether your lassitude craves her peace, your injured morality her harmony? Ask yourself, when art revolts you and the abuses in society drive you to lifeless nature in loneliness, whether it is society's deprivations, its burdens, its tedium, or whether it is its moral anarchy, its arbitrariness, its disorders that you despise in it? In the former your courage must joyfully rush in, and your compensation must be the freedom whence these evils derive. You may indeed retain the calm happiness of nature as your distant object, but only as one which is the reward of your worthiness. Then no more of complaints at the difficulties of life, of the inequality of stations, of the pressure of circumstances, of the uncertainty of possession, of ingratitude, oppression, persecution; with free resignation, you must subject yourself to all the *ills* of civilisation, respect them as the natural conditions of the only good; only its *evil* you must mourn, but not with vain tears alone. Rather, take heed that beneath that mire you remain pure, beneath that serfdom, free; constant in that capricious flux, acting lawfully in that anarchy. Be not afraid of the confusion around you, only of the confusion within you; strive after unity, but do not seek conformity; strive after calm, but through the equilibrium, not the cessation of your activity. That nature which you envy in the non-rational is worthy of no respect, no longing. It lies behind you, and must lie eternally behind you. Abandoned by the ladder that supported you, no other choice now lies open to you, but with free consciousness and will to grasp the law, or fall without hope of rescue into a bottomless pit.

But when you are consoled at the lost *happiness* of nature then let her *perfection* be your heart's example. If you march out toward her from your artificial environment she will stand before you in her great calm, in her naive beauty, in her childlike innocence and simplicity – then linger at this image, cultivate this emotion; this is worthy of your sublimest humanity. Let it no longer occur to you to want to exchange with her, but take her up within yourself and strive to wed her infinite advantage with your infinite prerogative,[10] and from both produce the divine. Let her surround you like an enchanting idyll in which you can always find yourself safe from the waywardness of art, and in which you accumulate courage and new confidence for the race, and which lights anew in your heart the flame of the ideal which is so easily extinguished in the storms of life.

If one recalls the beautiful nature that surrounded the ancient Greeks; if one ponders how familiarly this people could live with free nature beneath their fortunate skies, how very much closer their outlook, their manner of perception, their morals, were to simple nature, and what a faithful copy of this their poetry is, then the observation must be displeasing that one finds so little trace among them of the *sentimental* interest with which we moderns are attached to the scenes and characters of nature. The Greek is indeed to the highest degree precise, faithful, and circumstantial in describing them, yet simply no more so and with no more preferential involvement of his heart than he displays in the description of a tunic, a shield, a suit of armour, some domestic article, or any mechanical product. In his love of an object, he does not seem to make any distinction between those which appear of themselves, and those which arise as a result of art or the human will. Nature seems to interest his understanding and craving for knowledge more than his moral feeling; he does not cling to her with fervour, with sentimentality, with sweet melancholy, as we moderns do. Indeed, by hypostatising nature's individual phenomena, treating them as gods, and their effects as the acts of free beings, the Greek eliminates that calm necessity of nature precisely in virtue of which she is so attractive to us. His impatient fantasy leads him beyond nature to the drama of human life. Only the live and free, only characters, acts, destinies, and customs satisfy him, and if, *we,* in certain moral moods of the mind, might wish to surrender the advantage of our freedom of will, which exposes us to so much conflict within ourselves, to so much unrest and errant bypaths, to the choiceless but calm necessity of the non-rational, the fantasy of the Greek, in direct opposition to this, is engaged in rooting human nature in the inanimate world and assigning influence to the will where blind necessity reigns.

Whence derive these different spirits? How is it that we, who are in everything which is nature so boundlessly inferior to the ancients, offer tribute to nature just in this regard to such a higher degree, cling to her with fervour, and embrace even the inanimate world with the warmest sensibility? It is *because* nature in us has disappeared from humanity and we rediscover her in her truth only outside it, in the inanimate world. Not our greater *accord with nature*, but quite the contrary, the *unnaturalness* of our situation, conditions, and manners forces us to procure a satisfaction in the physical world (since none is to be hoped for in the moral) for the incipient impulse for truth and simplicity which, like the moral tendency whence it derives, lies incorruptible and inalienable in every human heart. For this reason the feeling by which we are attached to nature is so closely related to the feeling with which we mourn the lost age of childhood and childlike innocence. Our childhood is the only undisfigured nature that we still encounter in civilised mankind, hence it is no wonder if every trace of the nature outside us leads us back to our childhood.

It was quite otherwise with the ancient Greeks.[e] With them civilisation did not manifest itself to such an extent that nature was abandoned in consequence. The whole structure of their social life was founded on perceptions, not on a contrivance of art; their theology itself was the inspiration of a naive feeling, the child of a joyous imaginative power, not of brooding reason like the religious beliefs of modern nations; since, then, the Greek had not lost nature in his humanity, he could not be surprised by her outside it either and thus feel a pressing need for objects in which he might find her again. At one with himself and happy in the sense of his humanity he was obliged to remain with it as his maximum and assimilate all else to it; whereas *we,* not at one with ourselves and unhappy in our experience of mankind, possess no more urgent interest than to escape from it and cast from our view so unsuccessful a form.

The feeling of which we here speak is therefore not that which the ancients possessed; it is rather identical with that which *we have for the ancients.* They felt naturally; we feel the natural. Without a doubt the feeling that filled Homer's soul as he made his divine swineherd regale Ulysses was quite different from that which moved young Werther's soul as he read this song after an irritating evening in society.[12] Our feeling for nature is like the feeling of an invalid for health.

Just as nature began gradually to disappear from human life as *experience* and as the (active and perceiving) *subject,* so we see her arise in the world of poetry as *idea* and *object.* The nation that had brought this to the extremest degree both in unnaturalness and in reflection thereon must have been the first to be most moved by the phenomenon of the naive and to give it a name. This nation was, as far as I know, the French. But the feeling of the naive and interest in it is naturally much older and goes back even before the beginning of moral and aesthetic corruption. This change in the mode of perception is, for example, extremely obvious in Euripides, if one compares him with his predecessors, notably with Aeschylus, and yet the later poet was the favourite of his age. The same revolution can likewise be documented among the old historians. Horace, the poet of a cultivated and corrupt era, praises serene happiness in Tibur,[13] and one could call him the founder of this sentimental mode of poetry as well as a still unexcelled model of it. In Propertius, too, and Virgil, among others, one finds traces of this mode of perception, less so in Ovid, in whom the requisite fullness of heart was lacking and who in exile in Tomi painfully missed the happiness that Horace in Tibur so gladly dispensed with.

The poets are everywhere, by their very definition, the *guardians* of nature. Where they can no longer quite be so and have already felt within themselves the destructive influence of arbitrary and artificial forms or have had to struggle with them, then they will appear as the *witnesses* and *avengers* of nature. They will either *be* nature, or they will *seek* lost nature. From this arise two entirely different modes of poetry which, between them, exhaust and divide the whole range of poetry. All poets who are truly so will belong, according to the temper of the times in which they flourish, or according to the influence upon their general education or passing states of mind by fortuitous circumstances, either to the *naive* or to the *sentimental* poets.

The poet of a naive and bright youthful world, like the poet who in ages of artificial civilisation is closest to him, is severe and modest like virginal Diana in her forests; without intimacy he flees the heart that seeks his, flees the desire that would embrace him. The dry truth with which he deals with the object seems not infrequently like insensitivity. The object possesses him entirely, his heart does not lie like a tawdry alloy immediately beneath the surface, but like gold waits to be sought in the depths. Like the divinity behind the world's structure he stands behind his work; *he* is the work, and the work is *he;* to ask only for *him* is to be unworthy of it, inadequate to it, or sated with it.

Thus, for example, Homer among the ancients and Shakespeare among the moderns reveal themselves; two vastly different natures separated by the immeasurable distance of the years, but *one* in precisely this trait of character. When, at a very early age I first made the acquaintance of the latter poet, I was incensed by his coldness, the insensitivity which permitted him to jest in the midst of the highest pathos, to interrupt the heart-rending scenes in *Hamlet*, in *King Lear*, in *Macbeth*, etc., with a Fool; restraining himself now where my sympathies rushed on, then coldbloodedly tearing himself away where my heart would have gladly lingered. Misled by acquaintance with more recent poets into looking first for the poet in his work, to find *his* heart, to reflect in unison with *him* on his subject matter, in short, to observe the object in the subject, it was intolerable to me that here there was no way to lay hold of the poet, and nowhere to confront him. I studied him and he possessed my complete admiration for many years before I learned to love him as an individual. I was not yet prepared to understand nature at first hand. I could only support her image reflected in understanding and regulated by a rule, and for this purpose the sentimental poets of the French, and the Germans, too, of the period from 1750 to about 1780, were just the right subjects. However, I am not ashamed of this youthful judgement, since the old-established criticism had promulgated a similar one and was naive enough to publish it in the world.[14]

The same occurred to me with Homer also, whom I learned to know only at a later period. I recall now the curious point in the sixth book of the *Iliad* where Glaucus and Diomedes come face to face in the battle and, having recognised one another as guest-friends, afterwards exchange gifts. This touching depiction of the piety with which the rules of *hospitality* were observed even in battle can be compared with an account of the *knightly sense of nobility* in Ariosto, when two knights and rivals, Ferraù and Rinaldo, the latter a Christian, the former a Saracen, covered with wounds after a violent duel, make peace and in order to overtake the fleeing Angelica, mount the same horse. Both examples, as different as they may be otherwise, are almost alike in their effect upon our hearts, because both depict the beautiful victory of morals over passion and touch us by the naivety of their attitudes. But how differently the poets react in describing these similar actions. Ariosto, the citizen of a later world which had fallen from simplicity of manners, cannot, in recounting the occurrence, conceal his own wonderment and emotion. The feeling of the distance between those morals and those which characterised his own age overwhelms him. He abandons for a moment the portrait of the object and appears in his own person. This beautiful stanza is well known and has always been greatly admired:

> O nobility of ancient knightly mode!
> Who once were rivals, divided still
> In godly faith bitter pain still suffered,
> Bodies torn in enmity's wild struggle,
> Free of suspicion, together rode
> Along the darkling crooked path.
> The steed, by four spurs driven, sped
> To where the road in twain divided.[15]

And now old Homer! Scarcely has Diomedes learned from the narrative of Glaucus, his antagonist, that the latter's forefathers were guest-friends of his family, than he thrusts his lance into the ground, speaks in a friendly tone with him and agrees with him that in future they will avoid one another in battle. Let us, however, hear Homer himself:

In me you will now have a good friend in Argos, and I shall have you in Lycia, if ever I visit that country. So let us avoid each other's spears, even in the melee, since there are plenty of the Trojans and their famous allies for me to kill, if I have the luck and speed to catch them, and plenty of Achaeans for you to slaughter, if you can. And let us exchange our armour, so that everyone may know that our grandfathers' friendship has made friends of us. With no more said, they leapt from their chariots, shook hands, and pledged each other.[16]

It would hardly be possible for a *modern* poet (at least, hardly one who is modern in the moral sense of the word) to have waited even this long before expressing his pleasure at this action. We would forgive him this all the more readily because, even in reading, our hearts pause, and gladly detach themselves from the object in order to look within. But of all this, not a trace in Homer; as though he had reported something quite everyday; indeed, as though he possessed no heart in his bosom, he continues in his dry truthfulness:

But Zeus the son of Cronos must have robbed Glaucus of his wits, for he exchanged with Diomedes golden armour for bronze, a hundred oxen's worth for the value of nine.

Poets of this naive category are no longer at home in an artificial age. They are indeed scarcely even possible, at least in no other wise possible except they *run wild* in their own age, and are preserved by some favourable destiny from its crippling influence. From society itself they can never arise; but from outside it they still sometimes appear, but rather as strangers at whom one stares, and as uncouth sons of nature by whom one is irritated. As beneficent as such phenomena are for the artist who studies them and for the true connoisseur who is able to appreciate them, they yet elicit little joy on the whole and in their own century. The stamp of the conqueror is marked upon their brows; but we would rather be coddled and indulged by the Muses. By the critics, the true gamekeepers of taste, they are detested as trespassers whom one would prefer to suppress; for even Homer owes it only to the power of more than a thousand years of testimony that those who sit in judgement on taste permit him to stand; and it is unpleasant enough for them to maintain their rules against his example and his reputation against their rules.

The poet, I said, either *is* nature or he will *seek* her. The former is the naive, the latter the sentimental poet.

The poetic spirit is immortal and inalienable in mankind, it cannot be lost except together with humanity or with the capacity for it. For even if man should separate himself by the freedom of his fantasy and his understanding from the simplicity, truth and necessity of nature, yet not only does the way back to her remain open always, but also a powerful and ineradicable impulse, the moral, drives him ceaselessly back to her, and it is precisely with this impulse that the poetic faculty stands in the most intimate relationship. For this faculty is not forfeited along with the lost simplicity of nature; it merely assumes a new direction.

Even now, nature is the sole flame at which the poetic spirit nourishes itself; from her alone it draws its whole power, to her alone it speaks even in the artificial man entoiled by civilisation. All other modes of expression are alien to the poetic spirit; hence, generally speaking, all so-called works of wit[17] are quite misnamed poetic; although, for long, misled by the reputation of French literature, we have mistaken them as such. It is still nature, I say, even now in the artificial condition of civilisation, in virtue of which the poetic spirit is powerful; but now it stands in quite another relation to nature.

So long as man is pure – not, of course, crude – nature, he functions as an undivided sensuous unity and as a harmonious whole. Sense and reason, passive and active faculties, are not separated in their activities, still less do they stand in conflict with one another. His perceptions are not the formless play of chance, his thoughts not the empty play of the faculty of representation; the former proceed out of the law of *necessity,* the latter out of *actuality.* Once man has passed into the state of civilisation and art has laid her hand upon him, the *sensuous* harmony in him is withdrawn, and he can now express himself only as a *moral* unity, i.e., as striving after unity. The correspondence between his feeling and thought which in his first condition *actually* took place exists now only *ideally;* it is no longer within him, but outside of him, as an idea still to be realised, no longer as a fact in his life. If one now applies the concept of poetry, which is nothing but *giving mankind its most complete possible expression,* to both conditions, the result in the earlier state of natural simplicity is the completest possible *imitation of actuality* – at that stage man still functions with all his powers simultaneously as a harmonious unity and hence the whole of his nature is expressed completely in actuality; whereas now, in the state of civilisation where that harmonious cooperation of his whole nature is only an idea, it is the elevation of actuality to the ideal or, amounting to the same thing, the *representation of the ideal,* that makes for the poet. And these two are likewise the only possible modes in which poetic genius can express itself at all. They are, as one can see, extremely different from one another, but there is a higher concept under which both can be subsumed, and there should be no surprise if this concept should coincide with the idea of humanity.

This is not the place further to pursue these thoughts, which can only be expounded in full measure in a separate disquisition. But anyone who is capable of making a comparison, based on the spirit and not just on the accidental forms, between ancient and modern poets,[f] will be able readily to convince himself of the truth of the matter. The former move us by nature, by sensuous truth, by living presence; the latter by ideas.

This path taken by the modern poets is, moreover, that along which man in general, the individual as well as the race, must pass. Nature sets him at one with himself, art divides and cleaves him in two, through the ideal he returns to unity. But because the ideal is an infinitude to which he never attains, the civilised man can never become perfect in *his* own wise, while the natural man can in his. He must therefore fall infinitely short of the latter in perfection, if one heeds only the relation in which each stands to his species and to his maximum capacity. But if one compares the species

themselves with one another, it becomes evident that the goal to which
man *strives* through culture is infinitely preferable to that which he *attains*
through nature. For the one obtains its value by the absolute achievement
of a finite, the other by approximation to an infinite greatness. But only
the latter possesses *degrees* and displays a *progress;* hence the relative worth
of a man who is involved in civilisation is in general never determinable,
even though the same man considered as an individual necessarily finds
himself at a disadvantage compared with one in whom nature functions in
her utter perfection. But insofar as the ultimate object of mankind is not
otherwise to be attained than by that progress, and the latter cannot progress other than by civilising himself and hence passing over into the former category, there cannot therefore be any question to which of the two
the advantage accrues with reference to that ultimate object.

The very same as has been said of the two different forms of humanity
can likewise be applied to those species of poet corresponding to them.

Perhaps on this account one should not compare ancient with modern
– naive with sentimental – poets either at all, or only by reference to some
higher concept common to both (there is in fact such a concept). For
clearly, if one has first abstracted the concept of those species onesidedly
from the ancient poets, nothing is easier, but nothing also more trivial,
than to depreciate the moderns by comparison. If one calls poetry only
that which in every age has affected simple nature uniformly, the result
cannot be other than to deny the modern poets their title just where they
achieve their most characteristic and sublimest beauty, since precisely here
they speak only to the adherent of civilisation and have nothing to say to
simple nature.[g] Anyone whose temperament is not already prepared to
pass beyond actuality into the realm of ideas will find the richest content
empty appearance, and the loftiest flights of the poet exaggeration. It
would not occur to a reasonable person to want to compare any modern
with Homer where Homer excels, and it sounds ridiculous enough to find
Milton or Klopstock honoured with the title of a modern Homer. But just
as little could any ancient poet, and least of all Homer, support the comparison with a modern poet in those aspects which most characteristically
distinguish him. The former, I might put it, is powerful through the art of
finitude; the latter by the art of the infinite.

And for the very reason that the strength of the ancient artist (for what
has been said here of the poet can, allowing for self-evident qualifications,
be extended to apply to the fine arts generally) subsists in finitude, the
great advantage arises which the plastic art of antiquity maintains over that
of modern times, and in general the unequal value relationship in which
the modern art of poetry and modern plastic art stand to both species of
art in antiquity. A work addressed to the eye can achieve perfection only
in finitude; a work addressed to the imagination can achieve it also through

the infinite.[19] In plastic works the modern is little aided by his superiority in ideas; here he is obliged to *determine in space in the most precise way* the representation of his imagination and hence to compete with the ancient artists in precisely that quality in which they indisputably excel. In poetic works it is otherwise, and even if the ancient poets are victorious too in the simplicity of forms and in whatever is sensuously representable and *corporeal*, the modern can nonetheless leave them behind in richness of material in whatever is insusceptible of representation and ineffable, in a word, in whatever in the work of art is called *spirit.*

Since the naive poet only follows simple nature and feeling, and limits himself solely to imitation of actuality, he can have only a single relationship to his subject and in *this* respect there is for him no choice in his treatment. The varied impression of naive poetry depends (provided that one puts out of mind everything which in it belongs to the content, and considers that impression only as the pure product of the poetic treatment), it depends, I say, solely upon the various degrees of one and the same mode of feeling; even the variety of external forms cannot effect any alteration in the quality of that aesthetic impression. The form may be lyric or epic, dramatic or narrative: we can indeed be moved to a weaker or stronger degree, but (as soon as the matter is abstracted) never heterogeneously. Our feeling is uniformly the same, entirely composed of *one* element, so that we cannot differentiate within it. Even the difference of language and era changes nothing in this regard, for just this pure unity of its origin and of its effect is a characteristic of naive poetry.

The case is quite otherwise with the sentimental poet. He *reflects* upon the impression that objects make upon him, and only in that reflection is the emotion grounded which he himself experiences and which he excites in us. The object here is referred to an idea and his poetic power is based solely upon this referral. The sentimental poet is thus always involved with two conflicting representations and perceptions – with actuality as a limit and with his idea as infinitude; and the mixed feelings that he excites will always testify to this dual source.[h] Since in this case there is a plurality of principles it depends which of the two will *predominate* in the perception of the poet and in his representation, and hence a variation in the treatment is possible. For now the question arises whether he will tend more toward actuality or toward the ideal – whether he will realise the former as an object of antipathy or the latter as an object of sympathy. His presentation will, therefore, be either *satirical* or it will be (in a broader connotation of the word which will become clearer later) *elegiac;* every sentimental poet will adhere to one of these two modes of perception.

The poet is satirical if he takes as his subject alienation from nature and the contradiction between actuality and the ideal (in their effect upon the mind both amount to the same thing). But this he can execute either seri-

ously and with passion, or jokingly and with good humour, according as
he dwells in the realm of will or the realm of understanding. The former
is a function of punitive or pathetic satire, the latter of playful satire.

*   *   *

It has frequently been disputed which of the two, tragedy or comedy, merits precedence over the other. If the question is merely which of the two
treats of the more important subject matter, there can be no doubt that
the first has the advantage; but if one would know which of the two
demands the more significant poet, then the decision may rather fall to the
latter. In tragedy much is already determined by the substance, in comedy
nothing is determined by the substance and everything by the poet. Since
in judgements of taste the content is never taken into account it follows
naturally that the aesthetic value of these two artistic genres stands in
inverse proportion to their substantive significance. The tragic poet is supported by his theme, the comic poet on the other hand must raise his to
aesthetic height through his own person. The first may make a leap for
which, however, not much is required; the other must remain himself, he
must therefore already *be* there and be at home there where the first cannot attain without a starting leap. And it is precisely in this way that the
beautiful character is distinguished from the sublime.[20] In the first, all the
dimensions are already contained, flowing unconstrainedly and effortlessly
from its nature and it is, according to its capacity, an infinitude at every
point in its path; the other can elevate and exert itself to any dimension,
by the power of its will it can tear itself out of any state of limitation. The
latter is, then, only intermittently and with effort free, the former with
facility and always.

To promote and nourish this freedom of temperament is the fair task of
comedy, just as tragedy is destined to help to restore by aesthetic means
the freedom of temperament when it has been violently disrupted by emotion. In tragedy, therefore, freedom of temperament must be artificially
and experimentally disrupted, since it displays its poetic power in the res-
toration of that freedom; in comedy, on the other hand, care must be
taken to assure that that disruption of the freedom of temperament should
never occur. Hence the tragic poet always treats his subject practically, the
comic poet always treats his theoretically,[21] even if the former should
indulge the quirk (like Lessing in his *Nathan*)[22] of treating a theoretical
subject, or the latter of treating a practical subject. Not the sphere from
which the subject is drawn, but the forum before which the poet brings it
makes it tragic or comic. The tragedian must beware of calm reasoning and
always engage the heart; the comedian must beware of pathos and always
entertain the understanding. The former thus displays his art by the constant excitement of passion, the latter by constant avoidance of it; and this
art is naturally so much the greater on both sides the more the subject of
one is of an abstract nature, and that of the other tends toward the

pathetic.ⁱ Even if tragedy proceeds from a more significant point, one is obliged to concede, on the other hand, that comedy proceeds toward a more significant purpose and it would, were it to attain it, render all tragedy superfluous and impossible. Its purpose is uniform with the highest after which man has to struggle, to be free of passion, always clear, to look serenely about and within himself, to find everywhere more confidence than fate, and rather to laugh at absurdity than to rage or weep at malice.

* * *

If the poet should set nature and art, the ideal and actuality, in such opposition that the representation of the first prevails and pleasure in it becomes the predominant feeling, then I call him *elegiac*. This category, too, like satire, comprehends two species. Either nature and the ideal are an object of sadness if the first is treated as lost and the second as unattained. Or both are an object of joy represented as actual. The first yields the *elegy* in the narrower sense, and the second the idyll in the broader sense.ʲ

[Schiller explains that the force of the elegy must always reside in its lament for the loss of the ideal rather than of a merely finite object. The following poets are typical of the modern spirit.]

Among German poets of this order I will mention here only Haller, Kleist, and Klopstock.[25] The character of their poetry is sentimental; they touch us by ideas, not by sensuous truth; not so much because they are nature as because they are able to inspire enthusiasm in us for nature. Whatever, therefore, is true of the character of these as well as of all sentimental poets *in general* naturally does not by any means exclude the capacity *in particular* to move us by naive beauty; without this they would not be poets at all. But it is not their essential and predominant character to feel with serene, simple, and unencumbered senses and to present again what they have felt in like manner. Involuntarily imagination crowds out sense and thought feeling, and they close their eyes and ears to sink into internal reflection. The mind cannot tolerate any impression without at once observing its own activity and reflection, and yielding up in terms of itself whatever it has absorbed. In this mode we are never given the object, only what the reflective understanding has made of it, and even when the poet is himself the object, if he would describe his feeling to us, we never learn of his condition directly and at first hand, but rather how he has reflected it in his own mind, what he has thought about it as an observer of himself. When Haller is lamenting the death of his wife (in his well known poem), and begins as follows:

> Shall I sing of thy death?
> O Mariane, what a song!
> When sighs contest with words
> And one idea flees before the rest, etc.[26]

then we may indeed find this description exactly true, but we feel also that the poet has not actually communicated his feelings but his thoughts about them. He therefore moves us much more feebly also, because he must himself have been very much cooler to be an observer of his own emotion.

*   *   *

In the concept itself of poet, and only in this, lies the ground of that freedom which is merely contemptible licence as soon as it is not derived from the highest and noblest that constitutes him.

The laws of propriety are alien to innocent nature; only the experience of corruption has given them their origin. But as soon as that experience has been undergone and natural innocence has disappeared from morals, then they become sacred laws which a moral feeling may not contravene. They apply in any artificial world with the same right as the laws of nature rule in the world of innocence. But it is precisely this that denotes the poet: that he revokes everything in himself that recalls an artificial world, that he is able to restore nature within himself to her original simplicity. But having done this, then he is by the same token exempted from all laws by which a corrupted heart is protected against itself. He is pure, he is innocent, and whatever is permitted to innocent nature is permitted him too; if you, who read or listen to him, are no longer guiltless, and if you cannot become so for the moment through his purifying presence, then it is *your* misfortune, not his; you are forsaking him, he has not sung for you.

The following, then, may be said with reference to liberties of this kind:

First: only *nature* can justify them. Hence they may not be the product of choice or of deliberate imitation; for we can never allow to the will, which is always directed according to moral laws, to favour sensuousness. They must therefore be *naivety*. In order, however, to convince us that they are truly so, we must see them supported and accompanied by all else that is likewise grounded in nature, for nature can only be recognised by the rigorous consequence, unity, and uniformity of her effects. Only to a heart that despises all artificiality outright, and hence also even if it is useful, do we permit its exemption where it represses and limits; only to a heart that subordinates itself to all the shackles of nature do we permit that it make use of her freedom. All other feelings of such a person must in consequence bear the impress of naturalness; he must be true, simple, free, candid, full of feeling, upright; all deception, cunning, all caprice, all petty selfishness must be banished from his character, every trace of them from his work.

Second: only *beautiful* nature can justify liberties of this sort. Therefore they may not be onesided manifestations of appetite; for everything that originates in crude necessity is contemptible. From the totality and from the richness of human nature these sensuous energies must likewise derive. They must be *humanity*. But in order to be able to judge that the whole of human nature demands them and not merely a onesided and vulgar exigency of sensuousness, we must see that whole depicted of which they represent a single feature. In itself the sensuous mode of feeling is something innocent and indifferent. It displeases us in a human being only because it is animal and testifies to a lack of a more truly perfect humanity in him: it offends us in a work of art only because such a work makes a claim to please us and hence assumes that *we* are also capable of such a lack. But if we surprise in a person humanity functioning in all its remaining aspects, if we find in the work in which liberties of this species have been exercised all the realities of mankind expressed, then that ground of our disapproval is removed and we can delight with unequivocal joy in the naive expression of true and beautiful nature. The same poet, therefore, who may allow himself to make us participants in such basely human feelings, must on the other hand be able to elevate us to all that is humanly great and beautiful and sublime.

This, then, would provide us with the criterion to which we could with certainty submit every poet who offends somewhat against propriety, and forces his freedom in the depiction of nature to this extreme. His work is vulgar and low, reprehensible without exception, if it is *cold*, if it is *empty*, for this reveals its origin in intention and in vulgar exigency, and is a heinous assault on our appetites. On the other hand, it is beautiful, noble, and worthy of applause despite all the objections of frosty decency, if it is naive and binds spirit and heart together.[k]

*   *   *

Idyll

There remain only a few more words for me to say about this third species of sentimental poetry, because a more detailed development of them, which they surely require,[28] is reserved for another occasion.[l]

The poetic representation of innocent and contented mankind is the universal concept of this type of poetic composition. Since this innocence and this contentedness appear incompatible with the artificial conditions of society at large and with a certain degree of education and refinement, the poets have removed the location of idyll from the tumult of everyday life into the simple pastoral state and assigned its period before the *beginnings of civilisation* in the childlike age of man. But one can readily grasp that these designations are merely accidental, that they are not to be considered as the purpose of the idyll, simply as the most natural means to it. The purpose itself is invariably only to represent man in a state of innocence, i.e., in a condition of harmony and of peace with himself and with his environment.

But such a condition does not occur only before the beginnings of civilisation; rather it is also the condition which civilisation, if it can be said to have any particular tendency everywhere, aims at as its ultimate purpose. Only the idea of this condition and belief in its possible realisation can reconcile man to all the evils to which he is subjected in the course of civilisation, and were it merely a chimera the complaints of those would be justified who deplore society at large and the cultivation of the under-standing simply as an evil, and assume that superseded state of nature to be the true purpose of mankind.[29] For the individual who is immersed in civilisation, infinitely much therefore depends upon his receiving a tangi-ble assurance of the realisation of that idea in the world of sense, of the possible reality of that condition, and since actual experience, far from nourishing this belief, rather contradicts it constantly, here, as in so many cases, the faculty of poetic composition comes to the aid of reason in order to render that idea palpable to intuition and to realise it in individual cases.

[After explaining the limits of the pastoral, which because of its retrospective focus must tend to inspire regret rather than action, Schiller asks for an idyll of the future, leading us forward.]

The concept of this idyll is the concept of a conflict fully reconciled not only in the individual, but in society, of a free uniting of inclination with the law, of a nature illuminated by the highest moral dignity, briefly, none other than the ideal of beauty applied to actual life. Its character thus sub-sists in the complete reconciliation of *all opposition between actuality and the ideal* which has supplied material for satirical and elegiac poetry, and therewith of all conflict in the feelings likewise. Calm would then be the predominant impression of such a poetic type, but calm of perfection, not of inertia; a calm that derives from the balance not the arresting of those powers, that springs from richness and not emptiness, and is accompanied by the feeling of an infinite capacity. But for the very reason that all resis-tance vanishes it will then be incomparably more difficult than in the two former types of poetry to represent *motion*, without which, however, no poetic effect whatsoever can be conceived. The highest unity must prevail; but not at the expense of variety; the mind must be satisfied, but not so that aspiration ceases on that account. The resolution of this question is in fact what the theory of the idyll has to supply.

The following has been established on the relation of both modes of poetry to one another and to the poetic ideal:

To the naive poet nature has granted the favour of functioning always as an undivided unity, to be at every instant an independent and complete whole, and to represent mankind, in all its significance, in actuality. Upon the sentimental poet she has conferred the power, or rather impressed a lively impulse, to restore out of himself that unity that has been disrupted by abstraction, to complete the humanity within himself, and from a lim-ited condition to pass over into an infinite one.[m] But to give human nature its full expression is the common task of both, and without that they could not be called poets at all; the naive poet, however, always possesses the advantage of sensuous reality over the sentimental, since he implements as an actual fact what the other only strives to attain. And this it is too that everyone experiences in himself when he observes himself in the enjoyment of naive poetry. He feels all the powers of his humanity active in such a moment, he stands in need of nothing, he is a whole in himself; without distinguishing anything in his feeling, he is at once pleased with his spiritual activity and his sensuous life. It is quite another mood into which the sentimental poet casts him. Here he feels only a lively *impulse* to produce that harmony in himself which he there actually felt, to make a whole of himself, to give complete expression to the humanity within himself. Hence in the latter his mind is in motion, it is in tension, it wavers between conflicting feelings; whereas in the former it is calm, relaxed, at one with itself and completely satisfied.

But if the naive poet gains on the one hand in reality at the expense of the sentimental, and brings into actual existence what the latter can only arouse a lively impulse to attain, the latter for his part possesses the great advantage over the first that he can give the impulse a *greater object* than the former has supplied or could supply. All actuality, we know, falls short of the ideal; everything existing has its limits, but thought is boundless. From this limitation, to which everything sensuous is subjected, the naive poet therefore also suffers, whereas the unconditional freedom of the faculty of ideas accrues to the sentimental. The former therefore indeed fulfils his task, but the task itself is something limited; the latter indeed does not fulfil his, but his task is an infinite one. In this, too, everyone can learn from his own experience. From the naive poet one turns with facility and eagerness to the active environment; the sentimental will always for a few moments disaffect one for actual life. This is because our minds are here extended by the infinitude of the idea beyond their natural circumscription, so that nothing to hand can any longer be adequate to it. We fall back rather, lost in our thoughts, where we find nourishment for the impulse generated in the world of ideas instead of seeking outside ourselves, as with the former, for sensuous objects. Sentimental poetry is the offspring of retreat and quietude, and to them, too, it invites us; the naive is the child of life, and to life also it leads us back.

[Being rooted in nature, naive poetry does not encourage freedom as readily as does sentimental poetry. True naivety is not mere realism, but it can sponsor such among less gifted poets. The corresponding propensity of sentimental poetry is toward enthusiasm, excessive distance from nature. Each mode, as an extreme, can result in emptiness, respectively of spirit or of matter. After discussing at some length the decline of the sentimental into the "fantastic", Schiller goes on to inquire whether poetry has a moral or a merely recreational function.]

. . . The state of mind of most people is on the one hand intensive and exhausting *labour*, on the other, enervating *indulgence*. The former, we know, renders the sensuous need for spiritual calm and for cessation of

activity disproportionately more pressing than the moral need for harmony and for an absolute freedom of function, because above all else
nature must be satisfied before the *mind* can make its demands; the latter
confines and cripples the moral impulses themselves from which these
demands should originate. Hence nothing is more disadvantageous for
sensitivity to the truly beautiful than both these all-too-common frames of
mind among men, and from this it becomes clear why so few, even among
better men, possess correct judgement in aesthetic matters. Beauty is the
product of accord between the mind and the senses; it addresses itself at
once to all the faculties of man and can, therefore, be perceived and appreciated only under the condition that he employ all his powers fully and
freely. One must assemble clear senses, a full heart, a fresh and unimpaired mind, one's whole nature must be collected, which is by no means
the case with those who are divided in themselves by abstract thought,
hemmed in by petty business formalities, or exhausted by strenuous concentration. These persons yearn indeed for sensuous matter, not in order
to continue the play of their intellectual powers, but in order to stop it.
They want to be free, but only from a burden that fatigues their lassitude,
not from a barrier that blocks their activity.

Should one then still be amazed at the happiness of mediocrity and emptiness in aesthetic matters, or at the vengeance of weak minds upon the
truly and actively beautiful? They expected recreation from it, but a recreation to meet their need and in accordance with their feeble notion, and
they discover with dismay that they are now first expected to put out an
effort of strength for which they might lack the capacity even in their best
moments. There, on the contrary, they are welcome as they are; for as little
strength as they bring with them, still they need very much less to exhaust
the minds of their writers. Here they are at once relieved of the burden of
thought; and nature relaxed can indulge itself upon the downy pillow of
platitude in blessed enjoyment of nothingness. In the temple of Thalia and
Melpomene,[31] as it is established among us, the beloved goddess sits
enthroned receiving in her ample bosom the dull pedant and the tired
businessman, and lulls the mind into a mesmeric sleep, thawing out the
frigid senses and rocking the imagination in gentle motion.

And why should one not indulge vulgar individuals, when that is often
enough done for the best ones? The relaxation that nature demands after
every sustained effort and also takes without invitation (and only for such
moments does one reserve the enjoyment of beautiful works), is so little
favourable to aesthetic judgement that among those classes who are really
occupied only extremely few will be found who can judge in matters of
taste with certainty, and what is here more to the point, with consistency.
Nothing is more usual than that scholars, in contrast to cultivated mundane individuals, reveal themselves in judgements of beauty in the most
ridiculous light, and in particular the professional critics are the scorn of

all connoisseurs. Their neglected, sometimes exaggerated, sometimes coarse, feeling leads them astray in most cases, and even if they have seized upon something in theory in defence of it, they can only formulate *technical* (concerning the purposiveness of a work) not *aesthetic* judgements, which must always comprehend the whole, and in which, therefore, feeling must decide. If they at last voluntarily renounce the latter and rest content with the former, they may yet be of sufficient use, since the poet in his inspiration and the perceptive reader at the moment of enjoyment may only too easily overlook details. But it is an all the more laughable spectacle if these crude natures who, with all their painstaking efforts, at best attain the cultivation of a single skill, set up their paltry personalities as representative of universal feeling, and in the sweat of their brows pass judgement upon the beautiful.

The concept of *recreation*, which poetry is to provide, is as we have seen, usually beset by too narrow limits because one is accustomed to referring it too onesidedly to mere sensuous necessity. The notion of *ennoblement*, which the poet is supposed to aim at, is exactly the reverse; it is given too wide a scope because it is too onesidedly determined by the mere idea.

For, in accordance with the idea, ennoblement passes always into the infinite because reason in its demands is not bound by the necessary limits of the world of sense and does not stop short of the absolutely perfect. Nothing beyond which something still higher can be conceived can satisfy it; at its stern court no limitation of finite nature is acceptable in excuse; it acknowledges no other boundaries but those of thought, and of this we know that it soars beyond all the limits of space and time. Such an ideal of ennoblement which reason prescribes in its pure legislation may no more be established as his purpose by the poet as that base ideal of recreation which sensuousness sets up, since he should indeed liberate mankind from all accidental limitations, but without setting aside its concept or disrupting its necessary limitations. Whatever he allows himself beyond those limitations is exaggeration, and it is to just this that he is all too readily misled by a falsely construed concept of ennoblement. But the evil is that he can scarcely elevate himself to the true ideal of human ennoblement without in any case taking a few steps beyond it. For in order to attain to it he must abandon actuality, since he can draw upon it, as upon any ideal, only out of inner and moral sources. Not in the world that surrounds him nor in the tumult of everyday life, but only in his heart is it to be encountered, and only in the stillness of solitary contemplation can he find his heart. Yet this withdrawal from life will not only remove from his vision the accidental limitations of mankind – it will often remove the necessary and insurmountable limitations, and in seeking the pure form he stands in danger of losing the entire meaning. Reason will pursue its business much too isolated from experience, and whatever the contemplative spirit has discovered in the serene course of thought, the man of action will not be able

to realise in the tempestuous course of daily life. Thus the very same produces the fanatic that was solely able to engender the sage, and the advantage of the latter may perhaps subsist less in that he did not become the
former than in that he did not remain so.

It may therefore be left neither to the labouring classes of mankind to
determine the concept of recreation in accordance with their needs, nor
to the contemplative classes to determine the concept of ennoblement in
accordance with their speculation, if the former concept is not to become
too physical and too unworthy of poetry, nor the latter too hyperphysical
and too extravagant for poetry. But since both these concepts, as experience shows, govern common opinion of poetry and poetic works we must,
in order to interpret them, look for a class of men which, without toiling,
is active, and is capable of formulating ideals without fanaticism; a class
that unites within itself all the realities of life with its least possible limitations and is borne by the current of events without becoming its victim.
Only such a class can preserve the beautiful unity of human nature that is
destroyed for the moment by any particular task, and continuously by a
life of such toil, and decide, in everything that is purely human, by their
feelings the rule of common opinion. Whether such a class might actually
exist, or whether that class which actually does exist under the external
conditions described possesses the inner disposition corresponding to the
concept, is another question which I am not concerned with here. If it does
not correspond to it, then it has only itself to blame, since the contrasting
labouring class has at least the satisfaction of considering itself a victim of
its labour. In such a class of society (which, however, I offer here only as
an idea and by no means wish to have taken as a fact) the naive character
would be united with the sentimental so that each would preserve the other
from its own extreme, and while the first would save the mind from exag-
gerations the second would secure it against inertia. For, in the final analysis, we must concede that neither the naive nor the sentimental character,
each considered alone, quite exhausts that ideal of beautiful humanity that
can only arise out of the intimate union of both.

For so long as one exalts both characters as far as the *poetic,* as we have
thus far considered them, much of the limitation which adheres to them
falls away, and their antithesis becomes all the less noticeable the higher
the degree to which they become poetic; for the poetic mood is an independent whole in which all distinctions and all shortcomings vanish. But
for the very reason that it is only the concept of the poetic in which both
modes of perception can coincide, their mutual differences and limitations
become in the same degree more noticeable the more they are divested of
their poetic character; and this is the case in ordinary life. The more they
descend to this, the more they lose of their generic character which brings
them closer to one another, until finally in their caricatures only their specific character remains to oppose one to the other.

This leads me to a very remarkable psychological antagonism among men in a century that is civilising itself: an antagonism that because it is radical and based on inner mental dispositions is the cause of a worse division among men than any fortuitous clash of interests could ever provoke; one that deprives the artist and poet of all hope of pleasing and affecting universally, as is their task; which makes it impossible for the philosopher, even when he has done his utmost, to convince universally: yet the very concept of philosophy demands this; which, finally, will never permit a man in practical life to see his course of action universally approved – in a word, an antithesis that is to blame that no work of the spirit and no action of the heart can decisively satisfy one class without for that very reason bringing upon itself the damning judgement of the other. This antithesis is without doubt as old as the beginnings of civilisation and is scarcely to be overcome before its end other than in a few rare individuals who, it is to be hoped, always existed and always will; but among its effects is also this one, that it defeats every effort to overcome it because neither side can be induced to admit that there is any shortcoming on its part and any reality on the other; despite this, it still remains profitable enough to pursue so important a division back to its ultimate souce and thereby to reduce the actual point of the conflict at least to a simpler formulation.

One can best discover the true concept of this antithesis, as I have just remarked, by abstracting from both the naive and the sentimental character what each possesses of the poetic. Of the first, then, nothing remains (from the theoretical point of view) but a sober spirit of observation and a fixed loyalty to the uniform testimony of the senses, and (from the practical point of view) a resigned submission to the necessity (but not the blind necessity) of nature: an accession thus to what is and what must be. Of the sentimental character nothing remains (theoretically) but a restless spirit of speculation that presses on to the unconditional in all its knowledge, and (practically) a moral rigorism that insists upon the unconditional in acts of the will. The member of the first class can be called a *realist* and of the other class an *idealist;* but these names should not recall either the good or bad senses which are connected with them in metaphysics."

[After an exposition of the characters of the two classes, idealist and realist, the essay concludes as follows.]

To the attentive and impartial reader I will not, following the account just given (the truth of which can be admitted even by anybody who does not accept the outcome), have first to demonstrate that the ideal of human nature is divided between both, but is not fully attained by either. Experience and reason each has its own prerogatives and neither can infringe upon the area of the other without inflicting serious consequences upon either the inner or external condition of man. Experience alone can teach us what is under certain conditions, what follows upon certain antecedent circumstances, and what must occur for a certain purpose. Reason alone, on the other hand, can teach us what is unconditionally valid and what must necessarily be so. If we should presume to decide anything by our pure reason about the external existence of things we should be engaged in a merely empty game, and the results would amount to nothing; for all existence is conditional and reason determines unconditionally. If, however, we should permit an accidental occurrence to decide about something that is already involved in the very concept of our own being, then we make of ourselves an empty game of chance, and our personality would amount to nothing. In the first case we relinquish the *value* (the temporal content) of our lives, in the second the *dignity* (the moral content).

In our account thus far we have indeed allowed a moral value to the realist and a measure of experience to the idealist, but only insofar as both do not proceed consistently, and nature operates in them more powerfully than their systems. Even though both do not entirely correspond to the ideal of perfect humanity, yet between them the important difference subsists that although the realist in no individual case does justice to the rational concept of mankind, he never contradicts its concept of the understanding; and although the idealist in individual cases approaches the highest concept of humanity, he not infrequently falls short of even its lowest concepts. But in practical life much more depends upon the whole being *uniformly* humanly good, than upon the particular being *accidentally* divine – and even if the idealist is a more appropriate subject to arouse in us a lofty notion of what is possible for mankind, and to imbue us with respect for its vocation, still only the realist can carry it out in practice with constancy and maintain the race within its eternal boundaries. The former is indeed a more noble, but a disproportionately less perfect being; the latter may appear generally less noble, but he is on the other hand all the more perfect; for nobility is already present in the manifestation of a great potentiality, but the perfect lies in the conduct of the whole and in the actual deed.

What is true of both characters in their most favourable interpretation is even more noticeable in their respective *caricatures*. True realism is beneficent in its effects and only less noble in its origin; false realism is contemptible in its origin and only slightly less pernicious in its effects. For the true realist submits himself to nature and to her necessity – but to nature as a whole, to her eternal and absolute necessity, not to her blind and momentary *compulsions*. He embraces and follows her law in freedom, and will always subordinate the particular to the universal; thus he cannot fail to agree with the genuine idealist in the final result, however different the path which each takes to that end. The vulgar empiricist, however, submits himself to nature as a force, and in indiscriminate blind surrender. His judgements, like his efforts, are limited to the particular; he believes and grasps only what he touches; he esteems only what advances him sensuously. He is, therefore, no more than external impressions chance to make him; his individuality is suppressed and, as a human being, he possesses absolutely no worth and no dignity. But as a thing he is still something, he can still serve some purpose. For that same nature to which he blindly abandons himself does not let him sink altogether; her eternal boundaries protect him, her inexhaustible assistance rescues him, if only he surrenders his freedom without reservation. Although in this condition he knows no laws, yet they govern him unacknowledged, and as much as his individual efforts might be in conflict with the whole, yet that whole will infallibly be able to overcome them. There are men enough, even whole peoples, who live in this lamentable condition, who survive solely by the grace of the law of nature, without individuality, and hence are good only *for something;* but that they even live and survive demonstrates that this condition is not entirely without meaning.

If, in contrast to this, true idealism is insecure and often dangerous in its effects, false idealism is appalling in its effects. The true idealist abandons nature and experience only because he does not find in it the immutable and unconditional necessity for which his reason prompts him to strive; the fantast abandons nature out of mere caprice, in order to indulge with all the less restraint the wantonness of his desires and the whims of his imagination. He bases his freedom not on independence from physical duress, but on emancipation from moral compulsion. Thus the fantast renounces not only human character – he renounces all character, he is completely lawless, hence nothing in himself and fit for nothing. But for the very reason that his phantasmagoria is not an aberration of nature but of freedom, and thus develops out of a capacity in itself estimable and infinitely perfectible, it leads likewise to an infinite fall into a bottomless abyss and can only terminate in complete destruction.

Part 5

Friedrich Schlegel

Friedrich Schlegel

(1772–1829)

Friedrich Schlegel, major theorist of the romantic school, brought to the forefront of literary criticism Herder's earlier attempts to relate modern and ancient literature through an analysis of the 'essentially modern', with Shakespeare as the model and standard of the modern tendency in art. 'Über das Studium der griechischen Poesie' (1795, published 1797) was one of Schlegel's first published attempts to articulate the disparities between ancient and modern, 'interessante' literature. Schiller's article, 'Über Naiv und Sentimentalische Dichtung' (Dec. 1795), opened the way, through its admiration of modern techniques, for Schlegel's re-evaluation of his own critical position, a re-evaluation influenced by Kant's aesthetic relativism. By 1797, Schlegel had published his first fragments in the journal, *Lyceum der Schöne Künste*, in which he developed his idea of 'romantische Poesie' out of the earlier concept of 'interessante' literature, leaving behind his purist tendencies and embracing a non-objective, relativist aesthetic. In 1798, he published his critical masterpiece, 'Über Goethes *Meister*', in which he realized aesthetically many of his critical principles; by 1800 he had written his manifesto of Romanticism, *Gespräch über Poesie*. Many of his publications appeared first in the *Athenäum*, a journal founded in 1798 by himself and his brother, August Wilhelm, as an organ of criticism, and as Friedrich described it, 'an experiment, or series of experiments' on the possibility of communication, especially by means of irony. In the journal, several collections of fragments of mixed and unidentified authorship were published, including contributions from the Schlegels, Novalis, and Schleiermacher, the aphoristic genre having been inspired by the French writer, S.R.N. Chamfort (1741–94).

For Friedrich Schlegel, criticism should be concerned primarily with the literary text itself, and only secondarily with broad historical or literary generalizations. Schlegel distinguished between analytical and poetic criticism, the former producing only discursive 'Charakteristiks', the latter emphasizing the activity of interpretation as an endless play with the relations in the text and the infinite variety of meaningful responses possible. Poetic criticism sought to discover the 'central intellectual perspective' which unified the imaginative complexity of relations that constituted the text. Only once the initial enthusiasm of the critic (or poet) for his material had subsided could the detachment and ironic self-consciousness necessary for understanding the artifact emerge (the relation between enthusiasm and irony is one of the major topics of the Solger–Tieck letters). Schlegel rejected as improper and misguided any search by the critic for an objective (even if hidden) truth in the text, any privileged interpretation, and insisted upon the analysis of response as itself a crucial part of critical procedure, crucial because it was the means of 'self-cultivation', the ultimate aim of all art for Schlegel, and the other Romantics. The novel was seen by Schlegel as an absolutely new form of composition best expressing the modern sensibility, due in part to its all-inclusive content, its poetic-prose style, its mixed genre, and its emphasis on the particular and concrete. However, in order for modern literature to reach its highest possible achievement, Schlegel saw the need for a new mythology which would revitalize the language of poetry.

Schlegel's other major publications include a highly controversial novel, *Lucinde* (translated into English), attacked in its own time and later by Kierkegaard as 'lewd sensuality', but also criticized for its apparent disunity; 'Über Lessing' (1797), a critical study; and numerous essays on ancient literature as well as essays and lectures on contemporary literature and on philosophy.

Of the following selections, 'Critical Fragments' appeared in the journal, *Lyceum der Schöne Künste,* in 1797; the 'Athenäum Fragments' in *Athenäum,* 1798, as did 'On Goethe's *Meister*'. The 'Dialogue on Poetry' from which the 'Letter about the Novel' is taken, and 'On Incomprehensibility' appeared in *Athenäum,* 1800. The 'Ideas', inspired by Schleiermacher's *Reden Über die Religion* (1799), were also published in 1800, and all of these writings can be found in Jacob Minor, *Friedrich Schlegel, 1794–1802. Seine prosaischen Jugendschriften* (Vienna, 1882).

Further reading

See Dieckmann (1959), Eichner (1955, 1956, 1970), Handwerk (1985), Immerwahr (1951, 1957), Lange (1955), all in English. See also Henel (1945) and Szondi (1954).

KMW

On Incomprehensibility
Über die Unverständlichkeit

1800

English text from *Lucinde and the Fragments*, translated by Peter Firchow (1971), pp. 257–71.

Because of something either in them or in us, some subjects of human thought stimulate us to ever deeper thought, and the more we are stimulated and lose ourselves in these subjects, the more do they become a Single Subject, which, depending on whether we seek and find it in ourselves or outside of ourselves, we designate the Nature of Things or the Destiny of Man. Other subjects perhaps would never be able to attract our attention if we were to withdraw into holy seclusion and focus our minds exclusively on this subject of subjects, and if we did not have to be together with people and hence busy our minds with real and hypothetical human relationships which, when considered more carefully, always become more numerous and complex and thereby make us diverge into directions contrary to this single subject.

Of all things that have to do with communicating ideas, what could be more fascinating than the question of whether such communication is actually possible? And where could one find a better opportunity for carrying out a variety of experiments to test this possibility or impossibility than in either writing a journal like the *Athenaeum* oneself or else taking part in it as a reader?

Common sense which is so fond of navigating by the compass of etymologies – so long as they are very close by – probably did not have a difficult time in arriving at the conclusion that the basis of the incomprehensible is to be found in incomprehension. Now, it is a peculiarity of mine that I absolutely detest incomprehension, not only the incomprehension of the uncomprehending but even more the incomprehension of the comprehending. For this reason, I made a resolution quite some time ago to have a talk about this matter with my reader, and then create before his eyes – in spite of him as it were – another new reader to my own liking: yes, even to deduce him if need be. I meant it quite seriously and not without some of my old bent for mysticism. I wanted for once to be really thorough and go through the whole series of my essays, admit their frequent lack of success with complete frankness, and so gradually lead the reader to being similarly frank and straightforward with himself. I wanted to prove that all incomprehension is relative, and show how incomprehensible Garve,[1] for example, is to me. I wanted to demonstrate that words often understand themselves better than do those who use them, wanted to point out that there must be a connection of some secret brotherhood among philosophical words that, like a host of spirits too soon aroused, bring everything into confusion in their writings and exert the invisible power of the World Spirit on even those who try to deny it. I wanted to show that the purest and most genuine incomprehension emanates precisely from science and the arts – which by their very nature aim at comprehension and at making comprehensible – and from philosophy and philology; and so that the whole business shouldn't turn around in too palpable a circle I had made a firm resolve really to be comprehensible, at least this time. I wanted to focus attention on what the greatest thinkers of every age have divined (only very darkly, to be sure) until Kant discovered the table of categories[2] and there was light in the spirit of man: I mean by this a real language, so that we can stop rummaging about for words and pay attention to the power and source of all activity. The great frenzy of such a Cabala where one would be taught the way the human spirit can transform itself and thereby perhaps at last bind its transforming and ever transformed opponent in chains – I simply could not portray a mystery like this as naively and nakedly as, when with the thoughtlessness of youth, I made *Lucinde* reveal the nature of love in an eternal hieroglyph. Consequently I had to think of some popular medium to bond chemically the holy, delicate, fleeting, airy, fragrant, and, as it were, imponderable thought. Otherwise, how badly might it have been misunderstood, since only through its well-considered employment was an end finally to be made of all understandable misunderstandings? At the same time, I noted with sincere pleasure the progress of our country – not to speak of our age! The same age in which we too have the honour to live; the age that, to wrap it all up in a word, deserves the humble but highly suggestive name of the Critical Age,[3] so that soon now everything is going to be criticized, except the age itself, and everything is going to become more and more critical, and artists can already begin to cherish the just hope that humanity will at last rise up in a mass and learn to read.

Only a very short while ago this thought of a real language occurred to me again and a glorious prospect opened up before my mind's eye. In the nineteenth century, so Girtanner[4] assures us, in the nineteenth century man will be able to make gold; and isn't it now more than mere conjecture that the nineteenth century is shortly going to begin? With laudable confidence and some huffing and puffing, the worthy man says: 'Every chemist, every artist will make gold; the kitchen utensils are going to be made of silver, of gold.' How gladly all artists will now resolve to go on being hungry for the slight, insignificant remainder of the eighteenth century, and in future no longer fulfil this sacred duty with an aggrieved heart; for they know that in part they themselves, and in part also (and all the more certainly) their descendants will shortly be able to make gold. That he should specify precisely kitchen utensils is due to the fact that what this ingenious prophet finds really beautiful and great in this catastrophe is that we won't be swallowing so much vile vinegary wine out of ordinary, ignoble, base metals like lead, copper, iron, and suchlike.

I saw the whole thing from another point of view. I had often secretly admired the objectivity of gold, I might say even worshipped it. Among the Chinese, I thought, among the English, the Russians, in the island of Japan, among the natives of Fez and Morocco, even among the Cossacks, Cheremis, Bashkirs, and Mulattoes, in short, wherever there is even a little enlightenment and education, silver and gold are comprehensible and through them everything else. When it comes to pass that every artist possesses these materials in sufficient quantity, then he will be allowed only to write his works in bas-relief, with gold letters on silver tablets. Who would want to reject so beautifully printed a book with the vulgar remark that it doesn't make any sense?

But all these things are merely chimeras or ideals: for Girtanner is dead and consequently for the moment so far removed from being able to make gold that one might extract with all possible artistry only so much iron out of him as might be necessary to immortalize his memory by way of a little medallion.

Furthermore, the complaints of incomprehensibility have been directed so exclusively and so frequently and variously at the *Athenaeum* that my deduction might start off most appropriately right at the spot where the shoe actually hurts.

A penetrating critic in the *Berliner Archiv der Zeit* has already been good enough to defend the *Athenaeum* against these attacks and in so doing has used as an example the notorious fragment about the three tendencies. What a marvellous idea! This is just the way one should attack the problem. I am going to follow the same procedure, and so as to let the reader perceive all the more readily that I really think the fragment good, I shall print it once more in these pages:

The French Revolution, Fichte's philosophy, and Goethe's *Meister* are the greatest tendencies of the age. Whoever is offended by this juxtaposition, whoever cannot take any revolution seriously that isn't noisy and materialistic, hasn't yet achieved a lofty, broad perspective on the history of mankind. Even in our shabby histories of civilization, which usually resemble a collection of variants accompanied by a running commentary for which the original classical text has been lost; even there many a little book, almost unnoticed by the noisy rabble at the time, plays a greater role than anything they did.[5]

I wrote this fragment with the most honourable intentions and almost without any irony at all. The way that it has been misunderstood has caused me unspeakable surprise because I expected the misunderstanding to come from quite another quarter. That I consider art to be the heart of humanity and the French Revolution a marvellous allegory about the system of transcendental idealism is, to be sure, only one of my most extremely subjective opinions. But I have let this opinion be known so often and in so many different ways that I really might have hoped the reader would have gotten used to it by now. All the rest is mere cryptology. Whoever can't find Goethe's whole spirit in *Wilhelm Meister* won't be able to find it anywhere else. Poetry and idealism are the focal points of German art and culture; everybody knows that. All the greatest truths of every sort are completely trivial and hence nothing is more important than to express them forever in a new way and, wherever possible, forever more paradoxically, so that we won't forget they still exist and that they can never be expressed in their entirety.

Up to this point I have not been ironical and by all rights I ought not to be misunderstood; and yet it has happened, to the extent in fact of having the well-known Jacobin, Magister Dyk of Leipzig,[6] even find democratic leanings in it.

To be sure, there is something else in the fragment that might in fact be misunderstood. This lies in the word *tendencies* and this is where the irony begins. For this word can be understood to mean that I consider the *Theory of Knowledge,* for example, to be merely a tendency, a temporary venture like Kant's *Critique of Pure Reason* which I myself might perhaps have a mind to continue (only rather better) and then bring to completion; or else that I wish to use the jargon that is most usual and appropriate to this kind of conception, to place myself on Fichte's shoulders, just as he placed himself on Reinhold's[7] shoulders, Reinhold on Kant's shoulders, Kant on Leibniz's, and so on infinitely back to the prime shoulder. I was perfectly aware of this, but I thought I would like to try and see if anyone would accuse me of having had so bad an intention. No one seems to have noticed it. Why should I provide misunderstandings when no one wants to take them up? And so I now let irony go to the winds and declare point-blank that in the dialect of the *Fragments* the word means that everything now is only a tendency, that the age is the Age of Tendencies. As to whether or not I am of the opinion that all these tendencies are going to be corrected and resolved by me, or maybe by my brother or by Tieck, or by someone else from our group, or only some son of ours, or grandson, great-grandson, grandson twenty-seven times removed, or only at the last judgement, or never: that I leave to the wisdom of the reader, to whom this question really belongs.

Goethe and Fichte: that is still the easiest and fittest phrase for all the offence the *Athenaeum* has given, and for all the incomprehension it has provoked. Here too probably the best thing would be to aggravate it even more: when this vexation reaches its highest point, then it will burst and disappear, and then the process of understanding can set to work immediately. We haven't gotten far enough in giving offence; but what is not yet may still come to be. Yet, even those names are going to have to be named again – more than once. Just today my brother wrote a sonnet which I can't resist passing along to the reader because of the charming puns which he (the reader) loves almost more than he loves irony:

> Go, admire idols[8] that are finely made
> And leave us Goethe to be master, guide and friend:
> When his spirit's rosy dawns do fade
> Apollo's golden day no joy will send.
>
> He lures no new spring green from barren trunks,
> But cuts them down to give us warmth and fire.
> And so the time will come when all the Muse's clunks
> Will curse themselves to stone and stiffened mire.
>
> Not to know Goethe means to be a Goth.
> Fools are first blinded by every new, bright flame,
> Then too much light kills them, like the moth.
>
> Goethe, you who by the mercy of the gods came
> To us, an angel from the stars: we are not loth
> To call you godly in form, look, heart, and name.

A great part of the incomprehensibility of the *Athenaeum* is unquestionably due to the *irony* that to a greater or lesser extent is to be found everywhere in it. Here too I will begin with a text from the *Lyceum* [*Critical*] *Fragments:*

Socratic irony is the only involuntary and yet completely deliberate dissimulation. It is equally impossible to feign it or divulge it. To a person who hasn't got it, it will remain a riddle even after it is openly confessed. It is meant to deceive no one except those who consider it a deception and who either take pleasure in the delightful roguery of making fools of the whole world or else become angry when they get an inkling they themselves might be included. In this sort of irony, everything should be playful and serious, guilelessly open and deeply hidden. It originates in the union of *savoir vivre* and scientific spirit, in the conjunction of a perfectly instinctive and a perfectly conscious philosophy. It contains and arouses a feeling of indissoluble antagonism between the absolute and the relative, between the impossibility and the necessity of complete communication. It is the freest of all licenses, for by its means one transcends oneself; and yet it is also the most lawful, for it is absolutely necessary. It is a very good sign when the harmonious bores are at a loss about how they should react to this continuous self-parody, when they fluctuate endlessly between belief and disbelief until they get dizzy and take what is meant as a joke seriously and what is meant seriously as a joke. For Lessing irony is instinct; for Hemsterhuis it is classical study; for Hülsen it arises out of the philosophy of philosophy and surpasses these others by far.[9]

Another one of these fragments recommends itself even more by its brevity:

Irony is the form of paradox. Paradox is everything which is simultaneously good and great.[10]

Won't every reader who is used to the *Athenaeum* fragments find all this simply trifling – yes, even trivial? And yet at the time it seemed incomprehensible to many people because of its relative novelty. For only since then has irony become daily fare, only since the dawn of the new century has such a quantity of great and small ironies of different sorts sprung up, so that I will soon be able to say, like Boufflers,[11] of the various species of the human heart:

> J'ai vu des coeurs de toutes formes,
> Grands, petits, minces, gros, médiocres, énormes.

In order to facilitate a survey of the whole system of irony, we would like to mention here a few of the choicest kinds. The first and most distinguished of all is coarse irony. It is to be found in the real nature of things and is one of the most widespread of substances; it is properly at home in the history of mankind. Next there is fine or delicate irony; then extrafine. Scaramouche employs the last type when he seems to be talking amicably and earnestly with someone when really he is only waiting for the chance to give him – while preserving the social amenities – a kick in the behind. This kind of irony is also to be found in poets, as well as straightforward irony, a type that flourishes most purely and originally in old gardens where wonderfully lovely grottoes lure the sensitive friend of nature into their cool wombs only to be-splash him plentifully from all sides with water and thereby wipe him clean of delicacy. Further, dramatic irony; that is, when an author has written three acts, then unexpectedly turns into another man and now has to write the last two acts. Double irony, when two lines of irony run parallel side-by-side without disturbing each other: one for the gallery, the other for the boxes, though a few little sparks may also manage to get behind the scenes. Finally, there is the irony of irony. Generally speaking, the most fundamental irony of irony probably is that even it becomes tiresome if we are always being confronted with it. But what we want this irony to mean in the first place is something that happens in more ways than one. For example, if one speaks of irony without using it, as I have just done; if one speaks of irony ironically without in the process being aware of having fallen into a far more noticeable irony; if one can't disentangle oneself from irony anymore, as seems to be happening in this essay on incomprehensibility; if irony turns into a mannerism and becomes, as it were, ironical about the author; if one has promised to be ironical for some useless book without first having checked one's supply and then having to produce it against one's will, like an actor full of aches and pains; and if irony runs wild and can't be controlled any longer.

What gods will rescue us from all these ironies? The only solution is to find an irony that might be able to swallow up all these big and little ironies and leave no trace of them at all. I must confess that at precisely this moment I feel that mine has a real urge to do just that. But even this would only be a short-term solution. I fear that if I understand correctly what destiny seems to be hinting at, then soon there will arise a new generation of little ironies: for truly the stars augur the fantastic. And even if it should happen that everything were to be peaceful for a long period of time, one still would not be able to put any faith in this seeming calm. Irony is something one simply cannot play games with. It can have incredibly long-lasting after effects. I have a suspicion that some of the most conscious artists of earlier times are still carrying on ironically, hundreds of years after their deaths, with their most faithful followers and admirers. Shakespeare has so infinitely many depths, subterfuges, and intentions. Shouldn't he also, then, have had the intention of concealing insidious traps in his works to catch the cleverest artists of posterity, to deceive them and make them believe before they realize what they're doing that they are somewhat like Shakespeare themselves? Surely, he must be in this respect as in so many others much more full of intentions than people usually think.

I've already been forced to admit indirectly that the *Athenaeum* is incomprehensible, and because it happened in the heat of irony, I can hardly take it back without in the process doing violence to that irony.

But is incomprehensibility really something so unmitigatedly contemptible and evil? Methinks the salvation of families and nations rests upon it. If I am not wholly deceived, then states and systems, the most artificial products of man, are often so artificial that one simply can't admire the wisdom of their creator enough. Only an incredibly minute quantity of it suffices: as long as its truth and purity remain inviolate and no blasphemous rationality dares approach its sacred confines. Yes, even man's most precious possession, his own inner happiness, depends in the last analysis, as anybody can easily verify, on some such point of strength that must be left in the dark, but that nonetheless shores up and supports the whole burden and would crumble the moment one subjected it to rational analysis. Verily, it would fare badly with you if, as you demand, the whole world were ever to become wholly comprehensible in earnest. And isn't this entire, unending world constructed by the understanding out of incomprehensibility or chaos?

Another consolation for the acknowledged incomprehensibility of the *Athenaeum* lies in the very fact of this acknowledgment, because precisely this has taught us that the evil was a passing one. The new age reveals itself as a nimble and quick-footed one. The dawn has donned seven-league boots. For a long time now there has been lightning on the horizon of poetry; the whole thunderous power of the heavens had gathered together in a mighty cloud; at one moment, it thundered loudly, at another the cloud seemed to move away and discharge its lightning bolts in the distance, only to return again in an even more terrible aspect. But soon it won't be simply a matter of one thunderstorm, the whole sky will burn with a single flame, and then all your little lightning rods won't help you. Then the nineteenth century will indeed make a beginning of it and then the little riddle of the incomprehensibility of the *Athenaeum* will also be solved. What a catastrophe! Then there will be readers who will know how to read. In the nineteenth century everyone will be able to savour the fragments with much gratification and pleasure in the after-dinner hours and not need a nutcracker for even the hardest and most indigestible ones. In the nineteenth century every human being, every reader will find *Lucinde* innocent, *Genoveva*[12] Protestant, and A.W. Schlegel's didactic *Elegies*[13] almost too simple and transparent. And then too what I prophetically set forth as a maxim in the first fragments will hold true:

A classical text must never be entirely comprehensible. But those who are cultivated and who cultivate themselves must always want to learn more from it.[14]

The great schism between understanding and not understanding will grow more and more widespread, intense, and distinct. Much hidden incomprehension will still erupt. But understanding too will reveal its omnipotence: understanding that ennobles disposition into character, elevates talent into genius, purifies one's feelings and artistic perceptions. Understanding itself will be understood, and people will at last see and admit that everyone can achieve the highest degree and that up to now humanity has been neither malicious nor stupid but simply clumsy and new.

I break off at this point so as not to profane prematurely the worship of the highest divinity. But the great principles, the convictions on which this worship depends may be revealed without profanation; and I have attempted to express the essentials by adding on something myself, by way of what the Spanish call a gloss, to one of the profound and admirable verses of the poet. And now all I have left to wish for is that one of our excellent composers will find my lines worthy of being set to music. There is nothing more beautiful on earth than poetry and music mingled in sweet compliance for the greater ennoblement of mankind.[15]

> The rights of Jove are not for all.
> Don't go too far,
> Stay where you are,
> Look how you stand, or else you'll fall.
>
> One man is very humble,
> Another's cheeks swell up with pride;
> This one's brains are all a jumble,
> Another's still less well supplied.
> I love a fool, his hair and hide,
> I love it when he roars and rants,
> And love his languid, flowery dance.
> Forever will I now recall
> What in the master's heart I spied:
> The rights of Jove are not for all.

To keep the mighty pyre burning
A host of tender souls must be
Who fresh to every labour turning
Will make the heathen light to see.
Now let the din grow loud and louder:
Watch where you bite,
Watch what you write,
For when the fools with gun and powder
Crawl from their lairs, think who they are:
Don't go too far.

Some few have caught and kept the spark
That we have lighted.
The masses still are in the dark:
The dolts remain united.
Lack of understanding understood
Confers a lasting gloom
On all that issues from the womb.
The latest word brings lust for blood,
The wasps fly in from near and far:
Stay where you are.

Let them talk from now till doomsday
They never will understand.
Some are born to go astray,
Artists buried in the sand. –
There are sparrows every season
Exulting in their song:
Does this seem wrong?
Let them live by their own reason,
Just make sure you're big and tall:
Look how you stand, or else you'll fall.

From
Critical Fragments
[*Kritische Fragmente*]

1797

English text from *Lucinde and the Fragments,* translated by Peter Firchow (1971), pp. 143–159.

22. The flame of the most brilliantly witty idea should radiate warmth only after it has given off light; it can be quenched suddenly by a single analytic word, even when it is meant as praise.

23. Every good poem must be wholly intentional and wholly instinctive. That is how it becomes ideal.

25. The two main principles of the so-called historical criticism are the Postulate of Vulgarity and the Axiom of the Average. The Postulate of Vulgarity: everything great, good, and beautiful is improbable because it is extraordinary and, at the very least, suspicious. The Axiom of the Average: as we and our surroundings are, so must it have been always and everywhere, because that, after all, is so very natural.

26. Novels are the Socratic dialogues of our time. And this free form has become the refuge of common sense in its flight from pedantry.

27. The critic is a reader who ruminates. Therefore he ought to have more than one stomach.

28. Feeling (for a particular art, science, person, etc.) is divided spirit, is self-restriction: hence a result of self-creation and self-destruction.

29. Gracefulness is life lived correctly, is sensuality contemplating and shaping itself.

33. The overriding disposition of every writer is almost always to lean in one of two directions: either not to say a number of things that absolutely need saying, or else to say a great many things that absolutely ought to be left unsaid. The former is the original sin of synthetic, the latter of analytic minds.

37. In order to write well about something, one shouldn't be interested in it any longer. To express an idea with due circumspection, one must have relegated it wholly to one's past; one must no longer be preoccupied with it. As long as the artist is in the process of discovery and inspiration, he is in a state which, as far as communication is concerned, is at the very least intolerant. He wants to blurt out everything, which is a fault

188

of young geniuses or a legitimate prejudice of old bunglers. And so he fails to recognize the value and the dignity of self-restriction, which is after all, for the artist as well as the man, the first and the last, the most necessary and the highest duty. Most necessary because wherever one does not restrict oneself, one is restricted by the world; and that makes one a slave. The highest because one can only restrict oneself at those points and places where one possesses infinite power, self-creation, and self-destruction. Even a friendly conversation which cannot be broken off at any moment, completely arbitrarily, has something intolerant about it. But a writer who can and does talk himself out, who keeps nothing back for himself, and likes to tell everything he knows, is to be pitied. There are only three mistakes to guard against. First: What appears to be unlimited free will, and consequently seems and should seem to be irrational or supra-rational, nonetheless must still at bottom be simply necessary and rational; otherwise the whim becomes wilful, becomes intolerant, and self-restriction turns into self-destruction. Second: Don't be in too much of a hurry for self-restriction, but first give rein to self-creation, invention, and inspiration, until you're ready. Third: Don't exaggerate self-restriction.

42. Philosophy is the real homeland of irony, which one would like to define as logical beauty: for wherever philosophy appears in oral or written dialogues – and is not simply confined into rigid systems – there irony should be asked for and provided. And even the Stoics considered urbanity a virtue. Of course, there is also a rhetorical species of irony which, sparingly used, has an excellent effect, especially in polemics; but compared to the sublime urbanity of the Socratic muse, it is like the pomp of the most splendid oration set over against the noble style of an ancient tragedy. Only poetry can also reach the heights of philosophy in this way, and only poetry does not restrict itself to isolated ironical passages, as rhetoric does. There are ancient and modern poems that are pervaded by the divine breath of irony throughout and informed by a truly transcendental buffoonery. Internally: the mood that surveys everything and rises infinitely above all limitations, even above its own art, virtue, or genius; externally, in its execution: the mimic style of an averagely gifted Italian *buffo*.

44. You should never appeal to the spirit of the ancients as if to an authority. It's a peculiar thing with spirits: they don't let themselves be grabbed by the hand and shown to others. Spirits reveal themselves only to spirits. Probably here too the best and shortest way would be to prove one's possession of the only true belief by doing good works.

48. Irony is the form of paradox. Paradox is everything simultaneously good and great.

51. To use wit as an instrument for revenge is as shameful as using art as a means for titillating the senses.

55. A really free and cultivated person ought to be able to attune himself at will to bring philosophical or philological, critical or poetical, his-

torical or rhetorical, ancient or modern: quite arbitrarily, just as one tunes an instrument, at any time and to any degree.

56. Wit is logical sociability.

57. If some mystical art lovers who think of every criticism as a dissection and every dissection as a destruction of pleasure were to think logically, then 'wow' would be the best criticism of the greatest work of art. To be sure, there are critiques which say nothing more, but only take much longer to say it.

62. We already have so many theories about poetic genres. Why have we no concept of poetic genre? Perhaps then we would have to make do with a single theory of poetical genres.

65. Poetry is republican speech: a speech which is its own law and end unto itself, and in which all the parts are free citizens and have the right to vote.

70. People who write books and imagine that their readers are the public and that they must educate it soon arrive at the point not only of despising their so-called public but of hating it. Which leads absolutely nowhere.

73. What is lost in average, good, or even first-rate translations is precisely the best part.

85. Every honest author writes for nobody or everybody. Whoever writes for some particular group does not deserve to be read.

86. The function of criticism, people say, is to educate one's readers! Whoever wants to be educated, let him educate himself. This is rude: but it can't be helped.

108. Socratic irony is the only involuntary and yet completely deliberate dissimulation. It is equally impossible to feign it or divulge it. To a person who hasn't got it, it will remain a riddle even after it is openly confessed. It is meant to deceive no one except those who consider it a deception and who either take pleasure in the delightful roguery of making fools of the whole world or else become angry when they get an inkling they themselves might be included. In this sort of irony, everything should be playful and serious, guilelessly open and deeply hidden. It originates in the union of *savoir vivre* and scientific spirit, in the conjunction of a perfectly instinctive and a perfectly conscious philosophy. It contains and arouses a feeling of indissoluble antagonism between the absolute and the relative, between the impossibility and the necessity of complete communication. It is the freest of all licenses, for by its means one transcends oneself; and yet it is also the most lawful, for it is absolutely necessary. It is a very good sign when the harmonious bores are at a loss about how they should react to this continuous self-parody, when they fluctuate endlessly between belief and disbelief until they get dizzy and take what is meant as a joke seriously and what is meant seriously as a joke. For Lessing irony is instinct; for

Hemsterhuis[1] it is classical study; for Hülsen[2] it arises out of the philosophy of philosophy and surpasses these others by far.

109. Gentle wit, or wit without a barb, is a privilege of poetry which prose can't encroach upon: for only by means of the sharpest focus on a single point can the individual idea gain a kind of wholeness.

112. The analytic writer observes the reader as he is; and accordingly he makes his calculations and sets up his machines in order to make the proper impression on him. The synthetic writer constructs and creates a reader as he should be; he doesn't imagine him calm and dead, but alive and critical. He allows whatever he has created to take shape gradually before the reader's eyes, or else he tempts him to discover it himself. He doesn't try to make any particular impression on him, but enters with him into the sacred relationship of deepest symphilosophy or sympoetry.

114. There are so many critical journals of varying sorts and differing intentions! If only a society might be formed sometime with the sole purpose of gradually making criticism – since criticism is, after all, necessary – a real thing.

115. The whole history of modern poetry is a running commentary on the following brief philosophical text: all art should become science and all science art; poetry and philosophy should be made one.

From
Athenäum Fragments
[Athenäums Fragmente]

1798

English text from *Lucinde and the Fragments,* translated by Peter Firchow (1971), pp. 161–240.

1. Nothing is more rarely the subject of philosophy than philosophy itself.

24. Many of the works of the ancients have become fragments. Many modern works are fragments as soon as they are written.

43. Philosophy is still moving too much in a straight line; it's not yet cyclical enough.

44. Every philosophical review should simultaneously be a philosophy of reviews.

51. Naive is what is or seems to be natural, individual, or classical to the point of irony, or else to the point of continuously fluctuating between self-creation and self-destruction. If it's simply instinctive, then it's child-like, childish, or silly; if it's merely intentional, then it gives rise to affectation. The beautiful, poetical, ideal naive must combine intention and instinct. The essence of intention in this sense is freedom, though intention isn't consciousness by a long shot. There is a certain kind of self-infatuated contemplation of one's own naturalness or silliness that is itself unspeakably silly. Intention doesn't exactly require any deep calculation or plan. Even Homeric naiveté isn't simply instinctive; there is at least as much intention in it as there is in the grace of lovely children or innocent girls. And even if Homer himself had no intentions, his poetry and the real author of that poetry, Nature, certainly did.

77. A dialogue is a chain or garland of fragments. An exchange of letters is a dialogue on a larger scale, and memoirs constitute a system of fragments. But as yet no genre exists that is fragmentary both in form and in content, simultaneously completely subjective and individual, and completely objective and like a necessary part in a system of all the sciences.

116. Romantic poetry[1] is a progressive, universal poetry. Its aim isn't merely to reunite all the separate species of poetry and put poetry in touch with philosophy and rhetoric. It tries to and should mix and fuse poetry and prose, inspiration and criticism, the poetry of art and the poetry of nature; and make poetry lively and sociable, and life and society poetical;

192

poeticize wit and fill and saturate the forms of art with every kind of good, solid matter for instruction, and animate them with the pulsations of humour. It embraces everything that is purely poetic, from the greatest systems of art, containing within themselves still further systems, to the sigh, the kiss that the poetizing child breathes forth in artless song. It can so lose itself in what it describes that one might believe it exists only to characterize poetical individuals of all sorts; and yet there still is no form so fit for expressing the entire spirit of an author: so that many artists who started out to write only a novel ended up by providing us with a portrait of themselves. It alone can become, like the epic, a mirror of the whole circumambient world, an image of the age. And it can also – more than any other form – hover at the midpoint between the portrayed and the portrayer, free of all real and ideal self-interest, on the wings of poetic reflection, and can raise that reflection again and again to a higher power, can multiply it in an endless succession of mirrors. It is capable of the highest and most variegated refinement, not only from within outwards, but also from without inwards; capable in that it organizes – for everything that seeks a wholeness in its effects – the parts along similar lines, so that it opens up a perspective upon an infinitely increasing classicism. Romantic poetry is in the arts what wit is in philosophy, and what society and sociability, friendship and love are in life. Other kinds of poetry are finished and are now capable of being fully analysed. The romantic kind of poetry is still in the state of becoming; that, in fact, is its real essence: that it should forever be becoming and never be perfected. It can be exhausted by no theory and only a divinatory criticism would dare try to characterize its ideal. It alone is infinite, just as it alone is free; and it recognizes as its first commandment that the will of the poet can tolerate no law above itself. The romantic kind of poetry is the only one that is more than a kind, that is, as it were, poetry itself: for in a certain sense all poetry is or should be romantic.

149. The systematic Winckelmann[2] who read all the ancients as if they were a single author, who saw everything as a whole and concentrated all his powers on the Greeks, provided the first basis for a material knowledge of the ancients through his perception of the absolute difference between ancient and modern. Only when the perspective and the conditions of the absolute identity of ancient and modern in the past, present, and future have been discovered will one be able to say that at least the contours of classical study have been laid bare and one can now proceed to methodical investigation.

168. Cicero ranks philosophies according to their usefulness to the orator; similarly, one might ask what philosophy is fittest for the poet. Certainly no system at variance with one's feelings or common sense; or one that transforms the real into the illusory; or abstains from all decisions; or inhibits a leap into the suprasensory regions; or achieves humanity only by

adding up all the externals. This excludes eudaemonism, fatalism, idealism, scepticism, materialism, or empiricism. Then what philosophy is left for the poet? The creative philosophy that originates in freedom and belief in freedom, and shows how the human spirit impresses its law on all things and how the world is its work of art.

206. A fragment, like a miniature work of art, has to be entirely isolated from the surrounding world and be complete in itself like a porcupine.

216. The French Revolution, Fichte's philosophy, and Goethe's *Meister* are the greatest tendencies of the age. Whoever is offended by this juxtaposition, whoever cannot take any revolution seriously that isn't noisy and materialistic, hasn't yet achieved a lofty, broad perspective on the history of mankind. Even in our shabby histories of civilization, which usually resemble a collection of variants accompanied by a running commentary for which the original classical text has been lost; even there many a little book, almost unnoticed by the noisy rabble at the time, plays a greater role than anything they did.[3]

220. If wit in all its manifestations is the principle and the organ of universal philosophy, and if all philosophy is nothing but the spirit of universality, the science of all the eternally uniting and dividing sciences, a logical chemistry: then the value and importance of that absolute, enthusiastic, thoroughly material wit is infinite, that wit wherein Bacon and Leibniz, the chief representatives of scholastic prose, were masters, the former among the first, chronologically speaking, the latter among the greatest. The most important scientific discoveries are bons mots of this sort – are so because of the surprising contingency of their origin, the unifying force of their thought, and the baroqueness of their casual expression. But they are, of course, in respect to content, much more than the unsatisfied and evanescent expectation of purely poetical wit. The best ones are *echappées de vue* into the infinite. Leibniz's whole philosophy consists of a few fragments and projects that are witty in this sense. It may be that Kant – the Copernicus of philosophy – has even more natural syncretistic spirit and critical wit than Leibniz, but his situation and his education aren't as witty; and furthermore the same thing has happened to his ideas that happens to popular songs: the Kantians have sung them to death. Therefore it's quite easy to be unfair to him and think him less witty than he really is. Of course, philosophy will only be healthy when it no longer expects and counts on getting brilliant ideas, when it's able to make continuous progress, relying, naturally, on enthusiastic energy and brilliant art, but also on a sure method. But are we to despise the few still extant products of synthesizing genius because no unifying art and science exists as yet? And how could they exist as long as we still simply spell out most sciences like schoolchildren and imagine that we've achieved our object when we can decline and conjugate one of the many dialects of philosophy but have no notion of syntax and can't construct even the shortest periodic sentence?

238. There is a kind of poetry whose essence lies in the relation between ideal and real, and which therefore, by analogy to philosophical jargon, should be called transcendental poetry. It begins as satire in the absolute difference of ideal and real, hovers in between as elegy, and ends as idyll with the absolute identity of the two. But just as we wouldn't think much of an uncritical transcendental philosophy that doesn't represent the producer along with the product and contain at the same time within the system of transcendental thoughts a description of transcendental thinking: so too this sort of poetry should unite the transcendental raw materials and preliminaries of a theory of poetic creativity – often met with in modern poets – with the artistic reflection and beautiful self-mirroring that is present in Pindar, in the lyric fragments of the Greeks, in the classical elegy, and, among the moderns, in Goethe. In all its descriptions, this poetry should describe itself, and always be simultaneously poetry and the poetry of poetry.

247. Dante's prophetic poem is the only system of transcendental poetry, and is still the greatest of its kind. Shakespeare's universality is like the centre of romantic art. Goethe's purely poetical poetry is the most complete poetry of poetry. This is the great triple chord of modern poetry, the inmost and holiest circle among all the broad and narrow spheres of a critical anthology of the classics of modern poetry.

252. A real aesthetic theory of poetry would begin with the absolute antithesis of the eternally unbridgeable gulf between art and raw beauty. It would describe their struggle and conclude with the perfect harmony of artistic and natural poetry. This is to be found only among the ancients and would in itself constitute nothing but a more elevated history of the spirit of classical poetry. But a philosophy of poetry as such would begin with the independence of beauty, with the proposition that beauty is and should be distinct from truth and morality, and that it has the same rights as these: something that – for those who are able to understand it at all – follows from the proposition I = I. It would waver between the union and the division of philosophy and poetry, between poetry and practice, poetry as such and the genres and kinds of poetry; and it would conclude with their complete union. Its beginning would provide the principles of pure poetics; its middle the theory of the particular, characteristically modern types of poetry: the didactic, the musical, the rhetorical in a higher sense, etc. The keystone would be a philosophy of the novel, the rough outlines of which are contained in Plato's political theory. Of course, to the ephemeral, unenthusiastic dilettantes, who are ignorant of the best poets of all types, this kind of poetics would seem very much like a book of trigonometry to a child who just wants to draw pictures. Only a man who knows or possesses a subject can make use of the philosophy of that subject; only he will be able to understand what that philosophy means and what it's attempting to do. But philosophy can't inoculate someone with experience

and sense, or pull them out of a hat – and it shouldn't want to do so. To those who knew it already, philosophy of course brings nothing new; but only through it does it become knowledge and thereby assume a new form.

256. The basic error of sophistic aesthetics is to consider beauty merely as something given, as a psychological phenomenon. Of course, beauty isn't simply the empty thought of something that should be created, but at the same time the thing itself, one of the human spirit's original ways of acting: not simply a necessary fiction, but also a fact, that is, an eternally transcendental one.

275. People are always complaining that German authors write for such a small circle, and even sometimes just for themselves. That's how it should be. This is how German literature will gain more and more spirit and character. And perhaps in the meantime an audience will spring into being.

From
Ideas
[Ideen]

1800

English text from *Lucinde and the Fragments,* translated by Peter Firchow (1971), pp. 241–56.

19. To have genius is the natural state of humanity. Nature endowed even humanity with health, and since love is for women what genius is for men, we must conceive of the golden age as a time when love and genius were universal.

20. Everyone is an artist whose central purpose in life is to educate his intellect.

21. The need to raise itself above humanity is humanity's prime characteristic.

24. The symmetry and organization of history teach us that mankind, for as long as it existed and developed, has really always been and has always become an individual, a person. In the great person of mankind, God became a man.

33. The morality of a work is to be found not in its subject or in the relation of the speaker to his audience, but in the spirit of its execution. If this is infused with the whole wealth of humanity, then the work is moral. If it is only the product of a particular ability or art, then it is not.

34. Whoever has religion will speak in poetry. But to seek and find religion, you need the instrument of philosophy.

42. If one is to believe the philosophers, then what we call religion is simply intentionally popular or instinctively artless philosophy. The poets, however, seem to prefer to think of it as a variety of poetry which, unsure of its own lovely playfulness, takes itself too seriously and too onesidedly. Still, philosophy already admits and begins to recognize that it must start with religion and achieve perfection in religion, and poetry strives only for the infinite and despises worldly practicality and culture as the real opposites of religion. Hence eternal peace among artists is no longer a distant prospect.

43. What men are among the other creatures of the earth, artists are among men.

45. An artist is someone who carries his centre within himself.

Whoever lacks such a centre has to choose some particular leader and mediator outside of himself, not, to be sure, forever, but only to begin with. For a man cannot live without a vital centre, and if he does not yet have one within himself, then he can only seek it in another man, and only a man and a man's centre can stimulate and awaken his own.

46. Poetry and philosophy are, depending on one's point of view, different spheres, different forms, or simply the component parts of religion. For only try really to combine the two and you will find yourself with nothing but religion.

47. God is everything that is purely original and sublime, consequently the individual himself taken to the highest power. But aren't nature and the world also individuals?

48. Where philosophy stops, poetry has to begin. An ordinary point of view, a way of thinking, natural only in opposition to art and culture, a mere existing: all these are wrong; that is, there should be no kingdom of barbarity beyond the boundaries of culture. Every thinking part of an organization should not feel its limits without at the same time feeling its unity in relation to the whole.

54. The artist should have as little desire to rule as to serve. He can only create, do nothing but create, and so help the state only by making rulers and servants, and by exalting politicians and economists into artists.

55. Versatility consists not just in a comprehensive system but also in feeling for the chaos outside that system, like man's feeling for something beyond man.

60. Individuality is precisely what is original and eternal in man; personality doesn't matter so much. To pursue the cultivation and development of this individuality as one's highest calling would be a godlike egoism.

63. The really central insight of Christianity is sin.

64. Artists make mankind an individual by connecting the past with the future in the present. Artists are the higher organ of the soul where the vital spirits of all external humanity join together, and where inner humanity has its primary sphere of action.

65. Only by being cultivated does a human being, who is wholly that, become altogether human and permeated by humanity.

69. Irony is the clear consciousness of eternal agility, of an infinitely teeming chaos.

86. Beautiful is what reminds us of nature and thereby stimulates a sense of the infinite fullness of life. Nature is organic, and whatever is most sublimely beautiful is therefore always vegetal, and the same is true of morality and love.

95. The new, eternal gospel that Lessing prophesied will appear as a bible: but not as a single book in the usual sense. Even what we now call the Bible is actually a system of books. And that is, I might add, no mere

arbitrary turn of phrase! Or is there some other word to differentiate the idea of an infinite book from an ordinary one, than Bible, the book per se, the absolute book? And surely there is an eternally essential and even practical difference if a book is merely a means to an end, or an independent work, an individual, a personified idea. It cannot be this without divine inspiration, and here the esoteric concept is itself in agreement with the exoteric one; and, moreover, no idea is isolated, but is what it is only in combination with all other ideas. An example will explain this. All the classical poems of the ancients are coherent, inseparable; they form an organic whole, they constitute, properly viewed, only a single poem, the only one in which poetry itself appears in perfection. In a similar way, in a perfect literature all books should be only a single book, and in such an eternally developing book, the gospel of humanity and culture will be revealed.

96. All philosophy is idealism, and there exists no true realism except that of poetry. But poetry and philosophy are only extremes. If one were to say that some people are pure idealists and others very definitely realists, then that remark would be quite true. Stated differently, it means that there as yet exist no wholly cultivated human beings, that there still is no religion.

108. Whatever can be done while poetry and philosophy are separated has been done and accomplished. So the time has come to unite the two.

127. Women have less need for the poetry of poets because their very essence is poetry.

146. Even in their outward behaviour, the lives of artists should differ completely from the lives of other men. They are Brahmins, a higher caste: ennobled not by birth, but by free self-consecration.

148. Who unlocks the magic book of art and frees the imprisoned holy spirit? Only a kindred spirit.

149. Without poetry, religion becomes murky, false, and evil; without philosophy, extravagant in its lewdness and lustful to the point of self-emasculation.

153. All self-sufficiency is radical, is original, and all originality is moral, is originality of the whole man. Without originality, there is no energy of reason and no beauty of disposition.

155. I have expressed a few ideas pointing toward the heart of things, and have greeted the dawn in my own way, from my own point of view. Let anyone who knows the road do likewise in his own way, from his own point of view.

From
On Goethe's 'Meister'
[Über Goethes 'Meister']

1798

Translated from the German in *KFSA*, II, 126–46.

* * *

It is a beautiful and indeed necessary experience when reading a poetic work to give ourselves up entirely to its influence, to let the writer do with us what he will; perhaps only in matters of detail is it necessary to pause and confirm out emotional response with a moment's reflection, raise it into a thought, and where there is room for doubt or dispute, decide and amplify the matter. This is the prime, the most essential response. But it is no less necessary to be able to abstract from all the details, to have a loose general concept of the work, survey it en bloc, and grasp it as a whole, perceive even its most hidden parts, and make connections between the most remote corners. We must rise above our own affection for the work, and in our thoughts be able to destroy what we adore; otherwise, whatever our talents, we would lack a sense of the whole. Why should we not both breathe in the perfume of a flower and at the same time, entirely absorbed in the observation, contemplate in its infinite ramifications the vein-system of a single leaf? The whole man who feels and thinks in universal terms is interested not only in the brilliant outward covering, the bright garment of this beautiful earth; he also likes to investigate the layering and the composition of the strata far within; he would wish to delve deeper and deeper, even to the very centre, if possible, and would want to know the construction of the whole. So we gladly tear ourselves away from the poet's spell, after we have willingly let him cast his enchantment upon us; what we love most is to seek out what he has hidden from our gaze or was reluctant to reveal at first, what it is that most makes him an artist: the hidden intentions he pursues in secret. In a genius whose instinct has become will, there are many more intentions than we can take for granted.

* * *

Our feelings too protest against an orthodox academic judgment of this divine organism. Who would review a feast of the finest and choicest wit with all the usual fuss and formalities? An academic review of *Wilhelm Meister* would look like the young man who went walking in the woods with a book under his arm and drove away Philine as well as the cuckoo.

Perhaps then we should judge it, and at the same time refrain from judging it; which does not seem to be at all an easy task. Fortunately it turns out to be one of those books which carries its own judgement within it, and spares the critic his labour. Indeed, not only does it judge itself; it also describes itself. A mere description of the impression it makes, quite apart from being superfluous, would be bound to come off badly, even if it were not the worst of its kind. It would lose out not only to the poet, but also to the thoughts of the kind of reader who knows the highest when he sees it and has the capacity to worship, a reader who can tell at once without art or science what he should worship, and who responds to the real, right thing as though struck by lightning.

Our usual expectations of unity and coherence are disappointed by this novel as often as they are fulfilled. But the reader who possesses a true instinct for system, who has a sense of totality or that anticipation of the world in its entirety which makes Wilhelm so interesting, will be aware throughout the work of what we might call its personality and living individuality. And the more deeply he probes, the more inner connections and relations and the greater intellectual coherence he will discover in it. If there is any book with an indwelling genius, it is this. And if this genius could characterize itself in detail and as a whole, then there would be no need for anyone else to say what it is all about, or how it should be taken. A little elaboration is possible here, and some explanation need not seem unnecessary or superfluous, for despite this feeling of its wholeness, the beginning and the end of the work, as well as one or two parts in the middle, are generally felt to be superfluous and unrelated. Even the reader who is able to recognize the divine nature of its cultivated randomness, and do it honour, has a sense of something isolated at the beginning and the end as if despite the most beautiful coherence and innermost unity of the work, it lacked the ultimate interdependence of thoughts and feelings. Many readers, to whom one cannot deny this sense, are uneasy about several parts of the work, for in such developing natures, idea and feeling are mutually extended, sharpened and formed by one another.

The differing nature of the individual sections should be able to throw a great deal of light on the organization of the whole. But in progressing appropriately from the parts to the whole, observation and analysis must not get lost in over-minute detail. Rather analysis must pause, as if the detail were merely a matter of simple parts, at those major sections whose independence is also maintained by their free treatment, and by their shaping and transformation of what they have taken over from the previous section; and whose inner, unintentional homogeneity and original unity the poet himself has acknowledged in using the most various, though always poetic, means, in a deliberate effort to shape them into a rounded whole. The development within the individual sections ensures the overall coherence, and in pulling them together, the poet confirms their variety. And in this way each essential part of the single and indivisible novel becomes a system in itself. The means of connection and progression are more or less the same in all sections. In the second volume, Jarno and the appearance of the Amazons raise our expectations in the same way as the Stranger and Mignon had done in the first; and they likewise rouse our interest in the far distance and point forward to heights of education not yet visible. Here too, every book opens with a new scene and a new world; here too the old figures reappear with youth renewed; here too every book contains the germ of the next, and with vital energy absorbs into its own being what the previous book has yielded. And the third book, distinguished by the freshest and happiest colouring, is beautifully framed, as if by the blossoms of youth still burgeoning but already mature, first by Mignon's song 'Kennst du das Land . . . ' and at the end by Wilhelm's and the Countess's first kiss. Where there is so much to be noticed, there would be little point in drawing attention to something that has been there already, or recurs again and again with a few changes. Only what is quite new and individual requires commentary – but of the sort which should by no means make everything clear for everybody. It deserves the name of excellence only when the reader who understands *Wilhelm Meister* completely finds it utterly familiar and when the reader who does not understand it at all finds it as stupid and empty as the work it is supposed to elucidate. On the other hand, the reader who only half-understands the work would find such a commentary only half-comprehensible; it would enlighten him in some respects, but perhaps only confuse him the more in others – so that out of this disturbance and doubt, knowledge might emerge, or the reader might at least become aware of his incompleteness. The second volume in particular has least need of explanations. It is the fullest, but also the most charming. It is full of keen understanding, but still very understandable.

*   *   *

The view of *Hamlet* to be found scattered partly here and partly in the next [fourth] volume is not so much criticism as high poetry. What else but a poem can come into being when a poet in full possession of his powers contemplates a work of art and represents it in his own? This is not because his view makes suppositions and assertions which go beyond the visible work. All criticism has to do that, because every great work, of whatever kind, knows more than it says, and aspires to more than it knows. It is because the aims and approach of poetic criticism are something completely different. Poetic criticism does not act as a mere inscription, and merely say what the thing is, and where it stands and should stand in the world. For that, all that is required is a whole and undivided human being who has made the work the centre of his attention for as long as necessary. If he takes pleasure in communication, by word of mouth or in writing, he will enjoy developing and elaborating an insight which is fundamentally single and indivisible. That is how a critical characterization of a work actually comes into being. The poet and artist on the other hand will want to represent the representation anew, and form once more what has already been formed; he will add to the work, restore it, shape it afresh. He will only divide the whole into articulated parts and masses, not break it down into its original constituents, which in respect of the work are dead things, because their elements are no longer of the same nature as the whole; however, in respect of the universe they are certainly living, and could be articulated parts or masses there. The ordinary critic relates the object of his art to these, and so he is inevitably bound to destroy his living unity, sometimes breaking it down into its elements, sometimes regarding it as an atom itself within a greater mass.

Letter About the Novel
[Brief über den Roman]

1799

English text from *Dialogue on Poetry and Literary Aphorisms,* edited and translated by Ernst Behler and R. Struc (1968), pp. 94–105.

[Antonio, one of the main interlocutors of the *Dialogue,* speaks to Amalia.]

This is how I think of the matter. Poetry is so deeply rooted in man that at times, even under the most unfavourable circumstances, it grows without cultivation. Just as we find in almost every nation songs and stories in circulation and, even though crude, some kind of plays in use, so in our unfantastic age, in the actual estate of prose, and I mean the so-called educated and cultured people, we will find a few individuals who, sensing in themselves a certain originality of the imagination, express it, even though they are still far removed from true art. The humour of a Swift, a Sterne is, I believe, natural poetry of the higher classes of our age.

I am far from putting them next to the great ones; but you will admit that whoever has a sense for these, for Diderot, has a better start on the way to learning to appreciate the divine wit, the imagination of an Ariosto, Cervantes, Shakespeare, than one who did not even rise to that point. We simply must not make exaggerated demands on the people of our times; what has grown in such a sickly environment naturally cannot be anything else but sickly. I consider this circumstance, however, rather an advantage, as long as the arabesque is not a work of art but a natural product, and therefore place Richter over Sterne because his imagination is far more sickly, therefore far more eccentric and fantastic. Just go ahead and read Sterne again. It has been a long time since you read him and I think you will find him different. Then compare our German with him. He really does have more wit, at least for one who takes him wittily, for he could easily put himself in the wrong. And this excellence raises his sentimentality in appearance over the sphere of English sensibility.

There is another external reason why we should cultivate in ourselves this sense for the grotesque and remain in this mood. It is impossible in this age of books not to have to leaf through very many bad books, indeed, read them. Some of them always – one can depend on it – are fortunately of a silly kind, and thus it is really up to us to find them entertaining by looking at them as witty products of nature. Laputa is everywhere or nowhere, my dear friend; without an act of our freedom and imagination we are in the midst of it. When stupidity reaches a certain height, which we often see now when everything is more severely differentiated, stupidity equals foolishness even in the external appearance. And foolishness, you will admit, is the loveliest thing that man can imagine, and the actual and ultimate principle of all amusement. In such a mood I can often break out in almost incessant laughter over books which seem in no way meant to provoke it. And it is only fair that nature gave me this substitute, since I cannot laugh at all at many a thing nowadays called anecdote and satire. For me, on the other hand, learned journals, for example, become a farce, and the one called *Die Allgemeine Zeitung* I subscribe to very obstinately, as the Viennese keep their Jack Pudding.[1] Seen from my point of view, it is not only the most versatile of them all but in every way the most incomparable: having sunk from nullity to a certain triviality and from there to a kind of stupidity, now by way of stupidity it has finally fallen into that foolish silliness.

This in general is too learned a pleasure for you. If, however, you were to carry on what unfortunately you cannot stop doing, then I will no longer scorn your servant when he brings you the stacks of books from the loan library. Indeed, I offer myself as your porter for this purpose and promise to send you any number of the most beautiful comedies from all areas of literature.

* * *

What then is this sentimental? It is that which appeals to us, where feeling prevails, and to be sure not a sensual but a spiritual feeling. The source and soul of all these emotions is love, and the spirit of love must hover everywhere invisibly visible in romantic poetry. This is what is meant by this definition. As Diderot so comically explains in *The Fatalist,* the gallant passions which one cannot escape in the works of the moderns from the epigram to tragedy are the least essential, or more, they are not even the external letter of that spirit; on occasion they are simply nothing or something very unlovely and loveless. No, it is the sacred breath which, in the tones of music, moves us. It cannot be grasped forcibly and comprehended mechanically, but it can be amiably lured by mortal beauty and veiled in it. The magic words of poetry can be infused with and inspired by its power. But in the poem in which it is not everywhere present nor could be everywhere, it certainly does not exist at all. It is an infinite being and by no means does it cling and attach its interest only to persons, events, situations, and individual inclinations; for the true poet all this – no matter how intensely it embraces his soul – is only a hint at something higher, the infinite, a hieroglyph of the one eternal love and the sacred fullness of life of creative nature.

Only the imagination can grasp the mystery of this love and present it as a mystery; and this mysterious quality is the source of the fantastic in the form of all poetic representation. The imagination strives with all its might to express itself, but the divine can communicate and express itself only indirectly in the sphere of nature. Therefore, of that which originally was imagination there remains in the world of appearances only what we call wit.

One more thing resides in the meaning of the sentimental which concerns precisely the peculiar tendency of romantic poetry in contrast with ancient. No consideration is taken in it of the difference between appearance and truth, play and seriousness. Therein resides the great difference. Ancient poetry adheres throughout to mythology and avoids the specifically historical themes. Even ancient tragedy is play, and the poet who presented a true event of serious concern for the entire nation was punished. Romantic poetry, on the other hand, is based entirely on a historical foundation, far more than we know and believe. Any play you might see, any story you read – if it has a witty plot – you can be almost sure has a true story at its source, even if variously reshaped. Boccaccio is almost entirely true history, just as all the other sources are from which all Romantic ideas originate.

*   *   *

. . . there is otherwise so little contrast between the drama and the novel that it is rather the drama, treated thoroughly and historically, as for instance by Shakespeare, which is the true foundation of the novel. You claimed, to be sure, that the novel is most closely related to the narrative, the epic genre. On the other hand, I want to admonish you that a song can as well be romantic as a story. Indeed, I can scarcely visualize a novel but as a mixture of storytelling, song, and other forms. Cervantes always composed in this manner and even the otherwise so prosaic Boccaccio adorns his collections of stories by framing them with songs. If there is a novel in which this does not or cannot occur, it is only due to the individuality of the work and not the character of the genre; on the contrary, it is already an exception. But this is only by the way. My actual objection is as follows. Nothing is more contrary to the epic style than when the influence of the subjective mood becomes in the least visible; not to speak of one's ability to give himself up to his humour and play with it, as it often happens in the most excellent novels.

*   *   *

Part 6

Fichte

Johann Gottlieb Fichte

(1762–1814)

Along with Schelling, Fichte is among the great German Idealists the least known to the English-speaking world. After the conventional training in theology, he was inspired by Lessing and Spinoza, and above all by Kant, to turn to philosophy, and his first publication, the *Critique of all Revelation* (1792), was by virtue of its anonymous authorship widely mistaken for Kant's fourth critique.

In 1794 he took up a chair at Jena, which he abandoned in 1799 as a result of the notorious accusations of atheism directed at him: for an account of the controversy see Edwards (1967), article *Atheismusstreit*. He held a chair at Erlangen before moving to Berlin in 1809, dying of a fever five years later.

There are myths of Fichte just as there are myths of Kant. Lewes (1857) paints the picture of a meditative and solitary child, a transcendentalist *Wunderkind:* "He stands for hours, gazing into the far distance, or in mournful yearning at the silent sky overarching him" (p. 566). His popular lectures on the Germanic identity and on the moral obligation to freedom and resistance have often been taken as evidence of his political importance in the struggle against the French, but this too has been disputed: see Fichte (1968), p. xxvii. Perhaps most significantly of all, he was widely known as the leading spirit of the *Ichphilosophie* or ego-philosophy, itself mistakenly understood as a rationale for various forms of self-indulgence or self-obsession. Such a view quite misrepresents the scrupulous arguments of his great *Wissenschaftslehre* or *Science of Knowledge,* but it was supported by Goethe's and Schiller's habit of describing him as "the great *Ich* from Osmannstedt", and by the young Friedrich Schlegel's invocation of his system as a philosophical analogue of Romantic irony. As early as the 1798 *Sittenlehre (Science of Ethics)* Fichte differentiates himself from any affiliation with what was popularly recognized as irony, which he regarded simply as an elaborate self-protection and an avoidance of *action,* one of the most important obligations of enlightenment. Self-reflection is absolutely necessary to the personality caught up in the transcendental method, and it must indeed be continual, but it should never remain merely speculative. When it does, then such a man has

acquired an excellent knowledge of all the rules of that play of thoughts . . . but he does so only for the purpose of thereby producing another play in his mind. He causes good and noble sentiments and thoughts to arise in his mind; but merely in order to make these sentiments themselves an object of his enjoyment, and to amuse himself at the appearance of harmony . . . But he is and remains corrupt; for the whole interests him for his own enjoyment's sake; he has no serious interest in it, no interest lying beyond himself. Fichte (1907), p. 397

In the *Characteristics of the Present Age* (1804–5) Fichte does admit that a period of unsettled hovering [freie Schweben] between "authority and mere emptiness" is and has been a necessary step in the progress of the race, but it is only usefully so when it impels us toward determinate knowledge: see Fichte (1847), p. 82.

Throughout his career Fichte was emphatic about the need to convert the insights of the transcendental philosophy into action, and social action at that. In this ambition he had to face certain difficulties in the Kantian inheritance. Much of what Kant had to say about philosophy strictly conceived, and almost everything he had said about ethics and aesthetics, was premissed on the absence of an element of contingent interest in the highest states of mind. Fichte's task was thus to preserve the basic spirit and technique of Kant's arguments whilst somehow turning them into some form of social interventionism. Only through acting "in and for society" does man do his duty – see Fichte (1845), IV, 235 – and this generates the need for a community of scholars or learned men, in order that the freedom that each man has for himself "to question everything and to inquire freely and independently" shall be represented in some external and institutional form (IV, 248). Any healthily evolving society will have to throw aside the authority of merely received judgements; it thus becomes all the more important that there be a learned class to preserve some sense of direction, and one based on authenticated truth, even as this class must never be constrained in the subjects and conclusions of its inquiries.

Thus Fichte sought to establish the necessity of institutions based on freedom (Coleridge's ideas about the place of an enlightened clerisy might be compared here); a way of distributing through society the positive results of detached and interest-free individual speculations. His revision of Kant's method had of course much more technical manifestations, and they may be traced through the various versions of the *Wissenschaftslehre* appearing after 1794. Here Fichte sets going the gestures followed by so many others in his generation, aiming at closing the gaps or divisions in the mind argued for by Kant himself. He seeks to establish the grounds for a self-consciousness much more dynamic and exploratory, knowing itself not in the apparently timeless deploying of the categories of the understanding in repetitive ways, but in an ongoing positing of self and other through the biographical passage of time. This is to overstate the case somewhat, but it is worth doing to make clear the extent to which Fichte anticipates Hegel in this respect. Crudely put, the self becomes a more restless and aspiring entity, and it becomes so *for itself*, i.e. in its most important movements of self-recognition (as opposed to having these unstable elements excluded from critical attention, as they were by Kant). Interest and inclination, with a blurring of the divisions between the higher and lower faculties of desire, are readmitted in the cause of reuniting the activities of understanding and reason into a coherent personality. Thus, for Fichte, an aesthetic element is fundamental in all perception, and empirical inclinations are made continuous with our higher faculties of freedom and morality. Religion also reappears in places from which it had been carefully excluded by Kant.

In Fichte we can also see the awareness of a problem of audience, and he went perhaps further than any of his contemporaries in the search for popular epitomes of the critical philosophy. The wide range of his writings is not well represented in English translations, although the recent translation of the *Wissenschaftslehre* is an important step in the task of making his most important arguments available to a new audience: see Fichte (1970). Other major works available in English tend to exist only in somewhat outdated nineteenth-century translations: see Fichte (1889a, b), (1907). Revised or recent translations do exist of the *Addresses to the German Nation, The Vocation of Man,* and the *Critique of all Revelation:* see Fichte (1968), (1956), (1978). *On the Spirit and the Letter in Philosophy* is translated in DS, pp. 74–93.

Further reading

Again, apart from the accounts in the standard histories, e.g. Copleston (1965a), there is very little expository or interpretive work on Fichte in English. Exceptions are Engelbrecht (1933) and Seidel (1976). Two standard works in French should be mentioned: those of Léon (1922–7) and Guéroult (1930). See also the bibliography by Baumgartner & Jacobs (1968). A modern complete edition is in progress (1964–). There is also an edition of the letters (1967).

DS

Selections from

On the Nature of the Scholar,
and his Manifestations in the Sphere of Freedom
[Über das Wesen des Gelehrten und seine
Erscheinungen in Gebiete der Freiheit]

Lectures given at Erlangen in the summer of 1805

What follows is a heavily revised text of (selections from) the translation by William Smith in Fichte (1889a), I, 209–317. German text in *SW*, VI, 347–447.

Introductory note

These lectures constitute one of Fichte's public or exoteric statements of his philosophical priorities, and in many ways extend the themes of the 1794 lectures *On the Vocation of the Scholar:* see Fichte (1889a), I, 149–205; *SW*, VI, 289–346. Here he had emphasized the social function and identity of learning, arguing strongly against Rousseau's notion of the corrupting tendency of a scholar class (*SW*, VI, 335f.) whilst maintaining the ideal of minimal government.

The following lectures might seem in the first place to have very little to do with aesthetics, but it becomes apparent at a certain point in the argument that the scholar and the artist are defined each in terms of the other, and that what Fichte is working toward is some sort of socially manifested aesthetic identity. One might compare Shelley's broad and inclusive idea of poetry in *A Defence of Poetry*: it can exist in laws, in institutions, and in architecture, as well as in the literary mode commonly so named (which yet remains its pre-eminent form) – in short, in anything that is essentially creative and capable of inspiring cultural regeneration. Fichte would have said much the same of *Geist*, or, in this case, of *Genie* (genius).

If *Geist* has dropped out of the privileged place it occupied in the argument of *On the Spirit and the Letter in Philosophy*, it yet defines exactly what the scholar class must possess in order to function properly.

Various parts of the exposition in the later *Addresses to the German Nation* (1807–8) should also be consulted in this context. There, for example, he speaks of poetry in particular as having a special role in putting into action the principles of the transcendental philosophy. A living language "has within itself the power of infinite poetry, ever refreshing and renewing its youth, for every stirring of living thought in it opens up a new vein of poetic enthusiasm [*Begeisterung*]. To such a language, therefore, poetry is the highest and best means of flooding the life of all with the spiritual culture that has been attained." See Fichte (1968), p. 68; *SW*, VII, 334. The whole argument is very much in the spirit of Shelley.

From **Lecture IX**

OF THE ORAL SCHOLAR-TEACHER

Besides those possessors of the idea whose occupation it is to introduce the idea immediately into life by guiding and ordering the affairs of men,[1] there is yet another class, namely those who are strictly speaking and by pre-eminence called scholars; they express the idea directly in concepts, and their calling is to maintain among men the conviction that there is, in truth, a divine idea accessible to human thought, to raise this idea unceasingly to greater clarity and precision, and thus to transmit it from generation to generation fresh and radiant in ever-renewed youth.

The latter calling again divides itself into two very different occupations, according to the immediate purpose in view and the mode of its attainment. Either the minds of men are to be trained and cultivated to a capacity for receiving the idea, or the idea itself is to be produced in a definite form for those who are already prepared for its reception. The first occupation has particular men for its primary and immediate objects. In it the only use that is made of the idea is as a means of training and cultivating these men so that they may become capable of comprehending it through itself and by their own independent effort. In this occupation it follows that regard must be had solely to the men who are to be cultivated; to the level of their culture and their capacity for being cultivated. In this context an influence is valuable only in so far as it may be efficiently applied to those individuals for whom it is especially intended.[2] The second occupation has for its object the idea itself, and the developing and fashioning of it into a distinct concept. It has no reference whatsoever to any subjective disposition or capacity of men, and has no one especially in view as particularly called to or fitted for the reception of the idea in the form thus given to it. Its production [Werk] itself settles and determines by itself who shall grasp it, and it is addressed only to those who can grasp it. The first object will be best and most fittingly attained by the verbal discourses of the scholar-educator; the second through scholarly writings. . . .

Lecture X

OF THE AUTHOR [SCHRIFTSTELLER]

To complete and close our overall survey of the calling of the scholar, we have today to speak of the calling of the author.

I have hitherto contented myself with setting forth purely and clearly the idea of the specific objects of my inquiry, without turning aside to glance at the actual state of things in the present age. It is almost impossible to proceed in this way with the subject I am to discuss today. The concept of the author is as good as unknown in our age, and something most unworthy usurps its name. This is the particular disgrace of the time, and the true source of all its other evils in the realm of knowledge. The inglorious has become glorious and is encouraged, honoured and rewarded.

According to the almost universally received opinion it is a merit and an honour for a man to have printed something, merely because he has printed it and without any regard for what it is that is thus printed and what its consequences might be. And those who, as the phrase goes, review the works of others – who undertake to announce the fact that somebody has printed something and to describe it – also lay claim to the highest rank in the republic of learning. It is almost inexplicable that such an absurd opinion could have arisen and taken root, when we consider the subject in its true light.

This is how the matter stands: in the latter half of the last century reading took the place of some other amusements which had gone out of fashion. This new luxury from time to time demanded new fashionable goods, for it is of course quite impossible that one should read over again something one has already read, or those things our forefathers have read before us, just as it would be altogether unbecoming to appear frequently in fashionable society in the same costume, or to dress according to the notions of one's grandfather. The new want gave birth to a new trade, striving to nourish and enrich itself by supplying the wares now in demand: namely, bookselling. The success of those who first undertook this trade encouraged others to engage in it, until in our own days it has come to the point that this mode of obtaining a livelihood is greatly overextended, and the quantity of goods produced is much too large in proportion to the consumers. Like the dealer in any other commodity, the book-merchant orders his goods from the manufacturer solely with the view of bringing them to the market. At times also he buys uncommissioned goods which have been manufactured only on speculation. The author who writes for the sake of writing is this manufacturer. It is impossible to conceive of a reason why the book manufacturer should take precedence over any other manufacturer; he ought rather to feel that he is far inferior to the others, in that the luxury to which he panders is more pernicious than others. It may indeed be useful and profitable to him that he find a merchant for his wares, but how it should be an honour is not easy to discover. Of course, no value can be set on the judgement of the publisher, which is only a judgement on the saleableness or unsaleableness of the goods.[3]

Amid this bustle and pressure of the literary trade, a lucky thought struck someone: that is, to make one periodical book out of all the books which were printed, so that the reader of this book might be spared the trouble of reading any other. It was fortunate that this last purpose was not entirely successful, and that everybody did not take to reading this last book exclusively, since then no others would have been bought and consequently no others printed, so that this book itself, being constantly reliant upon other books for the possibility of its own existence, must likewise have remained unprinted.

He who undertook such a work, commonly called a 'learned library' or 'literary gazette' etc., had the advantage of seeing his work prosper by the charitable contributions of many anonymous individuals, and of thus earning honour and profit by the labour of others. To veil his own poverty of ideas he pretended to pass judgement on the authors whom he quoted – a shallow pretence to the thinker who looks below the surface. For either the book is a bad book, as most books are at present, and printed only that there might be one more book in the world (and in this case it ought never to have been written, and is a nullity, and so any judgement upon it is a nullity also); or the book is the sort of work that we shall describe below as a true literary [schriftstellerisch] work, and then is the result of a whole energetic life devoted to art or science, so that it would call for another entire life as energetic as the first to be employed in its judgement. Final judgement cannot be passed upon such a work in a couple of sheets put out within three or six months after its appearance. How can there be any honour in contributing to such collections? On the contrary, a good mind will rather be disposed to labour on a connected work, originated and planned out by itself, than to allow the current of its thoughts to be interrupted by every temporary phenomenon, lasting only until something else interrupts the interruption itself. The disposition to watch the thoughts of others continually, and to hang our own attempts at thinking, God willing, upon them, is a certain sign of immaturity and of a weak and dependent ability [Talent]. Or does the honour lie in the fact that those who undertake such works should consider us capable of filling the office of judge, actually making it over to us? In fact their judgement goes no deeper than that of a common unlettered printer, and applies to the saleableness or unsaleableness of the goods, and to the outward reputation which may thereby accrue to their critical academy [Recensions-Institute].[4]

I am aware that what I have now said might seem very paradoxical. All of us who are connected in any way with exact knowledge [Wissenschaft], which in this connection may be termed literature [Literatur], grow up in the belief that the literary industry is a blessing, an advantage, and an honourable distinction of our cultivated and philosophical age. Very few have the power to see through this presupposition and recognize its emptiness. The only apparent circumstance that can be adduced in defence of such perverted industry is in my opinion this: that thereby an extensive public is kept alive, roused to attention, and as it were held together, so that should anything of real value and importance be brought before it, a public shall be found already in existence, and will not have to be first called together. But I answer that, in the first place, the means appear much too extensive for the end contemplated. It seems too great a sacrifice that many generations should spend their time upon nothing in order that some future generation might be able to occupy itself with something. Moreover it is by no means true that a public is merely kept alive by this misdirected industry; it is at the same time perverted, vitiated and ruined for the appreciation of anything truly valuable. Much that is excellent has made its appearance in our age – I shall mention only the Kantian philosophy – but this very industriousness of the literary market has destroyed, perverted and degraded it so that its spirit has fled; now only a ghost of it stalks about, which no one can venerate.

The scholarly history [Gelehrten-Geschichte] of our own day shows the real thinker how writing for writing's sake may be honoured and applauded. A few only excepted, our authors have in their writings borne worse testimony against themselves than anyone else could have given against them. No even moderately well-disposed person would be inclined to consider the writers of our day so shallow, perverse and spiritless as the majority show themselves in their works. The only way to retain any respect for this age, or any desire to influence it, is to assume that those who proclaim their opinions aloud are inferior men, and that only among those who keep silence may be found some who are capable of teaching better things.

Thus, when I speak of the literary calling, it is not the literary trade of our age that I mean, but something quite other than that.

I have already set forth the concept of authorship, in distinguishing it from that of the oral teacher of prospective scholars. Both have to express and communicate the idea in language, the latter for particular individuals by whose capacity for receiving it he must be guided, and the former without regard to any individual and in the most perfect form that can be given to it in his age.

The author must represent the idea, and he must therefore be a partaker of it. All works of authorship are either works of art [Kunst] or of science [Wissenschaft]. Whatever may be the subject of a work of the first class, it is evident that since it does not directly express any special concept and thus teaches the reader nothing, it can only awaken the idea within him and furnish it with a fitting embodiment; otherwise it would be but an empty play of words and have no real content.[5] And whatever may be the subject of a scientific work, the author of it must not conceive of scientific knowledge in a merely historical fashion, only as it is received from others; he must have worked through it ideally and for himself in some one of its aspects, and produce in it a self-creative, new and hitherto unknown form. If he be but a link in the chain of historical tradition, and can do no more than hand down to others the doctrine as he himself has received it, and only in the form in which it already exists in the work whence he has obtained it, then let him leave others in peace to draw from the fountain from which he has drawn. What need is there of his officious mediation and meddling? To do over again that which has been done already is to do nothing, and no man who possesses common honesty and conscientiousness will allow himself to indulge in such idleness. Can his age then furnish him with no occupation suited to his powers, that he must thus employ himself in doing what he need not do? It is not necessary that he write an entirely new work in some branch of scientific knowledge, but only a better work than any hitherto existing. He who cannot do this should, emphatically, not write; it is a crime, a want of honesty to do so, which at the most can be excused only by his thoughtlessness and utter lack of any true concept of the business he has undertaken.

He must express the idea in language, in an intelligible manner and in a perfect form. The idea must therefore have become in him so clear, living and independent, that it of itself speaks out to him in words and, penetrating to the innermost spirit of his language, frames thence an embodiment for itself by its own inherent force. The idea itself must speak, not the author. His will, his individuality, his peculiar method and art, all must disappear from his page, so that only the method and art of his idea may live the highest life that it can attain in his language and in his time. As he is free from the obligation under which the oral teacher works – to accommodate himself to the capacities of others – so he does not have this excuse to plead before himself. He has no specific reader in view; he constructs his reader and lays down to him the law which he must obey. There may be printed productions addressed only to a certain age and certain circle – we shall see afterwards under what conditions such writings may be necessary – but these do not belong to the class of essentially literary [schriftstellerisch] works of which we now speak; they are printed discourses, which are printed because the circle to which they are addressed cannot be brought together.

In order that the idea may thus in his person become master of his language, it is necessary that the author shall first have acquired a mastery over that language. The idea does not seize upon the language directly, but only through him as its possessor. This indispensable mastery of the author over his language is acquired only by preparatory exercises, long continued and persevered in, which are studies for future works but have in themselves no essential value. The conscientious scholar writes them, indeed, but will never allow them to be printed. It requires, I say, long and persevering exercise; but happily these conditions mutually promote each other. As the idea becomes more vivid, language spontaneously appears, and as facility of expression is increased the idea flows forth in greater clarity.

These are the first and most necessary conditions of all true authorship. The idea itself – to express his idea in language in a particular way – is that which lives in him, and alone lives in him within whom the presentiment has arisen that he may one day send forth a literary work. It is this which drives him on in his preparations for that work, as well as in the future completion of his design.

By this idea he is inspired with a dignified and sacred conviction in the literary calling. The work of the oral scholar-teacher is in its immediate application only a work for its time, modified by the degree of culture possessed by those who are entrusted to his care. Only in so far as he can venture to suppose that he is cultivating future teachers worthy of their calling, who in their turn will train others for the same task, and so on without end, can he regard himself as working for eternity. But the work of the author is in itself a work for eternity. Even should future ages transcend the knowledge [Wissenschaft] expressed in his work, he has not therein recorded this knowledge alone, but also the fixed and settled character of his age in relation to it; and this will preserve its interest as long as the human race endures. Independent of all vicissitude and change, his characters [Buchstabe] speak in every age to all men who are able to make them live, and thus they continue their inspiring, elevating and ennobling work even to the end of time.[6]

The idea, in this its acknowledged sacredness, drives him on, and it alone drives him. He does not believe that he has attained anything until he has attained all, until his work stands before him in the purity and perfectness he has striven to attain. Devoid of love for his own person, and faithfully devoted to the idea by which he is constantly guided, he recognizes with certain vision and in its true character every trace of his former nature which remains in his expression of the idea, and strives unceasingly to free himself from it. As long as he is not conscious of this absolute freedom and purity, he has not attained his end, but still works on. In such an age as we have already described, where the quotation [Notiz] of knowledge has greatly increased and has even fallen into the hands of some who are better fitted for any occupation than for this one, it may be necessary for him to give some preliminary account of his labours. Other modes of communication, such as for example that of the oral scholar-teacher, may require such a preliminary account from him. But he will never put forth these required writings for anything else than what they are: preliminary announcements adapted to a certain age and certain circumstances. He will never regard them as finished works destined for immortality.

The idea alone drives him on, and nothing else. All personal concerns have disappeared from his sight. I do not speak of his own person, and of his having entirely forgotten himself in his purpose; this has already been sufficiently explained. But the personality of others has no more weight with him than his own, as against the truth and the idea. I do not mention his not encroaching upon the rights of other scholars or authors in their civic or personal relations. That is altogether below the dignity of one who has to do with real facts [Sache], and it is also below the dignity of these discourses to make mention of it.[7] But this I will say: that he will not allow himself to be restrained by forbearance towards any person whatsoever from demolishing error and establishing truth in its place. The worst insult that can be offered, even to a half-reasoning man, is to suppose that he can be offended by the exposure of an error he has entertained, or the proclamation of a truth which has escaped his notice. From this bold and open profession of truth as he recognizes it, without regard to any man, he will allow nothing to lead him away, not even the politely expressed contempt of the so-called fashionable world which can conceive of the literary calling only by analogy with its own social circles, and would impose the etiquette of the court upon the conduct of the scholar.

Here I close these lectures. If one of my thoughts has entered into any now present, and shall abide there as a guide to something better, then perhaps it may sometimes awaken the memory of these lectures and of me. Only in this way do I desire to live in your recollection.

Part 7

Schelling

Friedrich Wilhelm Joseph von Schelling

(1775–1854)

After a theological education during which he enjoyed the company and friendship of Hegel and Hölderlin (see Nauern, 1971), Schelling was appointed at the age of twenty-three to a professorship at Jena, where he became the colleague of Fichte and soon the friend of Schiller, Tieck, Goethe and others; he married A.W. Schlegel's divorced wife Caroline in 1803. After professorships at Würzburg, Munich, and Erlangen, he moved to Berlin in 1841.

Like Fichte, Schelling is relatively unfamiliar to the English-speaking tradition; it is only recently that a translation of the major work of his early period, the *System of Transcendental Idealism,* has appeared (1978). His thought is difficult, partly because it is more than usually uncongenial to English-speaking philosophical preoccupations, tending as it does toward a synthesis of everything (self, nature, science, and religion), and partly because scholars have had to concentrate on the task of plotting the different phases of Schelling's career, which has become something of a nightmare question for historians of philosophy. In the context of scientific theory Schelling is perhaps the major exponent of the *Naturphilosophie* (at least among the philosophers), purporting as it does to establish the grounds of an inner connection between all forms of life and expression on organic and dynamic principles. Although this may seem remote to us, its intentions are not totally at odds with the ambitions of those among modern physicists engaged in the search for a unified field theory, and it has been argued that Schelling's writings might have had a formative effect on, for example, the discovery of electromagnetism by Oersted: see Esposito (1977), pp. 137ff. In theology, Schelling's gradual elucidation of an element of evil was an important incorporation of a traditional problem into the spectrum of Idealism. In epistemology, his continuation and elaboration of Fichte's conviction of the simultaneous positing of self and other proved to be an important stage in the gradual bringing together of subjectivity and nature – a trend which indeed became much less gradual thanks to Schelling. In fact, it is with Schelling that German Romantic philosophy becomes most fully idealist, and it is also with Schelling that aesthetics are for the first and only time allowed to stand with philosophy as the ultimate and absolute expression of what is true and of value.

Further reading

Despite his obscurity and difficulty, it is also arguable that Schelling had a greater and more immediate influence on the English tradition than any of the other philosophers represented in this anthology, by virtue of Coleridge's famous borrowings. On his importance in this respect, see Wellek (1931), pp. 95–102; Orsini

223

(1969), pp. 192–237; McFarland (1969), pp. 146ff.; Ashton (1980), pp. 53–5; and for his typological suitability to an elucidation of English Romanticism, see Hirsch (1960). Lewes (1857), pp. 591f., may be consulted for a brief mid-century view of Schelling's general contribution to philosophy. For a more up to date account, see Copleston (1965a), pp. 121–82. Although they restrict their focus, much can be learned from two recent studies in English: Esposito (1977) and R.F. Brown (1977). See also Seidel (1976), Nauern (1971), and Fackenheim (1954).

At the time of the first appearance of the following selections in DS (1984), there was no extended account or translation into English of Schelling's lectures on aesthetics. At the present time of writing we may look forward to the publication of Douglas Stott's translation of the entire *Philosophy of Art*, forthcoming from the University of Minnesota Press. Wellek (1955), II, 74–82, summarizes a good deal in very little space; and Engell (1981) is helpful within its chosen limits. Michael Bullock has translated the 1807 oration, *Concerning the Relation of the Plastic Arts to Nature*, in Read (1968), pp. 323–58. There is a bibliography by Schneeberger (1954). For translations of others of Schelling's works into English, see the bibliography (Schelling, 1936, 1967, 1974, 1980).

DS

Conclusion to
System of Transcendental Idealism
[*System des transcendentalen Idealismus*]

1800

Concluding section

Translated by Albert Hofstadter (very slightly modified) in Hofstadter and Kuhns (1964), pp. 362–77.

German text in *Sämtliche Werke* (1856–61), III, 624ff.

Introductory note

By the time he published the *System of Transcendental Idealism* in 1800, Schelling had already initiated the exposition of his philosophy of nature, which removed the hypothetical element from the argument of Kant's 'Critique of Teleological Judgement' and put forward as a matter of fact that nature is a coherent and self-evolving system moving toward ends in a purposive way. In this work, broadly speaking, he explores the implications of this philosophy for self-consciousness, starting *from* self-consciousness in the true spirit of the transcendental method as maintained by Fichte. Before the final sections, here translated, Schelling has worked through all the primitive and developing stages of self-consciousness in its positing of the not-self, or objective world, and the consequent reflective intuition of self as free intelligence. The *System* is one of the masterpieces of German Idealism, both in itself and because of its important prefiguring of some of the central issues in Hegel's philosophy: it incorporates an argued recognition of other selves and the element of biographical and historical time, as well as a wider social dimension of ethics and politics – synthesizing into a single argument subjects which Fichte had tended to deal with separately, albeit synoptically.

What makes the *System* unique from our particular point of view is that it is the only major philosophical text to argue for aesthetics and the fine arts as the pinnacle and conclusive representation of its insights. As early as 1796, in his prospectus for a system of philosophy, Schelling had been emphatic about the role of aesthetics:

I am convinced that the highest act of reason, the one in which she encompasses all Ideas, is an aesthetic act . . . The philosopher must possess just as much aesthetic power as the poet . . . the poetic act alone will outlive all the arts and sciences.

Schelling (1966), pp. xii–xiii

225

Much of the thinking behind this assertion seems to have to do with the capacity of the art object to reach a wider public than abstract philosophy alone can do:

Unless we have made the Ideas aesthetic, i.e., mythological, they are of no interest to the people; and conversely, until mythology has been made rational, the philosopher can only be ashamed of it.   Schelling (1966), p. xiii

3. Corollaries

Having derived the nature and character of the art product as fully as was required for the present investigation, nothing remains but to give an account of the relation in which the philosophy of art stands to the whole system of philosophy in general.

1. Philosophy as a whole starts from, and must start from, a principle which, as the absolute identity, is completely nonobjective. How then is this absolutely nonobjective principle to be evoked in consciousness and understood, which is necessary if it is the condition of understanding the whole of philosophy? No proof is needed of the impossibility of apprehending or presenting it by means of concepts [Begriffe]. Nothing remains, therefore, but that it be presented in an immediate intuition; yet this itself seems incomprehensible and, since its object is supposed to be something absolutely nonobjective, even self-contradictory. If, however, there were nevertheless such an intuition, which had as object that which was absolutely identical, in itself neither subjective nor objective, and if on behalf of this intuition, which can only be an intellectual intuition, one were to appeal to immediate experience, by what means could this intuition be established as objective, i.e., how could we establish beyond doubt that it does not rest on a merely subjective illusion, unless there were an objectivity belonging to the intuition which was universal and acknowledged by all men? This universally acknowledged and thoroughly undeniable objectivity of intellectual intuition is art itself. For aesthetic intuition is precisely intellectual intuition become objective.[1] The work of art merely reflects to me what is otherwise reflected by nothing, that absolutely identical principle which has already divided itself in the ego. Thus what for the philosopher divides itself already in the first act of consciousness, and which is otherwise inaccessible to any intuition, shines back to us from its products by the miracle of art.

But not only the first principle of philosophy and the first intuition from which it proceeds, but also the whole mechanism which philosophy deduces and on which it itself rests, becomes objective for the first time through aesthetic production.

Philosophy starts out from an infinite dichotomy of opposed activities; but all aesthetic production rests on the same dichotomy, which latter is completely resolved [aufgehoben] by each artistic representation. What then is the marvellous faculty by which, according to the assertions of philosophers, an infinite opposition annuls itself [sich aufhebt] in productive intuition? We have until now been unable to make this mechanism fully comprehensible because it is only the faculty of art that can fully disclose it. This productive faculty under consideration is the same as that by which art also attains to the impossible, namely, to resolve [aufzuheben] an infinite contradiction in a finite product. It is the poetic faculty which, in the first potency, is original intuition, and conversely it is only productive intuition repeating itself in the highest potency that we call the poetic faculty.[2] It is one and the same thing that is active in both, the sole capacity by which we are able to think and comprehend even what is contradictory – the imagination [Einbildungskraft].[3] Hence also it is products of one and the same activity that appear to us beyond consciousness as real and on the hither side of consciousness as ideal or as a world of art. But precisely this fact, that under otherwise entirely identical conditions of origin, the genesis of one lies beyond consciousness and that of the other on this side of consciousness, constitutes the eternal and ineradicable difference between the two.

For while the real world proceeds wholly from the same original opposition as that from which the world of art must proceed (bearing in mind that the art world must also be thought of as a single great whole, and presents in all of its individual products only the one infinite), nevertheless the opposition beyond consciousness is infinite only to the extent that an infinite is presented by the objective world as a *whole* and never by the individual object, whereas for art the opposition is infinite in regard to *each individual object,* and every single product of art presents infinity. For if aesthetic production proceeds from freedom, and if the opposition of conscious and unconscious activity is absolute precisely for freedom, then there exists really only a single absolute work of art, which can to be sure exist in entirely different exemplars but which yet is only one, even though it should not yet exist in its most original form. To this view it cannot be objected that it would be inconsistent with the great freedom with which the predicate "work of art" is used. That which does not present an infinite immediately or at least in reflection is not a work of art. Shall we, e.g., also call poems works of art that by their nature present merely what is individual and subjective? Then we shall also have to apply the name to every epigram that records a merely momentary feeling or current impression.[4] Yet the great masters who worked in these literary types sought to achieve objectivity only through the *whole* of their writings, and used them only as means whereby to represent a whole infinite life and to reflect it by a many-faceted mirror.

2. If aesthetic intuition is only intellectual intuition become objective, then it is evident that art is the sole true and eternal organon as well as

document of philosophy, which sets forth in ever fresh forms what philosophy cannot represent outwardly, namely, the unconscious in action and production and its original identity with the conscious. For this very reason art occupies the highest place for the philosopher, since it opens to him, as it were, the holy of holies where in eternal and primal union, as in a single flame, there burns what is sundered in nature and history and what must eternally flee from itself in life and action as in thought. The view of nature which the philosopher composes artificially [künstlich] is, for art [Kunst], original and natural. What we call nature is a poem that lies hidden in a mysterious and marvellous script. Yet if the riddle could reveal itself, we would recognize in it the Odyssey of the spirit which, in a strange delusion, seeking itself, flees itself; for the land of phantasy [Phantasie] toward which we aspire gleams through the world of sense only as through a half-transparent mist, only as a meaning does through words. When a great painting comes into being it is as though the invisible curtain that separates the real from the ideal world is raised [aufgehoben]; it is merely the opening through which the characters and places of the world of fantasy, which shimmers only imperfectly through the real world, fully come upon the stage. Nature is nothing more to the artist than it is to the philosopher; it is merely the ideal world appearing under unchanging limitations, or it is merely the imperfect reflection of a world that exists not outside but within him.

What is the derivation of this affinity of philosophy and art, despite their opposition? This question is already sufficiently answered by the foregoing.

We conclude therefore with the following observation. A system is completed when it has returned to its starting point. But this is precisely the case with our system. For it is just that original ground of all harmony of the subjective and the objective which could be presented in its original identity only by intellectual intuition, that was fully brought forth from the subjective and became altogether objective by means of the work of art, in such a way that we have conducted our object, the ego itself, gradually to the point at which we ourselves stood when we began to philosophize.

But now, if it is art alone that can succeed in making objective with universal validity what the philosopher can only represent subjectively, then it is to be expected (to draw this further inference) that as philosophy, and with it all the sciences that were brought to perfection by it, was born from and nurtured by poetry in the childhood of science, so now after their completion they will return as just so many individual streams to the universal ocean of poetry from which they started out. On the whole it is not difficult to say what will be the intermediate stage in the return of science to poetry, since one such intermediate stage existed in mythology before this seemingly irresolvable breach occurred. But how a new mythology (which cannot be the invention of an individual poet but only of a new generation that represents things as if it were a single poet) can itself arise, is a problem for whose solution we must look to the future destiny of the world and the further course of history alone.[5]

General observation on the whole system

If the reader who has followed our progress attentively up to this point once more contemplates the organization of the whole, he will doubtless make the following observations.

The entire system falls between two extremes, of which one is characterized by intellectual and the other by aesthetic intuition. What intellectual intuition is for the philosopher, aesthetic intuition is for his object. The former, since it is necessary merely for the particular orientation of mind [Geist] adopted in philosophizing, does not at all occur in ordinary consciousness. The latter, since it is nothing but intellectual intuition become objective or universally valid, *can* at least occur in every consciousness. But this also makes it possible to see that and why philosophy *as* philosophy can never be universally valid. Absolute objectivity is given to art alone. If art is deprived of objectivity, one may say, it ceases to be what it is and becomes philosophy; give objectivity to philosophy, it ceases to be philosophy and becomes art. Philosophy, to be sure, reaches the highest level, but it brings only, as it were, a fragment of man to this point. Art brings *the whole man*, as he is, to that point, namely to a knowledge of the highest of all, and on this rests the eternal difference and the miracle of art.

Furthermore, the whole continuity of transcendental philosophy rests merely on a continuous potentiation of self-intuition, from the first, simplest stage in self-consciousness to the highest stage, the aesthetic.

The following are the potencies that the object of philosophy traverses so as to produce the total structure of self-consciousness.

The act of self-consciousness in which at the beginning the absolutely identical principle divides itself is nothing but an art of *self-intuition in general*. Consequently, nothing definite can yet be posited by this act in the ego, since it is only through it that all definiteness in general is posited. In this first act the identity first becomes subject and object simultaneously, i.e., it becomes in general ego – not for itself but for philosophizing reflection.

(What the identity is abstracted from and, as it were, might be *before* this act, cannot at all be asked. For it is that which can reveal itself *only* through self-consciousness and can in no way separate itself from this act).

The second self-intuition is that by which the ego intuits the definiteness posited in the objective aspect of its activity, which occurs in sensation. In this intuition the ego is *an object for itself*, whereas in the preceding one it was object and subject only for the philosopher.

In the third self-intuition the ego becomes an object for itself also as sensing, i.e., the previously subjective phase in the ego is transposed into an objective phase. Everything in the ego, consequently, is now objective, or the ego is *wholly* objective and *as* objective it is simultaneously subject and object.

From this moment of consciousness nothing will therefore be able to remain behind except what exists, in accordance with the consciousness that has already arisen, as the absolutely objective (the external world). In this intuition, which is already potentiated and for that very reason productive, there is contained in addition to the objective and subjective activities which are *both* objective here, still a third, a genuinely intuiting or *ideal* activity, the very same as later comes to view as *conscious* activity. But since it is merely the third of the other two, it cannot separate itself from them nor be set in opposition to them. Thus there is a conscious activity already comprised in this intuition, or the unconscious objective element is determined by a conscious activity, except that the latter is not differentiated as such.

The following intuition will be that by which the ego intuits itself as productive. However, since the ego is now *merely* objective, this intuition will also be *merely* objective, i.e., once again unconscious. There is indeed in this intuition an ideal activity which has as its objective the intuiting, virtually ideal activity comprised within the preceding intuition; the intuiting activity here is thus an ideal one to the second potency, i.e., a purposive activity which is, however, unconsciously purposive. What remains behind of this intuition in consciousness will thus indeed appear as purposive, but not as a purposively produced product. Such a result is *organization* [*Organisation*] throughout its entire range.[6]

By the way of these four stages the ego is completed as intelligence.[7] It is apparent that up to this point nature keeps pace with the ego, and hence that nature doubtless lacks only the final feature, whereby all the intuitions attain for it the same significance they have for the ego. But what this final feature may be will become evident from what follows.

If the ego were to continue to be *merely* objective, self-intuition could potentiate itself on and on to infinity; in this way the series of products in nature would merely be increased, but consciousness would never arise. Consciousness is possible only in so far as the merely objective element in the ego becomes objective *for the ego itself.* For the ego is absolutely identical with that *merely* objective phase. The ground, therefore, can only lie outside the ego, which is gradually narrowed, by progressive delimitation, to intelligence and even to individuality. *Outside* the individual, however, i.e., independent of it, there is only *intelligence itself.* But intelligence itself must (according to the deduced mechanism) limit itself, where it is, to individuality. The ground sought outside the individual can therefore lie only in *another individual.*

That which is absolutely objective can become an object *for the ego itself* only by means of the influence of another rational being. But the design of such an influence must already have lain in this latter being. Thus freedom is always already presupposed in nature (nature does not generate it), and where it is not already present as a first principle it can never arise. Here, therefore, it becomes evident that although nature is completely equal to intelligence up to this point and runs through the same potencies as intelligence, nevertheless freedom, *if* it exists (*that* it exists, however, cannot be proved theoretically), must be superior to nature (*natura prior*).

Hence a new sequence of actions, which are not possible by means of nature but leave it behind, begins at this point.

The absolutely objective element or the lawfulness of intuition becomes an object for the ego itself. But intuition becomes an object for the intuiting agent only by means of will [Wollen]. The objective element in will is intuition itself, or the pure lawfulness of nature; the subjective element is an ideal activity directed upon that lawfulness in itself; the act in which this happens is the *absolute act of will* [*absolute Willensakt*].

For the ego the absolute act of will itself becomes once more an object in that, for the ego, the objective element in will, directed toward something external, becomes object in the form of natural impulse, while the subjective element, directed toward lawfulness in itself, becomes object in the form of absolute will, i.e., categorical imperative.[8] But this, again, is not possible without an activity superior to both. This activity is *free choice* or *free will* [*Willkür*], or consciously free activity.

Now if this consciously free activity (which is opposed to the objective activity present in action, although it has to become one with it immediately) is intuited in its original identity with the objective activity (which is absolutely impossible by means of freedom) then there arises thereby the highest potency of self-intuition. Since this itself already lies above and beyond the *conditions* of consciousness and rather is itself consciousness self-creative from the beginning, it must appear to be simply accidental wherever it is; and this simply accidental feature in the highest potency of self-intuition is what is signified by the idea of *genius* [*Genie*].

These are the moments in the history of self-consciousness, invariable and fixed for all knowledge, which are expressed in experience by a continuous sequence of levels that can be exhibited and pursued from simple matter to organization (by which unconsciously productive nature returns into itself) and from that point through reason and free choice up to the highest union of freedom and necessity in art (by which nature, become consciously productive, closes and consummates itself in itself).

From *Philosophy of Art*
[*Philosophie der Kunst*]

Lectures given in Jena in the winter of 1802–3, and repeated in 1804–5 in Würzburg

Translated by Elizabeth Rubenstein and DS.

German text in *SW, V*, 718f.

Introductory note

Schelling's 1802–3 lectures are openly and consciously eclectic, drawing frequently upon the work of August Wilhelm and Friedrich Schlegel as well as upon other contemporaries and precursors. To try to recover all the borrowings and overlaps, and to assess the precise degree of Schelling's deviations from them, would be a considerable scholarly task, one which the present editor has not attempted. This is especially true of the account of Shakespeare, who had been widely translated into German (although the great Schlegel and Tieck translation was only 'under way' when Schelling was giving these lectures), and was already regarded as an adopted son by the German critics and theorists. Some account of the place of Shakespeare in German Romanticism can be gained by consulting Stahl (1947), Pascal (1937), and Ralli (1932), I, 108f.

Crabb Robinson (1929), p. 119, noted the remarks Schelling delivered at a dinner party in December 1802:

the Raptures with which he speaks of Shakespear are boundless – tho' he praises so mystically & so metaphysically that you wo^d not be able to comprehend one Word of his Eulogy And he does not scruple to say that not one of the Editors of Shakespear has the least presentim' or suspicion of his real Worth: Shakespear is a sealed book to the whole english Nation.

This mood of excessive praise does not however completely accord with the arguments of the lectures, given below.

On modern dramatic poetry

I shall continue with an exposition of tragedy and comedy in the modern dramatists. So as not to be completely submerged in this vast sea, I shall seek to draw attention to the few major points on which modern drama *differs* from the ancient, and to remark on its *coincidence* with it, and on its own specific features. I shall base these relationships once again on the determinate view [Anschauung] of what we must recognize as the most important phenomena in modern tragedy and comedy. Therefore in considering the major points I shall refer especially to Shakespeare.

The first thing which we must begin by considering is that the *combination [Mischung] of opposites*, thus of the tragic and comic especially, is the fundamental principle of modern drama. The following reflection will serve to make us grasp the importance of this combination: the tragic and the comic could be presented in a state of completeness as an unsublimated [nicht aufgehobenen] indifference,[1] but then the poetry [Poesie] would have to be neither tragic nor comic. It would be quite a different genre: it would be epic poetry. In epic poetry the two elements which are stressfully at variance in the drama are not united but yet not truly separate. The combination of these two elements in such a way that they do not appear at all separate cannot therefore be the distinguishing feature of modern tragedy, which entails rather a combination in which both are clearly differentiated and in such a way that the poet shows himself to be simultaneously master of both, as is Shakespeare, who focusses dramatic energy toward both opposite poles. And the *most heartrending* Shakespeare is in Falstaff and in Macbeth.

Yet we can consider this combination of opposing elements as the striving of modern drama to return to the epic, without thereby becoming epic; just as on the other hand the same poetry in the epic strives toward the dramatic through the novel. This poetry thus overcomes the pure limits of the higher art forms from both sides.

For this *combination* it is necessary that the poet has not simply got pieces of tragedy and pieces of comedy at his command, but that he should be a master of nuances; like Shakespeare, who in the comic is tender, adventurous and witty all at the same time, as in *Hamlet,* and earthy (as in the Falstaff plays) without ever being vulgar; just as in the tragic he is devastating (as in *Lear*), punishing (as in *Macbeth*), and stirring, touching and calming, as in *Romeo and Juliet* and in other plays in the mixed mode.

Let us now look at the subject matter of modern tragedy. This also had to have a mythological dignity [Würde], at least in its most perfect manifestation. There were therefore only three possible sources out of which the subject matter could be derived. The separate myths which, like those of Greek tragedy, had not unified themselves into epic wholes, remained outside the broad circle of the universal epic: they were expressed in the modern world through the *novellas*. Legendary or poetic history [Historie] provided a second source. The third source is made up of religious myths and legends and the stories of the saints. Shakespeare took material from the first two of these, since the third did not provide subject matter suited to his age and to his nation. It was especially the Spanish, among them Calderón, who took material from here. Shakespeare, therefore, found his material ready made. In this sense he was not an *inventor*, but in the way he used, arranged and brought to life his materials he showed himself in *his* sphere to be like the ancient dramatists and to be the wisest of artists. It has been remarked and it is a fact that Shakespeare committed himself to the exact details of the given material, especially that of the novellas; that he included everything, down to the most minor circumstance, and left nothing out (this is a practice which could perhaps often throw light on the apparently groundless elements in some of his plots), changing what he was given as little as possible.[2]

Here too he is like the ancients – except Euripides, who as the more frivolous poet deliberately distorts the myths.

The next undertaking is [to decide] how far or not the essence of ancient tragedy is present in the modern. Is there a true idea of fate to be found in modern tragedy? Indeed, of that higher fate which in itself incorporates freedom?

As observed, Aristotle defines the supreme instance of tragedy as occurring when a just man commits a crime by mistake [Irrthum]. It must be added that this mistake is inflicted by necessity or by the gods, possibly even *against* freedom.[3] According to the concepts of the Christian religion this last example would seem to be impossible. Those powers which undermine the will and inflict not only harm but *evil* are themselves evil and infernal powers.

At the very least if a mistake caused by divine decree were to bring about calamity and crime, then in that same religion according to which this were a possibility there would also have to be the possibility of a corresponding forgiveness. This is certainly there in Catholicism which, by its nature a mixture of the sacred and the profane, ordains sin in order to demonstrate the power of the means of grace in the forgiveness of sin. Thus in Catholicism the possibility of the *true* tragic fate existed, though it differed from that of the ancients.[4]

Shakespeare was a Protestant, and this possibility was not open to him. If there is a fate in his work it can only be of a twofold nature. Harm is brought about by conjuring up evil and demonic powers, but according to Christian concepts these cannot be invincible, and resistance to them should *and* can be made. The inescapability of their effect, in so far as it is made apparent, is reflected in and reverts to the character [Charakter] or subject. So it is with Shakespeare. Character takes the place of the ancient tragic fate [Schicksal], but he places within it such a mighty destiny [Fatum] that it can be no longer regarded as free. Indeed, it stands forth as insuperable necessity.

A demonic trickery lures Macbeth into murder but there is no objective need for the deed. Banquo does not allow himself to be beguiled by the voice of the witches, but Macbeth does. Therefore it is character which decides.

The childish folly of an old man is presented in Lear in the manner of a confusing delphic oracle, and the sweet Desdemona has to submit to the dark stain which is coupled with jealousy.

Because he had to place the necessity for the crime in the *character,* Shakespeare has had for the same reason to deal with the case *not* accepted by Aristotle as tragic, that of the criminal who plunges from happiness into misfortune with a terrible indifference.[5] In the place of fate in itself he has *nemesis* in all its forms, where horror is overwhelmed by horrors, one wave of blood drives the next one on, and the curse of the cursed is constantly being fulfilled, as the Wars of the Roses exemplify in English history. He *has* to show himself as a barbarian since he undertakes to show the worst kind of barbarity, such as the brutal battles of families amongst themselves, where all art [Kunst] seems at an end and brute force takes its place, as it is said in *Lear:*

> It will come,
> Humanity must perforce prey on itself,
> Like monsters of the deep.[6]

But here there are signs to be found that he has sent the grace [Anmuth] of art amongst the *furies,* who do not appear in their own shapes. Such is Margaret's love lament over the head of her unlawful and guilty lover and her parting from him.[7]

Shakespeare ends the sequence with Richard III, whom he makes pursue and attain his goal with monstrous energy, until he is driven from the heights of his achievement into the tight corner of despair. In the turmoil of the battle in which he is defeated he calls out, irretrievably lost:

> A horse! a horse! my kingdom for a horse![8]

In *Macbeth,* revenge forces its way step by step towards a nobler criminal led astray by an immoderate ambition, in such a way that, deceived by demonic illusions, he believes it to be far away.

A more gentle, indeed the mildest nemesis is to be found in *Julius Caesar.* Brutus does not perish so much because of avenging powers as because of the very mildness of a fine and tender disposition which moves him to take the wrong measures after the deed. He had made of his deed a sacrifice to virtue, as he believed he had to, and thereby sacrifices himself to it.

The difference between this nemesis and true *fate [Schicksal]* is however very significant. It comes from the real world and is rooted in *reality;* it is the nemesis that governs history, and Shakespeare found it *there* like the rest of his material. What brings it about is *freedom* quarrelling with *freedom;* it is a *sequence of events [Succession],* and the revenge is not immediately one with the crime.

In the cycle of the Greek presentations a nemesis also dominates, but here necessity is limited and punished directly by necessity, and each situation taken on its own was a completed action.

From the very beginning all the tragic myths of the Greeks belonged more to art, and a steady communication and interpenetration of gods and men, as of fate, was natural to them, as well as the concept of an irresistible influence. Perhaps *chance* [*Zufall*] itself plays a part in one of the most unfathomable of Shakespeare's plays *(Hamlet)*, but Shakespeare perceived it *with* its consequences: it is therefore intended by him and makes the greatest sense.

If after this we want to express in one word what Shakespeare is in relation to the sublime nature of ancient tragedy, then we will have to name him as the greatest inventor in *the realm of character* [*Charakteristischen*]. He cannot portray that sublime and as it were purified and transfigured beauty which proves itself against fate and becomes one with moral goodness – he cannot portray the beauty that he does portray in such a way that it appears in the *whole* and so that the totality of each work bears its image. He *knows* the highest beauty only as individual character. He has not been able to subordinate everything to it, because as a modern, who conceives of the eternal not within limits but in the unlimited, he is too diffuse in his universality. The ancients had a concentrated universality, a totality not in multiplicity but in unity.[9]

There is *nothing* in man that Shakespeare did not touch on, but he treats it individually whereas the Greeks treat it in its totality. The highest and the lowest elements in human nature lie dispersed in him: he knows *everything*, every passion, every state of mind, in youth and age, in the king and the shepherd boy. From the volumes of his works one would be able to recreate the lost earth. That ancient lyre on its own managed to draw the whole world out of *four* notes; the new instrument has a thousand strings.[10] It splits up the harmony of the universe in order to recreate it, and thus is always less soothing for the soul. The austere, all-assuaging beauty can only exist in simplicity.

In accordance with the nature of the romantic principle modern comedy does not present the action as pure or isolated, or with the representational limits [*plastischen Beschränkung*] of ancient drama, but it presents all that goes with it at the same time. Only Shakespeare has given his tragedy the most concentrated wealth of detail and succinctness in every part as well as in the broad whole, but yet without any arbitrary excess and in such a way that it appears as the richness of nature itself, apprehended by artistic necessity. The intention of the *whole* remains clear, but then again plunges to inexhaustible depths where all points of view can be absorbed.

It goes without saying that with this kind of universality Shakespeare's world is not a limited one, and is not an ideal world, in as much as the ideal world itself is a limited and closed one. But on the other hand it is not the world that is directly opposed to the ideal, the formal [conventionelle] world by which the miserable taste of the French has replaced the ideal.

Shakespeare never portrays either an ideal or a formal world but always the *real* world. The ideal appears in him in the construction of his plays. Moreover he is able to place himself with ease into every nationality and period as if it were his own, i.e. he draws them as *wholes* untroubled by less important details.

What men undertake, how and where they are able to do it, all this Shakespeare knew. He is therefore at home everywhere; nothing is strange or astonishing to him. He observes a much higher spectacle than that of customs and times. The style of his plays is determined by the subject and they differ one from another (in no way according to chronology) according to the harshness, softness, regularity or freedom of the verses, and the brevity and abruptness or the length of the sentences.

Now, to make mention of what remains to be said about the outward structure of modern tragedy, and in order not to waste time describing the necessary changes which must result from the differences already mentioned (such as the abandoning of the three unities, the division of the whole into scenes, etc.): so, again, the *combination* of prose and verse in modern drama is the outward expression of its inwardly mixed epic and dramatic nature. Leaving aside the so-called domestic or inferior tragedies [Trauerspielen] where the characters quite justifiably express themselves in prose, its use *from time to time* was necessary just because of the exposition of dramatic richness in secondary characters. Shakespeare has shown himself a master in this combination of prose and verse and in observing what is right as far as the language is concerned; not only in individual instances but in the work as a whole. Thus in *Hamlet* the structure of the sentences is confused, abrupt, troubled like the hero. In the historical plays based on early and more recent English and on Roman history, there prevails a very discrepant tone in terms of cultivation and purity. In the Roman plays there is almost no verse. On the other hand in the English plays, especially those based on early history, there is a great deal that is exceedingly picturesque [pittoresk].

The accusations of perversity and even coarseness that people make against Shakespeare are mostly not valid, and are only considered to be so by a narrow and feeble taste. Yet by no one does his true greatness go more unrecognized than by his fellow countrymen, the *English* critics and admirers. They cling to single presentations of passion or of a character; to the psychology, to scenes, to words, without any feeling for the whole, or for art. When one takes a look at the English critics, as Tieck says very tellingly, it is as if, travelling in a beautiful landscape, one were to pass by an inn in front of which drunken peasants were squabbling.[11]

That Shakespeare wrote by some happy inspiration and in completely unconscious mastery of his art is a very common error and a myth put about by a completely misinformed age, one which began in England with Pope.[12] Of course the Germans often misunderstood him, not just because they perhaps knew him only from a crude translation, but because the belief in art had disappeared altogether.

The poems of Shakespeare's youth – the *Sonnets*, *Adonis*, and *Lucrece* – testify to an extremely love-worthy nature and to a very *heartfelt, subjective* feeling, not to any unconscious genius-inspired storm or stress [Genie-Sturm oder Drang].[13] After this Shakespeare lived wholly in the world, as far as his environment allowed, until he began to reveal his existence in a world without any bounds, and to set it down in a series of works of art which truly portray the total infinity of art and nature.

Shakespeare's genius [Genius] is so all-encompassing that his name, like Homer's, could be taken to be a collective name; and as has indeed already happened, his works could be ascribed to different authors. (Here the individual is collective in the same way that the work is with the ancients.)

We might still view Shakespeare's art with a kind of hopelessness if we were absolutely bound to regard him as the zenith of romantic art in the drama; for barbarism must first be allowed him in order that he be seen as great, indeed divine within it. In his unboundedness Shakespeare cannot be compared with any of the ancient tragedians, but we must however be allowed to hope for a Sophocles of the differentiated [differenzürten] world, and to hope for appeasement in an art which is as it were *sinful*. At least the possibility of the fulfilment of this expectation seems to have been hinted at by a hitherto less well known source.[14]

On Dante in Relation to Philosophy
[Über Dante in philosophischer Beziehung]

1803

Translated by Elizabeth Rubenstein and DS.

German text in *SW*, V, 152–63. First published in *Kritisches Journal der Philosophie*, II (1803), 35–50.

Introductory note

Schelling's essay on Dante in many ways continues the themes outlined in the remarks on Shakespeare. Dante's importance as the prototype of the modern artist depends upon his creation of an individual mythology; thus he sets an example for other possible representations of the fragmented world.

Much of what Schelling says here is taken over (and acknowledged) by A.W. Schlegel in his *Lectures on Fine Art and Literature* (see 1962–74, IV, 169–81), who also finds Dante prophetic of the whole of modern poetry. Schlegel had written on Dante earlier, and had himself translated the *Inferno* along with sections of the other two parts of the *Divine Comedy*. Schelling's essay is apparently in reaction to Friedrich Bouterwek's negative judgement in his *Geschichte der Poesie und Beredsamkeit* (1801): see Wellek (1955), II, 80.

Those who love the past more than the present will not find it strange to find themselves drawn away from its not always rewarding aspects and taken back to such a distant monument of philosophy combined with poetry as the works of Dante, which have long been overshadowed by the sacrosanctness of antiquity.

As justification for the space which these thoughts here occupy, I demand for the time being no other admission than that the poem to which they refer presents one of the most remarkable problems concerning the philosophical and historical construction of art. What follows will show that this inquiry contains within it a far more general one, which concerns the circumstances of philosophy itself, and is of no less interest for philosophy than for poetry. Their reciprocal merging, to which the whole modern age is inclined, demands equally determinate conditions on both sides.[1]

> In the Holy of Holies,
> where religion and poetry ally,

stands Dante as the high priest and he who initiates the whole course of
modern art. Representing not just one single poem but the whole genre
of modern poetry, and even a genre in its own right, the *Divine Comedy*
stands so completely apart that no theory abstrated from individual models
is adequate to describe it. As a world of its own, it demands its own theory.
The author gave it the epithet 'divine' because it deals with theology and
divine things; he called it a 'comedy' according to the basic concepts of
this and of the opposite genre: because of the terrifying beginning and
happy outcome, and because the mixed nature of his poem, whose subject
matter is part sublime and part humble, makes a mixed kind of recitation
necessary.

But it is easy to see that it cannot be called 'dramatic' according to the
generally accepted concepts, because it does not portray a limited action.
In as much as Dante himself is viewed as the main protagonist, one who
serves as the link between the immeasurable series of visions and portraits,
and who behaves passively rather than actively, then the poem might seem
to approach the novel. But this definition does so little justice to the poem
that it could be called 'epic', after another more common view
[Vorstellung], since there is no sequential continuity in the objects portrayed.[2] To view it as a didactic poem is equally impossible, since it is written with a much more imprecise form and intention than that of the didactic poem. It is therefore not a particular example of any of the above, nor
is it merely a combination of various parts of each. It is a quite unique and
as it were organic fusion of all the elements of these genres, which cannot
be reproduced by any arbitrary skill [Kunst]. It is an absolutely individual
thing, not comparable to anything outside itself.

Broadly speaking, the subject matter of the poem is the clear-cut, essential identity of the whole age in which the poet lived, the imbuing of its
events with the ideas [Ideen] of religion, scientific knowledge
[Wissenschaft] and poetry [Poesie], conceived of in the most superior
mind of that century. But it is not our intention to look at the poem in its
immediate relation to its own time, but rather to see it in its universal validity [Allgemeingültigkeit] and in its role of archetype for the whole of modern poetry.

The necessary law governing the as yet undetermined, far-away point
where the great epic of modern times, which has revealed itself up to now
only rhapsodically and in single manifestations, emerges as a complete
totality, is this: that the individual moulds that part of the world revealed
to him into a whole, and creates his own mythology [Mythologie] from the
material of his age, from its history and its scientific learning. For just as
the ancient world is in general a world of types, so the modern is one of
individuals. There it is the general that is truly particular; the species acts
as a single individual. Here on the other hand the point of departure is
particularity, which is supposed to become general. For that reason every-

thing among the ancients is enduring and everlasting. Number seems to have no force, since the concept of the general fuses with that of the individual. Among the moderns change and alteration are a constant law. Not a completed, closed circle but one to be endlessly expanded through individuality determines its modifications, and because universality is of the essence of poetry, the necessary requirement is this: that through the most supreme uniqueness the individual should become universally valid again. Through fully developed particularity he must become once more absolute. It is through the sheer individuality of his poem, comparable to nothing else, that Dante is the creator of modern art, which cannot be conceived of without this arbitrary necessity and necessary arbitrariness.

From the very beginnings of Greek poetry, in Homer onwards, we see a poetry clearly distinct from scientific learning and philosophy, and this process of separation continued right up to the total polarization of poets and philosophers, who sought in vain to effect a harmony through allegorical explanations of the Homeric poems. In more recent times scientific knowledge has moved ahead of poetry and mythology, which indeed cannot be mythology without being universal and drawing into itself all elements of the existing culture – science, religion, art itself – and combining not just the material of the present but also that of the past to form a perfect unity. Since art demands the completed, the self-contained, and the limited, while the spirit of the modern world pushes towards the unlimited and tears down every barrier with unshakable determination, the individual must enter into this conflict, but with absolute freedom. He must seek to achieve lasting shapes out of the confusion of the age, and into the arbitrarily produced forms of the images of his poetry [Dichtung] he must again impart universal validity.

This Dante has done. He had the material of present as of past history in front of him. He could not work it into a pure epic, partly because of its nature, partly because by so doing he would have excluded other aspects of the culture of his time. Contemporary astronomy, theology and philosophy also belonged to this whole. He could not present them in a didactic poem because he would thereby limit himself once more, and in order to be universal his poem had to be at the same time historical. There was need of a completely freely willed [willkürlich] invention, emanating from the individual and able to combine this material and shape it organically into a whole. To present the ideas of philosophy and theology in symbols [Symbole] was impossible because there was no symbolic mythology in existence.[3] No more could he make his poem completely allegorical, because it would then no longer be historical. Therefore it had to be a completely unique mixture of the allegorical and the historical. In the exemplary poetry [Poesie] of the ancients no alternative of this kind was possible.[4] Only the individual was able to seize it, only free invention pure and simple could pursue it.

Dante's poem is not allegorical in the sense that the figures simply stand for something else, without being independent of this meaning and thus something in themselves. On the other hand none of them is independent of the meaning in such a way that it becomes one with the idea itself, and more than allegorical of it. There is thus in Dante's poem a quite unique middle point between allegory and symbolic-objective forms. For example, there is no doubt – and the poet has explained it himself elsewhere – that Beatrice is an allegory, namely of theology. So also her companions, and many other figures. However they still register in their own right and enter as historical characters, without for that purpose being symbols.

In this respect Dante is archetypal, since he has expressed what the modern poet must do in order to set forth in its entirety and in a poetic whole the history and culture of his time and the particular mythological material that is before him. He must combine the allegorical and the historical with absolute freedom of choice [Willkür]. He must be allegorical, and is so against his will, because he cannot be symbolic; and historical, because he must be poetic. The invention that he produces is in this respect unique every time, a world unto itself, wholly dependent on the personality.

In a similar way the one German poem of universal proportions joins together the most extreme aspects of the struggles of the age by the wholly individual invention of a partial mythology: the figure of Faust. However, this may be regarded as a comedy far more in the Aristophanic sense than is Dante's poem, and as divine in a different and more poetic sense.[5]

The energy with which the individual shapes the particular combination of the available materials of his life and times determines the extent to which it receives mythological force. Because of the place in which he sets them, which is eternal, Dante's characters already take on a kind of eternity. But not only the real events taken from his own times, like the story of Ugolino amongst others, but also what he has wholly invented, like the fate of Ulysses and his companions, take on in the context of his poem a truly mythological conviction.

To present Dante's philosophy, physics and astronomy purely in and for themselves would only be of minor interest, since his true uniqueness lies solely in the manner of their merging with poetry. The Ptolemaic cosmology, which is to some extent the basis of poetic edifice, already has a mythological colouring in itself; but if his philosophy is generally described as Aristotelian, then what must be understood here is not the purely peripatetic version but rather the particular connection current at that time between it and Platonic ideas, one which reveals itself on repeated investigations of the poem.[6]

We do not wish to dwell on the force and integrity of individual points, nor on the simplicity and infinite naivety of the individual images in which he expresses his philosophical ideas, such as the well-known one of the soul, which emerges from the hands of God as a little girl, childlike in its laughter and crying, an innocent little soul that knows nothing beyond what is controlled by its joyous creator, turning gladly to what amuses it.[7] We are only concerned with the generally symbolic form of the whole, in whose absoluteness the universal validity and eternal nature of this poem is more than anywhere else apparent.

If the union of philosophy and poetry even at the most elementary level of synthesis is viewed as didactic poetry then it is necessary, because the poem should be without any ulterior motive, that the intention to instruct is again in itself overcome and turned into an absolute, so that it can seem to exist for its own sake. This is however only conceivable if knowledge [Wissen], as image of the universe and in complete harmony with it, is in and for itself poetic, as with the most original and beautiful poetry. Dante's poem is a much more elevated interpenetration of scientific learning and poetry, and all the more must its form, even in its freer self-sufficiency, be attuned to the general paradigm of the world view [Weltanschauung].

The division of the universe and the arrangement of the subject matter into three realms, the *Inferno, Purgatorio,* and *Paradiso* is, independent of the particular significance of these concepts in Christianity, also a general symbolic form, so that one does not see why each age depicted in the same way could not have its divine comedy. Just as for recent drama the five-act form is regarded as usual, because each event can be seen in its beginning, continuation, culmination, progress to completion and actual ending; so for the higher prophetic poetry which expresses a whole age that trichotomy of Dante's is conceivable as a general form, but one whose filling out would be endlessly varied as it is revitalized by the power of original invention. That form is eternal, not only as outward form but also as sensuous [sinnbildlich] expression of the inner paradigm of all scientific knowledge and poetry, and is capable of containing within it the three great domains of science and culture: nature, history, and art. Nature, as the birthplace of all things, is eternal night, and as that unity through which they have their being in themselves, it is the aphelion of the universe, the place of distance from God as the true centre.[8] Life and history, whose nature is a succession of step by step advances, is simply a refining process, a transition to an absolute state. This is present only in art, which anticipates eternity, and is the *Paradiso* of life, truly at the centre.

Looked at from all sides Dante's poem is not therefore a single work of a particular time and stage of culture, but is archetypal through its universal validity, which it unites with absolute individuality. Its universality excludes no aspects of life and culture, and its form finally is not a particular paradigm but above all the paradigm of the contemplation of the universe.

The particular internal structure of the poem can certainly not have universal validity, since it is formed according to the concepts of the time and the particular intentions of the poet. On the other hand, as can only be

expected of such an artistic and totally deliberate work, the universal inner
paradigm is symbolized externally by the shape, colour and tone of the
three great sections of the poem.

Given the uncommon nature of his subject matter Dante needed a kind
of authentication for the detailed form of his inventions, which only the
scientific learning of his age could give him. This is for him, as it were, the
mythology and the general foundation which supports the bold edifice of
these inventions. But even in details he remains quite true to his intention
of being allegorical without ceasing to be historical and poetic. Hell, pur-
gatory and paradise are so to speak simply the physical and structural
expression of the system of theology. The measurements, numbers and
proportions which he observes within it were prescribed by scientific learning, and here he deliberately gave up freedom of invention in order to give
his poem, which was unlimited as far as the material was concerned, necessity and limitation through form. The universal sacredness and significance
of the numbers is another exterior form on which his poetry is based. Thus
for him all the logical and syllogistic erudition of his time is mere form,
which must be conceded to him if we are to arrive at that region in which
his poetry exists.

Nevertheless in this attachment to religious and scientific representations Dante never seeks any kind of common poetic probability as the most
universally valid thing that his age had to offer. Indeed, he overcomes all
inclination to pander to the coarser faculties [Sinnen]. His first entry into
hell takes place, as it had to, without any unpoetic attempt to motivate it
or make it comprehensible; it is a state similar to a vision, without there
being any intention of making this state account for it. His elevation
through the eyes of Beatrice, through which the divine force so to speak
transmitted itself to him, is expressed in a single line.[9] The wondrous
nature of his own encounters he turns directly into a figure of the secrets
of religion, and gives credence to them through the still higher mystery,
such as when he makes his absorption into the moon, which he compares
to a ray of light being in water but not cleaving it, into an image of God's
incarnation.[10]

To explain the fullness of art and the depth of intention in the internal
construction of the three parts of the world in detail would be a special
science in itself. This was recognized by his nation a short time after the
death of the poet, for they set up a special Dante Chair, which Boccaccio
was the first to take up.

What is universally meaningful in the first section shines through each
of the three parts of the poem, and not only in their particular inventions;
the law which applies to them expresses this meaningfulness still more precisely in the inner and spiritual rhythm through which they are set against
one another. Just as the *Inferno* is the most objectively terrible in its subject
matter, so it is the strongest in expression and the strictest in diction,

sombre and full of dread in its very choice of words. In one part of *Purgatorio* a deep stillness prevails, as the laments of the nether world grow silent, and on its hills, the forecourts of heaven, everything is glorious.[11] *Paradiso* is a true music of the spheres.

The diversity and variety of the punishments in the *Inferno* have been thought out with an almost unparalleled inventiveness. There is nothing other than a poetic connection between the crimes and the torments. Dante's spirit is not outraged by the horrific; indeed, he goes to the extreme limit of horror. But it can be shown in each individual case that he never ceases to be sublime and therefore truly beautiful. For what those who are not in a position to grasp the whole have singled out as base or inferior is not so in the sense that they mean but is a necessary element of the mixed nature of the poem, for which reason Dante himself calls it 'comedy'. The hatred of evil and the anger of a divine mind, as expressed in Dante's terrifying composition, are not the portion of ordinary souls. The generally held view is indeed very doubtful: that it was the exile from Florence, before which he had dedicated his poetry almost solely to love, that had first spurred on his mind (already inclined to the serious and the extraordinary) to the highest inventiveness, in which he breathed forth the whole of his life, the whole density of his heart and fatherland, together with his displeasure over them.[12] But the vengeance that he takes in the *Inferno* is taken in the name of the Last Judgement. He speaks with prophetic force as an authorized criminal judge; not from personal hatred, but as a pious soul outraged by the atrocities of the times, and with a love of the fatherland long since unknown. Thus he represents himself at one point in the *Paradiso*:

> If e'er the sacred poem, that hath made
> Both Heaven and earth copartners in its toil.
> And with lean abstinence, through many a year,
> Faded my brow, be destined to prevail
> Over the cruelty, which bars me forth
> Of the fair sheep-fold, where, a sleeping lamb
> The wolves set on and fain had worried me;
> With other voice, and fleece of other grain,
> I shall forthwith return; and, standing up
> At my baptismal font, shall claim the wreath
> Due to the poet's temples.[13]

He moderates the horrors of the torments of the damned by his own feeling, which at the final goal of so much misery almost so overcomes his vision that he desires to weep, and Virgil says to him: "Why are you afflicted?"[14]

It has already been remarked that most of the punishments in *Inferno* symbolize the crimes which are punished by them, but several are symbolic in a much more general context. One particular example of this type is the portrayal of a metamorphosis where two natures change into and through one another and, so to speak, exchange material identity.[15] None of the metamorphoses of antiquity can measure up to this in terms of invention, and if a naturalist or didactic poet were able to draw up with such force sensuous images of the eternal metamorphosis of nature, he might indeed call himself fortunate.

As already observed, the *Inferno* differs from the other parts not only in terms of the outward form of the presentation, but also because it is chiefly concerned with the realm of figures [Gestalten] and is thus the tangibly embodied [plastische] part of the poem. *Purgatorio* must be recognized as the picturesque. Not only are the penances which are here imposed on the sinners in part quite pictorially treated, even going so far as mirth; but the pilgrimage over the sacred mount of the place of penance in particular presents a rapid succession of fleeting views, scenes, and manifold effects of light.[16] At its final limits, after the poet has arrived at Lethe, the greatest splendour of painting and colour opens up in the descriptions of the ancient divine groves of that region, of the heavenly clarity of the waters that are clouded by their eternal shadows, of the virgin whom he encounters on the shore, and of the arrival of Beatrice in a cloud of flowers, under a white veil crowned with olives, wrapped in a green mantle, and clad in purple living flame.[17]

The poet has forced his way to the light through the centre of the earth. In the darkness of the underworld only shapes [Gestalt] could be distinguished. In *Purgatorio* the light is kindled by earthly matter, and becomes colour. In *Paradiso* only the pure music of light remains, the reflection ceases, and the poet raises himself gradually to the contemplation [Anschauung] of the transparent, pure substance of the Godhead itself.

The view of the cosmos at the time of the poet, and of the properties of the stars and the extent of their movement, is, invested with mythological dignity, the foundation upon which his inventions in this part of the poem rest. And if in this sphere of absoluteness he nevertheless allows gradations and differences to appear, then he overcomes [aufhebt] them with the splendid pronouncement which he has spoken forth by one of the sister souls he encounters on the moon: that every place in heaven is paradise.[18]

The structure of the poem requires that the highest principles of theology be discussed, precisely because of the elevation through paradise. The high respect for this science is exemplified by the love for Beatrice. It is necessary that in the same measure as contemplation [Anschauung] melts into the purely universal so poetry loses its forms and becomes music. In this respect the *Inferno* might appear as the most poetic part. But certainly nothing can be taken separately here, and the particular excellence of every part of the poem can only be understood and truly recognized in its harmony with the whole. If the relationship of the three parts is taken as a whole, then it has to be seen that the *Paradiso* is the purely musical and lyrical part by the very intention of the poet, who demonstrates this in external forms through the frequent use of the Latin words of church hymns.

The extraordinary greatness of this poem, which shines forth in the interpenetration of all elements of poetry and art, in this way fully reaches outward manifestation. This divine work is neither plastic, nor picturesque, nor musical, but all of these at the same time and in a mutual harmony. It is not dramatic, not epic, not lyric, but a completely individual and unparalleled combination of all of these.

At the same time I believe that I have shown that it is prophetic and exemplary [vorbildlich] for the whole of modern poetry. It contains all the attributes of modern poetry within it, and emerges from the frequently blended subject matter of the same as the first vintage to spread over earth to heaven, the first fruit of transfiguration. Those who want to get to know the poetry of more recent times at its source, rather than according to superficial concepts, may test themselves against this great and severe spirit [Geist], in order to know the means by which the totality of the modern age can be grasped, and that no easily created bond unites it. Those who are not called to do this may apply to themselves the words at the beginning of the first part:

All hope abandon, ye who enter here.[19]

Part 8

A.W. Schlegel

August Wilhelm von Schlegel

(1767–1845)

A.W. Schlegel was probably the most prominent critic of his time, being acquainted personally with the leading literary figures of Germany, including Schiller (to whose *Musen-Almanach* he frequently contributed), Goethe, and Tieck; he was also the close friend and tutor of Madame de Staël, whom he first met in 1805. He is probably best known to English readers for his Shakespeare criticism, but he also lectured and wrote extensively on contemporary German literature and its background, and also translated for publication many of Shakespeare's plays into German between 1797 and 1810. While lecturing on literature at Jena, he founded with his brother Friedrich the *Athenäum*, the journal which was to become the major vehicle of romantic criticism. Schlegel also wrote poems and plays, but his greatest success came as translator and critic; his translations include works from Spanish, Italian, and Portuguese. Toward the end of his life he became a well-known scholar of the Sanskrit language and literature, publishing the *Ramayana* (1825) and the *Bhagavad-Gita* (1829). He won considerable fame for his 1808 lectures on dramatic art and literature, and in 1827 he gave a successful series of lectures entitled 'Theory and History of the Fine Arts'.

Through his Shakespeare criticism and his founding of the *Athenäum* with his brother Friedrich, A.W. Schlegel was from the outset closely associated with the new romantic movement; indeed, he was seen as one of the original founders of it. But his relation to the theoretical aesthetics of, for example, tragedy and irony is more peripheral and even perhaps tenuous. Indeed, Karl Solger was some years later to discredit A.W. Schlegel's role in articulating the concept of romantic irony and theory of tragedy as misguided; his efforts to explain these theories to his audiences Solger saw as a watered down and even false account (see Solger's 'Resenzion von A.W. Schlegel's *Vorlesungen*', in *Erwin*, edited W. Henckmann (München, 1970), 394–471, and see Walzel (1938)). Hegel's rejection of romantic irony and his admiration for Solger's aesthetics may best be understood as a consequence of taking A.W. Schlegel as the main representative, and remaining (determinedly?) ignorant of the large difference between this simplistic version, designed for large audiences, and the sophisticated theory of his brother Friedrich.

The selection here is from the 'Lectures on Dramatic Art and Literature', given first in Vienna, in 1808, a mature account of the romantic principles of the 1790s which constituted the most powerful attack upon Neo-classicist criticism to be levelled since Herder. Herder's influence, particularly, as well as that of Lessing and Schiller, is evident both in the principles that inform them and in the lectures themselves. But the lectures also reveal the marked influence of English critics of Shakespeare, and it might be closer to the mark to suggest that Coleridge was indebted in his Shakespeare criticism less to his famous contemporary than to their common heritage, particularly that of Herder, Lessing, and Schiller.

The English text of the *Lectures on Dramatic Art and Literature* is from *Course of Lectures on Dramatic Art and Literature,* translated J. Black; revised A.J.W. Morrison (London, 1846), 17–29, 368–71, 404–7, 518–21. The standard edition is by Lohner (1962–74).

Further reading

See Ewton (1972).

KMW

Lectures on Dramatic Art and Literature
[*Vorlesungen über dramatische Kunst und Literatur*]

1808

Ancient and Modern, Classical and Romantic

The object of the present series of Lectures will be to combine the theory of Dramatic Art with its history, and to bring before my auditors at once its principles and its models.

It belongs to the general philosophical theory of poetry, and the other fine arts, to establish the fundamental laws of the beautiful. Every art, on the other hand, has its own special theory, designed to teach the limits, the difficulties, and the means by which it must be regulated in its attempt to realize those laws. For this purpose, certain scientific investigations are indispensable to the artist, although they have but little attraction for those whose admiration of art is confined to the enjoyment of the actual productions of distinguished minds. The general theory, on the other hand, seeks to analyse that essential faculty of human nature – the sense of the beautiful, which at once calls the fine arts into existence, and accounts for the satisfaction which arises from the contemplation of them; and also points out the relation which subsists between this and all other sentient and cognizant faculties of man. To the man of thought and speculation, therefore, it is of the highest importance, but by itself alone it is quite inadequate to guide and direct the essays and practice of art.

Now, the history of the fine arts informs us what has been, and the theory teaches what ought to be accomplished by them. But without some intermediate and connecting link, both would remain independent and separate from one and other, and each by itself, inadequate and defective. This connecting link is furnished by criticism, which both elucidates the history of the arts, and makes the theory fruitful. The comparing together, and judging of the existing productions of the human mind, necessarily throws light upon the conditions which are indispensable to the creation of original and masterly works of art.

Ordinarily, indeed, men entertain a very erroneous notion of criticism, and understand by it nothing more than a certain shrewdness in detecting and exposing the faults of a work of art. As I have devoted the greater part of my life to this pursuit, I may be excused if, by way of preface, I seek to lay before my auditors my own ideas of the true genius of criticism.

We see numbers of men, and even whole nations, so fettered by the conventions of education and habits of life, that, even in the appreciation of the fine arts, they cannot shake them off. Nothing to them appears natural, appropriate, or beautiful, which is alien to their own language, manners, and social relations. With this exclusive mode of seeing and feeling, it is no doubt possible to attain, by means of cultivation, to great nicety of discrimination within the narrow circle to which it limits and circumscribes them. But no man can be a true critic or connoisseur without universality of mind, without that flexibility which enables him, by renouncing all personal predilections and blind habits, to adapt himself to the peculiarities of other ages and nations – to feel them, as it were, from their proper central point, and, what ennobles human nature, to recognize and duly appreciate whatever is beautiful and grand under the external accessories which were necessary to its embodying, even though occasionally they may seem to disguise and distort it. There is no monopoly of poetry for particular ages and nations; and consequently that despotism in taste, which would seek to invest with universal authority the rules which at first, perhaps, were but arbitrarily advanced, is but a vain and empty pretension. Poetry, taken in its widest acceptation, as the power of creating what is beautiful, and representing it to the eye or the ear, is a universal gift of Heaven, being shared to a certain extent even by those whom we call barbarians and savages. Internal excellence is alone decisive, and where this exists, we must not allow ourselves to be repelled by the external appearance. Everything must be traced up to the root of human nature: if it has sprung from thence, it has an undoubted worth of its own; but if, without possessing a living germ, it is merely externally attached thereto, it will never thrive nor acquire a proper growth. Many productions which appear at first sight dazzling phenomena in the province of the fine arts, and which as a whole have been honoured with the appellation of works of a golden age, resemble the mimic gardens of children: impatient to witness the work of their hands, they break off here and there branches and flowers, and plant them in the earth; everything at first assumes a noble appearance: the childish gardener struts proudly up and down among his showy beds, till the rootless plants begin to droop, and hang their withered leaves and blossoms, and nothing soon remains but the bare twigs, while the dark forest, on which no art or care was ever bestowed, and which towered up towards heaven long before human remembrance, bears every blast unshaken, and fills the solitary beholder with religious awe.

Let us now apply the idea which we have been developing, of the universality of true criticism, to the history of poetry and the fine arts. This, like the so-called universal history, we generally limit (even though beyond this range there may be much that is both remarkable and worth knowing) to whatever has had a nearer or more remote influence on the present civilization of Europe: consequently, to the works of the Greeks and

Romans, and of those of the modern European nations, who first and chiefly distinguished themselves in art and literature. It is well known that, three centuries and a half ago, the study of ancient literature received a new life, by the diffusion of the Grecian language (for the Latin never became extinct); the classical authors were brought to light, and rendered universally accessible by means of the press; and the monuments of ancient art were diligently disinterred and preserved. All this powerfully excited the human mind, and formed a decided epoch in the history of human civilization; its manifold effects have extended to our times, and will yet extend to an incalculable series of ages. But the study of the ancients was forthwith most fatally perverted. The learned, who were chiefly in the possession of this knowledge, and who were incapable of distinguishing themselves by works of their own, claimed for the ancients an unlimited authority, and with great appearance of reason, since they are models in their kind. Maintaining that nothing could be hoped for the human mind but from an imitation of antiquity, in the works of the moderns they only valued what resembled, or seemed to bear a resemblance to, those of the ancients. Everything else they rejected as barbarous and unnatural. With the great poets and artists it was quite otherwise. However strong their enthusiasm for the ancients, and however determined their purpose of entering into competition with them, they were compelled by their independence and originality of mind, to strike out a path of their own, and to impress upon their productions the stamp of their own genius. Such was the case with Dante among the Italians, the father of modern poetry; acknowledging Virgil for his master, he has produced a work which, of all others, most differs from the Aeneid, and in our opinion far excels its pretended model in power, truth, compass, and profundity. It was the same afterwards with Ariosto, who has most unaccountably been compared to Homer, for nothing can be more unlike. So in art with Michael Angelo and Raphael, who had no doubt deeply studied the antique. When we ground our judgement of modern painters merely on their greater or less resemblance to the ancients, we must necessarily be unjust towards them, as Winckelmann undoubtedly has in the case of Raphael.[1] As the poets for the most part had their share of scholarship, it gave rise to a curious struggle between their natural inclination and their imaginary duty. When they sacrificed to the latter, they were praised by the learned; but by yielding to the former, they became the favourites of the people. What preserves the heroic poems of a Tasso and a Camoëns to this day alive in the hearts and on the lips of their countrymen, is by no means their imperfect resemblance to Virgil, or even to Homer, but in Tasso the tender feeling of chivalrous love and honour, and in Camoëns the glowing inspiration of heroic patriotism.

Those very ages, nations, and ranks, who felt least the want of a poetry of their own, were the most assiduous in their imitation of the ancients;

accordingly, its results are but dull school exercises, which at best excite a frigid admiration. But in the fine arts, mere imitation is always fruitless; even what we borrow from others, to assume a true poetical shape, must, as it were, be born again within us. Of what avail is all foreign imitation? Art cannot exist without nature, and man can give nothing to his fellow-men but himself.

Genuine successors and true rivals of the ancients, who, by virtue of congenial talents and cultivation have walked in their path and worked in their spirit, have ever been as rare as their mechanical spiritless copyists are common. Seduced by the form, the great body of critics have been but too indulgent to these servile imitators. These were held up as correct modern classics, while the great truly living and popular poets, whose reputation was a part of their nations' glory, and to whose sublimity it was impossible to be altogether blind, were at best but tolerated as rude and wild natural geniuses. But the unqualified separation of genius and taste on which such a judgement proceeds, is altogether untenable. Genius is the almost unconscious choice of the highest degree of excellence, and, consequently, it is taste in its highest activity.

In this state, nearly, matters continued till a period not far back, when several inquiring minds, chiefly Germans, endeavoured to clear up the misconception, and to give the ancients their due, without being insensible to the merits of the moderns, although of a totally different kind. The apparent contradiction did not intimidate them. The groundwork of human nature is no doubt everywhere the same; but in all our investigations, we may observe that, throughout the whole range of nature, there is no elementary power so simple, but that it is capable of dividing and diverging into opposite directions. The whole play of vital motion hinges on harmony and contrast. Why, then, should not this phenomenon recur on a grander scale in the history of man? In this idea we have perhaps discovered the true key to the ancient and modern history of poetry and the fine arts. Those who adopted it, gave to the peculiar spirit of *modern* art, as contrasted with the *antique* or *classical,* the name of *romantic.* The term is certainly not inappropriate; the word is derived from *romance* – the name originally given to the languages which were formed from the mixture of the Latin and the old Teutonic dialects, in the same manner as modern civilization is the fruit of the heterogeneous union of the peculiarities of the northern nations and the fragments of antiquity; whereas the civilization of the ancients was much more of a piece.[2]

The distinction which we have just stated can hardly fail to appear well founded, if it can be shown, so far as our knowledge of antiquity extends, that the same contrast in the labours of the ancients and moderns runs symmetrically, I might almost say systematically, throughout every branch of art – that it is as evident in music and the plastic arts as in poetry. This is a problem which, in its full extent, still remains to be demonstrated, though, on particular portions of it, many excellent observations have been advanced already.

Among the foreign authors who wrote before this school can be said to have been formed in Germany, we may mention Rousseau, who acknowledged the contrast in music, and showed that rhythm and melody were the prevailing principles of ancient, as harmony is that of modern music. In his prejudices against harmony, however, we cannot at all concur. On the subject of the arts of design an ingenious observation was made by Hemsterhuys,[3] that the ancient painters were perhaps too much of sculptors, and the modern sculptors too much of painters. This is the exact point of difference; for, as I shall distinctly show in the sequel, the spirit of ancient art and poetry is *plastic,* but that of the moderns *picturesque.*

By an example taken from another art, that of architecture, I shall endeavour to illustrate what I mean by this contrast. Throughout the Middle Ages there prevailed, and in the latter centuries of that æra was carried to perfection, a style of architecture, which has been called Gothic, but ought really to have been termed old German. When, on the general revival of classical antiquity, the imitation of Grecian architecture became prevalent, and but too frequently without a due regard to the difference of climate and manners or to the purpose of the building, the zealots of this new taste, passing a sweeping sentence of condemnation on the Gothic, reprobated it as tasteless, gloomy, and barbarous. This was in some degree pardonable in the Italians, among whom a love for ancient architecture, cherished by hereditary remains of classical edifices, and the similarity of their climate to that of the Greeks and Romans, might, in some sort, be said to be innate. But we Northerns are not so easily to be talked out of the powerful, solemn impressions which seize upon the mind at entering a Gothic cathedral. We feel, on the contrary, a strong desire to investigate and to justify the source of this impression. A very slight attention will convince us, that the Gothic architecture displays not only an extraordinary degree of mechanical skill, but also a marvellous power of invention; and, on a closer examination, we recognize its profound significance, and perceive that as well as the Grecian it constitutes in itself a complete and finished system.

To the application – The Pantheon is not more different from Westminster Abbey or the church of St. Stephen at Vienna, than the structure of a tragedy of Sophocles from a drama of Shakespeare. The comparison between these wonderful productions of poetry and architecture might be carried still farther. But does our admiration of the one compel us to depreciate the other? May we not admit that each is great and admirable in its kind, although the one is, and is meant to be, different from the other? The experiment is worth attempting. We will quarrel with no man for his predilection either for the Grecian or the Gothic. The world is wide, and affords room for a great diversity of objects. Narrow and blindly adopted prepossessions will never constitute a genuine critic or connoisseur, who ought, on the contrary, to possess the power of dwelling with liberal impartiality on the most discrepant views, renouncing the while all personal inclinations.

For our present object, the justification, namely, of the grand division which we lay down in the history of art, and according to which we conceive ourselves equally warranted in establishing the same division in dramatic literature, it might be sufficient merely to have stated this contrast between the ancient, or classical, and the romantic. But as there are exclusive admirers of the ancients, who never cease asserting that all deviation from them is merely the whim of a new school of critics, who, expressing themselves in language full of mystery, cautiously avoid conveying their sentiments in a tangible shape, I shall endeavour to explain the origin and spirit of the *romantic*, and then leave the world to judge if the use of the word, and of the idea which it is intended to convey, be thereby justified.

The mental culture of the Greeks was a finished education in the school of Nature. Of a beautiful and noble race, endowed with susceptible senses and a cheerful spirit under a mild sky, they lived and bloomed in the full health of existence; and, favoured by a rare combination of circumstances, accomplished all that the finite nature of man is capable of. The whole of their art and poetry is the expression of a consciousness of this harmony of all their faculties. They invented the poetry of joy.

Their religion was the deification of the powers of nature and of the earthly life: but this worship, which, among other nations, clouded the imagination with hideous shapes, and hardened the heart to cruelty, assumed, among the Greeks, a mild, a grand, and a dignified form. Superstition, too often the tyrant of the human faculties, seemed to have here contributed to their freest development. It cherished the arts by which it was adorned, and its idols became the models of ideal beauty.

But however highly the Greeks may have succeeded in the Beautiful, and even in the Moral, we cannot concede any higher character to their civilization than that of a refined and ennobled sensuality. Of course this must be understood generally. The conjectures of a few philosophers, and the irradiations of poetical inspiration, constitute an occasional exception. Man can never altogether turn aside his thoughts from infinity, and some obscure recollections will always remind him of the home he has lost; but we are now speaking of the predominant tendency of his endeavours.

Religion is the root of human existence. Were it possible for man to renounce all religion, including that which is unconscious, independent of the will, he would become a mere surface without any internal substance. When this centre is disturbed, the whole system of the mental faculties and feelings takes a new shape.

And this is what has actually taken place in modern Europe through the introduction of Christianity. This sublime and beneficent religion has regenerated the ancient world from its state of exhaustion and debasement; it is the guiding principle in the history of modern nations, and even at this day, when many suppose they have shaken off its authority, they still find themselves much more influenced by it in their views of human affairs than they themselves are aware.

After Christianity, the character of Europe has, since the commencement of the Middle Ages, been chiefly influenced by the Germanic race of northern conquerors, who infused new life and vigour into a degenerated people. The stern nature of the North drives man back within himself; and what is lost in the free sportive development of the senses, must, in noble dispositions, be compensated by earnestness of mind. Hence the honest cordiality with which Christianity was welcomed by all the Teutonic tribes, so that among no other race of men has it penetrated more deeply into the inner man, displayed more powerful effects, or become more interwoven with all human feelings and sensibilities.

The rough, but honest heroism of the northern conquerors, by its admixture with the sentiments of Christianity, gave rise to chivalry, of which the object was, by vows which should be looked upon as sacred, to guard the practice of arms from every rude and ungenerous abuse of force into which it was so likely to sink.

With the virtues of chivalry was associated a new and purer spirit of love, an inspired homage for genuine female worth, which was now revered as the acme of human excellence, and, maintained by religion itself under the image of a virgin mother, infused into all hearts a mysterious sense of the purity of love.

As Christianity did not, like the heathen worship, rest satisfied with certain external acts, but claimed an authority over the whole inward man and the most hidden movements of the heart; the feeling of moral independence took refuge in the domain of honour, a worldly morality, as it were, which subsisting alongside of, was often at variance with that of religion, but yet in so far resembling it that it never calculated consequences, but consecrated unconditionally certain principles of action, which like the articles of faith, were elevated far beyond the investigation of a casuistical reasoning.

Chivalry, love, and honour, together with religion itself, are the subjects of that poetry of nature which poured itself out in the Middle Ages with incredible fullness, and preceded the more artistic cultivation of the romantic spirit. This age had also its mythology, consisting of chivalrous tales and legends; but its wonders and its heroism were the very reverse of those of the ancient mythology.

Several enquirers who, in other respects, entertain the same conception of the peculiarities of the moderns, and trace them to the same source that we do, have placed the essence of the northern poetry in melancholy; and to this, when properly understood, we have nothing to object.

Among the Greeks human nature was in itself all-sufficient; it was conscious of no defects, and aspired to no higher perfection than that which it could actually attain by the exercise of its own energies. We, however, are taught by superior wisdom that man, through a grievous transgression, forfeited the place for which he was originally destined; and that the sole destination of his earthly existence is to struggle to regain his lost position, which, if left to his own strength, he can never accomplish. The old religion of the senses sought no higher possession than outward and perishable blessings; and immortality, so far as it was believed, stood shadow-like in the obscure distance, a faint dream of this sunny waking life. The very reverse of all this is the case with the Christian view: every thing finite and mortal is lost in the contemplation of infinity; life has become shadow and darkness, and the first day of our real existence dawns in the world beyond the grave. Such a religion must waken the vague foreboding, which slumbers in every feeling heart, into a distinct consciousness that the happiness after which we are here striving is unattainable; that no external object can ever entirely fill our souls; and that all earthly enjoyment is but a fleeting and momentary illusion. When the soul, resting as it were under the willows of exile, breathes out its longing for its distant home, what else but melancholy can be the key-note of its songs? Hence the poetry of the ancients was the poetry of enjoyment, and ours is that of desire: the former has its foundation in the scene which is present, while the latter hovers betwixt recollection and hope. Let me not be understood as affirming that everything flows in one unvarying strain of wailing and complaint, and that the voice of melancholy is always loudly heard. As the austerity of tragedy was not incompatible with the joyous views of the Greeks, so that romantic poetry, whose origin I have been describing, can assume every tone, even that of the liveliest joy; but still it will always, in some indescribable way, bear traces of the source from which it originated. The feeling of the moderns is, upon the whole, more inward, their fancy more incorporeal, and their thoughts more contemplative. In nature, it is true, the boundaries of objects run more into one another, and things are not so distinctly separated as we must exhibit them in order to convey distinct notions of them.

The Grecian ideal of human nature was perfect unison and proportion between all the powers – a natural harmony. The moderns, on the contrary, have arrived at the consciousness of an internal discord which renders such an ideal impossible; and hence the endeavour of their poetry is to reconcile these two worlds between which we find ourselves divided, and to blend them indissolubly together. The impressions of the senses are to be hallowed, as it were, by a mysterious connexion with higher feelings; and the soul, on the other hand, embodies its forebodings, or indescribable intuitions of infinity, in types and symbols borrowed from the visible world.

In Grecian art and poetry we find an original and unconscious unity of form and matter; in the modern, so far as it has remained true to its own spirit, we observe a keen struggle to unite the two, as being naturally in opposition to each other. The Grecian executed what it proposed in the utmost perfection; but the modern can only do justice to its endeavours after what is infinite by approximation; and, from a certain appearance of imperfection, is in greater danger of not being duly appreciated.

It would lead us too far, if in the separate arts of architecture, music, and painting (for the moderns have never had a sculpture of their own), we should endeavour to point out the distinctions which we have here announced, to show the contrast observable in the character of the same arts among the ancients and moderns, and at the same time to demonstrate the kindred aim of both.

Neither can we here enter into a more particular consideration of the different kinds and forms of romantic poetry in general, but must return to our more immediate subject, which is dramatic art and literature. The division of this, as of the other departments of art, into the antique and the romantic, at once points out to us the course which we have to pursue.

We shall begin with the ancients; then proceed to their imitators, their genuine or supposed successors among the moderns; and lastly, we shall consider those poets of later times, who, either disregarding the classical models, or purposely deviating from them, have struck out a path for themselves.

Of the ancient dramatists, the Greeks alone are of any importance. In this branch of art the Romans were at first mere translators of the Greeks, and afterwards imitators, and not always very successful ones. Besides, of their dramatic labours very little has been preserved. Among modern nations an endeavour to restore the ancient stage, and, where possible, to improve it, has been shown in a very lively manner by the Italians and the French. In other nations, also, attempts of the same kind, more or less earnest, have at times, especially of late, been made in tragedy; for in comedy, the form under which it appears in Plautus and Terence has certainly been more generally prevalent. Of all studied imitations of the ancient tragedy the French is the most brilliant essay, has acquired the greatest renown, and consequently deserves the most attentive consideration. After the French come the modern Italians; viz., Metastasio and Alfieri.[4] The romantic drama, which, strictly speaking, can neither be called tragedy nor comedy in the sense of the ancients, is indigenous only to England and Spain. In both it began to flourish at the same time, somewhat more than two hundred years ago, being brought to perfection by Shakespeare in the former country, and in the latter by Lope de Vega.

The German stage is the last of all, and has been influenced in the greatest variety of ways by all those which preceded it. It will be most appro-

priate, therefore, to enter upon its consideration last of all. By this course
we shall be better enabled to judge of the directions which it has hitherto
taken, and to point out the prospects which are still open to it.

When I promise to go through the history of the Greek and Roman, of
the Italian and French, and of the English and Spanish theatres, in the few
hours which are dedicated to these lectures, I wish it to be understood that
I can only enter into such an account of them as will comprehend their
most essential peculiarities under general points of view. Although I confine myself to a single domain of poetry, still the mass of materials comprehended within it is too extensive to be taken in by the eye at once, and
this would be the case were I even to limit myself to one of its subordinate
departments. We might read ourselves to death with farces. In the ordinary histories of literature the poets of one language, and one description,
are enumerated in succession, without any further discrimination, like the
Assyrian and Egyptian kings in the old universal histories. There are persons who have an unconquerable passion for the titles of books, and we
willingly concede to them the privilege of increasing their number by
books on the titles of books. It is much the same thing, however, as in the
history of a war to give the name of every soldier who fought in the ranks
of the hostile armies. It is usual, however, to speak only of the generals,
and those who may have performed actions of distinction. In like manner
the battles of the human mind, if I may use the expression, have been won
by a few intellectual heroes. The history of the development of art and its
various forms may be therefore exhibited in the characters of a number,
by no means considerable, of elevated and creative minds.

*   *   *

Shakespeare's Irony

If the delineation of all his characters, separately considered, is inimitably
bold and correct, he surpasses even himself in so combining and contrasting them, that they serve to bring out each other's peculiarities. This is the
very perfection of dramatic characterization: for we can never estimate a
man's true worth if we consider him altogether abstractedly by himself; we
must see him in his relations with others; and it is here that most dramatic
poets are deficient. Shakespeare makes each of his principal characters the
glass in which the others are reflected, and by like means enables us to
discover what could not be immediately revealed to us. What in others is
most profound, is with him but surface. Ill-advised should we be were we
always to take men's declarations respecting themselves and others for
sterling coin. Ambiguity of design with much propriety he makes to overflow with the most praiseworthy principles; and sage maxims are not unfre-
quently put in the mouth of stupidity, to show how easily such commonplace truisms may be acquired. Nobody ever painted so truthfully as he

has done the facility of self-deception, the half self-conscious hypocrisy towards ourselves, with which even noble minds attempt to disguise the almost inevitable influence of selfish motives in human nature. This secret irony of the characterization commands admiration as the profound abyss of acuteness and sagacity; but it is the grave of enthusiasm. We arrive at it only after we have had the misfortune to see human nature through and through; and when no choice remains but to adopt the melancholy truth, that 'no virtue or greatness is altogether pure and genuine', or the dangerous error that 'the highest perfection is attainable'. Here we therefore may perceive in the poet himself, notwithstanding his power to excite the most fervent emotions, a certain cool indifference, but still the indifference of a superior mind, which has run through the whole sphere of human existence and survived feeling.

The irony in Shakespeare has not merely a reference to the separate characters, but frequently to the whole of the action. Most poets who portray human events in a narrative or dramatic form take themselves a part; and exact from their readers a blind approbation or condemnation of whatever side they choose to support or oppose. The more zealous this rhetoric is, the more certainly it fails of its effect. In every case we are conscious that the subject itself is not brought immediately before us, but that we view it through the medium of a different way of thinking. When, however, by a dexterous manœuvre, the poet allows us an occasional glance at the less brilliant reverse of the medal, then he makes, as it were, a sort of secret understanding with the select circle of the more intelligent of his readers or spectators; he shows them that he had previously seen and admitted the validity of their tacit objections; that he himself is not tied down to the represented subject, but soars freely above it; and that, if he chose, he could unrelentingly annihilate the beautiful and irresistibly attractive scenes which his magic pen has produced. No doubt, wherever the proper tragic enters every thing like irony immediately ceases,[5] but from the avowed raillery of Comedy, to the point where the subjection of mortal beings to an inevitable destiny demands the highest degree of seriousness, there are a multitude of human relations which unquestionably may be considered in an ironical view, without confounding the eternal line of separation between good and evil. This purpose is answered by the comic characters and scenes which are interwoven with the serious parts in most of those pieces of Shakespeare where romantic fables or historical events are made the subject of a noble and elevating exhibition. Frequently an intentional parody of the serious part is not to be mistaken in them; at other times the connection is more arbitrary and loose, and the more so the more marvellous the invention of the whole, and the more entirely it is become a light revelling of the fancy. The comic intervals everywhere serve to prevent the pastime from being converted into a business, to preserve the mind in the possession of its serenity, and to keep off that gloomy and inert seriousness which so easily steals upon the sentimental, but not tragical, drama. Most assuredly Shakespeare did not intend thereby, in defiance to his own better judgement, to humour the taste of the multitude: for in various pieces, and throughout considerable portions of others, and especially when the catastrophe is approaching, and the mind consequently is more on the stretch and no longer likely to give heed to any amusement which would distract their attention, he has abstained from all such comic intermixtures. It was also an object with him, that the clowns or buffoons should not occupy a more important place than that which he had assigned them: he expressly condemns the extemporizing with which they loved to enlarge their parts.[6] Johnson founds the justification of the species of drama in which seriousness and mirth are mixed, on this, that in real life the vulgar is found close to the sublime, that the merry and the sad usually accompany and succeed one another.[7] But it does not follow that because both are found together, therefore they must not be separable in the compositions of art. The observation is in other respects just, and this circumstance invests the poet with a power to adopt this procedure, because every thing in the drama must be regulated by the conditions of theatrical probability; but the mixture of such dissimilar, and apparently contradictory, ingredients, in the same works, can only be justifiable on principles reconcilable with the views of art, which I have already described. In the dramas of Shakespeare the comic scenes are the antechamber of the poetry, where the servants remain; these prosaic attendants must not raise their voices so high as to deafen the speakers in the presence-chamber; however, in those intervals when the ideal society has retired they deserve to be listened to; their bold raillery, their presumption of mockery, may afford many an insight into the situation and circumstances of their masters.[8]

*   *   *

Shakespeare

Hamlet is singular in its kind: a tragedy of thought inspired by continual and never-satisfied meditation on human destiny and the dark perplexity of the events of this world, and calculated to call forth the very same meditation in the minds of the spectators. This enigmatical work resembles those irrational equations in which a fraction of unknown magnitude always remains, that will in no way admit of solution. Much has been said, much written, on this piece, and yet no thinking head who anew expresses himself on it, will (in his view of the connection and the signification of all the parts) entirely coincide with his predecessors. What naturally most astonishes us is the fact that with such hidden purposes, with a foundation laid in such unfathomable depth, the whole should, at a first view, exhibit an extremely popular appearance. The dread appearance of the Ghost takes possession of the mind and the imagination almost at the very commencement; then the play within the play, in which, as in a glass, we see reflected the crime, whose fruitlessly attempted punishment constitutes the subject-matter of the piece; the alarm with which it fills the King; Hamlet's pretended and Ophelia's real madness; her death and burial; the meeting of Hamlet and Laertes at her grave; their combat, and the grand determination; lastly, the appearance of the young hero Fortinbras, who, with warlike pomp, pays the last honours to an extinct family of kings; the interspersion of comic characteristic scenes with Polonius, the courtiers, and the grave-diggers, which have all of them their signification – all this fills the stage with an animated and varied movement. The only circumstance from which this piece might be judged to be less theatrical than other tragedies of Shakespeare is, that in the last scenes the main action either stands still or appears to retrograde. This, however, was inevitable, and lay in the nature of the subject. The whole is intended to show that a calculating consideration, which exhausts all the relations and possible consequences of a deed, must cripple the power of acting; as Hamlet himself expresses it:

> And thus the native hue of resolution
> Is sicklied o'er with the pale cast of thought;
> And enterprises of great pith and moment,
> With this regard, their currents turn awry,
> And lose the name of action.

With respect to Hamlet's character: I cannot, as I understand the poet's views, pronounce altogether so favourable a sentence upon it as Goethe does.[9] He is, it is true, of a highly cultivated mind, a prince of royal manners, endowed with the finest sense of propriety, susceptible of noble ambition, and open in the highest degree to an enthusiastic admiration of that excellence in others of which he himself is deficient. He acts the part of madness with unrivalled power, convincing the persons who are sent to examine into his supposed loss of reason, merely by telling them unwelcome truths, and rallying them with the most caustic wit. But in the resolutions which he so often embraces and always leaves unexecuted, his weakness is too apparent: he does himself only justice when he implies that there is no greater dissimilarity than between himself and Hercules. He is not solely impelled by necessity to artifice and dissimulation, he has a natural inclination for crooked ways; he is a hypocrite towards himself; his farfetched scruples are often mere pretexts to cover his want of determination: thoughts, as he says on a different occasion, which have

> but one part wisdom
> And ever three parts coward.

He has been chiefly condemned both for his harshness in repulsing the love of Ophelia, which he himself had cherished, and for his insensibility at her death. But he is too much overwhelmed with his own sorrow to have any compassion to spare for others; besides his outward indifference gives us by no means the measure of his internal perturbation. On the other hand, we evidently perceive in him a malicious joy, when he has succeeded in getting rid of his enemies, more through necessity and accident, which alone are able to impel him to quick and decisive measures, than by the merit of his own courage, as he himself confesses after the murder of Polonius, and with respect to Rosencrantz and Guildenstern. Hamlet has no firm belief either in himself or in anything else: from expressions of religious confidence he passes over to sceptical doubts; he believes in the Ghost of his father as long as he sees it, but as soon as it has disappeared, it appears to him almost in the light of a deception. He has even gone so far as to say, 'there is nothing either good or bad, but thinking makes it so'; with him the poet loses himself here in labyrinths of thought, in which neither end nor beginning is discoverable. The stars themselves, from the course of events, afford no answer to the question so urgently proposed to them. A voice from another world, commissioned, it would appear, by heaven, demands vengeance for a monstrous enormity, and the demand remains without effect; the criminals are at last punished, but, as it were, by an accidental blow, and not in the solemn way requisite to convey to the world a warning example of justice; irresolute foresight, cunning treachery, and impetuous rage, hurry on to a common destruction; the less guilty and the innocent are equally involved in the general ruin. The destiny of humanity is there exhibited as a gigantic Sphinx, which threatens to precipitate into the abyss of scepticism all who are unable to solve her dreadful enigmas.

As one example of the many niceties of Shakespeare which have never been understood, I may allude to the style in which the player's speech about Hecuba is conceived.[10] It has been the subject of much controversy among the commentators, whether this was borrowed by Shakespeare from himself or from another, and whether, in the praise of the piece of which it is supposed to be a part, he was speaking seriously, or merely meant to ridicule the tragical bombast of his contemporaries. It seems never to have occurred to them that this speech must not be judged of by itself, but in connection with the place where it is introduced. To distinguish it in the play itself as dramatic poetry, it was necessary that it should rise above the dignified poetry of the former in the same proportion that generally theatrical elevation soars above simple nature. Hence Shakespeare has composed the play in Hamlet altogether in sententious rhymes full of antitheses. But this solemn and measured tone did not suit a speech in which violent emotion ought to prevail, and the poet had no other expedient than the one of which he made choice: overcharging the pathos. The language of the speech in question is certainly falsely emphatical; but yet this fault is so mixed up with true grandeur, that a player practised in artificially calling forth in himself the emotion he is imitating, may certainly be carried away by it. Besides, it will hardly be believed that Shakespeare knew so little of his art, as not to be aware that a tragedy in which Aeneas had to make a lengthy epic relation of a transaction that happened so long before as the destruction of Troy, could neither be dramatical nor theatrical.

*   *   *

Goethe and Schiller

All must allow that Goethe possesses dramatic talent in a very high degree, but not indeed much theatrical talent. He is much more anxious to effect his object by tender development than by rapid external motion; even the mild grace of his harmonious mind prevented him from aiming at strong demagogic effect. *Iphigenia in Taurus* posseses, it is true, more affinity of the Greek spirit than perhaps any other work of the moderns composed before Goethe's; but is not so much an ancient tragedy as a reflected image of one, a musical echo: the violent catastrophes of the latter appear here in the distance only as recollections, and all is softly dissolved within the mind. The deepest and most moving pathos is to be found in *Egmont,* but in the conclusion this tragedy also is removed from the external world into the domain of an ideal soul-music.

That with this direction of his poetic career to the purest expression of his inspired imagining, without regard to any other object, and with the universality of his artistic studies, Goethe should not have had that decided influence on the shape of our theatre which, if he had chosen to dedicate himself exclusively and immediately to it, he might have exercised, is easily conceivable.

In the mean time, shortly after Goethe's first appearance, the attempt had been made to bring Shakespeare on our stage. The effort was a great and extraordinary one. Actors still alive acquired their first laurels in this wholly novel kind of exhibition, and Schröder,[11] perhaps, in some of the most celebrated tragic and comic parts, attained to the same perfection for which Garrick had been idolized. As a whole, however, no one piece appeared in a very perfect shape; most of them were in heavy prose translations, and frequently mere extracts, with disfiguring alterations, were exhibited. The separate characters and situations had been hit to a certain degree of success, but the sense of his composition was often missed.

In this state of things Schiller made his appearance, a man endowed with all the qualifications necessary to produce at once a strong effect on the multitude, and on nobler minds. He composed his earliest works while very young, and unacquainted with that world which he attempted to paint; and although a genius independent and boldly daring, he was nevertheless influenced in various ways by the models which he saw in the already mentioned pieces of Lessing, by the earlier labours of Goethe, and in Shakespeare, so far as he could understand him without an acquaintance with the original.

In this way were produced the works of his youth: *Die Räuber, Cabale und Liebe,* and *Fiesco.* The first, wild and horrible as it was, produced so powerful an effect as even to turn the heads of youthful enthusiasts. The defective imitation here of Shakespeare is not to be mistaken: Francis Moor is a prosaical Richard III, ennobled by none of the properties which in the latter mingle admiration with aversion. *Cabale und Liebe* can hardly affect us by its extravagant sentimentality, but it tortures us by the most painful impressions. *Fiesco* is in design the most perverted, in effect the feeblest.

So noble a mind could not long persevere in such mistaken courses, though they gained him applauses which might have rendered the continuance of his blindness excusable. He had in his own case experienced the dangers of an undisciplined spirit and an ungovernable defiance of all constraining authority, and therefore, with incredible diligence and a sort of passion, he gave himself up to artistic discipline. The work which marks this new epoch is *Don Carlos.* In parts we observe a greater depth in the delineation of character; yet the old and tumid extravagance is not altogether lost, but merely clothed with choicer forms. In the situations there is much of pathetic power, the plot is complicated even to epigrammatic subtlety; but of such value in the eyes of the poet were his dearly purchased reflections on human nature and social institutions, that, instead of expressing them by the progress of the action, he exhibited them with circumstantial fullness, and made his characters philosophize more or less on themselves and others, and by that means swelled his work to a size quite incompatible with theatrical limits.

Historical and philosophical studies seemed now, to the ultimate profit of his art, to have seduced the poet for a time from his poetical career, to which he returned with a riper mind, enriched with varied knowledge, and truly enlightened at last with respect to his own aims and means. He now applied himself exclusively to Historical Tragedy, and endeavoured, by divesting himself of his personality, to rise to a truly objective representation. In *Wallenstein* he had adhered so conscientiously to historical truth, that he could not wholly master his materials, an event of no great historical extent is spun out into two plays, with prologue in some degree didactical. In form he has closely followed Shakespeare; only that he might not make too large a demand on the imagination of the spectators, he has endeavoured to confine the changes of place and time within narrower limits. He also tied himself down to a more sustained observance of tragical dignity, and has brought forward no persons of mean condition, or at least did not allow them to speak in their natural tone, and banished into the prelude the mere people, here represented by the army, though Shakespeare introduced them with such vividness and truth into the very midst of the great public events. The loves of Thekla and Max Piccolomini form, it is true, properly an episode, and bear the stamp of an age very different from that depicted in the rest of the work; but it affords an opportunity for the most affecting scenes, and is conceived with equal tenderness and dignity.

Maria Stuart is planned and executed with more artistic skill, and also with greater depth and breadth. All is wisely weighed; we may censure particular parts as offensive: the quarrel for instance, between the two Queens, the wild fury of Mortimer's passion, & c.; but it is hardly possible to take any thing away without involving the whole in confusion. The piece cannot fail of effect; the last moments of Mary are truly worthy of a queen; religious impressions are employed with becoming earnestness; only from the care, perhaps superfluous, to exercise, after Mary's death, poetical justice on Elizabeth, the spectator is dismissed rather cooled and indifferent.

With such a wonderful subject as the *Maid of Orleans*, Schiller thought himself entitled to take greater liberties. The plot is looser; the scene with Montgomery, an epic intermixture, is at variance with the general tone; in the singular and inconceivable appearance of the black knight, the object of the poet is ambiguous; in the character of Talbot, and many other parts, Schiller has entered into an unsuccessful competition with Shakespeare; and I know not but the colouring employed, which is not so brilliant as might be imagined, is an equivalent for the severer pathos which has been sacrificed to it. The history of the *Maid of Orleans*, even to its details, is generally known; her high mission was believed by herself and generally by her contemporaries, and produced the most extraordinary effects. The marvel might, therefore, have been represented by the poet, even though the sceptical spirit of his contemporaries should have deterred him from giving it out for real; and the real ignominious martyrdom of this betrayed and abandoned heroine would have agitated us more deeply than the gaudy and rose-coloured one which, in contradiction to history, Schiller has invented for her. Shakespeare's picture, though partial from national prejudice, still possesses much more historical truth and profundity.[12] However, the German piece will ever remain as a generous attempt to vindicate the honour of a name deformed by impudent ridicule; and its dazzling effect, strengthened by the rich ornateness of the language, deservedly gained for it on the stage the most eminent success.

Part 9

Novalis

Novalis (Friedrich von Hardenberg)

(1772–1801)

Novalis, mystical philosopher-poet of the Romantic period and writer of fragments and novels, was a central figure of the Romantic School. He met Friedrich Schlegel in 1792 in Leipzig, and remained close friends with him for a decade; he met Tieck, with whom he shared a deep interest in Jakob Boehme and mysticism, in 1799, and he knew Herder, Goethe, Schelling, Schleiermacher, A.W. Schlegel, Henrik Steffens, and other prominent literati and scientists of the day. In the period 1797–8 Novalis worked closely with Friedrich Schlegel to develop a 'symphilosophy'. Their ideas arose in the midst of studies of Shakespeare, Kant, and Hemsterhuis, and from talks with Schelling and Hülsen, and at first took the form of fragments for publication. Novalis referred to his fragments as mystical, 'mystical' meaning something secret, hidden, and intuitively grasped. Novalis sought in his researches into chemistry, physics, and physiology to discover connections between sensible and intelligible experience. He developed mystical expressions and a 'special language' of tropes and enigmas in order to represent and communicate these connections. Nature Novalis saw as a hieroglyph for a hidden and other world of intelligence. Mysticism for Novalis and for the other Romantics was a symbol for the infinite, incomprehensible, and unknowable, that 'Urwelt' which must remain secret and mystical, but which forever enthralled the artist-thinker. Novalis valued his 'mystical fragment' as itself a formal symbol of the method necessary for communicating his own discoveries of that 'Urwelt' to others; he insisted that all communication was only a beginning, a push for the reader toward self-activity and self-discovery. He considered his fragments to be seeds that might become mature if nourished by his audience.

The 'Monologue' (composition date uncertain) is a concentrated and impressive example of romantic irony, fusing content and method, subject matter and style, and of the positive negation and self-criticism at the heart of irony.

Novalis' major publications include *Die Lehrlinge zu Sais* (1798), *Die Christenheit oder Europa* (1799), *Geistliche Lieder* (1799), *Heinrich von Ofterdingen* (1799–1800), and *Hymnen an die Nacht* (1800). The reader is referred to the critical edition of *Novalis Schriften*, edited by Paul Kluckhorn and Richard Samuel, 4 vols. (Stuttgart, 1960–75).

The source of the text is *Novalis Schriften*, II, 672–3.

Further reading

See Barrack (1971), Dyck (1960), Lewis (1960), Molnár (1987), Peacock (1952), and Schaber (1973), all in English. See also Fautek (1940), Haering (1954), and Ritter (1973).

KMW

Monologue

Uncertain date

Speaking and writing is a crazy state of affairs really; true conversation is just a game with words. It is amazing, the absurd error people make of imagining they are speaking for the sake of things; no one knows the essential thing about language, that it is concerned only with itself. That is why it is such a marvellous and fruitful mystery – for if someone merely speaks for the sake of speaking, he utters the most splendid, original truths. But if he wants to talk about something definite, the whims of language make him say the most ridiculous false stuff. Hence the hatred that so many serious people have for language. They notice its waywardness, but they do not notice that the babbling they scorn is the infinitely serious side of language. If it were only possible to make people understand that it is the same with language as it is with mathematical formulae – they constitute a world in itself – their play is self-sufficient, they express nothing but their own marvellous nature, and this is the very reason why they are so expressive, why they are the mirror to the strange play of relationships among things. Only their freedom makes them members of nature, only in their free movements does the world-soul express itself and make of them a delicate measure and a ground-plan of things. And so it is with language – the man who has a fine feeling for its tempo, its fingering, its musical spirit, who can hear with his inward ear the fine effects of its inner nature and raises his voice or hand accordingly, he shall surely be a prophet; on the other hand the man who knows how to write truths like this, but lacks a feeling and an ear for language, will find language making a game of him, and will become a mockery to men, as Cassandra was to the Trojans. And though I believe that with these words I have delineated the nature and office of poetry as clearly as I can, all the same I know that no one can understand it, and what I have said is quite foolish because I wanted to say it, and that is no way for poetry to come about. But what if I were compelled to speak? what if this urge to speak were the mark of the inspiration of language, the working of language within me? and my will only wanted to do what I had to do? Could this in the end, without my knowing or believing, be poetry? Could it make a mystery comprehensible to language? If so, would I be a writer by vocation, for after all, a writer is only someone inspired by language?

Part 10

Goethe

Johann Wolfgang von Goethe

(1749–1832)

Born in Frankfurt into a well-to-do bourgeois family, Goethe studied at Leipzig (1765–8) and Strasbourg (1770–1) Universities, taking a degree in Law at the latter. His meeting with Herder in Strasbourg provided the first major impetus in his literary career, introducing him to the folksong as a model for his own lyric poetry, and to Shakespeare, whose work inspired his historical drama *Götz von Berlichingen* (1773). Goethe became the leading figure of the *Sturm und Drang* movement, and his novel *The Sorrows of Werther* (1774) gave him a European reputation. His move to Weimar in 1775 led to his ennoblement (1782) and to high administrative office under Duke Karl August. His extended visit to Italy in 1786–8 completed his conversion, which had begun several years earlier, to classical ideals in art and literature, and allowed him to revise and complete his dramas *Iphigenie in Tauris* (1787), *Egmont* (1788), and *Torquato Tasso* (1790). His work on *Faust*, which he started before 1775, was not completed until 1831.

In the 1790s, Goethe devoted much time to his scientific studies; his chief publications in this area were *The Metamorphosis of Plants* (1790) and the *Theory of Colours* (1810). He also completed his novel *Wilhelm Meister's Apprenticeship* in 1795–6, the sequel to which *(Wilhelm Meister's Years of Wandering)* appeared in 1821. His friendship with Schiller from 1794 onwards led the two poets to formulate a joint scheme of classical values in poetry and art, which they defended against the young generation of Romantic poets and other non-classical tendencies in Germany. The essay *Winckelmann* (1805), written just before Schiller's death, marks the climax and end of this phase in Goethe's career.

The novel *The Elective Affinities* (1809) has some Romantic characteristics, in keeping with the older Goethe's increasing openness to multifarious literary influences, not all of them European ones. The *West-Eastern Divan* (1819), for example, is a collection of poems inspired by the fourteenth-century Persian poet Hafiz, and *Faust* embodies an encyclopaedic range of themes and forms of expression from the most disparate literary traditions.

Goethe's output was prodigious, and its diversity equally so. He tried his hand at almost every literary genre, and developed an enormous stylistic repertoire over his long career. He was less of a theorist than Schiller, and was temperamentally disinclined to philosophising. But his aesthetic principles carried the authority of the canonic works of literature in which he implemented them.

Goethe's criticism, scattered over a wide range, particularly of contemporary literature, was probably most influential (at least to an English audience) in the area of his writing on Shakespeare, about which it is sometimes exaggeratedly claimed that romantic criticism gained its original impulse from the *Hamlet* selections in *Wilhelm Meisters Lehrjahre* (1796). Romantic criticism certainly had centred upon

Shakespeare as the model and standard of modern literature in distinction from classical models. While the comparative approach of Lessing was transformed by Herder into a historical relativism, Goethe's own attitude to Shakespeare (and to Romanticism generally) was less stable, undergoing considerable transformation as he went from eager youthful admiration, to restrained criticism, and finally to a harsher and more general hostility toward Shakespeare's fundamental principles of structure and design. His attitude is charted in three essays and one translation: (1) 'Zum Shakespeares Tag' (1771); (2) the *Wilhelm Meister* sections (1796); (3) his translation of *Romeo and Juliet,* which substantially alters the play to fit his classicist theory; and, finally (4), 'Shakespeare und kein Ende' (1815), where Goethe argues against, for example, Tieck, that Shakespeare is no dramatic poet.

Further reading

The standard edition of Goethe's works and letters is the Weimar edition in 133 volumes (1887–1919). The Hamburg edition, edited by Trunz (1948–64), is selective but includes a helpful critical apparatus. The conversations are assembled in volumes 22 to 24 of the Gedenkausgabe (1948–60). Most of the main works have been translated into English. Readers of the present volume may find the *Literary Essays* translated by Spingarn (1964), the *Italian Journey* translated by Auden and Mayer (1962), the *Conversations and Encounters* translated by Luke and Pick (1966), and Eckermann's *Conversations with Goethe* translated by Oxenford (1971) of particular interest. Staiger (1952–9) and Conrady (1982–3) are general biographical studies, and biographies in English include Fairley (1947) and Friedenthal (1965). Reed (1980) gives an excellent account of Weimar classicism as a whole. Wilkinson (1984) contains a substantial bibliography of works on Goethe in English. See also Wilkinson and Willoughby (1970), and Gage's translation of the art criticism (Goethe, 1980). On Goethe's reading of Kant, see Molnár (1981–82).

HBN and KMW

From

Wilhelm Meister's Apprenticeship
[Wilhelm Meisters Lehrjahre]

1796

Translated by Thomas Carlyle (1824), II, 71–5, 176–81.

Loving Shakespeare as our friend did, he failed not to lead round the conversation to the merits of that dramatist. Expressing, as he entertained, the liveliest hopes of the new epoch which these exquisite productions must form in Germany, he ere long introduced his Hamlet, who had busied him so much of late.

Serlo declared that he would long ago have played the piece, had this been possible, and that he himself would willingly engage to act Polonius. He added, with a smile: 'An Ophelia, too, will certainly cast up, if we had but a Prince.'

Wilhelm did not notice that Aurelia seemed a little hurt at her brother's sarcasm. Our friend was in his proper vein, becoming copious and didactic, expounding how he would have Hamlet played. He circumstantially delivered to his hearers the opinions we before saw him busied with; taking all the trouble possible to make his notion of the matter acceptable, sceptical as Serlo shewed himself regarding it. 'Well then,' said the latter, finally, 'suppose we grant you all this, what will you explain by it?'

'Much; every thing,' said Wilhelm. 'Conceive a prince such as I have painted him, and that his father suddenly dies. Ambition, and the love of rule, are not the passions that inspire him. As a king's son, he would have been contented; but now he is first constrained to consider the difference which separates a sovereign from a subject. The crown was not hereditary; yet a longer possession of it by his father would have strengthened the pretensions of an only son, and secured his hopes of the succession. In place of this, he now beholds himself excluded by his uncle, in spite of specious promises, most probably forever. He is now poor in goods and favour, and a stranger in the scene which from youth he had looked upon as his inheritance. His temper here assumes its first mournful tinge. He feels that now he is not more, that he is less, than a private nobleman; he offers himself as the servant of every one; he is not courteous and condescending, he is needy and degraded.

'His past condition he remembers as a vanished dream. It is in vain that his uncle strives to cheer him, to present his situation in another point of view. The feeling of his nothingness will not forsake him.

'The second stroke that came upon him wounded deeper, bowed still more. It was the marriage of his mother. The faithful tender son had yet a mother, when his father passed away. He hoped, in the company of his surviving noble-minded parent, to reverence the heroic form of the departed; but his mother too he loses, and it is something worse than death that robs him of her. The trustful image, which a good child loves to form of its parents, is gone. With the dead there is no help, on the living no hold. She also is a woman, and her name is Frailty, like that of all her sex.

'Now first does he feel himself completely bent and orphaned; and no happiness of life can repay what he has lost. Not reflective or sorrowful by nature, reflection and sorrow have become for him a heavy obligation. It is thus that we see him first enter on the scene. I do not think that I have mixed aught foreign with the piece, or overcharged a single feature of it.'

Serlo looked at his sister, and said, 'Did I give thee a false picture of our friend? He begins well; he has still many things to tell us, many to persuade us of.' Wilhelm asseverated loudly, that he meant not to persuade, but to convince: he begged for another moment's patience.

'Figure to yourselves this youth,' cried he, 'this son of princes; conceive him vividly, bring his state before your eyes, and then observe him when he learns that his father's spirit walks; stand by him in the terrors of the night, when the venerable ghost itself appears before him. A horrid shudder passes over him; he speaks to the mysterious form; he sees it beckon him; he follows it, and hears. The fearful accusation of his uncle rings in his ears; the summons to revenge, and the piercing oft-repeated prayer, Remember me!

'And when the ghost has vanished, who is it that stands before us? A young hero panting for vengeance? A prince by birth, rejoicing to be called to punish the usurper of his crown? No! trouble and astonishment take hold of the solitary young man: he grows bitter against smiling villains, swears that he will not forget the spirit, and concludes with the expressive ejaculation:

> The time is out of joint: O! cursed spite,
> That ever I was born to set it right!

'In these words, I imagine, will be found the key to Hamlet's whole procedure. To me it is clear that Shakespeare meant, in the present case, to represent the effects of a great action laid upon a soul unfit for the performance of it. In this view the whole piece seems to me to be composed. There is an oak-tree planted in a costly jar, which should have borne only pleasant flowers in its bosom; the roots expand, the jar is shivered.

'A lovely, pure, noble, and most moral nature, without the strength of nerve which forms a hero, sinks beneath a burden which it cannot bear, and must not cast away. All duties are holy for him; the present is too hard. Impossibilities have been required of him; not in themselves impossibilities, but such for him. He winds, and turns, and torments himself; he advances and recoils; is ever put in mind, ever puts himself in mind; at last does all but lose his purpose from his thoughts; yet still without recovering his peace of mind.'

*   *   *

One evening a dispute arose among our friends about the novel and the drama, and which of them deserved the preference. Serlo said it was a fruitless and misunderstood debate; both might be superior in their kinds, only each must keep within the limits proper to it.

'About their limits and their kinds,' said Wilhelm, 'I confess myself not altogether clear.'

'Who *is* so?' said the other; 'and yet perhaps it were worth while to come a little closer to the business.'

They conversed together long upon the matter; and in fine, the following was nearly the result of their discussion:

'In the novel as well as in the drama, it is human nature and human action that we see. The difference between these sorts of fiction lies not merely in their outward form; not merely in the circumstance that the personages of the one are made to speak, while those of the other have commonly their history narrated. Unfortunately many dramas are but novels, which proceed by dialogue; and it would not be impossible to write a drama in the shape of letters.

'But in the novel, it is chiefly *sentiments* and *events* that are exhibited; in the drama, it is *characters* and *deeds*. The novel must go slowly forward; and the sentiments of the hero, by some means or another, must restrain the tendency of the whole to unfold itself and to conclude. The drama on the other hand must hasten, and the character of the hero must press forward to the end; it does not restrain, but is restrained. The novel hero must be suffering, at least he must not in a high degree be active; in the dramatic one, we look for activity and deeds. Grandison, Clarissa, Pamela, The Vicar of Wakefield, Tom Jones himself, are, if not suffering, at least retarding personages; and the incidents are all in some sort modelled by their sentiments. In the drama the hero models nothing by himself; all things withstand him, and he clears and casts away the hindrances from off his path, or else sinks under them.'

Our friends were also of opinion, that in the novel some degree of scope may be allowed to Chance; but that it must always be led and guided by the sentiments of the personages; on the other hand, that Fate, which by means of outward unconnected circumstances, carries forward men, without their own concurrence, to an unforeseen catastrophe, can have place only in the drama; that Chance may produce pathetic situations, but never tragic ones; Fate on the other hand ought always to be terrible; and is in the highest sense tragic, when it brings into a ruinous concatenation the guilty man, and the guiltless that was unconcerned with him.

These considerations led them to back the play of Hamlet, and the peculiarities of its composition. The hero in this case, it was observed, is endowed more properly with sentiments than with a character; it is events alone that push him on; and accordingly the piece has in some measure the expansion of a novel. But as it is Fate that draws the plan; as the story issues from a deed of terror, and the hero is continually driven forward to a deed of terror, the work is tragic in the highest sense, and admits of no other than a tragic end.

They were now to study and peruse the piece in common; to commence what are called the book-rehearsals. These Wilhelm had looked forward to as to a festival. Having formerly collated all the parts, no obstacle on this side could oppose him. The whole of the actors were acquainted with the piece; he endeavoured to impress their minds with the importance of these book-rehearsals. 'As you require', said he, 'of every musical performer that, in some degree, he shall be able to play from the book; so every actor, every educated man, should train himself to recite from the book, to catch immediately the character of any drama, any poem, any tale he may be reading, and exhibit it with grace and readiness. No committing of the piece to memory will be of service, if the actor have not in the first place penetrated into the sense and spirit of his author; the mere letter will avail him nothing.'

Serlo declared, that he would overlook all subsequent rehearsals, the last rehearsal itself, if justice were but done to these rehearsals from the book. 'For commonly,' said he, 'there is nothing more amusing than to hear an actor speak of study: it is as if freemasons were to talk of building.'

The rehearsal passed according to their wishes; and we may assert, that the fame and favour which our company acquired afterwards, had their foundation in these few but well-spent hours.

'You did right, my friend,' said Serlo, when they were alone, 'in speaking to our fellow-labourers so earnestly; and yet I am afraid that they will scarce fulfil your wishes.'

'How so?' asked Wilhelm.

'I have noticed', answered Serlo, 'that as easily as you may set in motion the imaginations of men, gladly as they listen to your tales and fictions, it is yet very rarely that you find among them any touch of an imagination you can call productive. In actors this remark is strikingly exemplified. Any one of them is well content to undertake a beautiful, praiseworthy, brilliant part; and seldom will any one of them do more than self-complacently transport himself into his hero's place, without in the smallest troubling his head, whether other people view him so or not. But to seize with vivacity what the author's feeling was in writing; what portion of your individual qualities you must cast off, in order to do justice to a part; how by your own conviction that you are become another man, you may carry with you the convictions of the audience; how by the inward truth of your conceptive power, you can change these boards into a temple, this pasteboard into woods; to seize and execute all this is given to very few. That internal strength of soul, by which alone deception can be brought about; that lying truth, without which nothing will affect us rightly, have by most men never even been imagined.

'Let us not then press too hard for spirit and feeling in our friends! The surest way is first coolly to instruct them in the sense and letter of the piece; if possible to open up their understandings. Whoever has the talent will then, of his own accord, eagerly adopt the spirited feeling and manner of expression; and those who have it not, will at least be prevented from acting or reciting altogether falsely. And among actors, as indeed in all cases, there is no worse arrangement than for any one to make pretensions to the spirit of a thing, while the sense and letter of it are not ready and clear to him.'

From
Winckelmann[1]

1805

Translated by H.B. Nisbet.

German text in *Goethes Werke*, edited by Trunz (1948–64), XII, 96–129.

Antiquity

Man may achieve much through the purposeful application of isolated faculties, and he may achieve the extraordinary by combining several of his
capacities; but he can accomplish the unique, the totally unexpected, only
when all his resources are uniformly united within him. The latter was the
happy lot of the ancients, especially of the Greeks in their best period; fate
has assigned the two former possibilities to us moderns.

When the healthy nature of man functions as a totality, when he feels
himself in the world as in a vast, beautiful, worthy, and valued whole, when
a harmonious sense of well-being affords him pure and free delight – then
the universe, if it were capable of sensation, would exult at having reached
its goal, and marvel at the culmination of its own development and being.
For what is the use of all the expenditure of suns and planets and moons,
of stars and galaxies, of comets and nebulae, of completed and developing
worlds, if at the end a happy man does not unconsciously rejoice in
existence?

Whereas modern man – as our own example has just demonstrated –
launches out into infinity almost every time he reflects, only to return eventually – if he is lucky – to a limited point, the ancients took a more direct
route from the outset: they felt a characteristic need to remain firmly
within the pleasant confines of the beautiful world. Here was their place,
here their vocation, here was scope for their activity, and here were objects
and food for their passions.

Why are their poets and historians the admiration of men of discern-
ment and the despair of all who would emulate them? Simply because the
persons whose actions they describe took so deep an interest in themselves,
in the narrow circle of their fatherland, in the allotted course of their own

and their fellow citizens' lives, and devoted all their senses, inclinations, and powers to acting upon the present; and for this reason, it was not difficult for a like-minded interpreter to render this present immortal.

Actual events were the only thing that mattered, whereas it is only what men have thought or felt that seems to hold any value for us today.

The ancient poet lived in the same way in his imagination as did the historians in the world of politics and the scientist in the natural world. All of them held fast to the immediate, the true, and the real, and even the products of their fancy have flesh and blood. Man and humanity were esteemed above all else, and all man's inner and outer relationships with the world were observed and depicted with the same breadth of vision. Feeling and reflection were not yet fragmented, that perhaps irreparable rift had not yet opened up within the healthy powers of man.[2]

But such natures as these were eminently equipped not only to enjoy happiness, but also to endure misfortune: for just as healthy fibres resist disease and rapidly recover from every attack of illness, so also can that healthy sense which distinguished the ancients recover quickly and easily from internal or external accidents. An antique nature of this kind – in so far as this can be said of any of our contemporaries – appeared once more in Winckelmann;[3] and it proved its mettle from the beginning by remaining unvanquished, unmoved, and unblunted by thirty years of abasement, malaise, and affliction. From the very moment when he won the freedom he required, he appeared whole and complete, entirely in the spirit of antiquity. Activity, enjoyment and privation, joy and sorrow, acquistion and loss, elevation and debasement – all of these were his lot; yet amidst these strange vicissitudes, he was always content with that happy earthly abode in which the whims of fate seek us out.

Just as he brought to his life a genuinely antique spirit, so also did it remain faithful to him in his studies. Yet whereas the ancients, in dealing with the sciences at large, already found themselves in a somewhat problematic situation – inasmuch as it is scarcely possible to comprehend the manifold objects of the extra-human world without a division of our powers and capacities, a fragmentation of the previous unity – modern man, in a similar situation, has an even more hazardous task. For when he looks in detail at the multifarious realm of the knowable, he runs the risk of dissipating his energies, of losing himself in disconnected facts, without being able, as the ancients were, to compensate for his shortcomings by the completeness of his own personality.[4]

However widely Winckelmann ranged over all possible and worthwhile knowledge, guided partly by love and desire, and partly by necessity, he always came back sooner or later to antiquity, and particularly to ancient Greece, with which he felt so close an affinity and with which he was to achieve so happy a union in his best years.

Paganism

The above description of the antique mentality and its concern with things of this world leads directly to the conclusion that the advantages it offered are compatible only with a pagan attitude.[5] That reliance of the ancients on the self, their concern with the present, their veneration of the gods as ancestors, their admiration for them, so to speak, only as works of art, their submission to an all-powerful fate, their high estimation of posthumous fame, which made even the future a function of this world – all of these factors are so essentially interrelated, form so indivisible a whole, and together constitute a human condition so clearly intended by nature itself, that we can detect, not only in the supreme moment of enjoyment but also in the darkest moment of self-sacrifice – or even extinction – an indestructible health.

This pagan mentality shines forth from Winckelmann's actions and writings, and is particularly evident in his early letters, when he is still embroiled in conflict with modern religious attitudes. This outlook of his, his remoteness from all Christian sentiments – indeed his revulsion against them – must be borne in mind when we come to assess his so-called religious conversion. The factions into which the Christian religion is divided were a matter of total indifference to him, for he did not by nature belong to any of the churches within it.

Friendship

But if, as we have claimed, the ancients were truly complete human beings who felt at one with themselves and with the world, they were also obliged to explore the whole range of human relationships; they could not deny themselves that rapturous pleasure which springs from the union of kindred natures.

Here again, a remarkable difference is apparent between ancient and modern times. Relations with women, which have become so tender and spiritualised in our era, scarcely rose in antiquity above the level of the most basic necessity. The relationship of parents to children seems to have been somewhat more affectionate. But more than all such sentiments, they valued friendship between members of the male sex (although Chloris and Thyia,[6] as females, also remained inseparable friends even in the underworld).

The passionate fulfilment of affectionate duties, the bliss of inseparability, the sacrifice of oneself for another, the explicit pledge of lifelong devotion, and the necessity of companionship even in death fill us with amazement when we encounter them in a relationship between two youths; we even feel ashamed when poets, historians, philosophers, and orators regale us with stories, events, sentiments, and attitudes of this variety.

Winckelmann felt he was born for this kind of friendship, for he was not only capable of it, but also eminently in need of it. He depended on friendship for his own self-awareness, and he could define his own identity only in relation to a whole for whose completion another person was necessary. At an early stage, he applied this idea to someone who may have been unworthy of it,[7] and dedicated himself to living and suffering for his sake; even in his poverty he found means to be generous towards his friend, to give and to sacrifice for him, and he did not hesitate to pledge to him his existence, indeed his life. Here it was that Winckelmann, even in the midst of oppression and privation, felt himself great, rich, generous, and happy, because he was able to do something for the person whom he loved above all else, and for whom he even had to make the supreme sacrifice of forgiving his ingratitude.

As time and circumstances changed, Winckelmann transformed all the worthy people who sought his company into friends on this model; and although many of the friendships he thereby created were easily and quickly dissolved, this admirable attitude won him the hearts of various excellent individuals, and he had the good fortune to enjoy the best of relations with the finest men of his age and circle.

Beauty

But while this profound need for friendship virtually creates and fashions its own object, the antique mentality can derive from it only a one-sided advantage of a moral variety; little is gained from the external world unless this need is happily complemented by a similar, related need which in turn finds an object to satisfy it; we mean by this the need for sensuous beauty, and sensous beauty itself: for the ultimate product of nature, in its constant process of self-enhancement,[8] is human beauty. Admittedly, nature can only rarely succeed in producing it, for too many limiting factors run counter to its ideas, and even the omnipotence of nature is unable to hold on to perfection for long and to confer any permanence on the beauty it has created. For strictly speaking, the beautiful human being is beautiful only for a moment.

But this is where art comes in: for although man is the culmination of nature, he also sees himself as a complete nature which must in turn achieve its own culmination. He raises[9] himself to this level by asserting all his perfections and virtues, bringing discrimination, order, harmony, and significance into play, until he at last ascends to the production of the work of art, which occupies a magnificent place among his other deeds and achievements. Once it is created and stands before the world in its ideal reality, it produces an enduring effect, indeed the highest effect of all: for since it is the spiritual product of all man's faculties, it becomes the vessel of everything glorious, admirable, and amiable about him; and by breathing life into the human figure, it raises man above himself, completes the cycle of his life and actions, and deifies him for the present moment, in which the past and future are also contained. Those who saw the statue of Zeus at Olympia[10] were inspired by such sentiments, as is evident from the descriptions, reports, and testimonies of the ancients. The god had become man, so that man might be raised to the level of a god. The highest dignity was there for all to see, and it fired them with enthusiasm for the highest beauty. In this sense, we may well agree with those ancients who declared, with full conviction, that it was a misfortune to die without having seen this work.

Winckelmann had a natural ability to appreciate this beauty, and he first encountered it in the writings of the ancients; but it confronted him face to face in works of visual art, which alone give us the knowledge we need to recognise and appreciate it in the products of living nature.

If these two needs, for friendship and for beauty, are satisfied simultaneously by the same object, the happiness and gratitude of the man in question will seem boundless, and he will gladly give away all his possessions as inadequate tokens of his devotion and reverence.

Thus we often find Winckelmann in the company of beautiful young men, and at no time does he appear more animated and engaging than in these often all-too-fleeting moments.

Part 11

Jean Paul Richter

Jean Paul Richter

(1763–1825)

Jean Paul, novelist of dream and fantasy literature, essayist, and reviewer, was a close friend and admirer of Herder; while warmly received by the Romantics he preferred to make his name apart from the Romantic School, though sharing many of their approaches to literature and criticism. Jean Paul is perhaps best known for his novel, *Hesperus* (1795), which won him a fame in his own day rivalled only by Goethe's *Werther*.

Jean Paul was well known in England to Crabb Robinson and Thomas Beddoes, and felt a particular affinity to English culture. He was influenced by Hartley's philosophy of associationism and Laurence Sterne's ironic, witty, style in *Tristram Shandy*, as well as by Fielding and many other English writers and critics. Not surprisingly, his analysis of the faculties is in important respects similar to that of his English contemporary, S.T. Coleridge. He distinguished 'Einbildungskraft' (Coleridge's 'fancy') from 'Phantasie' (creative imagination). The first was related to memory and association; the second was the faculty that makes parts into a coherent whole, which, like Coleridge and Shelley, Jean Paul insisted was necessary both to perception and to art. He also discussed the relation of instinct to judgment or reflectiveness in the two different types of genius which he distinguished from talent. Like Coleridge, he was aware of the role of the unconscious in creativity, and insisted furthermore that what appears to be spontaneous can in fact be attributed to our own unconscious activity.

Jean Paul maintained that good criticism must be based upon the 'analytic power of taste' and the 'synthetic power of good sense'. Like the other Romantics, he recommended beginning with the literary artifact (rather than with literary history or generalization), and then seeking to derive the principles embodied in it. Jean Paul's terminological differences from Friedrich Schlegel, Solger, and others ought not to be allowed to obscure the similarities of their insights. Jean Paul tends to use 'irony' for 'common irony' – sarcasm, satire, or hyperbole – and 'humour' for 'high irony', that is, the true Socratic-Platonic irony. Indeed, in the *Athenäum Fragment* 305, Friedrich Schlegel virtually defines 'humour' as 'irony'. Jean Paul, Friedrich Schlegel, and Solger all differ from A.W. Schlegel in insisting on the close relation of irony and tragedy, and on the affirmative and positive nature of irony, which appears purely negative and destructive only to those who misunderstand it. Solger best explains this 'positive negation', or 'cancellation', in *Erwin*. These three writers also shared the view that the paradoxical relation of play and seriousness was essential to their 'irony–humour' concept, as was the idea of self-criticism or self-parody. Like Solger, Jean Paul was deeply interested in the 'Bildung des Menschen' (cultivation of the human being) – the *School for Aesthetics* was originally written allegedly as a series of lectures for aesthetic education; Jean Paul however viewed his book as a work of art in the true Romantic tradition of criticism as poetry. While emphasizing practical criticism over theoretical aesthetics, the *School* nevertheless derives principles of criticism about the unity of art, the role of the spectator, the mental experience of aesthetic response, and the psychology of language as art.

Jean Paul's other major publications include the novels *Die unsichtbare Loge* (1793), *Siebenkäs* (1796) and *Titan* (1800); a study of immortality, *Das Kampaner Tal* (1797); a collection of essays, *Herbst-Blumen* (1810); and a theory of education, *Levana* (1807).

The reader is referred to the German critical edition, *Jean Pauls Sämtliche Werke*, edited by Eduard Berend (Weimar, 1927–44, Berlin, 1952–63), and organized into three sections: Part 1 contains material published during Jean Paul's lifetime, Part 2 manuscripts, and Part 3 letters. Also useful is the *Jean Paul-Bibliographie*, ed. E. Berend, revised J. Krogoll (Stuttgart, 1963).

The *School for Aesthetics (Vorschule über Aesthetik)* was first published in 1804; an enlarged second edition appeared in 1813, and in 1825 Jean Paul added the extension 'Kleine Nachschule' to the work. The English text is taken from *Horn of Oberon. Jean Paul Richter's School for Aesthetics,* translated by Margaret Hale (Detroit, 1973).

Further reading

Essays and discussions in English include Birzniks (1966), Brewer (1943), and Carlyle (1900). See also Berend (1909) and Profitlich (1968).

KMW

School for Aesthetics
[*Vorschule über Aesthetik*]

1804; revised 1813 and 1825

On the Poetic Faculties

§6

Reproductive imagination[1]

Reproductive imagination is the prose of creativity or imagination. It is only an intensified and more vividly coloured memory, which animals also have, for they both dream and fear. Its images are only fallen leaves wafted from the real world; fever, neurasthenia, drinks can so condense and materialize these images that they pass from the inner world into the outer and there stiffen into bodies.

§7

Creativity or imagination

But imagination or creativity is higher; it is the world-soul of the soul and the elemental spirit for the other faculties. Accordingly a great imagination can indeed be drained and diverted towards particular faculties, such as wit, judgement, etc., but none of these faculties can be extended into imagination. If wit is the playful *anagram* of nature, then imagination is its *hieroglyphic alphabet,* which expresses all nature in a few images. Whereas the other faculties and experience only tear leaves from the book of nature, imagination writes all parts into wholes and transforms all parts of the world into worlds. It totalizes everything, even the infinite universe. Hence its poetic optimism, the beauty of the figures who inhabit its realm, and the freedom with which beings move like suns in its ether. Imagination brings as it were the absolute and infinity of reason closer and makes them more perceptible to mortal man. To do this it uses much of the future and much of the past, its two creative eternities, because no other time can become an infinite or a whole. Not from a room full of air, but only from the whole height of an atmospheric column can the ethereal azure of a heaven be created. [...]

*   *   *

Imagination practises its cosmetic power already in life; it throws its light into the distant rainy past and surrounds it with the splendid rainbow or arch of peace, which we never reach. Imagination is the goddess of love, the goddess of youth. For the same reason that a life-sized head in a drawing seems larger than its original, or that a landscape engraved on copper promises more by its limitation than is held by the original, every memory of life shines in its distance like a planet in heaven; the imagination compresses the parts into a closed and serene whole. It could just as well compose a *gloomy* whole; but it places Spanish castles in the air full of torture chambers only in the *future* and only Belvederes in the past. Unlike Orpheus we win our Eurydice by looking back and lose her by looking ahead.

§8

Degrees of imagination

We want to accompany the imagination through its various degrees to the point where it creates poetically under the name of genius. At the lowest level it only receives. There can be no simple reception without production or creation, since every man receives poetic beauty only in parts, like chemical elements which he must compose organically into a whole, in order to contemplate it. Hence anyone who has ever said, 'That is beautiful,' has some imaginative creativity, even if he is wrong about the object. And how could a genius be tolerated or even exalted for so much as a month, not to mention thousands of years, by the multitude so unlike him, if there were not some understood family resemblance? Many works are like the *Clavicula Salomonis;* people may be reading them casually, without any intention of calling up an apparition, when suddenly the angry spirit steps out of the air before them.[2]

§9

Talent

In the second stage of imagination several faculties are prominent, such as acumen, wit, understanding, and the mathematical or historical reproductive imagination, while the faculty of creative imagination is minimal. This stage is that of *talent,* whose inner being is an aristocracy or monarchy, while that of the genius is a theocratic republic. Strictly speaking, talent, not genius, has instinct or the one-sided direction of all faculties; as a result it lacks the poetic reflectiveness by which the human being is distinguished from the animal. The reflectiveness of talent is only partial; it is mere separation of the inner from the external world, not that high separation of the self from its own whole inner world. The melodramatic *speaking voice* of talent drowns out the double choir of poetry and philosophy, which requires the whole singing voice of a man, so that talent is heard by the audience below as the only distinct music.

In philosophy mere talent is dogmatically exclusive, even mathematical, and hence intolerant. (True tolerance is present only in the man who mirrors all mankind.) The talented person numbers the doctrinal constructs and says he lives at number 1 or 99 or the like, while the great philosopher dwells in the wonder of the world, in that labyrinth of countless rooms half above, half below the earth. The talented philosopher, as soon as he has got his philosophy, naturally hates all philosophizing; for only he who is free loves free people. As he is only *quantitatively*[a] different from the multitude, he can completely amaze, please, dazzle, enlighten, and be all to the multitude, *timeless* within the *moment*. For however high the man of talent may stand and however long his measure, every other man need only apply himself as a yardstick to the man of talent to know at once his size. But the *fire* and *tone* of quality cannot be measured by the yardstick and scales of quantity. The poetry of talent affects people by particular strengths: by imagery, fire, abundance of ideas, or charms. Though such a poem is only a transfigured body with a Philistine soul, it deeply stirs the multitude, which easily recognizes limbs but not spirit, charms but not beauty. All Parnassus is full of verses which are only bright prose spread out upon verse as if on Leyden jars, or poetic petals which like botanic petals are simply juxtaposed leaves around a stalk. Since there is no image, no trope, no single thought produced by genius which talent may not also arrive at in its highest inspiration, except the poetic whole, talent may for a while be confused with genius. Indeed talent often blooms as a green hill next to the bald alp of genius, until it is destroyed by posterity, as every dictionary is by a better one. Men of talent, differentiated by degree, can destroy and replace one another; but geniuses, as genera, cannot. Images, witty, acute, profound thoughts, powers of expression, all charms in time change, as with polyps, from *food* into *colouring*. At first a few imitators steal, then the whole century does; thus the poem of talent dies in its diffusion like a talented philosophy which has more results than form. On the contrary, a whole, a spirit, can never be stolen; it lives on, great and young and alone even in a plundered work (in Homer, for example, or in Plato, repeated by rote). Talent has no excellence which cannot be imitated, as may be seen in the work of Ramler, the philosopher Wolff,[3] and others.

§10

Passive geniuses[4]

Allow me to call the third class feminine, receptive, or *passive geniuses*, or perhaps spirits written out into poetic prose.

I might describe them as being richer in receptive than in creative imagination, as commanding only weak subordinate faculties, and as lacking that reflectiveness of genius in their work which springs from the harmony of all faculties, and of great ones. But I feel that such definitions are either only systematizations of natural history according to stamens or teeth, or inventories of chemical analyses of organic corpses. There are men who, provided with a higher sensibility than that of the strong talent but with less strength, receive the great world-spirit into a holier, open soul, whether in their external life or in the inner life of poetry and thought. They cling and remain true to this spirit like the delicate woman to the strong man, disdaining mediocrity, yet when they want to express their love, torment themselves with broken and confused organs of speech and say something other than they wished. If the man of talent is the artistic actor and an ape happily miming genius, then these suffering borderline geniuses are the quiet, earnest, upright protohumans of the forest and the *night,* to whom destiny has refused speech. As animals are for Indians the mutes of the earth, they are the *mutes* of heaven. Let every man, whether inferior or superior, hold them sacred! For these very men are the mediators for the world between the common people and the genius. Like moons they cast upon the night the reconciling light of the sun.

They apprehend and comprehend the world and beauty with philosophical and poetical freedom. But when they themselves want to create, an invisible chain binds half their limbs and they create something other or smaller than they wanted. In their perceptions, they rule over all their powers with reflective imagination; in their invention, they are bound by a secondary faculty and yoked to the plow of mediocrity.

Why are their days of creation unsuccessful? Either their *reflectiveness,* which shines so brightly on the creations of others, becomes night above their own creations; they become lost in themselves and, despite all the levers in their hands, lack a standing place on a *second* world from which they could give motion to *their own.* Or their reflectiveness is not the genial sun whose light *generates* life but a moon whose reflected light *cools.* They give form to the materials of others rather than to their own and move more freely in foreign spheres than in their own, just as *flying* is easier than *running* for a man in a dream.[b]

The passive genius is unlike the man of talent, who can make us see only parts and bodies of a world but not world spirit, while for just this reason he can be compared to the genius, whose first and last distinguishing mark is contemplation of the universe. Nevertheless the world-view of the passive genius is only a continuation and development of the view of another genius.

I want to seek a few examples among the – dead, although, because of the inexhaustible mixtures and mezzotints of nature, examples always spill the colour outside the design. Where in philosophy does Diderot belong, and where in poetry Rousseau?[5] Evidently to the feminine border geniuses, although each produced more than he received, the former in poetry and the latter in philosophy.^c

In philosophy Bayle indeed belongs to the passive geniuses. But Lessing – as much his kin as his superior in erudition, freedom, and acumen – where does he, with his thought, belong? In my diffident opinion he is an active genius more as a man than as a philosopher. His versatile acumen dissected more than his profundity[6] established. Even his most ingenious conceptions had to be confined as it were in a coffin of Wolffian formulas. Without, of course, being like Plato, Leibniz, or Hemsterhuis, the creator of a philosophical world, he was nevertheless the prophetic son of a creator and consubstantial with him. Although endowed with the freedom and reflectiveness of a genius, he was a passively free poetic philosopher, whereas Plato was actively free. Lessing resembled the great Leibniz in that he let the rays of every other system pass into his own solid system, as the brilliant diamond, despite its hardness and density, allows the passage of every ray of light, and even holds sunlight fast. The ordinary philosopher resembles cork – flexible, light, porous, but incapable of transmitting or retaining light.

Among creative writers Moritz[7] should stand at the head of the feminine geniuses. He apprehended reality with a sense for the poetic, but he could not form any poetic life. Only in his *Anton Reiser* and *Hartknopf* is the rosy *midnight glow* of an overcast sun, if not a bright *aurora,* diffused over the veiled earth; but nowhere does his sun rise as a bright Phoebus, showing *heaven* and *earth* at once in splendour. How often Sturz,[8] on the contrary, cools us with the lustre of his magnificent prose, which has no new spirit to reveal, but only illuminates corners of the world and the court. When one has nothing to say, the style of the Diet and the Imperial gazette is better than the ostentatious, crowned, squandering style which has itself heralded: 'He comes!' For an official style can at least be interpreted as self-parody. Novalis and many of his models and eulogizers also belong among the men-women of genius, who think that in conceiving they are producing.

Such border geniuses can attain a certain height and freedom through years of cultivation and like a dissonant stroke on the lyre become ever more tender, pure and refined as they die away. But one will notice in them the imitation of the spirit, as one does the imitation of parts in talent.

Let no one distinguish too boldly. Every spirit is Corinthian brass, fused out of ruins and known metals in some unknown way. If peoples can grow straight upward and to a great height against the wall of the present, why not spirits, against the past? To mark off spirits is to change space into rooms and to measure the columns of air above, whose capitals cannot be separated from ether.

Are there not spiritual hybrids, first of *periods,* then of *countries?* And as two periods or two countries can be related at two poles, are there not extremes of both bad and good? The bad I will pass over. The German-French, the Jewish-Germans, the Papists, the Grecizers, in short the spiritual mediators of the lack of spirit are at hand in too glaring numbers. Let us turn rather to the geniuses and half-geniuses! As a mediator between *countries* we can cite Lichtenberg,[9] whose prose is an intellectual link between England and Germany. Pope is an alley crossing between London and Paris. Voltaire binds the two cities from the opposite direction on a higher level. Schiller is, if not the chord, still the dominant note between British and German poetry, on the whole a Young raised to a higher power and transfigured, with a preponderance of the philosophical and dramatic.

As a mediator between *periods* (which, of course, become *countries* in turn), Tieck is a fine baroque, flowering hybrid of ancient and modern Germany, although he is more closely related to the genial receivers than to the givers. Wieland[10] is an orange tree bearing French blossoms and German fruit at the same time. Goethe's tall tree puts down its roots in Germany and extends its canopy of blossoms over the Greek climate. Herder is a rich, blooming isthmus between the Orient and Greece.

Now, following the regular course of nature, in whose fords and ferries the stream can never be distinguished from the shore we have finally arrived among the active geniuses.

On Genius

§11

The multiplicity of its strengths

The belief in an instinctive, single faculty of genius could only arise and endure through a confusion of philosophical or poetic genius with the artistic instinct of the virtuoso. Painters, musicians, even the mechanic, must be endowed with an organ which supplies reality to them both as object and as tool of their artistic presentation. The predominance of one organ and one faculty, e.g., in Mozart, works then with the blindness and certainty of instinct.

Anyone who locates genius, the best thing the earth possesses, the awakener of slumbering centuries, in a 'marked strength of the lower psychological faculties', and who can imagine a genius lacking in understanding, as Adelung[11] does in his book on style, certainly is lacking in understanding. Our age presents me with every possible challenge to battle with sinners against the holy ghost. Shakespeare, Schiller, et al. distribute all the individual faculties among their individual characters, and often they must be within a single page witty, discerning, understanding, rational, fiery, learned, everything just so that the splendour of those faculties can shine like jewels, not like a candle-end lighting up poverty! Only the one-sided talent gives a single tone like a piano string struck by the hammer. Genius is like a string of an aeolian harp; one and the same string resounds in manifold tones in the manifold breezes. In genius[d] all faculties are in bloom at once, and imagination is not the flower, but the flower-goddess, who arranges the flower calyxes with their mingling pollens for new hybrids, as if she were the faculty of faculties. The existence of this harmony and of this harmonizer is demanded and guaranteed by two great phenomena of genius.

§12

Reflectiveness

The first is *reflectiveness*. It implies at every level a balance and a tension between activity and passivity, between subject and object. At its lowest level, which distinguishes man from animal, and waking from sleeping, it demands an equilibrium between inner and outer worlds. In the animal the external world swallows up the inner; in the man moved by passion, often the inner swallows up the external world. Then there is a higher reflectiveness which divides and separates the inner world itself into two parts, into a self and its realm, into a creator and his world. This divine reflectiveness is as far from the common kind as reason is from understanding, for these are their respective parents. The ordinary active reflectiveness is directed only outward, and is in the higher sense of the term always outside, never within itself. Its possessors have awareness rather than self-awareness, which is like a man's double contemplation of his complete self by facing one mirror and turning away from a second. The reflectiveness of genius differs so much from the other kind that it often appears as its very opposite. Like a burial lamp, this eternally burning lamp within is extinguished, if *outside* air and world touch it.[e] But what are the means of attaining it? Equality presupposes freedom more than freedom presupposes equality. The inner freedom of reflectiveness is secured and granted through the alternation and movement of great faculties, so that no single faculty can by dominating become an inferior self. The self is excited and calmed in such a way that the creator is never lost in the creation.

The poet, like the philosopher, is therefore an eye. All his pillars are pier-glasses. His is the free flight of a flame, not the explosion of an emotion-sprung mine. The wildest poet can therefore be a gentle man; one need only look into Shakespeare's heavenly clear face or, even better, into his great dramatic epic. Conversely, a man can be sold in the slave market of the moment every minute, yet raise himself gently and freely by writing poetry. Thus in the storm of his personality Guido Reni[13] rounded and curled his mild heads of children and angels, like the sea which despite its currents and waves breathes a calm clear dawn and sunset towards heaven.

Only the foolish youth can believe that the fire of genius burns like that of emotion, as the bust of Bacchus is passed off for the bust of the soberly poetic Plato. Alfieri,[14] who was always moved to the point of vertigo, found at the expense of his creations less repose within than without himself. The true genius is calm from within; not the upheaving wave but the smooth deep mirrors the world.

This reflectiveness of the poet, which we are inclined to presuppose also among philosophers, confirms the kinship of the two. In few poets and philosophers does it shine as brightly as in Plato, who was in fact both, from the clear-cut characterizations of his dialogues to his hymns and ideas, those constellations of a subterranean heaven. If we consider the reflective playful criticism with which Socrates dissects the eulogy to love in the *Phaedrus*, which condemns all our rhetorics, we can comprehend why twenty beginnings of the *Republic* were found after his death. The repose of genius is like the so-called 'unrest' or balance wheel in a watch, which works only to *moderate,* and hence to maintain the motion. What did our great Herder with his acumen, profundity, versatility and breadth of vision, lack in order to become a higher poet? Only the ultimate aspect of similarity to Plato; his steering tail-feathers *(pennae rectrices)* should have been in more just proportion to his flight feathers *(remiges).*

It is a misunderstanding and a prejudice to infer from this reflectiveness any limits to the poet's enthusiasm. For he must simultaneously cast flames upon the least detail and apply a thermometer to the flames; he must in the battle heat of all his faculties maintain the subtle balance of single syllables and must (to use another metaphor) lead the stream of his perceptions to the debouchment of a rhyme. Inspiration produces only the whole; calmness produces the parts. After all, does the philosopher, for instance, offend the god within because he tries to mount one vantage point after another as best he can in order to look into his inner light? Is philosophizing about the conscience without conscience? If reflectiveness as such could become excessive, then the reflective man would indeed be inferior to the senseless animal and the unreflective child; and the Infinite One, who although incomprehensible to us, cannot be anything which he does not know, would be inferior to the finite!

A certain understanding and judgement must, however, precede and underlie that misunderstanding and prejudgement. For according to Jacobi[15] man respects only what cannot be imitated mechanically; but reflectiveness always appears to imitate, wilfully and hypocritically to simulate divine inspiration and feeling and hence to cancel them out. Illustrations of an evil presence of mind need not be sought in the thought, poetry, and activity of the vacuous solipsists of the present day; the ancient learned world offers us a wealth of examples, above all in the field of rhetoric and the humanities, with their insolent cold instructions for presenting the finest feelings, like reflective skeletons taken from the grave. With self-satisfaction and vainglorious coldness, for example, the old pedagogue selects and moves the necessary muscles and tear glands (according to Peucer or Morhof)[16] in order to have a lachrymose mourning face for the benefit of the public when he looks down from the school window in making a threnody on the grave of his predecessor, while he complacently counts every drop with a rain gauge.

But how is divine distinguished from sinful reflectiveness? By the instinct of the unconscious and the love for it.

§13

Human instinct

The greatest power in the poet, breathing the good or the bad soul into his works, is precisely the unconscious. Therefore a great poet like Shakespeare will open up and distribute treasures as invisible to him as the heart in his body. For divine wisdom is always completely *immersed* upon the sleeping plant and animal instinct, and is *expressed* in the mobile soul. In general, reflectiveness does not see sight, but only the mirrored or dissected eye; and the reflection does not reflect itself. If we were completely aware of ourselves, then we would be our own creators, unlimited. An inextinguishable feeling within us places something dark, which is not our creation but rather our creator, above all our creations. So we come before God, as he commanded on Sinai, with a veil over our eyes.

If one dares to speak about the unconscious and unfathomable, one can undertake to determine only its existence, not its depth. In the following discussion, happily, I can plough with the Pegasi of Plato and Jacobi, although for the sake of my own seed.

Instinct or impulse is the sense of the future; it is blind, but only as the ear is blind to light and the eye deaf to sound. It signifies and contains its object just as the effect does the cause. If the secret were revealed to us, of how an effect which is necessarily given entirely and simultaneously with its cause nevertheless only follows the cause, then we would also understand how the instinct at the same time demands, determines, knows, and yet lacks its object. Every feeling of a deficiency supposes a relationship to that which is lacking and thus supposes its partial possession.[f] But only a true deficiency makes possible the impulse toward it, only distance allows direction. There are spiritually organic mutualisms, just as there are physically organic mutualisms; freedom and necessity, for example, or willing and thinking presuppose each other.

There is in the pure self as much a sense of the future, or an instinct, as there is in the impure self and in an animal, and its object is at once as remote as it is certain. Otherwise in the very heart of man the general truthfulness of nature would have lied for the first time. This instinct of the spirit – which eternally anticipates and demands its objects without consideration for time, because they exist beyond it – is what makes it possible for man to pronounce and understand the words *earthly, worldly, temporal,* and the like. For only that instinct gives them meaning through their opposites. If even the most ordinary man sees life and everything earthly as only a *piece,* as a *part,* then only a perception and assumption of a *whole* within him can posit and measure this partition. Even for the most ordinary realist, whose ideas and days crawl along on caterpillar feet and in caterpillar rings, something inexpressible limits the breadth of life. He is impelled to proclaim this life to be a game, confused and bestial, or painful and deceptive, or an empty *pastime.* Or like the older theologians, he compares it with a vulgar comic prologue to the heavenly, earnest play, or with a childish school for a future throne. He thus considers it the opposite of the future. In earthly, even earthy hearts, there is already something alien, like the coral islands in the Harz mountains which the earliest waters of creation may have deposited.

*   *   *

§15

The ideal of genius

If the ordinary man feels virtuous, then like every Christian in the past, he links by his faith this gross life directly to a second ethereal life after death. This fits the gross life as spirit does the body, yet is so little tied to it by *pre-established harmony, influence,* and *opportunity* that at first the body alone appears and governs, and only afterwards the spirit. The further any being stands from the centre, the greater the space he sees between the radii. A mute, hollow polyp, if he were to express himself, would surely find more contradictions in creation than any human seafarer.

And so one finds among the common people the inner and the outer world, time and eternity, as moral or Christian antitheses. In the philosopher these appear as a continued contrast, only with an alternating destruction of one world through the other; in the better man they appear as an alternating eclipse, like that which governs moon and earth; in the Janus-head of the man who faces opposite worlds, now one pair of eyes is closed or covered, now the other.

If, however, there are men in whom the instinct of the divine speaks more clearly and loudly than in others; if it teaches them to contemplate the earthly (instead of the earthly teaching them to contemplate it); if it provides and controls the perception of the whole; then will harmony and beauty stream back from both worlds and make them into *one* whole, for there is only *unity* before the divine and no contradiction in parts. That is genius; and the reconciliation of the two worlds is the so-called *ideal.* Only through *maps of heaven* can *maps of earth* be made; only viewed from above (for the view from below eternally divides heaven with the broad earth) does the whole sphere of heaven appear, and the sphere of earth itself will swim therein, small perhaps, but round and shining. For this reason, mere talent, which always degrades the divine world to a satellite or at most to the saturn-ring of an earthly world, can never round out any universe ideally or replace or build it with parts. When the old men of prose, petrified and full of earth[g] like men physically old, let us see poverty, the struggle of everyday existence or even its victories, we begin to feel as cramped and troubled at the sight as if we actually had to experience the adversity. One actually does experience the picture and its effect; their pain and even their joy lack a heaven. They trample down even the sublime in reality: love, friendship, and the grave, for example (as their funeral orations show), or the process of dying, this life between two worlds. In the wound-fever of reality, let us avoid those who would inoculate a new fever into the old by painting our wounds with their prosaic poetry, who make true poems necessary as antidotes to their false ones.

When, on the contrary, genius leads us over the battlefields of life, we survey them as freely as if glory or patriotism marched before us with flags fluttering behind; and next to genius poverty takes on an Arcadian form, as for a pair of lovers. Everywhere genius makes life free and death beautiful; on his sphere, as on the sea, we catch sight of the driving sails before the heavy ship. Like love and youth, he thus reconciles – indeed he weds – helpless life with ethereal sense, as at the edge of still water the real tree and its reflection seems to grow from a single root toward two heavens.

On Humorous Poetry

§31

Concept of humour

By our definition romantic poetry, as opposed to plastic poetry, delights in presenting the infinity of the subject in which the object-world loses its limits as in a kind of moonlight. But how will the comic become romantic, since it consists merely in contrasting the finite with the finite and cannot allow any infinity? The understanding and the object-world know only finitude. In the romantic we find only that infinite contrast between the ideas (or reason) and all finitude itself. But suppose just this finitude were imputed and lent as *subjective* contrast[h] to the idea (infinity) as *objective* contrast, and, instead of the sublime as an applied infinity, now produced a finitude applied to the infinite, and thus simply infinity of contrast, that is a negative infinity.

Then we should have humour or the romantic comic.

And so it happens in fact; and the understanding, although the atheist of an absolute infinity, must here face a contrast extending into infinity. To prove this, I will further differentiate the four components of humour.

§32

Humorous totality

Humour as the inverted sublime annihilates not the individual but the finite through its contrast with the idea. It recognizes no individual foolishness, no fools, but only folly and a mad world. Unlike the common joker with his innuendoes, humour does not elevate individual imbecility but lowers the great. It does so like parody, but with a different goal: to set the small beside the great. Humour raises the small like irony, but then sets the great beside the small. Humour thus annihilates both great and small, because before infinity everything is equal and nothing. 'Vive la bagatelle', the half-mad Swift cries sublimely, who at the end of his life preferred both to read and to compose bad works, because in this concave mirror foolish finitude, the enemy of the idea, appeared to him most tattered. In these bad books which he read and wrote, he enjoyed his own thoughts. The common satirist may on his travels or in his reviews pick up a few genuine examples of tastelessness and other faults and fix them on his pillory, to throw a few salty conceits at them instead of rotten eggs. The humorist, however, would almost rather take individual folly into protection, while taking the constable of the pillory together with all the spectators into custody; it is not civic folly but human folly, the universal that touches him within. His thyrsus-staff is no baton and no scourge; its blows are accidental. In Goethe's *Annual Fair at Plundersweilern* one must seek the goal either in specific satires on drovers, actors, and the like, which is absurd, or in the epic grouping and scorn of all earthly activity. Uncle Toby's campaigns do not make Toby himself or Louis XIV alone ridiculous; they are the allegory of all human hobbyhorses. There is a child's head kept in every man's head as in a hatbox, which at times still pops out into the open air despite any number of inner cases, and which in our old age often appears by itself with silver hair.

*   *   *

Humorous totality takes many forms. It is expressed, for example, in the structure of Sterne's periods, which bind with dashes not parts, but wholes. It will be expressed in any generalization from something which is strictly true only in a particular case; for example, in Sterne, 'Learned men, brother Toby, don't write dialogues upon long noses for nothing.' The common critic suffocates and materializes the truly humorous world spirit by contracting and confining it in partisan satires. Because he does not possess the buttress of the comic, namely the world-scorning Idea, this insignificant critic must consider the comic unfounded, even childish and purposeless, and almost laughable in its laughter; secretly but enthusiastically he must prefer the specious whimsy of Müller von Itzehoe[17] to the humour of Shandy, in more than one respect. Although Lichtenberg praised Müller (who may deserve it for his *Siegfried von Lindenberg*, at least in the first edition), and also, like a funeral orator, praised the Berlin wags and fireflies of his day too highly, and although he was somewhat constrained by a British and mathematical one-sidedness, he was still raised by his humorous faculties higher than he really knew. With his astronomical view of worldly activity and with his witty superabundance, Lichtenberg might perhaps have been able to show something better to the world than two wings in the ether which indeed move, but whose feathers are stuck together.

This totality of humour, furthermore, explains the mildness and tolerance of humour towards individual follies, because such follies in the mass are less significant and less harmful and because the humorist cannot deny his own kinship with humanity. The common mocker recognizes and reckons up only individual, abderitic[18] traits of both vulgar and learned existence, because they are alien to himself. He is narrowly and selfishly aware of his own superiority. And fancying that he rides as a hippocentaur through onocentaurs, he delivers from his horse that much the wilder a capuchin sermon against folly, like a matin and vesper preacher in this insane asylum of the earth. O what a difference between him and the man who simply laughs at everything, without excluding either the hippocentaur or himself!

But in the context of this general mockery, how is the humorist who warms the soul distinguished from the persifleur who chills it, since both laugh at everything? Shall the humorist, rich in feeling, be a neighbour of the cold persifleur who shows off only his lack of sensibility?[i] Impossible. The first is distinguished from the second as Voltaire from himself or from the rest of the French, by the annihilating idea.

§33

The annihilating or infinite idea of humour

This is the second component of humour as inverse sublimity. Whereas Luther calls our will a *lex inversa* [law of inverting] in an unfavourable sense, humour is a *lex inversa* in a good sense, and its descent to hell paves its way for an ascent to heaven. It is like the bird Merops, which indeed turns its tail towards heaven but still flies in this position up to heaven. This juggler, while dancing on his head, drinks his nectar *upwards*.

When man looks down, as ancient theology did, from the supernal world to the earthly world, it seems small and vain in the distance; when he mea-

sures out the small world, as humour does, against the infinite world and
sees them together, a kind of laughter results which contains pain and
greatness. Whereas Greek poetry, unlike modern poetry, made men cheerful, humour, in contrast to the ancient jest, makes men partly serious; it
walks on the low *soccus*,[19] but often with the tragic mask, at least in its hand.
For this reason not only have great humorists been very serious men, as
said before, but the best come from a melancholy people. The ancients
loved life too much to scorn it humorously. An underlying earnestness is
indicated in the old German farces by the fact that the devil is generally
the clown; even in the French farces a *grande diablerie* appears, a buffoon-
ing quadruple alliance of four devils. This is a significant idea! I can easily
think of the devil, the true reversed world of the divine world, the great
world-shadow which marks off the contours of the lightbody, as the greatest humorist and 'whimsical man!' But as the *arabesque* of an arabesque, he
would be far too unaesthetic; his laugh would have too much pain; it would
be like the colourful flowery garment of the – guillotined.

After all intense pathos man naturally craves humorous relaxation. Since
no feeling can desire its opposite, but only its own mitigation, there must
be a transitional element of seriousness in the jest which pathos seeks. And
this is found in humour. Even in Kalidasa's Sanskrit drama *Sakuntala*, as
in Shakespeare, there is a court jester, Madhawya. In Plato's *Symposium*
Socrates argues that the genius of tragedy is the same as that of comedy.
The Englishman adds to his tragedy a humorous epilogue and a comedy.
Similarly in the Greek tetralogy, the serious trilogy was followed by a satiric
drama (Schiller began with it),[j] and the parodists began their song after the
rhapsodists. In the old French mysteries, when a martyr or a Christ was to
be scourged, the old tenderness and goodness of heart interpolated this
advice: 'Here let Harlequin come on and speak, to cheer things up a bit
again.' But would anyone ever want to be let down suddenly from the
height of pathos to Lucian or Parisian persiflage? Mercier[20] says: 'For the
public to watch the sublimity of a Leander without laughing, it must be
permitted to expect as sequel the comic Bajazzo, with which it can kindle
and thus release the laughable matter won from the sublime.' The observation is fine and true; only what a double degradation of the sublime and
of humour at once, if the former relaxes and the latter stimulates! A heroic
poem is easy to parody and to transform into its opposite; but woe to a
tragedy which does not continue to have its effect even in its parody! One
can travesty Homer, but not Shakespeare; for the trivial is indeed destruc-
tively opposed to the sublime, but not to the pathetic. When to accompany
his travestied *Ariadne on Naxos* Kotzebue[21] proposes the music which
Benda wrote for the serious play by Gotter,[22] he forgets that the festive
earnestness of such music, armed with the powers of pathos and the sublime, would not serve but would conquer his burlesque. Like a serious goddess it would hurl the comic Ariadne more than once from a greater height

than that of Naxos. Much more sublimity arises from a simply low style, as in Thümmel's *Universal Tragedy or Paradise Lost*,[23] and everyone feels truth and untruth, the divine and human nature of man, working there with equal force.

In the title of this chapter I called the Idea 'annihilating'. This is demonstrated everywhere. In general, reason dazzles the understanding with light (e.g., by the idea of an infinite divinity), as a god dazzles, prostrates, and forcibly subverts finitude. Humour does the same; unlike persiflage, humour abandons the understanding and permits it to fall down piously before the Idea. Therefore humour often delights even in contradictions and impossiblities, for example in Tieck's *Zerbino*, in which the *dramatis personae* finally believe themselves to be merely fictive nonentities, thus drawing the audience themselves onto the stage and the stage under the press jack.[k] Hence comes that fondness of humour for the emptiest conclusions, while the serious closes epigrammatically with the most important, for example, the conclusion of the preface to Möser's *Defence of Harlequin*[25] or the pitiful conclusion of the funeral oration (by Fenk[26] of myself) on a prince's stomach. Thus, for example, Sterne several times speaks lengthily and reflectively about certain incidents, until in the end he concludes: 'All the same, 'tis not a word of it true.'

Something similar to the audacity of annihilating humour, an expression of scorn for the world, can be perceived in a good deal of music, like that of Haydn, which destroys entire tonal sequences by introducing an extraneous key and storms alternately between pianissimo and fortissimo, presto and andante. Scepticism is also similar to humour; according to Platner[27] it arises when the mind's eye surveys a frightful mass of conflicting opinions around it. It is a kind of psychic vertigo which suddenly transforms *our* own rapid motion into an *external* one affecting the whole steady world.

A third analogy appears in the humorous feasts of fools of the Middle Ages, which with a free hysteronproteron, an inner spiritual masquerade innocent of any impure purpose, reversed the worldly and the spiritual, inverted social ranks and moral values, and reduced all to one great equality and freedom of joy. For such life-humour, our taste is not so much too refined nowadays as our disposition is too corrupt.

§34

Humorous subjectivity
* * *

Since in humour the self is displayed parodically, several Germans dispensed twenty-five years ago with the first person pronoun 'ich' in order to emphasize it the more strongly through linguistic ellipsis. A better author has struck out the first person again in a parody of this parody, with thick, conspicuous strokes; he is the delightful Musäus, whose *Physiognomic Journeys* are true picturesque excursions of Comus and the reader. Soon afterwards the suppressed 'I's rose up again from the dead *en masse* in Fichtean aseity,[28] egoism, and a din of vowels. Why do only German jests have this grammatical suicide of the first person pronoun, but neither the related modern languages, nor the ancient? Probably because we are too polite, like the Persians and the Turks,[1] to have a first person before respectable people. For a German is glad to be anything except *himself*. While the Briton capitalizes his 'I' in the middle of a sentence, many Germans still write theirs small at the beginning of letters and wish in vain for a small italic *i* which would barely be visible and which would be more like the mathematical dot above than the line below. While the Briton always adds the 'self' to 'my', and the Frenchman 'même' to 'moi', the German only seldom says 'I myself' *(Ich selber)*, but gladly 'I for my part' *(ich meines Orts)*, which he hopes no one will interpret as unusual pomposity. In earlier times he never named himself from foot to navel without begging pardon for existing, so that he always carried about the polite half fit for company and church on a pitiful plebeian half as if on an organic pillory. If he boldly introduces the first person, the German does so when he can join it to a smaller one; the headmaster of the high school says modestly to the students 'we'. In addition, only the German possesses 'he' *(Er)* and 'they' *(Sie)* as forms of address; he can always thereby exclude the self which 'thou' and 'you' imply. There have been times when perhaps in all of Germany no letter passed through the mails containing the word 'I'. More fortunate than the French and British, whose languages allow no pure grammatical *inversion*, we Germans make the grammatical into a spiritual inversion, putting the most important first and the insignificant afterwards: 'Your Excellency', a German can write, 'am reporting or dedicating hereby.' Modern ages are allowed (perhaps as one of the fruits of the Revolution) to write directly: 'Your Excellency, *I* report, *I* dedicate.' Thus generally a weak but clear *'I'* is allowed in the middle of a letter or speech, but very reluctantly at the beginning and end.

This peculiarity now makes it uncommonly easy for us to be more comic than any other people. In humorous parody we poetically represent ourselves as fools and must therefore conceive ourselves to be such. By this very omission of the self, we can make the humorous self-reference not only, as said above, clearer, but also more ridiculous. For we are familiar with such an omission only in serious, polite cases.

This humour of the self extends even to small parts of speech. 'Je *m'étonne, je *me* tais', for example, means more than 'I am surprised' or 'I am silent.' Bode[29] often therefore translates 'myself' and 'himself' into German by 'Ich *selber*' or 'er *selber*'. Since in Latin the first person is hidden in the verb, it can only be emphasized by participles, as Doctor Arbuthnot did in concluding his *Virgilius Restauratus* directed against Bentley: *'majora moliturus'* [about to undertake greater things].[30]

* * *

A humorous character is an entity quite different from a humorous poet. The character is completely unconscious. He is ridiculous and serious, but he does not make others ridiculous; he can easily be the target, but not the rival of the poet. It is wholly false to attribute the Germans' lack of humorous poets to their lack of humorous fools; this would be explaining the rarity of wisemen through the rarity of simpletons. The true reason is the poverty and slavery of the true comic poetic spirit exhibited by the creating writers as well as the reading public, who know neither how to catch nor how to relish (enjoy) the privileged comic game which has been loosed and runs down from the Swiss mountains onto the Belgian plains. For the comic spirit thrives only on the open heath. One finds it wherever there is either inner freedom, among the young at universities or among old people, for example, or outer freedom, as in the very largest cities and in immense deserts, in manorial seats and in village parsonages, in free towns, among the rich, and in Holland. In private most men are originals; their wives know this. A passively humorous character is not in itself a satiric subject, for who would elaborate a satire or caricature about a single deformity? The deviation of the small human needle must be aligned with and indicate the deviation of the great earth-magnet. Thus old Shandy, however much he seems a portrait, is only the gaily painted plaster cast of all learned and philosophical pedantry;[m] the same is true in other ways for Falstaff, Pistol, et al.

§35

Humorous sensuousness

Since without sensuousness the comic cannot exist, the material element, as the exponent of applied finitude in humour, can never become too colourful. The representation should overflow with images and with witty and imaginative contrasts, both in grouping and in colouring. It should fill the soul with sensuousness and inflame it with that dithyramb[n] which opposes the idea to the material world, distorted and distended in art's concave mirror into a long and angular shape. While the understanding can dwell only in a properly ordered world-building, reason, like God, is not enclosed even in the greatest temple. Insofar as such a Day of Judgement precipitates the material world into a second chaos, simply in order to hold divine judgement, humour would conceivably seem to approach madness, which naturally renounces the senses and common sense, as the philosopher does artificially, and yet like the philosopher retains reason; humour is a raving Socrates, as the ancients called Diogenes.

Let us analyse further the metamorphic sensuous style of humour. First, it individualizes to the smallest detail, even the parts of a subject already individualized. Shakespeare is never more individual, i.e. sensuous, than in comic scenes. Aristophanes is more individual and sensuous than any other ancient.

As has been shown above, the serious always emphasizes the general and so spiritualizes things that we think, for example, of a poetic heart at the sight of an anatomic one rather than the reverse. The comic writer, however, fastens our minds narrowly upon physical detail, and does not fall on his knee, for example, but on both kneepans; he can even use the knee hough. Take the sentence, 'Modern man does not love well, although he is not stupid but rather quite enlightened.' The comic writer or I must translate the man into sensuous life: into a European, still more specifically, into a man of the nineteenth century – and limit this again to a country or to a city. In Paris or Berlin he must find a street and plant the man there. He or I must then also organically animate the second part of the sentence (most quickly accomplished by an allegory). He may be lucky enough to hit upon a man from Friedrichstadt writing by lamplight in a diving bell without any roommate or bellfellow in the cold sea and tied to the world on the ship only by the lengthened air-pipe of his windpipe. 'And so', the comic writer may conclude, 'the man from Friedrichstadt sheds light on himself alone and on his paper, scorning the monsters and fish around him completely.' This scene is our translation of the sentence above.

Comic individuation could be pursued into minutiae. For example: The English love the hangman and being hanged; we Germans prefer the devil, but only as the comparative of the hangman. 'He is for the hangman,' may be expressed more strongly as 'He is gone to the devil.' There is the same difference between 'Be hanged!' and 'To the devil!' To peers one might write, 'May the devil take him', but to superiors this would have to be moderated by the hangman. Among the French the devil and dog stand higher. 'Le chien d'esprit que j'ai', writes the splended Sévigné[32] (the French grandmother of Sterne, as Rabelais was his grandfather); like all French women she loves to use this animal. Similar sensuous details are: always to choose active verbs of motion, in figurative and literal presentation – to preface and conclude every action as Sterne and others do, even an internal one, with a brief physical action – always to give definite quantities in allusions to money, numbers, and all magnitudes, where one expects the indefinite: 'A chapter as long as my arm', or 'not worthy a curved farthing', etc. Comic sensuousness gains by the monosyllabic compression of the English language, as when Sterne says (*Tristram Shandy*, bk 11, chap. 10) that a French postilion has hardly mounted when he must dismount again, because there is always something missing about his coach: 'a tag, a rag, a jag, a strap'. These syllables, particularly their assonances, are not so easy

to translate into German as the Horatian *ridiculus mus* [ridiculous mouse].
Assonances forged in the comic fire occur not only in Sterne (e.g., bk 7,
chap. 31, 'all the frusts, crusts, and rusts of antiquity') but also in Rabelais,
Fischart, and others, like next-door neighbours to rhymes.

The comic writer should also take advantage of proper names and technical terms. No German perceives the want of a national or capital city
more sadly than one who laughs; for it hinders his individualization. 'Bed-
lam', 'Grubstreet', etc. pass current through all Great Britain and over the
sea; we Germans on the contrary must substitute for these the general
expressions 'madhouse', 'dirty writing-street', because without a national
capital the proper names in the scattered cities are both too little known
and less interesting. Thus it is fortunate for an individualizing humorist
that Leipzig has a blackboard, an Auerbach's celler, its Leipzig larks and
fairs,° which are sufficiently well known abroad to be used with success.
But the same familiarity would be desirable in more things and cities.

The paraphrase also belongs to humorous materiality, or the subdivision
of subject and predicate, which can often be carried on endlessly. It is most
easily copied from Sterne, who in turn most easily imitated Rabelais.
When, for example, Rabelais wants to say that Gargantua played, he begins
(1, 22):

> La jouoit
> au flux
> à la prime
> à la vole
> à la pille
> à la triumphe
> à la picardie
> au cent –
> etc. etc.

He names two hundred and sixteen games. Fischart[p] even adduces five
hundred and eighty-six games of children and society, which I counted up
with much haste and boredom. This humorous paraphrase, which Fischart
most often follows to the extreme, Sterne continues in his allegories,
whose abundance of sensuous details ranks next to the luxuriant painting
of Homeric similes and oriental metaphors. A similar colourful border or
margin of alien details surrounds even his witty metaphors; the imitation
of this boldness is *that* part, which Hippel[33] selected *particularly* and
reserved for himself to improve on (for everyone has spied out in Sterne
a side to copy: Wieland took over the paraphrase of subject and predicate,
others Sterne's unsurpassable periods, many his eternal 'said he', more
took nothing at all, and no one recaptured his airy grace). If one wanted
to discuss in the manner of Hippel this idea that the imitators are mere
transcendent translators, he would have to say, 'They are the origenic
Tetra-, Hexa-, and Octapla of Sterne.' An even clearer example is the

description of animals as a Carlsruhe and Viennese copy[34] of men on blotting paper. The mind is uncommonly refreshed when it is forced to contemplate in the particular nothing but the general or the light in the colour black.

Presentation of movement, particularly quick motion, or of rest beside movement, helps heighten the comic effect of humorous sensuousness. Presentation of a mass has a similar effect; through the predominance of the sensuous and the physical, it also produces the ridiculous appearance of the mechanical. Because of the mass of heads, we authors appear really ridiculous in all reviews in Meusel's *Learned Germany*.[35] Hence every reviewer jokes a little.

§45

Concise style

*   *   *

The French owe their *nonfigurative* or reflective wit to their precision of language and the latter to the former. What superior possibilities for witty relationship their simple particle *en* provides! English and German prose, which have not yet broken the chain of classic periods into single rings as much as the French has, combine with *chains* rather than *rings*.[q] When a certain Roman emperor asked a stranger, mocking their family resemblance, 'Was your mother not in Rome?' and the latter replied, 'No, but my father was', then the spark of wit in the answer springs from a collision less of the remotest similarities than of the closest. Translate this into a plain statement and you annihilate the entire witticism. But where then does wit lie? In brevity; the first chain of thought in the question and the suddenly reversing chain in the answer are run through in a few forceful words. If I said here (for the sake of the example rather than for the joke) that in ancient Rome temples preserved the libraries, but now libraries the temples,[r] I would be forcing the understanding in a few words and moments to the rapid reversal and retracing of the same mental sequence.

French conciseness conquers in prose, in so far as it is in the service of pure philosophy. Whereas imagination seeks living figures, conception seeks only relationships, in which no brevity is too brief,[s] for this is clarity. Most German – and English – philosophers should translate themselves into French, as Fichte's stylistic precision is manifestly modelled on Rousseau. Thus, while antithesis is not suitable to poetic presentation, it is through its abbreviation that much the more favourable to philosophic production; Lessing and Rousseau experienced this advantage. Kant and still more the Kantians become obscure by repeating themselves, as the transparent body becomes opaque when doubled. Many Germans say no word without adding an echo and re-echo, so that as in *resonating* churches the preacher's voice resounds completely muddled.

§50

Two forms of figurative wit

The French treasure of images contains, besides its mythological household store, little more than the common tragic military baggage and poetic service: throne, scepter, dagger, flower, temple, sacrificial victim and a few flames, gold, no silver, a bloody scaffold, and their own principal limbs. Because they always have this poetic set of tools at hand, especially the hands, feet, lips, and head, they use them as often and as boldly as Orientals and savages, who like the French materialists today construct the self out of physical members. 'Le sommeil caressé des *mains* de la nature' [sleep caressed by the hands of nature], said Voltaire. 'Ses mains cueillent des fleurs et ses *pas* les font naître' [his hands gather the flowers and his steps bring them forth], said another less badly. Thus with oriental boldness they assign and attach hands with splints to hope, time, or love, so long as the hands can in turn be opposed or attached to feet, lips, lap, or heart.

The poor heart! Among the brave Germans it is still at least the synonym of courage, but in French poetry, as in anatomy, it is the strongest muscle, although it has the smallest nerves. A comic writer might not scruple to call the compressed heart a 'globe de compression', the 'globulus hystericus' of the French muse,[36] or the steam chamber for the blast pipe, the firewheel of its works, its cylinder for playing music and for speech, its savings bank, the smelt, or anything else. But one needs little or no taste to find anything like that incompatible with the tone required for aesthetic courses.

On the Novel

§69

Its poetic value

The development of a pure novel form suffers from its breadth, in which almost all forms have room to lie and rattle about. Originally it is epic, but at times the hero or all the characters narrate, instead of the author. The epistolary novel, which is either simply a prolonged monologue or a dialogue, borders on the dramatic form or even on the lyric, as in the *Sorrows of Werther*. In one narrative the action moves with the confined limbs of the drama, as in Schiller's *Ghostseer;* in another it plays and dances over the entire surface of the earth as in the fairy tale. The freedom of prose is also detrimental, because its facility spares the artist an initial effort and discourages the reader from close study. Even its extent – for the novel surpasses all other artistic works in amount of paper – helps worsen it; the connoisseur readily studies and measures a drama of half a quire, but who can deal with one twenty times that size? Aristotle recommends that an epic be capable of being read within a day;[37] Richardson and the present author fulfil this rule in their novels, which are limited to a day's reading, except that since they live further north than Aristotle, it is the usual polar day, consisting of ninety and one-quarter nights. But critics do not sufficiently consider how hard it is for a single inspiration, spirit, and view of the whole and of a single hero to extend and be sustained through ten volumes. They do not consider how a good work must be created in the enveloping warmth and air of an entire climate, not in the narrow confines of a hothouse pot which might produce an ode.' Artists themselves do not reckon on it and, as a result, begin well, continue in a mediocre fashion, and then end miserably. People want only to study the smallest form, which actually requires less study.

Yet in the right hands the novel, the only permissible poetic prose, can flourish instead of wasting away. Why should there not be a poetic encyclopedia, a poetic license to use every poetic license? Let poetry come to us how and where she will, let her dress herself in some prosaic thin, poor body like the devil of hermits or the Jupiter of the heathens; if she is really present, we will welcome her masked ball. If a spirit is there, it may assume any form in the world, like the world-spirit, which it alone can use and wear. When Dante's spirit wanted to appear on earth, the epic, lyric and, dramatic eggshells and skulls were too narrow for him; he then dressed himself in vast night and in flame and in heaven's ether all at once and thus hovered only half-embodied among the strongest, sturdiest critics.

The most indispensable element in the novel is the romantic, into whatever form it may be hammered or cast. Up to now, however, the stylicists have demanded from a novel not the romantic spirit but its exorcism; the novel was supposed to repress and expel what little romanticism still glimmers in reality. The stylistic novel, an unversified didactic poem, became a thick almanac for theologians, philosophers, and housewives. The spirit became an agreeable dressing for the body. As the students in the old school-dramas of the Jesuits used to disguise themselves and act as verbs and their inflections, vocatives, datives, etc., so the stylicists' human characters presented paragraphs and moral applications and exegetic hints, words in season, and heterodox leisure hours. The poet gave his readers, as Basedow[38] gave children, cakes in the form of letters to eat.

Certainly poetry teaches and should teach, and the novel should do so as well, but only as a blossoming flower which through its opening and closing and even through its fragrance announces the weather and the times of day. Its tender stem will never be cut, carpentered, and confined to the wooden teacher's desk or preacher's pulpit; the wooden frame and the person standing therein do not replace the living breath of spring. And what does it mean to give lessons? Simply to give signs. But the whole world and all time are full of signs already. Yet these letters are not read; we need a dictionary and a grammar of the signs. Poetry teaches us to read, while the mere teacher belongs among the ciphers rather than among the deciphering chancery-clerks.

A man who expresses a judgement about the world gives us his world, a miniature fragment of world instead of the living extended one, a sum without the reckoning. Poetry is indispensable, because it renders to the spirit only the spiritually reborn world and does not impose any casual conclusion. In the poet humanity alone speaks to humanity alone, not this man to that man.

§70

The epic novel

While such degrees are somewhat arbitrary, the novel in its range around the two focuses of the poetic ellipse must approach either the *epic* or the *drama*. The common unpoetic class of novel produces mere biographies lacking the unity and necessity of nature and the romantic freedom of the epic, yet borrowing the limitations of nature and the caprice of the epic. These biographies ring all the changes of times and places in a common course of world and life until they run out of paper. I am almost ashamed to acknowledge that I found more in *Fortunatus' Wishing Hat*,[39] which I have just read, that is, more poetic spirit, than in the most famous novels of the stylicists. If the common copyists were to grasp at ether by reaching through earthly clouds, they would draw back a hand full of vapour; it is the enemies of romanticism who elevate on the far side of their earthly and vaporous sphere the most monstrous shapes and inorganic grotesques, even wilder than the true genius could ever produce, as it marches behind the flag of nature.

The *romantic-epic* form, or that spirit which resided in the Old French and Middle High German romances, was called back by Goethe's *Meister* with his magic wand as if out of collapsed ruins into fresh new pleasure palaces. True to the epic character, this resurrected spirit of a more romantic time allows a light, bright, high cloud to pass over which reflects or carries the world and the past rather than a single hero. The similarity between the dream and the novel in which Herder sees the essence of the novel[40] is true and subtle, also the similarity required now between fairy tale and novel. The fairy tale is the freer epic, the dream the freer fairy tale. Goethe's *Meister* has set the example for such better works as the novels of Novalis, Tieck, Ernst Wagner, La Motte Fouqué, and Arnim.[41] Of course, many of these novels, such as those of Arnim, despite all their brilliance have a form more like a divergent than a convergent lens, which does not sufficiently condense the warmth of interest.

§71

The dramatic novel

But the moderns want to forget that the novel can just as well assume a romantic dramatic form and that it has done so. I prefer this more precise form for the same reason that Aristotle recommends an approach to dramatic terseness in the epic,[42] certainly the freedom of prose makes a certain strictness of form necessary and wholesome for the novel. Richardson, Thümmel, Wieland, Schiller, Jacobi, Fielding, Engel, etc., and the present author have taken this path, which does not open into the playground of history so much as it contracts to the race track of the characters. This form produces scenes of emotional climax, words of the moment, intense expectation, precision of characters and motivations, strong knots, etc. The romantic spirit must be able to wear this more tightly laced body as easily as in the past it has born the heavy cothurnus and raised the tragic dagger.

Part 12
Solger

Karl Solger

(1780–1819)

Karl Solger, close friend of Ludwig Tieck and major theorist of aesthetics, was involved in a work on the religion and mythology of ancient peoples, influenced by his early enthusiasm for Spinoza and Schleiermacher, when he decided finally to write up in dialogue form his aesthetic philosophy. In *Erwin. Vier Gespräche über das Schöne und die Kunst*, finished in 1815, Solger began from Schelling's position that 'art is to the philosopher the highest concern', but then deviated from Schelling in insisting that art is the propaedeutic to philosophy, and plays a crucial role in the education of man. Like Schiller and Fichte before him, Solger was deeply concerned with the 'Bildung des Menschen'; he claimed that the philosopher's true role was to show men the way to raise themselves from ordinary life to a knowledge of reality in that life. Art for Solger was alone the means of opening the way to this ascent toward self-cultivation and knowledge. Both the influence of Plato and that of Solger's contemporary Schleiermacher can be seen in Solger's philosophy and in his choice of the dialogue form as the only adequate means of genuinely communicating his insights to his fellow man – a goal of the highest importance to these 'Symphilosophen', who rejected the abstract and inaccessible style of philosophizing for one more intelligible to a wider readership. Solger's aesthetic lectures, published posthumously by his student K.W.L. Heyse in 1829, discuss in lecture style many of the problems Solger grappled with artistically in *Erwin*.

Solger's aesthetic philosophy remained to his bitter disappointment almost unknown to his contemporaries outside his immediate circle of friends until, after his death, Tieck and Raumer published his *Nachgelassene Schriften* in 1826, and won him the attention and admiration of Goethe and Hegel. Both men quickly published appreciative reviews of the new edition of Solger's work; Hegel's article, in the *Berliner Jahrbücher für wissenschaftliche Kritik*, recognized Solger's contribution to the laying of the first speculative foundations of aesthetics, and particularly praised his analysis of allegory and symbol. After Hegel's pronouncements, Solger was seen as the main development between Schelling's 'Identitätsphilosophie' and Hegel's dialectic. Just over a decade after these reviews, Kierkegaard named Solger the 'metaphysical knight of Negation' in *The Concept of Irony* (1841).

Hegel, in his Solger review, insisted that Solger's aesthetics bore little if any relation to that of the school of romantic ironists, and denied any relation between Solger's concept of irony and that of Schlegel and Tieck. Both Hegel's and Kierkegaard's different comments raise the issue of the extent to which Solger's aesthetics are related to Romantic irony. Twentieth-century judgements, as for example those by Oskar Walzel and Ingrid Strohschneider-Kohrs, tend to reject Hegel's claim, recognizing a close affinity between Solger and Friedrich Schlegel's concepts of irony and art, while insisting on the divergence of both from A.W. Schlegel's popularized versions, especially on irony and tragedy. Solger's own extensive essay

319

(1819) on A.W. Schlegel's 'Lectures on Dramatic Art and Literature' reveals his disagreement with *this* Schlegel and clarifies his own position, particularly on tragedy (an essentially Hegelian conception of tragedy). At the same time the essay indicates close links with the Romantic concept of irony, of which A.W. Schlegel is hardly a representative (a distinction which Hegel failed to make, it seems). Nevertheless, his dialectical method and his abstract style will continue to link Solger with Hegel while his aesthetics link him with Friedrich Schlegel, as well as the English Romantic theorists such as Coleridge.

Solger's other most important writings include his correspondence with Tieck on art and mysticism – involving discussions of both irony in relation to enthusiasm and of the allegory/symbol distinction (1933). His essay 'Über Sophocles und die alte Tragödie' is of interest, particularly in connection with Solger's translations in verse of Sophocles, published in 1801. Goethe himself highly valued Solger's article on his *Wahlverwandschaften,* published first in *Nachgelassene Schriften,* where numerous discourses on philosophy, religion, and mythology are also to be found.

The text follows the German of *Erwin. Vier Gespräche über das Schöne und die Kunst,* edited by W. Henckmann (München, 1971), pp. 218–29. The following points should be noted about the translation of these selections from *Erwin.* First, 'Anschauung' has in the main been translated as 'intuition', though occasionally its meaning has been rendered by 'perception'. 'Phantasie' has been translated as 'Imagination'; 'Dasein' as 'existence'; 'Erkenntnis' as 'cognition'; 'Wesen' as 'nature', 'essence', or 'reality'; 'Darstellung' as 'representation' and 'Gegenstand' as 'object', or sometimes as 'subject matter'.

Further reading

There is little discussion in English of Solger's work, but see Mueller (1941). See also Boucher (1934), and Hegel's review in *Werke* (1949–59), XX.

KMW

From

Erwin, or *Four Dialogues on Beauty and Art*
[*Erwin. Vier Gespräche über das Schöne und die Kunst*]

1816

Translated by Joyce Crick.

On the Symbol

So in our view, I said, the symbol would be a thing of the imagination which, as such, would be the presence of the idea itself in existence.[1] But what distinguishes the idea from any subordinate cognition?

The unity of the universal and the particular.

Correct. And if we go on to make a further distinction between idea and symbol (not because each of them is in itself something different, but because our mode of cognition requires us to differentiate the relations of one and the same essence), should we not then give to this unity of the universal and the particular the name of symbol,[2] when we consider it from the point of view of the particular, but the name of idea, preferably, when we consider the unity from the point of view of the universal?

Certainly, he said. This is the best way for us to establish this distinction.

It is also certain, Erwin, I continued, that *all* art is symbolic in this sense – but only in this sense. The symbol is neither an arbitrary sign, nor yet an imitation of an original, from which it would be absolutely different, but the true revelation of the idea. For in revelation our innermost cognition is so closely intertwined with the apparently accidental external appearance that it is utterly impossible to separate them. So if someone were to ask us if the choice of the particular external object were *necessarily* given by means of the idea, and if they were to put it to us that artists will often select and then reject their subject matter, what would be our reply?

The same, I should think, rejoined the young man, as we gave to the question as to how far art could be learned – or something of that kind.

I would think so too, I said. We would remind him of our representation of the holy realm of the imagination: the moment the soul's activity emerges from the perfect light of our innermost being, this light also is already clothed in form and matter, and in this sense, at whatever point you may envisage in the transition from centre to surface, you always have

321

the complete symbol – the specific thing which is at the same time the eternal, universal thought of the light itself. The artist does in fact create this real thing out of his essential nature. But according to all we have learned so far, is not this essential nature at the same time also his real existence, which, regarded as 'given', and as coming from without in accordance with the relations and connections to other things on the dark surface, appears but accidental? For scarcely do we conceive this activity and creativity as in process of emerging, before it is already 'given' existence, because only in existence and through existence is it an activity of beauty. So anyone who looks merely at the process of creation will not acknowledge any subject matter to be a subject for art, if it did not arise from the free invention of the artist; and equally, on the other hand, anyone who, approaching the object from outside, comes upon it as already given, will regard it as accidental, because it will seem to him just one among all the thronging confusion of individual things. And there is no doubt that both types of spectators break apart art and symbol, and are speaking of entirely different things. If the artist chose his subject arbitrarily, it would be nothing but an image for a thought he had contrived; if it were thrust upon him by the blind necessity of accident, that would be an isolated fact without essential meaning or content. By contrast, art tells the truth just because the highest idea always appears to the artist in a real form and not otherwise, that is, because his subject matter is not chosen; nor does it freely emerge, but, by a mysterious inevitability, it is present both within him and without. This is why in true art traditional kinds of subject matter are so prevalent: they have a living existence in popular belief, and they surround the artist from his birth. So it is scarcely possible even to say that for the artist the world of imagination and the real world are one and the same; for the realm of imagination is itself reality – but in its essential and truly higher existence. This can perhaps be seen most clearly in truly poetic fairy-tales, whose first priority is often to present this unity as actual, present life. The most ordinary and everyday things fuse with the most marvellous, and the poet unites both, as if they were all located in one and the same world.

This peculiar nature of the symbol, observed Erwin, is no doubt the source of the inextricable contradictions into which it is possible to fall if we try to distinguish what was presented to the artist as a given fact in the ordinary meaning of the word, and what arose in his imagination.

And that, I rejoined, is because an attempt of that kind is entirely illegitimate, and can at the very least never lead to any insight into the work of art. For in the true symbol the external object has merged itself with the light of the inward essence, and is entirely one with it, so that this inner light is not to be found by itself in a particular part, nor even in the inner core of the thing, but equally over its entire external surface; and one could well say that it is the task of the artist to turn the inwardness of things into their outwardness.

Since I paused a little after these words, Erwin looked rather mischievously at his friend Bernhard and said, Bernhard, will you not take this opportunity to reestablish your old claims, now that Adalbert has declared so clearly that the artist turns inwardness into outwardness?

I would probably have done so myself, Bernhard replied, if I had not noticed, as I did recently when we spoke about the sublime, that though I could certainly make use of the expression, I would soon get caught up in a train of thought which was alien to my views. For I can see that we are talking not about pure cognition of the essential nature of phenomena, but about a world which, as Adalbert presents it, is supposed to float in the middle between the light of inwardness and the darkness of the surface.

And not only that, I interrupted. Have you not heard that the world of art is all-embracing? That it excludes neither the divine light which on first emerging assumes corporeal form, nor the particular body still charged with that light?

All the more strange, said Bernhard. And all the less appropriate to my argument. I have followed you up till now, and understood your symbol to unite idea and appearance, as it were giving equal rights to each – which certainly does not accord with my other views on appearance. I could not possibly ascribe the same truth to appearance as to idea.

Yes, resumed Erwin. I must confess that I too understand the symbol as Bernhard did. And yet you maintain that absolute Divinity and particular objects in reality are both taken up into the realm of art, and necessarily so. But this does not seem to accord with our conception of the symbol so far.

But, I replied, who bade you set to work so mechanically and connect the idea to the particular merely in the middle? Bear in mind, as I have just said, that the Godhead itself is something real, just as each individual thing is something eternal and essential.

That is my view too, he rejoined, with deep seriousness, for it is all too easy to lose the right path in this strange region we have entered. And yet always above me hovers the vague suspicion that we could attain perfect knowledge both of the place where idea and appearance saturate each other utterly, metaphysically and in reality, divinely and terrestrially, and of the place where the creative activity is as it were extinguished.

I am delighted to see from your remarks, I replied, that you have kept entirely to the right path. For when we were first identifying the symbol, we chose those terms for it which best served to distinguish it from other, related things. That is how it has come about that we have been regarding it from one aspect only. For you are not wrong to observe that everywhere in the symbol idea and appearance saturate each other, although I cannot agree with your remark that creative activity is extinguished in this.

True, he said. I should not say that it is extinguished, rather that it is wholly present in it.

That sounds better, I responded. But is not this activity itself the beautiful? And have we not observed that it must pass over into the real world if beauty is to be realized?

Indeed, he said. But this realized activity is art, is it not?

And is art, I rejoined, then so very different from the symbol? Rather, is not the symbol, as you will have perceived, completely present only in the work of art? For what is found in art must also be in the symbol. Consequently the symbol must not only appear as the consummate work of our powers, but also as the life and activity of those powers itself. Do you see that?

I certainly see that all this is a real consequence of the whole argument, he said. But I do not entirely understand what you mean by it.

What I mean, I answered, is that as far as creative activity is concerned we had still not entirely removed our conception of art from the refuge of the common view, where it is still lurking. For as long as we regarded the work of art as a symbol, as we did before, or as a real thing in which idea and appearance were one, we still did so with the silent reservation that we were pushing imagination, as a living activity, into the background, and cutting it off from existence. But now let us also summon forth imagination into the light of day and of real existence: how will it appear to us now, as it fills that holy realm? Will it not emanate out into reality as a divine energy, bursting forth from the light of the Holy of Holies? And on the other hand will it not soar up out of individual created things, purifying them and raising them to the light? And will not the divine *pneuma*, as it lives and moves and has its being in this holy world, be itself a work of art and the present actuality of the beautiful?

At this Erwin said, Now my insight into the inmost soul of the world of art has been marvellously extended. Yes, this is the only way beauty has passed wholly into reality. But I do not know how to carry this inner intuition, whose truth touches me so deeply, over into appearance. For I still require the outward form of a completed work in which this life-giving energy appears to me, and this, I fear, will make me revert to the old view of the symbol.

This, too, I replied, will resolve itself the moment you remember that even when we require the form of a real existence, we must free ourselves entirely from the bonds of sense-perception and gaze only with the eyes of the imagination. For this form seen by imagination is the real object, something that we perceive in our ordinary experience by every other cognitive means except the senses, that is, by energy, cause, will and the very inwardness of things. That activity itself then, that is, the dynamic life of the imagination as a whole, must at the same time also be its own revelation in the form of an object. Only now this whole activity seems to be filled with matter or object, whereas earlier in the symbol the object seemed to burst with energy. Now do you understand me more fully?

In general, I understand the train of thought so perfectly, he said, that I am quite convinced this is the only means by which the world of the imagination becomes complete in itself and a true world filled not merely with its own existence but also with its own creative power. But it would make me very happy, if you were to make it clearer to me how exactly to apply this to experience.

First, I said, I will have to explain it to you more fully in terms of our previous train of thought; for examples applied to philosophical subjects before the fundamental principles are completely clarified tend only to confuse. So in our earlier argument, when we considered the beautiful, as it lives in art, as symbol, we found it filling that whole world of the imagination from the beginning as a fully perfected existence, saturated with its own energy and activity. It was, you will recall, the idea in its full reality, appearing not only as a complete and definite presence, but enclosed within this presence by its own perfection, without any necessity or effort. That is why here the highest perfection of existence is united (in a way that can never occur in the ordinary world of appearance) with that veiled beatitude in which the inner relation of idea and appearance does not unfold gradually, but is immediately there as the most complete contentment in present actuality. But it will obviously be a very different matter if in this world, taken as a whole, we consider activity or creativity itself. This too cannot be present in art without an object or an actual form. But will there not have to be a striving and an efficacy present here in each form by which it takes into itself its opposite? For an activity can be known only by its effect in some particular direction, and this direction is still the governing and determining factor, even when such activity steps forth in a particular guise. Seen in these terms, if the essence of the Godhead clothes itself in form, it can do so only by actively lowering itself into existence, and through its omnipotent and eternal activity uniting the world of the individual and the particular with itself. Similarly, the individual can partake of this life only by lifting itself up in longing and aspiration to the splendour of the Divine. Whatever can enter the world of appearance only in this way includes within itself the perfect aspiration towards something other, and this dynamic effort and aspiration, already carrying the object of its striving perfected within itself, revolves it with all its powers from out of itself. If you would protest that in this scheme each one refers to another, or means the same thing as the other, I will concede the point, but only if you bear in mind that we cannot be speaking of a meaning in the sense ordinarily assumed by the understanding – even you would at least grant that. In order, however, to choose a particular term of art that corresponds to symbol, let us give the name of allegory to this kind of appearance of the beautiful in art where the beautiful constantly refers, in the way indicated, to something other.

Then according to this, said Erwin, allegory would be a relationship comprehending the entire realm of art, and not that subordinate mode of representation which we usually tend to understand by it, and which, if I am not mistaken, comes very close to being a mere sign.

I see there is no need to warn you against this misunderstanding, I responded, for you have rightly noted it yourself. Just as the symbol is commonly confused with the image, so the allegory is commonly confused with the sign.[3] It is childish and unworthy of art to try to indicate an idea by means of some external similarity, and still more ridiculous to treat a general concept as a particular personality as the French so often do. And that is what is usually called allegory. Certainly the truly allegorical work always says more than is to be found in its limited presence, but nothing more than it carries within itself and develops dynamically out of itself. This is why allegory is also given what is granted to the symbol: a comprehensible lucidity within and a completely delimited form without. On the other hand, its meaning penetrates the imagination in its innermost and outermost being all the more deeply, while neither the serene, unclouded light of the Godhead nor the multiform external surface of things is inaccessible to it. The inward being and acting of the divine powers, which the symbol veils in bodily form, are brought to light by allegory, and with conscious pleasure it penetrates that blissful state, still veiled, of the beautiful.

Now, said Erwin, I believe I have grasped the whole train of thought correctly, and, I beg you, give me the examples you promised.

Examples which would be adequate to my argument, I said, must doubtless be of the kind in which both aspects of the representation by art of the beautiful, namely symbol and allegory, would be fundamentally and completely revealed. For each must include in itself a whole world of art. You will recall that Anselm's argument recently led us to a paradoxical position in which the Godhead appeared on the one hand as a universal and eternal necessity of nature, but on the other hand as freedom and personality. On closer reflection you will discover that precisely in that paradox are to be found the most perfect examples. If you like, we might first consider in this light how the Greeks represented the Divine.

That would fulfil my warmest desire, he said.

Then turn your thoughts first, I continued, towards that perfect necessity of the universe, harmonious and coherent in itself, as it was in the beginning. Now this contains within itself no variety, no change, no contingent particularity, nor can it ever become for itself the object of art, because it cannot assume any definite form. That is why the moment we speak of its existence in terms of that pure universality, we conceive it first as the negation of all particular existence, as the opposite of the ordered world, as chaos. It does not enter the artistic imagination as form until it has been transformed by various particular tendencies into individual persons, and this – that the original universality can only become actual in particularity – is the basis of polytheism. But what is the essence of the symbol, if not this inner, indissoluble fusion of the general and the particular into one and the same reality? Through this marvellous fusion alone is it possible for the general tendencies into which the idea disintegrates to become not mere forms or concepts, but living, fully rounded persons. In the Greek gods, the bliss that consists in the unity with the universal coincides perfectly with the activity which is the attribute only of particular, impersonated, dynamic beings. This is also why their particular deeds, being the perfect expression of their nature, can be subjected to moral judgement. This coexistence of so many worlds in individual beings is the true nature of the symbol. And that in fact is what the symbol is: necessity and the eternal universe itself in its existence and in its reality – which after all has always been the aim and purpose of art. For in that view of the world which regards the universe and necessity as prior and original, creative activity vanishes as something in itself because it has from the beginning been bound up in existence by necessity. Where everything is from time immemorial already complete and eternal, there is no longer any possibility or need for an originating or perfecting power. But at the same time as real existence emerges out of the division of this universe (by contradiction and opposition into heaven and earth, active and passive, begetting and bearing), everything is already populated by real, separate persons from whose individual actions necessity shines forth; and real existence now recedes as a universal into the dark profundities of the universe. For this very power which with impartial rigour presses in upon the infinite variety of temporal existence, and subjects even the gods as individuals to the bondage of the law, at the same time makes their deeds perfect and infallible; and in so doing it fills their life with that untroubled serenity which repeatedly stirs our admiration and our longing. And just as this power, as it creates and determines, cannot endure anything accidental or inadequate in their appearance, it also gives the gods in their reality a thoroughly definite, limited form, perfect and full of life. So if anyone, led astray by the general characteristics in the personalities of these gods, looks underneath for general concepts (applying what is commonly thought of as allegory), he is on the wrong path, for each divinity contains an entire world of meaning within itself. We also note that in ancient art, the more the gods appear to signify quite separate concepts – Aphrodite, for example, or Ares, or others of that kind – the more they actively and effectively influence the affairs of men and the temporal world, so that they do not degenerate into general forms, but still remain thoroughly rounded persons.[4] On the other hand, there are gods, above all Zeus, who are more in control of the overall management of the world. This in itself makes them perfect as individuals, and they are able to give themselves up to a blissful serenity virtually indifferent to the tumult of the world. This is the symbolic world of ancient art, which in the symbol itself includes all tendencies in their universality. But where necessity is conceived by itself, without this fusion with the world of the individual, or where mere temporality appears without the indwelling power of the whole, there comes about a separation of the two extremes in whose interpenetration the symbol consists, and its kingdom hath an end. In this example, I hope, you will recognize what has been said about the nature of the symbol.[5]

Indeed, he answered. Now at last I understand how the symbol can be a wholly individual thing, and at the same time the Divine itself.

Part 13

Schopenhauer

Arthur Schopenhauer

(1788–1860)

At first sight Schopenhauer seems to articulate an entirely different kind of philosophy from that of his Idealist predecessors and contemporaries. Where Fichte and Schelling had spoken of the truth of the absolute and its relation to the divine idea, Schopenhauer puts forward the blind impulses of the will. He is deterministic where they aspired to an activity of ideal freedom, aggressively elitist where they tried to be democratic, and stoically pessimistic where they might seem improbably optimistic. In fact, that part of his exposition which comes closest to what we have traced so far as the 'tradition' is to be found in his case for the redeeming status of the aesthetic.

Unlike those he so bitterly attacked, Schopenhauer spent very little of his life within the universities. When he did start lecturing at Berlin in 1820, without holding a Chair, he pointedly arranged his courses to coincide with Hegel's, thus committing himself to a nearly non-existent audience. When these lectures failed he retired from the academic life and spent his time writing, remaining in almost complete obscurity until towards the very end of his life. Lewes (1857) does not even mention his name.

Schopenhauer placed himself directly in the tradition of Plato and Kant, declaring that most of what had been written since Kant was a waste of time. He had little time for Schelling, and Fichte was for him "a mere sophist and not a real philosopher"; Hegel was his favourite target, as the producer of "monstrous articulations of words that cancel and contradict one another", and that "gradually destroy so completely his ability to think, that henceforth hollow, empty flourishes and phrases are regarded by him as thoughts" (1974a, I, 141, 23; compare II, 501ff. and 1969, I, 429).

The first volume of his great work, *The World as Will and Representation*, was written in Dresden between 1814 and 1818, and published in 1819, although its significance did not begin to be appreciated until many years later. The second edition of 1844 appeared with a second volume of fifty chapters expanding on the content of the original, and a third edition, further revised, was published in 1859. Even in 1851 his obscurity was such that the two volumes of *Parerga and Paralipomena* were published in an imprint of 750. The author received ten free copies but no payment! (1974a, I, xi–xii).

As has been said, Schopenhauer saw himself as the only significant successor to Kant, though the movement away from concentration on the unchanging operations of mind towards the positing of some dynamic and practical version of what Schopenhauer calls the "will" is evident also in Fichte's treatment of the "drives" [Trieben] and Schelling's of "force" [Kraft]. Moreover, I have explained in the general introduction that one receives a very one-sided view of Kant if one reads

331

him only in the great *Critiques*. The writings on history and society, and above all the arguments of the *Anthropology*, reveal a mood of biologistic pessimism much closer to the spirit of Schopenhauer than to that of any other among Kant's successors; consider, for example, Kant's remarks on the inevitability of egotism, on the fundamental force of the sex drive and the urge for self-preservation, on the ubiquity of pain, and on the function of aggression and competition as nature's means of keeping the species in good health (1974, pp. 10, 100, 141ff.). These are the residual insights of Enlightenment materialism which are not allowed to impinge upon the founding of transcendental idealism, though they can occasionally be glimpsed behind it. And they were more or less ignored by Kant's followers, until Schopenhauer.

Apart from those on whom he exercised a direct influence – Hardy, Gissing, Thomas Mann, Wagner, Nietzsche, Freud, Wittgenstein and others – one looks to the tradition of Malthus and Darwin for analogues of the ideas we find explored in Schopenhauer. Striving and desiring are now the very essence of the human condition: we live in constant motion "without any possibility of that rest for which we are always longing. We resemble a man running down hill who would inevitably fall if he tried to stop" (1974a, II, 284). Schopenhauer means the simile to count. We are in contradiction with ourselves, wanting to rest even knowing that we cannot (it is Nietzsche who will try to insist on the joyousness or freedom of such a predicament), and the downhill road leads to dusty death. All forms of practical or scientific knowledge are expressions of the will, the inscrutable primary drive which is the true "thing in itself" and which forces us necessarily to obey its demands, whatever consoling fictions we may invent as responsible for our behaviour. Stridently contemptuous of theology, as he felt Kant to have been in spite of the efforts of his misty-minded followers (1974a, I, 188), Schopenhauer employs the "will" as the ground of a rigid determinism. The whole form and body of man is its outward manifestation (II, 176), and the differences between individuals which it creates are not to be mediated by the machinations of civil society (II, 229f.), which only imperfectly masks by legislation the nature of the egotistic drive (211f.). Where Schelling had put forward an idealist vitalism wherein all matter was infused with and impelled by the idea, Schopenhauer insists on a more materialized primary force:

the parts of the body must correspond completely to the chief demands and desires by which the will manifests itself. . . . Teeth, gullet, and intestinal canal are objectified hunger; the genitals are objectified sexual impulse; grasping hands and nimble feet correspond to the more indirect strivings of the will which they represent.

Schopenhauer (1969), I, 108

There are only two alternatives open to the individual – and only to the individual, for they can never be coordinated successfully into social forms – if he would escape total and continual subservience to the demands of the will: asceticism and art. Asceticism is in one sense the higher of the two, since it can endure through time as a subjective condition, and through it we may approach what can be salvaged of conventional ethics. Aesthetic creation or response is a more temporary source of relief, though its products do survive for others to experience. Art results from the individual's having an oversupply of will, a surplus beyond what is necessary to meet the demands of practical needs and desires. Thus it can produce a pure form of knowing, will-inspired indeed but not related to contingent necessities and therefore open to intersubjective consensus (as in Kant). The object is recognized as Platonic Idea, "as persistent form of the whole species of things", and the self as "pure, will-less subject of knowledge" (1969, I, 195).

Further reading

Schopenhauer's reading was extraordinarily broad, and unlike some of his predecessors with their emphasis on the *a priori*, he illustrates his case with abundant examples from the whole range of world literatures and religions. I have selected passages from the first volume of *The World as Will and Representation* (1819). The corresponding passages in volume two should also be consulted, as well as the essay 'On the Metaphysics of the Beautiful and Aesthetics' (1974a, II, 415–52). Useful preliminary accounts of Schopenhauer's aesthetics can be found in Copleston (1965b), pp. 43–8; Knox (1936); and Wellek (1955), II, 308–18. The recent bibliography by Arthur Hübscher (1981) is very helpfully arranged, and lists a wide range of works on Schopenhauer's aesthetics, as well as studies of his relation to and influence upon later literary writers, among them Beckett, Browning, Gissing, Hardy, Lawrence, and Melville. Sorg (1975) may also be consulted. Most of Schopenhauer's major writings are available in good English translations, thanks to the efforts of E.F.J. Payne. His philosophy in general is remarkable for its wholeness and coherence over the years of its exposition. For a recent overview, see Hamlyn (1980).

DS

Selections from
The World as Will and Representation
[Die Welt als Wille und Vorstellung]

Volume I, 1819

The translation is a very slightly modified reprint of that by E.F.J. Payne (1969).

German text in *Arthur Schopenhauers sämtliche Werke*, ed. Deussen, vol. I.

§36

History follows the thread of events; it is pragmatic in so far as it deduces them according to the law of motivation [Motivation], a law that determines the appearing will where that will is illuminated by knowledge [Erkenntniß]. At the lower grades of its objectivity, where it still acts without knowledge, natural science as etiology considers the laws of the changes of its phenomena, and as morphology considers what is permanent in them. This almost endless theme is facilitated by the aid of concepts [Begriffe] that comprehend the general, in order to deduce from it the particular. Finally, mathematics considers the mere forms, that is, time and space, in which the Ideas [Ideen] appear drawn apart into plurality for the knowledge of the subject as individual. All these, the common name of which is science, therefore follow the principle of sufficient reason in its different forms, and their theme remains the phenomenon, its laws, connexion, and the relations resulting from these.[1] But now, what kind of knowledge is it that considers what continues to exist outside and independently of all relations, but which alone is really essential to the world, the true content of its phenomena, that which is subject to no change, and is therefore known with equal truth for all time, in a word, the Ideas [Ideen] that are the immediate and adequate objectivity of the thing-in-itself, of the will? It is *art*, the work of genius [Genius]. It repeats the eternal Ideas apprehended through pure contemplation [Kontemplation],[2] the essential and abiding element in all the phenomena of the world. According to the material in which it repeats, it is sculpture, painting, poetry, or music. Its only source is knowledge of the Ideas; its sole aim is communication of this knowledge. Whilst science, following the restless and unstable stream of the fourfold forms of reasons or grounds and consequents, is with every end it attains again and again directed farther, and can never find an ultimate goal or complete satisfaction, any more than by running we can reach the point where the clouds touch the horizon; art, on the contrary, is everywhere at its goal. For it plucks the object of its contemplation from the stream of the world's course, and holds it isolated before it. This particular thing, which in that stream was an infinitesimal part, becomes for art a representative of the whole, an equivalent of the infinitely many in space and time. It therefore pauses at this particular thing; it stops the wheel of time; for it the relations vanish; its object is only the essential, the Idea. We can therefore define it accurately as *the way of considering things independently of the principle of sufficient reason,* in contrast to the way of considering them which proceeds in exact accordance with this principle, and is the way of science and experience. This latter method of consideration can be compared to an endless line running horizontally, and the former to a vertical line cutting the horizontal at any point. The method of consideration that follows the principle of sufficient reason is the rational method, and it alone is valid and useful in practical life and in science. The method of consideration that looks away from the content of this principle is the method of genius [geniale Betrachtungsart], which is valid and useful in art alone. The first is Aristotle's method; the second is, on the whole, Plato's. The first is like the mighty storm, rushing along without beginning or aim, bending, agitating, and carrying everything away with it; the second is like the silent sunbeam, cutting through the path of the storm, and quite unmoved by it. The first is like the innumerable violently agitated drops of the waterfall, constantly changing and never for a moment at rest; the second is like the rainbow silently resting on this raging torrent. Only through the pure contemplation described above, which becomes absorbed entirely in the object, are the Ideas comprehended; and the nature of *genius* consists precisely in the pre-eminent ability for such contemplation. Now as this demands a complete forgetting of our own person and of its relations and connexions, the *gift of genius* [*Genialität*] is nothing but the most complete *objectivity,* i.e., the objective tendency of the mind [Geist], as opposed to the subjective directed to our own person, i.e., to the will. Accordingly, genius is the capacity to remain in a state of pure perception, to lose oneself in perception [Anschauung],[3] to remove from the service of the will the knowledge which originally existed only for this service. In other words, genius is the ability to leave entirely out of sight our own interest, our willing, and our aims, and consequently to discard entirely our own personality for a time, in order to remain *pure knowing subject,* the clear eye of the world; and this not merely for moments, but with the necessary continuity and self-presence [Besonnenheit] to enable us to repeat by deliberate art what has been apprehended, and "what in wavering apparition gleams fix in its place with thoughts that stand for ever!"[4] For genius [Genius] to appear in an individual, it is as if a measure of the power of knowledge must have fallen to his lot far exceed-

ing that required for the service of an individual will; and this superfluity
of knowledge having become free, now becomes the subject purified of
will, the clear mirror of the inner nature of the world. This explains the
animation, amounting to disquietude, in men of genius, since the present
can seldom satisfy them, because it does not fill their consciousness. This
gives them that restless zealous nature, that constant search for new
objects worthy of contemplation [Betrachtung], and also that longing,
hardly ever satisfied, for men of like nature and stature to whom they may
open their hearts. The common mortal, on the other hand, entirely filled
and satisfied by the common present, is absorbed in it, and, finding everywhere his like, has that special ease and comfort in daily life which are
denied to the man of genius. Imagination [Phantasie] has been rightly recognized as an essential element of genius; indeed, it has sometimes been
regarded as identical with genius, but this is not correct. The objects of
genius as such are the eternal Ideas, the persistent, essential forms of the
world and of all its phenomena; but knowledge of the Idea is necessarily
knowledge through perception, and is not abstract. Thus the knowledge
of the genius would be restricted to the Ideas of objects actually present
to his own person, and would be dependent on the concatenation of circumstances that brought them to him, did not imagination extend his horizon far beyond the reality of his personal experience, and enable him to
construct all the rest out of the little that has come into his own actual
apperception [Apperception],[5] and thus to let almost all the possible
scenes of life pass by within himself. Moreover, the actual objects are
almost always only very imperfect copies of the Idea that manifests itself
in them. Therefore the man of genius requires imagination, in order to see
in things not what nature has actually formed, but what she endeavoured
to form, yet did not bring about, because of the conflict of her forms with
one another which was referred to in the previous book.[6] We shall return
to this later, when considering sculpture. Thus imagination extends the
mental horizon of the genius beyond the objects that actually present
themselves to his person, as regards both quality and quantity. For this
reason, unusual strength of imagination is a companion, indeed a condition, of genius. But the converse is not the case, for strength of imagination is not evidence of genius; on the contrary, even men with little or no
touch of genius may have much imagination. For we can consider an actual
object in two opposite ways, purely objectively, the way of genius grasping
the Idea of the object, or in the common way, merely in its relations to
other objects according to the principle of sufficient reason, and in its relations to our own will. In a similar manner, we can also perceive an imaginary object in these two ways. Considered in the first way, it is a means to
knowledge of the Idea, the communication of which is the work of art. In
the second case, the imaginary object is used to build castles in the air,
congenial to selfishness and to one's own whim, which for the moment

delude and delight; thus only the relations of the phantasms so connected are really ever known. The man who indulges in this game is a dreamer [Phantast]; he will easily mingle with reality the pictures that delight his solitude, and will thus become unfit for real life. Perhaps he will write down the delusions of his imagination, and these will give us the ordinary novels of all kinds which entertain those like him and the public at large, since the readers fancy themselves in the position of the hero, and then find the description very "nice".[7]

As we have said, the common, ordinary man, that manufactured article of nature which she daily produces in thousands, is not capable, at any rate continuously, of a consideration of things wholly disinterested in every sense, such as is contemplativeness [Beschaulichkeit] proper. He can direct his attention to things only in so far as they have some relation to his will, although that relation may be only very indirect. As in this reference that always demands only knowledge of the relations, the abstract concept of the thing is sufficient and often even more appropriate, the ordinary man does not linger long over the mere perception [Anschauung], does not fix his eye on an object for long, but, in everything that presents itself to him, quickly looks merely for the concept under which it is to be brought, just as the lazy man looks for a chair, which then no longer interests him. Therefore he is very soon finished with everything, with works of art, with beautiful natural objects, and with that contemplation of life in all its scenes which is really of significance everywhere. He does not linger; he seeks only his way in life, or at most all that might at any time become his way. Thus he makes topographical notes in the widest sense, but on the consideration [Betrachtung] of life itself as such he wastes no time. On the other hand, the man of genius [der Geniale], whose power of knowledge is, through its excess, withdrawn for a part of his time from the service of his will, dwells on the consideration of life itself, strives to grasp the Idea of each thing, not its relations to other things. In doing this, he frequently neglects a consideration of his own path in life, and therefore often pursues this with insufficient skill. Whereas to the ordinary man his faculty of knowledge is a lamp that lights his path, to the man of genius it is the sun that reveals the world. This great difference in their way of looking at life soon becomes visible even in the outward appearance of them both. The glance of the man in whom genius [Genius] lives and works readily distinguishes him; it is both vivid and firm and bears the character of contemplativeness [Beschaulichkeit], of contemplation [Kontemplation]. We can see this in the portraits of the few men of genius which nature has produced here and there among countless millions. On the other hand, the real opposite of contemplation, namely spying or prying, can be readily seen in the glance of others, if indeed it is not dull and vacant, as is often the case. Consequently a face's "expression of genius" consists in the fact that a decided predominance of knowing over willing is visible in it, and hence that there is manifested in it a knowledge without any relation to a will, in other words, a *pure knowing.*[8] On the other hand, in the case of faces that follow the rule, the expression of the will predominates, and we see that knowledge comes into activity only on the impulse of the will, and so is directed only to motives [Motive].

As the knowledge of the genius, or knowledge of the Idea, is that which does not follow the principle of sufficient reason, so, on the other hand, the knowledge that does follow this principle gives us prudence and rationality in life, and brings about the sciences. Thus individuals of genius will be affected with the defects entailed in the neglect of the latter kind of knowledge. Here, however, a limitation must be observed, that what I shall state in this regard concerns them only in so far as, and while, they are actually engaged with the kind of knowledge peculiar to the genius. Now this is by no means the case at every moment of their lives, for the great though spontaneous exertion required for the will-free comprehension of the Ideas necessarily relaxes again, and there are long intervals during which men of genius stand in very much the same position as ordinary persons, both as regards merits and defects.[9] On this account, the action of genius has always been regarded as an inspiration [Inspiration], as indeed the name itself indicates, as the action of a superhuman being different from the individual himself, which takes possession of him only periodically. The disinclination of men of genius to direct their attention to the content of the principle of sufficient reason will show itself first in regard to the ground of being, as a disinclination for mathematics. The consideration of mathematics proceeds on the most universal forms of the phenomenon, space and time, which are themselves only modes or aspects of the principle of sufficient reason; and it is therefore the very opposite of that consideration that seeks only the content of the phenomenon, namely the Idea expressing itself in the phenomenon apart from all relations. Moreover, the logical procedure of mathematics will be repugnant to genius, for it obscures real insight and does not satisfy it; it presents a mere concatenation of conclusions according to the principle of the ground of knowing. Of all the mental powers, it makes the greatest claim on memory, so that one may have before oneself all the earlier propositions to which reference is made. Experience has also confirmed that men of great artistic genius have no aptitude for mathematics; no man was ever very distinguished in both at the same time. Alfieri relates that he was never able to understand even the fourth proposition of Euclid. Goethe was reproached enough with his want of mathematical knowledge by the ignorant opponents of his colour theory.[10] Here, where it was naturally not a question of calculation and measurement according to hypothetical data, but one of direct knowledge by understanding cause and effect, this reproach was so utterly absurd and out of place, that they revealed their total lack of judgement just as much by such a reproach as by the rest of their Midas-utterances. The fact that even today, nearly half a century after the appearance of Goethe's colour theory, the Newtonian fallacies still remain in undisturbed possession of the professorial chair even in Germany, and that people continue to talk quite seriously about the seven homogeneous rays of light and their differing refrangibility, will one day be numbered among the great intellectual peculiarities of mankind in general, and of the Germans in particular. From the same above-mentioned cause may be explained the equally well-known fact that, conversely, distinguished mathematicians have little susceptibility to works of fine art. This is expressed with particular naivety in the well-known anecdote of that French mathematician who, after reading Racine's *Iphigenia,* shrugged his shoulders and asked: "Qu'est-ce que cela prouve?"[11] Further, as keen comprehension of relations according to the laws of causality and motivation really constitutes prudence or sagacity, whereas the knowledge of genius is not directed to relations, a prudent man will not be a genius in so far as and while he is prudent, and a genius will not be prudent in so far as and while he is a genius. Finally, perceptual knowledge generally, in the province of which the Idea entirely lies, is directly opposed to rational or abstract knowledge, which is guided by the principle of the ground of knowing.[12] It is also well known that we seldom find great genius united with pre-eminent rationality; on the contrary, men of genius are often subject to violent emotions and irrational passions. But the cause of this is not weakness of the faculty of reason, but partly unusual energy of that whole phenomenon of will, the individual genius. This phenomenon manifests itself through vehemence of all his acts of will. The cause is also partly a preponderance of knowledge from perception through the senses and the understanding over abstract knowledge, in other words, a decided tendency to the perceptual [Anschauliche]. In such men the extremely energetic impression of the perceptual outshines the colourless concepts so that conduct is no longer guided by the latter, but by the former, and on this very account becomes irrational. Accordingly, the impression of the present moment on them is very strong, and carries them away into thoughtless actions, into emotion and passion. Moreover, since their knowledge has generally been withdrawn in part from the service of the will, they will not in conversation think so much of the person with whom they are speaking as of the thing they are speaking about, which is vividly present in their minds. Therefore they will judge or narrate too objectively for their own interests; they will not conceal what it would be more prudent to keep concealed, and so on. Finally, they are inclined to soliloquize, and in general may exhibit several weaknesses that actually are closely akin to madness. It is often remarked that genius and madness have a side where they touch and even pass over into each other, and even poetic inspiration [Begeisterung] has been called a kind of madness; *amabilis insania,* as Horace calls it (*Odes,* iii, 4); and in the introduction to *Oberon*

Wieland speaks of "amiable madness". Even Aristotle, as quoted by Seneca (*De Tranquillitate Animi*, xv, 16 [xvii, 10]), is supposed to have said: "nullum magnum ingenium sine mixtura dementiae fuit."[13] Plato expresses it in the above-mentioned myth of the dark cave (*Republic*, Bk 7) by saying that those who outside the cave have seen the true sunlight and the things that actually are (the Ideas), cannot afterwards see within the cave any more, because their eyes have grown unaccustomed to the darkness; they no longer recognize the shadow-forms correctly. They are therefore ridiculed for their mistakes by those others who have never left that cave and those shadow-forms. Also in the *Phaedrus* (245a), he distinctly says that without a certain madness there can be no genuine poet, in fact (249d) that everyone appears mad who recognizes the eternal Ideas in fleeting things. Cicero also states: *Negat enim sine furore Democritus quemquam poetam magnum esse posse; quod idem dicit Plato (De Divinatione, i, 37).*[14] And finally, Pope says:

> Great wits to madness sure are near allied.
> And thin partitions do their bounds divide.[15]

Particularly instructive in this respect is Goethe's *Torquato Tasso*, in which he brings before our eyes not only suffering, the essential martyrdom of genius as such, but also its constant transition into madness. Finally, the fact of direct contact between genius and madness is established partly by the biographies of great men of genius, such as Rousseau, Byron, and Alfieri, and by anecdotes from the lives of others. On the other hand, I must mention having found, in frequent visits to lunatic asylums, individual subjects endowed with unmistakably great gifts. Their genius appeared distinctly through their madness which had completely gained the upper hand. Now this cannot be ascribed to chance, for on the one hand the number of mad persons is relatively very small, while on the other a man of genius is a phenomenon rare beyond all ordinary estimation, and appearing in nature only as the greatest exception. We may be convinced of this from the mere fact that we can compare the number of the really great men of genius produced by the whole of civilized Europe in ancient and modern times, with the two hundred and fifty millions who are always living in Europe and renew themselves every thirty years. Among men of genius, however, can be reckoned only those who have furnished works that have retained through all time an enduring value for mankind. Indeed, I will not refrain from mentioning that I have known some men of decided, though not remarkable, mental superiority who at the same time betrayed a slight touch of insanity. Accordingly, it might appear that every advance of the intellect beyond the usual amount, as an abnormality, already disposes to madness. Meanwhile, however, I will give as briefly as possible my opinion about the purely intellectual ground of the kinship between genius and madness, for this discussion will certainly contribute to the explanation of the real nature of genius, in other words, of that quality of the mind which is alone capable of producing genuine works of art. But this necessitates a brief discussion of madness itself.[16]

[Schopenhauer goes on to define madness as a malady of the memory, and to suggest its close relation to genius.]

§37

Now according to our explanation, genius consists in the ability to know, independently of the principle of sufficient reason, not individual things which have their existence only in relation, but the Ideas of such things, and in the ability to be, in face of these, the correlative of the Idea, and hence no longer individual, but pure subject of knowing. Yet this ability must be inherent in all men in a lesser and different degree, as otherwise they would be just as incapable of enjoying works of art as of producing them.[17] Generally they would have no susceptibility at all to the beautiful and to the sublime; indeed, these words could have no meaning for them. We must therefore assume as existing in all men that power of recognizing in things their Ideas, of divesting themselves for a moment of their personality, unless indeed there are some who are not capable of any aesthetic pleasure at all. The man of genius excels them only in the far higher degree and more continuous duration of this kind of knowledge. These enable him to retain that self-presence [Besonnenheit] necessary for him to repeat what is thus known in a voluntary and intentional work, such repetition being the work of art. Through this he communicates to others the Idea he has grasped. Therefore this Idea remains unchanged and the same, and hence aesthetic pleasure is essentially one and the same, whether it be called forth by a work of art, or directly by the perception [Anschauung] of nature and of life. The work of art is merely a means of facilitating that knowledge in which this pleasure consists. That the Idea comes to us more easily from the work of art than directly from nature and from reality, arises solely from the fact that the artist, who knew only the Idea and not reality, clearly repeated in his work only the Idea, separated it out from reality, and omitted all disturbing contingencies. The artist lets us peer into the world through his eyes. That he has these eyes, that he knows the essential in things which lies outside all relations, is the gift of genius and is inborn; but that he is able to lend us this gift, to let us see with his eyes, is acquired, and is the technical side of art. Therefore, after the account I have given in the foregoing remarks of the inner essence of the aesthetic way of knowing in its most general outline, the following more detailed philosophical consideration of the beautiful and the sublime will explain both simultaneously, in nature and in art, without separating them further. We shall first consider what takes place in a man when he is affected by the beautiful and the sublime. Whether he draws this emotion directly from nature, from life, or partakes of it only through the mediation of art, makes no essential difference, but only an outward one.

§38

In the aesthetic method of contemplation we found *two inseparable constituent parts:* namely, knowledge of the object not as individual thing, but as Platonic *Idea,* in other words, as persistent form of this whole species of things; and the self-consciousness of the knower, not as individual, but as *pure, will-less subject of knowledge.* The condition under which the two constituent parts appear always united was the abandonment of the method of knowledge that is bound to the principle of sufficient reason, a knowledge that, on the contrary, is the only appropriate kind for serving the will and also for science. Moreover, we shall see that the *pleasure* produced by contemplation of the beautiful arises from those two constituent parts, sometimes more from the one than from the other, according to what the object of aesthetic contemplation may be.

All *willing* [*Wollen*] springs from lack, from deficiency, and thus from suffering. Fulfilment brings this to an end; yet for one wish that is fulfilled there remain at least ten that are denied. Further, desiring [das Begehren] lasts a long time, demands and requests go on to infinity; fulfilment is short and meted out sparingly. But even the final satisfaction itself is only apparent; the wish fulfilled at once makes way for a new one; the former is a known delusion, the latter a delusion not as yet known. No attained object of willing can give a satisfaction that lasts and no longer declines; but it is always like the alms thrown to a beggar, which reprieves him today so that his misery may be prolonged till tomorrow. Therefore, so long as our consciousness is filled by our will, so long as we are given up to the throng of desires with its constant hopes and fears, so long as we are the subject of willing, we never obtain lasting happiness or peace. Essentially, it is all the same whether we pursue or flee, fear harm or aspire to enjoyment; care for the constantly demanding will, no matter in what form, continually fills and moves consciousness; but without peace and calm, true well-being is absolutely impossible. Thus the subject of willing is constantly lying on the revolving wheel of Ixion, is always drawing water in the sieve of the Danaides, and is the eternally thirsting Tantalus.

When, however, an external cause or inward disposition suddenly raises us out of the endless stream of willing, and snatches knowledge from the thraldom of the will, the attention is now no longer directed to the motives of willing, but comprehends things free from their relation to the will. Thus it considers things without interest, without subjectivity, purely objectively; it is entirely given up to them in so far as they are merely representations [Vorstellungen], and not motives. Then all at once the peace, always sought but always escaping us on that first path of willing, comes to us of its own accord, and all is well with us. It is the painless state, prized by Epicurus as the highest good and as the state of the gods; for that moment we are delivered from the miserable pressure of the will. We celebrate the Sabbath of the penal servitude of willing; the wheel of Ixion stands still.

But this is just the state that I described above as necessary for knowledge of the Idea, as pure contemplation, absorption in perception, being lost in the object, forgetting all individuality, abolishing [Aufhebung] the kind of knowledge which follows the principle of sufficient reason, and comprehends only relations. It is the state where, simultaneously and inseparably, the perceived individual thing is raised to the Idea of its species, and the knowing individual to the pure subject of will-less knowing, and now the two, as such, no longer stand in the stream of time and of all other relations. It is then all the same whether we see the setting sun from a prison or from a palace.[18]

Inward disposition, predominance of knowing over willing, can bring about this state in any environment. This is shown by those admirable Dutchmen who directed such purely objective perception to the most insignificant objects, and set up a lasting monument of their objectivity and spiritual peace in paintings of *still life*. The aesthetic beholder does not contemplate this without emotion, for it graphically describes to him the calm, tranquil, will-free frame of mind of the artist which was necessary for contemplating such insignificant things so objectively, considering them so attentively, and repeating this perception with such thought. Since the picture invites the beholder to participate in this state, his emotion is often enhanced by the contrast between it and his own restless state of mind, disturbed by vehement willing, in which he happens to be. In the same spirit landscape painters, especially Ruysdael, have often painted extremely insignificant landscape objects, and have thus produced the same effect even more delightfully.

So much is achieved simply and solely by the inner force of an artistic disposition; but that purely objective frame of mind is facilitated and favoured from without by accommodating objects, by the abundance of natural beauty that invites perception [Anschauen], and even presses itself on us. Whenever it presents itself to our gaze all at once, it almost always succeeds in snatching us, although only for a few moments, from subjectivity, from the thraldom of the will, and transferring us into the state of pure knowledge. This is why the man tormented by passions, want, or care, is so suddenly revived, cheered, and comforted by a single, free glance into nature. The storm of passions, the pressure of desire and fear, and all the miseries of willing are then at once calmed and appeased in a marvellous way. For at the moment when, torn from the will, we have given ourselves up to pure, will-less knowing, we have stepped into another world, so to speak, where everything that moves our will, and thus violently agitates us, no longer exists. This liberation of knowledge lifts us as wholly and completely above all this as do sleep and dreams. Happiness and unhappiness have vanished; we are no longer the individual; that is forgotten; we are only pure subject of knowledge. We are only that *one* eye of the world which looks out from all knowing creatures, but which in man alone can be wholly free from serving the will. In this way, all difference of individuality disappears so completely that it is all the same whether the perceiving eye belongs to a mighty monarch or to a stricken beggar; for beyond that boundary neither happiness nor misery is taken with us. There always lies so near to us a realm in which we have escaped entirely from all our affliction; but who has the strength to remain in it for long? As soon as any relation to our will, to our person, even of those objects of pure contemplation, again enters consciousness, the magic is at an end. We fall back into knowledge governed by the principle of sufficient reason; we now no longer know the Idea, but the individual thing, the link of a chain to which we also belong, and we are again abandoned to all our woe. Most men are almost always at this standpoint, because they entirely lack objectivity, i.e., genius. Therefore they do not like to be alone with nature; they need company, or at any rate a book, for their knowledge remains subject to the will. Therefore in objects they seek only some relation to their will, and with everything that has not such a relation there sounds within them, as it were like a ground-bass, the constant, inconsolable lament, "It is of no use to me." Thus in solitude even the most beautiful surroundings have for them a desolate, dark, strange, and hostile appearance.

Finally, it is also the blessedness of will-less perception [Anschauen] which spreads so wonderful a spell over the past and the distant, and by a self-deception presents them to us in so flattering a light. For by our conjuring up in our minds days long past spent in a distant place, it is only the objects recalled by our imagination, not the subject of will, that carried around its incurable sorrows with it just as much then as it does now. But these are forgotten, because since then they have frequently made way for others. Now in what is remembered, objective perception is just as effective as it would be in what is present, if we allowed it to have influence over us, if, free from will, we surrendered ourselves to it. Hence it happens that, especially when we are more than usually disturbed by some want, the sudden recollection of past and distant scenes flits across our minds like a lost paradise. The imagination recalls merely what was objective, not what was individually subjective, and we imagine that that something objective stood before us then just as pure and undisturbed by any relation to the will as its image now stands in the imagination; but the relation of objects to our will caused us just as much affliction then as it does now. We can withdraw from all suffering just as well through present as through distant objects, whenever we raise ourselves to a purely objective contemplation of them, and are thus able to produce the illusion that only those objects are present, not we ourselves. Then, as pure subject of knowing, delivered from the miserable self, we become entirely one with those objects, and foreign as our want is to them, it is at such moments just as foreign to us. Then the world as representation [Vorstellung] alone remains; the world as will [Wille] has disappeared.

In all these remarks, I have sought to make clear the nature and extent of the share which the subjective condition has in aesthetic pleasure, namely the deliverance of knowledge from the service of the will, the forgetting of oneself as individual, and the enhancement of consciousness to the pure, will-less, timeless subject of knowing that is independent of all relations. With this subjective side of aesthetic contemplation [Beschauung] there always appears at the same time as necessary correlative its objective side, the intuitive apprehension of the Platonic Idea. But before we turn to a closer consideration of this and to the achievements of art in reference to it, it is better to stop for a while at the subjective side of aesthetic pleasure, in order to complete our consideration of this by discussing the impression of the *sublime*, which depends solely on it, and arises through a modification of it. After this, our investigation of aesthetic pleasure will be completed by a consideration of its objective side.[19]

But first of all, the following remarks appertain to what has so far been said. Light is most pleasant and delightful; it has become the symbol of all that is good and salutary. In all religions it indicates eternal salvation, while darkness symbolizes damnation. Ormuzd dwells in the purest light, Ahriman in eternal night.[20] Dante's Paradise looks somewhat like Vauxhall in London, since all the blessed spirits appear there as points of light that arrange themselves in regular figures. The absence of light immediately makes us sad, and its return makes us feel happy. Colours directly excite a keen delight, which reaches its highest degree when they are translucent. All this is due to the fact that light is the correlative and condition of the most perfect kind of knowledge through perception, of the only knowledge that in no way directly affects the will. For sight, unlike the affections of the other senses, is in itself, directly, and by its sensuous effect, quite incapable of pleasantness or unpleasantness of *sensation* in the organ; in other words, it has no direct connexion with the will. Only perception [Anschauung] arising in the understanding can have such a connexion, which then lies in the relation of the object to the will. In the case of hearing, this is different; tones can excite pain immediately, and can also be directly agreeable sensuously without reference to harmony or melody. Touch, as being one with the feeling of the whole body, is still more subject to this direct influence on the will; and yet there is a touch devoid of pain and pleasure. Odours, however, are always pleasant or unpleasant, and tastes even more so. Thus the last two senses are most closely related to the will, and hence are always the most ignoble, and have been called by Kant the subjective senses.[21] Therefore the pleasure from light is in fact the pleasure from the objective possibility of the purest and most perfect kind of knowledge from perception. As such it can be deduced from the fact that pure knowing, freed and delivered from all willing, is extremely gratifying, and, as such, has a large share in aesthetic enjoyment. Again, the incredible beauty that we associated with the reflection of objects in water can be deduced from this view of light. That lightest, quickest, and finest species of the effect of bodies on one another, that to which we owe also by far the most perfect and pure of our perceptions [Wahrnehmungen], namely the impression by means of reflected light-rays, is here brought before our eyes quite distinctly, clearly, and completely, in cause and effect, and indeed on a large scale. Hence our aesthetic delight from it, which in the main is entirely rooted in the subjective ground of aesthetic pleasure, and is delight from pure knowledge and its ways.[22]

§39

All these considerations are intended to stress the subjective part of aesthetic pleasure, namely, that pleasure in so far as it is delight in the mere perceptual knowledge as such, in contrast to the will. Now directly connected with all this is the following explanation of the frame of mind which has been called the feeling of the *sublime*.

It has already been observed that transition into the state of pure perception occurs most easily when the objects accommodate themselves to it, in other words, when by their manifold and at the same time definite and distinct form they easily become representatives of their Ideas, in which beauty, in the objective sense, consists. Above all, natural beauty has this quality, and even the most stolid and apathetic person obtains therefrom at least a fleeting aesthetic pleasure. Indeed, it is remarkable how the plant world in particular invites one to aesthetic contemplation, and, as it were, obtrudes itself thereon. It might be said that such accommodation was connected with the fact that these organic beings themselves, unlike animal bodies, are not immediate objects of knowledge. They therefore need the extrinsic, intelligent individual in order to come from the world of blind willing into the world of the representation. Thus they yearn for this entrance, so to speak, in order to attain at any rate indirectly what directly is denied to them. For the rest, I leave entirely undecided this bold and venturesome idea that perhaps borders on the fanatic [Schwärmerei], for only a very intimate and devoted contemplation of nature can excite or justify it.[23] Now so long as it is this accommodation of nature, the significance and distinctness of its forms, from which the Ideas individualized in them readily speak to us; so long as it is this which moves us from knowledge of mere relations serving the will into aesthetic contemplation, and thus raises us to the will-free subject of knowing, so long is it merely the *beautiful* that affects us, and the feeling of beauty that is excited. But these very objects, whose significant forms invite us to a pure contemplation of them, may have a hostile relation to the human will in general, as manifested in its objectivity, the human body. They may be opposed to it; they may threaten it by their might that eliminates all resistance, or their immeasurable greatness may reduce it to nought. Nevertheless, the beholder may not direct his attention to this relation to his will which is so pressing and hostile, but, although he perceives and acknowledges it, he may consciously turn away from it, forcibly tear himself from his will and its relations, and, giving himself up entirely to knowledge, may quietly contemplate, as pure, will-less subject of knowing, those very objects so terrible to the will. He may comprehend only their Idea that is foreign to all relation, gladly linger over its contemplation, and consequently be elevated precisely in this way above himself, his person, his willing, and all willing. In that case, he is then filled with the feeling of the *sublime;* he is in the state of exaltation, and therefore the object that causes such a state is called *sublime*. Thus what distinguishes the feeling of the sublime from that of the beautiful is that, with the beautiful, pure knowledge has gained the upper hand without a struggle, since the beauty of the object, in other words that quality of it which facilitates knowledge of its Idea, has removed from consciousness, without resistance and hence imperceptibly, the will and knowledge of relations that slavishly serve this will. What is then left is pure subject of knowing, and not even a recollection of the will remains. On the other hand, with the sublime, that state of pure knowing is obtained first of all by a conscious and violent tearing away from the relations of the same object to the will which are recognized as unfavourable, by a free exaltation, accompanied by consciousness, beyond the will and the knowledge related to it. This exaltation must not only be won with consciousness, but also be maintained, and it is therefore accompanied by a constant recollection of the will, yet not of a single individual willing, such as fear or desire, but of human willing in general, in so far as it is expressed universally through its objectivity, the human body. If a single, real act of will were to enter consciousness through actual personal affliction and danger from the object, the individual will, thus actually affected, would at once gain the upper hand. The peace of contemplation would become impossible, the impression of the sublime would be lost, because it had yielded to anxiety, in which the effort of the individual to save himself supplanted every other thought. A few examples will contribute a great deal to making clear this theory of the aesthetically sublime, and removing any doubt about it. At the same time they will show the difference in the degrees of this feeling of the sublime. For in the main it is identical with the feeling of the beautiful, with pure will-less knowing, and with the knowledge, which necessarily appears therewith, of the Ideas out of all relation that is determined by the principle of sufficient reason. The feeling of the sublime is distinguished from that of the beautiful only by the addition, namely the exaltation beyond the known hostile relation of the contemplated object to the will in general. Thus there result several degrees of the sublime, in fact transitions from the beautiful to the sublime, according as this addition is strong, clamorous, urgent, and near, or only feeble, remote, and merely suggested. I regard it as more appropriate to the discussion to adduce first of all in examples these transitions, and generally the weaker degrees of the impression of the sublime, although those whose aesthetic susceptibility in general is not very great, and whose imagination is not vivid, will understand only the examples, given later, of the higher and more distinct degrees of that impression. They should therefore confine themselves to these, and should ignore the examples of the very weak degree of the above-mentioned impression, which are to be spoken of first.

[Schopenhauer presents a taxonomy of the sublime based upon the various degrees of its intensity.]

The impression of the sublime can arise in quite a different way by our imagining a mere magnitude in space and time, whose immensity reduces the individual to nought. By retaining Kant's terms and his correct division, we can call the first kind the dynamically sublime, and the second the mathematically sublime, although we differ from him entirely in the explanation of the inner nature of that impression, and can concede no share in this either to moral reflections or to hypostases from scholastic philosophy.[24]

[There follows an extended account of the two species of the sublime.]

§49

The truth which lies at the foundation of all the remarks we have so far made on art is that the object of art, the depiction of which is the aim of the artist, and the knowledge of which must consequently precede his work as its germ and source, is an *Idea*, in Plato's sense, and absolutely nothing else; not the particular thing, the object of common apprehension, and not the concept [Begriff], the object of rational thought and of science. Although Idea and concept have something in common, in that both as unities represent a plurality of actual things, the great difference between the two will have become sufficiently clear and evident from what was said in the first book about the concept, and what has been said in the present book about the Idea.[25] I certainly do not mean to assert that Plato grasped this difference clearly; indeed many of his examples of Ideas and his discussions of them are applicable only to concepts. However, we leave this aside, and go our way, glad whenever we come across traces of a great and noble mind, yet pursuing not his footsteps, but our own aim. The *concept* is abstract, discursive, wholly undetermined within its sphere, determined only by its limits, attainable and intelligible only to him who has the faculty of reason, communicable by words without further assistance, entirely exhausted by its definition. The *Idea,* on the other hand, definable perhaps as the adequate representative of the concept, is absolutely perceptual [anschaulich], and, although representing an infinite number of individual things, is yet thoroughly definite. It is never known by the individual as such, but only by him who has raised himself above all willing and all individuality to the pure subject of knowing. Thus it is attainable only by the man of genius, and by him who, mostly with the assistance of works of genius, has raised his power of pure knowledge, and is now in the frame of mind of the genius. Therefore it is communicable not absolutely, but only conditionally, since the Idea, apprehended and repeated in the work of art, appeals to everyone only according to the measure of his own intellectual worth. For this reason the most excellent works of any art, the noblest productions of genius, must eternally remain sealed books to the dull majority of men, and are inaccessible to them. They are separated from them by a wide gulf, just as the society of princes is inaccessible to the common people. It is true that even the dullest of them accept on authority works which are acknowledged to be great, in order not to betray their own weakness. But they always remain in silence, ready to express their condemnation the moment they are allowed to hope that they can do so without running the risk of exposure. Then their long-restrained hatred of all that is great and beautiful and of the authors thereof readily relieves itself; for such things never appealed to them, and so humiliated them. For in order to acknowledge, and freely and willingly to admit, the worth of another, a man must generally have some worth of his own. On this is based the necessity for modesty in spite of all merit, as also for the disproportionately loud praise of this virtue, which alone of all its sisters is always included in the eulogy of anyone who ventures to praise a man distinguished in some way, in order to conciliate and appease the wrath of worthlessness. For what is modesty but hypocritical humility, by means of which, in a world swelling with vile envy, a man seeks to beg pardon for his excellences and merits from those who have none? For whoever attributes no merits to himself because he really has none, is not modest, but merely honest.

The *Idea* is the unity that has fallen into plurality by virtue of the temporal and spatial form of our intuitive apprehension [intuitive Apprehension]. The *concept,* on the other hand, is the unity once more produced out of plurality by means of abstraction through our faculty of reason; the latter can be described as *unitas post rem,* and the former as *unitas ante rem.*[26] Finally, we can express the distinction between concept and Idea figuratively, by saying that the *concept* is like a dead receptacle in which whatever has been put actually lies side by side, but from which no more can be taken out (by analytical judgements) than has been put in (by synthetical reflection).[27] The *Idea*, on the other hand, develops in him who has grasped it representations that are new as regards the concept of the same name; it is like a living organism, developing itself and endowed with generative force, which brings forth that which was not previously put into it.

Now it follows from all that has been said that the concept, useful as it is in life, serviceable, necessary, and productive as it is in science, is eternally barren and unproductive in art. The apprehended Idea, on the contrary, is the true and only source of every genuine work of art. In its powerful originality it is drawn only from life itself, from nature, from the world, and only by the genuine genius. Genuine works bearing immortal life arise only from such immediate responsiveness [Empfängniß]. Just because the Idea is and remains perceptual, the artist is not conscious *in abstracto* of the intention and aim of his work. Not a concept but an Idea is present in his mind; hence he cannot give an account of his actions. He works, as people say, from mere feeling and unconsciously, indeed instinctively. On the other hand, imitators, mannerists, *imitatores, servum pecus*,[28] in art start from the concept. They note what pleases and affects in genuine works, make this clear to themselves, fix it in the concept, and hence in the abstract, and then imitate it, openly or in disguise, with skill and intention. Like parasitic plants, they suck their nourishment from the works of others; and like polyps, take on the colour of their nourishment. Indeed, we could even carry the comparison farther, and assert that they are like machines which mince very fine and mix up what is put into them, but can never digest it, so that the constituent elements of others can always be found again, and picked out and separated from the mixture. Only the genius, on the other hand, is like the organic body that assimilates, transforms, and produces. For he is, indeed, educated and cultured by his predecessors and their works; but only by life and the world itself is he made directly productive through the impression of what is perceived; therefore the highest culture never interferes with his originality. All imitators, all mannerists apprehend in the concept the essential nature of the exemplary achievements of others; but concepts can never impart inner life to a work. The generation, in other words the dull multitude of any time, itself knows only concepts and sticks to them; it therefore accepts mannered works with ready and loud applause. After a few years, however, these works become unpalatable, because the spirit of the times [Zeitgeist], in other words the prevailing concepts, in which alone those works could take root, has changed. Only the genuine works that are drawn directly from nature and life remain eternally young and strong, like nature and life itself. For they belong to no age, but to mankind; and for this reason they are received with indifference by their own age to which they disdained to conform; and because they indirectly and negatively exposed the errors of the age, they were recognized tardily and reluctantly. On the other hand, they do not grow old, but even down to the latest times always make an ever new and fresh appeal to us. They are then no longer exposed to neglect and misunderstanding; for they now stand crowned and sanctioned by the approbation of the few minds capable of judging. These appear singly and sparingly in the course of centuries,[29] and cast their votes, the slowly increasing number of which establishes the authority, the only judgement-seat that is meant when an appeal is made to posterity. It is these successively appearing individuals alone; for the mass and multitude of posterity will always be and remain just as perverse and dull as the mass and multitude of contemporaries always were and always are. Let us read the complaints of the great minds of every century about their contemporaries; they always sound as if they were of today, since the human race is always the same. In every age and in every art affectation [Manier] takes the place of the spirit, which always is only the property of individuals. Affectation, however, is the old, cast-off garment of the phenomenon of the spirit which last existed and was recognized. In view of all this, the approbation of posterity is earned as a rule only at the expense of the approbation of one's contemporaries, and *vice versa*.[30]

Part 14

Hegel

Georg Wilhelm Friedrich Hegel

(1770–1831)

Along with Kant, Hegel is the most important figure represented in this volume, not only because of the thoroughness with which he addresses the major issues of his time, but also because of the range of his influence on later thinkers. In this second context his influence has been perhaps even greater than that of Kant, whose writings outside the great *Critiques*, for example those on psychology, history, and natural science, are little known except to specialists. This is, as we have seen, the result of a conscious decision on Kant's part about the limits of exact philosophy; with Hegel, the discipline once again expands to include everything that Kant had excluded from the transcendental method. Closer knowledge of his contemporaries, especially Fichte and Schelling, would certainly persuade the English-speaking reader that Hegel was less 'original' than he often seems to be, but this in no sense detracts from his importance. The expansion of Fichte's basic epistemology of self and other into a model for the understanding of a whole range of forms of culture and behaviour; the idealist theory of history; the influence (or not) on the young Marx and the consequent interest in Hegel of theorists of both left and right – these and other priorities have ensured Hegel's continuing importance to debates in philosophy, psychology, and the political and social sciences.

Intended for theology, along with his friends and co-seminarians Schelling and Hölderlin, Hegel went through the usual apprenticeship as a private tutor before settling at Jena in 1801. There are famous stories of his fleeing the city with the manuscript of the *Phenomenology of Spirit* under his arm, following the seizure of the city by the French (1807). Between 1808 and 1816 he was the headmaster of a *Gymnasium* or 'grammar school' in Nürnberg, and this period produced his second major work, the *Science of Logic* (1812–16). After a brief period at Heidelberg (1816–18) he became a professor at Berlin, a post which he held until his death in 1831, and through which he dominated the world of German philosophy (much to Schopenhauer's disgust!). The other major published works are the *Philosophy of Right* (1821) and the *Encyclopaedia of the Philosophical Sciences* (1830). Thanks to his influence on the British Hegelians of the later nineteenth century and his continued interdisciplinary importance, most of his work can be read in English, including the lecture courses in the history of philosophy, on the philosophy of religion, and on aesthetics.

Most of the priorities in Hegel's thought will be signalled in the notes as they relate to the specific concerns of the selections reprinted below. His system is nothing if not holistic, and most things lead to most other things. Perhaps the most important thing to emphasize at once is the pervasiveness of Hegel's interest in and deduction of an evolutionary history. Human history is the record of the gradual emergence of *Geist* to self-consciousness and self-definition. This word, which had been central before (most significantly in Fichte), has been variously rendered as 'mind' or 'spirit' by Hegel's translators, and it is indeed mind-spirit, the essentially formative and self-forming element in the self. The end of history will be the consummation of philosophy, art and religion having been both left behind and gathered within along the way – the emergence of absolute *Geist*, self-knowledge of God through man, a realm of pure thinking unmarked by sensuous representation.

The notion of a progressive and refining principle operating through history was not original to Hegel; similar ideas can be found in Schelling (though with less emphasis upon the progressive), in Fichte's *Characteristics of the Present Age*, and also in Herder, where they were the focus of some pointed scepticism from Kant (see 1963, pp. 27f.). But it is Hegel who works out the idea most fully. He places all sorts of restrictions on the incidence of *Geist* in history, as indeed he must do if he is to explain the obvious presence of forms of incoherence in a system whose scope is nevertheless total. Whilst history is argued to be subject to a rational process, the *Geist* which is the medium of that rationality is not present at all times in all places. When it is present and operative, it is seldom understood as such, and does not provide conscious instructions or a prospectus for those engaged in living through particular moments of history. This is the 'tragical' element in Hegel's thought, whereby knowledge of what has been most important always comes after the event. Here he stands with the Greeks, and we should remember this when making assessments of his vocabulary of 'world historical' figures, and so forth. In all these ways, Hegel's analysis bears close comparison with that of Shelley in *A Defence of Poetry*. Here too the dynamic principle in history, which Shelley calls "poetry" in the widest sense, operates through the unconscious and is prone to disappear or lie dormant for long periods of time, so that poets are the *unacknowledged* legislators of the world.

As history is partial and even immediately unpredictable in the short term (though a pattern appears to retrospection in the long term), so it is not a sphere from which we may deduce any simple feeling of well-being: "It is possible to consider history from the point of view of happiness, but history is not the soil in which happiness grows. The periods of happiness in it are the blank pages of history" (1980, pp. 78–9). Anxiety is the correlative of the partial or selective appearance of *Geist*, and even when it does appear its transformations are strenuous ones: "Development, therefore, is not just a harmless and peaceful process of growth like that of organic life, but a hard and obstinate struggle with itself" (p. 127). Thus alienation is central to the theory. *Geist* indeed appears by positing itself as other in a moment of rupture (ideally to be overcome), whether in the course of culture and history at large or in the individual life experience which Hegel (at times awkwardly) makes parallel to it. This whole process is "mediated by consciousness and will" (p. 126), so that there is always the possibility of failure, of arrestation, of fixation – one which may be total for an individual or culture at a given moment, though of course not so for the whole course of history. Again, the comparison with the dynamics of Greek tragedy comes to mind: the curse of the God must play itself out, but none of the protagonists can know this, or know when. Consequently they behave freely, and bring about the crucial event in a cloud of unknowing. Thus also for Hegel we are creatures of our times, and can operate only within their limits, or just beyond them if we happen (through no conscious decision of our own) to be world-historical. The famous examples of literary criticism in the *Phenomenology* (not reprinted here), the account of Sophocles' *Antigone* and the various remarks on Diderot's *Rameau's Nephew*, must be read in this light.

Geist makes progress by a movement that is simultaneously cancellation and incorporation or sublimation, a process Hegel calls *Aufhebung*. Progress is by negation, but negation involves both a destruction and carrying over: Hegel himself celebrates the double reading of the word in the *Science of Logic* (1969, pp. 106–8). In this way the traces of past transitions are available for recollection, or *Erinnerung* – a far more active process than mere remembrance, and one involving re-enacting, as Schelling also makes clear:

It is certain that whoever could write the history of his own life from its very ground, would have thereby grasped in a brief conspectus the history of the universe . . . all history . . . can only be relived . . . Whoever wishes knowledge of history must make the long journey, dwell upon each moment, submit himself to the gradualness of the development.   Schelling (1967), pp. 93–4

And so to art and aesthetics. The main point to grasp is that, after the exalted estimation of art in the (different) theories of Schelling and Schopenhauer, art is once again relegated by Hegel, though not (according to the logic I have just explained) in any sense deprived of essential content. Art is an early stage in the development of *Geist* toward self-recognition, a process further refined in religion, which is for Hegel the proper realm of *Vorstellung* or representational thought, and then consummated in philosophy. The high point of art is to be found in the civilization of the Greeks, for at that point in history art was closest to the total world-view of its society, and most fully incorporated its religious representations. Before and after the Greeks, art is either approaching or declining from this moment of exemplary coherence. But because the Greeks were pagans, *Geist* did not require the inward self-consciousness and the dissolution of outward form that are demanded by its Christian manifestations, later stages in its coming into being. The perfection of Greek art is therefore founded upon an element of incompletion, and we must always bear this in mind when reading Hegel. Greek civilization could embody itself most successfully in art, because art is unconscious creation, and because its gods regularly and readily took on human form; the Greeks had not yet perceived the 'higher' demands of self-consciousness and alienation – as Nietzsche also realized in trying to re-establish the viability of a pre-Christian ethics.

This schema does not however do justice to the richness of Hegel's view of art. Although art reaches its high point with the Greeks, it yet always exists in other and less completed forms at all moments of history, and as such is always available as an index to its time. This notion of the historical significance of art, its capacity to publicize and embody the essential elements of the particular culture in which it exists, has clearly been of the greatest importance to aesthetic theory and to literary criticism. Far more than Kant, who is interested strictly in the nature of the subjective judgement of taste and not at all in the psychology of the artist or in the history of art, and who therefore deliberately eschews examples, Hegel (like Schelling before him) ignores nothing in the history of art that seems to bear upon his case.

Further reading

This has made the task of selection more difficult than usual. Fortunately, Hegel's major pronouncements on art and aesthetics, those made in his course of lectures on the subject, have been recently and admirably translated by T.M. Knox (Hegel,

1975), with a superbly detailed index. Wellek (1955), II, 318–34, as so often, offers a fine introductory summary of the range of Hegel's literary criticism; see also Knox (1936), Kaminsky (1962), and Karelis (1979). Copleston (1965a) has a good general introduction to Hegel's thought, and among the various longer studies C. Taylor (1975) may be especially recommended; this book provides not only an account of Hegel's philosophy *per se*, but a very clear and comprehensive outline of its historical context, and I have found it particularly useful in writing the notes to this section of the anthology. Schelling (1978), pp. 199–214, should also be consulted for its philosophy of history. There is a bibliography by Steinhauer (1980), and there is a lexicon by Glockner (1957).

Translations of Hegel into English began to appear only in the 1850s: see Muirhead (1927). Lewes (1857) had to cope with him in German: "Those who are utter strangers to German speculation will wonder, perhaps, how it is possible for such verbal quibbles to be accepted as philosophy" (p. 613). This response can be heard today, and is unlikely to disappear.

DS

Selections from
Aesthetics: Lectures on Fine Art
[Vorlesungen über die Aesthetik]

Lectures given in Berlin between 1823 and 1829

The following translation is by T.M. Knox (slightly modified) in Hegel (1975); sections reprinted here are found on pp. 30–55, 602–11, 959–70.

German text in *Sämtliche Werke*, Jubiläumsausgabe in 20 vols. (1949–59), vols. XII, XIII, XIV.

Introductory note

These lectures were first published after Hegel's death by H.G. Hotho (1835; 2nd revised edn 1842), who worked partly from Hegel's own manuscript notes and partly from transcripts made by others of the courses given in 1823, 1826, and 1828–9. Hotho dates the earliest manuscripts at 1818, though he does not use them in his edition: see *SW*, XII, 3, 7.

Despite the less than ideal integrity of the text, these extensive lectures (1237 pages in Knox's translation) are a very coherent exposition of Hegel's ideas about art, and an indispensable source of arguments and examples for anyone concerned with Romantic aesthetics, in particular and in general. Intended from the first for public consumption, they tend to be easier to follow than the terse final paragraphs of the *Encyclopaedia* – they even contain jokes! – and more orderly than the famous passages of 'literary criticism' found in the earlier *Phenomenology*.

My selections are necessarily partial and can in no sense represent the whole range of Hegel's arguments. In the excerpts here reprinted, the reader will find some of the most explicit and available of all Romantic speculations on the relation of art to desire and appetite (Hegel's attention to this issue may be taken to signal how prophetic was the direction Schopenhauer had sensed in philosophy at large); on the moral faculty and on didacticism; and on the immediate predicament of art and the art instinct in Hegel's own time.

From the Introduction

(d) Now granted that the work of art is made by man as the creation of his spirit [Geist], a final question arises, in order to derive a deeper result from the foregoing [discussion], namely, what is man's *need* to produce works of art? On the one hand, this production may be regarded as a mere play of chance and fancies which might just as well be left alone as pursued; for it might be held that there are other and even better means of achieving

359

what art aims at and that man has still higher and more important interests than art has the ability to satisfy. On the other hand, however, art seems to proceed from a higher impulse [Trieb] and to satisfy higher needs – at times the highest and absolute needs since it is bound up with the most universal views of life [Weltanschauungen] and the religious interests of whole epochs and peoples. This question about the non-contingent but absolute need for art, we cannot yet answer completely, because it is more concrete than an answer could turn out to be at this stage. Therefore we must content ourselves in the meantime with making only the following points.

The universal and absolute need from which art (on its formal side) springs has its origin in the fact that man is a *thinking* consciousness, i.e. that man draws out of himself and puts *before himself [für sich]* what he is and whatever else is. Things in nature are only *immediate* and *single*, while man as spirit *duplicates* himself, in that (i) he *is* as things in nature are, but (ii) he is just as much *for* himself; he intuits himself, represents himself, thinks, and only on the strength of this active placing himself before himself [Fürsichseyn] is he spirit. This consciousness of himself man acquires in a twofold way: *first, theoretically,* in so far as inwardly he must bring himself into his own consciousness, along with whatever moves, stirs, and presses in the human breast; and in general he must see himself, represent himself to himself, fix before himself what thinking finds as his essence, and recognize himself alone alike in what is summoned out of himself and in what is accepted from without. *Secondly,* man brings himself before himself by *practical* activity, since he has the impulse, in whatever is directly given to him, in what is present to him externally, to produce himself and therein equally to recognize himself. This aim he achieves by altering external things whereon he impresses the seal of his inner being and in which he now finds again his own characteristics [Bestimmungen].[1] Man does this in order, as a free subject, to strip the external world of its inflexible foreignness and to enjoy in the shape of things only an external realization of himself. Even a child's first impulse involves this practical alteration of external things; a boy throws stones into the river and now marvels at the circles drawn in the water as an effect in which he gains an intuition of something that is his own doing. This need runs through the most diversiform phenomena up to that mode of self-production in external things which is present in the work of art. And it is not only with external things that man proceeds in this way, but no less with himself, with his own natural figure which he does not leave as he finds it but deliberately alters. This is the cause of all dressing up and adornment, even if it be barbaric, tasteless, completely disfiguring, or even pernicious like crushing the feet of Chinese ladies, or slitting the ears and lips. For it is only among civilized people that alteration of figure, behaviour, and every sort of mode of external expression proceeds from spiritual development [Bildung].[2]

The universal need for art, that is to say, is man's rational need to lift the inner and outer world into his spiritual consciousness as an object in which he recognizes again his own self. The need for this spiritual freedom he satisfies, on the one hand, within, by making what is within him explicit to himself, but correspondingly by giving outward reality to this his explicit self [Fürsichseyn], and thus in this duplication of himself by bringing what is in him into intuition [Anschauung] and knowledge [Erkenntnis], for himself and others. This is the free rationality of man in which all acting and knowing, as well as art too, have their basis and necessary origin. The specific need of art, however, in distinction from other action, political and moral, from religious representation and scientific knowledge, we shall see later.

(ii) [The Work of Art, as being for Apprehension by Man's Senses, is drawn from the Sensuous Sphere]

So far we have considered in the work of art the aspect in which it is made by man. We have now to pass on to its second characteristic [Bestimmung], namely that it is produced for apprehension by man's *senses* [*Sinn*] and therefore is more or less derived from the sensuous sphere.

(a) This reflection has given rise to the consideration that fine art is meant to arouse feeling [Empfindung], in particular the feeling that suits us, pleasant feeling. In this regard, the investigation of fine art has been made into an investigation of the feelings, and the question has been raised, 'what feelings should be aroused by art, fear, for example, and pity? But how can these be agreeable, how can the treatment of misfortune afford satisfaction?' Reflection on these lines dates especially from Moses Mendelssohn's times and many such discussions can be found in his writings.[3] Yet such investigation did not get far, because feeling is the indefinite dull region of the spirit; what is felt remains enveloped in the form of the most abstract individual subjectivity, and therefore differences between feelings are also completely abstract, not differences in the thing itself. For example, fear, anxiety, alarm, terror are of course further modifications of one and the same sort of feeling, but in part they are only quantitative intensifications, in part just forms not affecting their content, but indifferent to it. In the case of fear, for example, something is present in which the subject has an interest, but at the same time he sees the approach of the negative which threatens to destroy what he is interested in, and now he finds unmediated in himself the interest and the negative, both as contradictory affections of his subjectivity. But such fear cannot by itself condition any content; on the contrary, it is capable of receiving into itself the most varied and opposite contents. Feeling as such is an entirely empty form of subjective affectivity [Affektion]. Of course this form may be manifold in itself, as hope, grief, joy, pleasure; and, again, in this variety it may encompass different contents, as there is a feeling for justice, moral feeling [Gefühl], sublime religious feeling, and so on. But the fact that such content is present in different forms of feeling is not enough to bring to light its essential and specific nature. Feeling remains a purely subjective emotional state of mind in which the concrete thing vanishes, contracted into a circle of the greatest abstraction. Consequently the investigation of the feelings [Empfindungen] which art evokes, or is supposed to evoke, does not get beyond vagueness; it is a study which precisely abstracts from the content proper and its concrete essence and concept. For reflection on feeling is satisfied with observing subjective emotional reaction in its particular character, instead of immersing itself in the thing at issue, i.e. in the work of art, plumbing its depths, and in addition relinquishing mere subjectivity and its states. But in the case of feeling it is precisely this empty subjectivity which is not only retained but is the chief thing, and this is why men are so fond of having feelings. But this too is why a study of this kind becomes wearisome on account of its indefiniteness and emptiness, and disagreeable by its concentration on tiny subjective peculiarities.

(b) But since the work of art is not, as may be supposed, meant merely in general to arouse feelings (for in that case it would have this aim in common, without any specific difference, with oratory, historical writing, religious edification, etc.), but to do so only in so far as it is beautiful, reflection on the beautiful hit upon the idea of looking for a *special feeling of the beautiful,* and finding a specific *sense for the same.* In this quest it soon appeared that such a sense is no blind instinct, made firmly definite by nature, capable from the start in and by itself of distinguishing beauty. Hence *education* [*Bildung*] was demanded for this sense, and the educated sense of beauty was called *taste* which, although an educated appreciation and discovery of beauty, was supposed to remain still in the guise of immediate feeling. We have already touched on how abstract theories undertook to educate such a sense of taste and how it itself remained external and one-sided.[4] Criticism at the time of these views was on the one hand deficient in *universal* principles; on the other hand, as the *particular* criticism of *individual works* of art, it aimed less at grounding a more *definite judgement* – the implements for making one being not yet available – than at advancing rather the education of taste in general. Thus this education likewise got no further than what was rather vague, and it laboured only, by reflection, so to equip feeling, as a sense of beauty, that now it could find beauty wherever and however it existed. Yet the depths of the thing remained a sealed book to taste, since these depths require not only sensing and abstract reflections, but the entirety of reason and the solidity of the spirit, while taste was directed only to the external surface on which feelings play and where one-sided principles may pass as valid. Consequently, however, so-called 'good taste' takes fright at all the deeper effects [of art] and is silent when the thing at issue comes in question and externalities and incidentals vanish. For when great passions and the movements of a profound soul are revealed, there is no longer any question of the finer distinctions of taste and its pedantic preoccupation with individual details. It feels genius [*Genius*] striding over such ground, and, retreating before its might, finds the place too hot for itself and knows not what to do with itself.

(c) For this reason the study of works of art has given up keeping in view merely the education of taste and proposing only to exhibit taste. The *connoisseur* [*Kenner*] has taken the place of the man of taste or the judge of artistic taste. The positive side of connoisseurship, in so far as it concerns a thorough acquaintance with the whole sweep of the individual character of a work of art, we have already described as necessary for the study of art.[5] For, on account of its nature, at once material and individual, the work of art issues essentially from particular conditions of the most varied sort, amongst them especially the time and place of its origin, then the specific individuality of the artist, and above all the technical development of his art. Attention to all these aspects is indispensable for a distinct and thorough intuition of, and acquaintance with, a work of art, and indeed for the enjoyment of it; with them connoisseurship is principally preoccupied, and what it achieves in its way is to be accepted with gratitude. Now while such scholarship is justly counted as something essential, it still may not be taken as the single and supreme element in the relation which the spirit adopts to a work of art and to art in general. For connoisseurship, and this is its defective side, may stick at acquaintance with purely external aspects, the technical, historical, etc., and perhaps have little notion of the true nature of the work of art, or even know nothing of it at all; indeed it can even disesteem the value of deeper studies in comparison with purely positive, technical, and historical information. Yet connoisseurship, if it be of a genuine kind, does itself strive at least for specific grounds and information, and for an intelligent judgement with which after all is bound up a more precise discrimination of the different, even if partly external, aspects of a work of art and the evaluation of these.

(d) After these remarks on the modes of study occasioned by that aspect of the work of art which, as itself a sensuous object, gave it an essential relation to men as sensuous beings, we propose now to treat this aspect in its more essential bearing on art itself, namely (α) in regard to the work of art as an object, and (β) in regard to the subjectivity of the artist, his genius, talent [*Genie, Talent*], etc., yet without our entering upon what in this connection can proceed only from the knowledge of art in its universal concept. For here we are not yet really on scientific ground and territory; we are still only in the province of external reflections.

(α) Of course the work of art presents itself to sensuous apprehension. It is there for sensuous feeling, external or internal, for sensuous intuition and representation, just as nature is, whether the external nature that surrounds us, or our own sensitive nature within. After all, a speech, for example, can exist for sensuous representation and feeling. But nevertheless the work of art, as a sensuous object, is not merely for *sensuous* apprehension; its standing is of such a kind that, though sensuous, it is essentially at the same time for *spiritual* apprehension; the spirit is meant to be affected by it and to find some satisfaction in it.

This vocation and purpose [Bestimmung] of the work of art explains at once how it can in no way be a natural product or have in its natural aspect a natural vitality, whether a natural product is supposed to have a higher or a lower value than a *mere* work of art, as a work of art is often called in a depreciatory sense.

For the sensuous element in a work of art should be there only in so far as it exists for the human spirit, regardless of its existing independently as a sensuous object.

If we examine more closely in what way the sensuous is *there* for man, we find that what is sensuous can be related in various ways to the spirit.

(αα) The poorest mode of apprehension, the least adequate to spirit, is purely sensuous apprehension. It consists, in the first place, of merely looking on, hearing, feeling, etc., just as in hours of spiritual fatigue (indeed for many people at any time) it may be an amusement to wander about without thinking, just to listen here and look round there, and so on. Spirit does not stop at the mere apprehension of the external world by sight and hearing; it makes it into an object for its inner being which then is itself driven, once again in the form of sensuousness, to realize itself in things, and relates itself to them as *desire [Begierde]*. In this appetitive relation to the external world, man, as a sensuous individual, confronts things as they are individuals; likewise he does not turn his mind to them as thinker with universal categories of determination [Bestimmungen]: instead, in accord with individual impulses and interests, he relates himself to the objects, individuals themselves, and maintains himself in them by using and consuming them, and by sacrificing them works his own self-satisfaction. In this negative relation, desire requires for itself not merely the superficial appearance of external things, but the things themselves in their concrete physical existence. With mere pictures of the wood that it might use, or of the animals it might want to eat, desire is not served. Neither can desire let the object persist in its freedom, for its impulse drives it just to cancel [aufzuheben] this independence and freedom of external things, and to show that they are only there to be destroyed and consumed. But at the same time the person too, caught up in the individual, restricted, and nugatory interests of his desire, is neither free in himself, since he is not determined by the essential universality and rationality of his will, nor free in respect of the external world, for desire remains essentially determined by external things and related to them.

Now this relation of desire is not the one in which man stands to the work of art. He leaves it free as an object [Gegenstand] to exist on its own account; he relates himself to it without desire, as to an object [Objekt] which is for the contemplative [theoretische] side of spirit alone.[6] Consequently the work of art, though it has sensuous existence, does not require in this respect a sensuously concrete being and a natural life; indeed it ought not to remain on this level, seeing that it is meant to satisfy purely spiritual interests and exclude all desire from itself. Hence it is true that practical desire rates organic and inorganic individual things in nature, which can serve its purpose, higher than works of art which show themselves useless to serve it and are enjoyable only by other forms of the spirit.

(ββ) A second way in which what is externally present can be *for* the spirit is, in contrast to individual sense-perception and practical desire, the purely theoretical relation to *intelligence*. The theoretical study of things is not interested in consuming them in their individuality and satisfying itself and maintaining itself sensuously by means of them, but in coming to know them in their *universality*, finding their inner essence and law, and conceiving them in accordance with their concept [und sie ihrem Begriff nach zu begreifen]. Therefore theoretical interest lets individual things alone and retreats from them as sensuous individualities, since this sensuous individualism is not what intelligence tries to study. For the rational intelligence does not belong to the individual person as such in the way that desires do, but belongs to him as at the same time inherently universal. In as much as man relates himself to things in accordance with his universality, it is his universal reason which strives to find itself in nature and thereby to re-establish that inner essence of things which sensuous existence, though that essence is its basis, cannot immediately display. This theoretical interest [Interesse], the satisfaction of which is the work of *science* [Wissenschaft], art does not share, however, in this scientific form, nor does it make common cause with the impulses of purely practical desires. Of course science can start from the sensuous in its individuality and possess an idea [Vorstellung] of how this individual thing comes to be there in its individual colour, shape, size, etc. Yet in that case this isolated sensuous thing has as such no further bearing on the spirit, in as much as intelligence goes straight for the universal, the law, the thought and concept of the object; on this account not only does it turn its back on the object in its immediate individuality, but transforms it within; out of something sensuously concrete it makes an abstraction, something thought, and so something essentially other than what that same object was in its sensuous appearance. This the artistic interest, in distinction from science, does not do. Just as the work of art proclaims itself *qua* external object in its sensuous individuality and immediate determinateness in respect of colour, shape, sound, or *qua* a single intuition, etc., so the reflection on the work of art accepts it like this too, without going so far beyond the imme-

diate object confronting it as to endeavour to grasp, as science does, the
concept of this object as a universal concept.

From the practical interest of desire, the interest in art is distinguished
by the fact that it lets its object persist freely and on its own account, while
desire converts it to its own use by destroying it. On the other hand, the
reflection on the work of art differs in an opposite way from theoretical
consideration [Betrachtung] by scientific intelligence, since it cherishes an
interest in the object in its individual existence and does not struggle to
change it into its universal thought and concept.

(γγ) Now it follows from this that the sensuous must indeed be present
in the work of art, but should appear only as the surface and as a pure
appearance [*Schein*] of the sensuous. For in the sensuous aspect of a work
of art the spirit seeks neither the concrete material stuff, the empirical
inner completeness and development of the organism which desire
demands, nor the universal and purely ideal thought. What it wants is sensuous presence which indeed should remain sensuous, but liberated from
the scaffolding of its purely material nature. Thereby the sensuous aspect
of a work of art, in comparison with the immediate existence of things in
nature, is elevated to a pure *appearance*, and the work of art stands in the
middle between immediate sensuousness and ideal thought. It is *not yet*
pure thought, but, despite its sensuousness, is *no longer* a purely material
existent either, like stones, plants, and organic life; on the contrary, the
sensuous in the work of art is itself something ideal, but which, not being
ideal as thought is ideal, is still at the same time there externally as a thing.
If spirit leaves the objects free yet without descending into their essential
inner being (for if it did so they would altogether cease to exist for it externally as individuals), then this pure appearance of the sensuous presents
itself to spirit from without as the shape, the appearance, or the sonority
of things. Consequently the sensuous aspect of art is related only to the
two *theoretical* senses of *sight* and *hearing*, while smell, taste, and touch
remain excluded from the enjoyment of art.[7] For smell, taste, and touch
have to do with matter as such and its immediately sensible qualities – smell
with material volatility in air, taste with the material liquefaction of objects,
touch with warmth, cold, smoothness, etc. For this reason these senses cannot have to do with artistic objects, which are meant to maintain themselves in their real independence and allow of no *purely* sensuous relationship. What is agreeable for these senses is not the beauty of art. Thus art
on its sensuous side deliberately produces only a shadow-world of shapes,
sounds, and sights; and it is quite out of the question to maintain that, in
calling works of art into existence, it is from mere impotence and because
of his limitations that man produces no more than a surface of the sensuous, mere *schemata*.[8] These sensuous shapes and sounds appear in art not
merely for the sake of themselves and their immediate shape, but with the
aim, in this shape, of affording satisfaction to higher spiritual interests,

since they have the power to call forth from all the depths of consciousness a sound and an echo in the spirit. In this way the sensuous aspect of art is *spiritualized,* since the *spirit* appears in art as made sensuous.

(β) But precisely for this reason an art-product is only there in so far as it has taken its passage through the spirit and has arisen from spiritual productive activity. This leads on to the other question which we have to answer, namely in what way the necessary sensuous side of art is operative in the artist as his objective productive activity. This sort and manner of production contains in itself, as subjective activity, just the same characteristics [Bestimmungen] which we found objectively present in the work of art; it must be a spiritual activity which yet contains at the same time the element of sensuousness and immediacy. Still it is neither on the one hand purely mechanical work, a purely unconscious skill in sensuous manipulation or a formal activity according to fixed rules to be learnt by heart, nor on the other hand is it a scientific production which passes over from the sensuous to abstract representations and thoughts or is active entirely in the element of pure thinking. In artistic production the spiritual and the sensuous aspects must be as one. For example, someone might propose to proceed in poetic composition by first apprehending the proposed theme as a prosaic thought and then putting it into poetical images, rhyme, and so forth, so that now the image would simply be hung on to the abstract reflections as an ornament and decoration. But such a procedure could produce only bad poetry, because in it there would be operative as *separate* activities what in artistic production has validity only as an undivided unity. This genuine mode of production constitutes the activity of artistic *imagination* [*Phantasie*].

This activity is the rational element which exists as spirit only in so far as it actively drives itself forth into consciousness, yet what it bears within itself it places before itself only in sensuous form. Thus this activity has a spiritual content which yet it configurates sensuously because only in this sensuous guise can it gain knowledge of the content. This can be compared with the characteristic mentality of a man experienced in life, or even of a man of quick wit and ingenuity, who, although he knows perfectly well what matters in life, what in substance holds men together, what moves them, what power dominates them, nevertheless has neither himself grasped this knowledge in general rules nor expounded it to others in general reflections. What fills his mind he always just makes clear to himself and others in particular cases, real or invented, in adequate examples, and so forth; for in his mode of representation anything and everything is shaped into concrete pictures, determined in time and space, to which there may not be wanting names and all sorts of other external circumstances. Yet such a kind of imagination [Einbildungskraft] rests rather on the recollection of situations lived through, of experiences enjoyed, instead of being creative itself. Recollection preserves and renews the individuality and the external fashion of the occurrence of such experiences, with all their accompanying circumstances, but does not allow the universal to emerge on its own account. But the productive imagination [Phantasie] of an artist is the imagination of a great spirit and heart, the apprehension and creation of representations and shapes, and indeed the exhibition of the profoundest and most universal human interests in pictorial and completely definite sensuous presentation.

Now from this it follows at once that, on one side, imagination [Phantasie] rests of course on natural gifts and talent in general, because its productive activity involves an aspect of sensuousness. We do indeed speak of 'scientific' talent too, but the sciences presuppose only the universal capacity for thinking, which, instead of proceeding in a natural way, like imagination, precisely abstracts from all natural activity; and so we are righter to say that there is no specifically scientific talent in the sense of a merely natural gift. Conversely, imagination has at the same time a sort of instinct-like productiveness, in that the essential figurativeness [Bildlichkeit] and sensuousness of the work of art must be present subjectively in the artist as a natural gift and natural impulse, and, as an unconscious operation, must also belong to the natural side of man.[9] Of course natural capacity is not the whole of talent and genius, since the production of art is also of a spiritual, self-conscious kind, yet its spirituality must somehow have in itself an element of natural picturing and shaping. Consequently almost anyone can get up to a certain point in an art, but to get beyond this point, where art proper only now begins, an inborn, higher talent for art is necessary.

As a natural gift, this talent declares itself after all in most cases in early youth, and it shows itself in the driving restlessness to shape a specific sensuous material at once in a lively and active way and to seize this mode of expression and communication as the only one, or as the most important and appropriate one. And so also an early technical facility, which up to a certain point is effortless, is a sign of inborn talent. For a sculptor everything turns into shapes, and from early years he lays hold of clay in order to model it. In short, whatever representations such talented men have, whatever rouses and moves them inwardly, turns at once into figure, drawing, melody, or poem.[10]

(γ) Thirdly, and lastly, the *subject matter* [*Inhalt*] of art is in a certain respect also drawn from the sensuous, from nature; or, in any case, even if the subject is of a spiritual kind, it can still be grasped only by displaying spiritual things, like human relationships, in the shape of phenomena possessed of external reality.

(iii) [The Aim of Art]

Now the question arises of what interest or *end* man sets before himself when he produces such subject matter in the form of works of art. This was the third point which we adduced with regard to the work of art,[11] and its closer discussion will lead us on at last to the true concept of art itself.

If in this matter we cast a glance at what is commonly thought, one of the most prevalent ideas [Vorstellungen] which may occur to us is

(a) the principle of the *imitation of nature*. According to this view, imitation, as facility in copying natural forms just as they are, in a way that corresponds to them completely, is supposed to constitute the essential end and aim of art, and the success of this portrayal in correspondence with nature is supposed to afford complete satisfaction.

(α) This definition [Bestimmung] contains, *prima facie*, only the purely formal aim that whatever exists already in the external world, and the manner in which it exists there, is now to be made over again as a copy, as well as a man can do with the means at his disposal. But this repetition can be seen at once to be

(αα) A *superfluous* labour, since what pictures, theatrical productions, etc., portray imitatively – animals, natural scenes, human affairs – we already possess in our gardens or in our own houses or in matters within our narrower or wider circle of acquaintance. And, looked at more closely, this superfluous labour may even be regarded as a presumptuous game

(ββ) which falls far short of nature. For art is restricted in its means of portrayal [Darstellungsmitteln], and can only produce one-sided deceptions, for example a pure appearance of reality for *one* sense only, and, in fact, if it abides by the formal aim of *mere imitation*, it provides not the reality of life but only a pretence of life. After all, the Turks, as Mahommedans, do not, as is well known, tolerate any pictures or copies of men, etc. James Bruce in his journey to Abyssinia showed paintings of a fish to a Turk; at first the Turk was astonished, but quickly enough he found an answer: "If this fish shall rise up against you on the last day and say: 'You have indeed given me a body but no living soul', how will you then justify yourself against this accusation?"[12] The prophet too, as is recorded in the Sunna, said to the two women, Ommi Habiba and Ommi Selma, who had told him about pictures in Ethiopian churches: "These pictures will accuse their authors on the day of judgement."[13]

Even so, there are doubtless examples of completely deceptive copying. The grapes painted by Zeuxis have from antiquity onward been styled a triumph of art and also of the principle of the imitation of nature, because living doves are supposed to have pecked at them. To this ancient example we could add the modern one of Büttner's monkey which ate away a painting of a cockchafer in Rösel's *Insektbelustigungen* [*Amusements of Insects*] and was pardoned by his master because it had proved the excellence of the pictures in this book, although it had thus destroyed the beautiful copy of this expensive work.[14] But in such examples and others it must at least occur to us at once that, instead of praising works of art because they have deceived *even* doves and monkeys, we should just precisely censure those who think of exalting a work of art by predicating so miserable an effect as this as its highest and supreme quality. In sum, however, it must be said that, by mere imitation, art cannot stand in competition with nature, and, if it tries, it looks like a worm trying to crawl after an elephant.

(γγ) If we stay within the context of the continual, though comparative, failure of the copy compared with the original in nature, then there remains over as an aim nothing but taking pleasure in the trick of producing something like nature. And of course a man may enjoy himself in now producing over again by his own work, skill, and assiduity what otherwise is there already. But this enjoyment and admiration become in themselves the more frigid and cold, the more the copy is like the natural original, or they may even be perverted into tedium and repugnance. There are portraits which, as has been wittily said, are "disgustingly like", and Kant, in relation to this pleasure in imitation as such, cites another example, namely that we soon get tired of a man who can imitate to perfection the warbling of the nightingale (and there are such men); as soon as it is discovered that it is a man who is producing the notes, we are at once weary of the song.[15] We then recognize in it nothing but a trick, neither the free production of nature, nor a work of art, since from the free productive power of man we expect something quite different from such music which interests us only when, as is the case with the nightingale's warbling, it gushes forth purposeless from the bird's own life, like the voice of human feeling. In general this delight in imitative skill can always be but restricted, and it befits man better to take delight in what he produces out of himself. In this sense the discovery of any insignificant technical product has higher value, and man can be prouder of having invented the hammer, the nail, etc., than of manufacturing tricks of imitation. For this enthusiasm for copying merely as copying is to be respected as little as the trick of the man who had learnt to throw lentils through a small opening without missing. He displayed this dexterity before Alexander, but Alexander gave him a bushel of lentils as a reward for this useless and worthless art.[16]

(β) Now further, since the principle of imitation is purely formal, *objective beauty* itself disappears when this principle is made the end of art. For if it is, then there is no longer a question of the character of *what* is supposed to be imitated, but only of the *correctness* of the imitation. The object and content of the beautiful is regarded as a matter of complete indifference. Even if, apart from this, we speak of a difference between beauty and ugliness in relation to animals, men, localities, actions, or characters, yet according to that principle this remains a difference which does not properly belong to art, to which we have left nothing but imitation pure and simple. So that the above-mentioned lack of a criterion for the endless forms of nature leaves us, so far as the choice of objects and their beauty and ugliness are concerned, with mere *subjective taste* as the last word, and such taste will not be bound by rules, and is not open to dispute. And indeed if, in choosing objects for representation, we start from what *people* find beautiful or ugly and therefore worthy of artistic representation, i.e. from their taste, then all spheres of natural objects stand open to us, and none of them is likely to lack an admirer. For among us, e.g., it may not be every husband who finds his wife beautiful, but he did before they were married, to the exclusion of all others too; and the fact that the subjective taste for this beauty has no fixed rule may be considered a good thing for both parties. If finally we look beyond single individuals and their capricious taste to the taste of *nations*, this too is of the greatest variety and contrariety. How often do we hear it said that a European beauty would not please a Chinese, or a Hottentot either, since the Chinese has inherently a totally different conception of beauty from the negro's, and his again from a European's, and so on. Indeed, if we examine the works of art of these non-European peoples, their images of the gods, for example, which have sprung from their imagination [Phantasie] as sublime and worthy of veneration, they may present themselves to us as the most hideous idols; and while their music may sound in our ears as the most detestable noise, they on their side will regard our sculptures, pictures, and music, as meaningless or ugly.

(γ) But even if we abstract from an objective principle for art, and if beauty is to be based on subjective and individual taste, we soon nevertheless find on the side of art itself that the imitation of nature, which indeed appeared to be a universal principle and one confirmed by high authority, is not to be adopted, at least in this general and wholly abstract form. For if we look at the different arts, it will be granted at once that, even if *painting* and *sculpture* portray objects that appear to be like natural ones or ones whose type is essentially drawn from nature, on the other hand works of *architecture*, which is also one of the *fine* arts, can as little be called imitations of nature as works of *poetry* can, in so far as the latter are not confined, e.g., to mere description. In any case, if we still wanted to uphold this principle in relation to these latter arts, we would at least find ourselves compelled to take a long circuitous route, because we would have to attach various conditions to the proposition and reduce the so-called 'truth' of imitation to probability at least. But with probability we would again encounter a great difficulty, namely in settling what is probable and what is not, and, apart from this, we would not wish or be able to exclude from poetry all purely arbitrary and completely fanciful [phantastischen] inventions.

The aim of art must therefore lie in something still other than the purely mechanical imitation of what is there, which in every case can bring to birth only technical *tricks*, not *works*, of art. It is true that it is an essential element in a work of art to have a natural shape as its basis because what it portrays it displays in the form of an external and therefore also natural phenomenon. In painting, e.g., it is an important study to get to know and copy with precision the colours in their relation to one another, the effects

of light, reflections, etc., as well as the forms and shapes of objects down
to the last detail. It is in this respect, after all, that chiefly in recent times
the principle of the imitation of nature, and of naturalism generally, has
raised its head again in order to bring back to the vigour and distinctness
of nature an art which had relapsed into feebleness and nebulosity; or, on
the other hand, to assert the regular, immediate, and explicitly fixed
sequences of nature against the manufactured and purely arbitrary con-
ventionalism, really just as inartistic as unnatural, into which art had
strayed. But whatever is right enough from one point of view in this endeavour, still the naturalism demanded is as such not the substantial and primary basis of art, and, even if external appearance in its naturalness constitutes one essential characteristic [Bestimmung] of art, still neither is the
given natural world the *rule* nor is the mere imitation of external phenomena, as external, the *aim* of art.

(b) Therefore the further question arises: what, then, is the *content* of
art, and why is this content to be portrayed? In this matter our consciousness confronts us with the common opinion that the task and aim of art is
to bring home to our sense, our feeling, and our inspiration everything
which has a place in the human spirit. That familiar saying "nihil humani
a me alienum puto" art is supposed to make real in us.[17]

Its aim therefore is supposed to consist in awakening and vivifying our
slumbering feelings, inclinations, and passions *of every kind,* in *filling* the
heart, in forcing the human being, educated or not, to go through the
whole gamut of feelings which the human heart in its inmost and secret
recesses can bear, experience, and produce, through what can move and
stir the human breast in its depths and manifold possibilities and aspects,
and to deliver to feeling and contemplation for its enjoyment whatever the
spirit possesses of the essential and lofty in its thinking and in the Idea
[Idee] – the splendour of the noble, eternal, and true: moreover to make
misfortune and misery, evil and guilt intelligible, to make men intimately
acquainted with all that is horrible and shocking, as well as with all that is
pleasurable and felicitous; and, finally, to let fancy [Phantasie] loose in the
idle plays of imagination [Einbildungskraft] and plunge it into the seductive magic of sensuously bewitching visions and feelings. According to this
view, art is on the one hand to embrace this universal wealth of subject
matter in order to complete the natural experience of our external existence, and on the other hand to arouse those passions in general so that
the experiences of life do not leave us unmoved and so that we might now
acquire a receptivity for all phenomena. But such a stimulus is not given
in this sphere by actual experience itself, but only through the appearance
of it, since art deceptively substitutes its productions for reality. The possibility of this deception through the pure appearance-status [Schein] of
art rests on the fact that, for man, all reality must come through the
medium of intuition and representation, and only through this medium

does it penetrate the heart and the will. Now here it is a matter of indifference whether a man's attention is claimed by immediate external reality or whether this happens in another way, namely through images, signs, and representations containing in themselves and portraying the material of reality. We can envisage things which are not real as if they were real. Therefore, it remains all the same for our feelings whether it is external reality, or only the appearance of it, whereby a situation, a relation, or, in general, a circumstance of life, is brought home to us, in order to make us respond appropriately to the essence of such a matter, whether by grief or rejoicing, whether by being touched or agitated, or whether by making us go through the gamut of the feelings and passions of wrath, hatred, pity, anxiety, fear, love, reverence and admiration, honour and fame.

This arousing of all feelings [Empfindungen] in us, this drawing of the heart through all the circumstances of life, this actualizing of all these inner movements by means of a purely deceptive externally presented object is above all what is regarded, on the view we have been considering, as the proper and supreme power of art.

But now since, on this view, art is supposed to have the vocation of imposing on the heart and the representational imagination [Vorstellung] good and bad alike, strengthening man to the noblest ideals and yet enervating him to the most sensuous and selfish feelings of pleasure, art is given a purely formal task; and without any explicitly fixed aim would thus provide only the empty form for every possible kind of content and worth.

(c) In fact art does indeed have this formal side, namely its ability to adorn and bring before perception and feeling every possible material, just as the thinking of ratiocination can work on every possible object and mode of action and equip them with reasons and justifications. But confronted by such a multiple variety of content, we are at once forced to notice that the different feelings and representations, which art is supposed to arouse or confirm, counteract one another, contradict and reciprocally cancel [aufheben] one another. Indeed, in this respect, the more art inspires to contradictory [emotions] the more it increases the contradictory character of feelings and passions and makes us stagger about like Bacchantes or even goes on, like ratiocination [Raisonnement], to sophistry and scepticism.[18] This variety of material itself compels us, therefore, not to stop at so formal a definition [of the aim of art], since rationality penetrates this jumbled diversity and demands to see, and know to be attained, even out of elements so contradictory, a higher and inherently more universal end. It is claimed indeed similarly that the final end of the state and the social life of men is that *all* human capacities and *all* individual powers be developed and given expression in every way and in every direction. But against so formal a view the question arises soon enough: into what *unity* are these manifold formations to be brought together, what *single aim* must they have as their fundamental concept and final end? As with the concept of the state, so too with the concept of art there arises the need (a) for a *common* end for its particular aspects, but (b) also for a higher *substantial* end. As such a substantial end, the first thing that occurs to reflection is the view that art has the capacity and the vocation to mitigate the ferocity of desires.

(α) In respect of this first idea, we have only to discover in what feature peculiar to art there lies the capacity to cancel crudity and to bridle and educate impulses, inclinations, and passions. Crudeness in general is grounded in a direct selfishness of the impulses which make straightaway, precisely, and exclusively for the satisfaction of their appetite [Begierlichkeit]. But desire is all the cruder and imperious the more, as single and restricted, it engrosses the *whole man,* so that he loses the power to tear himself free, as a universal being, from this determinateness and become aware of himself as universal. And if the man says in such a case, as may be supposed, "The passion is stronger than *I*", then for consciousness the abstract "I" *is* separated from the particular passion, but only in a purely formal way, since all that is pronounced with this cleavage is that, in face of the power of the passion, the "I" as a universal is of no account whatever. Thus the ferocity of passion consists in the unity of the "I" as universal with the restricted object of its desire, so that the man has no longer any will beyond this single passion. Now such crudeness and untamed force of passion is *prima facie* mitigated by art, in that it gives a man an image [vorstellig macht] of what he feels and achieves in such a situation. And even if art restricts itself to setting up pictures of passions for intuition, even if indeed it were to flatter them, still there is here already a power of mitigation, since thereby a man is at least made aware of what otherwise he only immediately is. For then the man contemplates his impulses and inclinations, and while previously they carried him reflectionless away, he now sees them outside himself and already begins to be free from them because they confront him as something objective.

For this reason it may often be the case with an artist that, overtaken by grief, he mitigates and weakens for himself the intensity of his own feeling by setting it forth. Tears, even, provide some comfort; at first entirely sunk and concentrated in grief, a man may then in this direct way utter this purely inward feeling. But still more of an alleviation is the expression of one's inner state in words, pictures, sounds, and shapes. For this reason it was a good old custom at deaths and funerals to appoint wailing women in order that grief might be brought to intuition in its expression. For by expressions of condolence the burden of a man's misfortune is brought before his mind; if it is much spoken about he has to reflect on it, and this alleviates his grief. And so to cry one's eyes out and to speak out has ever been regarded as a means of freeing oneself from the oppressive burden of care or at least of relieving the heart. The mitigation of the power of passions therefore has its universal ground in the fact that man is released from his immediate imprisonment in a feeling and becomes conscious of it as something external to him, to which he must now relate himself in an ideal way. Art by means of its presentations [Darstellungen], while remaining within the sensuous sphere, liberates man at the same time from the power of sensuousness. Of course we may often hear favourite phraseology about man's duty to remain in immediate unity with nature; but such unity, in its abstraction, is purely and simply crudeness and ferocity, and by dissolving this unity for man, art lifts him with gentle hands out of and above imprisonment in nature. For man's preoccupation with artistic objects remains purely contemplative [theoretisch], and thereby it educates, even if at first only an attention to artistic portrayals in general, later on an attention to their meaning and to a comparison with other subjects, and it opens the mind to a general consideration of them and the points of view therein involved.

(β) Now on this there follows quite logically the second characteristic [Bestimmung] that has been attributed to art as its essential aim, namely the *purification* of the passions, instruction, and *moral* improvement. For the theory [Bestimmung] that art was to curb crudeness and educate the passions, remained quite formal and general, so that it has become again a matter of what *specific* sort of education [Bildung] this is and what is its essential aim.

(αα) It is true that the doctrine of the purification of passion still suffers the same deficiency as the previous doctrine of the mitigation of desires, yet it does at least emphasize more closely the fact that artistic presentations need a criterion for assessing their worth or unworthiness. This criterion is precisely an effectiveness in separating pure from impure in the passions. Such effectiveness therefore requires a content which can exercise this purifying force, and, in so far as producing such an effect is supposed to constitute the substantial aim of art, the purifying content will have to be brought into consciousness in accordance with its *universality* and *essentiality*.

(ββ) From this latter point of view, the aim of art has been pronounced to be that it should *instruct*. On this view, on the one hand, the special character of art consists in the movement of feelings and in the satisfaction lying in this movement, lying even in fear, in pity, in grievous emotion and agitation, i.e. in the satisfying enlistment of feelings and passions, and to that extent in a gusto, a pleasure, and delight in artistic subjects, in their presentation and effect. But, on the other hand, this aim of art is supposed to have its higher criterion only in its instructiveness, in *fabula docet*,[19] and so in the useful influence which the work of art may exert on the individual. In this respect the Horatian aphorism *Et prodesse volunt et delectare poetae*[20] contains, concentrated in a few words, what later has been elaborated in an infinite degree, diluted, and made into a view of art reduced to the uttermost extreme of shallowness. Now in connection with such instruction we must ask at once whether it is supposed to be contained in the work of art directly or indirectly, explicitly or implicitly. If, in general, what is at issue is a universal and non-contingent aim, then this end and aim, in view of the essentially spiritual nature of art, can itself only be a spiritual one, and moreover one which is not contingent but existing in and for itself. This aim in relation to teaching could only consist in bringing into consciousness, by means of the work of art, an absolutely essential [an und für sich wesentlichen] spiritual content. From this point of view we must assert that the more highly art is ranked the more it has to adopt such a content into itself and find only in the essence of that content the criterion of whether what is expressed is appropriate or not. Art has in fact become the first *instructress* of peoples.

If, however, the aim of instruction is treated as an aim in such a way that the universal nature of the content represented is supposed to emerge and be explained directly and explicitly as an abstract proposition, prosaic reflection, or general doctrine, and not to be contained implicitly and only indirectly in the concrete form of a work of art, then by this separation the sensuous pictorial form, which is precisely what alone makes a work of art a work of *art,* becomes a useless appendage, a veil and a pure appearance [Schein], expressly pronounced to be a *mere veil* and a mere pure appearance. But thereby the nature of the work of art itself is distorted. For the work of art should put before our eyes [vor die Anschauung] a content, not in its universality as such, but one whose universality has been absolutely individualized and sensuously particularized. If the work of art does not proceed from this principle but emphasizes the universality with the aim of [providing] abstract instruction, then the pictorial and sensuous element is only an external and superfluous adornment, and the work of art is broken up internally; form and content no longer appear as coalesced. In that event the sensuously individual and the spiritually universal have become external to one another.

Now, further, if the aim of art is restricted to this usefulness for *instruction,* the other side, pleasure, entertainment, and delight, is pronounced explicitly to be *inessential,* and ought to have its substance only in the utility of the doctrine on which it is attendant. But what is implied here at the same time is that art does not carry its vocation [Bestimmung], end, and aim in itself, but that its essence lies in something else to which it serves as a *means.* In that event art is only one amongst several means which are proved useful for and applied to the end of instruction. But this brings us to the boundary at which art is supposed to cease to be an end in itself, because it is reduced either to a mere entertaining game or a mere means of instruction.

(γγ) This boundary is most sharply marked if in turn a question is raised about a supreme aim and end for the sake of which passions are to be purified and men instructed. As this aim, *moral [moralische]* betterment has often been adduced in recent times, and the end of art has been placed in the function of preparing inclinations and impulses for moral perfection and of leading them to this final end. This idea [Vorstellung] unites instruction with purification, in as much as art, by affording an insight into genuinely moral goodness and so by instruction, at the same time incites to purification and only so is to accomplish the betterment of mankind as its utility and its highest aim.

Now as regards art in relation to this moral betterment, the same must be said, in the first place, about the aim of art as instruction. It is readily granted that art may not take immorality and the intention of promoting it as its principle. But it is one thing to make immorality the express aim of the presentation, and another not to take morality as that aim. From every genuine work of art a good moral may be drawn, yet of course all depends on interpretation and on *who* draws the moral. We can hear the most immoral presentations defended on the ground that one must be acquainted with evil and sins in order to be able to act morally; conversely, it has been said that the portrayal of Mary Magdalene, the beautiful sinner who afterwards repented, has seduced many into sin, because art makes repentance look so beautiful, and sinning must come before repentance.[21] But the doctrine of moral betterment, carried through logically, is not content with holding that a moral may be pointed from a work of art; on the contrary, it would want the moral instruction to shine forth clearly as the substantial aim of the work of art, and indeed would expressly permit the presentation of none but moral subjects, moral characters, actions, and events. For art can choose its subjects, and is thus distinct from history or the sciences, which have their material given to them.

In order, in this aspect of the matter, to be able to form a thorough estimate of the view that the aim of art is moral, we must first ask what specific standpoint of morality this view professes. If we keep more clearly in view the standpoint of the 'moral' as we have to take it in the best sense of the word today, it is soon obvious that its concept does not immediately coincide with what apart from it we generally call virtue, conventional life [Sittlichkeit],[22] respectability, etc. From this point of view a conventionally virtuous man is not *ipso facto moral*, because to be moral needs *reflection* [*Reflexion*], the specific consciousness of what accords with duty, and action on this preceding consciousness. Duty itself is the law of the will, a law which man nevertheless freely lays down out of himself, and then he ought to determine himself to this duty for the sake of duty and its fulfilment, by doing good solely from the conviction he has won that it is the good. But this law, the duty chosen for duty's sake as a guide out of free conviction and inner conscience, and then carried out, is by itself the abstract universal of the will and this has its direct opposite in nature, in sensuous impulses, selfish interests, passions, and everything grouped together under the name of feeling and emotion. In this opposition it is perceived that one side *cancels* the other, and since both are present in the subject as opposites, he has a choice, since his decision is made from within, between following either the one or the other. But such a decision is a *moral* one, from the standpoint we are considering, and so is the action carried out in accordance with it, but only if it is done, on the one hand, from a free conviction of duty, and, on the other hand, by the conquest not only of the particular will, natural impulses, inclinations, passions, etc., but also of noble feelings and higher impulses. For the modern moralistic view starts from the fixed opposition between the will in its spiritual universality and the will in its sensuous natural particularity; and it consists not in the complete mediation [Vermittelung] of these opposed sides, but in their reciprocal battle against one another, which involves the demand that impulses in their conflict with duty must give way to it.[23]

Now this opposition does not arise for consciousness in the restricted sphere of moral action alone; it emerges in a thorough-going cleavage and opposition between what is in and for itself and what is external reality and existence. Taken quite abstractly, it is the opposition of universal and particular, when each is fixed over against the other on its own account in the same way; more concretely, it appears in nature as the opposition of the abstract law to the abundance of individual phenomena, each explicitly with its own character; in the spirit it appears as the contrast between the sensuous and the spiritual in man, as the battle of spirit against flesh, of duty for duty's sake, of the cold command against particular interest, warmth of heart, sensuous inclinations and impulses, against the individual disposition in general; as the harsh opposition between inner freedom and the necessity of external nature, further as the contradiction between the dead inherently empty concept, and the full concreteness of life, between theory or subjective thinking, and objective existence and experience.

These are oppositions which have not been invented at all by the subtlety of reflection or the pedantry of philosophy; in numerous forms they have always preoccupied and troubled human consciousness, even if it is modern culture [Bildung] that has first worked them out most sharply and driven them up to the peak of harshest contradiction. Spiritual culture, the modern intellect [Verstand], produces this opposition in man which makes him an amphibious animal, because he now has to live in two worlds which contradict one another. The result is that now consciousness wanders about in this contradiction, and, driven from one side to the other, cannot find satisfaction for itself in either the one or the other. For on the one side we see man imprisoned in the common world of reality and earthly temporality, borne down by need and poverty, hard pressed by nature, enmeshed in matter, sensuous ends and their enjoyment, mastered and carried away by natural impulses and passions. On the other side, he lifts himself to eternal ideas [Ideen], to a realm of thought and freedom, gives to himself, as *will* [*Wille*], universal laws and prescriptions

[Bestimmungen], strips the world of its enlivened and flowering reality and dissolves it into abstractions, since the spirit now upholds its right and dignity only by mishandling nature and denying its right, and so retaliates on nature the distress and violence which it has suffered from nature itself. But for modern culture and its intellect this discordance in life and consciousness involves the demand that such a contradiction be resolved. Yet the intellect [Verstand] cannot cut itself free from the rigidity of these oppositions; therefore the solution remains for consciousness a mere *ought* [*Sollen*], and the present and reality move only in the unrest of a hither and thither which seeks a reconciliation without finding one. Thus the question then arises whether such a universal and thorough-going opposition, which cannot get beyond a mere ought and a postulated solution, is in general the absolute [an und für sich] truth and supreme end. If general culture has run into such a contradiction, it becomes the task of philosophy to supersede the oppositions, i.e. to show that neither the one alternative in its abstraction, nor the other in the like one-sidedness, possesses truth, but that they are both self-dissolving; that truth lies only in the reconciliation and mediation of both, and that this mediation is no mere demand, but what is absolutely accomplished and is ever self-accomplishing. This insight coincides immediately with the ingenuous faith and will [Wollen] which does have precisely this dissolved opposition steadily present to its view [vor der Vorstellung], and in action makes it its end and achieves it. Philosophy affords a reflective insight into the essence of the opposition only in so far as it shows how truth is just the dissolving of opposition and, at that, not in the sense, as may be supposed, that the opposition and its two sides *do not exist at all*, but that they exist reconciled.

Now since the ultimate end, moral betterment, has pointed to a higher standpoint, we will have to vindicate this higher standpoint for art too. Thereby the false position, already noticed, is at once abandoned: the position, namely, that art has to serve as a means to moral purposes, and the moral end of the world in general, by instructing and improving, and thus has its substantial aim, not in itself, but in something else. If on this account we now continue to speak of a final end and aim, we must in the first place get rid of the perverse idea [Vorstellung] which, in the question about an end, clings to the accessory meaning of the question, namely that it is one about utility. The perversity here lies in this, that in that case the work of art is supposed to have a bearing on something else which is set before our minds as the essential thing or as what ought to be, so that then the work of art would have validity only as a useful tool for realizing this end which is independently valid on its own account outside the sphere of art. Against this we must maintain that art's vocation is to unveil the *truth* in the form of sensuous artistic configuration, to set forth the reconciled opposition just mentioned, and so to have its end and aim in itself, in this very setting forth and unveiling. For other ends, like instruction, purification, bettering, financial gain, struggling for fame and honour, have nothing to do with the work of art as such, and do not determine its nature.

* * *

(c) The End of the Romantic Form of Art[24]

Art, as it has been under our consideration hitherto, had as its basis the unity of meaning and shape and so the unity of the artist's subjective activity with his topic and work. Looked at more closely, it was the specific kind of this unification at each stage which provided, for the content and its corresponding portrayal, the substantial norm penetrating all artistic productions.

In this matter we found at the beginning of art, in the East, that the spirit was not yet itself explicitly free; it still sought for its Absolute [Absolute] in nature and therefore interpreted nature as in itself divine. Later on, the vision [Anschauung] of classical art represented the Greek gods as naive and inspired, yet even so essentially as individuals burdened with the natural human form as with an affirmative feature. Romantic art for the first time deepened the spirit in its own inwardness, in contrast to which the flesh, external reality, and the world in general were at first posited as negative [Nichtiges], even though the spirit and the Absolute had to appear in this element alone; yet at last this element could be given validity for itself again in a more and more positive way.

(α) These ways of viewing the world constitute religion, the substantial spirit of people and ages, and are woven into not art alone, but all the other spheres of the living present at all periods. Now just as every man is a child of his time in every activity, whether political, religious, or scientific, and just as he has the task of bringing out the essential content and the therefore necessary form of that time, so it is the vocation of art to find for the spirit of a people the artistic expression corresponding to it. Now so long as the artist is bound up with the specific character of such a worldview and religion, in immediate identity with it and with firm faith in it, so long is he genuinely in *earnest* with this material and its representation; i.e. this material remains for him the infinite and true element in his own consciousness — a material with which he lives in an original unity as part of his inmost self, while the form in which he exhibits it is for him as artist the final, necessary, and supreme manner of bringing before our intuition the Absolute and the soul of objects in general.[25] By the substance of his material, a substance immanent in himself, he is tied down to the specific mode of its exposition. For in that case the material, and therefore the form belonging to it, the artist carries immediately in himself as the proper essence of his existence which he does not imagine for himself but which he *is;* and therefore he only has the task of making this truly essential element objective to himself, to represent and develop it in a living way out of his own resources. Only in that event is the artist completely inspired by his material and its presentation; and his inventions are no product of caprice, they originate in him, out of him, out of this substantial ground, this stock, the content of which is not at rest until through the artist it acquires an individual shape adequate to its inner concept. If, on the other hand, we nowadays propose to make the subject of a statue or a painting a Greek god, or, Protestants as we are today, the Virgin Mary, we are not seriously in earnest with such material.[26] It is the innermost faith which we lack here, even if the artist in days when faith was still unimpaired did not exactly need to be what is generally called a pious man, for after all in every age artists have not as a rule been the most pious of men! The requirement is only this, that for the artist the content [of his work] shall constitute the substance, the inmost truth, of his consciousness and make his chosen mode of presentation necessary. For the artist in his production is at the same time a creature of nature, his skill is a *natural* talent; his work is not the pure activity of comprehension [Begreifen] which confronts its material entirely and unites itself with it in free thoughts, in pure thinking; on the contrary, the artist, not yet released from his natural side, is united directly with the subject matter, believes in it, and is identical with it in accordance with his very own self.[27] The result is then that the artist is entirely absorbed in the object; the work of art proceeds entirely out of the undivided inwardness and force of genius [Genie]; the production is firm and unwavering, and in it the full intensity [of creation] is preserved. This is the fundamental condition of art's being present in its integrity.

(β) On the other hand, in the position we have been forced to assign to art in the course of its development, the whole situation has altogether altered. This, however, we must not regard as a mere accidental misfortune suffered by art from without owing to the distress of the times, the sense for the prosaic, lack of interest, etc.; on the contrary, it is the effect and the progress of art itself which, by bringing before our intuition as an object its own indwelling material, at every step along this road makes its own contribution to freeing art from the content represented. What through art or thinking we have before our physical or spiritual eye as an object has lost all absolute interest for us if it has been put before us so completely that the content is exhausted, that everything is revealed, and nothing obscure or inward is left over any more. For interest is to be found only in the case of lively activity [of mind]. The spirit only occupies itself with objects so long as there is something secret, not revealed, in them. This is the case so long as the material is identical with the substance of our own being. But if the essential world-views [Weltanschauungen] implicit in the concept of art, and the range of the content belonging to these, are in every respect revealed by art, then art has got rid of this content which on every occasion was determinate for a particular people, a particular age, and the true need to resume it again is awakened only with the need to turn *against* the content that was alone valid hitherto; thus in Greece Aristophanes rose up against his present world, and Lucian against the whole of the Greek past, and in Italy and Spain, when the Middle Ages were closing, Ariosto and Cervantes began to turn against chivalry.[28]

Now contrasted with the time in which the artist owing to his nationality and his period stands with the substance of his being within a specific world-view and its content and forms of portrayal, we find an altogether opposed view which in its complete development is of importance only in most recent times. In our day, in the case of almost all peoples, criticism [die Kritik],[29] the cultivation of reflection, and, in our German case, freedom of thought have mastered the artists too, and have made them, so to say, a *tabula rasa* in respect of the material and the form of their productions, after the necessary particular stages of the romantic art-form have been traversed. Bondage to a particular subject matter and a mode of portrayal suitable for this material alone are for artists today something past, and art therefore has become a free instrument which the artist can wield in proportion to his subjective skill in relation to any material of whatever kind. The artist thus stands above specific consecrated forms and configurations and moves freely on his own account, independent of the subject matter and mode of conception in which the holy and eternal was previously made visible to human apprehension. No content, no form, is any longer immediately identical with the inwardness, the *nature*, the unconscious substantial essence of the artist; every material may be indifferent to him as long as it does not contradict the formal law of being simply beautiful and capable of artistic treatment. Today there is no material which stands in and for itself above this relativity [Relativität], and even if one matter be raised above it, still there is at least no absolute need for its representation by *art*. Therefore the artist's attitude to his topic is on the whole much the same as the dramatist's who brings on the scene and delineates different characters who are strangers to him. The artist does still put his genius into them, he weaves his web out of his own resources, but only out of what is purely universal or quite accidental there, whereas its more detailed individualization is not his. For this purpose he needs his supply of images, modes of configuration, earlier forms of art which, taken in themselves, are indifferent to him and only become important if they seem to him to be those most suitable for precisely this or that material. Moreover, in most arts, especially the visual arts, the topic comes to the artist from the outside; he works to a commission, and in the case of sacred or profane stories, or scenes, portraits, ecclesiastical buildings, etc., he has only to see what he can make of his commission. For, however much he puts his heart into the given topic, that topic yet always remains to him a material which is not in itself directly the substance of his own consciousness. It is therefore no help to him to adopt again, as that substance, so to say, past world-views, i.e. to propose to root himself firmly in one of these ways of looking at things, e.g. to turn Roman Catholic as in recent times many have done for art's sake in order to give stability to their mind and to give the character of something absolute [An-und-für-sich-seyenden] to the specifically limited character of their artistic product in itself.[30] The artist need not be forced first to settle his accounts with his mind or to worry about the salvation of his own soul. From the very beginning, before he embarks on production, his great and free soul must know and possess its own ground, must be sure of itself and confident in itself. The great artist today needs in particular the free development of the spirit; in that development all superstition [Aberglauben],[31] and all faith which remains restricted to determine forms of vision and presentation, is degraded into mere aspects and features. These the free spirit has mastered because he sees in them no absolutely sacrosanct conditions for his exposition and mode of configuration, but ascribes value to them only on the strength of the higher content which in the course of his re-creation he puts into them as adequate to them.

In this way every form and every material is now at the service and command of the artist whose talent and genius is explicitly freed from the earlier limitation to one specific art-form.

(γ) But if in conclusion we ask about the content and the forms which can be considered as *specific* to this stage of our inquiry in virtue of its universal standpoint, the answer is as follows.

The universal forms of art had a bearing above all on the absolute truth which art attains and they had the origin of their particular differences in the specific interpretation of what counted for consciousness as the Absolute and carried in itself the principle for its mode of configuration. In this matter we have seen in symbolic art natural meanings appearing as the *content*, natural things and human personifications as the *form* of the representation; in classical art spiritual individuality, but as a corporeal, not inwardized present over which there stood the abstract necessity of fate; in romantic art spirituality with the subjectivity immanent therein, for the inwardness of which the external shape remained accidental. In this final art-form too, as in the earlier ones, the divine is the absolute [an und für sich] subject matter of art. But the divine had to objectify itself, determine itself, and therefore proceed out of itself into the secular content of subjective personality. At first the infinity of personality lay in honour, love, and fidelity, and then later in particular individuality, in the specific character which coalesced with the particular content of human existence. Finally this cohesion with such a specific limitation of subject matter was cancelled by humour [Humor] which could make every determinacy waver and dissolve and therefore made it possible for art to transcend itself. Yet in this self-transcendence art is nevertheless a withdrawal of man into himself, a descent into his own breast, whereby art strips away from itself all

fixed restriction to a specific range of content and treatment, and makes
Humanus its new holy of holies: i.e. the depths and heights of the human
heart as such, universal humanity in its joys and sorrows, its strivings,
deeds, and fates. Herewith the artist acquires his subject matter in himself
and is the human spirit actually self-determining and considering, meditating, and expressing the infinity of its feelings and situations: nothing
that can be living in the human breast is alien to that spirit any more.[32]
This is a subject-matter which does not remain determined artistically in
itself and on its own account; on the contrary, the specific character of the
topic and its outward formation is left to capricious invention, yet no interest is excluded – for art does not need any longer to represent only what
is absolutely at home at one of its specific stages, but everything in which
man as such is capable of being at home.

In face of this breadth and variety of material we must above all make
the demand that the actual presence of the spirit today shall be displayed
at the same time throughout the mode of treating this material. The modern artist, it is true, may associate himself with the classical age and with
still more ancient times; to be a follower of Homer, even if the last one, is
fine, and productions reflecting the mediaeval veering to romantic art will
have their merits too; but the universal validity, depth, and special idiom
of some material is one thing, its mode of treatment another. No Homer,
Sophocles, etc., no Dante, Ariosto, or Shakespeare can appear in our day;
what was so magnificently sung, what so freely expressed, has been
expressed; these are materials, ways of looking at them and treating them
which have been sung once and for all. Only the present is fresh, the rest
is paler and paler.

The French must be reproached on historical grounds, and criticized on
the score of beauty, for presenting Greek and Roman heroes, Chinese, and
Peruvians, as French princes and princesses and for ascribing to them the
motives and views of the time of Louis XIV and XV; yet, if only these
motives and views had been deeper and finer in themselves, drawing them
into present-day works of art would not be exactly bad. On the contrary,
all materials, whatever they be and from whatever period and nation they
come, acquire their artistic truth only when imbued with living and contemporary interest. It is in this interest that artistic truth fills man's breast,
provides his own mirror-image, and brings truth home to our feelings and
representational imagination [Vorstellung]. It is the appearance and activity of imperishable humanity in its many-sided significance and endless all-
round development which in this reservoir of human situations and feelings can now constitute the absolute content of our art.

If after thus determining in a general way the subject matter peculiar to
this stage, we now look back at what we have considered in conclusion as
the forms of the dissolution of romantic art, we have stressed principally
how art falls to pieces, on the one hand, into the imitation of external

objectivity in all its contingent shapes; on the other hand, however, into the liberation of subjectivity, in accordance with its inner contingency, in humour. Now, finally, still within the material indicated above, we may draw attention to a coalescence of these extremes of romantic art. In other words, just as in the advance from symbolic to classical art we considered the transitional forms of image, simile, epigram, etc.,[33] so here in romantic art we have to make mention of a similar transitional form. In those earlier modes of treatment the chief thing was that inner meaning and external shape fell apart from one another, a cleavage partly superseded by the subjective activity of the artist and converted, particularly in epigram, so far as possible into an identification. Now romantic art was from the beginning the deeper disunion of the inwardness which was finding its satisfaction in itself and which, since objectivity does not completely correspond with the spirit's inward being, remained broken or indifferent to the objective world. In the course of romantic art this opposition developed up to the point at which we had to arrive at an exclusive interest, either in contingent externality or in equally contingent subjectivity. But if this satisfaction in externality or in the subjective portrayal is intensified, according to the principle of romantic art, into the heart's deeper immersion in the object, and if, on the other hand, what matters to humour is the object and its configuration within its subjective reflex, then we acquire thereby a growing intimacy with the object, a sort of *objective* humour. Yet such an intimacy can only be partial and can perhaps be expressed only within the compass of a song or only as part of a greater whole. For if it were extended and carried through within objectivity, it would necessarily become action and event and an objective presentation of these. But what we may regard as necessary here is rather a sensitive abandonment of the heart in the object, which is indeed unfolded but remains a *subjective* spirited movement of imagination [Phantasie] and the heart – a fugitive notion, but one which is not purely accidental and capricious but an inner movement of the spirit devoted entirely to its object and retaining it as its content and interest.

In this connection we may contrast such final blossomings of art with the old Greek epigram in which this form appeared in its first and simplest shape, the form meant here displays itself only when to talk of the object is not just to name it, not an inscription or epigraph which merely says in general terms what the object is, but only when there are added a deep feeling, a felicitous witticism [Witz], an ingenious reflection, and an intelligent movement of imagination [Phantasie] which vivify and expand the smallest detail through the way that poetry treats it.[34] But such poems to or about something, a tree, a mill-lade, the spring, etc., about things animate or inanimate, may be of quite endless variety and arise in any nation, yet they remain of a subordinate kind and, in general, readily become lame. For especially when reflection and speech have been developed, anyone may be struck in connection with most objects and circumstances by something or other which he now has skill enough to express, just as anyone is good at writing a letter. With such a general sing-song, often repeated even if with new nuances, we soon become bored. Therefore at this stage what is especially at stake is that the heart, with its depth of feeling, and the spirit and a rich consciousness shall be entirely absorbed in the circumstances, situation, etc., tarry there, and so make out of the object something new, beautiful, and intrinsically valuable.

A brilliant example of this, even for the present and for the subjective spiritual depth of today, is afforded especially by the Persians and Arabs in the eastern splendour of their images, in the free bliss of their imagination [Phantasie] which deals with its object entirely contemplatively [theoretisch]. The Spaniards and Italians too have done excellent work of this kind. Klopstock does say of Petrarch: "Petrarch sang songs of his Laura, beautiful to their admirer, but to the lover – nothing."[35] Yet Klopstock's love-poems are full only of moral reflections, pitiable longing [Sehnsucht], and strained passion for the happiness of immortality – whereas in Petrarch we admire the freedom of the inherently ennobled feeling which, however much it expresses desire for the beloved, is still satisfied in itself. For the desire, the craving, cannot be missing in the sphere of these subjects, provided it be confined to wine and love, the tavern and the glass, just as, after all, the Persian pictures are of extreme voluptuousness. But in its subjective interest imagination [Phantasie] here removes the object altogether from the scope of practical craving; it has an interest only in this imaginative occupation, which is satisfied in the freest way with its hundreds of changing turns of phrase and conceits, and plays in the most ingenious manner with joy and sorrow alike. Amongst modern poets those chiefly possessed of this equally ingenious freedom of imagination, but also of its subjectively more heartfelt depth, are Rückert, and Goethe in his *West-östliche Divan*.[36] Goethe's poems in the *Divan* are particularly and essentially different from his earlier ones. In *Willkomm und Abschied* [*Welcome and Farewell*], e.g., the language and the depiction are beautiful indeed, and the feeling is heartfelt, but otherwise the situation is quite ordinary, the conclusion trivial, and imagination and its freedom has added nothing further. Totally different is the poem called *Wiederfinden* [*Meeting Again*] in the *Divan*. Here love is transferred wholly into the imagination, its movement, happiness, and bliss. In general, in similar productions of this kind we have before us no subjective longing, no being in love, no desire, but a pure delight in the topics, an inexhaustible self-yielding of imagination, a harmless play, a freedom in toying alike with rhyme and ingenious metres – and, with all this, a depth of feeling and a cheerfulness of the inwardly self-moving heart which through the serenity of the outward shape lift the soul high above all painful entanglement in the restrictions of the real world.

With this we may close our consideration of the *particular* forms into which the ideal of art has been spread in the course of its development. I have made these forms the subject of a rather extensive investigation in order to exhibit the content out of which too their mode of portrayal has been derived. For it is the content which, in art as in all human work, is decisive. In accordance with its concept, art has nothing else for its function but to set forth in an adequate sensuous present what is itself inherently rich in content, and the philosophy of art must make it its chief task to comprehend [begreifen] in thought what this fullness of content and its beautiful mode of appearance are.

Chapter III
Poetry

INTRODUCTION

1. The temple of classical *architecture* needed a god to live in it; *sculpture* places him before us in plastic beauty and gives to the material it uses for this purpose forms which by their very nature are not external to the spirit but are the shape immanent in the selected content itself. But the body, sensuousness, and ideal universality of the sculptural figure has contrasted with it both the subjective inner life and the particular character of the individual; and the content alike of the religious and the mundane life must gain actuality in the subjective and particular by means of a new art. This subjective and particular characteristic mode of expression *painting* introduces within the principle of the visual arts themselves, because it reduces the real externality of the shape to a more ideal appearance in colour and makes the expression of the inner soul the centre of the representation. Yet the general sphere in which these arts move, the first symbolic in type, the second ideally plastic, the third romantic, is the sensuous *external shape* [*Außengestalt*] of the spirit and things in nature.[37]

But the spiritual content, by essentially belonging to the inner life of consciousness, has at the same time an existence external to that life in the pure element of external appearance and in the vision to which the external shape is offered. Art must withdraw from this foreign element in order to enshrine its conceptions in a sphere of an explicitly inner and ideal kind in respect alike of the material used and the manner of expression. This was the forward step which we saw *music* taking, in that it made the inner life as such, and subjective feeling, something for apprehension by the inner life, not in visible shapes, but in the figurations in inwardly reverberating sound. But in this way it went to the other extreme, to an undeveloped subjective concentration, the content of which found once again only a purely symbolic expression in notes. For the note, taken by itself, is without content and has its determinate character only in virtue of numerical relations, so that although the qualitative character of the spiritual content does correspond in general to these quantitative relations which open out into essential differences, oppositions, and modulation, still it cannot be completely characterized qualitatively by a note. Therefore, if this qualitative side is not to be missing altogether, music must, on account of its one-sidedness, call on the help of the more exact meaning of words and, in order to become more firmly conjoined with the detail and characteristic expression of the subject-matter, it demands a text which alone gives a fuller content to the subjective life's outpouring in the notes. By means of this expression of representations and feelings the abstract inwardness of music emerges into a clearer and firmer unfolding of them. Yet on the one hand what it develops in this unfolding is not representations and their artistically adequate form but only their accompanying inner sentiment; on the other hand, music simply snaps its link with words in order to move at will and unhampered within its own sphere of sounds. Consequently, on its side too, the sphere of representations, which transcend the rather abstract inner life of feeling as such and give to their world the shape of concrete actuality, cuts itself free from music and gives itself an artistically adequate existence in the art of poetry.[38]

Poetry, the art of speech, is the third term, the *totality*, which unites in itself, within the province of the spiritual inner life and on a higher level, the two extremes, i.e. the *visual* arts and *music*. For, on the one hand, poetry, like music, contains that principle of the self-apprehension of the inner life as inner, which architecture, sculpture, and painting lack; while, on the other hand, in the very field of inner ideas [Vorstellens], intuitions, and feelings it broadens out into an objective world which does not altogether lose the determinate character of sculpture and painting. Finally, poetry is more capable than any other art of completely unfolding the totality of an event, a successive series and the changes of the heart's movements, passions, representations, and the complete course of an action.

2. But furthermore poetry is the third of the *romantic* arts, painting and music being the other two.

(a) Poetry (i) has as its general principle *spirituality* and therefore it no longer turns to heavy matter as such in order, like architecture, to form it symbolically into an analogous environment for the inner life, or, like sculpture, to shape into real matter the natural form, as a spatial external object, belonging to the spirit; on the contrary, it expresses directly for its own apprehension the spirit with all its imaginative and artistic conceptions [Konceptionen der Phantasie und Kunst] but without setting these out visibly and bodily for contemplation from the outside. (ii) Poetry, to a still ampler extent than painting and music, can comprise in the form of the inner life not only the inner consciousness but also the special and particular details of what exists externally, and at the same time it can portray them separately in the whole expanse of their individual traits and arbitrary peculiarities.

(b) Nevertheless poetry as a totality is on the other hand to be essentially distinguished from the specific arts whose characters it combines in itself.

(α) *Painting*, in this connection, has an overall advantage when it is a matter of bringing a subject before our eyes in its external appearance. For, with manifold means at its command, poetry can indeed likewise illustrate, just as the principle of setting something out for intuition is implicit in imagination [Phantasie] generally, but since the element in which poetry principally moves, i.e. representational imagination [die Vorstellung], is of a spiritual kind and therefore enjoys the universality of thought, poetry is incapable of reaching the definiteness of sense-perception. On the other hand, the different traits, which poetry introduces in order to make perceptible to us the concrete content of the subject in hand, do not fall together, as they do in painting, into one and the same whole which completely confronts us with all its details simultaneously; on the contrary, they occur separately because the manifold content of a representation can be expressed only as a succession. But this is a defect only from the sensuous point of view, one which the spirit can always rectify. Even where speech is concerned to evoke some concrete intuition, it does not appeal to the sensuous perception of a present external object but always to the inner life, to *spiritual* intuition, and consequently even if the individual traits only follow one another they are transferred into the element of the inwardly harmonious spirit which can extinguish a succession, pull together a varied series into *one* image and keep this image firmly in mind [in der Vorstellung] and enjoy it. Besides, this deficiency of sensuous reality and external definiteness in poetry as contrasted with painting is at once turned into an incalculable wealth. For since poetry is exempt from painting's restriction to a specific space and still more to one specific feature of a situation or an action, it is given the possibility of presenting a subject in its whole inward depth and in the breadth of its temporal development. Truth is absolutely concrete in virtue of comprising in itself a unity of essential determinations. But these develop in their appearance not only as juxtaposed in space, but in a temporal succession as a history, the course of which painting can only present graphically in an inappropriate way. Even every blade of grass, every tree has in this sense its history, alteration, process, and a complete totality of different situations. This is still more the case in the sphere of the spirit; as actual spirit in its appearance, it can only be portrayed exhaustively if it is brought before our minds [vor die Vorstellung] as such a course of history.

(β) As we saw, poetry has sounds as an external material in common with *music*. The wholly external material (ordinarily, though not philosophically, called 'objective') slips away finally, in the progressive series of the partic-

ular arts, into the subjective element of sound which cannot be seen, with
the result that the inner life is made aware of itself solely by its own activity.
But music's essential aim is to shape these sounds as *sounds*. For although
in the course and progress of the melody and its fundamental harmonic
relations the soul presents to feeling the inner meaning of the subject matter or its own inner self, nevertheless what gives music its own proper character is not the inner life as such but the soul, most intimately interweaved
with its *sounding*, and the formation of this *musical* expression. This is so
much the case that music becomes music and an independent art the more
that what preponderates in it is the complete absorption of the inner life
into the realm of sounds, not of the spirit as such. But, for this reason, it
is capable only to a relative extent of harbouring the variety of spiritual
representations and intuitions and the broad expanse of a richly filled conscious life, and in its expression it does not get beyond the more abstract
and general character of what it takes as its subject or beyond vaguer deep
feelings of the heart. Now in proportion as the spirit transforms this
abstract generality into a concrete ensemble of ideas, aims, actions, and
events and adds to this process their inspection *seriatim*, it deserts the inner
sphere of imagination [Phantasie]. Consequently, simply on account of this
transformation, any attempt to express this new-won wealth of the spirit
wholly and exclusively through sounds and their harmony must be abandoned. Just as the material of sculpture is too poor to make possible the
portrayal of the richer phenomena which it is painting's business to call to
life, so now harmonious sounds and expression in melody cannot give full
reality to the poet's imaginative creations. For these possess the precise
and known definiteness of representations and an external phenomenal
form minted for inner intuition. Therefore the spirit withdraws its content
from sounds as such and is manifested by words which do not entirely forsake the element of sound but sink to being a merely external sign of what
is being communicated. The musical note being thus replete with spiritual
ideas becomes the sound of a word, and the word, instead of then being
an end in itself, becomes a self-unindependent means of spiritual expression. This gives us, in accordance with what we established earlier, the
essential difference between music and poetry. The subject matter of the
art of speech is the entire world of ideas developed with a wealth of imagination, i.e. the spirit abiding by itself in its own spiritual element and,
when it moves out to the creation of something external, using that only
as a sign, itself different from the subject matter. With music, art abandons
the immersion of the spirit in a tangible, visible, and directly present *shape;*
in poetry it gives up the opposite element of *sound* and hearing, at least in
so far as this sound is no longer formed into an adquate external object
and the sole expression of the subject matter. Therefore the inner life does
express itself [in music] but will not find its actual existence in the
sensibility[Sinnlichkeit] (even if more ideal) of the notes, because it seeks

this existence solely in itself, in order to express the content of the spirit as it is contained in the heart of imagination as imagination [Phantasie].

(c) If, *thirdly* and lastly, we look for the special character of poetry in its distinction from music, and from painting and the other visual arts, we find it simply in the above-mentioned subordination of the sensuous mode of presenting and elaborating all poetic subject matter. Since sound, as in music, or colour, as in painting, is no longer able to harbour and present that entire subject matter, the musical treatment of it by way of the beat, harmony, and melody necessarily disappears there and what is left is, in general, only the tempo of words and syllables, rhythm, and euphony, etc. And even these remain not as the proper element for conveying the subject matter but as a rather accidental externality which assumes an artistic form only because art cannot allow any external aspect to have free play purely by chance, arbitrarily, or capriciously.

(*a*) Granted the withdrawal of the spiritual content from sensuous material, the question arises at once: what, in default of sound, will now be the proper form of externality and objectivity in the case of poetry? We can answer quite simply: It is the *inner representational imagination* [*Vorstellen*] and *intuition* itself. It is *spiritual* forms which take the place of the sensuous ones and provide the material to be given shape, just as marble, bronze, colour, and musical notes were the material earlier on. For here we must not be led astray by the statement that representations and intuitions are in truth the *content* of poetry. This of course is true enough, as will be shown in detail later; but it is equally essential to maintain that representations, intuitions, feelings, etc., are the specific forms in which every content is apprehended and presented by poetry, so that, since the sensuous side of the communication always has only a subordinate part to play, these forms provide the proper material which the poet has to treat artistically. The thing in hand, the content, is to be objectified in poetry for the spirit's apprehension, yet this objectivity exchanges its previously external reality for an internal one, and it acquires an existence only within consciousness itself as something spiritually represented and intuited. Thus the spirit becomes objective to itself on its own ground and it has speech only as a medium, partly as a means of communication and partly as an external reality out of which, as out of a mere sign, it has withdrawn into itself from the very start. Consequently in the case of poetry proper it is a matter of indifference whether we read it or hear it read; it can even be translated into other languages without essential detriment to its value, and turned from poetry into prose, and in these cases it is related to quite different sounds from those of the original.[39]

(*β*) Further, this *second* question arises: granted that the inner representational imagination constitutes the material and form of poetry, *for what* is this material to be used? It is to be used for the absolute [an und für sich] truth contained in spiritual interests in general, yet not merely for their substance in its universality of symbolical meaning [in architecture] or its classical differentiation [in sculpture] but also for everything detailed and particular within this substance, and so for almost everything which interests and occupies the spirit in any way. Consequently the art of speech, in respect of its content and its mode of expounding it, has an enormous field, a wider field than that open to the other arts. Any topic, all spiritual and natural things, events, histories, deeds, actions, subjective and objective situations, all these can be drawn into poetry and fashioned by it.

(γ) But this most variegated material is not made poetic simply by being harboured in representation, for after all a commonplace mind can shape exactly the same subject matter into representations and have separate intuitions of it without achieving anything poetic. In this connection we previously called ideas the *material* and element which is only given a poetically adequate form when art has shaped it afresh, just as colour and sound are not already, as mere colour and sound, painting and music. We can put this difference in general terms by saying that it is not representation *as such* but the artistic imagination [Phantasie] which makes some material poetic; when, that is to say, imagination so lays hold of it that instead of confronting us as an architectural, sculptural, plastic, and painted shape or of sounding like musical notes, it can communicate with us in speech, in words and their beautiful spoken assembly.

The basic demand necessitated here is limited to this: (i) that the subject matter shall not be conceived either in terms of scientific or speculative *thinking* or in the form of wordless *feeling* or with the clarity and *precision* with which we perceive external objects, and (ii) that it shall not pass into representation with the accidents, fragmentations, and relativities of *finite* actuality. In this regard the poetic imagination has, for one thing, to keep to the mean between the abstract universality of thought and the sensuously concrete corporeal objects that we have come to recognize in the productions of the visual arts; for another thing, it has on the whole to satisfy the demands we made in the first part of these lectures in respect of any artistic creation, i.e. in its content it must be an end in itself and, with a purely contemplative [theoretische] interest, fashion everything that it conceives into an inherently independent and closed world. For only in this event does the content, as art requires, become by means of the manner of its presentation an organic whole which gives in its parts the appearance of close connection and coherence and, in contrast to the world of mutual dependence, stands there for its own sake and free on its own account.

3. The final point for discussion in connection with the difference between poetry and the other arts likewise concerns the changed relation which the poetic imagination introduces between its productions and the external material of their presentation.

The arts considered hitherto were completely in earnest with the sensuous element in which they moved, because they gave to a subject matter only a form which throughout could be adopted by and stamped on towering heavy masses, bronze, marble, wood, colours, and notes. Now in a certain sense it is true that poetry has a similar duty to fulfil. For in composing it must keep steadily in mind that its results are to be made known to the spirit only by communication in language. But this changes the whole relation to the material.

(a) The sensuous aspect acquires importance in the visual arts and in music. It follows that, owing to the specific *determinacy* of the material they use, it is only a *restricted* range of presentations that completely corresponds to particular real things existent in stone, colour, or sound, and the result is that the subject matter and the artistic mode of treatment in the arts considered hitherto is fenced in within certain limits. This was the reason why we brought each of the specific arts into close connection with only *one* of the *particular* art-forms which this and no other art seemed best able to express adequately – architecture with the symbolic art-form, sculpture with the classical, painting and music with the romantic. It is true that the particular arts, below and above their proper sphere, encroached on the other art-forms too, and for this reason we could speak of classical and romantic architecture, and symbolic and Christian sculpture, and we also had to mention classical painting and music. But these deviations did not reach the real summit of art but either were the preparatory attempts of inferior beginning or else displayed the start of a transition to an art which, in this transition, seized on a content, and a way of treating the material, of a type that only a further art was permitted to develop completely.

In the expression of its content on the whole, architecture is poorest, sculpture is richer, while the scope of painting and music can be extended most widely of all. For with the increasing ideality and more varied particularization of the external material, the variety of the subject matter and of the forms it assumes is increased. Now poetry cuts itself free from this importance of the material, in the general sense that the specific character of its mode of sensuous expression affords no reason any longer for restriction to a specific subject matter and a confined sphere of treatment and presentation. It is therefore not linked exclusively to any specific form of art; on the contrary, it is the *universal* art which can shape in any way and express any content capable at all of entering the imagination [Phantasie], because its proper material is the imagination itself, that universal foundation of all the particular art-forms and the individual arts.

This is the point that we reached at the close of our treatment of the particular art-forms. Their culmination we looked for in art's making itself independent of the mode of representation peculiar to *one* of the art-forms and in its standing above the whole of these particular forms. Among the specific arts, the possibility of such a development in every direction lies from the very beginning in the essence of poetry alone, and it is therefore actualized in the course of poetic production partly through the actual exploitation of every particular form, partly through liberation from imprisonment in any exclusive type and character of treatment and content, whether symbolic, classical, or romantic.

(b) From this point of view too the position we have assigned to poetry in our philosophical development of the arts can be justified. Since poetry is occupied with the universal element in art as such to a greater extent than is the case in any of the other ways of producing works of art, it might seem that a philosophical explanation had to begin with it and only thereafter proceed to particularize the ways in which the other arts are differentiated by their sensuous material. But, as we have seen already in connection with particular art-forms, the process of development, regarded philosophically, consists on the one hand in a deepening of art's spiritual content, and on the other in showing that at first art only *seeks* its adequate content, then *finds* it, and finally *transcends* it. This conception [Begriff] of beauty and art must now also be made good in the *arts* themselves. We began therefore with architecture, which only strove after the complete representation of spiritual material in a sensuous element, so that art achieved a genuine fusion of form and content only in sculpture; with painting and music, on account of the inwardness and subjectivity of their content, art began to dissolve again the accomplished unification of conception and execution in the field of sense. This latter character poetry displays most strikingly because in its artistic materialization it is essentially to be interpreted as a withdrawal from the real world of sense-perception, and as a subordination of that world; yet not as a production that does not dare to embark yet on materialization and movement in the external world. But in order to expound this liberation philosophically it is first necessary to explain what it is from which art undertakes to free itself, and, similarly, how it is that poetry can harbour the entire content of art and all the forms of art. This too we have to regard as a struggle for a totality, a struggle that can be demonstrated philosophically only as the cancellation [Aufheben] of a restriction to the particular, which in turn implies a previous consideration of the one-sided stages, the unique value possessed by each being negated in the totality.

Only as a result of considering the series of the arts in this way does poetry appear as that particular art in which art itself begins at the same time to dissolve and acquire in the eyes of philosophy its point of transition to religious pictorial thinking [religiösen Vorstellung] as such, as well as to the prose of scientific thought. The realm of the beautiful, as we saw earlier, is bordered on one side by the prose of finitude and commonplace thinking, out of which art struggles on its way to truth, and on the other side the higher spheres of religion and philosophy [Wissenschaft] where there is a transition to that apprehension of the Absolute which is still further removed from the sensuous sphere.

(c) Therefore, however completely poetry produces the totality of beauty once and for all in a most spiritual way, nevertheless spirituality constitutes at the same time precisely the deficiency of this final sphere of art. In the system of the arts we can regard poetry as the polar opposite of architecture. Architecture cannot so subordinate the sensuous material to the spiritual content as to be able to form that material into an adequate shape of the spirit; poetry, on the other hand, goes so far in its negative treatment of its sensuous material that it reduces the opposite of heavy spatial matter, namely sound, to a meaningless sign instead of making it, as architecture makes its material, into a meaningful symbol. But in this way poetry destroys the fusion of spiritual inwardness with external existence to an extent that begins to be incompatible with the original conception of art, with the result that poetry runs the risk of losing itself in a transition from the region of sense into that of the spirit. The beautiful mean between these extremes of architecture and poetry is occupied by sculpture, painting, and music, because each of these arts works the spiritual content entirely into a natural medium and makes it intelligible alike to sense and spirit. For although painting and music, as romantic arts, do adopt a material which is already more ideal, yet on the other hand for the immediacy of tangible objects, which begins to evaporate in this enhanced ideality of the medium, they substitute the wealth of detail and the more varied configuration which colour and sound are capable of providing in a richer way than can be called for from the material of sculpture.

Poetry for its part likewise looks for a substitute: it brings the objective world before our eyes in a breadth and variety which even painting cannot achieve, at least on a single canvas, and yet this always remains only a real existence in the inner consciousness; and even if poetry in its need for an artistic embodiment makes straight for a strengthened sensuous impression, still it can produce this only by means foreign to itself and borrowed from painting and music; or else, in order to maintain itself as genuine poetry, it must always put these sister arts in the background, purely as its servants, and emphasize instead, as the really chief thing concerned, the spiritual idea, the imagination [Phantasie] which speaks to inner imagination [Phantasie].

So much in general about the conceptual relation of poetry to the other arts. The more detailed consideration of the art of poetry must be arranged as follows:

We have seen that in poetry both content and material are provided by our inner representational imagination. Yet this, outside art, is already the commonest form of consciousness and therefore we must in the first place undertake the task of distinguishing poetic from prosaic representation. But poetry should not abide by this inner poetical representation alone but must give its creations an expression in *language*. Here once again a double duty is to be undertaken. (i) Poetry must so organize its inner images that they can be completely adapted to communication in language; (ii) it must not leave this linguistic medium in the state in which it is used every day, but must treat it poetically in order to distinguish it from expressions in prose by the choice, placing, and sound of words.

But despite its expression in language, poetry is free in the main from the restrictions and conditions laid on the other arts by the particular character of their medium, and consequently it has the widest possibility of completely developing all the different genres that a work of art can permit of, independently of the one-sidedness of any particular art. For this reason the most perfect articulation of the different genres of poetry comes into view.

Accordingly our further course is

> *First,* to discuss poetry in general and the poetic work of art;
> *Secondly,* poetic expression;
> *Thirdly,* the division of this art into epic, lyric, and dramatic poetry.

*   *   *

Notes
Bibliography

Notes

LESSING

Laocoon

[These notes are from HBN.]

1 There is a useful commentary on the *Laocoon* in Lessing's *Werke,* edited by Herbert G. Göpfert, 8 vols. (Munich, 1970–9), VI, 861–917. The fullest collection of drafts, variants, and background materials is still that in Hugo Blümner's edition of Lessing's *Laokoon,* second edition (Berlin, 1880). In the present translation, those of Lessing's long and learned footnotes which are now of only antiquarian interest are omitted. Where his footnotes contain material essential to his argument or to an understanding of the text, their substance is incorporated in the notes which follow here.

2 Greek painters of the fourth century B.C.

3 The Greek lyric poet Simonides of Ceos, 556–467 B.C.

4 'They differ in their objects and mode of imitation.' The quotation, used by Lessing as a motto on the title page of his work, is from Plutarch, 'Whether the Athenians were more Famous for their Martial Accomplishments or for their Knowledge', Chapter 3.

5 This claim is not strictly true.

6 Alexander Gottlieb Baumgarten (1714–62), the founder of aesthetics as a philosophical discipline (*Aesthetica,* 1750).

7 Johann Matthias Gesner (1691–1761), humanist and antiquary; the work referred to is his *Novus linguae et eruditionis romanae Thesaurus.*

8 Jacopo Sadoleto (1477–1547), Italian cardinal and author of a Latin poem on the Laocoon group.

9 Metrodorus of Athens, a philosopher and painter of the second century B.C. On his dual accomplishment cf. Pliny's *Natural History,* XXV, 135.

10 J. J. Winckelmann, *Thoughts on the Imitation of the Painting and Sculpture of the Greeks* (1755). For this passage, see HBN, p. 42.

11 Exclamations of pain.

12 Danish hero and legendary founder of the town of Jomsburg.

12 'Shedding hot tears.'

14 'But the great Priam forbade them to weep.'

15 Anne Lefèvre Dacier (1654–1720), philologist and translator of classical texts, including the *Iliad* (Paris, 1711).

16 'I in no way condemn weeping.'

17 In the *Trachiniae* of Sophocles.

18 The French.

19 Jean Baptiste Vivien de Chateaubrun (1686–1775), author of the drama *Philoctète* (1775).

20 Lessing adds a learned footnote, in which he tries to prove that supposed representations of the Furies in ancient art are in fact of other mythological figures.

21 Greek painter (c. 420–380 B.C.).

22 Bernard de Montfaucon (1655–1741), *L'antiquité expliquée et représentée en figures*, 5 vols. (Paris, 1710–24), I, 50.

23 Valerius Maximus, Roman historian of the first century A.D., and author of *De factis dictisque memorabilibus libri IX*.

24 Greek sculptor of Rhegium, fifth century B.C.

25 Julien Offray de La Mettrie (1709–51), materialistic philosopher and author of *L'homme machine* (1748); Democritus of Abdera (c. 460–370 B.C.), 'the laughing philosopher', traditionally opposed in iconography to the mournful Heracleitus.

26 Greek painter of the Hellenistic period.

27 Flavius Philostratus, second to third century A.D., author of the *Life of Apollonius of Tyana;* Lessing's reference is to Book II, Chapter 22 of this work.

28 'He raises terrible shouts to the stars above' (*Aeneid*, II, 222).

29 Figure of Greek mythology, whose life depended on a piece of wood rescued from the fire by his mother. His mother, when Melaeger slew her brothers, cast the wood upon the fire and Meleager was himself consumed.

30 See note 19 above.

31 Lessing's footnote refers to the *Mercure de France*, April 1755, p. 177.

32 Or rather, a Scotsman: Adam Smith (1723–90), *The Theory of Moral Sentiments* (London, 1761).

33 In Lessing's day, Seneca's authorship of the tragedies traditionally attributed to him was doubted.

34 Lessing's error; intended is probably Cresilas, an artist of the first century A.D. to whom Pliny (XXXVI, 77) attributes a statue of a dying gladiator.

35 Chateaubrun; see note 19 above.

36 The actor David Garrick (1717–79) was revered in Germany, where he had appeared on tour in 1763, no less than in England.

37 Tiberius Claudius Donatus (fourth century A.D.), author of *Interpretationes Vergilianae*, a commentary on Virgil. Lessing's footnote quotes Donatus's comment on *Aeneid*, II, 227, which confirms his own reconstruction of the serpents' attack on Laocoon as described by Virgil.

38 *Aeneid*, II, 220: 'His hands strove frantically to wrench the knots apart.'

39 *Aeneid*, II, 218–19: 'twice round his middle, twice round his throat; and still their heads and necks towered above him'.

40 Franz Cleyn (1590–1658), Dutch painter and engraver who died in London.

41 (London, 1697).

42 *Aeneid*, II, 221: 'Filth and black venom drenched his priestly bands.'

43 On 'arbitrary' and 'natural' signs, see Lessing's explanations in Chapter XVII below (p. 54).

44 Jonathan Richardson (1665–1745), author of *The Theory of Painting* (1715), which Lessing's footnote cites in a French translation of 1728.

45 'The one snake darts upwards and seizes Laocoon, winds round him from top to bottom and wounds him in the side with a furious bite. . . . But the slippery serpent turns downward in repeated circles and binds his knees in a tight knot.'

46 Jacopo Sadoleto (1477–1547), cardinal and poet, author of the poem *De Lao-coontis statua* from which the quotation here is taken.

47 See note 39 above.

48 Joseph Spence (1699–1768), historian and antiquary, author of *Polymetis: or, An Enquiry concerning the Agreement between the Works of the Roman Poets and the Remains of the Antient Artists* (London, 1747). Characteristically, Lessing develops his own views by attacking those of another, just as he subsequently does with Caylus in Chapter XI. That he is far from fair to Spence, misrepresenting his arguments when it suits him, has been shown by Donald T. Siebert, 'Laokoon and *Polymetis*: Lessing's Treatment of Joseph Spence', *Lessing Yearbook*, 3 (1971), 71–83.

Joseph Addison (1672–1719), *Dialogues upon the Usefulness of Ancient Medals* (1702); Lessing's lengthy footnote discusses Spence's and Addison's comments on Juvenal, *Satires*, XI, 100–7 and related images on antique coins.

49 Lessing adds a long footnote in which he criticises Spence on further points of detail.

50 Anne Claude Philippe de Tubières, Comte de Caylus (1692–1765), antiquarian and author of *Tableaux tirés de l'Illiade* (Paris, 1757), the work with which Lessing here takes issue. His greatest work, however, was the monumental *Recueil d'antiquités*, 7 vols. (Paris, 1752–67). Lessing adds a footnote in which he takes issue with Caylus on the manner in which ancient artists depicted death. He later devoted a separate treatise to this problem, entitled *How the Ancients portrayed Death* (1769).

51 Lessing's footnote quotes Caylus, *Tableaux*, Avertissement, p. v, as follows: 'On est toujours convenu, que plus un Poëme fournissoit d'images et d'actions, plus il avoit de supériorité en Poësie. Cette réflexion m'avoit conduit à penser que le calcul des differens Tableaux, qu'offrent les Poëmes, pouvoit servir à comparer le merite respectif des Poëmes et des Poëtes. Le nombre et le genre des Tableaux que presentent ces grands ouvrages, auroient été une espèce de pierre de touche, ou plutôt une balance certaine du mérite de ces Poëmes et du Genie de leurs Auteurs.'

52 *Iliad*, IV, 105–26

53 The following deductive argument had in fact formed the basis of Lessing's plan for the whole work.

54 *Iliad*, V, 722–31: 'Hebe quickly put to the car on either side the curved wheels of bronze, eight-spoked, about the iron axle-tree. Of these the felloe verily is of gold imperishable, and thereover are tyres of bronze fitted, a marvel to behold; and the naves are of silver, revolving on this side and on that; and the body is plaited tight with gold and silver thongs, and two rims there are that run about it. From the body stood forth the pole of silver, and on the end thereof she bound the fair golden yoke, and cast thereon the fair golden breast-straps.'

55 *Iliad*, II, 42–6: 'He put on his soft tunic, fair and glistening, and about him cast his great cloak, and beneath his shining feet he bound his fair sandals, and about his shoulders flung his silver-studded sword; and he grasped the sceptre of his fathers, imperishable ever.'

56 *Iliad*, II, 101–8: ' . . . bearing in his hands the sceptre which Hephaestus had wrought with toil. Hephaestus gave it to king Zeus, son of Cronos, and Zeus gave it to the messenger Argeiphontes; and Hermes, the lord, gave it to Pelops, driver of horses, and Pelops in turn gave it to Atreus, shepherd of the host; and

Atreus at his death left it to Thyestes, rich in flocks, and Thyestes again left it to Agamemnon to bear, so that he might be lord of many isles and of all Argos.'

57 A 'natural' sign resembles the object it signifies, as do the shapes and colours of figurative sculpture and painting. An 'arbitrary' sign (and all language, with a few rare exceptions such as onomatopoeic words, consists of 'arbitrary' signs) has no necessary connection with its object: the connection is a purely conventional one. For a discussion of this aspect of Lessing's theory, see HBN, pp. 9–10, and the 'Letter to Nicolai,' p. 65, below.

58 The following quotation consists of stanzas 39 and 40 of the didactic poem *The Alps (Die Alpen, 1729)* by the Swiss poet and scientist Albrecht von Haller (1708–77): 'There the high head of the noble gentian towers far above the lowly chorus of the vulgar herbs. A whole nation of flowers serves under his banner, and even his blue brother [a lesser species of gentian] bows low and honours him. The bright gold of the flowers, radiating outwards [centaury], ascends the stalk and crowns its grey garment; the smooth white of the leaves, streaked with dark green, shines with the coloured sparkle of the dewy diamond. Most equitable law! That strength should join with ornament; in a beautiful body there dwells a more beautiful soul.

Here creeps a lowly herb [antirrhinum], like a grey mist, whose leaf nature has formed in a cross; the lovely flower displays the two gilded beaks of a bird made of amethyst. There a gleaming leaf, its edges divided into fingers, casts its green reflection on a bright rivulet; the delicate snow of the flowers, dyed with crimson, surrounds a striped star with its white rays [Astrantia major, masterwort]. Emerald and roses bloom even on the trodden heath [wild rosemary], and rocks are clothed in a dress of purple [campion].' (Haller himself, in footnotes to the poem, elucidates the botanical references.)

59 The praise of Haller quoted here is by his fellow Swiss, Johann Jakob Breitinger (1701–76), in his *Kritische Dichtkunst (Critical Poetics* (Zurich, 1740)), Part II, p. 407 (Lessing's reference).

60 Jan van Huysum (1682–1749), one of the most famous Dutch flower-painters of his day.

61 Virgil, *Georgics*, III, 51–9:

> In a cow the following
> Points should be looked for – a rough appearance, a coarse head,
> Generous neck, and dewlaps hanging from jaw to leg;
> Flanks as roomy as you like; everything built on a large scale,
> Even the hoof; and shaggy ears under the crooked horns.
> I have nothing against an animal of prominent white markings,
> Or one that rejects the yoke and is hasty at times with her horn –
> More like a bull to look at,
> Tall all over, dusting the ground with her tail as she goes.
> > Virgil, The *Eclogues, Georgics and Aeneid,* translated by
> > C. Day Lewis (London, 1966)

62 Virgil, *Georgics*, III, 79–81:

> He shows a proud neck,
> A finely tapering head, short barrel and fleshy back,
> And his spirited chest ripples with muscle.
> > Translated by C. Day Lewis

63 Horace, *Ars Poetica*, lines 16–18: 'they describe Diana's grove and altar, the meanderings of a stream through a pleasant landscape, or the River Rhine, or a rainbow'.

64 Alexander Pope (1688–1744); Lessing's reference to his *Epistle to Arbuthnot (Prologue to the Satires)*, lines 148 f. and 340 f. Lessing's footnote shows that he is aware that Warburton, in his commentary on the poem, is the author of the culinary reference he cites, but he (Lessing) maintains that Warburton is merely echoing Pope's own sentiments.

65 Christian Ewald von Kleist (1715–59), poet and officer in Frederick the Great's army, who died of wounds received in the Seven Years' War. His descriptive poem *Der Frühling (The Spring)* was greatly admired in Lessing's day. Kleist had been a close friend of Lessing's.

66 Jean François de Marmontel (1723–99), French critic, author of a *Poétique française* (1763); Lessing's reference is to Part II, p. 501, of his work.

67 The reference is to Kleist's (not Marmontel's) Ecologues or pastoral poems.

68 Francesco Mazzola Parmigianino (1503–40), Italian painter.

69 Anton Raphael Mengs (1728–79), painter and friend of Winckelmann in Rome, author of *Gedanken über die Schönheit und über den Geschmack in der Malerei* (Zurich, 1762); Lessing's reference is to p. 69 of that work.

70 *Iliad*, V, 722 f.

71 *Iliad*, XII, 296.

72 See note 15 above.

73 'The round, brazen, eight-spoked'.

74 'Wheels'.

75 Virgil, *Aeneid*, VIII, 447–53: 'They shape an enormous shield. . . . Others, with bellows full of wind, draw in and discharge the air. Others again temper the hissing bronze in a vessel of water. The cave resounds with the blows on the anvils. They powerfully raise their arms together in rhythm and turn the mass of metal with the grip of their tongs.'

76 *Aeneid*, VIII, 730: 'he delights in the image, though ignorant of the things represented'.

77 That is, Vulcan.

78 *Iliad*, III, 156–8: 'Small blame that Trojans and well-greaved Achaeans should for such a woman suffer woes for so long; for she is indeed like an immortal goddess to look upon.'

79 Sappho (c. 600 B.C.), poetess of Lesbos.

80 Ovid, *Amores*, I, 5, lines 19–22:

> What arms and shoulders did I touch and see,
> How apt her breasts were to be press'd by me!
> How smooth a belly under her waist saw I!
> How large a leg, and what a lusty thigh!
>
> Translation by Christopher Marlowe

The name of Ovid's mistress was in fact Corinna; Lesbia was the mistress of Catullus.

81 Ariosto, *Orlando furioso* (canto VII): 'A pair of apples, not yet ripe, fashioned in ivory, rose and fell like the sea-swell at times when a gentle breeze stirs the ocean.'

82 'In the dimple of her soft chin and round her marble neck let all the Graces play.'

83 'Impressed by Amor's finger.'
84 Zeuxis (fifth century B.C.), Greek painter of Heraclea.
85 Town in southern Italy; the painting was for the temple of Hera there.

Letter to Nicolai

1 The first paragraph, in which Lessing briefly discusses his current publications and a projected journey to Austria, is omitted in this translation.
2 The review was by Christian Garve (1742–98), and it appeared in 1769 in the *Allgemeine Deutsche Bibliothek*, a journal edited by Lessing's friend Christoph Friedrich Nicolai (1733–1811), to whom the present letter is addressed. The review is reprinted in *Lessings Laokoon*, edited by Hugo Blümner, second edition (Berlin, 1880), pp. 683–703.
3 Lessing refers to the planned continuation of the *Laocoon*, in which he intended to deal, among other things, with music, dance, and mime, and to elaborate at greater length his theory of 'natural' and 'arbitrary' signs in the arts. The continuation, which was never written, would have consisted of two further parts.
4 On Lessing's theory of signs, see note 57, p. 402.
5 The philosopher Moses Mendelssohn (1729–86), a close friend of Lessing and Nicolai.
6 The concluding paragraph, in which Lessing criticises a review of an unrelated work, is omitted from this translation.

HERDER

Extract from a Correspondence on Ossian and the Songs of Ancient Peoples

(These notes are from HBN.)

1 This work was first published in an anonymous collection of five essays, edited by Johann Gottfried Herder, entitled *Von deutscher Art und Kunst. Einige fliegende Blätter (On German Character and Art. A Collection of Broadsheets)* (Hamburg, 1773). Herder's epistolary essay on Ossian was the first item in the collection. His essay on Shakespeare was the second. The remaining contributions were Johann Wolfgang Goethe's *Von deutscher Baukunst (On German Architecture)*, a eulogy of Gothic architecture, and of Strasbourg Cathedral in particular; Paolo Frisi's *Versuch über die Gotische Baukunst (Essay on Gothic Architecture)*, translated from the Italian original of 1766; and Justus Möser's *Deutsche Geschichte (German History)*, an extract from the preface to Möser's *History of Osnabrück* (1768). The present translation of Herder's essay on Ossian omits the numerous folksongs and ballads from various countries which Herder cites as examples of folk poetry, as well as sections in which he discusses Klopstock and various lesser poets of the time.
   The correspondent is fictitious. His supposed contempt for folk poetry is a rhetorical device which enables Herder to defend such literature in a direct and vigorous manner.
2 James Macpherson's *The Works of Ossian, the Son of Fingal*, 2 vols. (London, 1765) appeared in the German translation of Michael Denis as *Die Gedichte Ossians, eines alten celtischen Dichters*, 3 vols. (Vienna, 1768–9).

3 The references are to Olaus Wormius (1588–1654), author of *Danica litteratura antiquissima volga gothica dicta* (Copenhagen, 1636) and other works on ancient Norse poetry; Thomas Bartholinus (died 1690), author of *Antiquitatum de causis contemptae a Danis adhuc gentilibus mortis libri tres* (Copenhagen, 1689); Johann Peringer de Peringskiöld (1654–1720), author of *Monumenta Sueo-Gothica* (Stockholm, 1710–19); and Olaus Verelius (1618–82), editor of the *Hervarar-Saga* (Upsala, 1672) and other Norse sagas.

4 The following short discussion of alliterative verse-forms in Old Norse poetry is omitted here.

5 Pierre François Xavier de Charlevoix (1682–1761), *Histoire et description générale de la Nouvelle-France* (Paris, 1744); Joseph François Lafiteau, *Moeurs des Sauvages Amériquains, comparées aus moeurs des premiers temps* (Paris, 1723); Woodes Rogers (died 1732), *A Cruising Voyage Round the World* (London, 1712); Cadwallader Colden (1688–1776), *The History of the Five Indian Nations* (New York, 1727).

6 Henry Timberlake, *Memoirs of Lt Henry Timberlake . . .* (London, 1765).

7 In his letter to Rousseau of 30 August 1755, Voltaire ironically distanced himself in such terms from Rousseau's praise of primitive society in his *Discours sur les origines et les fondements de l'inégalité parmi les hommes*.

8 A long section follows, in which Herder describes how his appreciation for primitive poetry was first awakened by reading it in an appropriately 'natural' environment (on board ship, in stormy weather, on his voyage from the Baltic to France in 1769). He then describes hearing Latvian folksongs at first hand, and, after further criticisms of Denis's hexameter translation of Ossian, quotes a selection of folk poems from various countries, including the ballad 'Edward' from Thomas Percy's *Reliques of Ancient Poetry*.

9 'Poets' or 'singers.'

10 Greek Painter of the fourth century B.C., renowned for the lifelike quality of his work.

11 'Sweet William's Ghost', which Herder has just quoted in full in his own German translation.

12 Lessing edited and published a collection of epigrams by the German baroque poet Friedrich von Logau (1604–55) in 1759 and a collection of poems by Andreas Scultetus (c. 1622–47) in 1771.

13 Justus Friedrich Wilhelm Zachariae (1726–77), a friend of Lessing's and himself a poet, published a two-volume anthology (Brunswick, 1766–71) of German poetry which included works by the baroque poets Martin Opitz (1597–1639), Paul Fleming (1609–40), and Andreas Gryphius (1616–64).

14 Herder proceeds, in the following (omitted) passage, to quote German poems, including Goethe's famous 'Heidenröslein', which is presented as an anonymous folksong like the rest. He praises its popular language and elisions as the antithesis of over-polished modern verse.

15 Herder goes on to quote further examples of the free use of language in popular poetry, and praises Luther's hymns in particular. He again attacks slavish adherents of (neo-classical) poetic rules, and defends Klopstock's odes for their bold inversions and innovative language.

16 Thomas Gray (1716–71), *Odes* ('The Progress of Poesy', 'The Bard') (Strawberry Hill, 1757); Mark Akenside (1721–70), author of *The Pleasures of the Imagination* (1744) and of various odes which appeared in his collected poems in 1772; William Mason (1725–97), a friend of Gray and author of *Poems* (London, 1764).

17 The essay concludes with a 'Postscript', in which Herder ecstatically praises Klopstock's newly published *Odes* (1771), and laments the inadequacy of recent musical settings of German poetry.

Shakespeare

1 On the original edition of this essay, see note 1 to the preceding essay by Herder (above).

2 The image is taken from Mark Akenside's didactic poem *The Pleasures of the Imagination* (1744), III, 550–9, which Herder paraphrases; cf. also note 16 to Herder's essay on Ossian (above).

3 That is, the French. Herder's contemptuous remarks on French neo-classicism echo Lessing's strictures on it in his *Hamburg Dramaturgy* of 1767–9.

4 Prosper Jolyot de Crébillon (1674–1762), French tragedian whose dramas include *Idoménée* (1705), *Rhadamiste et Zénobie* (1711), and *Catilina* (1748).

5 *Astrée*, a pastoral romance in five volumes (Paris, 1607–28) by Honoré d'Urfé (1567–1615).

6 *Clélie*, a romance in ten volumes (Paris, 1654–60) by Madeleine de Scudéry (1607–1701).

7 *Aspasia:* the name of more than one French novel of the eighteenth century. It is uncertain whether Herder is referring to one of them in particular, or to them all as a class. Aspasia is also, however, a character in Madeleine de Scudéry's romance of chivalry *Artamène ou le Grand Cyrus* (1648).

8 'The Britons, divided from the rest of the world'; after Virgil, *Eclogues*, I, 66.

9 'Pupil [literally 'chicken'] of Aristotle'.

10 Henry Home (Lord Kames) (1696–1782); author of *Elements of Criticism* (Edinburgh, 1762). Richard Hurd (1720–1808), editor of *Q. Horatii Flacci Ars Poetica. Epistola ad Pisones* (London, 1749), the commentary to which contained an analysis of the different kinds of drama.

11 The young Herder was already studying the much decried heretic Spinoza. Along with Lessing and Goethe, he was shortly to initiate a wave of enthusiasm in Germany for Spinoza's nature pantheism, an enthusiasm which was shared by Schelling, Novalis, and other German Romantics: see David Bell, *Spinoza in Germany from 1670 to the Age of Goethe* (London, 1984), especially pp. 38–70 and 97–146.

12 Herder's criticisms here are directed in particular at Pierre Corneille's *Discours des trois unités (Théâtre de Pierre Corneille*, vol. III (Amsterdam, 1664)).

13 Mohammed's dream of his assumption into heaven.

14 Order of succession and simultaneity (order in time and space); cf. Lessing's use of these categories in Chapter 16 of his *Laocoon* (pp. 51–4 above).

KANT

The Critique of Judgement

[These notes are from DS.]

1 Kant's "faculty of desire" is to be understood in a precise sense as that through which we generate the wish that our representation [Vorstellung] should correspond to an object in the empirical world. We have, i.e., a mental image of something that we want to convert into actual experience. Such desire is of

course not always satisfied (see the long footnote to *CJ*, I, 16, not included here), and in fact in its capacity for projection in advance of and even in despite of actual experience, it is a valuable signal of the independence of the mind and its capacity to generate the laws of freedom and practical reason. Kant distinguishes in this context between the lower and higher faculties of desire, the latter identical with reason in its capacity to determine the will without reference to empirical inclinations.

2 Kant uses two words which we have to translate as 'object', namely *Object* and *Gegenstand*. Meredith distinguishes between them by capitalizing the first letter of the former: "an object, regarded as merely presented to the mind, is *Gegenstand;* whereas an object, regarded as already something for the mind – a thought-object – is *Object*" (Meredith (1911), p. 229). (See also the long entry under *Objekt* in Eisler (1961).) I have preserved this distinction – though not his capitalization of the translation of *das Subject* – so that in what follows *Gegenstand* appears as 'object' and *Object* as 'Object'.

3 The "concept" [*der Begriff*] is one of the two or three most important terms in the vocabulary of the critical philosophy. For Kant, experience is composed by a synthesis of mental (*a priori*) and objective (contingent) elements. The concept is that "through which an object in general is thought (the category)", and in all acts of perception it is joined with the empirical "intuition" [*Anschauung*] through which it is given (Kant (1933), p. 162; B 146). Intuitions, which are sensible, would fail to 'produce' intelligible experience without the concepts of the understanding, and *vice versa*. For the "interest" of pure practical laws, see Kant (1956), p. 124; *Ak.* V, 120.

4 Kant's usual term for "universal" is *allgemein*, but here he incorporates the English words straight into German. The most likely source would seem to be Hume, for whom "general" is a familiar adjective, used both in opposition and loose apposition to "universal". Compare Kant with Hume in 'Of the Standard of Taste': "But though all the general rules of art are founded only on experience and on the observation of the common sentiments of human nature, we must not imagine, that on every occasion, the feelings of men will be conformable to these rules" (Hume (1912), I, 270).

5 "Properly speaking, an idea [*Idee*] signifies a concept of reason, and an *ideal* [*Ideale*] the representation of an individual existence as adequate to an idea" (*CJ*, I, 76; and below, §17). Compare the distinction between aesthetic and rational ideas, neither of which are convertible to cognitions, made in the first remark appended to §57 (*CJ*, I, 209–10). Ideas are always to be distinguished from representations, which are mental pictures or images, although *Vorstellung* is often translated as "idea" in a non-specialized context. Kant's *Idee* is not Platonic: it is a guide to experience but has no metaphysical power.

6 Kant's term *Einbildungskraft*, or "imagination", signifies a faculty absolutely basic to all perception, and not an elevated or specifically artistic capacity, for which he tends to use *Genie* or *Phantasie*. But it is not a passive operation; it works to synthesize intuitions, though doing so in a normative way, at least in healthy and sane minds. See Kant (1933), pp. 141f., (A 115f.), and compare *CJ*, I, 30–2, 84–9. Imagination may be productive, rather than reproductive, when it is the "originator of arbitrary forms of possible intuitions" (*CJ*, I, 86), as it is in the judgement of taste. But this still does not make it 'creative' in any *exceptional* sense of the term. As ever, Kant is interested in the normal aesthetic response rather than the psychology of genius.

For arguments about a confusion in Kant's use of the term *Einbildungskraft*, see Engell (1981), pp. 128–39, and his mentor in this respect, Kemp-Smith (1923), pp. 227–34, 264–70. See also §§23, 49 of *CJ*.

7 A difficult but important point: Kant is extending the case made at the beginning of §9 about the dependence of aesthetic pleasure upon the assumed communicability of the state of mind to which it relates. If it were itself prior, then we would be back in the realm of empirical verification.

8 I.e. in the *Critique of Pure Reason*, wherein "schematism" is the term for the activity or process by which concepts and intuitions are mediated through representations. See Kant (1933), pp. 180f.; A 137f., B 176f.

9 Kant is not suggesting a tradition of exemplary works of art handed down through the generations as evidence of the universality of taste, but rather the fact that in any culture or moment of history there are going to be some things looked upon as exemplary, even if not the same things at all times. It is the universality of the *response*, or faculty of *mind*, that concerns him here.

10 "Models of taste with respect to the arts of speech must be composed in a dead and learned language; the first, to prevent their having to suffer the changes that inevitably overtake living ones, making dignified expressions become degraded, common ones antiquated, and ones newly coined after a short currency obsolete; the second to ensure its having a grammar that is not subject to the caprices of fashion, but has fixed rules of its own." [Kant's own note.] Compare Hegel's much more developed argument for the use of the classics in *On Classical Studies*, in DS, pp. 201–5.

11 I am not sure that Kant makes a strong or clear distinction between *Sittlichkeit* and *Moralität*, as Hegel does (see below, p. 438, note 22), but he does tend to use the latter when emphatically self-prescribed behaviour is indicated. Kant's remarks on the physiological manifestations of the moral and aesthetic identity in the human form contain the seeds of the argument pursued by Schiller in his 1793 treatise *On Grace and Dignity* [*Über Anmuth und Würde*]. Meredith (1911), p. 256, cites an interesting passage from Hugh Blair's *Lectures on Rhetoric and Belles Lettres* in this context; they were translated into German between 1785 and 1789.

12 "As telling against this explanation, the instance may be adduced, that there are things in which we see a form suggesting adaptation to an end, without any end being cognized in them – as, for example, the stone implements frequently obtained from sepulchral tumuli and supplied with a hole, as if for [inserting] a handle; and although these by their shape manifestly indicate a finality, the end of which is unknown, they are not on that account described as beautiful. But the very fact of their being regarded as art-products involves an immediate recognition that their shape is attributed to some purpose or other and to a definite end. For this reason there is no immediate delight whatever in their contemplation. A flower, on the other hand, such as a tulip, is regarded as beautiful, because we meet with a certain finality in its perception which, in our estimate of it, is not referred to any end whatever." [Kant's own note.] "Artifact" would be a better translation of *Kunstwerk* here, given that Kant clearly means an object produced for a purpose and not a work of fine art. Modern interests in various kinds of functional or primitive art would not *necessarily* be incompatible with Kant's argument that the perception of purpose precludes the feeling of delight; delight could, e.g., precede such a perception and remain

distinct from it. But we would have to reassemble the details of this case to bring it round to this position!

13 William Marsden's *The History of Sumatra* (1783) had been translated as *Natürliche und bürgerliche Beschreibung der Insel Sumatra in Ostindien* (Leipzig, 1785).

14 Two (rare) examples of Kant's exposition, and it is significant that neither has anything to do with works of fine art. We may infer the contaminating presence of *interest* in the distinction between the bird's song and the human imitation, which has trained itself purposively to perfect an illusion. Compare *Anthropology*, §13; and *CJ*, I, 162.

15 In *CJ*, §13 Kant has already argued that the *pure* judgement of taste is independent of charm, which he regards as a quality additive or ornamental to form. But §14 suggests that there can be an empirical judgement of taste involving the merely agreeable – charm and emotion.

16 It is hard to follow Kant here in his assertion that the sublime is "less important and rich in consequences" than the beautiful, unless we limit the terms of the comparison, emphasizing the qualification *for nature*. For, given that the sublime is not concerned with *form*, it must function more readily than does the beautiful in referring us back to our own inner tendency to *introduce* sublimity into nature. As such it seems even more closely analogous to the operations of the moral faculty. Compare §27 below, and see also my comments in the general introduction.

For accounts of the importance of the sublime in eighteenth-century aesthetics, see Hipple (1957), Monk (1935), and Weiskel (1976).

17 Even the mathematically sublime, i.e., is related to the ideas of reason rather than to the concepts of the understanding, in that what is at work is an expanding act of perceiving relations, and never the specific computation of ratios – the onset of which, always possible, would be the passage out of the experience of the sublime. In this way the mathematically sublime does not allow the assumption of finality, and remains in accord with the argument that sublimity applies not to things in nature but to the mental processes operative upon them.

18 This habit of or tendency toward reifying our active powers, attributing them falsely to the material things through which we recognize them, is a very important Romantic concern, shared explicitly by Wordsworth and Coleridge among others. As far as I know Kant is the first to use the term *Subreption* in a philosophical sense, taking it from the vocabulary of ecclesiastical law, where it denotes the concealment of facts.

19 The sublime and the beautiful taken together thus demonstrate the connection between the imagination and the faculties identified as transcendental by the first two *Critiques:* understanding and reason. As well as showing the symmetry of *CJ* with its two predecessors, this formulation again implies the closer relation of the sublime to moral experience, as compared to that of the beautiful. There is a stoical character to Kant's ethics, involving us as it does in an experience of subjective isolation before an unknowable or non-existent finality for which we are yet compelled to legislate. This is very much the spirit of his analysis of the sublime.

20 I.e. in the mathematically sublime. The dynamically sublime, now being discussed, concerns the imbalance of power, rather than magnitude, between nature and ourselves.

21 Once again, we see the emphasis on the need to avoid the rule of outer forms over inner spirit. Given the way in which institutions tend to employ such outer forms to represent their power, we can trace a strong analogy between Kant's argument (more fully developed for theology in *Religion Within the Limits of Reason Alone*) and those of Godwin against factions and parties, and that of Wordsworth against poetic diction. The common inheritance is that of the Enlightenment attack on various forms of superstition. See Simpson (1982a, 1982b). And compare Fichte in 1792:

> Should we not be more intent in education on developing the feeling for the sublime? This is a way that nature herself opens to us to pass over from sensibility to morality; and in our age it is usually checked very early in us by frivolities and trinkets – and also, among other things, by theodicies and doctrines of happiness.   Fichte (1978), p. 51

22 Kant's use of the English *enthusiasm* signals his awareness of its place in the British tradition from at least Shaftesbury onwards. I have discussed the polemic against *Schwärmerei* in the general introduction.

23 Compare Burke (1759), Pt I, §11. This argument of Kant's accords with the frequently gloomy view (from the position of particular individuality) he expresses about history and civil society in the non-critical writings. Issues surrounding retirement, and the migration from the city to the country, provide some of the most important political–aesthetic themes in eighteenth-century English literature, as any perusal of Pope, Thomson, Cowper, Smollett, Crabbe, Goldsmith, etc. will demonstrate.

Translations of the various parts of *Robinson Crusoe*, and even theatrical adaptations thereof, were enormously popular in Germany: see Price and Price (1934), pp. 78–80. Kant mentions the Crusoe fantasy also in his *Conjectural Beginnings of Human History* (1786), as part of an attack on the myth of primitive innocence (see Kant (1963), pp. 67–8). Burke's treatise on the sublime and beautiful had been translated into German in 1773 (Riga), and again in 1784 (Erfurt). Meredith (1911) footnotes some of the parallels.

24 Against this exemplary statement of the Enlightenment case against superstition, we may quote Matthew Arnold's assimilation of Goethe in *Literature and Dogma*:

> . . . 'Aberglaube', *extra-belief,* belief beyond what is certain and verifiable. Our word 'superstition' had by its derivation this same meaning, but it has come to be used in a merely bad sense, and to mean a childish & craven religiosity. With the German word it is not so; therefore Goethe can say with propriety and truth '*Aberglaube* is the poetry of life' . . .   Arnold (1960–78), VI, 212

25 "We readily see that enlightenment, while easy, no doubt, *in thesi, in hypothesi* is difficult and slow of realization. For not to be passive with one's reason, but always to be self-legislative is doubtless quite an easy matter for a man who only desires to be adapted to his essential end, and does not seek to know what is beyond his understanding. But as the tendency in the latter direction is hardly avoidable, and others are always coming and promising with full assurance that they are able to satisfy one's curiosity, it must be very difficult to preserve or restore in the mind (and particularly in the public mind) that merely negative attitude (which constitutes enlightenment proper)." [Kant's own note.] See also

Kant's essay of 1784, *An Answer to the Question: What is Enlightenment?* in DS, pp. 29–34.

26 Note that in its relation to the other two *Critiques* judgement is here related most centrally to the question of consensus.

27 Yet another formulation of the relation between the beautiful and the moral. Note that it is the beauty of *nature*, and not that of art, which arouses an interest akin to the moral. Kant has already made the point that as soon as an interest is aroused then the judgement of taste ceases to be pure, but there he had in mind empirical interest (see §§13–14).

The "beautiful soul", which Kant defines as marking the preference for nature over art and for pure properties over social distinctions (*CJ*, I, 159), was to become a *leitmotiv* in German Romanticism. Most famously, Schiller makes it the centrepiece of his essay *On Grace and Dignity* (1793). Here, what is for Kant a somewhat off-handed expression is developed into a fully argued concept, providing an alternative to what Schiller regarded as the excessive severity and abstractness of Kantian ethics. In Schiller's "beautiful soul" the moral instinct is so surely developed that the promptings of the will can be passively followed in the confidence that they will spontaneously embody moral action. Morality is thus taken out of the sphere of anxious self-consciousness. More common in women than in men, this reconciliation of freedom and determination is visibly embodied in *grace*. See Schiller (1943–), XX, 287–9.

The "beautiful soul" appears again in the title to Part II, book VI of Goethe's *Wilhelm Meister* (though one would not infer this from Carlyle's translation), and in Hegel, *Phenomenology of Spirit*, §632f. Although it is likely that Schiller's exact argument was not itself a determining influence on the British consciousness, at least in the early years of the nineteenth century, we can nevertheless observe variously weighted investigations of the relation between morality and spontaneity, ones which bear very close comparison with Schiller's case. For example, in the preface to *Lyrical Ballads* Wordsworth insists that the spontaneous overflow of powerful feelings that is poetry can only be proper if the poet has also thought long and deeply; it is the *habitual* discipline of the poet's thoughts and feelings that gives his statements the quality of apparent intuitions. Toward the end of chapter 13 of Austen's *Sense and Sensibility*, Marianne Dashwood tries to get away with a more fragile correlation of ethics with intuition. And by the time of the anti-self-consciousness crusade of Carlyle and Mill, the rational ingredient of Schiller's model (itself of course much less rational than Kant's) has been largely left aside.

28 An extreme statement of the opposite position would be by e.g. Brecht: that the artist take every opportunity to dramatize his presence in order to *prevent* his audience from reposing in the illusion of the natural. But if Kant and Brecht stand at opposite ends of this spectrum, it must be said that the movement away from Kant begins very quickly. Though few if any of the romantics would have subscribed wholeheartedly to the idea of art as a form of bad faith requiring our being regularly reminded of its status as mere appearance (indeed they are generally concerned with the positive aspects of this fact), yet in Hegel we can see an emphasis on the importance of the very self-consciousness, and its appearance in labour, that Kant here ideally excludes. We should register also the strong formal incidence of themes of self-presence in Romantic poetry, often accompanied by anxieties about isolation or misunderstanding, even as we recognize other aspirations as its declared goals.

29 Compare Shelley (1977), pp. 486, 504:

> A Poet is a nightingale, who sits in darkness and sings to cheer its own solitude
> with sweet sounds; his auditors are as men entranced by the melody of an
> unseen musician, who feel that they are moved and softened, yet know not
> whence or why . . . this power arises from within . . . and the conscious portions
> of our natures are unprophetic either of its approach or its departure.

30 Meredith's (1911) notes on this whole discussion of genius are especially full,
   and should be consulted for suggestions about Kant's relation to the British
   tradition. I have however altered his translation of *Geist* as "soul". This important section is obviously what Fichte has before him when he writes *On the Spirit
   and the Letter in Philosophy* (translated in DS, pp. 74–93). What follows is Kant's
   most important definition of the aesthetic imagination.

31 Kant here means simply to subsume the particular under the general, and to
   explain that artistic genius is essentially connected to a faculty normal to the
   human mind (imagination). The term "talent" has no connotations of inferi-
   ority here.

32 Kant here – "und mit der Sprache, als bloßem Buchstaben, Geist verbindert"
   – specifically prefigures the title and subject of Fichte's essay (see above, note
   30), and expounds that aspect of the imagination so popular among the Romantics: its capacity for renovation and discovery, for going beyond inherited associations and for producing new configurations.

33 Because the aesthetic idea now passes into an empirically available form – as
   poem, painting, statue – it must embody a concept, even though in its original
   apprehension no concept was adequate to it. We can distinguish between the
   concepts of the understanding necessary for the *existence* of a work of art and
   the indeterminate concepts to which it gives rise once it is in existence, and
   which were presumably in the artist's mind at the time of composition. See
   H.W. Cassirer (1938), pp. 278–85.

34 The desire to preserve the communicability of art and the continuity between
   the artist's faculties and those of ordinary human beings is central to Kant's
   purpose here; it is through the common possession of the understanding that
   shared experience of this sort is possible.

35 Compare Schiller on *Schein*, in *AE*, pp. 191–203; and see note 7 to Hegel's
   Aesthetics, below. The declaration of poetry as the first among the fine arts, a
   view shared by Schelling and (ambiguously) by Hegel, has been felt to consort
   awkwardly with the emphasis on the visual arts in earlier parts of the *CJ*. The
   point is, I think, that the visual arts were more conducive to those parts of the
   argument stressing the absence of *interest* in the aesthetic response, painting
   and statuary being more prone to appetitive associations than the reading of
   words (for Kant, that is).

36 Once again, Kant's example makes clear that he has in mind the lower meaning
   of *Kunst* as "artifact".

37 For the very synthesis of art and nature that Kant here keeps apart, compare
   Coleridge (1972), p. 30:

> a Symbol . . . always partakes of the Reality which it renders intelligible; and
> while it enunciates the whole, abides itself as a living part in that Unity, of which
> it is the representative.

38 "We may, on the other hand, make use of an analogy to the above mentioned
   immediate physical ends to throw light on a certain union, which, however, is

to be found more often in idea than in fact. Thus in the case of a complete transformation, recently undertaken, of a great people into a state, the word *organization* has frequently, and with much propriety, been used for the constitution of the legal authorities and even of the entire body politic. For in a whole of this kind certainly no member should be a mere means, but should also be an end, and, seeing that he contributes to the possibility of the entire body, should have his position and function in turn defined by the idea of the whole." [Kant's own note.]

39 Behind this emphasis is of course Kant's desire to pre-empt any hint of an argument for the existence of God from the evidence of a design in the created world. It is worth stressing yet again that in most of this exposition Kant has in mind our capacity to produce artifacts rather than fine art; he is interested in our production of things with a *purpose*, which we will be most tempted to relate to the productions of nature. (The beautiful, it will be remembered, is by definition never purposive.) This is important in view of the tendency of Kant's followers to apply these arguments to fine art, where they never belonged for their founder.

40 Meredith (1928), p. 170, notes as follows:

The reference to 'objective reality' in this passage . . . is certainly somewhat misleading . . . Kant presumably only means that organisms first give teleology a point of attachment in nature. The passage is one of several that are responsible for misinterpretations of Kant's teleology.

41 Any adequate footnote to this section of *CJ* would have to be of book-length proportions, and "splendid misery" would indeed be a suitable title. Within the general model of a fall both fortunate and unfortunate, many eighteenth-century thinkers were exploring the problems of the divisions in civil society (of labour, interest, wealth) and within the individual mind. Suffice it to say here that Kant is closer to the spirit of Hobbes and Mandeville, and to what will become the spirit of Malthus and the social Darwinists, than he is to the liberal sociologists of the nineteenth century. Kant (1963) should also be consulted for its arguments for the disjunctive relation of individual and species and the emergence of culture from strife. Evidence, if any were needed, that the arguments of the 'Critique of Teleological Judgement' are to be applied strictly to their declared contexts!

SCHILLER

On the Aesthetic Education of Man

[Wilkinson and Willoughby's notes are designated W&W. Other notes are by DS.]

1 For the complex textual history of this work, see *AE*, pp. 334–7. The first complete version was published in three segments in *Die Horen* between January and June, 1795, although Schiller had been working on it since 1793. The following selections are taken from the revised text of 1801.

2 Schiller has just described the spirit of the age as "wavering between perversity and brutality", and kept within bounds "only through an equilibrium of evils" (*AE*, p. 29).

3 *Die Vernunft*, Kant's term for "reason". Schiller's treatise is formulated as, among other things, a debate with the legacy of Kant, which he saw as a divisive one, setting up unnecessary tensions and distinctions between the operations

of the understanding (empirical experience), reason (moral experience), and the aesthetic sense.

4 Schiller's term is *Verstand*, the Kantian "understanding", i.e. the faculty governing the understanding of empirical knowledge.

5 An allusion to Rousseau's *Premier discours*, on the deleterious effects of the arts and sciences; the next three paragraphs allude to the second *Discourse*, where Rousseau discusses the negative effects of a government based on blind force and mere need (W&W).

6 I.e., the Venus who presides over profane and the Venus who presides over sacred love (W&W).

7 Compare Rousseau's description of the degeneration of government into despotism in *De l'inégalité* (W&W).

8 *Der Geschäftsgeist*, the spirit of trade, business, worldly vocation, i.e. it has nothing to do with Kant's definition of the "practical" as pertaining to the moral.

9 With our translation of this first sentence we have committed Schiller to a purely logical statement. But it is by no means certain that he is not referring to the circularity inherent in the process of education as well as to the apparently vicious circle of his own argument (W&W).

10 Orestes, who murdered his mother Clytemnestra to avenge her complicity in the murder of Agamemnon.

11 See *AE*, p. 241, where the editors note the Pietist aura of Schiller's vocabulary in this and in the following paragraph.

12 See letter X and letter XIII (*AE*, pp. 63, 91–93).

13 See Kant, *CJ*, §29 (W&W).

14 *Begriffen*. Schiller means to allude to the Kantian concepts of the understanding as well as to 'thought' in general.

15 This, the key sentence of the whole treatise, should make us adjust our image of an 'idealist' Schiller (W&W).

16 *Selbsttätigkeit*, a key term in Fichte's vocabulary. In a footnote to letter XIII (*AE*, p. 85), Schiller tells us that he has been reading Fichte's *Wissenschaftslehre*.

17 This is one of Schiller's various answers to the problem that he and his contemporaries regarded as the most painful legacy of the *Critique of Judgement*: Kant's skeptical or over-complex idea of the relation of the aesthetic to the moral. In what follows, Schiller typically locates the argument in the context of the debate about consensus stimulated by the widespread concern over the effects of division of labour and division of interest.

18 *Durch die Bestimmtheit seines Begriffs*. Again, Schiller's language alludes to Kant's system (for Kant on music, see *CJ*, §54). Because sculpture and painting rely upon visual images of things in the world, they are necessarily associated with the concepts of the understanding, and as such are tinged with the aspiration to scientific knowledge (which derives from those concepts). In this complex paragraph, Schiller suggests that no form of art, however perfect, is able to rid itself completely of the limits of its particular form, to the degree that we might move effortlessly across the whole spectrum of psychic drives. Once again, the point is that the pure aesthetic effect is not in the world.

19 No doubt an oblique reference to the triumph of form over subject-matter in Goethe's *Roman Elegies* (W&W).

20 *Einer totalen Revolution*. Schiller's Francophone vocabulary makes it even clearer that he means to affirm that a spiritual change is more important than any change in the worldly political order – which would indeed become unnec-

essary if such spiritual change were ever to come about. This whole paragraph is prophetic of Schopenhauer's aesthetic theory.

21 The word here is *Umwälzung*, also translated as "revolution" by W&W.

22 An allusion to the Third Kingdom, or Third Age, dreamed of by mystics since Joachim de Fiore (W&W). The editors go on to discuss ideas about the earthly incarnation of this "third *Reich* of play and of semblance", alluding to the obvious sinister consequences. But such consequences are completely contrary to Schiller's argument, as paragraph 10 (below) makes clear.

23 This is a difficult passage, because of the way in which it seems to conflate knowledge *(Erkenntnis)* and reason *(Vernunft)* as sharing a distinction from sense *(Sinn)*. Because most of Kant's discussions of *Erkenntnis* emphasize its relation to empirical experience and to the categories of the understanding, rather than those of reason, it might seem that Schiller is departing from or negating Kant's logic. But Kant was always clear that there is nothing merely passive about *Erkenntnis*, which is always the result of an *a priori* element in experience; and, close to the end of the *Critique of Pure Reason* he explicitly discusses a "rational" knowledge in philosophy and mathematics *(Verunfterkenntnis)* that would fit precisely the terms of the distinction here made by Schiller (see Kant, *Ak.*, III, 540f.; A 838f., B 866f.). Schiller's formulation might then describe both the basic cognitive psychology of ordinary experience, which belongs to us as a species at the normative level, and also the higher moral faculty which is similarly available but which (Kant had stressed) few of us attain. Both involve the assumption that other individualities will, if purged of peculiar dispositions and interests, correspond to our own; but, empirically, we cannot bring this about. Compare also Kant in *CJ*, §§9, 21.

On Naive and Sentimental Poetry

Schiller's own notes

a Kant, who was the first, as far as I know, who began to reflect purposefully upon this phenomenon, remarks that if we were to hear the song of the nightingale imitated with the utmost deception by a human voice and had abandoned ourselves to the impression with all our feelings, our entire delight would disappear with the destruction of the illusion. See the chapter on the intellectual interest in the beautiful in the *Critique of Aesthetic Judgement*.[2] Anyone who has learned to admire the author only as a great thinker will be pleased here to come upon a trace of his heart and be convinced by this discovery of the man's high philosophical calling (which absolutely requires the combination of both characteristics).

b In a note appended to the 'Analytic of the Sublime' (*Critique of Aesthetic Judgement*, p. 225, 1st edition) Kant likewise distinguishes these threefold ingredients in the feeling of the naive, but he supplies another explanation. 'Something compounded of both (the animal feeling of pleasure and the spiritual feeling of respect) is found in naivety, which is the bursting forth of that sincerity originally natural to mankind in opposition to the art of dissimulation that has become second nature. We laugh at a simplicity that does not yet understand how to conceal itself, yet we are delighted at the simplicity of nature which here thwarts that art. We expected some routine mode of utterance, artificial and carefully contrived to make a fine impression, and yet we see unspoiled innocent nature which we no more expected to see than he who displayed it intended it to be exposed. That the fair but false impression which ordinarily weighs so much in our judgement is now suddenly transformed into nothing – that the scoundrel in us, as it were, is revealed – sets the mind in motion in two opposed directions one after the other, giving the body a salutary shock. A mixture of solemnity and high esteem appears in this play of the faculty of judgement, because something infinitely superior to all conventional manners, namely, purity of thought (or at least an inclination thereto) is, after all, not wholly extinguished in human nature. But since it appears only fleetingly and the art of dissimulation swiftly draws a veil before it, there is at the same time an admixture of regret, which is an emotion of tenderness; an emotion which, taken as a joke, is very easily combined with good-humoured laughter (and in fact is usually so combined), and which simultaneously compensates for the embarrassment of whoever gave rise to the occasion for not yet being experienced in the ways of men.'[8] – I confess that this mode of explanation does not entirely satisfy me, and this principally because it asserts of the naive as a whole what is at most true only of a species of it, the naive of surprise, of which I shall speak later. It certainly arouses laughter if somebody exposes himself by naivety, and in some cases this laughter may derive from a preceding expectation that fails to materialise. But even naivety of the noblest sort, the naive of temperament, arouses a smile always, which however is scarcely due to any expectation that comes to nothing, but that can only be explained by the contrast between certain behaviour and the conventionally accepted and expected forms. I doubt also whether the regret which is mingled in our feeling about the latter kind of naivety refers to the naive person and not rather to ourselves or to humanity at large, whose decay we are reminded of in such cases. It is too clearly a moral regret which must have some nobler object than the physical ills by which sincerity is threatened in the ordinary course of things, and this object can hardly be any other than the loss of truth and simplicity in mankind.

c Perhaps I should say quite briefly: *truth victorious over deceit;* but the concept of the naive seems to me still more inclusive, since any form of simplicity that triumphs over artifice, and natural freedom over stiffness and constraint, excites a similar emotion in us.

d A child is badly behaved if, out of greediness, foolhardiness, or impetuosity, it acts in opposition to the prescripts of a good education but it is naive if its free and healthy nature rids it of the mannerisms of an irrational education, such as the awkward posturings of the dancing master. The same occurs with the naive in its wholly figurative meaning, when it is transferred from the human to the inanimate. Nobody would find naive the spectacle of a badly tended garden in which the weeds have the upper hand, but there is certainly something naive when the free growth of spreading branches undoes the painstaking work of the topiarist in a French garden. Likewise, it is in no way naive if a trained horse performs its lessons badly out of natural stupidity, but something of the naive is present if it forgets them out of natural freedom.

e But also only with the Greeks; since just such an active motion and such a rich fullness of human life as surrounded the Greeks was required to breathe life even into the lifeless and to pursue the image of humanity with this avidity. For example, the world peopled by Ossian was shabby and uniform;[11] the inanimate world that surrounded it, however, was broad, colossal and powerful, so it imposed itself and asserted its rights even over the people. In the songs of this poet, therefore, inanimate nature (in contrast with the people) figures much more as an object of sentiment. Yet even Ossian complains of a decline of humanity and, as small among his people as the extent of civilisation and its perversions was, yet the awareness of it was still lively and penetrating enough to drive the emotion-laden moral poet back to the inanimate and to pour out in his songs that elegiac tone that makes them so moving and attractive to us.

f It is perhaps not superfluous to remark that if here the modern poets are set over against the ancients, the difference of manner rather than of time is to be understood. We possess in modern times, even most recently, naive works of poetry in all classes, even if no longer the purest kind and, among the old Latin, even among the Greek poets, there is no lack of sentimental ones. Not only in the same poet, even in the same work one often encounters both species combined, as, for example, in *The Sorrows of Werther,* and such creations will always produce the greater effects.

g Molière, as a naive poet, is said to have left it in every case to the opinion of his chambermaid what should stand or fall in his comedies; it might also be wished that the masters of the French buskin had occasionally tried the same experiment with their tragedies. But I would not advise that a similar experiment be undertaken with Klopstock's *Odes,* with the finest passages in the *Messiah,* in *Paradise Lost,* in *Nathan the Wise,* or in many other pieces.[18] Yet what am I saying? – the test has really been undertaken, and Molière's chambermaid chops logic back and forth in our critical literature, philosophical and belletristic journals and travel accounts, on poetry, art and the like, except that, as is proper, she does so less tastefully on German soil than on French, as only becomes the servants' hall of German literature.

h Anyone who observes the impression that naive poetry makes on him and is able to separate from it that part which is due to the content will find this impression always joyous, always pure, always serene, even in the case of very pathetic objects; with sentimental poetry it will always be somewhat solemn and intense. This is because with naive accounts, regardless of their subject matter, we always rejoice in the truth, in the living presence of the object in our imagination, and seek nothing further beyond these; whereas with the sentimental we have to reconcile the representation of imagination with an idea of reason and hence always fluctuate between two different conditions.

i In *Nathan the Wise* this is not the case; here the frosty nature of the theme has cooled the whole art work. But Lessing himself knew that he was not writing a tragedy and simply forgot in his own case, humanly enough, his own doctrine propounded in the *Hamburg Dramaturgy*[23] that the poet is not permitted to employ the tragic form for other than a tragic purpose. Without very substantial changes it would hardly be possible to transform this dramatic poem into a good tragedy; but with merely incidental changes it might have yielded a good comedy. For the latter purpose the pathetic would have to be sacrificed, for the former its reasoning, and there can be no question upon which of the two the beauty of the poem most depends.

j That I employ the terms satire, elegy, and idyll in a wider sense than is customary, I will hardly have to explain to readers who penetrate deeper into the matter. My intention in doing so is by no means to disrupt the boundaries which have been set for good reasons by usage hitherto for satire and elegy as well as idyll; I look merely at the *mode of perception* predominant in these poetic categories, and it is sufficiently well known that this cannot be accommodated at all within those narrow limits. We are not moved elegiacally solely by the elegy which is exclusively so called: the dramatic and epic poets can also move us in the elegiac manner. In the *Messiah*,[24] in Thomson's *Seasons*, in *Paradise Lost*, in *Jerusalem Delivered*, we find numerous depictions which are otherwise proper only to the idyll, the elegy, and to satire. Likewise, to a greater or lesser degree, in almost every pathetic poem. But that I account the idyll as an elegiac category does seem to require justification. It should be recalled, though, that here I speak only of that kind of idyll that is a species of sentimental poetry, to the essence of which belongs the notion that nature is *opposed* to art, and the ideal to actuality. Even if this is not rendered explicit by the artist and he offers to our view a pure and spontaneous portrait of unspoiled nature or of the ideal fulfilled, yet that opposition is still within his heart and will betray itself in every stroke of the brush, even against his will. For even if this were not so, then the very language which he must employ, because it bears the spirit of the age and has undergone the influence of art, would serve to remind us of actuality and its limitations, of civilisation with its mannerism; indeed, our own heart would oppose to that picture of pure nature its experience of corruption and thus render the mode of perception elegiac in us even though this had not been sought by the poet. This last is so unavoidable that even the highest delight which the finest works of the naive genus of ancient and modern times assure to the cultivated individual does not for long remain pure, but sooner or later will be accompanied by an elegiac mood. Finally, I would still observe that the division attempted here, for the very reason that it is simply based on the distinction of mode of perception, should by no means whatever determine the division of poetry itself nor the derivation of poetic genres; since the poet is in no way bound, even in a single work, to the same mode of perception, that division therefore cannot be based upon it, but must be taken from the form of the presentation.

k And *heart:* for the merely sensuous ardour of the portrayal and the luxuriant richness of imagination do not by far make it so. Thus *Ardinghello*[27] remains, despite all its sensuous energy and all the fire of its coloration, only a sensuous caricature without truth and without aesthetic dignity. Still, this unusual production will always remain remarkable as an example of the almost poetic impetus which *mere appetite* was capable of supplying.

l I must repeat once again that satire, elegy, and idyll, as they are here laid down as the only three possible species of sentimental poetry, have nothing in common with the three particular genres of poem which are known by these names, other than the *modes of perception* which are proper to the former as well as to the latter. But that, beyond the limits of naive poetry, only this tripartite mode of perception and poetic composition is possible, consequently that the area of sentimental poetry is completely exhausted by this division, can be easily deduced from the concept of the latter.

Sentimental is distinguished from naive poetry, namely, in that it refers actual conditions, at which the latter halts, to ideas, and applies ideas to actuality. Hence it has always, as has already been observed above, to contend simultaneously with two conflicting objects, i.e., with the ideal and with experience, between which neither more nor less than just these three following relationships can be conceived of. Either it is the *contradiction* with actual conditions, or it is its *correspondence* with the ideal, which is the preferred attitude of mind, or it is divided between the two. In the first case it is satisfied by the force of the inner conflict, by *energetic movement;* in the second, it is satisfied by the *harmony* of the inner life, by *dynamic calm;* in the third, conflict *alternates* with harmony, calm alternates with motion. This triadic state of feeling gives rise to three different modes of poetry to which the customary names, *satire, idyll, elegy,* correspond exactly, provided only that one recalls the mood into which the poetic species known by these names place the mind, and abstracts from the means by which they achieve it.

Anyone who could now still ask me to which of the three species I assign the epic, the novel, the tragedy, etc., would not have understood me at all. For the concept of these last, as individual *genres of composition,* is either not at all or at least not solely determined by the mode of perception; it is clear, rather, that they can be executed in more than one mode of perception, consequently in more than one of the species of poetry I have established.

Finally, I have still to remark that if one is inclined to take sentimental poetry, as is reasonable, as a genuine order (and not simply as a degenerate species) and as an extension of true poetic art, then some attention must be paid to it in the determination of poetic types as well as generally in the whole of poetic legislation, which is still onesidedly based on the observances of the ancient and naive poets. The sentimental poet deviates too radically from the naive for those forms which the latter introduced to accommodate him at all times without strain. In such cases it is indeed difficult to distinguish correctly always the exceptions which the differentiation between the species demands, from the subterfuges to which incompetence resorts: but this much we learn from experience, that in the hands of sentimental poets (even the most outstanding) no single type of composition has ever remained entirely what it was among the ancients, and that often very new types have been executed under the old names.

m For the reader whose scrutiny is critical I add that both modes of perception considered in their ultimate concepts are related to one another like the first and third categories, in that the last always arises by the combination of the first with its exact opposite.[30] The opposite of naive perception is, namely, reflective understanding, and the sentimental mood is the result of the effort, *even under the conditions of reflection,* to restore naive feeling according to its content. This would occur through the fulfilled ideal in which art again encounters nature. If one considers those three concepts in relation to the categories one will always find *nature* and the naive mood corresponding to her in the first; *art,* as the overcoming of nature by the freely functioning understanding, always in the second; the *ideal,* in which consummated art returns to nature, in the third category.

n I note, in order to forestall any misunderstanding, that this division is by no means undertaken in order to promote a choice between them or therewith the preference of one to the exclusion of the other. It is just this *exclusion* which is found in experience that I am combatting; and the result of the present observations will be the proof that only by completely equal *inclusion* of both can justice be done to the rational concept of mankind. Moreover, I take both in their most dignified sense and in the whole wealth of the connotations which can only subsist together with their purity and the retention of their specific differences. It will also be apparent that a high degree of human truth is compatible with each and that their diversion from one another may indeed make a difference in detail but not in the whole; in the form perhaps, but not in the content.

Editor's notes (HBN)

1 Commentaries to the work can be found in *Schillers Werke. Nationalausgabe*, edited by Petersen and others (1943–), XXI, 278–314 and in Schiller, *Über naive und sentimentalische Dichtung*, edited by William F. Mainland (Oxford, 1957).

2 Kant, *The Critique of Judgement (Kritik der Urteilskraft)* Part I, *Critique of Aesthetic Judgement*, §42. Kant says of such artificial nightingales, employed to entertain guests at country houses: 'But as soon as the deception is discovered, no one will for long be able to endure listening to this song which had previously seemed so enrapturing; and the same applies to all other songbirds. It has to be nature, or to be taken for nature by us, for us to be able to take an immediate interest in the beautiful as such' (Ak., V, 302).

3 Schiller alludes to the vogue for *sensibilité* in European literature of the later eighteenth century, as in Rousseau's novel *La nouvelle Héloïse* (1761), Goethe's *The Sorrows of Werther* (1774), Laurence Sterne's *A Sentimental Journey through France and Italy* (1768), etc.

4 'Determination' and 'determinability' (*Bestimmung* und *Bestimmbarkeit*): one of Schiller's key conceptual antitheses, between the extent to which an individual's potential is already determined or realised, and the extent to which it exists as infinite and unfulfilled possibility. Schiller develops this antithesis at greater length in his *Aesthetic Letters*, letters 19–21.

5 'Determination' (*Bestimmung*) is used here in a rather different sense from above, closer to its common eighteenth-century meaning of 'destiny'. In the child, its (future) destiny is as yet unrealised; in the adult, it is fulfilled. This is a characteristic instance of Schiller's use of the same term in shifting senses.

6 'Understanding' and 'reason' (*Verstand* and *Vernunft*) are used by Schiller in the Kantian sense of the faculties of (conceptual) explanation and judgement on the one hand and of (*a priori* or moral) reason on the other. Reason is the higher of the two, in that it brings general principles to bear upon the operations of the understanding. The understanding relates to the empirical world, reason to the world of ideas and principles.

7 *'Theoretical'* . . . *'practical'*: Schiller adopts Kant's antithesis, in which the terms refer to the spheres of cognition and morality respectively.

8 The passage occurs at the end of Part I of *CJ*, §54 (Ak., V, 335).

9 'Affect' (*Affekt*): spontaneous feeling or reaction.

10 That is, freedom of the will.

11 It is noteworthy that Schiller, who was unaware that the poems of Ossian were largely a modern forgery (by James Macpherson), has recognised their essentially modern and 'sentimental' character. Compare Herder's assessment of them, in his essay on Ossian (pp. 71–6 above), as primitive and 'natural' poetry.

12 Homer, *Odyssey*, XIV, 72ff, and Goethe, *The Sorrows of Werther*, Book II, letter of 15 March.

13 The modern Tivoli, where Horace had his rural retreat.

14 Schiller is probably referring to Johann Christoph Gottsched (1700–66), who had on various occasions roundly condemned Shakespeare for failing to observe the rules of French neo-classical poetics: for examples of his censures, see *Shakespeare-Rezeption. Die Diskussion um Shakespeare in Deutschland*, edited by Hansjürgen Blinn, vol. I (Berlin, 1982), pp. 40f. and 62f.

15 *Orlando Furioso*, Canto I, verse 22.

16 *Iliad*, VI, 224–33 (translation by E.V. Rieu).

17 Schiller's 'wit' *(Witz)* translates the French *esprit;* note the continuity with Lessing and Herder in Schiller's anti-French sentiments.

18 *'Messiade . . . Nathan the Wise'*: Friedrich Gottlieb Klopstock's (1724–1803) religious epic *Der Messias* and Lessing's drama on religious tolerance *Nathan der Weise.*

19 Schiller builds here on Lessing's antithesis, in his *Laocoon,* between the circumscribed sphere of visual art and the unlimited sphere of poetry, and links it to his own antithesis between 'naive' (finite) and 'sentimental' (infinite) modes of perception.

20 Schiller was not the first to associate the sublime with tragedy and the beautiful with comedy. Kant had already done so in his essay 'Observations on the Feelings of the Sublime and the Beautiful' in 1764 (Ak., II, 205–56, and Kant, 1960). Schiller's own theory of tragedy, as expressed in his *On Pathos (Über das Pathetische)* of 1793, is based on the principle of sublimity. The tragic hero attains sublimity by asserting his moral freedom, in situations of suffering, over the weakness of the senses.

21 'Theoretically' and 'practically': cf. note 7 above.

22 *Nathan:* cf. note 18 above.

23 The reference here is to §80 of the *Hamburg Dramaturgy.*

24 See note 18 above.

25 Albrecht von Haller (1708–77), Swiss poet and scientist whose descriptive poem *The Alps* was criticised by Lessing in the *Laocoon,* section XVII. He was also the writer of satrical verse, akin to that of Pope, e.g., 'The Falseness of Human Virtues' (1730) and 'On the Origin of Evil' (1734). Christian Ewald von Kleist (1715–59) was a writer of pastoral poems and a friend of Lessing. On Klopstock, see note 18 above.

26 From Haller's 'Ode of Mourning' ('Trauer-Ode') of 1736.

27 Wilhelm Heinse's (1746–1803) novel *Ardinghello* (1787) glorifies Renaissance amoralism and sensuality.

28 This plan was never carried out.

29 The reference is, of course, to Rousseau.

30 Schiller is referring to the doctrine of categories formulated by Kant in §11 of the *Critique of Pure Reason.* In his later years Schiller frequently structures his arguments on the triadic model outlined here.

31 Thalia and Melpomene: the Muses of comedy and tragedy, respectively.

FRIEDRICH SCHLEGEL

On Incomprehensibility

[All notes on F. Schlegel are from KMW.]

1 Christian Garve (1742–98), German popularizer of philosophy.

2 Immanuel Kant (1724–68); the 'table of categories' refers to section 3, chapter 1 of Book I of the 'Transcendental Analytic' under the first main section, 'Transcendental Doctrine of Elements' (p. 113 of Kemp-Smith's translation).

3 'Critical Age', parodying the name given to Kant's Critical Philosophy.

4 Christoph Girtanner (1760–1800), German physician whose publications included research into medicine and chemistry.

5 This is Fragment 216 of the *Athenäum* collection.

6 Johann Dyk (1750–1813), Leipzig bookseller and translator of French popular comedies.

7 Karl Leonard Reinhold (1758–1823), German philosopher and follower of Kant. See *Critical Fragment 66* on Reinhold.

8 'Götzen' in the German, probably referring to Goethe's play *Götz von Berlichingen*.

9 *Critical Fragment* 108.

10 *Critical Fragment* 48.

11 Stanislas, Chevalier de Boufflers (1738–1815), French poet.

12 *Genoveva:* Tieck's play, *Leben und Tod der Heiligen Genoveva* (1799), based on a medieval legend.

13 A.W. Schlegel's didactic 'Elegies' in *Sämtliche Werke* (1846–7), vols. 1–2.

14 Critical Fragment 20.

15 Schlegel's gloss takes off from the last stanza of Goethe's poem 'Beherzigung'.

Critical Fragments

1 François Hemsterhuis (1721–90), Dutch aesthetician and moral philosopher influenced by the Neoplatonic tradition.

2 August Ludwig Hülsen (1765–1810), German philosopher and educator, friend of Fichte and the Schlegels.

Athenäum Fragments

1 This is probably the most famous, most frequently quoted of all Schlegel's fragments.

2 Johann Joachim Winckelmann (1717–68), German aesthetician and archaeologist, famous for his work *Die Geschichte der Kunst im Altertum* (1762), which had a profound impact upon the development of aesthetics in Germany over the next several decades.

3 See the foregoing essay, 'On Incomprehensibility', for a discussion of this fragment.

Letter About the Novel

1 *Die Allgemeine Zeitung,* a contemporary newspaper published by Cotta. 'Jack Pudding' – a literal rendering of the German 'Hanswurst', the traditional name for the clown in comedy. The clown was formally banished from the German stage of Leipzig in the 1730s by Gottsched, in an attempt to raise the tone of the drama; the Viennese, on the other hand, obstinately clung to the Hanswurst right into the following century.

FICHTE

On the Nature of the Scholar

[These notes are from DS.]

1 Fichte has discussed the obligations of the governing class in the previous lecture.

2 Because it is an important part of Fichte's case that all essential truths be self-realized, consisting as they indeed often do in the very *experience* of self-realiza-

tion, then the worldly career of the scholar-teacher who is in direct contact with students must be largely a propaedeutic one, clearing the ground of errors rather than simply putting forth 'truth' in a didactic way. This avoids the paradox of the student passively receiving the incitement to self-activity. On the propaedeutic method generally – which of course has a distinguished history from at least Socrates onwards – see the prefaces to the two editions of the *Critique of Pure Reason*. Fichte's description of the two kinds of scholar-teacher should also be compared with Kant's distinction, in *What is Enlightenment?*, between public and private.

3 For a longer polemic against the contemporary situation, and the habits of lazy reading similarly deplored by Wordsworth and Coleridge and related by them specifically to novel reading, see Fichte (1968), p. 94f; *SW*, VII, 86f. Fichte's positioning of the book trade within the spectrum of an economy founded on luxuries and commodities taps a deep vein in eighteenth-century moral rhetoric. Fichte himself wrote a treatise *On the Closed Commercial State* (1800); see *SW*, III, 387–513.

4 This is not simply an arbitrary complaint on Fichte's part: the reliance upon a prefigured or second-hand literature is at odds with the whole imperative of *Selbstthätigkeit* in his philosophy in general.

5 Again, compare Kant in *CJ*, §34. That the aesthetic is not tied to concepts is of course the received doctrine.

6 For the full exposition of this notion of a historical evolution and a series of specific historical variants of the idea, see Fichte (1847), *The Characteristics of the Present Age*. This explains the presence of a *Weltplan*, beginning in blind instinct and moving through reason to a condition of freedom, while at the same time "these epochs and fundamental paradigms [Grundbegriffe] of different ages can only be properly understood by and through each other, realizing their connection to the whole of history". It is in this work that Fichte is closest to Hegel, whose analysis of the work of art in its relation to a historical identity is much more thorough and much more famous, and to Schelling's writings on *Mythologie*.

7 It had not, we are to recall, been beneath the dignity of those who attacked Fichte on charges of atheism during his years at Jena.

SCHELLING

System of Transcendental Idealism

[These notes are from DS.]

1 "Philosophy as a whole proceeds, and must proceed, from a principle that, as the absolute principle, is also at the same time the simply identical. An absolutely simple, identical entity cannot be apprehended or communicated by description or, in general, by concepts. It can only be intuited. Such an intuition is the organ of all philosophy. But this intuition, which is not sensuous but intellectual and which has for its object not the objective or the subjective but the absolutely identical, the in-itself neither subjective nor objective, is itself merely something inward which cannot again become objective for itself: it can become objective only through a second intuition. This second intuition is aesthetic intuition." [Alternate version by Schelling.] At this point Schelling's argument becomes very hard to follow without some account of his placing of the "intellectual intuition" [intellektuelle Anschauung]. Despite hints to the

contrary, Kant had not favoured this term, limiting all intuitions to sensible ones, whether pure (mere space and time) or empirical: see Kant (1933), B 147f. This did not of course interfere with the necessary appending of the 'I think' to all representations, and the deduction of the transcendental unity of self-consciousness (B 131ff.; see also A 287ff.). It is the discussion of the noumenon, or thing as thought in itself (see A 287f., and *CJ*, §77), which as it were opens the field for Fichte, whose use of the term in the *Wissenschaftslehre* never entirely loses the Kantian restraint: intellectual intuition is "the immediate consciousness that I act, and what I enact: it is that whereby I know something because I do it". It can never be apprehended in isolation, but is "an inference from the obvious facts of consciousness" (*SK*, pp. 38–9). Schelling took the case much further, and regarded Fichte as having stopped short, owing to the limits of his method, sooner than he need have. For Schelling, at this stage of his career, intellectual intuition is still partial, still too dialectically unresolved, and not yet totally objective, shifting between freedom and necessity. It is "the organ of all transcendental thinking" (1978, p. 27), without which all philosophy would be unintelligible, but requires the aesthetic intuition for its final expression: see the "General Observation" below. Harris and Cerf give useful accounts of the whole controversy over the "intellectual intuition", and its place in the development of Idealism, in Hegel (1977), pp. xxv–xxxv, 11–12, 69 n. 32. Hegel later attacked this entire terminology in his predecessors, though the grounds for this attack have themselves been queried (see Esposito (1977), pp. 175–8).

2 "Potency" is a (necessarily) ungainly translation of Schelling's *Potenz*, one of the key terms in his vocabulary. He worked with a model of three *Potenzen*, each embodying an ideal stage in the development of the absolute, which is the totality of all three. The clearest account of the *Potenzen* is in the introduction to the *Philosophy of Art* (*SW*, V, 366f.), the leading points of which are translated in Hegel (1977), pp. 53–4. There is also a useful schema in Engell (1981), pp. 307–8, where the three stages are related to the empirical, the productive (leading the intellectual) and the aesthetic intuitions.

3 Schelling would seem to be the source for Coleridge's fascination with this word and its cognates, taking it as he does much further than Kant had in his predominantly normative epistemology. See *SW*, V, 386:

Through art the divine creation comes to be presented objectively, for it devolves through the same synthesis [Einbildung] of the infinite ideality into reality as does art. The excellent German word "Einbildungskraft" actually signifies the force of *making into one [Ineinsbildung]*, upon which in fact all creation depends. It is the force whereby an ideal is similarly a reality, and the soul is a body; the force of individuation, which is the truly creative principle.

There is an important note some pages later (V, 395);

In relation to *Phantasie* I define *Einbildungskraft* as that wherein the products of art are conceived and brought forth; *Phantasie* is that which intuits them outwardly, works them out of itself, so to speak, and thus presents them. In reason, and from its material, as it were, ideas [Ideen] are formed; the intellectual intuition is the inner presentational faculty. *Phantasie* is then the intellectual intuition in art.

4 One may suspect here another comment on the popularity of the aphoristic mode among the Romantic ironists.

5 The arguments and imagery of the two preceding paragraphs are very close to those of Shelley in *A Defence of Poetry*. For a different emphasis of the relation between philosophy and art, see (1966), p. 147: "because both are absolute, each can be the archetype of the other". The *Philosophy of Art*, written two years later than the *System*, is also less rhapsodic about the primacy of art over philosophy: see *SW*, V, 364f.

Given that art is here the most complete "objectivation" of philosophy, which is itself "a progressive history of self-consciousness" (1978, p. 2), we can see the potential in Schelling's system for a historical analysis of art as an index of the genetic development of the absolute – the kind of analysis made famous by Hegel. In the *Philosophy of Art* Schelling defines *Mythologie* as the "necessary condition and primary material of all art" (*SW*, V, 405), and it is the Greeks who provide the exemplary case. In his later writing on "mythology" Schelling employs the term to define religious doctrines prior to revelation – necessary to such revelation but superseded by it. Here, as in the essay on Dante and the comments on Shakespeare (see below), the word seems to suggest a unifying body of representations held in common by an artist, his public, and the idea which he objectifies; i.e., a body of material from which art may emerge and in whose terms it may be understood.

6 Compare *CJ*, §65, on "organization".

7 Schelling's exposition seems confused here because the other models of the *Potenzen* (see note 2 above) include only three stages. It might be pointed out that in this case simple sensation is the second stage, preceded (for the philosophical consciousness only) by an act of uncontingent self-intuition; and that the third stage includes the other two and yet another, which leads into the fourth stage, the union of the purposive and the unconscious. Schelling goes on to describe the importance of the recognition of other persons in a way clearly important for Hegel, and for the general passage of Idealist epistemology out of its Kantian focus on a single exemplary subjectivity operating with objects in the world.

8 The categorical imperative is the famous centrepiece to Kant's second *Critique* (1956), p. 30: "So act that the maxim of your will could always hold at the same time as a principle establishing universal law." Schelling (1978), p. 188, puts it slightly differently: "thou shalt will only what all intelligences are able to will".

Philosophy of Art

1 I.e. an opposition or indifference not reconciled, not sublimated into a higher unity.

2 Schelling is here noticeably at odds with the notion of Shakespeare as a wild and untutored genius transforming everything he touches into things rich and strange; this may be a reaction to *Sturm und Drang* priorities.

3 In his explanation of the famous ἁμαρτία or "mistake" in Aristotle's *Poetics* (1453a) Schelling shows himself to be at one with more recent scholarship, which emphasizes the irrelevance of meditated and conscious decisions emanating from free will. Philoctetes, for example, wanders unknowingly into a forbidden place, making no decision of his own to do so.

4 Compare the extended comparison of the Greek and Christian worlds pursued earlier in the lectures, *SW*, V, 430–57. Among Christian cultures, "only Catholicism lives in a mythological world" (p. 443), but it can never achieve totality therein: "Catholicism is a necessary element of all modern poetry and mythol-

ogy, but it is not the whole of it, and in the purpose of the world spirit
[Weltgeist] it can doubtless only be a part thereof" (p. 442).

5 *Poetics*, 1452b–1453a.

6 *King Lear*, IV, ii, 40–, or so I assume. Schelling's prose rendering of this passage
is a long way from Shakespeare's verse, and seems to conflate various images
from Albany's speech, the end of which I quote: "Wenn die Tiger des Waldes
oder die Ungeheuer der See aus der Dumpfheit heraustäten, so würden sie
auf solche Weise wirken." There were several extant translations or adaptations
of the play from which Schelling might have drawn: see Price and Price (1934),
pp. 209–10.

7 *Henry VI, Part II*, IV, iv.

8 *Richard III*, V, iv, 7.

9 The identification of the modern with the fragmentary was a commonplace in
Romantic thought and is explored elsewhere in Schelling, for example in the
essay on Dante (below). Elsewhere in the lectures he comments that "the modern world generally can be called a world of individuals: the ancient world a
world of species" (*SW*, V, 444); "*Originality* is the fundamental law of modern
poetry . . . each truly creative individual has to create his own mythology" (p.
446). Protestantism is the symptom and analogue of this fact, and it is from
Protestantism that Shakespeare's art emanates. Christianity as a whole had
already broken apart the unity of the finite and the infinite by its preoccupation
with the ideal at the expense of the mundane; Protestantism, being "essentially
anti-universal", carries this trend even further. See Schelling (1966), pp. 89, 98.
Compare p. 66:

The modern world is in general a world of antitheses, whereas in antiquity,
except for individual stirrings, the finite and the infinite were united under a
common veil. The spirit of the modern era tore this veil and showed the one in
absolute opposition to the other.

It is central to Schelling's reasoning here that the Greek gods easily and frequently took on human form.

10 Pythagoras was said to have deduced all the ratios of the octave as recognized
by the Greeks in relation to a series of numbers from 1 to 4.

11 In the *Letters on Shakespeare* (1800), Tieck speaks of "a whole gallery of English
commentators, whom perhaps one ought rather to pass over, since when I read
Shakespeare and from time to time chance to cast an eye over the notes, then
I am in exactly the same spirits as if, journeying through a beautiful romantic
landscape, one were to go by a tavern in which drunken peasants were bickering
and fighting". See Tieck (1848–52), I, 147. Tieck's residence in England seems
to have left him with an abiding disrespect for the English common man.

12 Perhaps a reference to Pope's remark about a "fluent Shakespear" who "scarce
effac'd a line" ('Imitations of Horace', Ep. II, i, 279), or to his contrast of
"Shakespear's nature" with "Johnson's art" (*The Dunciad*, Bk II, A 216, B 224).
For Pope, the whole case for the spontaneity of Shakespeare as against any
element of premeditation was evidence to be adduced in the quarrel between
the ancients and the moderns, and in the support of his particular polemic
against Theobald and other 'learned' editors.

13 Schelling means to rescue not only the mature Shakespeare, for whose
mediated and derivative genius he has already argued, but also the youthful

poet from the *Sturm und Drang* image of him as the vehicle of an unconscious emotional outpouring.

14 By "sinful" Schelling presumably means an art not based on recognition of or reconciliation with the gods; "unboundedness" is in this sense not a positive quality, and it is Sophocles who is for him the pinnacle of the dramatic art. The "less well-known source" is Spain, and it is Calderón (whom Schelling knew in A.W. Schlegel's translation) especially who is, so to speak, the "Catholic Shakespeare" (V, 726), and who has less need of the "characteristic" because he can deploy a "true fate" (p. 729): "this highest and absolute composure [Besonnenheit], this ultimate indifference of intention and necessity, is achieved in such a way by Calderón alone among the moderns" (p. 729).

On Dante in Relation to Philosophy

1 This recapitulates the end of the argument of the *System of Transcendental Idealism* (1800), where art is presented as the consummation of philosophy, each being the complement of the other. The lectures on the *Philosophy of Art* (1802–3), had made poetry the highest among the arts:

> Poetry . . . permits the absolute act of cognition [Erkenntnißakt] to appear immediately as an act of cognition, and is thus the highest potency [Potenz] of the plastic arts, as it maintains in synthesis both nature and the character of the ideal, of essence, of the universal. That through which plastic art expresses its ideas is something in itself concrete; the speaking art does it through something in itself *universal*, namely language.   *SW*, V, 631

2 Schelling elsewhere defines the epic as the unity of freedom and necessity without any opposition between finite and infinite. Its action is "timeless" because it does not involve the difference between possibility and actuality which is the basis of time. See *SW*, V, 646, 648.

3 Compare *SW*, V, 554–5:

> An image is *symbolic* when its object not only signifies the idea, but *itself* is the idea, . . . the most completely symbolic representation is afforded by the static and independent poetic form of a particular *mythology*. So St Mary Magdalene not only *signifies* repentance, but she is herself living repentance.

4 Nor, indeed, was it necessary, Schelling means to imply.

5 See also the discussion of *Faust* in *SW*, V, 731–4.

6 For an account of the limited number of Aristotle's texts available to mediaeval scholars, and the consequent Platonized versions of this thought in circulation, see Edwards (1967), article "Aristotelianism".

7 The history of the birth of the soul is recounted by Statius in *Purgatorio*, XXV, 52ff.

8 The aphelion is that part of a planet's orbit when it is furthest from the sun.

9 In the first printing of these notes (DS, 1984) I was unsure whether any single line would fit the literal terms of Schelling's paraphrase. Ronald Martinez suggested *Purgatorio*, VI, 45, reasoning persuasively that the reference would be to the second book of the *Comedy*, since in this and the preceding paragraph Schelling refers to all three books in sequence (see DS, p. 272). Rachel Jacoff has since pointed out to me that most of the references to Beatrice's eyes occur

in *Purgatorio* XXX and XXXI. And indeed there is one line, XXXI, 119, which does seem to correspond to the terms of Schelling's description.

10 *Paradiso*, II, 34f.

11 Presumably in the first canto of the *Purgatorio*, describing the ascent out of hell. Schlegel translated ll. 1–28.

12 Schelling himself repeats this view in *SW*, V, 644.

13 *Paradiso*, XXV, 1–9. I cite from Henry Cary's translation (1805–6, reprinted 1814), which became the one most familiar to nineteenth-century English readers.

14 *Inferno*, XXIX, 1–8.

15 Schelling may have in mind the famous meeting with Paolo and Francesca in *Inferno*, V, or perhaps the wood of the suicides, where men have become trees (*Inferno*, XIII).

16 *Purgatorio*, III–XXVII.

17 *Purgatorio*, XXV.

18 *Paradiso*, III, 88–90.

19 *Inferno*, III, 9.

A.W. SCHLEGEL

Lectures on Dramatic Art and Literature

[These notes are from KMW.]

1 Johann Joachim Winckelmann (1717–68), archaelogist and aesthetician, whose *History of Ancient Art* (1762) powerfully influenced German criticism.

2 Here Schlegel follows closely Herder in his 'Shakespeare' essay in *Von Deutscher Art und Kunst*.

3 François Hemsterhuis (1721–90), Dutch aesthetician and moral philosopher.

4 Pietro Antonio Domenico Buonaventura Metastasio (Pietro Trapassi, 1698–1782), Italian poet. Vittorio Alfieri (1749–1803), Italian dramatist.

5 Schlegel's point is at variance with the views of Friedrich Schlegel and Solger. See Walzel (1938) for discussion of this and other of Schlegel's most important deviations from romantic irony theory.

6 As for example in *Hamlet*, Act III, scene ii, in Hamlet's instructions to the actors.

7 Samuel Johnson, *Preface to Shakespeare*, ed. W.K. Wimsatt (Harmondsworth, 1969), p. 62ff.

8 Here again Schlegel would seem to be in disagreement with his brother, and with Novalis, Solger, and Jean Paul, all of whom had a more synthetic notion of the relation of humour and seriousness. For a discussion of this, see KMW, p. 20ff.

9 See Goethe's 'Zum Shakespeares Tag' (1771) and the *Hamlet* discussion from *Wilhelm Meister* included in this anthology; Goethe's own views underwent considerable change between the writing of these two pieces.

10 The player's speech about Hecuba occurs in *Hamlet*, Act III, scene ii, ll. 270–5.

11 Friedrich Ludwig Schröder (1744–1816), German actor, in charge of the Hamburg Theatre for many years at the end of the century, published alterations and translations of plays.

12 For Shakespeare's handling of the Maid of Orleans legend, see *The First Part of King Henry VI.*

GOETHE

Winckelmann

[These notes are from HBN.]

1 J.J. Winckelmann (1717–68), author of *Thoughts on the Imitation of the Painting and Sculpture of the Greeks* (1755), which marked the beginning of the passion for the Hellenic ideal in German culture. The text is translated in HBN (1985), pp. 32–54.

2 Compare Schiller's parallel distinction between ancients and moderns in his essay *On Naive and Sentimental Poetry.*

3 Winckelmann's role here as an antique spirit in the modern age recalls, and is doubtless to some extent modelled on, that of Goethe himself as portrayed in Schiller's essay.

4 The dire consequences of over-specialisation and the division of labour are a frequent theme in the late eighteenth century in Germany. This problem is discussed at length, with suggested remedies, by Schiller in his *On the Aesthetic Education of Man: In a Series of Letters* (1795): see the bilingual edition of this work, with an excellent introduction and commentary, by Elizabeth M. Wilkinson and L. A. Willoughby (Oxford, 1967), and the selections in the present volume.

5 The following glorification of pagan attitudes is doubtless intended by Goethe in part as a counterblast to the Catholicising tendencies of the German Romantics, which he deplores on various occasions around this time.

6 Mythological figures: Chloris, the only surviving daughter of Niobe, and Thyia, who became by Apollo the mother of Delphus.

7 Friedrich Wilhelm Lamprecht, a pupil of Winckelmann in his school-teaching days, with whom he subsequently lived for a time.

8 *Der sich immer steigernden Natur.* Goethe's concept of *Steigerung* (enhancement, intensification) is evident in many of his poetic works – particularly those which culminate on an ideal or transcendental plane – from *Egmont* to *Faust*, Part II. In the present essay it is combined with the triadic model favoured by Schiller, as in the section on *Antiquity* (above).

9 *Steigert:* see previous note.

10 Lost work by Phidias in gold and ivory, among the most celebrated sculptures of antiquity.

JEAN PAUL RICHTER

School for Aesthetics

Richter's own notes

a Only the majority and minority, the minimum and maximum permit this expression. For no man actually differs qualitatively from another. Like the rise and fall of peoples, the transition from servile childhood to morally free adulthood, which clearly demonstrates evolution through degrees, confutes the proud man who prefers to consider himself distinguished by genus rather than by degree.

b Because he wishes to use the usual muscles for walking on the ground and cannot, while in the heavenly air, he feels no need of muscles for flying.

c Since even in ethics the two classes of *moral sense* and *moral strength* can be distinguished, Rousseau should also be classed as passive.

d This is equally true of the philosophical genius, whom I (unlike Kant) cannot specifically distinguish from the poet.[12] See the reasons for this in *The Campan Valley*, p. 51, which have not yet been refuted. The *inventive* philosophers were all poetic, that is, the truly systematic ones. Something different are the *sifting* philosophers, who never create an organic system, but at best clothe, nourish, amputate, etc. The difference in application between related kinds of genius, however, merits a special, difficult investigation.

e For unreflectiveness in action, i.e., the forgetting of personal relations, agrees so well with poetic and philosophic reflectiveness, that reflection and writing poetry often occur in dream and in madness, where such forgetfulness governs most strongly. The genius is in more than one sense a somnambulist: In his bright dream he can do more than he who is awake, and he climbs every dark height of reality. But rob him of the world of dream, and he tumbles in the real world.

f For pure negation or emptiness would exclude every opposed effort, and negative magnitude would have the same effect as positive.

g As is well known, the vessels in old age become cartilage and the cartilage bones, and earth enters into the body until the body enters the earth.

h Let it be remembered that I have given above the name of *objective* contrast to the contradiction between the ridiculous effort and the sensuously perceived circumstance, but the name *subjective* to a second contradiction, which we attribute to the ridiculous being when we lend *our* knowledge to *its* action.

i *Empfindselig (sensible)*, a coinage of Hamann's, is better than *empfindelnd (sentimental)*, and not merely for the sake of euphony; the former means simply an excessive luxuriating frequency of feeling according to the analogies *redselig, saumselig,* and *friedselig;* but the latter indicates, although incorrectly, a feeling both petty and false.

j But incorrectly, for the comic prepares the pathetic as little as relaxation does tension; rather the reverse is true.

k In this technique he imitated Holberg,[24] Foote, Swift, etc.

l The Persians say, 'Only God can have a self'; the Turks, 'Only the devil says "I".' *Bibliothèque des Philosophes,* by Gautier.

m Every absurdity in *Tristram Shandy*, although for the most part micrological, is a product of human nature not of accidental individuality. If the general, however, is lacking, as in Peter Pindar,[31] no wit can save a book from death. That for many years Walter Shandy has been resolving every time the door creaks to oil it, etc., is our nature, not his alone.

n The further the reader gets into *Tristram Shandy*, the more lyric Sterne's humour becomes. Thus his marvellous journey in the seventh book, the humorous dithyramb in the eighth book (chaps. 11, 12), etc.

o Therefore, as many named particularities as could be tolerated should be made current for *every* German city (they already have their beers). The prime goal would be to place in the hands of the comic writer over a period of time a dictionary and *cadastre flora* of comic individuation. Such a Swabian league of cities would join the separate cities into the very slips or boards of a comic national theatre. The Comicus would then be able to describe more easily and the reader would understand more easily. The lindens, the Tiergarten, the Charité, the Wilhelmshöhe, the Prater, and the terrace of Brühle fortunately provide arable latitude for every individualizing comic poet. But if, for example, the present author chose the proper names of places and circumstances which should be best for comic individuation, because they are best known and well named, from among the few cities where he has lived (Hof, Leipzig, Weimar, Meinungen, Coburg, Bayreuth), he would be little understood and as a result poorly appreciated in any other place.

p In philological, figurative, and sensuous fullness Fischart far surpasses Rabelais and he equals Rabelais in erudition and Aristophanic word-coining. He is more Rabelais's regenerator than his translator; his Pactolus deserved to be panned for gold by the investigators of languages and customs. Here are some traits from his picture of a pretty maid, from his *Historical Sketch* (1590), p. 142: 'Her little cheeks bloomed with roses, and illuminated more brightly the circumfluent air with their reflection like a rainbow, like women coming out of a bath in pictures of the ancients; through her swan-white throat tube one might see the red wine slip as through a Moorish glass; she had a truly alabaster little gullet, a prophyry skin, through which all the veins appeared, like the white and black little stones in a clear little fountain; apple-round and sweetly hard breasts of marble, true apples of Paradise and alabaster balls, finely *decorated* near her heart and nicely *elevated*, not too high like the Swiss and Cologner, not too low like the Dutch, but like the French, etc.' His prose frequently rhymes, sometimes, as in chapter 26, p. 351, to fine effect. The fifth chapter about married people is a masterpiece of sensuous description and observation, but chaste and free as the Bible and our ancestors.

q I.e., more with a series of figurative similies than with an antithesis, as will be shown further in the discussion of figurative wit.

r For our divine service is now mostly held in books.

s The only exception is Hamann, whose commas at times form planetary systems, whose periods become solar systems, and whose words (like those of primitive languages, according to Herder) are whole sentences. Often brevity is easier to write than to read; the author arrives at the expressed thought by merely eliminating incidental ones; the reader must supply the latter from the former.

t An ode can be created in a single day, but *Clarissa*, despite its flaws, cannot be completed even in one year. The ode reflects a single side of the world or of a spirit, while the true novel reflects every side.

Editor's notes (KMW)

1 'Reproductive Imagination' is Hale's rendering of 'Eindildungskraft' in contrast to 'Phantasie', rendered 'imagination', to distinguish active and passive imagination. Jean Paul may be influenced here by the tradition traced by McFarland (1972), in reference to Coleridge's distinction between primary and secondary imagination and fancy. Jean Paul's interest in eighteenth-century English literature, and particularly the influence of Sterne on his style, in conjunction with many Coleridgean theories, is an important reminder of the flow of ideas between Germany and England at this time, and of the fact that the English tradition provided both Jean Paul and Coleridge with a heritage of crit-

ical ideas, more theoretically systematized no doubt by the German tradition, but nevertheless present in the prose and fiction, as Sterne's writings vividly illustrate.

2 *Clavicula Salomonis* refers to the *Key of Solomon*, a Hebrew manuscript ascribed to King Solomon of Israel (tenth century B.C.), supposedly dictated to him by the angels; the treatise is an introduction to the magical arts, full of Greek, Babylonian, Egyptian, and other ancient traditions. It is sometimes known as the 'Secret of Secrets'. Jean Paul further refers to the legend of Solomon's seal or ring, an amulet supposed to control and protect from evil spirits.

3 Karl Ramler (1725–98), aesthetician and editor of *Batteaux, Cours de Belles Lettres* (1756–8). Christian Wolff (1679–1754), follower of Leibniz's philosophy and an important precursor of Kant.

4 M. Hale notes that Edward Young in *Conjectures on Original Composition* (1759), and Alexander Gerard, in *An Essay on Genius* (1764), set precedents for this 'passive genius' concept.

5 Jean Paul probably read Diderot's *Le Neveu de Rameau* in a German translation by Goethe. Jean Paul's *Levana* (1807) may be taken as a reply to Jean Jacques Rousseau's (1712–78) *Emile* (1762).

6 In German 'acumen' is 'Scharfsinn', 'profundity' is 'Tiefsinn'.

7 Karl Philipp Moritz (1757–93), philosopher, author of *Anton Reiser* and *Andreas Hartknopf,* and friend of Goethe and Jean Paul.

8 Helferich Peter Sturz (1757–79), prose writer.

9 Georg Christian Lichtenberg (1742–80), satirist, known for his description of Hogarth's engravings.

10 Christoph Martin Wieland (1733–1813), major critic and creative writer.

11 J.C. Adelung (1732–1806).

12 Kant, *Kritik der Urteilsraft,* §47.

13 Guido Reni (1575–1642), Italian painter.

14 Vittorio Alfieri (1749–1803), Italian dramatist.

15 Friedrich Heinrich Jacobi (1743–1819), German philosopher and novelist, and friend of Jean Paul, well known especially for his *Über die Lehre des Spinoza* (Breslau, 1789).

16 Daniel Peucer (1699–1756), rhetorician, and Daniel Morhof (1639–91), literary historian.

17 Johann Gottwerth Müller von Itzehoe (1743–93).

18 Echo of the title of Wieland's novel *Der Prozess um des Esels Schaffen – Die Geschichte der Abderifen* (The Republic of Fools; being the history of the state and people of Abdera) satirizing philistinism.

19 *Soccus,* the low shoe worn by comic actors, as the *cothurnus* was worn by tragic actors.

20 Louis Sébastien Mercier (1740–1814), *Tableaux de Paris* (1781–90).

21 August von Kotzebue (1761–1819), German dramatist, author of over two hundred plays, many achieving great contemporary popularity.

22 Friedrich Gotter (1746–97).

23 Moritz August von Thümmel (1738–1817), novelist influenced by Sterne, and author of *Reise in die mittägliche Provinzen von Frankreich* (1791–1805).

24 Ludwig von Holberg (1684–1754), Danish comedian.

25 Justus Möser (1720–94).

26 Refers to Jean Paul's *Dr. Fenks Leichenrede.*

27 Ernst Platner, *Gespräch über den Atheismus* (Leipzig, 1783).

28 Fichte used the term to refer to pure selfhood.
29 J.J. Bode (1730–93), translator of numerous English novelists.
30 John Arbuthnot (1667–1735), friend of Pope and Swift.
31 Pseudonym of John Wolcot (1738–1819), physician and author of satires.
32 Marquise Marie de Sévigné (1626–96), whose letters were published in 1726.
33 T.G. von Hippel (1741–96), German humorist.
34 Noted centres of pirated editions; an unauthorized edition of Jean Paul's *School* was published in Vienna in 1815, according to Hale.
35 J.G. Meusel (1743–1820), author of a literary *Who's Who?*
36 Jean Paul refers to the mine invented by de Belidor in 1756, called 'globe de compression'; 'Globulus hystericus' describes a delusion of suffering (according to Hale).
37 *Poetics*, chapter 24.
38 J.B. Basedow (1723–90), *Philalethie* (1764), I, 286.
39 A folk book of 1504.
40 Herder, *Adrastea*, ed. Suphan, XXIII, 295–7.
41 Ernst Wagner (1769–1812), novelist influenced by Jean Paul in, for example, *Wilibalds Ansichten des Lebens* (1804). Friedrich, Baron de la Motte-Fouqué (1777–1843), author of *Undine* (1811), a work that charmed Fouqué's contemporaries from Goethe to Walter Scott, and later Heinrich Heine. Achim von Arnim (1718–1831), novelist noted for his collection of old German folksongs and author of *Aphorismen über die Kunst* (1802).
42 *Poetics*, chapters 23–4.

KARL SOLGER

Erwin

[These notes are from KMW.]

1 Compare Coleridge's definition of the symbol, in the *Statesman's Manual*, almost exactly contemporary with Solger's *Erwin* publication.
2 Henckmann compares Goethe, 'Maxims and Reflections', numbers 279, 1112, 1113; in 314 Goethe writes: 'This is the truly symbolic, where the particular represents the universal, not as dream or shadow, but as the living, momentary revelation of the inscrutable.' And compare Schelling, *Philosophie der Kunst*, §39. For a brief discussion of the relation between Schelling and Solger's aesthetics, see Strohschneider-Kohrs (1960) under the section on Solger. Hegel's relation to Solger is discussed by Kahlert (1846).
3 These comments and the continuation of the passage show that Solger is distinguishing allegory from symbol in a way quite different from that familiar to English readers. That is, he defines 'allegory' differently from, say, Coleridge; his distinction between allegory and symbol implies then either a different valuation of allegory or a quality that falls within our category of the symbol usually not distinguished by us. In the *Vorlesungen*, for example, Solger speaks of the necessity of seeing beauty from two points of veiw depending upon whether the linguistic expression charts movement from appearance to reality (as allegory does) or from reality to appearance (as symbol does); instead, the distinction might be better understood by English readers as between 'allegorical symbol' and 'plastic (tending toward concrete) symbol'. See below, note 4.

4 One might risk suggesting that for Solger 'mere allegory' was 'mere' only because its symbolical energy had suffered 'semantic entropy', and had become inaccessible to later cultures. His discussion here of the Greek gods as symbols bears out this view, and also shows that Solger was aware of the difference between 'what is commonly thought of as allegory' – that is, general concepts or forms or abstractions represented by persons or images – and what *he* defined true allegory to be. The relation between allegory and symbol as basic forms of art is discussed in the Tieck-Solger letters on art and mysticism; see KMW, pp. 154–8.

5 Hegel continues the problem of symbolical versus allegorical art in his discussion of the three world-historical stages of the development of art; symbolical art he links to the Orient, while art developed its highest revelation of essence in the classical art of the Greeks; finally, with romantic, Christian art the plasticity of sensuous appearance is achieved in an internalized, spiritualized fullness.

SCHOPENHAUER

The World as Will and Representation

[Payne's notes are indicated by the initial P. Other notes are by DS.]

1 For Schopenhauer's particular formulation of the relation between concepts and ideas, see below, §49. For the moment it is enough to say that he regards art as capable of expressing (his version of) the Plantonic Idea: that which is essential, eternal, archetypal. His first published work of 1813, *On the Fourfold Root of the Principle of Sufficient Reason* (see 1974b), had taken up the exposition of the inherited maxim or principle of sufficient reason (found in Leibniz among others), that "nothing is without a reason why it is thus and not otherwise"; i.e. everything that there is can be explained by reference to its relation to other things. The fourfold division of the principle covers, for Schopenhauer, all empirical phenomena. Schopenhauer often demanded that all his works be read as a whole, and he here presumes acquaintance with this earlier work.

2 One of the hallmarks of Schopenhauer's style is his frequent use of words of English or French origin (he did briefly attend school in London), e.g. "Inspiration", "Motivation". Sometimes the foreign word and the German word alternate with apparent synonymity, e.g. "Kontemplation" will alternate with "Betrachtung". One can sense here a conscious campaign against the ideas expressed in Fichte and Hegel about the need to produce an authentic German Language in philosophy (not that they always obeyed the rule themselves).

3 Schopenhauer does intend to preserve the Kantian use of *Anschauung* and its compounds, as referring to an empirical experience, and the translation "intuition" which I have generally adopted throughout this anthology is admitted by Payne (1969, I, viii-ix) as a possible alternative.

4 Goethe's *Faust*, Bayard Taylor's translation [P]. The citation is from the end of the prologue in heaven (*Faust*, Pt. I). God is addressing the archangels, and bestowing creative power upon them.

5 Kant had defined both an empirical and a transcendental "apperception" as making possible the synthesis that constitutes experience.

6 I.e. Bk. II, the selections here being taken from Bk. III. The idea of art going

beyond nature, and perfecting what nature alone can never perfect because it is the forum of the various struggles of objectified will, is a point of contrast between Schopenhauer and Schelling.

7 The word used by Schopenhauer is *gemütlich* [P]. In his remarks on the imagination [Phantasie] Schopenhauer does not invoke the Kantian *Einbildungskraft*, which is the connective principle in ordinary perception, but refers to the distinction between true perception of the Idea and mere loose association or interest-dominated representation. See below.

8 For Schopenhauer, the whole physical form of a person is the expression of the will, and this leads him at times to a completely 'scientific' model of the relation between human organs and the kind of will they express. Thus

it must really be possible to understand and deduce not only the nature of his intellect from that of his brain and from the blood-flow that excites this, but also the whole of his moral character with all its traits and peculiarities from the more specific nature of all the rest of his corporization, thus from the texture, size, quality, and mutal relation of heart, liver, lungs, spleen, kidneys, and so on, although, of course, we shall never succeed in actually achieving this. But the possibility of doing this must exist objectively.   (1974a), II, 176

Speculations about the scientific credibility of phrenology and physiognomy were widespread in the eighteenth and nineteenth centuries. Compare Schiller's case for the outward visibility of inner moral identity in *On Grace and Dignity* (1943–), XX, 251f.

9 Compare Shelley (1977), p. 507:

But in the intervals of inspiration, and they may be frequent without being durable, a poet becomes a man, and is abandoned to the sudden reflux of the influences under which others habitually live.

10 One of Schopenhauer's earlier works, *On Vision and Colours* (1816), was a defence of Goethe's theory of colours against the Newtonian tradition; see also (1974a), II, 177–200. The argument about the applicability of a notion of genius to the sciences or to mathematics recalls Schelling in the *System*. It might also be noted that Kant had seen mathematics as offering important evidence for the deduction of synthetic *a priori* propositions (then as now the subject of debate), i.e. as independent of and prior to the recombination of memorized or previously experienced data.

11 "What does all that prove?"[P].

12 I.e. by the principle of sufficient reason [Satz vom Grunde]. Schopenhauer's 'proof' of the relation between genius and madness, and his argument for the necessary eccentricity of the genius, would not have pleased those of his predecessors who were concerned, as Kant had been, to regulate the energies of genius by the rules of the understanding, without which no shared experience could occur.

13 "There has been no great mind without an admixture of madness" [P].

14 "For Democritus asserts that there can be no great poet without madness, and Plato says the same thing" [P].

15 From Dryden's *Absalom and Achitophel*, I, 163; not from Pope as attributed by Schopenhauer [P]. Schopenhauer quotes in English.

16 Compare vol. II, ch. 31 [P].

17 It is worth pointing out how much of Schopenhauer's exposition so far has concentrated on the artist, the man of genius. Kant's priority had always been the analysis of the aesthetic *response* and of the judgement involved therein.

18 Compare (1974), I, 317:

Differences of rank and wealth give everyone his part to play, but there is certainly not an internal difference of happiness and satisfaction that corresponds to that role. On the contrary, here too there is in everyone the same poor wretch with his worries and wants. Materially these may be different in everyone, but in form and thus in their essential nature they are pretty much the same in all, although with differences of degree which do not by any means correspond to position and wealth . . .

19 I.e. of particular kinds of art and objects.

20 The two polar principles of the Zoroastrian religion, always at war with one another until the eventual expulsion of the evil by the good (but Schopenhauer would not have gone this far!).

   The relation between light and spirituality (see also (1969), I, 216) was of course traditional and commonplace, but it was also of special interest to the Romantic generation. Schelling, in the *Philosophy of Art* (*SW*, V, 507), declares that "Light is the ideal appearing in nature, the first breakthrough of idealism. The *idea itself* is *light*, but *absolute* light."

21 In the *Anthropology*; see (1974), pp. 33f. (§16). See also Hegel's remarks in the *Aesthetics* (*SW*, XII, 67–8), below.

22 Compare vol. II, ch. 33 [P].

23 "I am now all the more delighted and surprised, forty years after advancing this thought so timidly and hesitatingly, to discover that St Augustine had already expressed it: 'Arbusta formas suas varias, quibus mundi hujus visibilis structura formosa est, sentiendas sensibus praebent; ut, pro eo quod NOSSE non possunt, quasi INNOTESCERE velle videantur.' (*De Civitate Dei*, xi, 27.)" [Schopenhauer's own note.] "The trees offer to the senses for perception the many different forms by which the structure of this visible world is adorned, so that, because they are unable to *know*, they may appear, as it were, to want to *be known*" [P]. Since the perfection of plant forms cannot be attributed to an active intelligence contemplating itself, an extrinsic intelligence (in the beholder) is required for these forms to appear as representations. Compare §42.

24 For Kant's relation of morality and the sublime, see *CJ*, §29, and my remarks in the general introduction. The reference to scholasticism may be in reaction to Kant's use of the distinction between *apprehensio* and *comprehensio* (*CJ*, §26f.).

25 See §§30–5 on the Idea, and the early sections of the work for the explanation of the concept. The argument is briefly summarized in what follows.

26 I.e. "unity after the fact" and "unity before the fact".

27 The distinction between analytical and synthetic is a Kantian one; see Kant (1933), pp. 48ff. (A 7f., B 11f.).

28 "Imitators, the slavish mob" [P]. Horace, *Epist.*, I, xix, 19.

29 *Apparent rari, nantes in gurgite vasto.* [Schopenhauer's own note.] "Singly they appear, swimming by in the vast waste of waves." Virgil, *Aeneid*, I, 118 [P]. Appropriately, given Schopenhauer's view of the fate of excellence, the reference is to the wreck of Aeneas' ships and to the sight of his crew trying to save themselves from drowning.

30 Compare vol. II, ch. 34 [P].

HEGEL

Aesthetics: Lectures on Fine Art

[Knox's notes are indicated by the inital K. Other notes are by DS.]

1 By "theoretical" and "practical" Hegel does not invoke the strict Kantian use of the terms, where they would correspond respectively to the laws of the empirical understanding and of the moral faculty. His idea of the "practical" would seem to include the modifications wrought by Fichte in connecting ordinary purposive activity or mere appetite with the higher faculty of desire, the one preparing the way for the other. The "theoretical" activity is, roughly, contemplative activity. See *SW*, XII, 65 (below):

The theoretical study of things is not interested in consuming them in their individuality and satisfying itself and maintaining itself sensuously by means of them, but in coming to know them in their *universality*, finding their inner essence and law, and conceiving them in accordance with their concept.

Hegel's *Begriff* (concept) is also much more active than Kant's, and should be thought of as a necessary principle actually bringing into being that in which it is perceived or thought.
2 See also Kant, *CJ*, §41. Hegel makes clear his negative attitude toward an undifferentiated primitive condition, and his conviction that the development of socially implicated forms of self-representation (the recognition of self as and through other) is a necessary step beyond it. This process may however involve perverse forms and is not always instinct with *Geist*. On *Bildung*, see Gadamer (1975), pp. 10–19.
3. See, for example, *Briefe über die Empfindungen* (1755), or *Betrachtungen über die Quellen und die Verbindungen der schönen Künste und Wissenschaften* (1757) [K]. The following remarks against the aesthetics of mere "feeling" had been paralleled in Britain by the arguments of the Romantic generation against the literature of "sensibility".
4 See *Aesthetics* (1975), pp. 16ff. [K].
5 See *Aesthetics* (1975), pp. 14f. [K].
6 Hegel's use of *Objekt* and *Gegenstand* here would seem to be symmetrical with Kant's: see note 2 to *CJ*.
7 On this division of the senses, see Kant, *Anthropology*, §15f. The status of art as appearance [*Schein*] had been important to Kant, and also to Schiller, for example in *AE*. For Hegel's general placing of *Schein*, see *Phenomenology*, paragraphs 132f.; *Science of Logic* (1969), pp. 394–408; *Encyclopaedia*, §§131ff. See also Taylor (1975), pp. 273–9, and compare *SW*, XII, 78–9 (below). *Schein* has an integral status but one which is yet recognized and thought beyond. Unlike Schelling, who had dignified both mind and nature as instinct with spirit and with the ideal, and who could celebrate art precisely because it fuses the two together, Hegel operates with a model of the evolution of spirit *from* nature and matter.
8 Or, roughly, ideal prototypes to which actual objects never precisely correspond. For the technical functions of schemata in Kant, not very specifically invoked here, see Kant (1933), A 137ff, B 176ff.
9 *SW*, XII, 70, reads "als bewußtes Wirken", which makes no sense; Hotho and other reprints of his text read "bewußtloses", i.e. "unconscious". There had been much speculation on the presence or absence of genius in scientific inves-

tigation: see note 10 to Schopenhauer, *The World as Will and Representation*; and Fichte, *On the Nature of the Scholar*, lecture III, in DS, pp. 97–102.

10 Knox notes the apparent contradiction with *Aesthetics*, p. 28:

> In poetry . . . the spirit and heart must be richly and deeply educated by life, experience, and reflection before genius can bring into being anything mature, of sterling worth, and complete in itself. The first productions of Goethe and Schiller are of an immaturity, yes even of a crudity and barbarity, that can be terrifying.

But Hegel is not necessarily implying here that youthful energies produce works of genius – just that they forecast its development.

11 *Aesthetics*, p. 25 [K].

12 *Travels to Discover the Source of the Nile*, 3rd edn (London, 1813), VI, 526–7. Hegel quotes from memory, and usually inaccurately, but here he has given the gist of the story accurately enough for his purposes [K]. The first edition of Bruce's work had been translated into German, at Leipzig, in 5 volumes (1790).

13 The Sunna is a body of traditions incorporating the history of Mahomet's life and so is a sort of supplement to the Koran [K].

14 For Zeuxis, see e.g. Pliny, *Natural History*, XXXV, 36. J.F. Blumenbach told a story of an old fellow-student of Linnaeus called Büttner [?C.W., 1716–81, professor at Göttingen], who put all his money into books and acquired a copy of Rösel's book (published 1746–55) with coloured plates [K]. Both these examples of the deceptive power of art are cited within a few lines of each other by Goethe in his dialogue "On Truth and Probability in Works of Art", *Propyläen*, I, ii (1798). See Goethe (1980), p. 29.

15 *CJ*, §42 [K]. See also the remark following §22 (*CJ*, I, 89).

16 I have been unable to trace the source of this story [K].

17 Terence, *Heauton Timorumenos*, I, i, 25. "I count nothing human indifferent to me." As usual Hegel quotes inaccurately [K].

18 Hegel uses the French word, and presumably means to invoke the achievement of the French Enlightenment in removing superstition, and this in both positive and negative moments. See the discussion in *Phenomenology*, paragraphs 538ff. While clearing the ground of prejudices and mysteries, the Enlightenment still bears within it "the blemish of an unsatisfied yearning" (paragraph 573).

19 "The story teaches." *Aesthetics*, p. 385, shows that Hegel regarded these words in the Greek text of Aesop's fables (ὁ μῦθος δηλοῖ) as a corrupt, later addition.

20 "Poets wish alike to benefit and to please"; *Ars Poetica*, 1. 333 [K].

21 I have not been able to discover a precise source for this view, which is yet frustratingly familiar. The reference is most probably to a comment made about Correggio's Dresden Magdalene, to which Hegel himself alludes (*Aesthetics*, p. 868; cf. pp. 549–50). The inherent graciousness and beauty of the painting had often been noted, e.g. by Raphael Mengs and by Friedrich Schlegel (1849), p. 24. But there were also many seventeenth-century versions of the subject, any one of which might have inspired this ironic remark.

22 Hegel makes a clear distinction between *Sittlichkeit* and *Moralität*. The former indicates the conventional values of a community, to which we owe allegiance as its members (the other meaning of *sittlich* is thus "customary"). *Moralität* is that which pertains to us as universal, independent rational wills, rather in the spirit of the Kantian categorical imperative. See C. Taylor (1975), pp. 365–88.

23 This is a restatement (further expounded in the next two paragraphs) of

Hegel's view of the effects of Kant's system on the ethical thinking of his generation, instituting a radical separation or strife between the empirical and the moral will. Hegel generally regarded Kant as having bequeathed a series of unfortunate dualisms to philosophy; but he also saw these divisions as a necessary historical moment, an expression of the spirit of the late Enlightenment. Like Fichte and Schelling before him, Hegel saw his own function to be the reconciliation of these divisions between ideal and empirical, noumena and phenomena, independent selfhood and wider community. Alienation has a central and inevitable place, but through time it can prospectively be overcome. In what follows, Hegel declares for the truthfulness of Kant's claim for art as standing outside didactic limitations, but insists that it has an essential content in itself: the setting forth of the reconciled opposition between spirit and nature. For Hegel on Kant and the Kantian inheritance, see *Aesthetics*, pp. 56–61; *Encyclopaedia*, §§40ff.; Hegel (1892), III, 423ff.; and Taylor (1975), pp. 29–36.

24 With this discussion we rejoin the lectures after Hegel has been through not only the theoretical analysis of the aesthetic but also the various (roughly) historical genres of art: the symbolic (early, pre-classical and oriental art), the classical, and the romantic, which begins in the middle ages (as it had for Schelling and others). This evolution is summarized in the following paragraph, and Hegel then goes on to describe the contemporary situation.

25 This is an important statement of the relation of the artist to his *Weltanschauung*. The standard translation of this term, as "world-view", unfortunately loses the foothold that Hegel's use of *Anschauung* always has in its Kantian context: it signifies an embodied, empirical intuition. This is why the artist, when in earnest, is at one with the actuality of this world-view; he *is* its empirical expression. This actualized intuition also explains why art is understood as significant by its wider community. Schelling's idea of *Mythologie* should be compared here.

26 Schiller and Schelling, among others, had also insisted on the futility of merely reproducing or copying rather than in some way recreating the spirit of ancient art, or of any art of the past. Behind the whole discussion we may sense the spectre of Winckelmann, who had declared ((1765), p. 2) that "There is but one way for the moderns to become great, and perhaps unequalled; I mean, by imitating the antients."

27 Consequently for Hegel, unlike Schelling in the *System*, a further stage is necessary in which release from the 'natural side' may take place. As Hegel goes on to explain, it is this longing which Romantic art dramatizes, signalling as it does so the imminent end of all art and the passage into pure thought, or philosophy (Romantic art being itself the expression of a religious world-view, as it is religion which precedes the emergence of philosophy in Hegel's scheme).

28 It would seem to follow from this that, whatever the relative status of art as a whole (highest in classical civilization), the individual artist is yet the most sensitive barometer of the changes happening or about to happen in the world-view. Similarly for Shelley (1977), p. 508, poets are "the mirrors of the gigantic shadows which futurity casts upon the present". Shelley does however accord the poetic more formative power than does Hegel, for whom the whole relation of the artist to his times is more potentially disjunctive or tragical.

29 Kant and his followers were often spoken of as the exponents of the "critical philosophy", and Kant himself had stressed the nature of the *Kritik* as a 'neg-

ative' analysis, narrowing the limits of what can properly be thought or argued by exposing what cannot be so thought or argued.

30 There had been a widespread fashion for Catholicism during the early years of the nineteenth century. The most famous conversion was that of Friedrich Schlegel, who began as the exponent of Romantic irony, seeking to avoid (in Hegel's eyes) all accountable relations to any form of worldly engagement or dogma, and then went through a period of pantheist idealism (around 1804–6) before declaring for Catholicism in 1808.

31 See note 24 to Kant, *CJ*.

32 See note 17, above.

33 See *Aesthetics* (1975), pp. 421ff.

34 *Witz* and *Phantasie* were among the major conceptual terms in Solger's *Vorlesungen über Aesthetik* (Leipzig, 1829), first delivered in 1819. It is not clear that a direct allusion is intended, and the terms are certainly common elsewhere, but Hegel did respect Solger as a serious exponent of the spirit of the age, and gave him much more credit than he extended to other theorists of irony. For Hegel's views on irony, see *Aesthetics*, pp. 64–9; Hegel (1967), pp. 101–2; and the review of Solger in Hegel (1956), pp. 155ff.

35 In *Die künftige Geliebte* (*The Future Sweetheart*), 1747 [K].

36 Goethe's *West-östliche Divan*, composed under the inspiration of the very Persian and Arabic poetry just commended by Hegel, was begun in 1814 when the poet was sixty-five.

37 This is another summary of the evolution of art through history, and it conflates the formal or theoretical sequence (symbolic–classical–romantic) with particular art forms (architecture–sculpture–painting). This relation of the historical and the generic has caused some debate. Karelis (1979), pp. lxi-lxiii, xlviii-xlix, has argued (following R.S. Lucas) for an 'affinity thesis' in which specific art forms correspond significantly to the historical trichotomy, but do not exhaust it, nor are they exclusively determined by it. Thus architecture is predominantly related to the symbolic, sculpture to the classical, and painting, music and poetry to the romantic; though there obviously can be and has been a classical poetry or a romantic architecture, and so forth, the point is that certain art forms best express the major moments in the evolution of *Geist*. See Hegel's own explanation; *SW*, XIV, 230, below. In what follows, it should be understood that poetry inaugurates the final stage in romantic art as it tends toward its own dissolution.

38 Unlike Schopenhauer, who was ready to define music as the highest of the arts because it is the pure expression of will, not limited by embodiment in an Idea, Hegel insists on the relation of art to self-consciousness. Thus, because of its existence in language, the most appropriate medium of self-consciousness, poetry is the genre through which art most efficiently cancels itself. Music does not provide any material for self-consciousness; thus Kant had remarked that by music, "all said and done, nothing is thought" (*CJ*, §54; compare *Anthropology*, §71).

39 Hegel carries his case for the importance of the (spiritual) content of poetry so far as to suggest that it can even survive translation – not a view shared by many Romantic critics or writers, even where they accept some unifying principle for poetry and prose, as Wordsworth and Shelley do. Indeed, for Hegel, the self-consciousness of spirit achieved in poetry could be said to be already translating itself into the prose of thought, which (as incorporating revealed religion) is the goal of his system.

Bibliography

Abrams, M.H. 1953. *The Mirror and the Lamp: Romantic Theory and the Critical Tradition*. London, Oxford, New York.

1971. *Natural Supernaturalism: Tradition and Revolution in Romantic Literature*. New York.

Allison, Henry E. 1966. *Lessing and the Enlightenment*. Ann Arbor, Michigan.

Arnold, Matthew. 1960–78. *The Complete Prose Works of Matthew Arnold*. Ed. R.H. Super, 11 vols. Ann Arbor.

Ashton, Rosemary. 1980. *The German Idea: Four English Writers and the Reception of German Thought, 1800–1860*. Cambridge.

Barnard, F.M. 1965. *Herder's Social and Political Thought. From Enlightenment to Nationalism*. Oxford.

Barrack, C.M. 1971. 'Novalis' Metaphysic of the Poet'. *Germanic Review* 46, 257–81.

Baumgartner, Hans Michael and Jacobs, Wilhelm G. 1968. *J. G. Fichte-Bibliographie* Stuttgart–Bad Canstatt.

Bell, David. 1984. *Spinoza in Germany from 1670 to the Age of Goethe*. London.

Bennett, Jonathan. 1966. *Kant's Analytic*. Cambridge.

1974. *Kant's Dialectic*. Cambridge.

Berend. E. 1909. *Jean Pauls Aesthetik*. Berlin.

1963. *Jean Paul-Bibliographie*. Rev. J. Krogoll. Stuttgart.

Berlin, Isaiah. 1976. *Vico and Herder: Two Studies in the History of Ideas*. New York.

Birzniks, Paul. 1966. 'Jean Paul's Early Theory of Poetic Communication'. *Germanic Review*, 41, 186–201.

Blackall, Eric A. 1959. *The Emergence of German as a Literary Language, 1700–1775*. Cambridge.

Boucher, Maurice. 1934. *K.W.F. Solger: esthétique et philosophie de la présence*. Paris.

Brewer, Éduard V. 1943. 'The New England Interest in Jean Paul'. *Modern Philology*, 27, 1–25.

Brown, F. Andrew, 1971. *Gotthold Ephraim Lessing*. New York.

Brown, Marshall. 1979. *The Shape of German Romanticism*. Ithaca and London.

Brown, Robert F. 1977. *The Later Philosophy of Schelling: The Influence of Boehme on the Works of 1809–15*. Lewisburg and London.

Bruford, W.H. 1935. *Germany in the Eighteenth Century: The Social Background of the Literary Revival*. Cambridge. Reprinted 1965.

1949 'Goethe's Reputation in England Since 1832', in *Essays on Goethe*, ed. William Rose, pp. 187–206. London.

1962. *Culture and Society in Classical Weimar, 1775–1806*. Cambridge. Reprinted 1975.

Burke, Edmund, 1759. *A Philosophical Enquiry into the Origin of our Ideas of the Sublime and Beautiful.* 2nd edn. London.

Carlyle, Thomas. 1845. *The Life of Friedrich Schiller.* 2nd edn. London.

1900. *Critical and Miscellaneous Essays.* New York.

Cassirer, Ernst. 1945. *Rousseau, Kant, Goethe.* Trans. James Gutmann, Paul Oskar Kristeller, and John Herman Randall Jr. Princeton.

1951. *The Philosophy of the Enlightenment.* Trans. F.C.A. Koelln and J.P. Pettegrove. Princeton.

1953–57. *The Philosophy of Symbolic Forms.* Trans. Ralph Manheim. 3 vols. New Haven.

1981. *Kant's Life and Thought.* Trans. James Haden. New Haven and London.

Cassirer, H.W. 1938. *A Commentary on Kant's 'Critique of Judgement'.* London.

Clark, R.T. 1955. *Herder: His Life and Thought.* Berkeley and Los Angeles.

Coleman, Francis X.J. 1974. *The Harmony of Reason: A Study in Kant's Aesthetics.* Pittsburgh.

Coleridge, Samuel Taylor. 1972. *Lay Sermons.* Ed. R.J. White. London and Princeton.

Conrady, Karl-Otto. 1982–83. *Goethe: Leben und Werk.* 2 vols. Königstein/Taunus.

Copleston, Frederick, S.J. 1964a. *A History of Philosophy. Vol. VI, Pt 1: The French Enlightenment to Kant.* Garden City, N.Y.

1964b. *A History of Philosophy. Vol. VI, Pt 2: Kant.* Garden City, N.Y.

1965a. *A History of Philosophy. Vol. VII, Pt 1: Fichte to Hegel.* Garden City, N.Y.

1965b. *A History of Philosophy. Vol. VII, Pt 2: Schopenhauer to Nietzsche.* Garden City, N.Y.

Crawford, Donald W. 1974. *Kant's Aesthetic Theory.* Madison and London.

Dante Alighieri. 1908. *The Divine Comedy.* Trans. Henry Cary. London and New York.

De Quincey, Thomas. 1889–90. *The Collected Writings of Thomas de Quincey.* Ed. David Masson. 14 vols. Edinburgh.

Dewhurst, Kenneth, and Reeves, Nigel. 1978. *Friedrich Schiller: Medicine, Psychology and Literature.* Oxford.

Dieckmann, Liselotte. 1959. 'Friedrich Schlegel and the Romantic Concepts of the Symbol'. *Germanic Review,* 34, 276–83.

Drummond, Rt. Hon. William. 1805. *Academical Questions. Volume One.* London.

Dyck, Martin. 1960. *Novalis and Mathematics. A Study of Friedrich von Hardenberg's 'Fragments on Mathematics' and its Relation to Magic, Music, Religion, Philosophy, Language and Literature.* Chapel Hill.

Edwards, Paul. Ed. 1967. *The Encyclopaedia of Philosophy.* London and New York.

Eichner, Hans. 1955. 'The Supposed Influence of Schiller's *Naive and Sentimental Poetry* on Friedrich Schlegel's *Ueber das Studium der griechischen Poesie'. Germanic Review,* 30, 260–64.

1956. 'Friedrich Schlegel's Theory of Romantic Poetry'. *PMLA,* 71, 1018–41.

1970. *Friedrich Schlegel.* New York.

Eisler, Rudolf. 1961. *Kant Lexicon.* 1930; rpt. Hildesheim.

Ellis, J.M. 1969. *Schiller's 'Kalliasbriefe' and the Study of his Aesthetic Theory.* The Hague and Paris.

Engelbrecht, H.C. 1933. *Johann Gottlieb Fichte: A Study of his Political Writings with special reference to his Nationalism.* New York.

Engell, James. 1981. *The Creative Imagination: Enlightenment to Romanticism.* Cambridge, Mass. and London.

Esposito, Joseph L. 1977. *Schelling's Idealism and Philosophy of Nature.* Lewisburg and London.

Ewton, R.W. 1972. *The Literary Theories of August Wilhelm Schlegel.* The Hague.

Fackenheim, Emil L. 1954. 'Schelling's Philosophy of the Literary Arts'. *Philosophical Quarterly*, 4, 310–26.

Fairley, Barker. 1947. *A Study of Goethe.* Oxford.

Fautek, H. 1940. 'Die Sprachtheorie Friedrich von Hardenbergs'. *Neue Forschungen.* 34. Berlin.

Fichte, Johann Gottlieb. 1845. *Johann Gottlieb Fichtes sämmtliche Werke.* Ed. I.H. Fichte. 8 vols. Berlin.

1847. *The Characteristics of the Present Age.* Trans. William Smith. London.

1889a. *The Popular Works of Johann Gottlieb Fichte.* Trans. William Smith. 4th ed. 2 vols. London.

1889b. *The Science of Rights.* Trans. A.E. Kroeger. Preface by William T. Harris. London.

1907. *The Science of Ethics as Based on the Science of Knowledge.* Trans. A.E. Kroeger. Ed. W.T. Harris. London.

1956. *The Vocation of Man.* Ed. Roderick M. Chisholm. Indianapolis and New York.

1964–. *J.G. Fichte: Gesamtausgabe der Bayerischen Akademie der Wissenschaften.* Ed. Reinhard Lauth, Hans Jacob, Hans Gliwitzky etc. In progress. Stuttgart and Bad Canstatt.

1967. *J.G. Fichte: Briefwechsel.* Ed. Hans Schulz. 2 vols. Hildesheim.

1968. *Addresses to the German Nation.* Trans. R.F. Jones & G.H. Turnbull. Ed. and revised George Armstrong Kelly. New York and Evanston.

1970. *Fichte: 'Science of Knowledge' (Wissenschaftslehre).* Ed. and trans. Peter Heath and John Lachs. New York.

1978. *Attempt at a Critique of all Revelation.* Trans. Garrett Green. Cambridge.

Friedenthal, Richard. 1965. *Goethe: His Life and Times.* London.

Gadamer, Hans-Georg. 1975. *Truth and Method.* Trans. Garrett Barden and John Cumming. New York.

Garland, H.B. 1949. *Schiller.* London.

1962. *Lessing: The Founder of Modern German Literature.* 2nd edn. London.

Gay, Peter. 1966. *The Enlightenment, An Interpretation. Volume I: The Rise of Modern Paganism.* New York.

1969. *The Enlightenment, An Interpretation. Volume II: The Science of Freedom.* New York.

Gillies, Alexander. 1945. *Herder.* Oxford.

Glockner, Herman. 1957. *Hegel-Lexicon.* 2nd (revised) edn. 2 vols. Stuttgart.

Goethe, Johann Wolfgang von. 1824. *Wilhelm Meister's Apprenticeship.* Trans. Thomas Carlyle. 3 vols. Edinburgh and London.

1887–1919. *Werke.* 133 vols. Weimar.

1948–60. *Goethes Werke, Briefe und Gespräche.* Gedenkausgabe. Ed. Ernst Beutler. 24 vols. Zurich.

1948–64. *Goethes Werke.* Ed. Erich Trunz. 14 vols. Hamburg.

1962. *The Italian Journey, 1786–88.* Trans. W.H. Auden and Elizabeth Mayer. New York and London.

1964. *Literary Essays.* Ed. J.E. Spingarn. New York.

1966. *Conversations and Encounters.* Trans. David Luke and Robert Pick. Chicago and London.

1971. *Eckermann's Conversations with Goethe.* Trans. John Oxenford, ed. J.K. Moorhead. London and New York.

1974. *The Autobiography of Johann Wolfgang von Goethe.* Trans. John Oxenford. 2 vols. Chicago and London.

1980. *Goethe on Art.* Ed. John Gage. Berkeley and Los Angeles.

Guéroult, Martial. 1930. *L'évolution et la structure de la doctrine de la science chez Fichte.* 2 vols. Paris.

Guyer, Paul. 1979. *Kant and the Claims of Taste.* Cambridge, Mass., and London.

Haering, T. 1954. *Novalis als Philosoph.* Stuttgart.

Hamlyn, D.W. 1980. *Schopenhauer: The Arguments of the Philosophers.* London, Boston, and Henley.

Handwerk, Gary. 1985. *Irony and Ethics in Narrative: From Schlegel to Lacan.* New Haven and London.

Hatfield, Henry. 1964. *Aesthetic Paganism in German Literature from Winckelmann to the Death of Goethe.* Cambridge, Mass.

Haym, Rudolf. 1880–85. *Herder.* 2 vols. New edition, Berlin, 1954.

Hazlitt, William. 1930. *Selected Essays of William Hazlitt.* Ed. Geoffrey Keynes. New York and London.

1930–34. *The Complete Works of William Hazlitt.* Ed. P.P. Howe. 21 vols. London and Toronto.

Hegel, George Wilhelm Friedrich. 1892. *Hegel's Lectures on the History of Philosophy.* Trans. E.S. Haldane. 3 vols. Rpt. London and New York, 1963.

1949–59. *Sämtliche Werke.* Jubiläumsausgabe in 20 vols. 3rd printing. Ed. Ludwig Boumann etc., newly arranged by Herman Glockner. Stuttgart.

1956. *Berliner Schriften, 1818–31.* Ed. J. Hoffmeister. Hamburg.

1967. *Hegel's Philosophy of Right.* Trans. T.M. Knox. 1952; rpt. Oxford, London, New York.

1969. *Hegel's Science of Logic.* Trans. A.V. Miller. Introduction by J.N. Findlay. London and New York.

1971. *Hegel's Philosophy of Mind.* Trans. William Wallace. Oxford.

1975. *Hegel's Aesthetics: Lectures on Fine Art.* Trans. T.M. Knox. 2 vols. continuously paginated. Oxford.

1977. *The Difference Between Fichte's and Schelling's System of Philosophy.* Trans. H.S. Harris and Walter Cerf. Albany, New York.

1979. *Phenomenology of Spirit.* Trans. A.V. Miller. Introduction by J.N. Findlay. Oxford.

1980. *Lectures on the Philosophy of World History. Introduction: Reason in History.* Trans. H.B. Nisbet. Introduction by Duncan Forbes. 1975; rpt. Cambridge.

Henel, H. 1945. 'Friedrich Schlegel und die Grundlagen der modernen literarischen Kritik'. *Germanic Review,* 20, 81–93.

Herder, Johann Gottfried. 1877–1913. *Sämtliche Werke.* Ed. B. Suphan. 33 vols. Berlin.

1962. *God. Some Conversations.* Trans. Frederick H. Burkhardt. Third ed. Indianapolis and New York.

1967. *Essay on the Origin of Language* [with Rousseau, *Essay on the Origin of Languages*]. Trans. John H. Moran and Alexander Gode. New York.

1968. *Reflections on the Philosophy of the History of Mankind.* Trans. T.O. Churchill (1800). Ed. Frank E. Manuel. Chicago and London.

1969. *J.G. Herder on Social and Political Culture.* Trans. and ed. F.M. Barnard. Cambridge.

1977–85. *Briefe. Gesamtausgabe* 1763–1803. Ed. Karl-Heinz Hahn. 8 vols. Weimar.

Hipple, W.J. 1957. *The Beautiful, the Sublime and the Picturesque in Eighteenth-Century British Aesthetic Theory.* Carbondale, Illinois.

Hirsch, E.D., Jr. 1960. *Wordsworth and Schelling: A Typological Study of Romanticism.* New Haven.

Hofstadter, Albert, and Kuhns, Richard. 1964. Eds. *Philosophies of Art and Beauty: Selected Readings in Aesthetics from Plato to Heidegger;* rpt. Chicago, 1976.

Howard, William Guild, ed. 1910. *'Laokoon': Lessing, Goethe, Herder.* New York.

Hübscher, Arthur. 1981. *Schopenhauer-Bibliographie.* Stuttgart–Bad Canstatt.

Hume, David. 1912. *Essays Moral, Political, and Literary.* Ed. T.H. Green and T.H. Grose. 2 vols. London.

Immerwahr, Raymond. 1951. 'The Subjectivity or Objectivity of Friedrich Schlegel's Poetic Irony'. *Germanic Review,* 26, 173–91.

1957. 'Friedrich Schlegel's Essay "On Goethe's *Wilhelm Meister*"'. *Monatsheft,* 49, 1–22.

Kahlert, B.A. 1846. *System der Aesthetik.* Leipzig.

Kaminsky, Jack. 1962. *Hegel on Art: An Interpretation of Hegel's Aesthetics.* New York.

Kant, Immanuel. 1900–42. *Kants gesammelte Schriften.* Published by the Königlich Preussische Akademie der Wissenschaften. 22 vols. Berlin.

1933. *Immanuel Kant's Critique of Pure Reason.* Trans. Norman Kemp Smith. 2nd impression with corrections. London.

1935. *Immanuel Kant on Philosophy in General.* Trans. Humayun Kabir. Calcutta.

1952. *The Critique of Judgement.* Trans. James Creed Meredith. Two parts in one volume. Oxford.

1956. *Critique of Practical Reason.* Trans. Lewis White Beck. Indianapolis and New York.

1960. *Observations on the Feeling of the Beautiful and Sublime.* Trans. John T. Goldthwait. Berkeley and Los Angeles.

1963. *Kant on History.* Trans. Lewis White Beck. Indianapolis and New York.

1974. *Anthropology from a Practical Point of View.* Trans. Mary J. Gregor. The Hague.

Karelis, Charles. 1979. *Hegel's Introduction to Aesthetics.* Trans. T.M. Knox. Ed. with an interpretative essay by Charles Karelis. Oxford.

Kemp-Smith, Norman. 1923. *A Commentary to Kant's 'Critique of Pure Reason'.* 2nd (revised) edn. New York.

Kerry, S.S. 1961. *Schiller's Writings on Aesthetics.* Manchester.

Klapper, M. Roxana. 1975. *The German Literary Influence on Shelley.* Salzburg Studies in English Literature; Romantic Reassessment. Salzburg.

Knox, Israel. 1936. *The Aesthetic Theories of Kant, Hegel, and Schopenhauer.* New York.

Kohlschmidt, Werner. 1975. *A History of German Literature, 1760–1805.* Trans. Ian Hilton. London.

Körner, Stephan. 1955. *Kant.* Harmondsworth, Middx.

Lange, Victor. 1955. 'Friedrich Schlegel's Literary Criticism'. *Comparative Literature,* 7, 289–305.

1982. *The Classical Age of German Literature, 1740–1815.* London.

Léon, Xavier. 1922–27. *Fichte et son temps.* 2 parts in 3 vols. Paris.

Lessing, Gotthold Ephraim. 1880. *Lessings 'Laokoon'.* Ed. Hugo Blümner. 2nd edn. Berlin.

1886–1924. *Sämtliche Schriften.* Ed. Karl Lachmann and Franz Muncker. 23 vols. Stuttgart and Leipzig.

1930. *Laocoon, Nathan the Wise, Minna von Barnhelm.* Ed. William A. Steel. Rpt. London and New York, 1967.

1956. *Theological Writings.* Trans. Henry Chadwick. London.

1962. *Hamburg Dramaturgy.* Trans. Helen Zimmern. New York.

1968. *Gesammelte Werke.* Ed. Paul Rilla. 2nd edn. 10 vols. Berlin and Weimar.

1970–79. *Werke.* Ed. Herbert G. Göpfert. 8 vols. Munich.

Lewes, George Henry. 1857. *The Biographical History of Philosophy, from Its Origins in Greece down to the Present Day.* Revised ed. London.

Lewis, L.J. 1960. 'Novalis and the Fichtean Absolute'. *German Quarterly,* 35, 464–74.

Lukács, Georg. 1971. *History and Class Consciousness: Studies in Marxist Dialectics.* Trans. Rodney Livingstone. Cambridge, Mass.

McFarland, Thomas. 1969. *Coleridge and the Pantheist Tradition.* Oxford.

1972. 'The Origin and Significance of Coleridge's Theory of the Secondary Imagination', pp. 195–246 in *New Perspectives on Coleridge and Wordsworth.* Ed. G.H. Hartman. New York.

Marx, Karl, and Engels, Friedrich. 1970. *The German Ideology.* Trans. and ed. C.J. Arthur. New York.

Mehennet, A. 1973. *Order and Freedom: German Literature and Society,* 1720–1805. London.

Meredith, James Creed. 1911. *Kant's Critique of Aesthetic Judgement.* Oxford.

1928. *Kant's Critique of Teleological Judgement.* Oxford.

Minor, Jacob. 1890. *Schiller, sein Leben und seine Werke.* 2 vols. Berlin.

Mitchell, W.J.T. 1986. *Iconology: Image, Text, Ideology.* Chicago and London.

Molnár, Géza von. 1981–82. 'Goethe's Reading of Kant's *Critique of Esthetic Judgement:* A Referential Guide for Wilhelm Meister's Aesthetic Education'. *Eighteenth-Century Studies,* 15, 402–20.

1987. *Romantic Vision, Ethical Context: Novalis and Artistic Autonomy.* Minneapolis.

Monk, Samuel Holt. 1935. *The Sublime: A Study of Critical Theories in Eighteenth-Century England.* New York.

Mueller, G.E. 1941. 'Solger's Aesthetics: A Key to Hegel'. In *Corona: Studies in Celebration of the Eightieth Birthday of Samuel Singer,* ed. A. Schirokauer, pp. 212–27. Durham, N.C.

Muirhead, J.H. 1927. 'How Hegel Came to England'. *Mind,* 36, 423–47.

Nauern, Franz-Gabriel. 1971. *Revolution, Idealism and Human Freedom: Schelling, Hölderlin and Hegel and the Crisis of Early German Idealism.* The Hague.

Nisbet, H.B. 1970. *Herder and the Philosophy and History of Science.* Cambridge.

1979. 'Laocoon in Germany: The Reception of the Group Since Winckelmann'. *Oxford German Studies,* 10, 22–63.

1985. *German Aesthetic and Literary Criticism: Winckelmann, Lessing, Hamann, Herder, Schiller and Goethe.* Cambridge.

Nivelle, Armand. 1955. *Les théories esthétiques en Allemagne de Baumgarten à Kant.* Paris.

Novalis (Friedrich von Hardenberg). 1960–75. *Novalis Schriften.* Ed. Paul Kluckhorn and Richard Samuel. 4 vols. Stuttgart.

Orsini, Gian N.G. 1969. *Coleridge and German Idealism: A Study in the History of Philosophy, with unpublished materials from Coleridge's Notebooks.* Carbondale, Illinois.

Pascal, Roy. 1937. *Shakespeare in Germany, 1740–1815*. Cambridge.

1953. *The German Sturm und Drang*. Manchester.

Peacock, Ronald. 1952. 'Novalis and Schopenhauer: A Critical transition in Romanticism'. In *German Studies Presented to L.A. Willoughby*. Oxford.

Pick, Robert. 1961. 'Schiller in England, 1787–1960: A Bibliography'. *Publications of the English Goethe Society*, 30, 1–123.

Pochmann, Henry A. 1957. *German Culture in America*. Madison, Wisconsin.

Price, Lawrence Marsden. 1932. *The Reception of English Literature in Germany*. Berkeley.

Price, Mary Bell, and, Price, Lawrence Marsden. 1934. *The Publication of English Literature in Germany in the Eighteenth Century*. Berkeley.

1955. *The Publication of English Humaniora in Germany in the Eighteenth Century*. Berkeley and Los Angeles.

Profitlich, Ulrich. 1968. *Der seelige Leser: Untersuchungen zur Dichtungstheorie Jean Pauls*. Bonn.

Ralli, Augustus. 1932. *A History of Shakespearean Criticism*. 2 vols. London.

Read, Herbert, 1947. *The True Voice of Feeling: Studies in English Romantic Poetry* rpt. London. 1968.

Reed, T.J. 1980. *The Classical Centre: Goethe and Weimar, 1775–1832*. London.

Richter, Jean Paul. 1927–44. *Sämtliche Werke*. Ed. Eduard Berend. 37 vols. in three parts. Weimar. Rpt. Berlin, 1952–53.

1973. *Horn of Oberon. Jean Paul Richter's School for Aesthetics*. Trans. Margaret R. Hale. Detroit.

Ritter, H. 1973. *Novalis in Zeugnissen seiner Zeitgenossen*. Stuttgart.

Robertson, John G. 1939. *Lessing's Dramatic Theory*. Cambridge. 2nd edn. 1965.

Robinson, Henry Crabb. 1869. *Diary, Reminiscences, and Correspondence of Henry Crabb Robinson*. Ed. Thomas Sadler. 3 vols. London.

1929. *Crabb Robinson in Germany, 1800–1805*. Extracts from his correspondence. Ed. Edith J. Morley. London.

Schaber, S.C. 1973. 'Novalis' Theory of the work of Art and Hieroglyph'. *Germanic Review*, 48, 35–44.

Schelling, Friedrich Wilhelm Joseph von. 1856–61. *Sämmtliche Werke*. Ed. K.F.A. von Schelling. 14 vols. Stuttgart and Augsburg.

1936. *Of Human Freedom*. Trans. James Gutman. Chicago.

1966. *On University Studies*. Trans. E.S. Morgan. Ed. Norbert Guterman. Athens, Ohio.

1967. *The Ages of the World*. Trans. Frederick de Wolfe Bolman Jr., 1942, rpt. New York.

1974. *Schelling's Treatise on 'The Deities of Samothrace'*. Trans. Robert F. Brown American Academy of Religion, Studies in Religion. Missoula, Montana.

1978. *System of Transcendental Idealism (1800)*. Trans. Peter Heath. Introduction by Michael Vater. Charlottesville, Virginia.

1980. *The Unconditional in Human Knowledge: Four Early Essays (1794–96)*. Trans. Fritz Marti. Lewisburg and London.

1988. *The Philosophy of Art*. Trans. Douglas Stott. Foreword by David Simpson. Minneapolis and London.

Schiller, Johann Christoph Friedrich von. 1892–96. *Schillers Briefe*. Ed. Fritz Jonas. 7 vols. Stuttgart.

1943–. *Schillers Werke. Nationalausgabe*. Ed. Julius Petersen and others. In progress. Weimar.

1957. *Über naive und sentimentalische Dichtung.* Ed. William F. Mainland. Oxford.
1958–59. *Sämtliche Werke.* Ed. Gerhard Fricke and Herbert G. Göpfert. 5 vols. Munich.
1966. *'Naive and Sentimental Poetry' and 'On the Sublime'.* Trans. Julius A. Elias. New York.
1967. *On the Aesthetic Education of Man, in a Series of Letters.* Ed. and trans. Elizabeth M. Wilkinson and L.A. Willoughby. Oxford.
1969. *Mary Stuart.* In *Five German Tragedies.* Ed. F.J. Lamport. Harmondsworth, Middlesex.
1979. *The Robbers, Wallenstein.* Trans. F.J. Lamport. Harmondsworth, Middlesex.
Schlegel, August Wilhelm. 1846. *Course of Lectures on Dramatic Art and Literature.* Trans. J. Black. Rev. A.J.W. Morrison. London.
1962–74. *Kritische Schriften und Briefe.* Ed. E. Lohner. 7 vols. Stuttgart.
Schlegel, Friedrich. 1849. *The Aesthetic and Miscellaneous Works of Friedrich von Schlegel.* Trans. E.J. Millington. London.
1882. *Prosaische Jugendschriften.* Ed. J. Minor. 2 vols. Vienna.
1958–67. *Kritische Friedrich–Schlegel–Ausgabe.* Ed. Ernst Behler, with J.J. Anstett and Hans Eichner. 22 vols. Munich.
1968. *Dialogue on Poetry.* Trans. Ernst Behler and Roman Struc. Pennsylvania and London.
1971. *'Lucinde' and the 'Fragments'.* Trans. Peter Firchow. Minneapolis.
Schmidt, Erich. 1923. *Lessing: Geschichte seines Lebens und seiner Schriften.* 2 vols. Fourth ed. Berlin.
Schneeberger, Guido. 1954. *Frans Wilhelm Josef Schelling: eine Bibliographie.* Bern.
Schopenhauer, Arthur. 1911. *Arthur Schopenhauers sämtliche Werke.* Vol. 1. Ed. Paul Deussen. Munich.
1969. *The World as Will and Representation.* Trans. E.F.J. Payne. 2 vols. 1958; rpt. New York.
1974a. *Parerga and Paralipomena.* Trans. E.F.J. Payne. 2 vols. Oxford.
1974b. *On the Fourfold Root of the Principle of Sufficient Reason.* Trans. E.F.J. Payne. Introduction by Richard Howard. La Salle, Illinois.
Seidel, George J. 1976. *Activity and Ground: Fichte, Schelling and Hegel.* Hildesheim & New York.
Shaffer, Elinor S. 1975. *'Kubla Khan' and the Fall of Jerusalem.* Cambridge.
Shaper, Eva. 1979. *Studies in Kant's Aesthetics.* Edinburgh.
Shelley, Percy Bysshe. 1977. *Shelley's Poetry and Prose.* Ed. Donald H. Reiman and Sharon B. Powers. New York and London.
Simpson, David. 1982a. *Wordsworth and the Figurings of the Real.* London and Atlantic Highlands, N.J.
1982b. *Fetishism and Imagination: Melville, Dickens, Conrad.* Baltimore and London.
1984. *German Aesthetic and Literary Criticism: Kant, Fichte, Schelling, Schopenhauer, Hegel.* Cambridge. Rpt. 1987.
Solger, Karl. 1826. *Nachgelassene Schriften und Briefwechsel.* Ed. L. Tieck and F. von Raumer. 2 vols. Leipzig.
1829. *Vorlesungen über Aesthetik.* Ed. K.W.L. Heyse. Leipzig.
1933. *Tieck and Solger: The Complete Correspondence.* Ed. Percy Matenko. New York and Berlin.
1971. *Erwin. Vier Gespräche über das Schöne und die Kunst.* Ed. W. Henckmann. Munich.

Sorg, Bernhard. 1975. *Zur literarischen Schopenhaur-Rezeption im 19. Jahrhundert.* Heidelberg.

Staël, Madame de (Baroness de Staël-Holstein). 1813. *Germany.* 3 vols. London.

Stahl, Ernest L. 1947. *Shakespeare und das deutsche Theater.* Stuttgart.

Staiger, Emil. 1952–59. *Goethe.* 3 vols. Zurich and Freiburg.

Steinhauer, Kurt. 1980. *Hegel Bibliography-Bibliographie.* Background Material on the International Reception of Hegel within the context of the History of Philosophy. München, New York, London, Paris.

Stewart, Dugald. 1854. *The Collected Works of Dugald Stewart.* Ed. Sir William Hamilton. 11 vols. Edinburgh.

Stockley, V. 1929. *German Literature as Known in England, 1750–1830.* London.

Stokoe, F.W. 1926. *German Influence in the English Romantic Period, 1788–1818.* Cambridge.

Strawson, P.F. 1966. *The Bounds of Sense.* London.

Strohschneider-Kohrs, Ingrid. 1960. *Die Romantische Ironie im Theorie und Gestaltung.* Tübingen.

Szondi, Peter. 1954. 'Friedrich Schlegel und die romantische Ironie: Mit einem Anhang über Ludwig Tieck'. *Euphorion,* 48, 397–411.

Taylor, Charles. 1975. *Hegel.* Cambridge.

Taylor, Mark C. Ed. 1986. *Deconstruction in Context: Literature and Philosophy.* Chicago and London.

Tieck, Ludwig. 1848–52. *Kritische Schriften.* 4 vols. Leipzig.

Trotsky, Leon. 1972. *On Literature and Art.* Ed. Paul N. Siegel. 2nd edn. New York.

Vogel, Stanley, M. 1955. *German Literary Influences on the American Transcendentalists.* New Haven.

Walzel, O. 1938. 'Methode? Ironie bei F. Schlegel und bei Solger'. *Helicon,* 1, 33–50.

Ward, Albert. 1974. *Book Production, Fiction and the German Reading Public, 1740–1800.* Oxford.

Weiskel, Thomas. 1976. *The Romantic Sublime: Studies in the Structure and Psychology of Transcendence.* Baltimore and London.

Wellbery, David E. 1984. *Lessing's 'Laocoon': Semiotics and Aesthetics in the Age of Reason.* Cambridge.

Wellek, René. 1931. *Immanuel Kant in England, 1793–1838.* Princeton.

1955. *A History of Modern Criticism, 1750–1955.* 4 vols. New Haven.

1965. *Confrontations: Studies in the Intellectual and Literary Relations between Germany, England and the United States during the Nineteenth Century.* Princeton.

Wells, George A. 1959. *Herder and After: A Study in the Development of Sociology.* The Hague.

Wheeler, Kathleen M. 1980. *Sources, Processes and Methods in Coleridge's 'Biographia Literaria'.* Cambridge.

1984. *German Aesthetic and Literary Criticism: The Romantic Ironists and Goethe.* Cambridge.

Wiese, Benno von. 1978. *Friedrich Schiller.* Fourth ed. Stuttgart.

Wilkinson, Elizabeth M. Ed. 1984. *Goethe Revisited: A Collection of Essays.* London and New York.

and L.A. Willoughby. 1970. *Goethe, Poet and Thinker.* 2nd edn. London.

Winckelmann, Johann Joachim. 1765. *Reflections on the Painting and Sculpture of the Greeks.* Trans. Henry Fuseli. London.

Witte, William. 1949. *Schiller.* Oxford.